The Wine Regions of France

D1316232

On the wine trail...

France is without doubt at the centre of gravity of the world of wine. At a time when there have never been so many challenges from the vineyards of the New World, France, with its wide range of soils and its rich history of viticulture, remains the landmark and absolute point of reference in the field of wine production.

A quick glance through a list of the French regions reveals the huge influence of the vine on French life and customs. The vineyard is often the focal point of a village, a showcase for its heritage, and wines produced there serve as the cornerstone of the regional identity.

Let us guide you around this unique cultural heritage, through beautiful scenery and along picturesque lanes. Take the time to wander through vineyards, to contemplate their secrets, to learn the science behind it all, and of course, to savour the results...

Our team of editors have travelled the length and breadth of France to bring you the most interesting itineraries, encompassing the best selection of restaurants and hotels, with the care and attention to detail which have characterised Michelin guides for over a century.

We welcome comments and suggestions from our readers, which will serve to enhance the next edition of the guide.

So turn the page and open a window on the vineyards of France. Join the Green Guide in the spirit of discovery.

The Michelin Green Guide Team
TheGreenGuide-uk@uk.michelin.com

Michelin Pilot Sport guarantees you ultimate driving precision. Built to fit with sports car requirements, Michelin Pilot Sport equips Audi Quattro, BMW Motorsport, Mercedes-Benz AMG, Porsche...

MICHELIN PILOT SPORT
ULTIMATE DRIVING PRECISION.

A better way forward

Contents

A **general map** of the wine regions of France is on the inside front cover of this guide and a **table** of the wine regions of France appears on the inside back cover.

Practical Points

Understanding and Tasting Wine

S. Sauvignier / MICHELIN

S. Sauvignier / MICHELIN

Tours of the Wine Regions

S. Sauvignier / MICHELIN

S. Sauvignier/MICHELIN

Maps

Road maps

All Michelin publications are cross-referenced and the reference for each French wine region is given at the start of the chapter. From our range of products we recommend the following:

– **Local Maps,** on a scale of 1:150 000 or 1:180 000, with detailed information on a small scale for those who want to fully discover all that one or two *départements* have to offer. Michelin local maps have an alphabetical index of places and plans of principal towns and are numbered from 301 to 345 *(see map below).*

– **Regional Maps,** on a scale of 1:250 000 to 1:300 000, cover the regions of France and show the primary and secondary road networks, together with tourist information. They are useful when covering a large area or travelling longer distances between towns and have an alphabetical index of places and plans of principal towns.

Internet users can access personalised route plans, Michelin maps and town plans, and addresses of hotels and restaurants featured in the Michelin Guide France through the website at **www. ViaMichelin.com**

Maps of the Wine Regions

Maps of each wine region are to be found on the following pages:

How to use this guide

Finding your way round the guide

There are several ways to find the wine regions of your choice in the guide.

The number on the top right-hand corner of each page corresponds to the number of the wine region on the **general map** on the inside front cover of the guide.

The **contents page** also lists the wine regions covered in the guide, with the corresponding page number.

The **reference table of the wine regions of France** on the inside back cover of the guide enables you to narrow down your choice by region, tour or alternative activity.

Before you go

Practical Points – A few useful chapters at the start of the guide with advice on how to get to the French wine regions, practical information for your stay in France and tips on how to source and cellar your wine.

Understanding and Tasting Wine – This section of the guide deals with the world of wine and tasting wine. Before walking among the vineyards, learn how to recognise the different soils and how the quality of the soil influences the taste of the wine, and find out how to recognise the vintage when tasting the wine. Discover more about the intricacies of wine growing/viticulture.

Chapter by chapter

In each chapter relating to a wine region, we introduce the region, its wines and its appellations. The **background** section explains the history or specificity of the region. Then the wine routes are described, with an indication of the mileage you will cover en route, together with the map references of Michelin maps.

Directories

Each wine region covered in the guide has a directory section with a selection of **restaurants, hotels** and **guesthouses,** together with **stores offering local**

specialities to accompany the wines you will be tasting and buying. Finally, we list the most interesting **markets** of the region.

OUR LISTINGS

We have scoured the wine regions of France to find the best hotels, guesthouses, and restaurants. We have favoured those establishments which are set in the heart of the vineyards, in wine-producing villages or on our wine routes.

Comfort, tranquillity and the quality of the food were at the top of our list of essentials and every establishment in the guide has been visited by our inspectors and chosen with the greatest of care. However, things may have changed since our last visit, so please let us know if any establishment is not up to standard: your comments and suggestions are always very welcome.

Hotel and guesthouse prices are for a double room in high season; cheaper rates are often available in low season – contact the proprietor for more information.

If necessary, we give directions for how to reach the establishment from the nearest town.

Our selection is divided into three price brackets: for those on a budget of 42€ or under, choose from the simple, convivial accommodation listed under the ☺ category. Good, honest food at a reasonable price is available for 16€ or under in this category.

Those on a slightly more generous budget should look to the ☺☺ category for food and accommodation. This price bracket allows up to 76€ a night for accommodation and up to 31€ for a meal. A hotel or restaurant in this category will be run by proprietors keen to share with you the specialities of their region. Your stay in a hotel in this category should be comfortable and particularly pleasant. Note that booking is often necessary for a hotel or restaurant in this category.

The ☺☺☺ category is for those looking to splash out on the highest standards of accommodation and cuisine. When eating in any of these establishments, note that there is often a smart dress code.

Directory key

20rm: 38/57€ – Number of rooms: price of a single/double room

half-board or full board – Price per person, based on 2 people sharing a double room

☕ **6€** – Price of breakfast, when this is not included in the price of the room

12€ lunch – Price of the set menu served at lunchtime

16/38€ – Lowest/highest price of a meal (set menu or à la carte) served at lunchtime or in the evening

table d'hôte 15€ – Price of a meal served for residents only

reserv – Booking advised

✄ – Credit cards not accepted

P – Parking reserved for hotel patrons only

EATING OUT

We have selected restaurants which serve local specialities, as well as those which serve classical French cuisine and themed food. We have also included some *fermes-auberges* (farmhouse B&Bs), which often serve traditional French country food round the farmhouse table.

ACCOMMODATION

Hotels – Prices are per night and do not normally include breakfast. Some hotels have an on-site restaurant.

Chambres d'hôte – You are normally welcomed by the owners who open their home to you. Prices are per night and normally include breakfast. Some establishments also serve dinner for residents only *(table d'hôte)*. Given the increasing popularity of this type of accommodation it is advisable to book in advance. Note that some establishments do not accept dogs, or request a supplement. Ask when reserving.

Shopping Guide

We include a buying guide in each wine region chapter. This section is devoted to buying wine. Under the **Information** heading we list the addresses of professional wine bodies and representatives of the wine industry to help you learn more about the vineyards and wines of the local area.

The **Overview** section presents the characteristics of the wines of the region, how long they should be kept and an indication of price, wine by wine.

The **Buying** section brings you the addresses of quality wine merchants, cooperatives and estates on our wine routes. These addresses are listed in alphabetical order of the town where they are situated. Don't hesitate to ask the proprietor's advice – they know their wine. On-site tasting sessions are probably the best way for you to judge the wine available. However, remember that the consumption of alcohol should be avoided if you're driving. In any case, as a general rule, wine should be spat out after tasting.

Finally, look to the **Wine Festivals** section for details of the main celebrations of wine or see **The "Fêtes du vin"** on p. 30 – this chapter brings together all the fêtes, festivals and other celebrations of wine, by time of year and by location.

Vintages

	1993	1994	1995	1996	1997	1998	1999	2000	2001	2002	2003
Alsace	Good	Good	Good	Good	Vintage	Good	Good	Vintage	Vintage	Good	Vintage
Bordeaux (white)	Good	Good	Good	Vintage	Good	Good	Good	Vintage	Good	Average	Good
Bordeaux (red)	Good	Good	Vintage	Good	Average	Good	Good	Vintage	Good	Good	Good
Burgundy (white)	Good	Good	Vintage	Good	Vintage	Good	Good	Good	Average	Vintage	Good
Burgundy (red)	Good	Good	Vintage	Good	Good	Good	Vintage	Good	Good	Vintage	Good
Beaujolais	Good	Good	Vintage	Good	Good	Good	Vintage	Average	Good	Good	Vintage
Champagne	Good	Good	Good	Vintage	Good	Good	Good	Average	Good	Good	Vintage
Côtes du Rhône North	Good	Good	Good	Vintage	Good	Good	Vintage	Good	Good	Good	Good
Côtes du Rhône South	Good	Good	Good	Vintage	Vintage	Good	Good	Vintage	Vintage	Good	Good
Provence	Good	Good	Good	Good	Good	Average	Good	Good	Vintage	Good	Good
Languedoc Roussillon	Vintage	Good	Vintage	Good	Good	Good	Good	Good	Good	Good	Good
Loire Valley Muscadet	Good	Good	Vintage	Good	Good	Good	Good	Good	Good	Good	Vintage
Loire Valley Anjou-Tourraine	Good	Good	Vintage	Good	Good	Good	Good	Good	Good	Good	Vintage
Loire Valley Pouilly-Sancerre	Good	Good	Good	Good	Vintage	Good	Good	Vintage	Good	Good	Vintage

- ■ Vintage year
- ■ Good year
- ■ Average year

The large wine storehouse at Chateau Mouton Rothschild.

A. Thuillier / MICHELIN

Practical Points

Planning your Trip

Useful Addresses

INTERNET

www.ambafrance-us.org
The French Embassy in the USA has a web site providing basic information (geography, demographics, history), a news digest and business-related information. It offers special pages for children, and pages devoted to culture, language study and travel, and you can reach other selected French sites (regions, cities, ministries) with a hypertext link.

www.franceguide.com
The French Government Tourist Office/Maison de la France site is packed with practical information and tips for those travelling to France. The home page has a number of links to more specific guidance, for American or Canadian travellers for example, or to the FGTO's London pages.

www.FranceKeys.com
This sight has plenty of practical information for visiting France. It covers all the regions, with links to tourist offices and related sites. Very useful for planning the details of your tour in France.

www.fr-holidaystore.co.uk
The French Travel Centre in London has gone on-line with this service, providing information on all of the regions of France, including updated special travel offers and details on available accommodation.

www.visiteurope.com
The European Travel Commission provides useful information on travelling to, and around, 27 European countries, and includes links to some commercial booking services (ie vehicle hire), rail schedules, weather reports and more.

Tourist Organisations
For information, brochures, maps and assistance in planning a trip to France travellers should apply to the official French Tourist Office or Maison de France in their own country.

Australia and New Zealand – BNP Building, 12 Castlereagh Street, Sydney, New South Wales 2000; ☎ (02) 9231 5244; Fax (02) 9221 8682.

Canada – Montreal – 1981 Avenue McGill College, Suite 490, Montreal, PQ H3A 2W9; ☎ (514) 288-4264; Fax (514) 845 4868.
Toronto – 30 St Patrick's Street, Suite 700, Toronto, Ontario; ☎ (416) 979 7587.

Ireland – 10 Suffolk Street, Dublin 2; ☎ (01) 679 0813; Fax (01) 679 0814.

South Africa – P.O. Box 41022, Craig Hall 2024; ☎ (011) 880 8062.

United Kingdom – 178 Piccadilly, London, WIV 0AL; ☎ 0906 8244 123 (60p per minute at all times); Fax 020 7493 6594; info.uk@franceguide.com; www.franceguide.com

United States – East Coast – New York – 444 Madison Avenue; 16th Floor, NY 10022-6903; ☎ (212) 838-7800; Fax (212) 838-7855. Mid West – Chicago – 676 North Michigan Avenue, Suite 3360, Chicago, IL 60611-2819; ☎ (312) 751-7800; Fax (312) 337-6339.
West Coast – Los Angeles – 9454 Wilshire Boulevard, Suite 715, Beverly Hills, CA 90212-2967; ☎ (310) 271-6665; Fax (310) 276-2835. Information can also be requested from France on Call, ☎ (202) 659-7779.

EMBASSIES AND CONSULATES IN FRANCE

Australia: Embassy – 4 rue Jean-Rey, 75015 Paris; ☎ 01 40 59 33 00; Fax 01 40 59 33 10.
Canada: Embassy – 35 avenue Montaigne, 75008 Paris; ☎ 01 44 43 29 00; Fax 01 44 43 29 99
Ireland: Embassy – 4 rue Rude, 75016 Paris; ☎ 01 44 17 67 00; Fax 01 44 17 67 60.
New Zealand: Embassy – 7 ter rue Léonard-de-Vinci, 75016 Paris; ☎ 01 45 01 43 43; Fax 01 45 01 43 44.
South Africa: Embassy 59 quai d'Orsay, 75007 Paris; ☎ 01 53 59 23 23; Fax 01 53 59 23 33.
UK: Embassy – 35 rue du Faubourg St-Honoré, 75008 Paris; ☎ 01 44 51 31 00; Fax 01 44 51 31 27. Consulate – 16 rue d'Anjou, 75008 Paris; ☎ 01 44 51 31 01 (visas).
USA: Embassy – 2 avenue Gabriel, 75008 Paris; ☎ 01 43 12 22 22; Fax 01 42 66 97 83.
Consulate – 2 rue St-Florentin, 75001 Paris; ☎ 01 42 96 14 88.

Formalities

DOCUMENTS

PASSPORT
Nationals of countries within the European Union entering France need only a national identity card (or in the case of the British a passport). Nationals of other countries must be in possession of a valid national **passport**. In case of loss or theft, report to your embassy or consulate and the local police.

VISA

No entry visa is required for Canadian, US or Australian citizens travelling as tourists and staying less than 90 days, except for students planning to study in France. If you think you may need a visa, apply to your local French Consulate. US citizens should obtain the booklet *Safe Trip Abroad* (US$1), which provides useful information on visa requirements, customs regulations, medical care etc for international travellers. Published by the Government Printing Office, it can be ordered by phone – ☎ (202) 512-1800 – or consulted on-line (www.access.gpo.gov). General passport information is available by phone toll-free from the Federal Information Center (item 5 on the automated menu), ☎ 800-688-9889. US passport application forms can be downloaded from http://travel.state.gov

DRIVING LICENCE

Travellers from other European Union countries and North America can drive in France with a valid national or home-state driving licence. An international driving licence is useful because the information on it appears in nine languages (keep in mind that traffic officers are empowered to fine motorists). A permit is available (US$10) from the National Automobile Club, 1151 East Hillsdale Blvd., Foster City, CA 94404, ☎ 650-294-7000 or www.nationalautoclub.com; or contact your local branch of the American Automobile Association.

REGISTRATION PAPERS

If you are taking your own vehicle to France, it is necessary to have the registration papers (logbook) and a nationality plate of the approved size.

VEHICLE INSURANCE

Certain motoring organisations (AAA, AA, RAC) offer accident insurance and breakdown service schemes for members. Check with your current insurance company in regard to coverage while abroad. If you plan to hire a car using your credit card, check with the company, which may provide liability insurance automatically (and thus save you having to pay the cost for optimum coverage).

HEALTH

First aid, medical advice and chemists' night service rotas are available from chemists and drugstores *(pharmacie)* identified by the green cross sign. All prescription drugs should be clearly labelled; it is recommended that you carry a copy of the prescription. It is advisable to take out comprehensive insurance coverage as the recipient of medical treatment in French hospitals or clinics must pay the bill. Nationals of non-EU countries should check with their insurance companies about policy limitations. Reimbursement can then be negotiated with the insurance company according to the policy held. Citizens of EU countries should apply to the relevant Department of Health and Social Security before travelling for the European Health Insurance Card (valid one year), which entitles the holder to urgent treatment for accident or unexpected illness in EU countries. A refund of part of the costs of treatment can be obtained on application in person or by post to the local Social Security Offices *(Caisse Primaire d'Assurance Maladie)*. Americans concerned about travel and health can contact the International Association for Medical Assistance to Travelers, which can also provide details of English-speaking doctors in different parts of France: ☎ (716) 754-4883.

The American Hospital of Paris is open 24hr for emergencies as well as consultations, with English-speaking staff, at 63 boulevard Victor-Hugo, 92200 Neuilly-sur-Seine, ☎ 01 46 41 25 25. Accredited by major insurance companies.

The British Hospital is just outside Paris in Levallois-Perret, 3 rue Barbès, ☎ 01 46 39 22 22.

CUSTOMS REGULATIONS

Apply to the Customs Office (UK) for a leaflet on customs regulations and the full range of duty-free allowances; available from HM Customs and Excise, Thomas Paine House, Angel Square, Torrens Street, London EC1V 1TA, ☎ 08450 109 000. The US Customs Service offers a publication *Know Before You Go* for US citizens: for the office nearest you, consult the phone book, Federal Government, US Treasury (www.customs.ustreas.gov). There are no customs formalities for holidaymakers bringing their caravans into France for a stay of less than six months. No customs document is necessary for pleasure boats and outboard motors for a stay of less than six months but the registration certificate should be kept on board. Americans can take home, tax-free, up to US$400 worth of goods (limited quantities of alcohol and tobacco products); Canadians up to CAN$300; Australians up to AUS$400 and New Zealanders up to NZ$700.

Residents from a member state of the European Union are not restricted with regard to purchasing goods for private use, but the recommended allowances for alcoholic beverages and tobacco are as follows :

Spirits (whisky, gin, etc) – 10 litres
Cigarettes – 800
Fortified wines (port etc) – 10 litres

Cigars – 200
Wine – not more 90 litres than 60 sparkling
Smoking tobacco – 1 kg
Beer – 110 litres

Seasons

THE BEST TIME
Spring, summer and autumn are the best seasons to visit France but there is a region for every season. The summer period can be beautiful but attracts crowds, so it would be wiser to travel either in June or September when French children are still at school.

PUBLIC HOLIDAYS
Public services, museums and vineyards may be closed or may vary their hours of admission on the following public holidays:
1 January – New Year's Day (jour de l'An)
            – Easter Day and Easter Monday (Pâques)
1 May – May Day (Fête du Travail)
8 May – VE Day (Anniversaire 1945)
Thurs 40 days after Easter – Ascension Day (Ascension)
7th Sun-Mon after Easter – Whit Sunday and Monday (Pentecôte)
14 July – France's National Day (Fête Nationale)
15 August – Assumption (Assomption)
1 November – All Saints' Day (Toussaint)
11 November – Armistice Day (Armistice 1918)
25 December – Christmas Day (Noël)

TIME DIFFERENCE
France is 1hr ahead of Greenwich Mean Time (GMT). France goes on daylight-saving time from the last Sunday in March to the last Sunday in October.

Budget

PRICES AND TIPS
Since a service charge is automatically included in the prices of meals and accommodation in France, it is not necessary to tip in restaurants and hotels. However, if the service in a restaurant is especially good or if you have enjoyed a fine meal, an extra tip (this is the *pourboire*, rather than the *service*) will be appreciated. Usually 1.50€ to 3.50€ is enough, but if the bill is big (a large party or a luxury restaurant), it is not uncommon to leave 7€ to 8€ or more.

As a rule, the cost of staying in a hotel and eating in restaurants is significantly higher in Paris than in the French regions. However, by reserving a hotel room well in advance and taking advantage of the wide choice of restaurants, you can enjoy your trip without breaking the bank.

Restaurants usually charge for meals in two ways: a *menu*, that is a fixed price menu with 2 or 3 courses, sometimes a small pitcher of wine, all for a stated price, or *à la carte*, the more expensive way, with each course ordered separately.

Cafés have very different prices, depending on where they are located. The price of a drink or a coffee is cheaper if you stand at the counter (*comptoir*) than if you sit down (*salle*) and sometimes it is even more expensive if you sit outdoors (*terrasse*).

EXCHANGE RATE
At the time of going to press, the exchange rate for one euro (1€) was: US$1.31; GB£0.69; CAN$1.63; AUS$1.68.

Special Needs

On TGV and Corail trains operated by the national railway (SNCF), there are special wheelchair slots in 1st class carriages available to holders of 2nd-class tickets. On Eurostar and Thalys, special rates are available for accompanying adults. All airports are equipped to receive physically disabled passengers.

Web-surfers can find information for slow walkers, mature travellers and others with special needs at www.access-able.com

The *Michelin Guide France* and the Michelin *Camping France* guide indicate hotels and camp sites with facilities suitable for physically handicapped people.

Transport

Getting there

By Air

The various national and other independent airlines offer services to one of Paris' two airports (Roissy-Charles-de-Gaulle to the north, and Orly to the south), Bordeaux, Lyon, Mulhouse, Toulouse, Marseille, Nice, Montpellier and Perpignan. North American airlines usually operate flights to Paris. Regional airports are well connected to both Parisian airports. Contact airline companies and travel agents for details of package tour flights with a rail or coach link-up as well as Fly-Drive schemes.

By Sea

From the UK or Ireland. There are numerous cross-Channel services (passenger and car ferries, hovercraft) from the United Kingdom and Ireland. To choose the most suitable route between your port of arrival and your destination use the Michelin Tourist and Motoring Atlas France, Michelin map 726 (which gives travel times and mileages) or Michelin maps from the LOCAL series (with the yellow cover). For details apply to travel agencies or to:

Stena Line Ferries – Charter House, Park Street, Ashford, Kent TN2 8EX. Reservations for all UK routes: ☎ 08705 70 70 70; Internet: www.stenaline.co.uk

Hoverspeed – In the UK: ☎ 0870 240 8070; In France: ☎ 00800 1211 1211; Internet: www.hoverspeed.co.uk

Brittany Ferries – In the UK: ☎ 08703 665 333; In France: ☎ 0825 828 828; Internet: www.brittany-ferries.com

Irish Ferries – In the UK: ☎ 08705 17 17 17; In Ireland: ☎ 0818 300 400; In France: ☎ 01 43 94 46 94; In the US: ☎ (772) 563 2856; Internet: www.irishferries.com

Seafrance – In the UK: ☎ 08705 711 711; In France: ☎ 03 21 46 80 00 Internet: www.seafrance.fr

By Train

Eurostar runs via the Channel Tunnel between London (Waterloo) and Paris (Gare du Nord) in under 3hr (bookings and information ☎ 0870 518 6186 in the UK; ☎ 1-888-EUROSTAR in the US). In Paris it links to the high-speed rail network (TGV). Eurailpass, Flexipass, Eurailpass Youth, EurailDrive Pass and Saverpass are three of the travel passes which may be purchased by residents of countries outside the European Union. Contact your travel agent or, in the US, Rail Europe 2100 Central Ave, Boulder, CO, 80301, ☎ 1-800-4-EURAIL. If you are a European resident, you can buy an individual country pass, if you are not a resident of the country where you plan to use it. In the UK, call Rail Europe, ☎ 0870 584 8848. Information on schedules can be obtained on web sites for these agencies and the SNCF, respectively: www.raileurope.com, www.eurail.on.ca, www.raileurope.co.uk, www.sncf.fr At the SNCF site, you can book ahead, pay with a credit card, and receive your ticket at home. There are numerous discounts available when you purchase your tickets in France, from 25-50% below the regular rate. These include discounts for using senior cards and youth cards (cards with a photograph must be purchased – 44€ and 41€, respectively), and lower rates for 2-9 people travelling together (no card required, advance purchase necessary). There are a limited number of discount seats available during peak travel times, and the best discounts are available for travel during off-peak periods.

Tickets must be validated *(composter)* by using the orange automatic date-stamping machines at the platform entrance (failure to do so may result in a fine).

The French railway company SNCF operates a telephone information, reservation and prepayment service in English from 7am to 10pm (French time). In France call ☎ 08 36 35 35 39 (when calling from outside France, drop the initial 0).

By Coach/Bus

Eurolines (London), 4 Cardiff Road, Luton, Bedfordshire, LU1 1PP, ☎ 08705 143219, Fax 01582 400694.

Eurolines (Paris), 22 rue Malmaison, 93177 Bagnolet, ☎ 01 49 72 57 80, Fax 01 49 72 57 99.

www.eurolines.com is the international web site with information about travelling all over Europe by coach (bus).

By Car

Drivers from the British Isles can easily take their car to France via the cross-Channel services *(see above)* or via the Eurotunnel. Contact Eurotunnel Customer Relations Department, P.O. Box 2000, Folkestone, Kent CT18 8XY; ☎ 08705 35 35 35 (reservations); ☎ 08000 969 992 (customer information). *(See also Motoring, below.)*

Wine Tours

Arblaster & Clarke, ☎ 01730 893 344; www.winetours.co.uk - Wine tours specialist, with various tours available, including vineyard walks and champagne tasting weekends.

Gourmet Touring, ☎ 00 33 6 32 80 04 74; www.gourmet-touring.com - Based in the Gironde,this company offers a selection of options based around food, wine and classic cars.

Grape Escapes, ☎ 0870 766 7617, www.grapeescapes.net - Self-drive wine holidays in the Loire and Burgundy.

Orpheus & Bacchus, ☎ 00 33 5 57 47 48 80, www.orpheusandbacchus.com - Music, wine and food festivals set on estate near Bordeaux.

Getting about

MOTORING

HIGHWAY CODE

The minimum driving age is 18. Traffic drives on the right. All passengers must wear seat belts. Children under the age of 10 must ride in the back seat. Headlights must be switched on in poor visibility and at night; use side-lights only when the vehicle is stationary.

In the case of a breakdown, a red warning triangle or hazard warning lights are obligatory. In the absence of stop signs at intersections, cars must yield to the right. Traffic on main roads outside built-up areas (priority indicated by a yellow diamond sign) and on roundabouts has right of way. Vehicles must stop when the lights turn red at road junctions and may filter to the right only when indicated by an amber arrow.

Speeding regulations are rigorously enforced – usually by an on-the-spot fine and/or confiscation of the vehicle. The legal level of alcohol in the blood is strictly limited to 0.5g/litre.

SPEED LIMITS

Although liable to modification, these are as follows:

– toll motorways (*autoroutes*) 130kph/ 80mph (110kph/68mph when raining);
– dual carriageways and motorways without tolls 110kph/68mph (100kph/ 62mph when raining);
– other roads 90kph/56mph (80kph/ 50mph when raining) and in towns 50kph/31mph;
– outside lane on motorways during daylight, on level ground and with good visibility – minimum speed limit of 80kph/50mph.

PARKING REGULATIONS

In town there are zones where parking is either restricted or subject to a fee; tickets should be obtained from the ticket machines (*horodateurs* – small change necessary) and displayed inside the windscreen on the driver's side; failure to display may result in a fine, or towing and impoundment. Other parking areas in town may require you to take a ticket when passing through a barrier. To exit, you must pay the parking fee (usually there is a machine located by the exit – *sortie*) and insert the paid-up card in another machine which will lift the exit gate.

ROAD TOLLS

In France, most motorway sections are subject to a toll (*péage*). You can pay in cash or with a credit card (Visa, MasterCard).

PETROL/GAS

French service stations dispense: *sans plomb 98* (super unleaded 98), *sans plomb 95* (super unleaded 95), *diesel/gazole* (diesel) and *GPL* (LPG). Petrol is considerably more expensive in France than in the USA. Prices are listed on signboards on the motorways; it is usually cheaper to fill up after leaving the motorway.

CAR RENTAL

There are car rental agencies at airports, railway stations and in all large towns throughout France. European cars usually have manual transmission; automatic cars are available in larger cities only if an advance reservation is made. Drivers must be over 21; between ages 21-25, drivers are required to pay an extra daily fee; some companies allow drivers under 23 only if the reservation has been made through a travel agent. It is relatively expensive to hire a car in France; Americans in particular will notice the difference and should make arrangements before leaving; take advantage of fly-drive offers when you buy your ticket, or seek advice from a travel agent, specifying requirements. Nova can be contacted at www. rentacar-europe.com or ☎ 0800 018 6682 (freephone UK) or ☎ 44 28 4272 8189 (calling from outside the UK). All of the firms listed below have internet sites for reservations and information. In France, you can call the following numbers:

Avis: ☎ 08 20 05 05 05
Europcar: ☎ 08 25 82 54 57
Budget France: ☎ 08 25 00 35 64
Hertz France: ☎ 01 47 03 49 12
SIXT-Eurorent: ☎ 08 20 00 74 98
National-CITER: ☎ 01 45 22 77 91.
A Baron's Limousine:
☎ 01 45 30 21 21 provides cars and drivers (English-speaking drivers available).

Overseas Motorhome Tours Inc organises escorted tours and individual rental of recreational vehicles: in the US ☎ 800-322-2127; outside the US
☎ 1-310-543-2590; www.omtinc.com

Services

BANKS

Although business hours vary from branch to branch, banks are usually open from 9am to noon and 2pm to 5pm and are closed either on Mondays or Saturdays. Banks close early on the day before a bank holiday. A passport is necessary as identification when cashing travellers cheques in banks. Commission charges vary and hotels usually charge more than banks for cashing cheques.

One of the most economical ways to use your money in France is by using ATM machines to get cash directly from your bank account (with a debit card) or to use your credit card to get a cash advance. Be sure to remember your PIN number, you will need it to use cash dispensers and to pay with your card in shops, restaurants etc. Code pads are numeric; use a telephone pad to translate a letter code into numbers. Pin numbers have 4 digits in France; inquire with the issuing company or bank if the code you usually use is longer. Visa is the most widely accepted credit card, followed by MasterCard; other cards, credit and debit (Diners Club, Plus, Cirrus etc) are also accepted in some cash machines. American Express is more often accepted in premium establishments. Most places post signs indicating which card they accept. Cards are widely accepted in shops, hypermarkets, hotels and restaurants, at tollbooths and in petrol stations. Before you leave home, check with the bank that issued your card for emergency replacement procedures. Carry your card number and emergency phone numbers separate from your wallet and handbag; leave a copy of this information with someone you can easily reach. If your card is lost or stolen while you are in France, call one of the following 24-hour hotlines:

American Express: ☎ 01 47 77 72 00
Mastercard/Eurocard:
☎ 0 800 901 387
Visa: ☎ 0 800 901 179
Diners Club: ☎ 0 810 314 519
These numbers are subject to change, but you can also check at ATM machines, where they are usually listed. You must report any loss or theft of credit cards or travellers cheques to the local police who will issue you with a certificate.

CURRENCY

Since 2002, **euros** have been the only currency accepted as a means of payment in France.
There are no restrictions on the amount of currency visitors can take into France. Visitors carrying a lot of cash are advised to complete a currency declaration form on arrival, because there are restrictions on currency export.

ELECTRICITY

The electric current is 220 volts. Circular two-pin plugs are the rule. Adapters and converters (for hairdryers, for example) should be bought before you leave home; they are on sale in most airports. If you have a rechargable device (video camera, portable computer, battery recharger), read the instructions carefully or contact the manufacturer or shop. Sometimes these items only require a plug adapter, in other cases you must use a voltage converter as well or risk ruining your appliance.

EMERGENCIES

Police: ☎ 17
SAMU (Paramedics): ☎ 15
Fire *(Pompiers)*: ☎ 18

POST

Main post offices open Monday to Friday 8am to 7pm, Saturday 8am to noon. Smaller branch post offices generally close at lunchtime between noon and 2pm and at 4pm.
Postage via air mail:
UK: letter (20g) 0.50€
North America: letter (20g) 0.90€
Australia and NZ: letter (20g) 0.90€
Stamps are also available from newsagents and *bureaux de tabac*. Stamp collectors should ask for *timbres de collection* in any post office.

TELEPHONE

Most public phones in France use pre-paid phone cards *(télécartes)*, rather than coins. Some telephone booths accept credit cards (Visa, MasterCard/Eurocard). *Télécartes* (50 or 120 units) can be bought in post offices, branches of France Télécom, bureaux de tabac (cafés that sell cigarettes) and newsagents and can be used to make calls in France and abroad. Calls can be received at phone boxes where the blue bell sign is shown; the phone will not ring, so keep your eye on the little digital screen.
National calls – French telephone numbers have 10 digits. Paris and Paris region numbers begin with 01; 02 in Northwest France; 03 in Northeast France; 04 in Southeast France and Corsica; 05 in Southwest France.
International calls – To call France from abroad, dial the country code (33) + 9-digit number (omit the initial 0).

When calling abroad from France dial 00, then dial the country code followed by the area code (minus the initial 0) and number of your correspondent.

International dialling codes (00 + code):

Australia –   ☎ 61
Canada –   ☎ 1
Ireland –   ☎ 353
United Kingdom – ☎ 44
United States – ☎ 1

To use your personal calling card dial:

AT&T –   ☎ 0-800 99 00 11
Sprint –   ☎ 0-800 99 00 87
MCI –   ☎ 0-800 99 00 19
Canada Direct – ☎ 0-800 99 00 16
International information, US/Canada: ☎ 00 33 12 11
International operator: ☎ 00 33 12 + country code
Local directory assistance: ☎ 12

Choosing your Wine

Wine Classifications

VINS DE TABLE

The first and most general of the categories of wine is the "vin de table", which takes in all wines described as "vin de pays" or "vin de table".

A vin de pays comes from a specific geographic area, frequently a *département* or region. It must meet strict standards which govern the planting of grape varieties, the yield per hectare and the wine's alcohol content; once the classification has been given, the wine must be of a consistent quality level. The label on the bottle usually shows the grape variety used. *Vins de pays* are widely available and very affordable.

Vins de table are often sold under a brand name. For the most part, they are produced by mixing wines from France or other European Union countries. Producers are not required to use the term "vin de table" on the label.

VINS DE QUALITÉ PRODUITS DANS UNE RÉGION DÉTERMINÉE

This category, usually abbreviated to VQPRD, covers wines described as appellations d'origine vins de qualité supérieure (AOVDQS) and the appellations d'origine contrôlée (AOC).

The AOVDQS classification – In terms of quality, these wines are between the vins de table and the AOCs, and have to pass an official analysis and tasting. AOVDQS status is often short-lived, as the best wines in the category are developed into AOCs.

The AOCs – Particularly rigorous monitoring surrounds the production of the AOC wines. The grape varieties grown and the percentage of each variety must be approved by the Comité national des vins et des eaux-de-vie, part of the Institut national des appellations d'origine, or INAO. There is a minimum and maximum yield and a minimum alcohol content, measured as the minimum sugar content of the wine before its ageing begins. Standards are also set for cultivation methods, the size of the vines and the vinification process. A tasting must also take place before AOC status can be confirmed: such careful control ensures that the AOC label is a mark of quality. As of 2004, there were 467 appellations d'origine contrôlée.

AOCs in detail – An appellation is a defined geographical area of France which produces wine; the word, and particularly the phrase "appellation contrôllée", is sometimes also used to mean a standard of wine, or the actual wine itself. The appellation name may refer to a region (Bordeaux or Burgundy, for example), sub-regional areas (the Entre-deux-mers appellation) or a smaller district or commune (Volnay). This is the standard throughout the country. However, four regions of France classify their wines in a particular way.

Wines from Alsace always show the grape variety on the label: only Riesling, Gewürztraminer, Muscat and Tokay-Pinot Gris grapes can be used to make an Alsace grand cru. This term signifies a wine from one of 50 terroirs which have a particularly strong reputation, among the most famous being Bruderthal, Hatschbourg and Rosacker.

In the Bordelais region, the oldest official classification, based on the ranking of the wine estates, dates back to 1855, and recognises 61 Médocs, one Graves red wine (Haut-Brion) and 26 Sauternes. Today, the Médoc crus are divided into five categories, while the Pessac-Léognan and Sauternes-Barsac wines fall into one of three categories, and those from Saint-Emilion one of two. Only Pomerol wines are not classified in this way

In Burgundy, the term "climat" is used to refer to the best plots of vines, named after a part of a locality or group of localities.

In Burgundy there are:
- 22 regional appellations, which indicate that the wine is from the region;
- 45 appellations communales (or appellations villages). These are labelled with the name of the place where they are produced;
- Appellations Premiers Crus: a further distinction awarded to localities or climats within a village;
- 33 appellations Grands Crus designate exceptional wine from a single climat, which gives its name to the wine.

Beaujolais-villages, Bourgogne-aligoté and crémant de Bourgogne are examples of regional AOCs.

Pommard, Meursault and Fixin belong to the category of appellations communales.

Chablis 1er Cru Fourchaumes and Pommard 1er Cru Les Rugiens are appellations communales for which the climats are classified as Premier Cru.

A Montrachet is a grand cru from the communes Puligny-Montrachet and Chassange-Montrachet.

In the Champagne region, the appellation is applied to 320 communes which are listed in a "scale of crus". Within this ranking, the "Premiers Crus" from 50 communes are given a percentage score from 90 to 99%. This information may well appear on a Champagne label, but producers are not obliged to use the term AOC on their bottles. In the case of good vintages, you may find bottles of champagne marked with a year, indicating a blend of wines from this one year.

VINS DE GARAGE

This unflattering-sounding term was first used in the 1990s in the Bordeaux region: it refers to wines produced in small quantities, blended in new barrels and stored in a garage because the producer has no storehouse and only a small plot of land. Vinification techniques count for more than the inherent quality of the terroir, but the dense, concentrated wines produced in this way can fetch high prices.

Marks of Excellence

THE PRIZE WINNERS

When you buy a bottle of wine, you may see that it has won prizes or medals at tasting competitions. Some of these competitions are very prestigious, like the Concours general agricole, held at the Salon international de l'agriculture in Paris. Another name you may see or hear is Les Citadelles du Vin, organised by the Office international de la vigne et du vin as part of the Vinexpo in Bordeaux, a trade fair for wine professionals.

At these *concours*, the wines are presented in identical bottles, marked only with numbers: the range of wines is tasted "blind" by professional tasters who, judging by taste, smell and sight, mark the elements of the wines according to a scorecard agreed in advance. A gold, silver or bronze medal at these events gives a wine prestige and a commercial edge in a competitive market. Since 2000, an award for excellence has been given to producers in recognition of their results at the previous five events: a list of these producers can be found at www.concours-agricole.com or www.citadellesduvin.com

THE GREAT VINTAGES

A wine's vintage, or *millésime* in French, is the year it was produced. The key to a great vintage is the weather: a hot, dry, sunny end of May and early June to give good, early flowering, then a warm spell from mid-August to harvest-time. But good years differ from region to region, as you can see from the grid on p. 9, and the quality will vary even within a region: a storm, or an over-hasty harvest can change everything. Among the best years were 1900, 1921, 1929, 1937, 1945, 1947, 1949, 1955, 1959, 1961, regarded as the vintage of the century, 1964, 1966, 1967, 1970, 1985, 1989, 1990, 1996, 1999, 2000 and 2003, when exceptionally hot weather brought on a very early harvest.

Buying your Wine

Where to Buy

FROM THE PRODUCERS

A visit to a *vigneron récoltant* – a wine-grower who produces his own wine – is a good way to try wines and buy a few bottles, or even a case or two, but always arrange the trip beforehand. The grower will take the time to talk you through a tasting, from most modest wines to the best. As you would expect, the prices follow the same upward curve, but are always lower than you would expect from a retailer. There are a few points to remember on a first visit. The tasting itself is usually free, so make sure you don't abuse your host's hospitality. Even at the risk of seeming impolite, decline any nuts or cheese, both of which can flatter a poor wine and mislead your taste buds. Spit out the wines you try: you'll need a clear head when it's time to talk about prices! Even if you don't find any huge bargains, you'll still save money on transport costs, and the pleasure of the experience is well worthwhile in itself. Many estates also ship wine to retailers in the UK and the USA. It can be worth asking the producer if their wine is exported abroad as it may be more economical and convenient to buy in bulk at home than take it back with you.

Producers' addresses are listed in the "buying guide" section in each chapter.

FROM A CAVE COOPERATIVE

There are around 850 of these wine cooperatives in France, producing wine for their 110 000 members and selling it by the bottle or in bulk. On the whole, their production techniques are steadily improving.

The addresses of these cooperatives can be found in the "buying guide".

Coteaux du Layon
Anjou Villages

S. Sauvignier / MICHELIN

FROM A WINE MERCHANT

A good wine merchant should be willing and able to offer personalised advice to the customer, particularly when it comes to the combination of food and wine. Wine merchants need to know the characteristics of the wine region and the specific appellation, and be able to buy and sell at the right price. Their wine tastings are a chance to introduce customers to new wines and bring together clients and producers. There are 450 members of the Fédération nationale des cavistes independents, which is well-known in the world of wine for its choice and good value for money. The national chains Nicolas and Repaire de Bacchus also have a good reputation.

Wine merchants' addresses can be found in the "buyer's guide".

FROM A SUPERMARKET WINE EVENT

Special wine sales, or "foires aux vins", are organised by major supermarket chains such as Auchan, Carrefour, Leclerc, Intermarché, usually in September. The choice, or at least the quantity, is enormous, even if the discounts may be less generous than you might expect. There are interesting wines to be found, especially from the Bordeaux region, but do your research first: study the catalogues, prices, vintages and appellation, arrive early on the opening day and check that the wine on the shelf is the one you're after.

FROM A REGIONAL WINE EVENT

Regional wine fairs give you the chance to try wines sold by the producers, while sampling local delicacies. You may find regional arts and crafts on display too. It's a pleasant way to learn more about local wine, and the people who make and drink it!

FROM A WINE CLUB

The idea is simple and, to many people, very appealing: members receive a monthly choice of wines chosen by sommeliers, chefs and other wine experts, as well as invitations to wine events. And if you don't like the wine you've bought, you can send it back. Before joining one of the many wine clubs, it's worth comparing the terms of membership and the savings offered.

AT A WINE AUCTION

In the heady excitement of the auction rooms, the prices paid for wine range from the reasonable to the extravagant. You'll be bidding against professionals – wine brokers and restaurateurs – as well as amateur wine-lovers, for lots from restaurant cellars, private owners or groups of investors. The greatest wine auctions take place at Christie's, Sotheby's and Drouot, and in Burgundy, at the famous Hospices de Beaune wine sale which takes place on the 3rd Sunday of November every year. If you're tempted, take a copy of one of the French-language reference books: *La Cote des grands vins de France* or the *Guide Bettane & Desseauve*. During the viewing, find out as much as you can on the provenance of the bottles and how they have been stored. Check the corks and the level of the wine, and ask to see inside unopened crates. Remember that there is a fee to pay for every lot sold, for the buyer as well as the seller.

Find out more on the internet: www.idealwine.com; www.iencheres.com

In bulk from the barrel

You can buy wine "on tap" from the producer, at a cooperative and from some wine merchants, and there is a saving to be made: wine costs 25% less from the barrel than in the bottle. But there are drawbacks, too. You'll generally be buying *vin ordinaire*: make sure you check where it's come from. Wine in plastic containers is very susceptible to heat, so bottle it as soon as you can, and remember to take the price of bottles and corks into account.

Vins Primeurs

Combining a knowledge of wine with an instinct for the futures market, buyers of new "vin primeur" pay half the price of their wine before it has been aged and bottled: acquiring 2005 vintage wine in Spring 2006, for example. This method of buying wine is most common in Bordeaux, but vins primeurs are also sold in Burgundy, on a smaller scale. The dealers' prices when the subscription opens in April gives buyers a fair idea of the prospects of the year's vintage: the balance of the cost is paid on delivery. Wine traders, growers and wine clubs may all offer the chance to buy wine this way, but remember that not every year can be a *grande année*.

On the Internet

Once again, take time to research and compare. Keep an eye out for special offers and you'll find that there are some good deals to be had. Vins primeurs are purchased directly, so these wines will be the same price everywhere, but prices for older wines depend on demand, supply and the reputation of the vintage. Here are a few Internet sites you may wish to try:
www.1855.com
www.chateaunet.com
www.chateauonline.com
www.millesima.com
www.chateauinternet.com

Transport and Tax

The bottles of wine or spirits you buy should have a metallic sticker over the cork, stamped with the image of a woman's head: the Marianne logo. This disc (known as a *capsule representative des droits*) is proof of your right to transport the wine within France and is obligatory by order of the French tax and excise service. It is green for AOC and AOVDQS, blue for vins de pays, orange for unfortified sweet wines and yellow for Cognac and Armagnac. If you buy the wine in a bulk container, you should instead be given a paper authorisation called a "congé". This transport document, issued by the French customs authorities, is the equivalent of the *capsule*.

The regulations surrounding the importation of wine for personal consumption or as a gift to Canada and the USA can seem confusing at first sight. Both nations' border authorities classify wine as a restricted import: you may bring in a limited quantity – 1 litre to the USA, 1.5 litres into Canada – in accompanied baggage as part of your personal exemption (currently valued at US$800 and CAN$750). Duty must be paid for higher volumes, but customs officials can, and do, decide to impound large quantities if they suspect the wine is for resale. If you plan to bring a significant quantity of alcohol back with you, you are strongly advised to find out about taxes and limitations on unlicensed imports in your home state or province, contact the relevant government authority *(www.customs.ustreas.gov; www.cbsa-asfc.gc.ca)* and make arrangements in advance at the port of entry. Alternatively international shipping agents may be able to undertake some of these arrangements for you. Alcohol may not be sent by mail.

Storing your Wine

Any lover of fine wine dreams of having their own cellar; a store of carefully chosen bottles, slowly taking on their full character and kept in perfect condition. The pleasure of a wine cellar blends memory and personal taste with a sense of anticipation and discovery.

The Perfect Cellar

Wine Cabinets

Mini-cellars – or wine cabinets – may be expensive and most take up space, but they do provide an ideal storage environment. Make sure that the model you buy keeps out UV light, and that there is no noise or vibration from its motor to disturb the wine. A good cabinet will store wine at different temperatures and be fitted with anti-odour and anti-mould filters. Leading brand names include Electolux, EuroCave, Tastvin, Liebherr, Vinosafe and Climadiff.

An Underground Cellar

The ultimate way to stock young wines and allow them to develop to a flavourful maturity: wine is a fragile, living product which needs to be handled carefully, and there really is an art to cellaring it well. The first rule is that the cellar should be clean and should be used for storing wine and nothing else. Don't keep household cleaning products, cheese, vinegar, paints or solvents in the cellar, as all of these can affect the flavour of the wine.

If you want to build yourself an underground cellar, companies like Côté Cave will sell you a prefabricated cellar which is quick and easy to install. When planning the size of your cellar, you should allow 1.5m³ per 100 bottles.

Temperature

White wines are more sensitive to changes in temperature than reds, but wines of any kind are best stored at a constant temperature of 10-14C: within this, 11-12C is ideal. If the room is too warm, the wine ages too quickly; too cold an environment slows the process and can lead to tartrate crystals forming. Below -4C, the wine will freeze. The cellar is best located where it will not be affected by changes of temperature. If possible, it should face northeast and be ventilated by ducts at the foot of the north wall and the top of the east wall. Air conditioning is another option. At the very least, it is worth investing in a **thermometer**.

Humidity

Ideally, a cellar should have whitewashed walls, a dry solid floor covered with gravel, and a steady humidity of between 70 and 80%. Wines prefer moist rather than dry air, which may dry out the corks and lead to leaks. The only disadvantage of the damp atmosphere of a cellar is that wine labels may peel off: you can protect them using cling film or clear adhesive plastic. If the humidity of the cellar falls below 50%, either water the gravel or place a basin filled with water and charcoal in a corner of the room. To make sure your wine is being kept in the best conditions, you should consider buying a **hygrometer**.

Light

Over-exposure to light affects the tannins in wine and disturbs the ageing process. Neon lights are far too harsh for a cellar – choose lighting which is muted and, if possible, indirect. Your third purchase should be a supply of **40W bulbs**.

Vibrations and Noise

Passing trucks and trains cause vibrations which unsettle the molecules of the wine and prevent it from ageing as it should. A simple way around the problem is to place anti-vibration rubber pads or "feet" at the base of the racks, if they are not fitted with these already.

Organising your Cellar

Wine Racks

Storage racks come in a wide range of materials, including metal, wood, lava rock, reinforced concrete or conglomerate: stability should be your first priority.

Metal racks which hold bottles on wavy metal bars are affordable, easy to fit and are a very economical use of cellar space. Before filling the rack with bottles, fix it firmly to the wall and make sure it is absolutely stable. Wine racks with compartments made out of wood, bricks or plywood make it easier to arrange your wine in batches, according to age or type, which in turn simplifies the job of managing a larger cellar. If you opt for wooden construction, which looks most elegant but also costs more, make sure that the wood has been given a water-resistant finish and reject any structure made from timber that has been sprayed with a chlorophenol-based pesticide, as the chemical residue may affect the taste of your wine.

STANDING OR IN THE RACK?
The bottles should be laid flat, as this keeps the wine in contact with the cork and stops the cork from drying out. You will notice that, in most cellars, the bottles are stored with their necks facing the wall, which makes it easier to read their labels. Spirits and sweet wines should be stored standing up, to prevent the alcohol from damaging the cork.

ARRANGING THE BOTTLES
There are two reasons why bottles of wine should be left in cardboard boxes for as little time as possible. You should unpack them at the earliest opportunity to check that they are in the correct condition and, unlikely as it sounds, storing wine in the box may affect the flavour. Wine delivered in a wooden case, on the other hand, is best left in its original packaging, particularly if the wine is to be stored for some time. Even wines which are meant to be drunk young will be much better after "resting" for two weeks or even for a month, and distinguished vintages need to be left for a few months at least if they are to be enjoyed at their best.

The temperature in your cellar will be slightly lower near the floor, because hot air rises, so Champagnes should be placed at the bottom level of the racks, with other white wines above them. Next should be the bottles of rosé, followed by reds which require only a short storage, and finally the reds to be laid down for long maturation. Within this arrangement, you may wish to group your wines by region or appellation. If you have a large cellar, you will be able to find a dark corner to store vintages that need to be forgotten, then "rediscovered" in a few years' time.

MANAGING YOUR CELLAR
The best way to stay on top of your changing collection of wines is to buy a cellar book, sold in some stationers and specialist bookshops. Alternatively you can make your own by printing out standard forms on a computer and collecting these in a folder or binder. Each page should have a space for the name of the wine, its appellation, its region, its colour, its vintage, the year before which it should be drunk, the time and place of purchase, the price and the details of the producer and supplier. You can then note down the number of bottles in stock and tick them off as they leave the cellar. Finally, jot down your own notes on the wine after the tasting or meal. You could even add a score or rating, or stick the label at the foot of the page. A number of internet sites, including www.idealwine.com, offer an online cellar-management facility or a wine manager application, allowing you to sort through your wines by type or region.

INSURANCE
Unfortunately, few insurers offer a policy insuring your wines against theft. It may be safer to trust to discretion rather than advertising a valuable cellar by fitting reinforced doors. In the case of your most jealously guarded wines, consider removing the labels and identifying them by code instead.

RENTING CELLAR SPACE
A number of storage companies and wine merchants now offer more or less specialised cellarage for the food and wine trade or for larger private collections. If you need to store large stocks of wine in the Paris region before transporting it home, two of the many cellars providing this service are:

La Cave – *7 impasse Charles-Petit, 75011 Paris.*

Les Crayères des Montquartiers – *5 chemin des Montquartiers, 92130 Issy-les Moulineaux.*

Learning More

Tastings, Courses and Holidays

If you've always wanted to find out more about the ideal blend of fine food and drink, or just put a love of wine into words, France is the place to perfect your appreciation and knowledge, and find out more about what you like. Courses for beginners and experts take place around the country. A professional expert – an *oenologue* – will first talk you through the language of wine in a relaxed atmosphere. The best way to learn, though, is hands-on: comparing a series of wines chosen to bring out the variation between, or within, one or more regions, grape varieties or vineyards. You'll be tasting them "blind", just like the experts do. Finally, all is revealed and your wine tutor guides you through the subject of wine and gastronomy. On average, expect to pay 50€ for a 2-3 hour course, while a wine weekend in Burgundy, including food and accommodation will cost around 380€.

Outside France

The American Wine Society – *www.americanwinesociety. com* – Accreditation, awards and competitions, wine events, travel, publications and much more.
International Food and Wine Society – *www.iwfs.org* – Promoting a "knowledge and understanding of wine and food", the IWFS has branches in 40 countries.
The Wine Society – *www. thewinesociety.com* – Organises tastings and offers buying advice to its members. Sales by phone and online.
The Wine & Spirit Education Trust – *www.wset.co.uk* – This UK-based charity oversees qualifications and runs courses for wine enthusiasts and professionals.

Around France

Prodegustation – ☎ *0820 82 10 20* – *www.prodegustation.com* A training organisation which aims to demystify wine and teach people to talk about it in everyday words. Tasting sessions, wine weekends and vineyard tours.
Savour Club – ☎ *0820 72 03 33* – *www.lesavourclub.fr* Tasting sessions of six wines, in a gastronomic setting.

In Paris

École du vin de Paris – *25 r de la Félicité – 17ᵉ arr* – ☎ *01 43 41 33 94* – *www.ecoleduvin.fr* Founded by Olivier Thiénot, the School of Wine is open to professionals and individuals.
Centre Jaques-Vivet – *48 r de Vaugirard – 6ᵉ arr* – ☎ *01 43 25 96 30* – *info@jvivet.com* A well-known wine school founded over 20 years ago.
Explorateurs des vins – *Restaurant Chez Pierrette, 30 r Émile-Lepeu – 11ᵉ arr* – ☎ *01 43 73 72 33* – *info@explorateursduvin.com* A team of sommeliers, specialising in Champagnes, enliven your tastebuds.
Flavouries – ☎ *01 39 89 25 29* – *http://flavouries.free.fr* A relatively new company which organises wine evenings and weekends in your home, with the aim of making wine accessible to everyone.
Grains Nobles – *5 r Laplace – 5ᵉ arr* – ☎ *01 43 54 93 54* – *www.grainsnobles. fr* A team of young wine enthusiasts organises introductory courses at this Parisian wine cellar.
Union des oenologues de France – *21-23 r Croulebarbe – 13ᵉ arr* – ☎ *01 58 52 20 20* – *www.oenologuesdefrance.fr* Introductions to wine tasting and more specialised training courses offer an introduction to the great wine regions of France and the rest of the world.
Vinissime – *35 r de l'Espérance – 13ᵉ arr* – ☎ *01 45 81 26 36* – *www.vinissime.fr* Advisers on all things wine, Vinissime organises wine events and themed dinners.

In the French Regions

The Shopping Guide in each regional chapter of this book gives details of the major wine traders and the local *écoles des vins* run by wine trade organisations.

At the Wine Merchant's

Many wine merchants organise tastings as a way of introducing the wines they sell, often enlisting the help of the producers or even bringing along an *oenologue* to conduct the event. Every autumn, the **Fédération nationale des cavistes independents** organises tastings to coincide with the Fête du vin. *177 av Charles-de-Gaulle, 92200 Neuilly-sur-Seine* – ☎ *01 46 37 88 45.*

Talking about Wine

Acidity - *Fr.: Acidité.* Lends freshness and a vigorous quality called "nervosité" in French. If too acidic, a wine is aggressively sharp; if lacking in acidity, it tastes "flat".

Alcoholic Content - *Fr.: Titre alcoométrique.* Percentage of alcohol in a volume of wine at 20°C. This must be stated on the label.

Ampelography - The science of grape varieties.

Appellation - Name of a region or district, denoting a wine which is typical of the area and reflects the local geographic and human factors of production.

Aroma - Scent of a wine at the moment of tasting. In young wines, the primary aromas – flowery, fruity or vegetal – reflect the grape variety. Secondary aromas develop during fermentation; the wine may take on undertones of banana, boiled sweets or candy, wax or butter. Tertiary aromas, linked to the wine's ageing, may suggest smoke, wood or game: they make up a wine's "bouquet".

Assemblage - A blend of wines of the same origin and quality, producing a better wine than the sum of its parts. Also called a cuvée.

Astringency - The quality of a wine that gives the sensation of the drying of the mucous membranes. Linked to high tannin content; most noticeable in younger wines.

Ban des vendanges - Official proclamation of the date on which the harvest starts.

Botrytis cinerea - A type of fungus which, in wet weather, can lead to grey rot *(pourriture grise)* – a disaster for the grower – but in dry, sunny conditions causes noble rot *(pourriture noble)*. This latter concentrates the grape sugars and is a vital element in the production of certain sweet wines.

Bouquet - The combination of aromas developed by ageing. A taster experiences elements of the scent in the nose and the aromas in the mouth.

Cépage - The type of vine which produces the grapes. The French term for variety.

Chai - A wine storehouse, above ground, as opposed to the *cave*, or cellar.

Chaptalisation - The adding of sugar to the wine must.

Château - Word often used to designate a wine-producing property, even if it does not have a château in its grounds. The term may only be used of an AOC or AOVDQS.

(vin) Crémant - A sparkling wine.

Cru - Literally "growth": a wine's geographical origin.

Encepagement - Planting with (a particular variety of) vines. The overall varietal composition of a wine-making area.

Egrappage - Removal of the grape stalks during the wine-making process.

Lees - *Fr.: Lie.* Solid deposit in wine, left by the yeast, which appears after fermentation. Leaving the wine "on the lees" can enhance the aroma of white wines and lend them extra character. When a Muscadet is produced this way, its label will say "mise en bouteille sur lie".

Liquoreux - Sweet wine with sugars at a concentration of over 40g/l, produced from a harvest affected by noble rot. Examples include Sauternes, Gewürztraminer, Coteaux-du-Layon.

Lutte raisonnée - Environmentally friendly farming using non-chemical treatments.

Moelleux - A full, mellow wine, not usually as sweet as a *vin liquoreux*. It contains 12-45g/l of unfermented sugars.

Mousseux - Effervescent wine under 3-6 bar pressure at 20°C.

Oenology / Enology - *Fr.: Oenologie, un oenologue.* The science of wine, as studied by an oenologist.

Passerillage - Process in which grapes are sun-dried at the foot of the vine or on a bed of straw *(paille)*. This increases the sugar content of the grape. The method is used to make wines known as *vin de paille.*

Perlant - A very lightly sparkling wine, made so by the natural presence of carbon dioxide, is said to be "pearling" when poured: a few fine bubbles stick to the side of the glass.

Pétillant - This describes wines which are less effervescent than a *vin mousseux*, with a gas pressure of between 1 and 2.5 bar.

Phylloxera - A plant-louse that devastated Europe's vineyards from the 1860s, attacking the roots and leaves of the vine.

Polyphenol - A type of chemical compound that gives wine its colour and includes tannins.

Primeur - Wine from the last harvest sold from 3rd November. To be drunk very young. All such wines must be labelled "vin nouveau" or "vin primeur".

Récoltant - Literally "harvester" – a grower, either one who sells his grapes or one who makes his own wine.

Robe - The colour of a wine.

Sommelier - More than just a wine-waiter: a sommelier is also responsible for the choice, purchase and storage of wines.

Storage - *Fr.: Garde.* Over time, a fine wine meant for long storage – a *vin de garde* – develops the mature qualities of a great wine.

Surmaturation - Literally "over-ripening" – this makes for a concentration of sugars in the grapes, a necessary element in the production of *vins doux naturels*, *vins de paille*, and *vendages tardives*, fine wines from Alsace made from late-picked grapes.

Tannins - Organic substances found in the pips, skins and stems of the grape: they play an important part in the ageing of red wines and the development of their bouquet. A tannin-rich wine often has a strongly astringent quality.

Terroir - The combination of a vineyard's natural elements; soil, subsoil, climate, exposure... and the grower's input that makes the most of them.

Vendanges vertes - Literally, "green harvests": the trimming-off of leaves and picking of unripe grapes to encourage the remaining crop to ripen.

Véraison - The final stage of grape-ripening.

Vigneron - A wine-grower: someone who cultivates vines and produces wine.

Vin Doux Naturel - Sweet fortified wine.

Vintage - *Fr.: Millésime.* The year of the grape harvest – a wine's date of birth.

M. Paygnard/MICHELIN

St-Vincent procession, Champlitte, Haute-Saône.

Further Reading

WINE GUIDES
Hugh Johnson's Pocket Wine Book by Hugh Johnson (Mitchell Beazley)
Wine Report by Tom Stevenson (Dorling Kindersley)

REFERENCE
The Art and Science of Wine by James Halliday, Hugh Johnson (Mitchell Beazley)
The Heart of Burgundy: A Portrait of French Countryside by Robert Parker, Andy Katz (Simon & Schuster)
Terroir: Role of Geology, Climate and Culture in the Making of French Wines by James Wilson (Mitchell Beazley)
The Wine Lover's Guide to Burgundy by Michael Busselle (Pavilion)
The Wine Lover's Guide to the Rhone and South West France by Michael Busselle (Pavilion)
The Wines and Winelands of France: Geological Journeys by Charles Pomerol (Seven Hills Books)

WINE TASTING
The Taste of Wine: Art and Science of Wine Appreciation by Emile Peynaud, translated by Michael Schuster (Wine Appreciation Guild)

WINE AND CUISINE
An Omelette and a Glass of Wine by Elizabeth David (Penguin)
Recipes from the French Wine Harvest: Vintage Feasts from the Vineyards by Rosi Hanson (Cassell Illustrated)

PERIODICALS
Decanter Magazine – available from selected wine shops and online (www.decanter.com)
Food and Wine – available from selected wine shops, on subscription and online (www.foodandwine.com)
The Wine Advocate – Robert Parker's newsletter, available on subscription and online from www.erobertparker.com
Wine Spectator – available from selected wine shops, on subscription and online (www.winespectator.com)

WEBSITES
To prepare your trip, visit the official French wines website: www.wines-france.com
Three very likeable characters, a wine-maker, an oenologue and a sommelier, provide answers to all your questions: which French wine to choose for which occasion? Which vintage to drink?
Understanding France's regions, climates, grape varietals and wine labels, and how we use our senses to taste wine.

FICTION
Blackberry Wine by Joanne Harris (Black Swan)
The Voyage by Charles Morgan (Ballantine)

TRAVELOGUE
In the Vine Country by Edith Somerville and Martin Ross (Vintage)
Long Ago in France by MFK Fisher (Pocket Books)

BIOGRAPHY
Chateaux of the Heart of France by Alex Dingwall-Main (Ebury)
The Ripening Sun: One Woman and the Creation of a Vineyard by Patricia Atkinson (Arrow)
The Vine Garden: A Life-changing Summer in the Gardens, Vineyards and Virgile's Vineyard: A Year in the Languedoc Wine Country by Patrick Moon (John Murray)

FILMS
Mondovino, Jonathon Nossiter, 2004 (in French with English subtitles)
Le Festin de Babette, Gabriel Axel, 1987 (in French)

BOOKSHOPS
Books for Cooks – 4 Blenheim Crescent, London, W11 1NN – ☎ 020 7221 1992; fax 020 7221 1517; info@booksforcooks.com; www.booksforcooks.com
Librairie Gourmande – 4 r Dante, 75005 Paris – ☎ 01 43 54 37 27; www.librairie-gourmande.fr

Sales, Fairs and Markets

Events are listed by month, then venues are given in alphabetical order.

January
Marché aux vins (3rd Sun and Mon).

Blaye (Bordelais)

February
Salon des vins du Tricastin (2nd weekend).

St-Paul-Trois-Châteaux
(vallée du Rhône)

Salon des vins (2nd weekend).

Tain-l'Hermitage
(vallée du Rhône)

March
Vente des Hospices de Beaujeu (4th weekend), at the municipal theatre. The world's oldest charity sale dates back to 1797. ☎ 04 74 04 31 05.
Trade fair for owners of private cellars (2nd weekend).

Beaujeu (Beaujolais)

Bordeaux
(Bordelais)

Foire aux vins (1st weekend).

Bourgueil, Saint-Nicolas-de-Bourgueil
(vallée de la Loire)

Salon des vins de La Bourdaisière (2nd weekend).

Montlouis-sur-Loire
(vallée de la Loire)

Hospices de Nuits-St-Georges sale (last weekend). ☎ 03 80 62 67 00.
Expo-Vall (mid-March): a large sales event for regional wines.
Saveurs et vins de Vouvray (2nd weekend).

Nuits-Saint-Georges
(Bourgognes)
Vallet
(vallée de la Loire)
Vouvray
(vallée de la Loire)

Easter
Foire aux vins.

Reuilly
(vallée de la Loire)

Foire du Grand Jeudi (Thu before Easter): every aspect of wine culture and cultivation under one roof in Ricey-Haut.

Les Riceys
(Champagne)

April
Foire-exposition des vins du Var et de Provence (3rd Sat)
Foire aux vins de Chinon (1st two weeks).

Brignoles
(Provence).
Chinon
(vallée de la Loire)

Open-house day at the Châteaux (3rd weekend).

Lalande-de-Pomerol
(Bordelais)

Salon des vins d'Onzain.

Onzain
(vallée de la Loire)

May
Côtes de Blaye open day (3rd or 4th Sun).
Open-day at the Côtes de Bourg châteax (2nd weekend).

Blaye (Bordelais)
Bourg-sur-Gironde
(Bordelais)

Foire des eaux-de-vie (Ascension day).
Foire aux vins (Ascension day).
Foire nationale des vins de France (mid-May).
Foire du pain, du vin et du fromage écobiologiques: an organic food event. (Ascension weekend).
Open day at St-Émilion châteaux (1st weekend).

Eauze (Sud-Ouest)
Guebwiller (Alsace)
Mâcon (Bourgogne)
Rouffach (Alsace)

St-Émilion
(Bordelais)

Graves de Vayres open day (2nd Sun).

Vayres (Bordelais)

Whitsun *(Pentecôte)*
Open day: premières côtes de Bordeaux et Cadillac.
Foire aux vins et à la gastronomie.

Cadillac (Bordelais)
Mailly-Champagne
(Champagne)

Foire aux vins de Sancerre.

Sancerre
(vallée de la Loire)

July

Foire aux vins (on or around 14th). — **Barr** (Alsace)

Foire aux vins (3rd weekend). — **La Chartre-sur-le-Loir** (vallée de la Loire)

Foire du vin (1st weekend). — **Luri** (Corse)
Foire aux vins (Sunday after 14th July). — **Ribeauvillé** (Alsace)
Foire aux vins de l'Entre-Deux-Mers (3rd Sat). — **Sauveterre-de-Guyenne** (Bordelais)

August

Foire aux vins d'Alsace (from 2nd Fri). — **Colmar** (Alsace)
Foire aux vins et aux produits régionaux (14th-15th). — **Duravel** (Sud-Ouest)
Cellar open day (weekend before 15th). — **Menetou-Salon** (vallée de la Loire)

Foire aux vins (weekend nearest 15th). — **Obernai** (Alsace)
Foire aux vins (15th). — **Pouilly-sur-Loire** (vallée de la Loire)

Foire aux vins et aux produits naturels (1st weekend). — **Ste-Foy-la-Grande** (Bordelais)

Foire aux vins de France, (last weekend). — **Sancerre** (vallée de la Loire)

September

Foire aux vins de Champagne (1st weekend). — **Bar-sur-Aube** (Champagne)

Foire aux vins de France et gastronomie (1st and 2nd weekend). — **Belfort** (Jura)
Foire internationale vins, fromages et pains (2nd weekend). — **Langon** (Bordelais)

October

Open day (last Sun). — **Cérons et Graves** (Bordelais)

Châteaux open day (3rd weekend). — **Fronsac** (Bordelais)
La Sauve open day (1st weekend). — **La Sauve** (Bordelais)

November

"Les Trois Glorieuses" (3rd weekend): auction of Hospices de Beaune wines. www.hospices-de-beaune.tm.fr — **Clos de Vougeot, Beaune, Meursault** (Bourgogne)
Open day (last weekend). — **Loupiac** (Bordelais)

December

Open weekend (2nd weekend). — **Pessac-Léognan** (Bordelais)

Marché du réveillon at the Caves de Bailly (24th). www.caves-bailly.com — **St-Bris-le-Vineux** (Bourgogne)

Auction of Hospices de Beaune wines by candlelight.

S. Sauvignier / MICHELIN

The "Fêtes du vin"

Saint Vincent

Quite how Vincent came to be the patron saint of wine-producers, no-one really knows: perhaps it was because he has the word "vin" in his name. Over the centuries, however, the saint has become the figurehead of France's proud culture of wine, and given his name to the *sociétés de saint Vincent*, which began as mutual aid groups, uniting fellow *vignerons* long before the age of benefit, or "friendly", societies.

The feast of St Vincent is celebrated in many wine producing regions, either on 22nd January, the "*fête*" itself, or on the nearest weekend. The day is usually marked by the procession of the saint, a church service, and a wine tasting and meal for the wine-growers.

In **Burgundy**, between Dijon and Beaune, the St Vincent's day celebrations are "*tournant*": held in a different wine growing village from year to year. The same is true of events in **Savoie**, in the **Côte Chalonnaise**, around **Auxerre**, in the **Chablis** region, in the **Bourgeuil** appellation, in the vineyards around **Nantes**, and in **Champagne**.

Other regions always hold their festivities in the same place. "*Les Saint-Vincent fixes*" are annual highlights in **Arlay** and **Champlitte** (Jura), **Villié-Morgon** and **Visan** (Rhône Valley), **Savignac-de-Duras** (South West), **Puy-Notre-Dame** (Loire Valley), **St-Amour** (Beaujolais), and **Assignan** and **Villespassans** (St-Chinian/ Languedoc).

Other Celebrations

January
Wine and truffle festival (last Sun)

Fête des amis des vins de Chitry (weekend before Saint Vincent's day). ☎ 03 86 41 41 28.
Ampélofolies du Cabardès (nearest Sun to Saint Vincent's day): wine, truffle and foie gras festival; truffle market.

February
The "Percée du vin jaune" (1st weekend): celebrates the tapping of the first barrel of *vin jaune* after six years and three months of maturation. A different village is chosen each year.
Fête des Gosiers Secs (1st Sun): "The dry throats festival".

March
"Nuit de la blanquette" (Sun after Palm Sun) marks the end of *Carnaval*. ☎ 04 68 31 11 82. www.limoux.fr
Fête des vins de Bourgueil (3rd Sat).

April
Printemps des Châteaux du Médoc (1st and 2nd weekend).
National Book and Wine Days (Apr-May).

Les Vinées tonnerroises (2nd weekend). ☎ 03 86 55 14 48. www.vignerons-tonnerrois.com
Fête de Saint-Marc (last weekend): a vine branch is tied with ribbons and paraded through the town.

May
"Le Bon air est dans les caves" (Sat after Ascension): music and wine in the local cellars.
Fête des crus du Beaujolais: the host village is chosen by lot (1st weekend).

Carpentras
(vallée du Rhône)
Chitry (Bourgogne)

Moussoulens
(Languedoc)

Jura
(location varies)

Vaux-en-Beaujolais
(Beaujolais)

Limoux
(Languedoc)

Tours
(vallée de la Loire)

Médoc (Bordelais)

Saumur
(vallée de la Loire)
Tonnerre
(Bourgogne)
Villeneuve-lès-Avignon
(vallée du Rhône)

Albas (Sud-Ouest)

Beaujolais
(location varies)

"Circuit des Châteaux" cycle tours (2nd Sun of May).
☎ 05 56 64 81 56.
Festival de Rablay-sur-Layon (Whitsun Weekend).

Pessac-Léognan (Bordelais)
Rablay-sur-Layon (vallée de la Loire)

"Randonnée des cadoles" (1st): Country walk
(c 20km) and picnic. Admission charge.
Fête des vins des coteaux d'Aix (end of May).
Fête du clairet (mid-May).
Rondes en Sauternais (Thu of Ascension): Tours on
foot or by bike. Admission charge.
Les Prémices de la vigne (Sat of Ascension).

Les Riceys (Champagne)
Rognes (Provence)
Quinsac (Bordelais)
Sauternes (Bordelais)

Vitiloire: festival of Loire and Centre wines
(3rd weekend).

Séguret (vallée du Rhône)
Tours (vallée de la Loire)

June

Apéritif à la française – French cocktail Hour (1st Thu):
"l'Apéritif à la française" is celebrated all over the world.
For more information on events near you, visit
www.aperitifalafrancaise.com

All over the world

Fête du vin (last weekend June or 1st in Aug –
even-numbered years): tastings and concerts.
☎ 05 56 00 66 00.

Bordeaux (Bordelais)

Procession of the flasks (1st): hymn to Saint Marcellinus
and blessing of the wine.
Fête des vins du Roussillon (3rd Fri and Sat).

Boulbon (Provence)

Perpignan (Roussillon)

"Jurade" (3rd Sun): Church service, wine council
ceremonies and proclamation of the verdict
on the "vin nouveau". ☎ 05 57 55 50 51.
www.vins-saint-emilion.com

St-Émilion (Bordelais)

Morgon et fanfares (2nd weekend).

Villié-Morgon (Beaujolais)

July

Fêtes Henri IV (1st weekend: even-numbered years)
Fête musicale des vins d'Arbois (last weekend): music,
processions in folk costume and cheese and wine tastings
in the streets of the town.

Ay (Champagne)
Arbois (Jura)

La Table de Cyrano (mid-Jul, even-numbered years):
wines, gastronomy and a programme of concerts.
Fête du vin (4th Sun).

Bergerac (Sud-Ouest)
Cairanne (vallée du Rhône)
Faugères (Languedoc)

Fête vigneronne du Grand St-Jean (1st Sun): Procession
of the wine brotherhoods, auctions and presentation
of the wines.
Festival du muscat (3rd and 4th weeks)
☎ 04 67 18 50 04. www.tourisme-frontignan.com
Les Vignades, tastings and sales (3rd Sat).
Balade gourmande (1st Sun): vineyard walks,
picnic and music. Admission charge.
Fête du vin (last weekend). ☎ 03 88 08 01 66.

Frontignan (Languedoc)
Hyères (Provence)
Ladoix-Sérigny (Bourgogne)
Mittelbergheim (Alsace)

Wine-growers pilgrimage to Brouilly chapel (1st Sat).
☎ 04 74 66 82 19.
La nuit du Muscadet (1st weekend).

Mont Brouilly (Beaujolais)
Mouzillon (vallée de la Loire)

Fête du vin et du terroir (3rd weekend).
Fête des caves (2nd weekend).

Pauillac (Bordelais)
Pfaffenheim (Alsace)

Fête des peintres de vignes en caves (3rd weekend).
☎ 03 86 53 31 79. www.saint-bris.com
Fête du cru St-Chinian (1st Sun after 14th Jul).

St-Bris-le-Vineux (Bourgogne)
St-Chinian (Languedoc)

Fête des vins et de l'andouillette (2nd Sun):
tastings of chitterling and white wine sausages;
race through the vineyards. ☎ 02 41 78 42 75.
Musique aux caves.

St-Lambert-du-Lattay (vallée de la Loire)
Sancerre (vallée de la Loire)

Fête de la fontaine (1st weekend):
the village fountain flows with wine (11am-12.30pm).

Wangen (Alsace)

July-August
Les Grandes Heures de Cluny: concerts followed by tastings in the wine cellars. — **Cluny** (Bourgogne)

La Grande Tablée du Saumur-Champigny (end Jul – early Aug). — **Saumur** (vallée de la Loire)

July-September
Festival musical des Grands Crus de Bourgogne. — **Villages du vignoble** (Bourgogne)

August
Fête du vin au pays du Brand (1st weekend). — **Andlau** (Alsace)

Fête du vin (weekend of 15th). ☎ 03 89 47 90 26. — **Bennwihr** (Alsace)

La Table de Roxane (mid- August, odd-numbered years): similar to the Table de Cyrano *(see above in July)*: the events centre on the place de la Republique. — **Bergerac** (Sud-Ouest)

Fête médiévale de la véraison (1st weekend): The "grape ripening" festival — **Châteauneuf-du-Pape** (vallée du Rhône)

Eurovin (on or around 15th): wine tasting, food, crafts and music *à l'alsacienne*. ☎ 03 88 92 42 57. — **Dambach-la-Ville** (Alsace)

Fête des vins de Duras (2nd weekend), in the courtyard of the château. Hot-air balloon flights. ☎ 05 93 94 13 48. — **Duras** (Sud-Ouest)

Fête des vignerons (last week). ☎ 03 89 23 40 33. — **Eguisheim** (Alsace)

Fête du raisin (1st weekend): celebration of the first grapes of the year, with wine tasting, the "Grape Mass" and traditional dances. — **Fréjus** (Provence)

Fête des vins (2nd weekend). — **Gaillac** (Sud-Ouest)

Fête du vin et de l'amitié (3rd weekend): open day at the wine cellars. — **Gueberschwihr** (Alsace)

Fête du klevener (weekend of 15th). ☎ 03 88 08 02 49. — **Heiligendtein** (Alsace)

Fête du vin de Madiran (14th and 15th). — **Madiran** (Sud-Ouest)

Jazz in Marciac (1st two weeks): wine-growers organise event to coincide with the festival. — **Marciac** (Sud-Ouest)

Fête du vin de Jurançon (1st weekend). ☎ 05 59 21 30 06. — **Monein** (Sud-Ouest)

Fête du trousseau (3rd weekend every two years): open cellars, wine events, wine-growers dinner to celebrate the local grape variety. — **Montigny-lès-Arsures** (Jura)

Fête du vin de Buzet (2nd weekend). — **Nérac** (Sud-Ouest)

Festival des vins de Savoie (3rd Fri): programme of events introducing Savoie wines. ☎ 04 79 31 61 40. — **Notre-Dame-de-Bellecombe** (Savoie)

"Jazz, Wine and Cinema, Pauillac" (3rd Fri). — **Pauillac** (Bordelais)

Fête du poulsard (3rd weekend, alternates with la Fête du trousseau). — **Pupillin** (Jura)

Journée de l'Océan (last weekend). — **Quincy** (vallée de la Loire)

Fête des amis de Brouilly (last Sat): Huge picnic on the slopes of mont Brouilly. — **St-Lager** (Beaujolais)

Fête Art, artisanat et riesling (weekend after 15th). — **Scherwiller** (Alsace)

Nuit des grands crus du zinnkoepflé (1st Sat). — **Soultzmatt** (Alsace)

Fête du vin (1st weekend). ☎ 03 88 08 93 01. — **Turckheim** (Alsace)

September
Fête du Biou (1st Sun): a procession carries a giant bunch of grapes through the village, ☎ 03 84 66 55 50. — **Arbois** (Jura)

Vendanges à l'ancienne (2nd Sun): a procession of villagers in traditional dress parade from the church to château Pecauld. — **Arbois** (Jura)

Fête du vin de Cassis (1st Sun): ban des vendanges. — **Cassis** (Provence)

Fête du pressurage (last Sun in Sep or 1st in Oct): grape pressing using the old *pressoir*. — **Champvallon** (Bourgogne)

Fête des vendanges (odd-numbered years). ☎ 05 45 82 48 14. — **Cognac**

Marathon des Châteaux du Médoc et des Graves (Sat before the *ban des vendanges*). ☎ 05 56 5901 91. — **Médoc** (Bordelais)

Fête du Biou (3rd Sun): *see Arbois above.* — **Pupillin** (Jura)

Fête des ménétriers or Pfifferdaj (1st weekend): historical parade, free tastings at the *fontaine du vin*. — **Ribeauvillé** (Alsace)

Ban des vendanges (3rd Sun). — **St-Émilion** (Bordelais)

Foué Avaloue (1st weekend).

St-Père
(vallée de la Loire)
Scherwiler (Alsace)

Sentier gourmand (1st Sun): a series of tastings on a walk around the vineyard.
Fête des vendanges (3rd weekend).

Tain-l'Hermitage
(vallée du Rhône)
Vadans (Jura)
Vinsobres
(vallée du Rhône)

Fête du Biou (4th Sun). ☎ 03 84 66 20 01. *See Arbois above.*
Ban de vendanges (1st weekend).

October

Fête des vendanges (3rd weekend).

Banyuls-sur-Mer
(Languedoc)

Fête des vendanges (1st weekend).
Randonnée du vin nouveau (1st Sun).
Fête du vin nouveau (4th Thu): the dance of the vines and the blessing of the new wine.
Les Écrits Vins: a literary programme on the theme of wine.
Fête du pressurage (3rd Sun).

Barr (Alsace)
Beaujeu (Beaujolais)
Béziers (Languedoc)

Paulée de la côte chalonnaise (4th Sun).

Cairanne
(vallée du Rhône)
La Caunette
(Languedoc)
Côte chalonnaise
(Bourgogne)

Grand cochelet des vendanges (last day of harvest): wine-growers' dinner. ☎ 03 26 55 27 49.
Fête des vendanges (3rd Sun).
Fête du vin nouveau (2nd Sun).
Fête des vendanges à l'ancienne (2nd weekend) ☎ 05 57 32 41 03.
Fête des vendanges (3rd weekend).

Épernay
(Champagne)
Joigny (Bourgogne)
Jullié (Beaujolais)
Marcillac (Bordelais)

Fête du raisin (2nd weekend). ☎ 03 88 49 58 37.
Vendanges à l'ancienne au domaine de Carcher. (1st Sat). ☎ 05 58 98 69 27.

Marlenheim
(Alsace)
Molsheim (Alsace)
Montfort-en-Chalosse
(Sud-Ouest)

Fête du vin bourru (last weekend). ☎ 03 80 62 11 17.

Nuits-Saint-Georges
(Bourgogne)

Fête des vendanges (3rd Sun).
Fête du paradis (2nd Sun): wine tasting and outdoor events.
Auction of "grands vins du Languedoc-Roussillon", vineyard walks, tastings and other events (last weekend).

Obernai (Alsace)
Odenas (Beaujolais)

Saint-Jean-de-Cuculles
(Languedoc)

Vendanges à l'ancienne (3rd weekend: odd numbered years). ☎ 03 26 03 12 62.

Massif de St-Thierry
(Champagne)

Fête des vendanges (3rd Sat). ☎ 05 56 76 69 13.

Sauternes
(Bordelais)

November

Les Sarmentelles de Beaujeu (3rd Wed)
Beaujolais nouveau at midnight.
Tapping of the first cask of Beaujolais nouveau in the municipal cellars of the town hall. (midnight, 3rd Wed).
Fête des vins de Chablis (last weekend). ☎ 03 86 42 80 80.

Beaujeu
(Beaujolais)
Belleville
(Beaujolais)
Chablis
(Bourgogne)

Fête des vins (2nd or 3rd weekend). ☎ 04 74 04 41 87.
Pressing of the Beaujolais nouveau (3rd Thu): tasting of the local wine from 6pm. Cellar open day on Fri
Fêtes des vins de l'Auxerrois (weekend before 11th). ☎ 03 86 53 66 76. Admission charge.
Fête du Beaujolais nouveau (3rd Wed).

Juliénas (Beaujolais)
Pommiers
(Beaujolais)
Saint-Bris-le-Vineux (Bourgogne)
Tarare (Beaujolais)

December

Fête du millésime (1st Sun).
Concours des vins (1st Sun.): public tasting on Sat and Sun.

Bandol (Provence)
Villefranche-sur-Saône (Beaujolais)
Viella (Sud-Ouest)

Vendanges du pacherenc de la St-Sylvestre: (New Year's Eve) midnight harvest of air-dried grapes for sweet wine. Admission charge: book in advance by calling Les Producteurs Plaimont, ☎ 05 62 69 62 87.

Understanding and Tasting Wine

Soil and Climate

When wine-producers in France, or anywhere else, want to talk about all the natural elements of the vineyard, they use the word "terroir". It means the sum total of an area's climate, geology, geography and ecology, and the special character it brings to the wine produced in that locality. To make the best of a good terroir, the grower must understand its soil and subsoil, the aspect of its slopes and the particular grape varieties that will flourish there.

The Importance of the Soil

The history of the terroir begins with the ancient Egyptians and Romans, who marked the origin of their wines on the side of their jars and amphorae. The monks of the Middle Ages also noticed that the quality of the grapes they grew varied from one plot of the vineyard to another. In modern times, geographers and geologists have confirmed what the monks long suspected: the defining quality of good wine-producing land is its hydrology, the way it supplies water to the vine. Of course, there is no single, ideal type of soil: many different types can all produce Grand Crus. A single grape variety can also produce many subtly different styles of wine, depending on soil type and ageing method. The character of a Chardonnay comes out very differently in a Corton-Charlemagne, a Chablis and an Arbois.

Even an overview of France gives some idea of the great variation of soils and rock from region to region. Alsace's vineyards, for instance, are on a geological mosaic of schist, red sandstone and igneous rocks like granite and gneiss. Champagne's soil is chalky, whereas Burgundy's calcareous rock is intermixed with clay. Chinon and Bourgueil are particularly chalk-rich, while in Beaujolais we again find granite and shale. In the Rhône valley, the vines grow on shale and rounded, cobble-like stones, or *galets*, which are also characteristic of Languedoc, and Saint-Chinian and Faugères in particular. Médoc wines are produced from vines grown in a distinctive gravelly combination of pebbles, sand, flint and quartz which is known as *"graves"*. St-Emilion wines come from chalkier land, whereas the famous Petrus vineyard is on a weald of clay, which retains water extremely well.

A "Favourite" Type of Ground

A grape variety will only reveal its full potential in a place that suits it: marl and chalk for Chardonnay or Pinot, *graves* for Cabernet-Sauvignon and clay for Merlot. Gamay and Syrah call for granite, and Grenache prefers shale. Two wines from the same grape, but grown in different soil, may reveal discernible differences in colour and aroma. Wines from chalky ground stand out as mellow, smooth and "round"; clay, on the other hand instils a depth and strength of colour, and strong tannic character. The finesse and lightness derived from silica soil is as distinctive in its way as the bold robe of a wine from iron-rich ground. The pebbly, alluvial *graves* brings out the rich fruit flavours of a wine: if aged well, its rugged, emphatic tannins will mellow into a broad and aromatic palette of greater complexity.

Climate, prevailing winds and the bioculture of the area also affect the vines: the plants of the surrounding area, be they oaks, mimosas, pines or cypress trees, add and take away different soil nutrients. Even the colour of the soil is a factor. Dark-coloured soils, which absorb more solar radiation, are particularly suitable for red-wine varieties which need plenty of sunlight to encourage the assimilation of

Terraced vineyard near Cassis.

chlorophyll and boost the production of tannins. Pale coloured earth is better for whites. Sauvignon, for example, flourishes in the chalky marl of Sancerre whereas, in Corbières, the Grenache grape enjoys the shale-rich earth and makes excellent, dark-red *vins doux naturels*.

Just Enough Water

The vine is a Mediterranean plant and copes well with dry conditions; in fact, the traditional wisdom of the grower holds that vines need to suffer a little if they are to give good results. As the vine grows, it absorbs water through its roots and expels it through the leaves, a process known as evapotranspiration. The level of groundwater below the vineyard's soil will vary from one year to the next, and the lower it is, the better the harvest will be, as it is the shortage of water that stops the plant's growth and allows the grapes to start absorbing sugars. As the vines grow older, the roots push deeper into the well-drained ground in their search for water and nutrients, and as a consequence the plant becomes less vulnerable to hard drought or sustained downpours. Young vines, on the other hand, have shallow root formations; they are more likely to rot in an exceptionally wet year, or struggle for moisture in a long, dry season.

The Right Exposure

Wine-growers dread the hazards of extreme weather. Hail shreds the vine leaves and damages the bunches of grapes beneath them. An icy winter may kill off the plant completely, while a sudden rainstorm just before harvest can be the ruin of a good crop. Even a less dramatic change can have an effect. A year with lower than average sunshine means unripe grapes; a cold growing season results in a more astringent wine.

Growers usually plant their vines on hillsides, usually facing southeast: if it rains heavily, the water runs away down the slope, and of course growers can optimise the conditions of the terroir by improving its drainage. A good example of the complementary elements of a good terroir is the Bandol-producing Château de Pibarnon estate, planted on chalky land with blue marl beneath. Its southeast-facing slope curves round the inside of a cirque, which protects it from the force of the mistral. The grapes ripen slowly and the chalky soil gives them great tannic finesse in the bottle.

Soil type is crucial to the quality of the wine.

Varieties and Appellations

*"What is there in this bottle, Babette?"
she asked in a low voice. "Not wine?"
"Wine, Madame!" Babette answered.
"No, Madame, it is a Clos Vougeot
1846!" Martine had never suspected
that wines could have names to them.
(Karen Blixen, "Babette's Feast")*

The Science of Variety

Ampelography – from the Greek word *ampelos*, or vine – is the study of grape
varieties. These varieties, referred to in French as *cépages*, can be identified by
sight by their different shoots, flowers, early and mature leaves and the shapes of
their grape-bunches, as well as their development through the year – the emer-
gence of their buds, their flowering, and the colouring of their leaves in autumn.
Varieties also differ in their ability to resist an attack of oidium, mildew or grey rot,
or a parasite like phylloxera. One characteristic shared by all varieties, however,
is the fivefold nervation of the leaves: the patterning is clearest on the underside
of the leaf.

We know from Pliny the Elder's writings that descriptions of grape varieties played
a part of Roman cultivation, but although Olivier de Serres's *Théâtre d'Agriculture*,
published in 1600, does mention various *cépages*, it was not until the mid-18C that
the great Swedish botanist Carl von Linné, better known as Carolus Linnaeus,
published precise taxonomic descriptions of the different types of vine. By the
end of the 1780s, botanical collections had been planted in Béziers, Dijon and
Pessac-Léognan and, in the century that followed, the study of ampelography was
to spread from Spain to Russia. In 1951, the Office International de la Vigne et
du Vin produced a standardised code for assessing grape varieties which is still
the recognised guide.

The last 25 years have seen great changes in the distribution of varieties around
France. The viticultural map has been redrawn in the Languedoc, where growers
have planted Syrah and Mourvedre alongside their traditional Grenache and
Carignan. Some varieties, Cinsault and Folle Blanche among them, have fallen
out of favour, while others, such as Chardonnay, Sauvignon, Merlot and Syrah,
are grown in greater quantities than ever
before.

VARIETAL OR CUVÉE?

Varietal wines, or "vins de
cépage", are made from a single
kind of grape; famous examples
include Muscadet, Beaujolais,
Sancerre, Montlouis and
Meursault. Cuvees are made by
blending different varieties; they
include Bandols, Saint-Chinians
and Pomerols. Châteauneuf-
du-Pape can be made with
thirteen different types.
Traditionally, varieties are only
named on the label in Alsace
though Bourgogne-Aligoté
from Burgundy and Muscadet,
from the Nantes region are two
notable exceptions.

Not all grape varieties have the potential to make
great wines: growers make a formal distinction between poor, medium-quality or so-called
"noble" grapes. Only the last of these are used
for wines today, and these are classed in one of
two further groups. Those termed "cépages uni-
versels" adapt to different growing conditions
with relative ease and produce wines with consistent and identifiable character wherever they
are grown. Cabernet-Sauvignon, Cabernet Franc,
Gamay, Syrah and Merlot all belong to this category, as do white wine varieties like Chardonnay,
Gewürztraminer, Muscat, Sauvignon and Riesling.
Other *cépages*, including Chenin, Mourvèdre
and Pinot Noir, will only grow well in particular
areas, but these too may be considered "noble"
varieties.

Matching Variety and Terroir

The growers' and oenologists' choice of vines is in part made for them by the INAO's legislation, which determines which varieties are to be grown in the appellation region. Beyond this, all the factors of the terroir, and the quality of wine to be produced are crucial considerations. Early varieties can be grown in colder areas, while later ones need a long, hot growing season.

To get an idea of the range of *encépagement*, imagine a cross drawn over a map of France, from the Pas-de-Calais to the eastern Pyrenees, and from the north of Charente-Maritime, on the Atlantic coast, to Haute Savoie in the Alps. In the northwest quarter, which includes the Loire Valley vineyards, Gamay and Cabernet Franc are grown for red wines and Muscadet, Pineau de la Loire and Sauvignon supply the white.

To the Southwest, reds are made from Cabernet-Franc too, but also Cabernet-Sauvignon, Merlot and Malbec, while the trio of Sauvignon, Semillon and Muscadelle dominate white wine production. The northeast quarter, covering the great vineyards of Champagne, Burgundy and Alsace, grows Pinot Noir and Gamay for varietal reds. Burgundy's whites are made from Chardonnay and Aligoté, while an Alsatian white may be produced from Riesling, Gewürztraminer, Tokay-Pinot Gris, Sylvaner, Muscat, Pinot Blanc or Pinot Noir. Finally, the reds of Southeast France are made from Syrah, Grenache, Mourvèdre, Cinsault and Carignan and the region's whites from Roussanne, Marsanne and Ugni Blanc.

But how many more varieties could you name? The studies of the great ampelographer Pierre Galet cover some 9 600 grape types, making up 99% of the world's grapes, yet only 20 varieties account for around 87% of France's viticulture.

Red Varieties

Cabernet Franc – Well represented in the vineyards of the Southwest, Dordogne and around Bordeaux, where it is grown at St-Emilion and Pomerol, Cabernet Franc can also be found in Languedoc and in the Loire Valley, notably in AOC Bourgueil, Saint-Nicolas-de-Bourgueil and Chinon.

Cabernet Franc likes hot, sandy, gravelly soil. Its little bunches are made up of round, blue-black grapes. The young wine's cherry-red robe deepens with age; a strongly aromatic nose combines the red-fruit aromas of strawberry and cherry with liquorice or pepper; it sometimes has a little acidity to it, but its tannic character is invariably smooth and fine.

Cabernet-Sauvignon – The classic Médoc grape, Cabernet-Sauvignon is also cultivated in Languedoc and the Loire Valley. A late variety, the vine gives of its best in hot, dry soil like the gravelly mix of the Graves appellation: its little, deep-violet grapes produce wines with good ageing potential.

Pinot noir.

S. Sauvignier / MICHELIN

Its intense colour may range from dark ruby to deep garnet shades, and when under-matured can be recognised by its unmistakeable peppery aroma. A well-aged example, however, combines blackberry with tertiary notes of smoke and leather. Rich in tannins, these wines reward longer cellarage.

Gamay – The 36 000 hectares of Gamay grown in France include 99% of the Beaujolais vineyards. In Bourgogne it is combined with Pinot Noir to make Bourgogne-Passetoutgrain, and is also grown on the Loir around Vendôme, on the Côte Roannaise, in Savoie and in the Estaing, Entraygues and Fel appellations. An early variety, most at home in granitic soils, the Gamay vine produces blackish-violet grapes. Its light robe is a brilliant red with a blueish-purple tint. A strongly fruity nose, full of red fruit, combines with a lively, faintly acidic taste without noticeable tannins.

Grenache – Grenache covers almost 100 000ha of Provence, the Rhône Valley (Gigondas, Lirac) and Languedoc-Roussillon (Banyuls, Rivesaltes, Maury). It is often blended with Syrah and Mourvèdre. Resistant to dry and windy weather, it thrives on steep, shale-rich terrain and hot, dry, stony soil. Its black grapes grow in tight-packed bunches.

The intense red of younger wines tends towards dark brick or mahogany in older vintages and *vins doux naturels*. A ripe, red-fruit nose also has notes of spice, and a taste reveals a robust, round wine, rich in alcohol, which echoes the fruity, spicy character of the bouquet.

Merlot – The third most common red grape after Carignan and Grenache. It is most common in its area of origin, the Bordeaux region, and is particularly associated with Saint-Emilion, Médoc and Pomerol (Pétrus), but can also be found in Languedoc-Roussillon. This sturdy early variety is usually planted in areas of clay and chalk. Merlot grapes are blue-black.

Look for a garnet red robe and a bouquet which combines violets, red fruit, and spices, sometimes a hint of prunes or plums. Complex and powerful in the mouth, it is smoother when blended with Cabernet-Sauvignon.

Mourvèdre – Provence (Bandol), the Rhône Valley and Languedoc-Roussillon all produce Mourvèdre's close clutches of little, late-maturing black grapes. It lends structure to heady *vins de garde* which will improve with age for up to a decade. Mourvèdre is recognisable by its deep, dense colour, between crimson and dark purple. An intense, spicy aroma of forest fruit, blackberry and liquorice sets off a refined tannic quality, spicy fruit and a good, long finish in well-aged wines.

Pinot Noir – A noted Burgundian grape, it is also used, on its own or in a blend, to make Alsatian wine, Champagne, Rosé-des-Riceys and Loire wines from the Menetou-Salon and Sancerre appellations. Jura and Savoie also produce Pinot Noir. Its "personality" varies from one terroir to another, but the grapes are always the same in appearance: blueish black, in very tight bunches. The vine prefers chalky soil.

Whatever Pinot Noir may lack in vibrancy of colour, it more than makes up for with its perfumed aroma and good cellaring potential. A frequently powerful nose, where strawberry, blackcurrant and cherry scents predominate, is matched by a rich fruit flavour; after a few years of storage, the tannins mellow pleasantly.

Syrah – A fine variety with strong links to the upper Rhône valley, where its varietals and cuvees include Grand Crus (Côte-rôtie, Hermitage, Cornas). Saint-Chinian and Faugères are the names most associated with it in Languedoc-Roussillon. Like Gamay, it grows well in granitic soil, but it flowers and fruits late: the grapes are oval in shape, with a blue-black colour.

Syrah wines have a strong, dark colour and, being rich in tannins, are generally powerful. Their initial aroma is marked by spicy red fruit, with violet and pepper notes coming through.

White Grapes

Aligoté – A Burgundian grape, much admired in varietal wines from the Bourgogne-Aligoté and Bouzeron appellations, and in cuvées including the well-

Chardonnay grapes.

known Crémant de Bourgogne. Planted over 1 700ha in Burgundy, Jura, Savoie and around Die, the early-flowering vine should be grown on chalk. Its little round grapes are off-white with an orange tone, and flecked with brown.

Its dry, fresh, light white wines should be drunk young. Poured over a measure of crème de cassis, it makes a typically Burgundian aperitif. Its robe, pale gold or sometimes a light straw-yellow, has a fine green tint to it. Its floral bouquet of acacia or honeysuckle mixed with apple also has a mineral note to it. It tastes fruity, round and slightly dry.

Chardonnay – In its native Burgundy, Chardonnay makes refined *vins de garde* including Corton-Charlemagne, Montrachet, Meursault and Chablis, while in Champagne it is used to make blanc des blancs. It is also cultivated in the Loire Valley, Savoie, Jura and Limoux. At home on lime-rich or clay soil, as well as the chalky Côte des Blancs south of Épernay, it buds early, making it vulnerable to spring frosts, and bears little bunches of golden yellow or amber grapes.

The typical result is a nicely balanced wine which ages well and combines a brilliant, subtly green-tinted colour with acidity, intense, complex aromas and an all-round elegance. Tasters catch the scent of nuts, almonds, lime tea, toast and a faint aroma of butter, sometimes accompanied by honey or citrus notes. Depending on the nature of the terroir, Chardonnay may take on a mineral character, as at Sancerre, a more fruity quality in a Meursault, or even suggest a hint of woodland undergrowth in wines from the slopes of Corton.

Chasselas – A white variety grown in the Crépy and Pouilly-sur-Loire appellations, but is best known as a table grape called "Chasselas de Moissac". It is grown less and less in France, increasingly replaced by the Sauvignon grape, and now covers no more than 500ha, but produces enjoyable wine in the Valais and Vaud cantons of Switzerland, where it is known as Fendant and Dorin respectively. It is an early, delicate variety; its round, pale green grapes with russet speckles are used to make a dry white.

The wine's robe is very light yellow, almost transparent, with a hint of green. Depending on the terroir from which it comes, the lightly *perlant* young wine may have a slightly more floral or mineral balance, or a fruity or spicy quality.

Chenin – Also known as *pineau de la Loire*, it is the Anjou region's foremost variety, grown at Saumur, Vouvray and Montlouis. The whites produced may be dry, *moelleux*, *liquoreux* or sparkling: Coteaux-de-Layon, Quarts-de-Chaume, Bonnezeaux and Savennières number among the most popular Chenin wines.

This characterful variety will flower and fruit early, and flourishes in pebbly schist soil. Noble rot develops easily on its closely grouped golden grapes.

Dry Chenin wines are round and lively, and some will improve with age for up to ten years, by which time its pale yellow robe will have turned a rich golden shade. A very floral wine, with acacia notes to the fore and a suggestion of honey or quinces, it is known for its delicate and well-balanced flavours.

The sweeter wines are meant to be stored: their green-gold colour sometimes deepening to a warm amber. The fruit-and-flower tones of pear and may-blossom are joined by the aroma of polished wood. Expect an ample, developed flavour with the taste of exotic fruits in the finish.

Gewürztraminer – The celebrated *cépage noble* of Alsace produces comparable, strongly characteristic dry or sweet wines in the Moselle region. A hardy vine, early to flower, it comes into its own in clay soil, producing bunches of little, oval grapes in a pretty shade of pink.

Given time, golden Gewürztraminer wines take on a richer amber robe. The smooth, round taste is matched by an intense and elegant nose, and it is here that the variety lives up to its name, combining *Gewürz*, or spice, with lychee scents.

Marsanne – Marsanne is much cultivated in the northern Rhône valley where, blended with Roussanne, it makes some very fine wines: Hermitage, Crozes-Hermitage, Saint-Joseph and Saint-Péray. Many terroirs of Languedoc are also to its liking, and it is grown successfully in the Cassis appellation of Provence. It is vigorous and late-growing, but oxidises easily. Happiest in a mixture of silt and pebbles, it bears round, white grapes with a touch of gold.

The colour of a Marsanne varies from pale and faintly green to a mid-gold. The unmistakeable may-blossom in the nose of an early wine gives way to spice and honey notes and the scent of wax. It is marked by a sense of vivacity and "roundness" and, in certain well-aged vintages, a delightfully long finish that just goes on and on...

Muscadet – Originally from Burgundy, the Muscadet or melon grape was introduced to the area around Nantes at the beginning of the 18C, where it is now found in the appellations Muscadet-de-Sèvre-et-Maine, Muscadet-Côteaux–de-la-Loire and Muscadet-Côtes-de-Grand-Lieu. Here, its iodine character shows the influence of the shale soil and the Atlantic Ocean. As an early variety, it is vulnerable to a late frost, and it is also susceptible to disease. Its little grapes are a golden yellow.

When matured on its lees, Muscadet develops a slightly *perlant* character. It is conspicuously pale, with an iodine nose. The mineral quality of a young wine is joined by a bouquet of floral scents after a few years. Its taste is pleasantly light and lively.

Muscat blanc à petits grains – This is the variety which makes the sparkling Clairette-de-Die and sweet Muscats from Frontignan, Saint-Jean-de-Minervois, Lunel, Mireval, Beaumes-de-Venise, le cap Corse and Rivesaltes: it is an early grape which is best grown in pebbly soil and likes a hot terroir. For the production of *vins doux naturels*, the yield is limited to 28 hl/ha. The amber yellow grapes are closely clustered in long bunches.

Muscat wines are recognisable by their pale gold colour and a bouquet which combines roses, citronella, a touch of citrus fruit and a slight menthol note.

Petit Manseng – This variety is most at home among the round stones of Béarn, where it yields only 20 hl/ha but lends a mellow tone to Juraçon whites, and is part of the blend in wines of the Béarn, Irouléguy and Pacherenc-du-Vic-Bilh appellations. A vigorous and early vine, it may nonetheless fall victim to oidium and mildew. The thick-skinned little grapes are harvested by sorting or by *passerillage*. Petit Manseng produces rich and expressive wines, which may rise from 12% to 16% in strength. They have a golden robe, a nose of honey and cinnamon with ripe, peachy fruit, and a delicate quality on the tongue.

Riesling – The noble grape of Alsace par excellence! It accounts for almost a quarter of the region's viticulture. This late variety grows well on exposed slopes and is equally well suited to sandstone or granitic sand. The Riesling grape, a spherical, speckled fruit, may be anything from light green to yellow-gold, and grows in distinctive cylindrical bunches.

A good Riesling can be stored for ten years, or even longer, in which case its brilliant pale yellow colour, tinctured with green, will have had time to darken to a deep gold. Flowers, peaches, citronella and mineral notes predominate in a lively bouquet. A very aromatic wine, it has good balanced acidity and the vivacious keenness the French refer to as "nervosité".

UNDERSTANDING THE LABEL

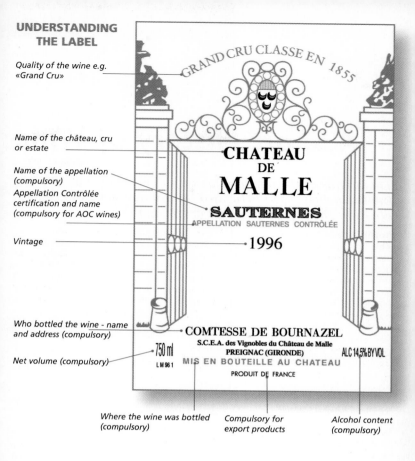

Quality of the wine e.g. «Grand Cru»

Name of the château, cru or estate

Name of the appellation (compulsory)

Appellation Contrôlée certification and name (compulsory for AOC wines)

Vintage

Who bottled the wine - name and address (compulsory)

Net volume (compulsory)

GRAND CRU CLASSE EN 1855

CHATEAU DE MALLE

SAUTERNES

APPELLATION SAUTERNES CONTRÔLÉE

1996

COMTESSE DE BOURNAZEL
S.C.E.A. des Vignobles du Château de Malle
PREIGNAC (GIRONDE)

750 ml

LM 961

MIS EN BOUTEILLE AU CHATEAU

PRODUIT DE FRANCE

ALC 14,5% BY VOL

Where the wine was bottled (compulsory)

Compulsory for export products

Alcohol content (compulsory)

Sauvignon – Although it originates in the Bordelais, Sauvignon is now far more widespread, grown for cuvees or varietals in Southwest France, the Loire Valley (AOC Sancerre), Provence and Languedoc as well as the Entre-deux-mers appellation. Vigorous and adaptable, the vine grows with equanimity in flinty clay, limestone and calcareous marl, bearing golden-yellow oval grapes in small bunches.

Sauvignon makes pale-coloured wines with a faint green glint to them. Though quick to take on the character of the terroir, which determines their robust or softer body, most have traces of blackcurrant and boxwood in their bouquet, often accompanied by a smoky character and sometimes with an accent of gunflint.

Semillon – Another Bordeaux *cépage*, it makes both fine sweet wines (Sauternes, Loupiac, Monbazillac), and notable dry whites (Graves), some sparkling: in both cases in combination with Sauvignon and Muscatel. A robust variety with a preference for *graves* and calcareous clay, Semillon is France's second most common white variety after Ugni Blanc (Cognac and Armagnac). Its round, whitish gold grapes grow pinker as they ripen.

Semillon makes a straw-coloured wine with a golden edge to it, and a discreet scent of dried fruit and honey, the latter being reflected on the palate. A big, powerful wine. A sweet Semillon is opulence itself: brilliant gold in colour with a bouquet of honey and citrus, round and well-defined to the taste.

A Look at the Label

Even before you open the bottle, you can tell a lot about a wine's provenance and style. French and European law insists on six items of information on the label. Most important is the name of the appellation followed, as the case may be, by the words "appellation d'origine contrôlée", "appellation d'origine, vin délimité de qualité supérieure" (AOVDQS) or the classification "vin de pays". Then comes the name and address of the bottler, the alcoholic content, the net volume, country of origin and a batch number.

Optional information includes the name of the vineyard, Cru or Château, a brand name, the vintage, grape variety, the colour of the wine, and any medals awarded at professional tastings. The label on the back gives advice on serving temperature, storage, suggested dishes to accompany the wine, and more about the grapes.

A Short History of Wine

The origins of the vine are lost in the mists of time. But the Bible tells how Noah cultivated the ground and planted vines after the Flood – and then got drunk on the wine...

In the beginning

The first images of wine harvests – In 2000 BC vines were a common sight in many of the gardens of **Egypt**. They were grown for their black fruit and also for their red wine, which was drunk at feasts and celebrations. The best wines came from west of the Nile Delta, Memphis and Fayoum. Tomb paintings show each step in the wine-making process: bunches of grapes being picked, the grapes being pressed by foot in large vats, fermentation of the wine in earthenware jars and finally consumption of the wine at a celebratory feast.

In Ancient Egypt, wine was aged in pottery jars with a straw stopper sealed with clay. The jars were each identified by an inscription on the neck which indicated the content, origin, quantity, year and names of the wine-maker and proprietor – the same information, in fact, that is shown on many modern-day wine labels.

From Egypt to Greece – The Egyptians taught the arts of viticulture and fermentation to the Greeks. As Phoenician trading posts sprang up throughout the Mediterranean – from Asia Minor to Gaul, Southern Italy and Sicily – so this knowledge spread. The best wines came from the Greek islands of Chios, Thrace and Samos, as well as from Capua and Falerna in Italy. The wine was transported by sea throughout the Phoenician Empire in amphorae similar to the Egyptian jars, but with 2 handles and a rounded base. Wine made from ripe grapes dried on straw was fermented in pithoi, large earthenware jars which were buried underground; this wine was diluted with sea water, flavoured with herbs, honey and spices and served at banquets.

Roman times – In around 200 BC, the Romans began to take an interest in viticulture and wine, even describing wine from Falerna, which took on a golden hue as it aged, as a Grand Cru.

The works of Pliny the Elder, Cato the Elder, Columella and Galen contain a mine of information on Roman viticulture, with opinions on vine varieties, vineyard locations, wine presses, how best to announce the start of the grape harvest, fining using egg white, fermentation and aging the wine in amphorae and *dolia* (large earthenware jars). The Romans enthusiastically built up huge cellars and Pliny recounts that a certain Hortensius left no less than 10 000 amphorae of wine on his death. Pompeii was a great wine-trading town and counted no less than 200 taverns. It was from here that

> **UNDER THE AEGIS OF BACCHUS**
> At Mas des Tourelles in Beaucaire, Diane and Hervé Durant produce Roman wine with the help of specialists from the French National Scientific Research Centre (Centre National de la Recherche Scientifique, CNRS). Inspired by Pliny the Elder, Cato the Elder and Columella, they have reconstructed a Gallo-Roman cellar and produce wines such as *turriculæ* (to the recipe of the Roman agriculturist Columella), *mulsum* (made with honey) and *carenum* (a sweet white wine). The grapes are trodden by foot, squeezed in presses similar to those used in Ancient times, then the juice is left ferment in *dolia*. As 2000 years ago, they stabilise and flavour the wine with plants, aromatics, spices, sea water and honey.

In ancient times, Amphorae were used to transport wine.

S. SAUVIGNIER / MICHELIN

Mosaic of Infant with Grapes (Musée de l'Arles antique, Arles).

Wine and Religion

The aphrodisiac qualities of wine are associated with fertility and rebirth and as such the vine has always been an important religious symbol. Ancient religions each had their wine God: the Egyptians had Osiris; the Greeks Dionysos and the Romans Bacchus. In the 1C AD, wine was adopted as a symbol by Christianity; Jesus turns water into wine at a Jewish wedding in Cana and shares bread and wine with the disciples at the Last Supper.

amphorae were exported to Narbonne, Toulouse and Bordeaux to be filled. It was the Romans who, tired of the amphorae's tendency to shatter, started using barrels to transport the wine.

French Wine

The Greeks, who established a colony at Marseille (Massalia), taught the Gauls the art of wine-making in around 600 BC. But it wasn't until the 1C AD, that Gaul passed from being mainly an importer of wine to being the largest exporter of wine in the Roman Empire. During the Pax Romana, wines from the Narbonnaise (Languedoc), Bordeaux and Rhône valley developed formidable reputations. Gaulish domination of the wine trade led Emperor Domitian to forbid the creation of new vineyards and to decree that half the vineyards of the Roman provinces be uprooted. In spite of this, the French vineyards prospered and extended along the Rhone Valley, to Burgundy and the Moselle. In 280 AD vine cultivation was again legitimised by Emperor Probus.

Archaeological excavations of Roman settlements in France have uncovered scores of earthenware jars, sarcophagi and mosaics decorated with scenes of the grape harvest. Pruning knives, amphorae and barrels (which were invented by the Gauls) have also been discovered. Many of these items are on show in the archaeological museums of Lyon, St-Romian-en-Gal, Narbonne, Istres, Nîmes and Cap-d'Agde. During construction work in Marseille in 1947 the remains of a commercial Roman warehouse used for storing *dolia* were uncovered. Some examples are display in the Musée des Docks Romains in the city. Archaeologists have carried out excavations in some of the great French wine *domaines*, including Molard in Donzère in the Drôme, the villa of Sauvian near Béziers and the Mas des Tourelles villa in the Beaucaire region.

From 1000 AD to the present day

The fall of the Roman Empire led to the decline of many vineyards. But wine production continued in the monasteries, where it was an indispensable part of everyday life, used in the celebration of Mass and for consumption at mealtimes. After the Norman invasions, peace returned, towns grew and churches and vineyards were established throughout France. The Church played an important part in the propagation of the vine and the advancement of wine-making techniques. From the 12C, Cistercian monks were responsible for the creation of renowned vineyards at Beaune, Pommard, Vosne and Le Clos de Vougeot.

The spectacular winepress at Champvallon, Yonne. The design dates from the 12C and it was built in the early 14C.

The Cistercians observed how the vines grew, pruning them, taking cuttings and grafting, and noticed how the colour and aroma of the wines were influenced by the soil, location and aspect.

By the Middle Ages, wine was a feature of everyday life: on the tables of the rich and poor, on the shelves of the apothecary and next to the sick-bed, in the Church and the Synagogue. Wine became a valuable economic commodity which could be sent further than ever before because of advances in transport. La Rochelle became famous for the export of wine and salt to England and Holland. At the beginning of the 13C, the region of Bordeaux was exempted by King John Lackland (1167-1216) from taxes on exported wines and the English quickly developed a taste for that region's wine.

The end of the Middle Ages and the Renaissance saw land reform which put vineyards into the hands of city-dwelling aristocrats and the bourgeoisie. The growth in the towns and cities – where the water was not always safe to drink – led to unprecedented demand for *vin ordinaire*. Cabarets and open-air cafés serving wine sprang up, to cater for the common people.

Agricultural and oenological advances made during the 18C form the basis of modern-day viticulture techniques: grape varieties and soil types were defined and the procedure for making champagne was established. The English opened important trading houses at the gates of Bordeaux for the export of red wine to Great Britain and white to Holland. After the French Revolution (1789), the largely aristocratic and ecclesiastically-owned vineyards fell into the hands of the peasants and middle classes and the *vignobles* took on something of the appearance they have today. The quality of the wine also improved.

Science enters the world of wine

The 19C saw the publication of numerous treatises on vines and grape varieties. Increasing industrialisation of the wine-making process led to vineyards being set up and expanded in the Languedoc, Bordeaux and the French colony of Algeria, where large quantities of cheap, poor-quality wine were produced. The advent of the railway meant that wine barrels could be easily transported.

Disastrously, the fungal disease oidium appeared in 1851 in Bordeaux, having come to France from America. This was followed by severe bouts of phylloxera (vine louse) and mildew, culminating in the destruction of almost the whole of the French vine stock in the late 19C. The scientists Pasteur, Planchon and Gayon, as well as explaining the science behind fermentation, recommended the grafting of French vines on to phylloxera-resistant New World rootstock.

The 20C was dominated by legislation: the government outlawed fraudulent labelling and laws were passed regulating viticulture with the aim of improving wine quality and limiting production levels. The *appellation contrôlées* were established by decree in 1935.

In the last hundred years, increasing mechanisation of wine-making has made it much more of a scientific process. The use of heating cables, aromatic compound chemical fertilisers, biochemical processes and the advent of cloning techniques has radically changed the way the industry operates.

Unfortunately the 20C also brought troubles to the French wine trade. French domestic spending on alcoholic beverages dropped from 12.4% in 1960 to 9.6% in 2002 and at the same time the consumption of alcohol went down by more than a third. There has been a huge increase in wine-growing regions throughout the world; vineyards now take up nearly 8 million ha. The New World vineyards of Australia, New Zealand, South Africa, Chile and California are producing more and more first-class wines. In the face of this unprecedented international competition and the domestic slump in sales, the French wine industry is undoubtedly feeling the pinch.

In spring 2004, the president of the INAO, René Renou, proposed reforms of the AOCs to respond to the crisis in the French wine trade. He proposed the creation of an *Appellation d'origine contrôlée d'excellence* (AOCE) which would be reserved for "luxury wines to long for and dream about". The *Appellation d'origine contrôlée* would be used on "easy-drinking, reasonably priced wines" and labels would indicate the grape type. These proposals would require a complete revision of all the appellations, backed up by a rigorous system of controls.

Despite these upheavals, wine-making is the second largest agricultural industry in France, with an annual turnover of 9€ billion and wine continues to be the country's principal foodstuff export. France maintains its position as number one wine producer in the world, just ahead of Italy.

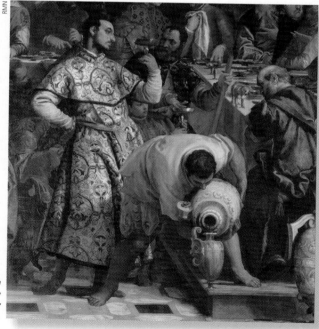

RMN

Detail from "The Marriage at Cana" by Veronese.

Wine Crafts and Professions

Vineyard in Vézeley.

From grafting the vine to pouring the first glass, dedicated experts ensure our enjoyment of wine. Each of them needs a knowledge and love of their craft, whether they are making a local vin de pays or a Grand Cru.

The People

Viticulteurs and Vignerons – The distinction between a viticulteur – traditionally a cultivator of vines – and the vigneron, who turns the juice into wine, has never been as simple as these definitions suggest. Modern-day vignerons need to play a part in the whole of the process, tending the plants, taking charge of the vinification and putting the wine on the wholesale or retail market. Most of their working day is spent in the open air, but they must put in long hours in the chais or the cellars. To do the job well, a vigneron needs to understand the soil and climate, and take the responsibility of being an owner, manager and his own boss. A 21C viticulteur needs at least a professional school-leavers' certificate in agriculture and farm management, and many study for a further technical degree.

Nadia Bourgne plays a full part in her husband Cyril's job as a wine grower, achieving professional qualifications in wine production and sales and marketing. Since the couple acquired La Madura estate in the Saint-Chinian appellation of the Languedoc back in 1998, Nadia's job has been to orchestrate their accounts and financial affairs, and the orders and shipping, to organise tastings and to keep up their working relationship with wine merchants, restaurateurs and other customers. As if that were not enough, she also lends a hand with the harvest, like everyone else. It took real entrepreneurial energy and courage to restructure the vineyard's varieties by planting Mourvèdre and Syrah, but their efforts have paid off with the production of well-balanced and hugely characterful wines. No-one is more pleased with the results than Nadia herself who, even after a long working day that revolves around the grape, likes to relax with her friends over a glass of red...

The oenologist – Official qualifications in oenology have been recognised in French law since 1955, defining its graduates as "scientists of wine" from its production to its storage. The Universities of Dijon, Montpellier, Reims, Bordeaux and Toulouse offer four-year degree courses which are renowned for their teaching of scientific and technical expertise.

The oenologist is far more than just a taster: he or she advises the viticulteur on the choice of grape varieties and the cultivation of vines, takes part in the vinification process itself, conducts chemical and bacteriological analyses of the grapes, both in their raw and fermenting states and passes on his or her knowledge to wine brokers and sommeliers.

The sommelier – A sommelier is in charge of the wine at a gastronomic restaurant, a wine bar or even a specialist delicatessen and wine shop, where tasks include not only choosing which wines to buy, but also monitoring stock and purchases, taking delivery of the bottles and maintaining ideal storage conditions in the cellar. In a restaurant, it is the sommelier's responsibility to keep the cellar book and discuss the best food and wine combinations with the head chef. All of this is done with one eye on value for money for the customer, who is the focal point of the sommelier's profession. Knowing how best to serve the wine – at the correct temperature, in the right shape and size of glass

– may seem simple, but these skills require a knowledge of Crus, vintages and varieties, an acute nose and palate, and an ability to be discreetly helpful and on hand.

The profession has come a long way from the status of the nobleman's *échanson*, the cupbearer or steward who had charge of his lord's linen and plate as well as his bread and wine. These days, a sommelier will have taken a formal qualification from a catering college. In 2000, the job joined the list of trades recognised in the Meilleur Ouvrier de France awards, given to top professionals in their fields, but competitions to find the best sommelier in France, Europe and the world have existed for much longer, as have the keenly contested regional titles. Among those to have made a name for themselves in the world of wine are Philippe Faure-Brac, Olivier Poussier, Éric Baumard, David Biraud, Arnaud Chambost and the 2004 world champion Enrico Bernardo. Although the roll of honour may suggest otherwise, the profession is by no means a male preserve.

Nor even a French one: the master of the cellars at the Michelin-starred restaurant La Tour d'Argent in Paris is an Englishman, David Ridgway. Most modern-day sommeliers would recognise his description of a fascinating and seemingly limitless professional world, a day-to-day life spent keeping track of wine legislation, balancing the budget, updating the list, working out a long-term buying plan for *vins de garde*, discovering new Crus and making weekly visits to the vineyards. Most, too, would agree that sommeliers and their wine-drinkers 'have never had it so good!' Contrary to the old stereotype, David comes across as modest and cultivated, a sound judge of character in the matter of customers as well as wines. He trains his juniors and advises his diners, dealing patiently with the occasional 'buveurs d'étiquettes', "label drinkers" who would rather have a status symbol on their table than appreciate the wine in their glass. Since 1986, he has held the keys to a treasure-trove of around 500 000 bottles, including a Chambertin 1865, a Romanée 1874, a Château-Gruaud-Laros 1870 and a Château-d'Yquem 1871, names and vintages to make any oenophile's heart beat faster!

The merchant – The professional privileges of a medieval Bordeaux wine merchant were generous indeed: exemption from excise and the king's taxes, the right to form guilds and even mint money. From the 17C onwards, the wine trader was at the head of a new mercantile class, distinguished by the prestige of an international trade in massive quantity. Nowadays, wine traders buy wine from independent producers, which they bottle when they judge the time is right. Some even produce their own cuvees.

Bottles of Champagne, from the Nebuchadnezzar to the quarter-litre.

From Cask to Glass

The barrel – The wooden barrel began to replace the heavier, more fragile terracotta amphorae and flasks of the Ancient World in the 3C AD. Modern day production may involve more precision engineering alongside the traditional work of the craftsman, but the design and principle of the wooden cask have remained almost totally unchanged. A boost for the industry came in 2004, when five workers from the Rousseau cooperage in the Côte des Nuits region were awarded the title of Meilleur Ouvrier de France. Between 1995 and 2000, the industry grew by 250% in France, as oenologists and vignerons began to rediscover the added quality of the wooden barrel compared to metallic containers.

Barrel-makers have been using the sessile oaks *(quercus petraea)* from the forests of Tronçais, Loche and Jupille, in the Centre region, for as long as anyone can remember. The slow-growing, fine-grained trees are much sought-after, and have more suitable aromatic and tannic properties than the common oak *(quercus pedunculata)*, but this latter variety is considered a good choice for the more naturally robust wines from the southwest corner of France.

To ensure that they work only with the best materials, most cooperages make the barrel from start to finish, beginning with the choosing and felling of the tree. The staves are split, shaped and dried before the machine tool stage. They are then assembled and given a first firing while the cooper checks the curve of the barrel. The second firing, the *'contre-chauffe'*, 'torrefies' the barrel, conditioning it for either red, white or rosé wines. Finally, the bases, or heads, are fitted, a bunghole is cut and water-tightness is checked.

Among the many different names for a wine barrel are those that describe its contents – *muid, demi-muid or foudre* – and others that vary with the regions. *Barrique* is originally a Bordeaux term, while a Burgundian barrel is a *pièce* or *feuillette*.

The bottles and the box – When it first appeared in the 13C, the word "bouteille" meant a leather wineskin. Unlikely as it seems, the credit for the first long-necked, cork-sealed bottles goes to the English craftsmen of the 17C. By 1730, glass bottles strong enough to store champagne were in common use and by 1735, the French royal court was issuing royal edicts announcing the correct shape of the champagne bottle and the official method of sealing the cork. The familiar model, with rounded shoulders and long neck, quickly became the standard before different regions began to diversify their shapes by the end of the century: Alsace developed the *flûte*, Anjou the *fillette*, Burgundy its *pot* and Jura the distinctive *clavecin*, not to mention the magnum and jeroboam in Champagne. The Saint-Gobain glassworks now produces around 4 000 million bottles a year.

Most bottles contain 75cl, but other sizes are half (37.5cl), magnum (2 bottles), jeroboams (4 bottles), methuselah (8 bottles), salmanazar (12 bottles), Balthazar (16 bottles) and Nebuchadnezzar (20 bottles). The sizes influence the development of the wines in the bottles: it is quicker in halves, but much less noticeable in anything larger than a magnum.

The new arrival, the wine box, is often referred to as a "Bib" in French. The vacuum-sealed plastic bag stops the wine from oxidising for several weeks and typically holds 3 to 20 litres. Wine boxes are unbreakable, recyclable and easy to transport: could this spell the end for glass bottles in the long run?

Corks – Drinkers, producers and professional appreciators are all divided on the subject of natural corks. Perhaps the only undisputed argument in favour of a "real" cork is an environmental one: only commercial cork-oak cultivation will preserve the rich natural habitat of the oak forests

A cork-oak can live for two hundred years or more, but cork can only be harvested after 25 years: bark grows by 1 to 1.5mm per year. Every nine years, in spring, a piece of oak is carefully taken from the tree. The area around Céret, in the Pyrenees, is France's main cork-producing region, but 54% of the world's corks come from Portugal.

Synthetic corks and screw-caps eliminate the problem of "corked" wine, but many producers insist that these solutions are more suited to young-drinking wines than *vins de garde*: the traditional wisdom, difficult to disprove, is that only a natural cork allows for the transfer of gases which is a vital part of the wine's maturation.

Glass and crystal – The technique of blowing glass is almost two thousand years old, but drinking glasses were a rarity until the 13C, when returning crusaders brought them home from Damascus. Then the wars and political divisions of 16C Italy made the country unsafe and unprofitable for peacetime crafts, and soon the French court imported not only precious Venetian glassware, but the glassblowers themselves, who set up workshops in Nevers. Fashions changed again a century later, when only pewter, gold and silver vessels were thought fit for a noble table, but Louis XIV's sumptuary laws brought glass back again.

In 1764, the Bishop of Montmorency-Laval petitioned Louis XV for the right to build a glassworks to compete with the glassware imported from Bohemia. By 1816 it employed 3 000 people and had installed the first crystal kiln; crystal production was to be one of the industrial successes of post-Napoleonic France.

For wine-lovers, however, the most famous name in crystal is that of a 19C Austrian manufacturer, Riedel. Today the firm makes over 80 different styles of glass: evocative names include "Bourgogne Grand Cru", "Champagne millésimé" and "Sauvignon Blanc". Each one is designed, with the help of oenologists and viticulteurs, to bring the best out of a particular wine, in the nose and on the palate.

Cork-oak bark.

From the Vine to the Bottle

Tending the vine demands care and effort in every season, but late summer's long ripening is the making of the vintage: the grapes, laden with scents and rich in sugars, are ready for their transformation to begin.

The Domesticated Vine

Left to develop naturally, the vine grows as a creeper, like the lianas of the rainforest and other members of the Vitaceae family. When pruned, its growth is brought under control, but vines trained up a wall can reach impressive sizes. The "treille du Roy" in the gardens of the Château de Fontainebleau covered 1.5km: the espalier-trained vine was a Chasselas.

During the growing season, the viticulteur trains the vine, and in winter he prunes it: the vine grows in diameter and becomes more knotty with age. In spring, buds appear on the vine-branches (or *sarments* in French), and from these grow the stems, their tendrils, leaves and flowers. Only 10% of these will be pollinated and turn into fruit. In August, the stems undergo a change; they in turn become branches, developing a bark. The spiralling tendrils wrap around anything that will support them.

A truly Mediterranean plant, the vine survives happily on only 500-600mm of rain per year, and needs this water most during the period of growth from April to July. A vine may live for between 40 and 60 years: younger plants produce large volumes of light, acidic wine, while older ones give a lower yield of more concentrated grapes.

In colder regions, early-fruiting varieties can be picked before the first frosts of autumn. The northern vineyards are more suitable for white grape production: black grapes need too much calorific energy, and therefore sunshine, to take on their full colour.

The art of making Champagne.

THE VIGNERON'S CALENDAR		
Winter	No vegetable growth between November and February	Trimming the branches Clearing the stones from the foot of the vine (*épierrage*) and protecting the base of the plant from frost with a covering of earth
Spring	Sap rises, growth of buds in March-April Blossoming May-June	Uncovering the foot of the vine Trimming and training the branches Trimming off the buds to concentrate production Ploughing to aerate the soil Harrowing out weeds
Summer	First development of the fruit *(nouaison)* in July Final ripening stage *(véraison)*	*Vendange verte*: cutting off some of the unripe bunches to limit the yield Cutting off leaves to give the grapes more sun Disease and pest treatments
Autumn	Harvest time in September-October	

Planting the Vineyard

New vines are always planted in springtime; but deciding "when" is easier than answering the questions "what?" and "why?" In both cases, the viticulteur is limited by regulations from ONIVINS, an organisation which ultimately answers to the French Ministry of Agriculture. New planting is only allowed during the restructuring of a vineyard, to improve production, for example, or to replace vines which have become too old and unproductive. Only the varieties authorised for local use may be planted and, in every case, the number of plants per hectare is regulated too. Ever since the phylloxera crisis of the 19C, almost all plants are the result of grafting and varieties propagated by taking cuttings, which preserves their individual characteristics.

The size of the vine influences the quality and quantity of the yield: vines are cut high or low, depending on the risk of frost and the richness of the soil. They may be pruned and trained to fit a steel-wire trellis, either "en cordon de Royat" with two equal branches running horizontally along the wire or "en Guyot", with one long and one short, or grown "en gobelet", with five or six branches without a wire support. This last method, more common in the Mediterranean, is less suited to mechanised farming and more work must be done by hand.

When harvest-time comes, the harvesters pick off the whole bunch of grapes. The bunch is made up of a stalk and the grapes themselves. The stalk is fibrous and contains, among other things, water, tannins and naturally occurring organic acids. The fruit itself is surrounded by an outer skin which is itself covered by a kind of waxy powder or dust. This substance, known as "bloom", or "*pruine*" in French, forms a water-resistant layer on the fruit and keeps in its yeasts. The skin contains elements which lend colour and aroma to the wine, the pips are rich in oil and tannins and the grape pulp gives a colourless juice made up of water, sugar and more organic acids. The percentage of sugars in the grape rises as summer draws on. When the grapes are ripe and ready to be picked, they change colour: this final stage of ripening is called "*la véraison*".

September: the moment of truth

Between the flowering of the vine, one hundred days before the harvest, and the *vendange* itself, important chemical changes take place inside the plant. These can make a big difference to the fruit it produces. A cold spring usually means a smaller crop. Too much heat will "burn off" the aroma of the grape by speeding up its growth. Old vines show greater resistance in hot weather whereas the grapes of a younger vine dry out, but wines gain in concentration when the grapes are subjected to a strong heat. The ideal recipe for aromatic grapes is sun, heat and a little humidity, but ice, storms and drought can be devastating. The correct temperature is most vital in August and September, just before the harvest, but even if these months go according to plan, it is vital to check the sugar content – and thus the ripeness – of the grapes before picking them.

S. Sauvignier / MICHELIN

The Organic Estate

The changing attitudes to organic food and farming over the last few decades has not followed the same course on both sides of the Atlantic, nor even among the nations of Europe: consumers' demands and producers' interests have brought different expectations to the trend towards sustainable farming, healthier food and drink and a healthier environment.

France and the French wine industry are no exception. Despite the long-acknowledged influence of a healthy terroir on the quality of the wine, growers have differed greatly in their approach to their soil, but the existence of organisations like the Syndicat international des vignerons en culture biodynamique have helped to make organic methods a viable and desirable possibility for producers.

Biodynamic farming – This approach to farming was first given a name and a systematic philosophy by Rudolf Steiner who, in 1924, published what was to be a prescient and influential work explaining his ecological system of thought. Stressing the importance of the soil and the natural environment, he recommended treating the cultivated plant with products from animal, vegetable and mineral sources, at particular times in the annual growth cycle, and stressed the importance of tilling and preparing the ground. The application of liquid herbal preparations, animal and vegetable composts and rock crystals in place of chemical herbicides and pesticides is current practice on many estates around France, and the positive effects of this "gentler" approach to the soil is reflected in insect populations, the local flora and the purity of the ground water.

Organic farming – Organic farming is similarly concerned with respecting the environment and protecting the quality of the land. Its mode of production is based on managing the microbiotic activity and balance of the soil, the recycling of organic waste and the protection of natural vegetation, like hedgerows and the uncultivated land around a plot. Chemical herbicides, fungicides, insecticides and fertilisers are not used: instead vegetable extracts and treatments derived from copper and sulphur are used to dispel pests and ward off diseases. The vinification process should involve as few preserving and stabilising elements as possible and limit the use of sulphur. However, far from being an invitation to "let nature take its course", organic farming means a greater investment in human effort as well as organic products and materials.

To be sold as an "organic product", the wine must be monitored and given a certificate by one of the independent, state-approved organisations set up for the purpose. European Union legislation rightly covers many aspects of food production, but the vinification process is not yet one of them. Wines may therefore only be described as "produced from organic grapes".

Visitors to an environmentally conscious French estate are almost certain to hear the term *"lutte raisonnée"*. The words literally mean something like "considered, measured struggle" in defence of the vine and sum up a move away from heavy-handed chemical cure-alls for blights and parasites. This ecologically responsible approach to cultivation prefers natural, biological solutions for pest and disease control. Vines are not routinely dosed: the grower only treats them when help is really needed.

The "Vendange"

The harvest is an exciting but anxious time for everyone involved with wine: until the grapes are safely gathered in, the year's vintage is still at risk from a sudden hailstorm or a torrential downpour out of the blue.

Although an institution of ancient origin, the "ban des vendanges", or official declaration of the start of the harvest, is more than just a quaint old tradition: it stops over-eager viticulteurs from picking their crop before it is ripe. The declaration now comes from the *préfecture*, the local governmental authority, but in certain areas the more visible indication of the "harvest banns" is a procession in traditional costume, still to be seen at Saint-Étienne in Alsace, during the Jurade festival in Saint-Emilion, and in Burgundy, performed by the Chevaliers du Tastevin.

When the crop is gathered by hand, the bunches are cut by the harvesters using secateurs, placed in a solid plastic carrying-box or a bucket worn on their backs, then transferred to a big grape-pannier called a *benne*. Harvesting machines shake the vines and gather the grapes while leaving the stalks. This method costs between a half and two-thirds the price of a manual harvest, but not all areas are accessible to machines, and some regions, including Champagne and Beaujolais, do not allow them to be used.

Wine Production

From harvest to fermentation – Once the grapes are picked, the stems are removed from red varieties. This process, known as *égrappage*, is common practice in almost every vineyard, except those in Beaujolais and Champagne. This method is used to make "softer", less tannic wines, but varieties which are naturally low in tannins, such as Pinot Noir, are all the better for being fermented with a part of their stalk.

Red grapes may also be pressed in a machine which bursts the grape without crushing the pips or stalk: the pressing mixes up the grape skins, juice and natural yeasts and helps to induce maceration.

Vinification consists in the fermentation of fresh grapes, grape must and grape juice. During this natural process, the yeast makes the sugars in the grape turn to alcohol and causes the mixture to release carbonic gas.

Making a red wine – In the case of nearly all of the grape varieties, the juice of the fruit is almost completely colourless. A longer or shorter maceration allows red or rosé wines to take on colour from the pigment in the skins of black grape varieties. Once the grapes are de-stalked or pressed, the pips, skins and in some cases the stalks are put in the fermenting vat with the juice. Sulphur dioxide is

The oenologists at work.

The vigneron tastes the wine at intervals until it is perfect.

S. Sauvignier / MICHELIN

added to prevent oxidisation and act on the fermenting yeast. Fermentation and maceration take place simultaneously. As maceration goes on, the percentage of juice in the mixture rises to up to 70% of the volume. Hours of maceration will produce a rosé and a few days will make a light red for drinking young, but *vins de garde* need two to three weeks of this treatment to take on the necessary tannic character.

During fermentation it may be necessary to displace the must which has settled at the bottom of the vat in order to dissolve more of the materials at the top, which will give the wine its colour and aroma. During this *remontage*, the must is run off into another vat and the solids are put into the press. The *vin de presse* obtained in this way may or may not then be blended back in, and the wine continues its malolactic fermentation which softens the wine by reducing its acidity.

Making a rosé – The only rosé made by mixing red and white wines is pink champagne. All of the others are produced in one of two ways. The first, called "pressurage", makes very pale *vins gris*; the red or pink tint of the grape skins colour the wine in the press, but there is no extra maceration.

The more common *"saignée"* method follows the procedure for red wine, but requires the wine-maker to draw off the juice after a few hours of maceration and separate the juice from the solid matter. The juice then continues to ferment at a low temperature, and the resulting wine is deeper in colour than *vin gris*.

Making a white wine – Making white wine starts with particularly careful harvesting. The vinification process is the same as for red wine, except that no maceration takes place. The grapes are put straight into the pressoir, drained and pressed. The grape juice is then separated from the solids – a process known as *débourbage* in French – and sulphur dioxide added to destroy the yeasts which do not play a part in the fermentation. Fermentation takes place at a low temperature.

Sparkling wine and the "méthode traditionnelle" – Until recently this process was known as "méthode champenoise" or the "Champagne method". Although there are now geographical restrictions which determine which wines may be referred to by this name, the technique is used in other parts of France as well. The grapes are picked with particular care and transported immediately to the pressoir before they have a chance to oxidise. The initial stage is identical to the standard white wine method. Then sugar and yeast are added to a blend of still white wines, and a second fermentation takes place inside the bottle: sugar turns to alcohol and carbon dioxide is produced. This development, which gives champagne its fizz, traditionally takes place in sloped, A-frame racks called *pupitres*, in which the bottles are held with their necks tilted downwards. Every day, for up to two months, they are given a quarter-turn and moved further towards the upside-down vertical. Finally it is time for the *dégorgement*: by freezing the neck of the bottle then removing its cap, the wine-maker can extract the yeast solids which have collected in the neck without losing the pressure in the bottle. After a top up of champagne and sugar, called *liqueur d'expedition*, the bottle can be sealed with a cork and wrapped with all its distinctive trimmings at the neck. After bottling, the wine may only be sold after a minimum of 15 months in the cellars.

VIN DOUX NATUREL

In the 17C, a Catalan physician called Arnau de Vilanova discovered a way of halting the fermentation of wine, but still retaining the aromas of the grape, by an admixture of liqueur. The method, known as mutage to oenologists, is used to make wines known as *vins doux naturels,* produced from over-ripe Muscat, Grenache or Malvoisie grapes. The grape juice, or "must" should contain more than 252g of sugar per litre. During fermentation, the wine is enriched with alcohol of 95° or more, in a quantity equal to 5%-10% percent of the grape must. Against all usual wine wisdom, these *vins doux naturels* are normally exposed to the air and, in the case of Banyuls or Maury, are even left out in the sun in glass containers. In fact, this unusual treatment lends them an interesting oxidised character and a wonderful colour with a hint of deep amber-brown.

Wine Production

Once the maceration has taken place, the wine is stored in barrels or vats which must be kept full to prevent their contents from oxidising. The amount of liquid lost by evaporation is known as ullage and the process of topping-up is referred to in French as *ouillage*, supposedly from the *oeil*, the "eye" or bunghole of the barrel. Wine is added once or twice a week.

The next task is to clarify the wine by removing any undesirable particles in it; this may involve the use of a filter or the addition of substances known as finings. The latter method dates back to Roman times and involves adding gelatine, egg-white or a substance called isinglass, taken from a fish's swim bladder, to the wine in the barrel. The impurities gather at the bottom of the barrel and the wine should then be racked, or drawn off, to avoid the risk of contaminating tastes or smells. A second racking takes place in spring and the third in the September after harvest.

Now the wine can undergo one last, delicate operation: the bottling process. The wine is drawn by gravity into a bottling machine and the filled bottles are given their label and sealed with a cork. Once the wine has rested for a while, it's time to taste it.

S. Savignier / MICHELIN

Mechanical harvesting.

Wine Tasting

"First, one takes the glass in the hollow of the hand, to warm it, then one swirls it with a circular motion, so that the alcohol may release its scent. Then one raises the glass to one's nose and gently breathes in. Then one places the glass back down and talks about it."
(Charles-Maurice de Talleyrand, statesman and gourmet, 1754-1838)

Pleasure and Discovery

What is wine tasting? Who can do it? And how do you start?

Wine tasting is a bit like a game; one that stimulates the senses, demands awareness and concentration, tests your memory, and can be taken more or less seriously. For a professional, tasting means judging in some way: appraising a wine's quality, evaluating its potential in a blend or ranking it among others as part of a competition. For an amateur, it can be a way of learning to notice more about what you're drinking, doing justice to a good wine by appreciating what is good about it, and analysing it purely for the enjoyment of doing so. David Ridgway, chief sommelier at La Tour d'Argent, is a real believer in the "convivial, relaxing side of wine; you shouldn't have to try too hard to enjoy it, or forget the pleasure of wine": a philosophy to which we can all raise a glass.

S. Sauvignier / MICHELIN

DIFFERENT TYPES OF TASTING
Describing a wine is easier when you have something to compare it to. A paired tasting means comparing wines in twos. Are they the same? If not, how are they different? For a triangular tasting, three glasses are poured: two contain the same wine. The three are tasted in random order, with no going back to re-taste. A vertical tasting means trying a number of different vintages from the same appellation and noting the way the wines change with age.

Putting it into words

Finding the best way to express a wine's impression and sensations is a question of taste in itself. A description of a wine, or the idea of describing it at all, might discourage or confuse one person, while another is enthusiastic and intrigued. Some wine talk comes across as over-scientific, too remote from our sociable experience of wine round the table; other tasters' free-associations sound exaggerated or too far-fetched. Taste is subjective, individual, and yet the experts seem to understand each other, know what to look for, and recognise the same sensations that their fellow experts find.

Judging a wine by its "robe": an important first step in the tasting process.

The taste experiences which oenologists draw on to express themselves are really no different from everyone else's, and are based on comparisons with things we have all experienced ourselves: the way our senses respond to fruits, plants, spices, materials or even places.

The four basic kinds of taste are the starting point. Sweetness is detected by the tip of the tongue, and acidity just behind and underneath the tip. The salt receptors are on the sides of the tongue, and at the back is where we sense astringency or bitterness. This is why it is important to taste from the right kind of glass, one which will guide the wine on to the tongue.

The recognition of scents, like that of tastes, is something we use in everyday life: the first step to improving your skill is simply to be more aware of it. Practice your ability to recall different aromas. Try thinking about the smell of fresh bread in a bakery, flowers in a garden, fruit or herbs in the kitchen, or coffee and chocolate. Practice at home with jars of spices. You can even train your senses with wine tasting scent kits, although these are only synthetic approximations, and tend to fade over time.

Organising a tasting

The best time to taste wine is before a meal, when the taste buds are best able to sense the wine's different qualities. Choose a room which is around 20°C and lit by natural light, or at least a light which will not distort colours. The tasting room needs to be free from the smell of cigarettes, flowers, perfume or food.

You should have a spittoon ready if you are planning to taste a large number of wines, but most tasters will not rinse their mouth out if tasting a series of similar wines. This said, some people find it helps to have some bread and water during the tasting. On a plain white tablecloth, set out transparent, non-coloured glasses, ideally ones with a tulip-shaped bowl and a long stem. Glasses this shape will allow the aroma to concentrate and will prevent the wine from being heated by the warmth of the taster's hand. Remember that too small a glass leaves too little of the wine in contact with the air and makes it harder to smell it properly. Once you have practiced a little, try tasting the same wine in different-shaped glasses; you'll find the experience, to the nose and on the palate, is not quite the same! Young wines should be opened one hour before tasting and left to stand upright, but an older wine should ideally be in a wine basket, in the same position in which it was stored in the cellar.

Tasting in Three Steps

Looking at wine

At a "blind" wine tasting, the label and sometimes even the shape of the bottle are concealed, so your first sight of the wine will be in the glass. Pour out a third of a glass and look at the wine. How would you describe its "robe"? What can you say about the intensity and brilliance of this colour? These first observations can tell you something about the vinification and storage of the wine as well as its age and its alcohol content.

Tilt the glass, at eye level, hold a sheet of plain white paper behind it and observe the wine's clarity. A wine should always be clear, but it may occasionally be opaque or cloudy.

Look at the wine at the top of the glass: a brilliant colour is a good sign, particularly in a white wine, when it is indicative of a wine's acidity, but wine can also be lustreless and dull.

What can you discover about its age? A white wine is pale, lemon- or straw-yellow when young and becomes more golden with age. If it is brown or brownish with age it is said to be maderized. Young reds frequently have an off-blue note to their cerise, garnet or ruby colour, but they may take on a hint of brown, orange or even mahogany. Rosés can range from pale *vin gris* – the lightest rosés with only a hint of colour to them – to a tint of peony red, but develop an orange, salmon or apricot shade over time.

A fine wine with concentrated flavours clings to the side of the glass when lightly swirled and then runs back down in fine drops: it is said to have "legs".

The aroma in the glass

Take the glass by the base and smell the wine while moving it as little as possible in the glass. Then lightly swirl it to aerate it and smell it again: some people close their eyes to concentrate better. Now swing the wine round the glass more vigorously before stopping it sharply with a reverse twist, thus "breaking" it. This releases new aromas from the wine, perhaps including some, like the scent of sulphur, which do not belong there.

Not all wines are strongly aromatic. Oenologists refer to primary aromas, characteristic of the grape type, and secondary ones, which vary in character according to the manner of fermentation. Tertiary aromas, those arising from the ageing in the barrel or bottle are known collectively as the "bouquet". Some varieties have distinctive aromas: Cabernet Sauvignon smells of boxwood, Pinot Noir is suggestive of strawberries, cherries and blackcurrants. In white wines these primary aromas usually fall into three categories: floral scents, recalling acacia, honeysuckle or fruit-blossom, fresh fruits such as apple, peach, pear or lemon, and mineral scents like flint.

Reds and rosés are often reminiscent of violets, roses, orange-blossom or peonies. Their scents may also call to mind a whole basketful of fruit and vegetable associations including figs, apricots, peppers, mushrooms or truffles as well as red fruits like cherry, strawberry, blackcurrants or mulberries, and spicy tones like pepper.

Secondary aromas are produced by the action of the yeast: tasters might identify banana, candy or boiled-sweet flavours, butter, candle wax, beeswax or wheat.

The bouquet of white wines is characterised by the scent of wood, honey and dried fruit and flowers. Red wine bouquets may have a touch of red fruit or preserved fruit, wood, game, spice (clove or cinnamon) as well as "balsamic" scents like pine resin, cedar and juniper, and roasted or burnt aromas of coffee, tobacco, cocoa, smoke, or toast.

Analysing these aromas is not easy, particularly at first. Sometimes it is hard to pick out any particular smell; at other times the scent "jumps out at you" and the identification is clear and immediate: Burgundy blackcurrants, or a flinty Sancerre.

Tasting the wine

Take a sip of wine and move it around your mouth, then open your lips, take a "sip" of air and inhale it into your nose, amplifying the aromas.

What are the flavours in your mouth? First sweetness, then acidity, then astringency. The qualities of the wine? Structure, balance, harmony and "length", the word used to describe the quality of a lingering but undistorted aftertaste. The taste should confirm the impression in the nose. It should allow you to gauge the alcoholic content of the wine, the smoothness of a wine, related to the presence of glycerine, sugar and alcohol, which can make it seem pleasantly substantial and well-tempered or else too thick and heavy in the mouth. A red wine is thin or robust. A white is dry, medium or sweet, these last two definitions being more general approximations of the French *moelleux* and *liquoreux*. The right degree of acidity is very important. When the balance is just right, the acidity makes a wine lively, but too much makes it seem undesirably tart and piquant, but too little leaves it tasting flat and uninteresting.

Finally, consider the wine's finish after spitting or swallowing. If the exact flavour persists pleasantly in the mouth, that is an indication of a fine wine.

Champagne:
a special kind of tasting

Much of this technique applies equally to appreciating a glass of champagne, but there are certain special things to look out for. Do not fill the flute completely. Take time to observe the colour of the champagne: is it pale straw-yellow or a deeper shade? Does it have a greenish edge to it? It may even be pink. Look at the size of the bubbles. The smaller they are, and the more slowly they rise up the glass, the better the champagne. Smell the champagne, then give it the lightest of swirls and gauge the aroma again. Can you pick out vanilla, rose petals, peach, citrus, honey or spices? Now taste it, holding it in your mouth but without rolling it around your tongue. Now swallow. Elegant, delicate, floral? You decide...

A wine tasting session in a cellar in Beaune: the tasters are using special wine-tasting cups, like the one shown at the start of the chapter.

Ph. Gajic / MICHELIN

Serving Wine

The beauty of the bottle and its label, the crystal glasses, the smooth white tablecloth, fine food and the company of good friends: all of these things add to the convivial enjoyment of wine.

An Art in itself

Opening the bottle

Wine may improve with age, but it does not become any less fragile after long storage: quite the reverse. The older the wine is, the more care must be taken when bringing it out of the cellar.

The next task is to open the bottle without disturbing the contents. The corkscrew, an invention for which the English wine-lovers of the mid 17C can take the credit, has been designed and redesigned in thousands of different ways, but nearly all have a 'queue de cochon', the "pigtail" spiral, and a handle. Some also have a knife or capsule cutter and a lever. Pulltap, Kalao and the famous cutler, Château Laguiole, are among the brand names favoured by some French sommeliers.

Cut the capsule just below the ring, remove it and wipe the top of the neck with a clean cloth, and screw into the middle of the cork without putting the screw right through the cork. Only *vins de garde* have a long cork. If you are right-handed, hold the lever of the corkscrew to the edge of the neck with your left index finger as you ease the cork out in a slow, continuous movement.

Now smell the cork. If you detect an unpleasant odour of must, the wine is corked: this is caused by fungus which has survived the sterilisation of the cork. If the cork does not smell bad, wipe the neck of the bottle again and, to prevent drops of wine staining your tablecloth, insert a non-drip pourer into it.

If the cork gets stuck in the bottle and breaks off, try to reinsert the corkscrew at an angle and then pull carefully. If this doesn't work, push the cork down into the bottle, but make sure you don't spray wine over yourself, or anyone else. This method of opening a wine doesn't alter its flavour, but it is one more reason to have a decanter at the ready. If sealed with a vacuum-sealing cork, any leftover wine in a bottle will keep for at least 48 hours.

Champagne

Of course, if you find yourself without a corkscrew, you may have no choice but to drink champagne! The most theatrical and dangerous way to open a bottle of champagne is with a cavalry sabre, slicing through the cork where its mush-room bulb meets the mouth of the

An elegant and practical way to serve wine (carafes from the Cristallerie de Bayel).

Red wine in a wine basket.

bottle and allowing the pressure of the wine to push out the base. Expensive and hazardous to practice, this party-piece should only be attempted by the experienced.

The more conventional method involves tearing off the capsule, unwrapping the cork from the iron wire *"muselet"* holding it in place, holding the cork with your thumb and turning the bottle, not the cork, with your left hand. Always make sure that the bottle is pointing towards the wall, at an angle of 45 degrees. Serve the champagne immediately, holding the bottle at the bottom and filling each glass gradually, with two or three pours, so that they do not overflow. A special kind of cork, which compresses the air, can be used to reseal a bottle of champagne and keep in its effervescence.

Decanting wine

Over many years, the question of whether or not it is necessary to decant wine has become confused by questions of status and etiquette. Decanting is only really necessary when there are deposits in the bottle. These may form in older wines, particularly those reds which are particularly rich in tannins. Decanting oxygenates a tannic red wine by exposing it to the air as much as possible. As white wines are usually free of these deposits, with the exception of some in which tartar crystals may form during storage in the refrigerator, and whites are not tannic, it seems unnecessary to decant them.

Decant your bottle by pouring the wine slowly but steadily into a carafe held at an angle, stopping as the sediment reaches the neck. A lighted candle or a torch may be held under the neck to illuminate it and help the pourer see more clearly. Some sommeliers use a funnel and a piece of muslin to filter the wine.

The wide base of the carafe allows the wine to breathe, its long neck holds the aromas and the glass, or crystal, sets off the colour of the wine.

Wine Temperatures

These are given as a guide only. It is not uncommon for reds to be served too warm and whites too cold, which does not show them at their best.

16 to 18°C Mature, tannic reds
14 to 16°C Younger reds
13 to 15°C Red *vins doux naturels*
12 to 14°C Young, light reds
11 to 13°C Dry white wines, champagne, rosé, red *primeurs*
8 to 9°C *Vins liquoreux*; light, dry whites; sparking wines
8°C White *vins doux naturels*
6°C *Vins liquoreux*

A young *grand vin* (two to four years) will benefit from being decanted two to three hours before the meal: during this time, the tannins will soften and the bouquet will become fuller and more enjoyable. On the other hand, an older vintage, particularly a burgundy, may lose some of its bouquet: it's much better to leave it in the bottle, which should be opened only a few minutes before serving.

The perfect temperature

Serving wine at the correct temperature is not just a point of wine etiquette, it's a vital part of appreciating the delicate components of a wine. If it is too cold, it will be harder to appreciate the bouquet in all its breadth and character and the acidity will seem disproportionately strong. Too warm, and the alcoholic taste of the wine tends to drown out the other flavours. In any case, your bottles should leave the cellar some hours before they are due to be served and should be kept as still as possible during that time.

A Chavignol goat's cheese and a glass of Sancerre make a perfect combination.

It is worth remembering that, once at the table, the wine will increase in temperature by one or two degrees, or more in summer.

If you want to be sure of serving wines at precisely the right temperature, you might consider investing in a wine thermometer. Whites and rosés should be kept in a champagne bucket filled with cold water rather than packed with ice. You should never put champagne, or any other wine, in the freezer compartment, and once a bottle has been put in the refrigerator, it is best to leave it there until the day it is to be opened.

As a guide, remember that young wines are served colder than old ones: to chill a young red, place the bottle in a bucket of cold water. A wine is said to be "chambré" – at room temperature – at 18°C.

Fine glasses for fine wines

For those who could afford them, wine glasses began to be widely used in the 17C. Two hundred years later, they had become part of the formal dinner service, and it was this grand era of social etiquette which originated the custom of arranging different glasses by size according to the drink, from water by way of red wine to liqueurs. During the 20C, different shapes of glass became increasingly associated with different regions: a long green stem and a round bowl in Alsace, a generously rounded bowl narrowing at the top in Burgundy, the classic tulip form of Bordeaux and the narrow Champagne flute.

A brilliant, perfectly transparent crystal glass seems literally to cast new light on the wine, magnifying all the nuances of its colour. The shape and finesse of the glass can alter the way we experience the combination of bouquet, flavours, acidity and tannins.

The bowl of the glass should be wide and round enough to allow the aromas to open up properly when you swirl the wine in it. The glass also needs to be large enough for you to be able to smell the wine as your lips touch it. And for the wine purist, an elegant, slender stem is all part of the aesthetic appreciation!

Baccarat, Saint-Louis, Cristalleries royals de Champagne, Cristal de Sèvres, Daum, Lalique and Riedel are among the major glassmakers who produce superb, mouth-blown wine glasses. When investing in fine wine glasses, it is a good idea to test them, so far as you can in a shop: lift them up, turn them around in your hand and go through the motions of drinking with them. Test several, and you'll probably find that one or two styles feel less stable, too heavy or too narrow.

The best way to look after your glasses and carafes is to wash them by hand, in very hot water but without any liquid soap or other cleaning products. As soon as they have dripped dry, wave them gently to and fro through the steam from a pan or kettle: this helps to keep them shiny. Then wipe them with a canvas cloth washed in boiling water and used only for wiping glassware. The best way to store glasses is hanging upside down, to stop them retaining dust or odour.

Food and wine

A time and place for everything

If you are serving more than one wine with a meal, there are a few practical things to remember if you want to avoid overpowering your taste buds. A young red or a lighter Grand Cru should be served before a richer one. In general, younger wines come before older ones, dry wines before sweet ones and whites before reds. If you're serving fish, white wines are usually a sound choice; reds traditionally accompany red meat. If all of these rules have their own flavourful and successful exceptions, there is one other which you should always keep to: each new wine should be a delicious improvement on the last.

Simple food and sumptuous wines

A cook can plan a meal in one of two ways, choosing wines which will go well with the cuisine or preparing dishes which will suit the wines. One way of planning a menu is to pair simple wines with more complex dishes and vice versa. Another, an even more sure-fire success, is to compose a meal by region.

A region in harmony – Wines and food from the same area – from the same terroir – nearly always bring the best out of each other. Try a cassoulet with a Madiran or Fitou, foie gras with Gewürztraminer, Sauternes or Jurançon, *magret de canard* with a Tursan, oysters and Picpoul-de-Pinet, entrecote bordelaise with St-Emilion, *boeuf bourguignon* and a Volnay, chicken à la basquaise with an Irouléguy, grilled andouillette with Chablis, bouillabaisse and a white from Cassis, Alsatian *choucroute* with a Pinot Blanc, a crottin de Chavignol goat's cheese with a Sancerre, Sainte-Maure, a Touraine goat's cheese, with a Cour-Cheverny, tarte Tatin and a Saumur-Champigny, and strawberries with a red Bergerac.

The perfect menu – As these examples show, it would be easy to plan a meal with a different glass of wine accompanying each course, moving from light, acidic wines to rich, tannic ones, and even finishing off with an Armagnac, a Calvados or an eau-de-vie. Although this would be difficult to do at home, many French restaurants make this sort of *tour de force* a point of gastronomic pride.

Wine in a culinary classic: coq au vin.

J. Damase / MICHELIN

What to drink with ... Shellfish: a dry white wine like a Sylvaner, a Riesling, an Entre-deux-mers, a Chablis, a Mâcon-Villages, St-Joseph, Cassis, Palette, Picpoul-de-Pinet, Muscadet or Montlouis.

Fish: again, a dry white, perhaps a Riesling, a Pessac-Léognan, a Graves, Meursault, Chassagne-Montrachet, Hermitage, Condrieu, Bellet, Bandol, Patrimonio, Coteaux-du-Languedoc, Sancerre, Menetou-Salon.

Poultry or charcuterie: red or a light white. Try a Tokay-Pinot Gris, Pinot Noir d'Alsace, Coteaux-Champenois, Côtes-de-Bourg, Côtes-de-Blaye, Côtes-de-Castillon, Mâcon, Beaujolais-Villages, St-Romain, Tavel (a rosé), Côtes-du-Ventoux, Faugères, Coteaux-d'Aix-en-Provence, Ajaccio, Corse-Porto-Vecchio, Anjou or Vouvray.

Red meat: Médoc, St-Emilion, Buzet, Volnay, Hautes-Côtes-de-Beaune, Moulin-à-Vent, Morgon, Vacqueyras, Gigondas, Bandol, Côtes-de-Provence, Fitou, Minervois, Bourgueil or Saumur.

Game: a full-bodied red such as a Pauillac, St-Estèphe, Madiran, Pommard, Gevrey-Chambertin, Côte-Rôtie, Cornas, Corbières, Collioure or Chinon.

Salad: traditionally wines are not served with dressed salads, as the conflicting tastes of wine and vinaigrette disagree with one another. As with all such rules, there are exceptions, but most sommeliers would recommend a fine (French!) mineral water.

Cheese: a white or a red wine, but avoid heavily tannic reds, as the combination of full-fat cheese and tannins can be unpleasant to the taste. Try a Gewürztraminer (with Munster cheese), St-Julien, Pomerol, Margaux, Pouilly-Fuissé, Santenay, St-Amour, Fleurie, Hermitage, Châteauneuf-du-Pape, St-Chinian, a *vin jaune* from the Jura (with a Comté cheese from the same region), Pouilly-Fumé or a Valençay. In a rare example of the influence of British taste, you may well be offered a port or Banyuls with blue cheese. Dry white wines, on the other hand, are generally excellent with goat's cheese.

Desserts can only be improved by a good dessert wine: try a Muscat-d'Alsace, Crémant-d'Alsace, white or rosé champagne, Sauternes, Monbazillac, Jurançon, Crémant-de-Bourgogne, a vin de paille, Cerdon, Muscat-de-Beaumes-de-Venise, Banyuls, Maury, any Muscat, a Limoux, Coteaux-du-Layon or Bonnezeaux. Red *vins doux naturels* such as Maury or Banyuls go deliciously with chocolate.

When cooking with wine, the golden rule is to serve the wine that was used in preparing the dish. If you are planning to serve a Grand Cru, then use a less distinguished wine of the same region in the recipe. Once you have finished cooking, add a little drop of the wine to the dish: you'll find it brings out the flavours superbly.

BRIDGEMAN / GIRAUDON

Great dinners and everyday pleasures

"A drink for the king!"

In the days of the French monarchy, high fashions in food, wine and etiquette, as in everything else, often followed the king and court, although royal tastes were often surprisingly frugal. When King Louis XIV dined in company, his cupbearer would fetch his plate, cutlery and carafe of wine and water from the buffet. It was not until the reign of his successor, Louis XV, that bottles, in individual buckets, appeared before the royal diners. The custom was keen enough for a courtier at the King's château in Choisy to record that "the King was graciously pleased to serve several glasses of wine to Monseigneur the Archbishop of Paris, as the bottles were on the table". The wine buckets also allowed the diners to rinse out their glasses between drinks.

At Louis XVI's *grand souper*, the King would be presented with a single bottle of still wine from Champagne, on ice, followed by a bottle of Clos-Vougeot. This selection never varied, from one meal and season to the next, and nor did the manner of service: the king would pour himself a single glass and then pass the bottle to the other diners at table, and would take a small glass of Madeira with dessert.

Napoleon was no lover of leisurely gastronomy, regarding time at the table as wasted. The Emperor would take lunch alone and dine with the Empress Josephine, yet even he kept up the form and grandeur of the Ancien Régime banquet. Little record survives of the dishes served at these Imperial dinners, but we know that the guest of honour was fond of a glass of Chambertin.

The glory days of gastronomy

The Exposition Universelle, held in Paris in 1867, drew many of the crowned heads of Europe to the French capital. In June, Wilhelm I, King of Prussia and later the German Kaiser, invited Alexander II, Tsar of all the Russias, the Tsarevich

"The Wedding Banquet at Yport", by Albert-Auguste Fourie (Musée des Beaux-Arts de Rouen).

Alexander, the future Alexander III, and Bismarck to dinner at the Café Anglais. The meal was to be a truly memorable one, later to go down in culinary history as The Dinner of the Three Emperors.

The chef of the Café Anglais, Adolphe Dugléré, had trained under the great Antonin Carême, who had been the head of many royal kitchens, including the Prince Regent's. Acclaimed as "The Mozart of cuisine", the Bordeaux-born Dugléré was in fact no *enfant terrible*. Described by one contemporary as "a taciturn artist who revelled in contemplative isolation", he nonetheless composed menus on a typically splendid Second Empire scale.

Dugléré's kitchen prepared a rich potage à l'Impératrice and a potage Fontanges, made with consommée, peas and sorrel; a soufflé à la reine, sole à la vénetienne – in a white sauce with tarragon and other herbs; a saddle of lamb à la bretonne – with a bean purée; poulet à la portugaise; a warm quail terrine; a cold truffled lobster "parisienne" and Champagne sorbets. These were followed by duck à la rouennaise, canapés of ortolan (bunting) with aubergine, asparagus and a casso-lette princesse. They finished with bombes glacées.

Claudius Burdel's selection of wines earned the *maître de cave* the patronage of all three of the royal diners, who made him their buyer by appointment. The wines served included an 1810 Madeira, an 1821 sherry, an 1846 Chambertin, the 1847 vintages of Châteaux Margaux, Yquem and Latour and a Châteaux Lafite from 1848.

Sadly, we will never know exactly how the Emperors' wines must have tasted. The list is a snapshot in time. It not only confirms the pedigree of some of the most enduringly famous names in the world of wine but also reminds us of how much that world has changed since the days before phylloxera. In 1867 that destroyer of traditional wine-growing, still unidentified, had not spread beyond the lower Rhône, and the wealth and patience of the wine market had yet to be depleted by the social cataclysm of the World Wars, before it was in turn transformed and reinvigorated by the world wine revolution of the last decades.

"À Votre Santé!"

Wine has been used for the treatment of a variety of ills since Ancient times. More recently, numerous scientific studies have pointed to the health benefits of regular (moderate) consumption of good quality wine.

"Wine is the most healthful and most hygienic of beverages", Louis Pasteur (1822-1895)

The Ancient Egyptians recognised the medicinal and antiseptic virtues of wine: the Edwin Smith papyrus explains how to heal an open wound using a balm prepared with wine and honey. In Ancient Greece, Hippocrates (c 460-c 375 BC) prescribed white wine for the treatment of diuretic conditions and red wine for the treatment of diarrhoea. Claudius Galen (c AD 130-c 200), physician to the Roman Emperor Marcus Aurelius, treated gladiators' injuries by washing them with wine.

In the Middle Ages, wine was used as a disinfectant and in the preparation of numerous remedies. A 13C herbalist advised that those wishing to eliminate body odour should wash with wine and rosewater. Aniseed and sage wines were recommended to aid the digestion. The famous Medical School of Salerno pronounced: "[Who] would not be sea-sick when seas do rage, Sage-water drink with wine before he goes". This preparation was also recommended for the treatment of anxiety, trembling hands and fever.

In the 17C, Guy Patin, Professor at the Royal College of Pharmacy and Anatomy, regarded consumption of *vin cuit* as the ideal way to settle the stomach. Under Louis XV, the Duke of Richelieu drank a glass of Bordeaux with each meal to prevent intestinal troubles.

In recent years, regular consumption of a moderate amount of wine has been advocated for the prevention and cure of a number of health problems.

WINE THERAPY

Among the vineyards of Chateau Smith-Haut-Lafitte, the Spa de Vinotherapie Caudalie offers beauty treatments founded on the health benefits of wine. Here you can enjoy red wine baths, a "Sauvignon" massage, or a honey and wine body wrap while sipping on a red wine infusion. The antioxidant properties of the polyphenols found in wine, together with the benefits of the local spring water – which is rich in iron, fluoride and sulphur – combine to help fight against the effects of free radicals, responsible for 80% of the ageing of the skin. Wine polyphenols and resveratrol, a compound found largely in the skins of red grapes and recognised for its effect on the elasticity of the skin, are used in Caudalie's range of beauty products.

The French Paradox

In 1990 an article appeared in *Health* magazine which put forward the baffling observation that the French, while famous for their rich cuisine (eg foie gras, cassoulet, confit de canard) and good wine, experienced very low levels of cardiovascular disease. Research by the American cardiologist Arthur Klatsky revealed that those who consumed a moderate amount (2-3 glasses a day) of tannic red wine (Bordeaux and other wines from southwest France) had a lower incidence of cardiovascular disease than those who drank no wine at all. He reported that this was due to the remarkable antioxidant action of the polyphenols present in the wine.

What's in wine? – Wine contains 80-90% water and around 1 000 other components, including alcohol, polyphenols (tannin, anthocyanin and flavonoids), acids, minerals (including potassium and sodium), vitamins and trace elements (including copper, zinc and manganese). In fact, the composition of wine has been found to be similar to that of the gastric juices thus promoting digestion of proteins and fat. The presence of resveratrol – known to stimulate cell multiplication – may also protect the body against certain cancers. Studies have indicated that moderate consumption of wine increases good cholesterol and lowers blood-clotting levels and, for people over 65, a regular glass of wine has been shown to reduce the onset of senile dementia and Alzheimer's disease. And as the physicians of Antiquity suspected, wine has powerful anti-bacterial properties.

Wine and Weight Loss – For more than thirty years, the French cordon bleu chef Michel Guérard has advocated that gastronomy and dietetics should go hand in hand. At his restaurant in Eugénie-Les-Bains, southwest France, diners are encouraged to enjoy a single glass (10cl) of wine as part of the "slimmers" menu". The chef at the Sources de Caudalie Spa *(see above)* uses Bordeaux to bring rich flavour to dishes which are still low in calories. According to a Danish study, wine drinkers suffer far fewer obesity-related health problems than do those who drink beer and spirits. The calorie content of wine compares well with beer and spirits: a 10cl glass of red wine at 12% contains 89.5 kilocalories, a glass of rosé 86.8 kilocalories, a glass of white wine 86.4 kilocalories and a flute of champagne 80.6 kilocalories. It is said that when Marlene Dietrich wanted to lose a little weight, she took to a diet of yoghurt and champagne!

Drinking and driving

Driving under the influence of alcohol is a serious offence in France. The police have the right to check the level of alcohol in the blood of anyone driving a vehicle, either by conducting a blood test or by using a breathalyser. Note that there is as much alcohol in a 10cl glass of wine at 12% volume as there is in a 25cl glass of beer at 5% volume or a 2cl measure of spirits. Each "glass" increases the level of alcohol by around 0.2g per litre of blood. For drivers, the blood/alcohol limit is 0.5g per litre of blood or 0.25mg per litre of expired air. Drivers who refuse to give a breath test are treated in the same way as would be a driver with a level equivalent to or higher than 0.8g per litre of alcohol in the blood. Drink driving offences are usually punishable by a fine (up to a maximum of €4 500), disqualification from driving and up to two years' imprisonment.

THE PHYSIOLOGICAL EFFECTS OF ALCOHOL

Alcohol...
...narrows the field of vision
...can cause dizziness
...alters judgement of distances
...affects the reflexes
...reduces concentration levels
...has a disinhibiting effect.
Someone in good health metabolises 0.1g-0.15g of alcohol per hour.

S. Sauvignier311/MICHELIN

Tours of the Wine Regions

Alsace

After such a troubled past, it seems only right that Alsace should live out its pleasures to the full, enjoying its position at the heart of modern-day Europe, whilst remaining true to its time-honoured traditions. The Alsatian wine-producing region is remarkable for the diversity of its varieties of grape vines which produce highly distinctive wines. However, its delightful flower-decked villages and row upon row of vineyards, lined up as if on parade across the foothills of the Vosges mountains, also bear witness to a longstanding tradition of hospitality which its wine-growers are keen to uphold. Here, the cellar is much more than just a place to store or buy wine; it is a place where enthusiastic wine-growers take the time to explain the distinctive character of each individual wine. Alsace's vineyards, which date back to Roman times, owe much to the loving care of the region's monasteries, but it was not until after the Second World War that today's quality regulations were applied across the board. The systematic planting of noble varieties of vines was sanctioned in 1962 by the creation of an Alsace AOC, after which time it became mandatory to bottle wine in the region in which it was grown. The distinctive qualities of Alsatian wines were rewarded in 1975 with the creation of an Alsace Grand Cru AOC awarded to fifty or so terroirs with precise geological and climatic characteristics.

The terroir

Michelin Local Map 315 – Bas-Rhin (67) and Haut-Rhin (68)
Surface area: 15 000 hectares stretching from north to south along a strip of land 120km long and 2 to 5km wide, 40% of which is in Bas-Rhin and 60% of which is in Haut-Rhin. It also comprises an enclave in the northernmost tip of Alsace around Wissembourg.
Production: approximately 1.2 million hectolitres per year.
The vineyards are planted in terraces extending from the Vosges foothills down to the plain at altitudes from 150 to 400m.
The climate is semi-continental with rainy springs, cold winters and very sunny summers and autumns. Geologically, the soil is varied including limestone-marl, loess, sandstone, schist, volcanic sediment and numerous conglomerates of marl.

The wines

Alsatian wines are defined primarily in terms of the variety of grape, or *cépage*.
Alsace AOC: Chasselas, Gewürztraminer, Muscat, Pinot Blanc, Pinot Gris, Riesling, Sylvaner for white wines and Pinot noir for red and rosé wines.
Alsace Grand Cru AOC: Gewürztraminer, Muscat, Pinot Gris, Pinot Noir and Riesling.
Crémant-d'alsace AOC: Auxerrois, Pinot Blanc, Pinot Noir, Chardonnay and Pinot gris.
"Vendanges tardives" and "Sélection de grains nobles": since 1984, *"Vendange tardive"* (late harvest) or *"Sélection de grains nobles"* can be found on wine labels to designate grapes affected by what is known as noble rot, meaning that they have a sugar content of over 14° in the case of late harvests and over 18.3° in

The village and vineyards of Blienschwiller.

that of *"grains nobles"*. The production of such wines is very carefully controlled; they may only come from a single grape variety and chaptalisation (the addition of sugar) is totally forbidden.

Useful tip

The grape harvest generally takes place between late September and mid-October depending on the grapes' maturity. During the harvest period, access to the trails through the vineyards can be restricted and it is best to check which are open on arrival.

Alsace Wine Road

180km itinerary. Allow two days taking your time.

In addition to being one of France's most famous Wine Roads, the Alsace Wine Road is without doubt its most attractive. It zigzags for 180km from Wissembourg to Thann offering a multitude of delights for the eye and the palate, including vineyards, flower-decked villages, old castles, wine cellars, excellent restaurants and inns, animal parks, tiny chapels and wine-growing festivals. The region deserves its reputation for varied talents and for its *Gemütlichkeit*, a delightful, if untranslatable, feeling of warm conviviality and pleasant lifestyle.

WISSEMBOURG'S VINEYARDS

17km N of Haguenau on the D 263. Michelin Local Map 315, L2.

The tiny vineyards of Wissembourg, at the northernmost tip of Alsace, are exceptional both by their distance from the rest of Alsace's vineyards and because the majority of the grapes harvested in the area are in fact made into wine in Germany where they become Baden wines.

Despite a troubled past, the border town of **Wissembourg★★** has retained a great deal of its rich heritage and a stroll through its appealing streets and lanes is most enjoyable.

The Protestant **Eglise St-Jean** dates back to the 15C although the belfry is 13C.

The **Eglise St-Pierre et St-Paul★**, built in sandstone, is 13C Gothic. Inside, the enormous 15C fresco depicting Saint Christopher is the largest painted statue in France; it measures 11m in height.

Those interested in finding out more about the history of everyday life in Alsace should make a point of visiting the **Westercamp Museum**, located in a 16C wine-grower's house steeped in tradition. The visit begins in the cosy kitchen and continues through the house's snug rooms furnished with magnificent old wardrobes, traditional costumes and souvenirs from the 1870 battlefield. Prehistoric and Roman artefacts are also displayed and there is a weapons room. *Closed for renovation.* ☎ *03 88 94 10 11 (tourist office).*

The bridge over the Lauter commands a fine view of the historic **Bruch district**. A walk around the old **ramparts** offering views of the old town's weather-worn roofs is a splendid way to finish a visit to the town.

CLEEBOURG'S VINEYARDS

6km S of Wissembourg on the D 77. Michelin Local Map 315, L2.

Unlike Wissembourg, Cleebourg's vineyards have remained French and a cooperative cellar handles practically all the production of the 190 hectares of vineyards spread over the towns Wissembourg, Cleebourg, Rott, Steinseltz and Riedseltz. Peter Jülg in Seebach is the only independent wine producer in the area.

The hospitable **wine cellar of Cleebourg**, near to which is a stork sanctuary, offers a good selection of attractively priced wines and some excellent Pinot Gris *(see Shopping Guide).*

FROM MARLENHEIM TO CHATENOIS

68km. Michelin Local Map 315, I 5-7. See itinerary **1** *on the map p. 79.*

As far as Rosheim, the route skirts the Vosges foothills where the villages are more representative of the plain.

Marlenheim

The welcoming town of Marlenheim is a well-known wine-producing centre boasting a vast choice of restaurants. The vineyards date back to Merovingian times. The Steinklotz Grand Cru is produced here from Pinot Gris, Riesling and Gewürztraminer which thrive so well on steep limestone slopes.

The imposing wine merchant's **Metz-Laugel (Marlenberg cellar)** is open to visitors *(guided tour: admission charge)* with a fine choice of regional wines. *102, rue du Général-de-Gaulle, 67520 Marlenheim, 03 88 59 28 69. Open 10.30am-12.30pm and 2-7pm (afternoons only Sat-Sun). Closed public holidays and Sun from Jan-Mar.*

Directory

WHERE TO EAT

AROUND BARR

Au Bœuf Rouge – *6 r. du Dr-Stoltz – 67140 Andlau – ☎ 03 88 08 96 26 – closed 21 Jun to 12 Jul, 7 to 17 Feb, Wed evening and Thu - 15-35€.* Set in a 17C post house, this typical Alsatian restaurant serves tasty traditional dishes in an elegant wainscoted dining room or summer terrace, while the winstub offers regional specialities including its famed *flammekeuches*.

Am Lindeplatzel – *71 r. Principale – 67140 Mittelbergheim – closed Feb holidays, 20 to 31 Aug, Mon lunchtime, Wed evening and Thu – ☎ 03 88 08 10 69 – ⏞ - 21/59.50€.* An excellent address whose à la carte menu offers delights such as sautéed artichokes in peanut oil and fried goose liver, vanilla flavoured sea bass and French toast with cardamom ice cream. Set menus feature wafer-thin onion tarts, crispy fillets of quail and pistou sauce and other enticing dishes.

AROUND COLMAR

Chez Hansi – *23 r. des Marchands – 68000 Colmar – ☎ 03 89 41 37 84 – closed 5 Jan to 5 Feb, Wed and Thu - 18/44€.* The lively atmosphere of old Colmar can be felt in this inn next door to the former Custom's and Pilgrim's houses. Within its half-timbered façade lies a traditional, very popular, Alsatian dining room. Tasty regional dishes (choucroute with all the trimmings, smoked shoulder of ham and *kouglof*) are served by a team in traditional dress.

Restaurant des Halles – *11 r. Wickram – 68000 Colmar – ☎ 03 89 23 61 10 – closed 14 Jul to 15 Aug, 24 Dec to 4 Jan, Sat and Sun – lunch 11.50€ - 18/34€.* Fresh market produce takes pride of place in this restaurant, next-door to the Lauch Canal and the former wholesale fruit and vegetable market. The young chef changes the menus daily depending on his inspiration and what is in season. The dining room is also treated to a fresh coat of paint several times a year.

Taverne Alsacienne – *99 r. de la République – 68040 Ingersheim – 4km NW of Colmar on the N 83 – ☎ 03 89 27 08 41 – closed 1-8 Jan, 23 Jul to 13 Aug, Sun evening and Mon except public holidays – lunch 15€ - 18/53€.* On the banks of the Fecht, this establishment specialises in traditional Alsatian fare to the delight of its customers who also appreciate its excellent value for money. Choucroute, duck, fish and farmhouse Munster cheese complemented by a fine wine list with a wide choice of regional wines.

Aux Trois Poissons – *15 quai de la Poissonnerie – 68000 Colmar – ☎ 03 89 41 25 21 – closed 15 Jul to 1 Aug, 23 to 27 Dec, 5 to 18 Jan, Sun evening, Tue evening and Wed - 21/42€.* Naturally enough this establishment on the banks of the Lauch Canal specialises in fish dishes – oysters from Marennes-Oléron, mussels, sole, sea bream, pike quenelles and fried carp are just some of the delights awaiting you in this half-timbered house in Little Venice.

Bartholdi – *2 r. des Boulangers – 68000 Colmar – ☎ 03 89 41 07 74 – closed 4 to 18 Jun, 12 to 20 Nov, Sun evening and Mon – 21/49€.* Everything in this excellent establishment reminds you that you are in Alsace, from the painted sign, traditional winstub decor and furnishings, friendly atmosphere and the regional cuisine (fresh foie gras, choucroute, onion tart, trout in Riesling). Terrace in a paved courtyard alongside the famous Maison des Têtes.

Winstub Flory – *1 r. Mangold – 68000 Colmar – ☎ 03 89 41 78 80 – closed Tue, Wed except Jul-Aug and Dec - 21.50/23€.* This is your chance to discover the convivial atmosphere of the Alsacian *Stammtisch*: a communal table, usually for regulars. Ringing the little bell in the centre means another round of good white wine for everyone! The faultless regional fare and wall fresco are both worth the visit.

La Grangelière – *59 r. du Rempart-Sud – 68420 Eguisheim – ☎ 03 89 23 00 30 – closed mid-Feb to mid-Mar, Sun evening from Nov to Apr and Thu - 22/65€.* Before taking charge of his own establishment, Alain Finkbeiner learnt his trade in a number of prestigious restaurants. Customers can choose between an unfussy brasserie-style decor serving regional dishes or the restaurant which offers a more elaborate menu and personalised service.

Au Vieux Porche – *16 r. des Trois-Châteaux - 68420 Eguisheim – ☎ 03 89 24 01 90 – closed 27 Jun to 6 Jul, 8 to 16 Nov, 15 Feb to 15 Mar, Tue and Wed - 23/60€.* This welcoming house built in 1707 stands under the protection of Bacchus. The owner's family still owns vineyards, the produce of which can be found on the fine wine list. Guests tuck into an interesting blend of regional dishes and personal recipes.

Au Crocus – *14 pl. de l'Ecole – 68000 Colmar – ☎ 03 89 23 32 49 – closed 15 to 29 Aug, 13 to 20 Feb, Wed evening and Sun – lunch 13.50€ - 23/40€.* This period house next door to the Dominican Church and former guardroom is now a welcoming restaurant. In the kitchens, the chef focuses on fresh seasonal produce to concoct interesting tasty dishes served in the attractive, country-style, timbered dining room.

La Maison des Têtes – *19 r. des Têtes – 68000 Colmar – ☎ 03 89 24 43 43 – closed Feb, Sun evening and Mon - 24.20/65€.* Take the time before you cross the threshold to look up and admire the superb façade of this restaurant, one of Colmar's architectural gems adorned with at least a hundred sculpted masks. Indoors an enthusiastic staff prepares and serves excellent traditional French and a few regional dishes.

AROUND MOLSHEIM

Auberge du Cerf – *120 r. du Général-de-Gaulle – 67560 Rosheim – ☎ 03 88 50 40 14 – closed 7 to 18 Jan, 21 Jun to 7 Jul, Sun evening and Mon – lunch 11€ - 14/35€.* What better way to savour the local wines at their best than with a tasty "snack" at this auberge. Delicious, regional classics – such as presskopf, foie gras and choucroute – take pride of place at this food lovers' favourite.

Winstub O'Baerenheim – *46 r. du Général-Gouraud – 67210 Obernai – ☎ 03 88 95 53 77 – closed 4 to 23 Mar, 16 to 30 Nov, Tue evening, Thu lunch and Wed – lunch 13.50€ - 22/50€.* As you enter, notice the barrels above the main door. Once inside, seated near a warm open hearth, you can choose from a selection of very reasonably-priced regional dishes including a wide range of meat, fish, seafood and shellfish courses and an appealing set menu.

La Petite Auberge – *41 r. du Général-de-Gaulle – 67560 Rosheim – ☎ 03 88 50 40 60 – closed 30 Jun to 12 Jul, 19 to 26 Nov and 16 to 28 Feb - 21/46€.* Whether in the comfortable wood-panelled dining room or on the summer terrace, the Petite Auberge treats its guests to a delicious selection of regional dishes. Famed for its *baeckeofe*, the house is also known for its meat cooked in Riesling or Sylvaner, homemade foie gras and fresh fruit soup flavoured with Crémant-d'Alsace.

AROUND RIQUEWIHR

Auberge St-Alexis – *68240 Kayserberg – ☎ 03 89 73 90 38 – closed Fri - 11-16€.* A magnificent forest of fir trees surrounds this farmhouse inn decorated in a warm country style. The simple, wholesome fare relies heavily on produce from the local farms: savoury vegetable soup, tasty choucroute and delicious homemade apple, red fruit and cherry plum pies.

Caveau du Vigneron - *5 Grand-Rue – 68150 Hunawihr – 2km from Ribeauvillé on the D 1 – ☎ 03 89 73 70 15 – closed 20 Dec to 7 Feb and Wed – lunch 7€ - 13/27€.* The new owner, Christophe Bruault, is in fact not a newcomer to the establishment because he worked here as a chef for five years. The interior decoration – that of the cellar of a 17C house – is unchanged and regional Alsatian dishes continue to take pride of place on the menu: onion tart, choucroute, duck in Riesling, and braised ham.

A l'Arbre Vert – *7 r. des Cigognes – 68770 Ammerschwihr – 4km SE of Kayserberg on the N 415 – ☎ 03 89 47 12 23 – closed 1 to 12 Mar, 15 to 26 Nov - 14/46€.* In the dining room decorated with wooden carvings inspired by wine and vineyards, the Gebel-Tournier family is rightly proud of its carefully prepared, tasty local cuisine: choucroute, coq au Riesling, and roasted pikeperch garnished with a traditional horseradish sauce and *spätzle*, a kind of noodle.

Winstub du Château – *38 r. du Général-de-Gaulle – 68240 Kayserberg – ☎ 03 89 78 24 33 – closed 17 Jan to 4 Feb, 23 Jun to 1 Jul, 2 to 11 Nov, Wed evening and Thu - 16/30€.* Popular all year round, the Kohler family's restaurant is even more so around Christmas time because Kayserberg's Christmas market is one of the best known in Alsace. On the faultless regional menu are local specialities such as snails à l'alsacienne, choucroute royale, smoked fillet of trout with horseradish sauce.

La Vieille Forge – *11 r. des Ecoles – 68240 Kayserberg – ☎ 03 89 47 17 51 – closed Feb holidays, 1 to 21 Jul, Mon, Tue and Thu, except evenings in Sep-Oct and Wed - 18.50/35€.* A charming dining room welcomes tourists and regulars, drawn by the establishment's flavourful country cooking. How about a preview of the menu to set your taste buds tingling? Pikeperch in Riesling, choucroute, tournedos of beef in Pinot Noir, Munster cheese, iced *kouglof* with cherries or warm plums.

R. Mattes / MICHELIN

Aux Trois Merles – *68770 Ammerschwihr – 4km SE of Kayserberg on the N 415 – ☎ 03 89 78 24 35 – closed Feb holidays, Wed evening, Sun evening and Mon - 19.80/40€.* A menu slanted towards fish and seafood is served in a cosy dining room and comfortable terrace – roasted pikeperch and bacon, mixed fish in a beurre blanc or tuna steak à la plancha. The menu is composed with seasonal produce and also features a number of Alsatian favourites such as choucroute and *baeckeofe*.

Winstub du Sommelier – *68750 Bergheim – 3km N of Ribeauvillé on the D 1 – ☎ 03 89 73 69 99 – closed 15 to 29 Jul, 20 to 29 Jan, Tue evening and Wed - 19.90€.* This house built in 1746 reveals an elegant *winstub* atmosphere, perfectly matched by its refined regional cuisine. Diners can choose between a daily set menu or a more elaborate choice which evolves with the seasons. Handsome wine list and selection of wines by the glass.

Le Sarment d'Or – *4 r. du Cerf – 68340 Riquewihr – ☎ 03 89 86 02 86 – closed 5 Jan to 11 Feb, 28 Jun to 6 Jul, Sun evening, Tue lunchtime and Mon - 20/52€.* The enchanting village of Riquewihr is home to many lovely houses including this 17C building, now a restaurant. Wood panelling, beams, open fireplace and tasteful furnishings set the scene for the pleasant dining rooms where traditional dishes are spiced up by a few sprigs of modernity.

Auberge du Froehn – *route d'Ostheim – 68340 Zellenberg – 2km S of Ribeauvillé on the D 1 – ☎ 03 89 47 81 57 – closed 1-16 Jul, 9 Feb to 5 Mar, Tue and Wed – 21/35€.* An attractive flower-decked façade announces a pleasantly rustic inn, noted for its friendly atmosphere. The regulars seem to appreciate the innkeeper's smile as much as they do the tasty dishes prepared by her husband who has added his own personal touch to regional specialities.

Au Relais des Ménétriers – *10 avenue du Général-de-Gaulle – 68150 Ribeauvillé – ☎ 03 89 73 64 52 – closed 29 Jun to 17 Jul, 23 Dec to 2 Jan, Thu evening, Sun evening and Mon – lunch 11€ - 22/32€.* The fiddle-playing tradition is far from dead in Ribeauvillé and the sound of the violin may well guide your footsteps to this restaurant in which the terroir is all important. Spacious dining rooms decorated in full-blown Alsatian style. Regional tasty cooking made with fresh local produce.

Caveau Morakopf – *7 rue des Trois-Epis – 68230 Niedermorschwihr – 7km SE of Kaysersberg on N 415 then on D 107 – ☎ 03 89 27 05 10 – closed 7-20 Jan, 23 Jun to 7 Jul, Mon lunchtime and Sun – lunch 20€ - 23/53€.* A warm atmosphere greets the visitor to this establishment located in the cellar of an 18C building with a terrace garden. Alsatian specialities such as *Schwina Zingala* (boiled pork tongue) or *fleischschnaka* are just a few of the delights on the menu prepared by Mrs Guidat.

IN THANN

La Gare – *68800 Thann – ☎ 03 89 82 51 29 – closed 27 Jul to 14 Aug, 15 Feb to 4 Mar, Tue evening and Wed - 22/58€.* This former village café, run by the same family for four generations, is proud of its wine list which boasts no less than 800 references. A wide choice of set menus featuring traditional and local dishes. The dish of the day is served simply in the bistro area.

AROUND WISSEMBOURG

Auberge du Pfaffenschlick – *Col de Pfaffenschlick – 67510 Climbach – 12km SW of Wissembourg on the D 3, towards Lembach, take the pass road on D 51 – ☎ 03 88 54 28 84 – closed 15 Jan to 15 Feb, Mon and Tue - 16/32€.* Deep in the forest, opposite a cabin which served as a canteen during the construction of the Maginot Line, stands an inn: at one time, only walkers came here, but now its wholesome and plentiful cooking is deservedly better known. Pleasant terrace.

Hostellerie du Cygne – *67160 Wissembourg – ☎ 03 88 94 00 16 - 25/55€.* Two terraced houses, one dating from the 14C, the other already an inn in the 16C, have been put together. The more modern dining rooms feature woodwork and inlaid ceiling. Local produce comes into its own in dishes like boar stew, *presskopf* of pork, and stuffed young rabbit with oxtail.

WHERE TO STAY

IN BARR

Château d'Andlau – *113 Vallée St-Ulrich – 67140 Barr – ☎ 03 88 08 96 78 – Closed 2-20 Jan, Sun evening and Mon – 22rm: 50/63€ - 8€ – restaurant 21/32€.* This low-lying half-timbered inn surrounded by high trees stands on the banks of the Kirneck on the road to Mont Ste-Odile. Enjoy a peaceful night's sleep and awaken to the lovely flowered garden in the morning. New restaurant with a wine list of over 1 000 bottles, including many Champagnes, the house speciality.

R. Mattes / MICHELIN

AROUND COLMAR

Chambre d'Hôte les Framboises - *128 rue des Trois-Epis – 68230 Katzenthal – 5km NW of Colmar, towards Kaysersberg on the D 10 - ☎ 03 89 27 48 85 – sarl. amrein@wanadoo.fr - 4rm: 35/45€.* Leave the bustle of Colmar and relax in the peace and quiet of this village set in the heart of vineyards. The owner distils marc, a sort of brandy, from Gewürztraminer, and offers guests comfortable panelled rooms under the eaves. Don't miss the puppet show in the morning.

Hôtel au Moulin – *Route d'Herrlisheim – 68127 Ste-Croix-en-Plaine – 10km S of Colmar on the A 35 then the D 1 – ☎ 03 89 49 31 20 – closed 5 Nov to 31 Mar – 17rm: 40/80€ - 8€.* This old flour-mill, dating from 1880, offers a real sanctuary for tired travellers within its flowered courtyard and surrounding half-timbered buildings. Some of the rooms, which are spacious and tastefully decorated, overlook the Vosges, while the others have a view of the plain. All are gloriously quiet. Quick snacks and mini Alsace museum.

A la Vigne – *5 Grande-Rue – 68280 Logelheim – 6km SE of Colmar, on the D 13 and the D 45 – closed 23 Jun to 10 Jul and 23 Dec to 8 Jan – 9rm: 50/68€ - 6€.* A welcoming establishment with a red-painted façade and fully renovated interior. This quiet hotel offers tasteful, spotlessly clean rooms providing an excellent stopover point just 10min from Colmar. Classical recipes served in the family dining room and tartes flambées at the bar.

⊖⊖ **Turenne** – *10 route de Bâle – 68000 Colmar –* ☎ *03 89 21 58 58 – ⋈ - 85rm: 59/68€ - ⋤ 8€.* Ideally located two minutes from Little Venice, it is impossible to miss the bright pink and yellow façade of this large establishment. The spacious rooms have been treated to a makeover and some are furnished with regional pieces. Breakfasts are served in a traditional Alsatian room. Friendly staff.

⊖⊖ **Hostellerie du Château** – *2 rue du Château – 68420 Eguisheim –* ☎ *03 89 23 72 00 – info@hostellerieduchateau.com - closed 2 Jan to 10 Feb – 11rm: 63/120€ - ⋤ 9.50€.* On the main square of this picture postcard town, this old house has been entirely renovated by the owner himself, an architect by training. The contemporary, personalised rooms blend in well with the old structure and the bathrooms are a joy.

⊖⊖ **Château de la Prairie** – *Allée des Maronniers – 68500 Guebwiller –* ☎ *03 89 72 28 57 – ⋈ - 18rm: 59/89€ - ⋤ 8€.* This modest manor-house, built in 1858 for a local industrialist, features spacious bedrooms whose original moulding and wooden parquet floors have been retained and enhanced by rustic furniture. Some have a terrace. A number of wood-lined sitting rooms with fireplaces. Two hectares of fenced parkland.

⊖⊖ **Hôtel le Colombier** – *7 rue de Turenne – 68000 Colmar – 6km S of Colmar on the D 13 then the D 45 –* ☎ *03 89 23 96 00 – info@hotel-le-colombier.com - closed Christmas holidays – 24rm: 75/180€ - ⋤ 10€.* In historic Colmar, this lovely 15C house combines old stonework and contemporary finishings. Italian-designed furniture, modern artwork, a superb Renaissance staircase and peaceful patio are just a few of its appeals. Immaculate rooms.

AROUND RIQUEWIHR

⊖ **Chambre d'hôte Schmitt Gérard** – *3 chemin des Vignes – 68340 Riquewihr –* ☎ *03 89 47 89 72 – closed Jan-Mar – ⋈ - 2rm: 35/45€.* Mr Schmitt's home and garden stand in the upper part of the village on the edge of the vineyards. The wood-panelled rooms are under the eaves. Impeccable cleanliness and faultless prices are just some of its appeal.

⊖ **Chambre d'hôte Maison Thomas** – *41 Grand'Rue – 68770 Ammerschwihr –* ☎ *03 89 78 23 90 – www.maisonthomas.com - ⋈ - 4rm and 4 gîtes: 38/46€.* The turquoise blue façade of this former wine-grower's house stands in the most picturesque part of the village, near a fortified gate. Its large functional rooms are all equipped with a small kitchen and some have a mezzanine. Several apartments also available. Pleasant garden.

⊖⊖ **Fief du Château** – *67600 Orschwiller – 7km N of Ribeauvillé on the D 1 –* ☎ *03 88 82 56 25 – fiefduchateau@evc.net - closed 30 Jun to 5 Jul, 3-8 Nov, 17 Feb to 3 Mar and Wed –* **P** *- 8rm: 45€ - ⋤ 7€ – restaurant 18/30€.* The resplendently Alsatian façade of this late 19C house is adorned with brightly coloured geraniums in summer. Indoors a welcoming interior reveals a beamed dining room where the local dishes do full justice to the region's wines.

⊖⊖ **Domaine Bouxhof** – *Rue du Bouxhof – 68630 Mittelwihr – 2km S of Riquewihr on the D 3 –* ☎ *03 89 47 93 67 – closed Jan – 3rm: 50€.* A delightful 17C house set in the midst of wine-growing estate. The owners are only too pleased to take you on a tour of their magnificent listed cellar and introduce you to the estate's production. Spacious, well-equipped gîtes and modern guestrooms – minimum 2 nights' booking. Breakfast is served in the 15C chapel.

⊖⊖ **Hôtel de la Tour** – *1 rue de la Mairie – 68150 Ribeauvillé –* ☎ *03 89 72 72 73 – hoteldelatour@aol.com - closed late Dec to mid-Mar –* **P** *– 33rm: 53/76€ - ⋤ 7€.* This former wine-growing farm converted into a hotel is tucked away in the heart of the town, a stone's throw from the Butchers' Tower. The renovated rooms are bright and practical. Those overlooking the inner courtyard and its half-timbered façade are very quiet. Small fitness room.

⊖⊖ **Hôtel l'Oriel** – *3 rue des Ecuries-Seigneuriales – 68340 Riquewihr –* ☎ *03 89 49 03 13 – info@hotel-oriel.com - 19rm: 65/90€ - ⋤ 9.50€.* A double oriel window and an amusing wrought-iron sign adorn the frontage of this 16C house. Indoors, a maze of corridors and staircases take guests up to rustic rooms furnished in Alsatian style. Several have a mezzanine. A recent wing also offers accommodation.

⊖⊖ **Hostellerie Schwendi** – *2 place Schwendi – 68240 Kientzheim –* ☎ *03 89 47 30 50 – hotel-schwendi@wanadoo.fr - closed 20 Dec to 15 Mar –* **P** *– 17rm: 65/78€ - ⋤ 7.50€ – restaurant 23/54€.* In summer, the terrace is laid around an old well, against the backdrop of a pale yellow half-timbered façade. This 17C hostelry offers renovated rooms, all of which have retained their original beams. In the dining room, tasty regional fare is served with wines made on the family estate.

⊖⊖ **Aux Armes de France** – *1 Grand'Rue – 68770 Ammerschwihr –* ☎ *03 89 47 10 12 – closed Wed and Thu – ⋈ –10rm: 65/80€ - ⋤ 12€ – restaurant 18/93€.* Countless chefs started their careers in this attractive house whose reputation for culinary excellence dates back to the time when the current chef's grandmother was behind the stove. Warm Alsatian decor, spacious rooms and delicious up-to-date cooking. What more could you want!

AROUND THANN

⊖ **Moschenross** – *42 rue du Général-de-Gaulle – 68800 Thann –* ☎ *03 89 37 00 86 – info@le-moschenross.com - closed 1-20 Jul – 23rm: 31/52€ - ⋤ 6.50€*

– *restaurant 16/46€*. Behind the smart red walls of this 19C hotel, opposite the station, you'll find a fully renovated interior. The rooms are small, but modern, practical and well soundproofed. Some offer a view of the famous sloping vineyard of Rangen. Charming staff.

AROUND WISSEMBOURG

⊖ Chambre d'hôte Klein – *59 rue Principale – 67160 Cleebourg – 7km SW of Wissembourg on the D 7 – ☎ 03 88 94 50 95 – annejp.klein@laposte.net – ⊭ - 4rm: 27/40€ – meals 12€*. This 18C-19C Alsatian abode in the heart of the village of Cleebourg, renowned for its wine, will appeal to all those in search of authenticity and calm. All the ground-floor rooms are furnished with lovely antique pieces. Pleasant rear garden. Regional cooking.

⊖⊖ Moulin de la Walk – *2 rue Walk – 67160 Wissembourg – ☎ 03 88 94 06 44 – info@moulin-walk.com - closed 2-23 Jan – ₽ – 25rm: 55/90€ - ⊒ 6.50€ – restaurant 30/38€*. A riverside setting for these three buildings grafted onto the remains of the old water mill, the wheel of which still turns. Most of the rooms feature practical modern fixtures and fittings. Welcoming dining room lined in wood and flowered terrace. Classical dishes.

GOURMET SHOPPING

Ferme l'Hirondelle – *Route de Guémar – 68150 Ribeauvillé – ☎ 03 89 73 62 32 – Tue-Fri 2-6pm, Sat 9am-noon and 2-6.30pm, Sun and public holidays noon-7pm; daily Jul-Aug 10am-7pm*. In the Hirondelle boutique, over 100 cheeses, cooked meats, jams and dairy products are attractively displayed. The star of the show is Ribeaupierre, a local cheese which this farm has begun producing again.

Windholtz – *31 avenue du Général-de-Gaulle – 68150 Ribeauvillé – ☎ 03 89 73 66 61 – Mon-Sat 9am-midday and 2-6pm*. Mr Windholtz makes eaux de vie for true connoisseurs. His brandies are distilled according to old traditions to ensure that they retain all their character and taste. His special plum, pear and cherry Réserve brandies are particularly worthy of note.

Wangen

The twisting lanes lined with handsome old houses and arched porches make Wangen a typical wine-growing village. Don't miss the medieval fortifications including two towers, one of which is called the "Niederturm".

Westhoffen

This wine-growing village, also famed for its cherries, still boasts a number of 16C and 17C houses as well as a Renaissance fountain. In Eglise St-Martin, look out for the 14C chancel and stained-glass windows. An unusual 19C oriental-style synagogue can also be seen, while in the heart of the village, wedged in between two churches, the **Etienne Loew Estate**, open to the public *(no charge)* sells sought-after wines including a Grand Cru Altenberg from Bergbieten. *28 r. Birris, 67310 Westhoffen, ☎ 03 88 50 59 19, etienneloew@hotmail.com 8am-noon, 2-6pm. By appointment.*

The surrounding vineyards reach as far as the towns of **Bergbieten** and **Traenheim**. At Bergbieten, the **Roland Schmitt** organic wine-growing estate, produces extremely subtle wines *(see Shopping Guide)*. The equally well-known **Frédéric Mochel** estate in Traenheim possesses an old 17C wine press and is open to the public. *56 r. Principale, 67310 Traenheim, ☎ 03 88 50 38 67, infos@mochel.net. Mon-Sat, 8am-noon, 1.30-6pm. By appointment.*

Avolsheim

Chapelle St-Ulrich, adorned with handsome 13C **frescoes★**, is thought to be one of the oldest sanctuaries in Alsace and is a former baptistery built c 1000. The neighbouring village of Wolxheim, whose terroir is particularly suited to Riesling, produces the Grand Cru Altenberg of Wolxheim that was one of Napoleon's favourites.

Molsheim★

Forced to leave the Protestant states, Benedictine, Carthusian, Capuchin and Jesuit monks fled to Molsheim, making it the capital of the Counter-Reformation in Alsace. Although dating from the early 17C, the **Jesuit Church★** was built in the Gothic style and its graceful interior proportions are truly remarkable. As was often the case elsewhere, the region's vineyards flourished under the care and attention lavished by these religious communities. Molsheim boasts a Grand Cru classé, Bruderthal, where Riesling and Gewürztraminer do particularly well. It can be tasted at the **Gérard Neumeyer** estate *(see Shopping Guide)*.

Another of Molsheim's claims to fame is the presence in the 1920s of the factory of the legendary Italian car manufacturer, **Ettore Bugatti**. As a result, every year in early September the town hosts a parade of vintage automobiles during the Bugatti Festival. The **Musée de la Chartreuse**, on the site of a former Charterhouse (1598-

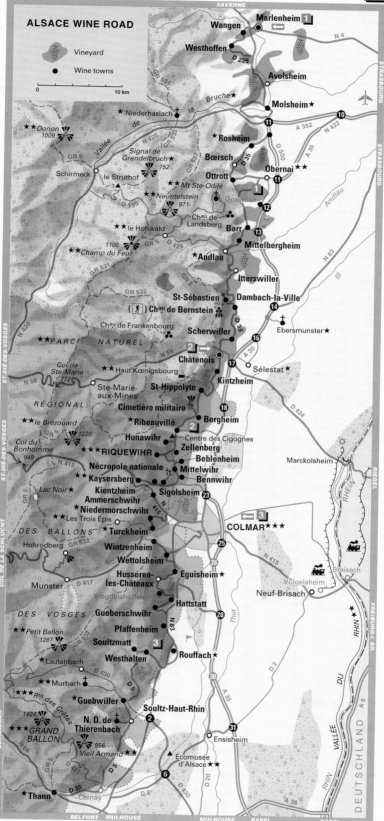

ALSACE WINE ROAD

Vineyard

Wine towns

0   10 km

SAVERNE

Marlenheim 1
Wangen

Westhoffen
D 225

Avolsheim

Molsheim ★

Niederhaslach ★

la Bruche ★

★★ Donon 1009

Signal de Grendelbruch ★ 752

le Struthof

★ Rosheim

Bœrsch

Ottrott ★

Obernai ★★

★★ Mt Ste-Odile

Neuntelstein 971

Goxwiller

Ch^au de Landsberg

Barr

Mittelbergheim

★★ le Hohwald

1100

★★ Champ du Feu

★ Andlau

Itterswiller

St-Sébastien

Dambach-la-Ville

Ch^au de Bernstein

Ebersmunster ★

Ch^au de Frankenbourg

Scherwiller

★★ PARC NATUREL

Col de Ste-Marie 772

★★ Haut Kœnigsbourg

Châtenois

Sélestat ★

Kintzheim

RÉGIONAL

Ste-Marie-aux-Mines

St-Hippolyte

Cimetière militaire

★★ le Brézouard 1228

★ Ribeauvillé

Bergheim

Col du Bonhomme 949

Hunawihr

Centre des Cigognes

★★★ RIQUEWIHR

Zellenberg

Marckolsheim

Nécropole nationale

Beblenheim

★★ Kaysersberg

Mittelwihr

Lac Noir ★

Kientzheim

Bennwihr

Ammerschwihr

Sigolsheim

Niedermorschwihr

★★ Les Trois Épis

DES BALLONS

★ Turckheim

COLMAR ★★★

Hohrodberg

Wintzenheim

Wettolsheim

Vœlgelsheim

Munster

Husseren-les-Châteaux

Eguisheim ★

Neuf-Brisach

Breisach

DES VOSGES

Vœgtlinshoffen

Hattstatt

★★ Petit Ballon 1267

Gueberschwihr

Pfaffenheim

★ Lautenbach

Soultzmatt

★★ Murbach

Westhalten

Rouffach ★

★★★ Rte des Crêtes

1424

Guebwiller

★★★ GRAND BALLON

N.D. de Thierenbach

Soultz-Haut-Rhin

956

Vieil Armand ★★

Ensisheim

Écomusée d'Alsace ★★

★ Thann

Cernay

BELFORT MULHOUSE

MULHOUSE

BASEL

DEUTSCHLAND

RHIN

FREIBURG I. BR.

STRASBOURG

SAVERNE

1792), exhibits several of the models built in the town between the two World Wars. *Open mid-Jun to mid-Sep, daily except Tue 10am-noon and 2-6pm, Sat-Sun and public holidays 2-5pm.* 3€. ☎ 03 88 38 25 10.

Rosheim★

The tourist office has created a historic walk around the town.

It begins on a **wine trail** offering a splendid panorama of the vineyards. **Eglise St-Pierre-et-St-Paul★**, built in yellow sandstone in the 12C, features an octagonal belfry; the gable on the west front depicts humans being devoured by lions. The **Romanesque house**, located on Rue du Général-de-Gaulle between n°21 and n°23, is Alsace's oldest stone edifice dating from the second half of the 12C.

Leave Rosheim. From here on, the route becomes much hillier, rising to reveal a view of the plain of Alsace where the ruins of numerous castles, such as Ottrott, Ortenbourg, Ramstein and Landsberg, can be seen perched on hilltops.

Boersch

Three old gates provide access to the town of Boersch. The Porte du bas (lower gate) leads into a **square★** lined with old houses, the most remarkable of which is the 16C town hall. Leave Boersch through the Porte du Haut (upper gate).

Stop at the **Spindler marquetry workshop** to see an exhibition and an audio-visual presentation of its work. *Open daily except Sun, 9am-noon and 2-6pm. Closed public holidays. No charge.* ☎ 03 88 95 80 17.

Ottrott

This characterful village stands on a steep slope at the foot of Mount Ste-Odile and is famed for its red Pinot noir wine. Ottrott is equally proud of its two châteaux, Lutzelbourg (12C) with a square building and round tower and the larger and more elaborate 13C Rathsamhausen castle.

Further on the road towards Klingenthal, the huge **Naïades aquarium** is home to over 3 000 fish from all over the world. ♿ *Open daily 10am-6.30pm (last entrance 1hr prior to closing time); 24 and 31 Dec 10am-4pm; 1Jan and 25 Dec 1.30-6.30pm.* 10€ (3-10 year olds 7.50€). ☎ 03 88 95 90 32. www.parc-les-naides.com

Obernai★★

Visitors run no risk of dying of thirst in Obernai, because in addition to being in the heart of wine-growing country, it is also home to the famous Kronenbourg beer brewery. Storks, old houses with multicoloured roofs, flower-decked lanes, painted shop signs and legions of tourists: Obernai has everything you would expect to find in Alsace!

Place du Marché★★ (market square) is lined with houses whose gold-coloured hues sometimes border on crimson, bathing the streets of Obernai in a distinctive luminosity. The former covered market of the **Halle aux Blés★** dates from 1554 and served at one time as the town's butchers. The 13C **Tour de la Chapelle★** belfry is home to a chancel which is all that remains of the former chapel; the 16C Gothic spire rises to a height of 60m. When the **town hall★** was rebuilt in 1848, it was decided to retain a number of architectural elements (14C-17C) such as an oriel window and a beautifully carved balcony, both added to the façade in 1604.

Countless **old houses★** add charm to the area between the market square and Place des Etoiles, particularly on Ruelle des Juifs. Look out for the 13C three-storey stone house on Rue des Pèlerins.

The regularly rebuilt **ramparts**, the best conserved section of which is the Maréchal-Foch rampart, offer tourists and residents the opportunity of a pleasant stroll.

🚶 The 3.6km-long **Schenkenberg wine trail** (1hr 30min) enables walkers to discover some 250 hectares of vineyards. Park your car at the ADEIF memorial, a 12m-high cross. In summer, weekly guided tours are organised on Wednesday mornings followed by a visit to a cellar. Enquire at the tourist office.

Return to the D 35 via Bernardswiller.

Heiligenstein

This village is famed for its Klevener, a dry white wine made from a variety of Traminer similar to the Savagnin rosé that is used to make Jura wines.

Jean and Hubert Heywang's wine estate is an excellent place to discover this wine *(see Shopping Guide).*

Barr

Barr is both an industrial centre, famous for its tanneries, and a major wine-producing centre, reputed for its Kirchberg Grand Cru. The Gewürztraminer, Riesling and Pinot Gris varieties produce heady wines, the best examples of which can be sampled at **Martine and Vincent Stoeffler's estate** *(see Shopping Guide).* The **Klipfel estate** is open to the public with wine-tasting sessions organised combined with the chance to sample local specialities or a full meal. *6 av. de la Gare, 67140 Barr* ☎ 03 88 58 59 00, *alsacevin@klipfel.com.*

Open 10am-noon and 2-6pm. By appointment.

Take the time to venture into the courtyard of the 17C **town hall**, adorned with a carved loggia and balcony, to admire the rear section.

Folie Marco, an 18C nobleman's house, is home to a museum where 17C-19C furniture, porcelain, china, pewter and mementoes of local history are exhibited. *Guided tours Jul-Sep, open daily except Tue, 10am-noon and 2-6pm; May-Jun and Oct, Sat-Sun, 10am-noon and 2-6pm; tours start on the hour every hour. 3€. ☎ 03 88 08 66 66.*

The village and vineyards of Andlau.

R. Mattes / MICHELIN

Mittelbergheim

The houses of this delightful town are built on a hillside. The town hall square is lined with handsome Renaissance edifices. The Zotzenberg Grand Cru vineyard (on limestone-marl soil) stands at an altitude of 320m above the village. It is reputed for its Sylvaner, but other varieties do equally well here.

Andlau★

The two belfries of Andlau can be seen from a distance rising above the roofs and surrounding forest. The town boasts three Grands Crus, Wiebelsberg, Muenchberg and Kastelberg. If you need to know more, **Marc Kreydenweiss**, one of the pioneers of biodynamic wine making, is a useful place to start *(see Shopping Guide)*.

Eglise St-Pierre-et-St-Paul★★, rebuilt in the 12C, has retained a magnificent **door-way★★** entirely decorated with bas-relief from the Romanesque period. These represent scenes of the Creation and the Garden of Eden, in addition to the abbey's benefactors. Inside, the chancel which stands over the **crypt★** is adorned with some fine 15C stalls.

Itterswiller

This charming flower-decked village clings to a hillside of vineyards. The church boasts a 13C or 14C mural. Itterswiller does not possess a Grand Cru, but the locality of Fruhemes is noted for its Riesling.

🚶 A **wine trail** *(c 1hr walk)* leads to a splendid viewpoint with an orientation table.

Dambach-la-Ville

The historic town centre, encircled by ramparts of which three town gates still remain, is stunningly picturesque. The Frankstein Grand Cru is justly famous for its excellent Rieslings and Gewürztraminers. The town is a thriving wine-producing centre.

The **Ruhlman estate** is one of many places worth a halt offering a visit of the cellars, the vineyards and a tour of the medieval city in a small train, all to the commentary of the wine-grower. Wine tasting takes place in a 17C cellar. *34 rue du Maréchal-Foch, 67650 Dambach-la-Ville, ☎ 03 88 92 41 86. Open Mon-Sat 9am-noon and 1.30-7pm. By appointment. Admission charge.*

For a splendid view of the Alsace plain and the vineyards, turn left 400m past the Porte Haute (upper gate). At the top of the road, turn right onto a trail which goes as far as Chapelle St-Sébastien. Inside the chapel is an ornate late 17C Baroque altar caved in wood.

🚶 Continue along the trail *(2hr walk there and back)* to the **ruins of the castle of Bernstein**. Built in the 12C and 13C on a granite ridge, all that remains today are the main building and a pentagonal keep, but it does command a wonderful panorama of the plain.

Scherwiller

At the foot of the fortified castles of Ortenbourg and Ramstein, an old guardroom with an oriel and a number of fine 18C houses can still be seen in the town, as can some former wash-houses along the banks of the Aubach.

🚶 An 18C crucifix can be seen along the **wine trail**.

The **André Dussourt Estate**, at the foot of Ortenbourg castle, has opened its 18C cellars, which boast hundred-year-old barrels among other curiosities, to the public. *2 rue de Dambach, 67750 Scherwiller, ☎ 03 88 92 10 27. Open Mon-Sat 8am-noon and 1-7pm (6pm Sat). Sun by appointment. Admission charge.*

Châtenois

An unusual Romanesque belfry with a spire and four timber watchtowers is one of the more eye-catching sights of this town. Look out for the stork's nest over a 15C gateway, known as the Tour des Sorcières (Witches' Tower). ⚡ A **wine trail** leading up to the summit of the Hahnenberg *(3hr walk there and back)* commands fine views.

FROM CHATENOIS TO COLMAR

54km. Michelin Local Map 315, I 7-8. See itinerary **2** *on map p. 79.*

As far as Ribeauvillé, the road is dominated by countless castles, among them the imposing mass of Haut-Koenigsbourg and the ruins of Kintzheim, Frankenbourg, St-Ulrich, Girsberg and Haut-Ribeaupierre.

Kintzheim

At the foot of Haut-Koenigsbourg Castle, Kintzheim (not to be confused with Kientzheim in Haut-Rhin) is a major tourist centre with two animal parks.

The **Volerie des Aigles** (Eagle Aviary) is located in the courtyard of the old feudal castle where awnings provide shelter to some 80 birds of prey. *30min walk there and back. Open daily, mid-Jul to mid-Aug 10am-5pm, rest of the year 2-5pm, closed mid-Nov to late Mar.* & *Shows (40min): enquire as to times. 8€ (children: 5€).* ☎ *03 88 92 84 33. www.voleriedesaigles.com*

Return to your car and continue driving along the forest road then on the D 159. Turn left after 2km onto a lane which leads to the electrified fence encircling the **Montagne des Singes** (Monkey Mountain).

On 20 hectares of parkland planted with pine trees, Monkey Mountain is home to 300 barbary apes from the Atlas mountains who live wild in the park and have apparently had no difficulty adapting to the Alsatian climate. *Open Jul-Aug, 10am-6pm; May-Jun and Sep 10am-noon and 1-6pm; Apr and early Oct to 11 Nov, 10am-noon and 1-5pm. Closed 12 Nov to late Mar. 7.50€ (children 5-14 years: 4.50€).* ☎ *03 88 92 11 09.*

Straddling the neighbouring town of Orschwiller, the Praelatenberg Grand Cru, formerly the property of the monks of Ebermunster Abbey, is planted with Riesling, Gewürztraminer, Muscat and Pinot Gris varieties and its siliceous soil produces very full-bodied wines.

Saint-Hippolyte

Fountains adorned with flowers in summer and a handsome Gothic 14C and 16C church add to the appeal of Saint-Hippolyte which is renowned for its red wines. The Gloeckelberg Grand Cru, astride the towns of St-Hippolyte and Roedern, produces Gewürztraminers and Pinots Gris of remarkable subtlety.

Bergheim

The lime tree said to date back to 1300 and the 14C Porte Haute (upper gate) which stands just two minutes away both bear witness to the great age of this wine-growing town. Inside the medieval wall around the town, flanked by three slender round towers, a large number of fine old houses can be seen. Look out for the fountain in the market square and an imposing 19C synagogue.

The 18C **church**, built out of red sandstone like the town hall, still retains a number of 14C architectural features. *Open daily Jul-Aug; rest of the year enquire at the presbytery, 1 rue de l'Eglise,* ☎ *03 89 73 63 20.*

The Altenberg vineyards of Bergheim, at an altitude of 320m, dominate the town below, producing Gewürztraminers and Rieslings, a fine selection of which can be found on the **Gustave Lorentz estate** *(see Shopping Guide).*

Ribeauvillé★

The ancient towers of Ribeauvillé, dominated by the three Ribeaupierre castles (12C-13C), are topped by several stork nests. This pleasant stop along the Wine Road boasts no less than three Grands Crus: Osterberg, Kirchberg and Geisberg. Many reputable wine-growing estates are located in Ribeauvillé, among them **Trimbach**; the **Ribeauvillé Cave Vinicole** (cooperative cellar) is another ideal place to find out more about the region's Grands Crus *(see Shopping Guide).*

The semi-pedestrian **Grand'Rue★★** extends the entire length of the town and is lined with timber-framed houses, their window boxes laden with geraniums. The **Pfifferhüs** (Ménétriers restaurant) at n°14, **Halle au blé** (corn exchange) and **Tour des Bouchers★** (Butchers' Tower) are particularly worthy of note.

Beyond Ribeauvillé, the road rises half way up the hillside, offering a wider panorama of the Alsatian plain. Between Ribeauvillé and Colmar, you are in the heart of Alsace's vineyards, whose plentiful hillsides are dotted with famous wine-growing villages and towns.

Hunawihr

Hunawihr is one of the gems of the Wine Road.

⚡ The Rosacker Grand Cru vineyard, which you can walk through on a **wine trail**, is planted mainly with Riesling, but Gewürztraminer does equally well in this soil.

The atmosphere of this peaceful, welcoming village is summed up by its 16C fortified church, which alternates between Protestant and Catholic ceremonies. The **Mittnacht Frères** wine estate is well worth a trip *(see Shopping Guide).*

Centre de réintroduction des cigognes et des loutres (Stork and Otter Park) ♿ *Open Jun-Aug, 10am-7pm (6pm Jun, 6.30pm Jul); Apr (late Mar depending on the weather) to May and Sep-11 Nov, 10am-12.30pm and 2-6pm (5.30pm Apr, 5pm Oct), Sat-Sun and public holidays open all day; 1-11 Nov, Sat-Sun, public and school holidays, 10am-12.30pm and 2-5pm. 7.50€ (children: 5€).* ☎ *03 89 73 72 62. www. cigogne-loutre.com*

Alsace wouldn't be Alsace without storks! Since 1976, the centre has been trying to suppress the migratory instinct of Alsace's storks which was endangering them for a number of reasons: hunting, high-voltage lines, droughts in Africa, etc. It is possible to suppress this instinct among some adult birds, but when summer draws to a close the majority of young birds can't wait to take wing southwards, from whence only a few return the following spring. The reintroduction centre allows visitors to get a closer look at the nesting process and observe several couples as they raise their newly-hatched fledglings during the spring and summer season. Over 200 storks are raised here. In 1991 an otter reintroduction centre was added to the site and the otter, which had disappeared from French rivers, is gradually returning to the region as are beavers and salmon.

Zellenberg

A historic tour of this high-perched village, which commands a superb view of Riquewihr and its vineyards, will take you about 40min on foot (enquire at the town hall or tourist offices of Ribeauvillé or Riquewihr for the leaflet). ⓘ On leaving the village, a **wine trail** leads through the Froehn Grand Cru vineyards which are particularly suited to Gewürztraminer, Muscat and Pinot gris.

Riquewihr★★★

Where the warring invaders of yesteryear failed to take Riquewihr by force, the peaceful hordes of tourists have succeeded and each year its ramparts are stormed by some 2 million visitors. Spared by the many wars which ravaged the region, the town looks just as it did in the 16C. Since the Middle Ages, wine has been the backbone of Riquewihr's prosperity and the town has two Grands Crus, Sporen, suited to Gewürztraminer and Pinot gris, and Schoenenbourg, devoted primarily to Riesling. Riquewihr is home to a number of renowned wine firms including **Dopff et Irion** and **Hugel et Fils** *(see Shopping Guide).*

Mullioned windows, gables crowned with antlers and a turreted staircase bring to mind a picture of the **Wurtemberg Ducal Palace** finished in 1540. It is home to the **Musée de la Communication en Alsace** devoted to exhibitions of the different means of communication used throughout the region over the centuries. *Open Apr-Oct and during the Christmas market, daily except Tue, 10am-1pm and 2-5.30pm. 4€ (children: 2.50€).* ☎ *03 89 47 93 80. www.shpta.com*

Walk down Rue du Général-de-Gaulle. At n°12 is Irion House, dating from 1606 with a corner oriel and opposite an old 16C well. Next-door is the ornately carved house of Jung-Selig, built in 1561.

Riquewihr, surrounded by vineyards.

Liebrich House (cour des Cigognes) dates from 1535 with a picturesque courtyard with balustraded wooden galleries (mid-17C), a well dating from 1603 and an immense wine press (1817). **Hansi House** is reached through a souvenir shop. Upstairs are watercolours, lithographs, decorated ceramics and posters by the talented Colmar-born artist and caricaturist Jean-Jacques Waltz, known as Hansi. *Open Mar-Dec 10am-6pm (Mon 2-6pm); Jan-Feb, 2-6pm. Closed 1 Jan, 25 Dec. 2€ (children under 16: no charge). ☎ 03 89 47 97 00.*

At the end of Rue Kilian, admire the door (1618) of Brauer House. Continue on as far as **Place des Trois-Eglises** along the road of the same name. The square is flanked by two former churches, Saint-Erard and Notre-Dame, converted into houses, and a 19C Protestant church.

Preiss-Zimmer House★ is Riquewihr's best known sight. After crossing over several successive courtyards, you will reach the last but one courtyard which fronts this house that belonged to a wine-makers guild.

Further on to the left is the former **Cour Dimière** (tithe court) of the lords of Ribeaupierre. At the end of Rue du Général-de-Gaulle, on Place de la Sinn, admire the lovely **Sinnbrunnen fountain** dating from 1580.

The tiny **Rue des Juifs** leads into the unusual Jewish courtyard, a former ghetto, at the end of which is a narrow passage and a wooden staircase which leads up to the ramparts and the Musée de la **Tour des Voleurs** (Thieves' Tower) devoted to a somewhat gruesome subject with a torture chamber, dungeon, guardroom and living quarters of the warden of this former prison. Not for the faint-hearted! *Open daily 10am-12.30pm and 2-6.30pm. Closed early Nov to Easter. 2€ (combined ticket with Dolder Museum: 3€, children under 10: no charge). ☎ 0 820 36 09 22 or 03 89 49 08 40.*

Built in 1291, **Dolder Door★** was reinforced in the 15C and 16C and the portcullis and position of the old drawbridge (1600) can still be seen. To the left the ramparts of the Cour des Bergers (shepherds' courtyard) comprise a defence tower. The staircase to the left of Dolder Door leads to the **Dolder Museum** which contains mementoes, engravings, weapons and artefacts relating to local history. *Open daily Jul-Aug, 10am-12.30pm and 2-6.30pm; Apr-Jun and Sep-Oct, Sat-Sun and public holidays, 10am-12.30pm and 2-6.30pm. Closed early Nov to Easter. 2€ (combined ticket with Thieves' Museum: 3€, children under 10: no charge). Tourist office: ☎ 0 820 36 09 22 or 03 89 49 08 40.*

At n°2 Rue du Cerf, note the semi-circular door of **Kiener House★** *(not open to the public)* built at an angle to make it easier for vehicles to enter. The traditional courtyard features a spiral staircase, corbelled storeys and a well dating from 1576. Opposite, the former Stag Inn dates from 1566. Continue along Rue du Cerf and left into Rue Latérale, where you can admire some fine houses among which n°6, the house of the merchant Tobie Berger, still has an original 1551 oriel and in the courtyard a fine Renaissance doorway.

At n°16 Rue de la Première Armée, **Bouton d'Or House** dates back to 1566. At the corner of the house, a cul-de-sac leads to what is known as **Cour de Strasbourg** (1597), which was formerly the tithe court of the chapter of Strasbourg Cathedral.

Opposite **Jung House** (1683) on Rue de la Couronne is an old well called the **Kuhlebrunnen** (cool fountain). At n°6, the stone-built **Dissler House★** (1610) with scrolled gables and loggia is an interesting example of Renaissance architecture in the Rhine.

Beblenheim

This village, which boasts a late 15C Gothic fountain, stands on the hillside of the vineyards of the Sonnenglantz Grand Cru whose 35 hectares are planted with Pinot gris, Muscat and Gewürztraminer. 🚶 **Wine trail**.

The **Bott-Geyl** biodynamic wine estate produces excellent wines *(see Shopping Guide)*. The **Espace Alsace Coopération** is also worth a visit: *68980 Beblenheim, ☎ 03 89 47 91 33.* Made up of 17 cooperative cellars on the Alsace Wine Road, it offers a wide range of Alsatian wines and local specialities.

Mittelwihr

At the southern exit of the village stands the Mur des Fleurs Martyres (destroyed in 1944) which was planted with blue, white and red flowers during the Occupation in token of Alsace's loyalty to France. The area's mild climate explains the presence of almond trees.

🚶 A **wine trail** winds its way through the Mandelberg vineyard that Mittelwihr shares with Bennwihr. Primarily devoted to Riesling and Gewürztraminer, it is known for its particularly fruity wines.

Bennwihr

This village, in the heart of which is a monumental fountain devoted to Saint Odile, was destroyed in 1944 and later rebuilt in keeping with local architectural traditions. Bennwihr shares the Marckrain Grand Cru vineyards with Sigolsheim, whose joint micro-climate particularly favours Gewürztraminer and Pinot gris.

Sigolsheim

This village was also badly damaged during the fighting around Colmar between 1944 and 1945, although the 12C **Eglise St-Pierre-et-St-Paul** still remains. Sigolsheim is proud to possess three Grands Crus: part of Marckrain, part of Furstentum, shared with Kientzheim, and Mambourg, renowned for its strong Gewürztraminer. The estates of **Stirn** and **Pierre Sparr et Fils** offer a fine selection of Grands Crus and other local wines *(see Shopping Guide)*.
Go down Rue de la Première Armée to the national necropolis 2km away to the northeast past the Capuchin Convent.

National necropolis

From the car park, 5min walk there and back. 124 steps. A great many soldiers of the First French Army are buried here, alongside their comrades from North-Africa, also killed in 1944. A central platform commands a **panoramic view★** of the neighbouring peaks and châteaux, as well as of Colmar and the Alsatian plain.

Kientzheim

The profusion of timber-framed houses, old wells and sun dials in Kientzheim is such that visitors often feel they've stepped back in time to the Middle Ages. Schlossberg, Alsace's first Grand Cru vineyard created in 1975, culminates at an altitude of 350m to the northwest of Kientzheim and is characterised by its rich floral Riesling. The **Cave Vinicole de Kientzheim** represents some 150 producers and offers excellent value-for-money wines, including Grands Crus; we also recommend the **Paul Blanck** wine estate *(see Shopping Guide)*.
Originally built in the Middle Ages, the **old castle** was transformed in the 16C. Today it is the headquarters of the **Confrérie St-Etienne**, the official body in charge of controlling the quality of Alsace wines awarding them a seal-style label. The three-storey **Museum of Alsatian Wine and Vineyards** possesses a well-stocked wine library and interesting pieces such as an immense wine press and countless rare tools. *Open daily Jun-Oct, 10am-noon and 2-6pm; May, Sat-Sun and public holidays, 10am-noon and 2-6pm. 3€.* ☎ *03 89 48 21 36.*
As you pass through **Porte Basse** (lower gate), known as the Lalli, look up and admire the carved head poking his tongue out at passers-by. It is believed that his defiant grin was intended to mock assailants who had broken through the first wall of defence.
The Gothic tower of the **church** has been greatly restored. Inside notice the 14C statue of the Virgin on the north side altar, next to which is the **tombstone** of Lazare de Schwendi. In the sacristy are a former ossuary, 14C frescoes and statues of the Virgin Mary from the 14C and 17C.

Kaysersberg★★

The small town remains fiercely proud of one of its sons, **Albert Schweitzer** (1875-1965), Nobel Peace Prize winner in 1952. Missionary surgeon, organist, musicologist and writer, he is above all remembered for his tireless fight in Africa against under-development and illness. He died in September 1965 in Lambaréné, Gabon. The **Albert-Schweitzer Museum**, next door to his birthplace, displays documents, photos, personal items and souvenirs which retrace his life. ⌕ *Open daily Easter to 11 Nov, 9am-noon and 2-6pm; Sat-Sun of Christmas fair (from late Nov), 9am-noon and 2-6pm. 2€ (children: 1€).* ☎ *03 89 47 36 55.*
The town's medieval character is still strong, making its Christmas market one of the most famous of Alsace. The **Weinbach estate**, located in the former Capuchin vineyard, is also one of the best known in Alsace *(see Shopping Guide)*.
The **town hall★**, built in traditional Rhenish style, has a pleasant façade, peaceful courtyard and carved wooden gallery.
The square in front of **Eglise Ste-Croix★** is adorned with a fountain dating from 1521, restored in the 18C, representing Emperor Constantine. Look out for the mermaids and pelicans around the church's Romanesque doorway and in the nave, keep an eye open for the polychrome carved figures and lovely 15C glass roof. In the chancel is a magnificent **altarpiece★★** (1518) by Master Jean Bongartz of Colmar depicting the Crucifixion and the Stations of the Cross.
Chapelle St-Michel, the former chapel of the cemetery, dates from 1463 and comprises two storeys. The lower chamber, turned into an ossuary, is most striking with a font whose base represents a skull. A fresco (1464) and to the right an unusual 14C crucifix can be seen in the upper chapel.
Rue de l'Eglise, Rue de l'Ancien-Hôpital and Rue de l'Ancienne Gendarmerie all boast ornately carved timber-framed **houses★**, one of the town's main architectural attractions in addition to those of Grand'Rue.
The **fortified bridge★** possesses a crenellated parapet and even a small chapel. As soon as you reach the other side, look for **Brief House★**, also known as the "Maison du Gourmet" and admire its richly sculpted and painted wood panels and covered gallery.

R. Mattes/MICHELIN

Ammerschwihr at the foot of hills covered in vineyards.

The **Musée communal** (town museum) is located in a Renaissance house with turreted staircase. On display are religious artefacts (a rare opening 14C statue of the Virgin, a 15C Christ with branches of palms), traditional arts and crafts (coopery) and archaeological finds from Bennwihr. *Open daily Jul-Aug, except Tue, 10am-noon and 2-6pm. 2€.*

Ammerschwihr

After being destroyed by fire following bombing in December 1944 and January 1945, the town was entirely rebuilt in keeping with regional traditions. Eglise St-Martin, whose chancel is lit by modern stained-glass windows, the Renaissance façade of the old town hall, Porte Haute (upper gate) and two fortified towers (Thieves' Tower and Bourgeois Tower) are the only relics of the town's past.

Ammerschwihr shares the Wineck-Schlossberg Grand Cru vineyard with Katzenthal, but the town's other vineyards also produce a number of high quality local wines such as that made by the Sibler estate *(see Shopping Guide).*

Niedermorschwihr★

The modern church of this charming village tucked away in a landscape of vineyards has retained its 13C corkscrew belfry, the only one in Alsace. The oriel windows and wooden balconies of the old houses which line the main street set the scene. The jam and confectionery shop of Catherine Ferber, whose reputation has reached as far as Japan, is not to be missed. The Sommerberg Grand Cru, which lies to the north of the village on a very steep granite slope, produces Rieslings which are ideal for laying down. We recommend **Albert Boxler's** wine estate *(see Shopping Guide).*

Turckheim★

The road out of Niedermorschwihr winds its way through acres of vineyards until the ramparts of the picturesque town of Turckheim come into view. Old roofs, the multi-coloured tiles of its belfry and nests of storks complete the picture of this town that enjoys upholding ancient traditions; from May 22 to October, a night-watchman in traditional dress patrols the town every evening.

The Brand Grand Cru, overlooking the town, produces Riesling, Pinot gris and Gewürztraminer on its granite soil. The **Zind-Humbrecht estate** offers a fine selection of local produce *(see Shopping Guide).*

For a pleasant walk through the vineyards *(1hr there and back)*, leave the town through the Porte du Brand to the **wine trail** which bears right after 30m, level with a small chapel. This 2km-walk through vines with signposted explanations will give you a crash course in how the vines are tended and the different varieties.

Opposite Quai de la Fecht, **Porte de France** leads through a massive 14C quadrangular tower complete with stork's nest. **Porte de Munster** is typical of the town's three other gates. **Place Turenne** is lined with old houses. On the right stands the guardroom with a fountain in front, while the gabled Renaissance town hall is to the rear. Behind is the old church whose tower of Romanesque origins is still visible. **Grand'Rue** is also flanked by countless old houses which date back to the late 16C and early 17C.

Wintzenheim

Nestling in the heart of vineyards which include the Hengst Grand Cru, this village located at the start of the Munster Valley has old fortifications (1275), a number of old houses on Rue des Laboureurs, a lovely 18C fountain depicting the Virgin Mary and the former manor-house of the Order of the Knights of Malta, now the town hall.

The Hengst Grand Cru is famed for its Gewürztraminer which acquires rich spicy aromas on ageing.

Colmar★★★

Whether it be on foot or by boat along the canals of Little Venice, the profusion of fountains, storks, half-timbered houses and window boxes overflowing with brightly coloured geraniums leave the visitor in no doubt as to the town's Alsatian heritage.

Neither war nor time seems to have left a scar or even a wrinkle on the town and its cultural legacy is fully equal to the copious delights that await hungry travellers in its inns and restaurants. Undisputed capital of Alsatian wine, Colmar not only hosts a magnificent wine fair every year, it is also home to the headquarters of the **Maison des vins d'Alsace** *(see Shopping Guide)*.

If interested in buying wines, you could not do better than make a beeline for **Robert Karcher's cellar** *(see Shopping Guide)*.

A tour of the historic town is the perfect way to discover its many sights *(the tour leaves from Place d'Unterlinden, near the tourist office)*. As you go down Rue des Clefs, admire the beautiful pink sandstone tiles on the 18C town hall.

At Place Jeanne d'Arc, turn right into Grand'Rue. The **Protestant church** is in a former Franciscan church (13C-14C), which has been restored to its former beauty after several years of work. Make a short detour to Place du 2-Février to admire the **old 18C hospital** whose high roof is dotted with dormer windows. Back on Grand'Rue, you will go past the lovely Renaissance-style **Maison des Arcades★**, flanked on each corner by two octagonal turrets and then past **Schwendi fountain**.

You now reach **Place de l'Ancienne-Douane**. The former Customs square is one of the most picturesque of Colmar, lined with countless timber-framed houses such as the **Maison au Fer rouge**. The former **Customs House★** (or Koifhus) is an impressive building whose roof is covered in colourful tiles. Merchandise subject to town taxes was stocked on the ground-floor of the main building (1480) while the members of the league of ten free cities met upstairs. The rear section, added in the late 16C, features a turreted staircase crowned with a pinnacle which leads into the attractive wooden gallery.

Continue down Rue des Marchands. **Pfister House★★**, a gem of local architecture, was built in 1357 for a hatter from Besançon: painted façade, a corner oriel on the first floor cleverly built into ornately carved and decorated second floor gallery. In the same street, look out for the 15C **Schongauer or Viola House**, which belonged to the painter's family and the **Cygne (Swan) House**, where he is said to have lived; at n°9 a wooden sculpture depicts a merchant (1609).

The downstairs floors of the birthplace of sculptor **Auguste Bartholdi** (1834-1904) are now a **Local History Museum**. It traces the life and work of the sculptor of the Lion of Belfort, Clermont-Ferrand's Vercingétorix and, most famously of all, The Statue of Liberty. One of the rooms is devoted to a collection of Jewish art. *Open daily except Tue, Mar-Dec, 10am-noon and 2-6pm (last entrance 30min before closing time). Closed 1 May, 25 Dec. 4.10€ (children under 12: no charge).* ☎ 03 89 41 90 60. *www.musee-bartholdi.com*

An arcaded passage opposite the Bartholdi Museum will take you to Place de la Cathédrale. It is on this square that Colmar's oldest house, **Adolphe House** (1350), stands, as does the **town's former guardroom★** (1575). The latter boasts a superb loggia from where the magistrates took their oath and proclaimed infamous sentences. The **collegiate church of St-Martin★**, commonly referred to as the "cathedral", is built out of red sandstone and its main door is flanked by two towers. A sundial can be seen on the south tower. St-Nicolas' Door, the work of Master Humbret, depicts the legend of St Nicolas. Good quality furnishings inside (18C organ by Silbermann).

Leave Place de la Cathédrale along Rue des Serruriers. The **Dominican church** is a quite remarkable and surprisingly slender building whose tall capital-free pillars and 14C and 15C **stained-glass windows★** provide the setting for the famous painting by Schongauer, **The Virgin of the Rose Bower★★**. *Open daily Apr-Dec, 10am-1pm and 3-6pm, 1.30€ (children: 0.50€).*

Now walk along Rue des Boulangers and turn right into Rue des Têtes. The street's name and that of the **Maison des Têtes** (House of Heads) come from the numerous carved heads that adorn the façade of this fine Renaissance building. Continue on to **Place d'Unterlinden**. The Logelbach (Canal des Moulins) cuts

Shopping Guide

INFORMATION

Maison des vins d'Alsace – Civa –
*12 av. de la Foire-aux-Vins – BP 1217, 68000
Colmar – ☎ 03 89 20 16 20 –
www.vinsalsace.com - Mon-Fri 9am-noon
and 2-5pm – closed Christmas to New Year's
Day.* A major centre devoted to Alsace
wines comprised of 5 regional wine-growing
bodies. Relief maps showing villages and
Grands Crus, interactive screens explaining
the wine-grower's work and the wines of
Alsace, brochures, posters, souvenirs. An
answer to all your questions about Alsatian
wines.

USEFUL TIPS

While 2002 proved to be an exceptional
vintage, particularly in the case of
Rieslings, 2003 was more varied; the
heatwave, never very favourable to white
wines, forced many producers to add
acidity to their wines, an almost unheard
of practice in Alsace.
Overall, yields remain high, leading many
wine-producers to chaptalise their wine
(addition of sugar to raise the degree of
alcohol). There are still too many "sweet"
wines which, while they might appeal to the
palate, make it impossible to distinguish the
character of each individual terroir.

FUN AND GAMES

**Jeux de pistes dans le vignoble (A
vineyard treasure hunt)** – *Aglaé – 36 r.
de la Forêt – 67280 Urmatt – ☎ 03 88 47
36 71 – www.coccinellerusee.free.fr - Open
Jul-Aug, Wed-Fri and Apr-Jun and Sep-
Dec on Sun.* Join a group in the towns of
Obernai, Dambach-la-Ville and Turckheim
and take part in an amusing question and
answer treasure hunt (in French) through the
vineyards. Programme on the web site and in
tourist offices.

OVERVIEW

CHARACTERISTICS

White wines – Powerful aroma. They can
be dry, sweet or liquoreux.
Riesling: exuberant, with floral notes and
hints of menthol and citrus fruits when
young; on ageing, takes on a distinctive
"kerosene" note.
Tokay-Pinot Gris: full-bodied, often sweet
with linden, exotic fruit and smoked notes.
Sylvaner: exuberant, slightly dry and fruity.
Pinot Blanc: fruity and tender.
Gewürztraminer: very aromatic, with hints of
rose, violet and exotic fruits, particularly in
the late harvest vintages.
Muscat: generally dry, very fruity, with lemon
notes.
Red wines – The Pinot Noir can range from
a light near-rosé to a dark, ruby-red colour.
A fruity, generally low in tannin, wine.
Sparkling wines – The exuberant Crémant-
d'Alsace has lasting bubbles and notes of
hawthorn blossom and sometimes ripe
grapes.

STORAGE

White wines – Excellent cellar life with
the exception of Sylvaner and Pinot Gris
which should be drunk within three to five
years. Good Rieslings can be kept for twenty
years and more, most of the other wines for
ten years.
Red wines – Most of the Pinot Noir should
be drunk within three to five years.

PRICES

After a period of sharp price increases, most
of the prices have steadied out.
Alsace AOC – 3€ to 8€
Alsace Grand Cru AOC and some special
vintages – 8€ to 12€
**Vendanges tardives and Sélection de
grains nobles** – 20€ to 40€ (50cl)
Crémant-d'Alsace – 5€ to 8€

BUYING

WINE MERCHANTS AND COOPERATIVES

Cave vinicole de Cleebourg – *Route du
Vin – 67160 Cleebourg – ☎ 03 88 94
50 33 – www.cave-cleebourg.com - daily
8am-noon and 2-6pm, Sun and public
holidays from 10am – closed Christmas, New
Year's Day and Easter.* The estate, recreated
in 1946 as a cooperative in the first land
consolidation programme, grows the seven
traditional Alsace grape varieties. Its two
blue-chip values are Tokay-Pinot Gris and
Pinot Blanc. Each year one of the vintages of
the Confrèrerie is selected from the wines of
Cleebourg.
La Sommelière – *2 rue des Tourneurs
– 68000 Colmar – ☎ 03 89 41 20 38
– Open Tue-Fri 9.30am-noon and 2-6.30pm,
Sat 9.30am-6pm.* Mr and Mrs Tempé have
personally tasted 90% of the wines on offer
and visited every single estate. This first-
hand knowledge of their catalogue makes it
possible for them to offer highly personalised
advice to customers who appreciate the
excellent range of Alsace wines including
Marc Tempé's own production.
Cave cooperative Wolfberger –
*6 Grand'Rue – 68420 Eguisheim – ☎ 03 89
22 20 20.* Under the Wolfberger brand, the
cooperative sells a selection of wines from all
over Alsace, including a dozen or so Grands
Crus.
Cave vinicole de Kientzheim – *10 rue des
Vieux-Moulins – 68240 Kientzheim –
☎ 03 89 47 13 19 – www.vinsalsace-
kaysersberg.com - open Mon-Fri 8am-noon
and 2-6pm, Sat, Sun and public holidays
from 10am.* Thanks to high wine-making
standards and strict quality controls, the
distinctive character of the wines of this
cooperative is regularly singled out by wine
specialists. The Grands Crus Schlossberg,
Furstentum and Altenberg are among
Alsace's most prized vineyards.
Cave vinicole de Ribeauvillé – *2 route de
Colmar – 68150 Ribeauvillé – ☎ 03 89 73
61 80 – cave@cave-ribeauville.com - daily
9am-noon and 2-6pm by appointment.* The
cellar produces the wine of ten Grands Crus

and several other well-known vineyards. The grapes are hand-picked and selected minutely. The wine-makers working in the cellar have all signed a charter by which they agree to implement ecologically-friendly techniques. All the vats are stainless steel.

ESTATES

Domaine Sibler – *8 rue du Château – 68770 Ammerschwihr – ☎ 03 89 47 13 15 – jm.sibler@wanadoo.fr – open daily (forewarning preferred).* The Sibler family has been in the wine-making business for three generations. Their estate grows all the authorised Alsatian varieties except for Sylvaner. One of the house's best-sellers is its Kaefferkopf wine. The cellar has been furnished with benches and a vat has been turned into a tasting table.

Domaine Marc Kreydenweiss – *12 rue Deharbe – 67140 Andlau – ☎ 03 88 08 95 83 – marc@kreydenweiss.com - open Mon-Sat 8am-noon and 2-6pm.* Born into a family that has been making wine in Alsace for over three centuries, Marc Kreydenweiss has been at the head of this estate since 1971. In the company of his wife and son, he runs his 12-hectare vineyard, implementing biodynamic growing methods for the last 15 years. A happy blend of modern wine-making techniques and traditional wine-lore, such as temperature control by a water circulation regulation system; the estate produces several Grands Crus and is renowned for its distinctive wines with character.

Domaine Martine and Vincent Stoeffler – *1 rue des Lièvres – 67140 Barr – ☎ 03 88 08 52 50 – info@vins-stoeffler.com - open Mon-Sat 8am-noon and 1.30-6pm.* Martine and Vincent Stoeffler are both descended from several generations of wine-growing families. The current 13-hectare estate is the fruit of the merger between each spouse's individual estate, that they been have running together since 1986. They implement ecologically responsible techniques and since 2002 have been using organic methods certified by Ecocert. The estate produces no less than 35 wines.

Domaine Bott-Geyl – *1 rue du Petit-Château – 68980 Beblenheim – ☎ 03 89 47 90 04 – bottgeyl@libertysurf.fr – open Mon-Tue 8.30-11.30am and 2-6pm.* Heir to a family tradition which dates back to 1795, Jean-Christophe Bott has been running the Bott-Geyl estate since 1993. The 13-hectare estate is home to 70 vineyards spread over seven towns. Biodynamic farming methods, low yields, severe and systematic pruning even during the growing stage. After the entirely manual harvest, the grapes are pressed by gravity and not in pneumatic presses. The wine is then left on the lees until being bottled.

Domaine Roland Schmitt – *35 rue des Vosges – 67310 Bergbieten – ☎ 03 88 38 20 72 – rschmitt@terre-net.fr - open Mon-Sat.* Anne-Marie Schmitt, born in Naples, has thrown herself body and soul into maintaining the high standards set by her late husband, helped by her son Bruno since June 2003. The estate's 9.5 hectares

of vineyards is planted with seven traditional Alsatian varieties.

Gustave Lorentz – *68750 Bergheim – ☎ 03 89 83 22 22 – info@gustvelorentz. com - open Mon lunchtime to Sat 9am-noon and 2-6pm.* A family business begun in 1750; the Lorentz family now owns some thirty hectares and also buys grapes from other growers. The vines, planted on clayey limestone soil, enjoy a south-southeast facing aspect with maximum sunshine.

R. Mattes / MICHELIN

Caveau Robert-Karcher – *11 rue de l'Ours – 68000 Colmar – ☎ 03 89 41 14 42 – www.vins-karcher.com - open daily 8am-noon and 1.30-7pm – closed Good Friday, Easter, 25 and 26 Dec and 1 Jan and Sun afternoons.* The Karcher's wine-growing estate stands on the site of an old farm (1602) in the heart of old Colmar. The wines sold come exclusively from the vineyard known as the Harth de Colmar (6km from the centre). Seven varieties of grapes and regular prizes and awards. Tasting and tours of the property possible.

Charles Baur – *29 Grand'Rue – 68420 Eguisheim – ☎ 03 89 41 32 49 – cave@vinscharlesbaur.fr - open Mon-Sat 8am-noon and 1-7pm, Sun 9am-noon (afternoon by appointment) – closed at Christmas.* The Baur family makes the famous Grands Crus Eichberg and Pfersigberg, "vendanges tardives" from Gewürztraminer, Crémant-d'Alsace and eaux-de-vie. Its wines regularly win medals in national competitions. Tours of the cellar, tasting and sales.

Maison Léon Beyer – *8 place du Château – 68420 Eguisheim – ☎ 03 89 23 16 16 – www.leonbeyer.fr – open Thu-Tue 10am-noon and 2-6pm.* This establishment, one of the oldest in Alsace, (it is said to date back to 1580), enjoys a particularly fine reputation among many top restaurants in Europe and America for its dry white wines. The house's pride and joy are its Réserve maison and above all the Grandes Cuvées Comtes d'Eguisheim wines.

Domaine Ernest Burn – *8 rue Basse – 68420 Gueberschwihr – ☎ 03 89 49 20 68 – jf.burn@wanadoo.fr – open Mon-Sat 9-11am – 2-6pm by appointment.* Following in the footsteps of their father, Ernest Burn, his two sons now run the estate, one in charge of the cellar, the other the vines. The wine is made from low yield grapes which are always harvested as late as possible for maximum quality. The wine is aged in barrels for at least a year.

Domaine Schlumberger – *100 rue Théodore-Deck – 68501 Guebwiller Cedex – ☎ 03 89 74 27 00 – dvschlum@aol.com* A single domain of 140 hectares of vineyards, 70 hectares of which are Grands Crus, make up the Schlumberger estate, one of the largest in Alsace. The estate instigated a local quality charter for the Grands Crus Kitterlé and Kessler which has been applied since the harvest of 2001. In December 2000, a modernisation process has been implemented with the inauguration of new vats and other renovation works.

Jean et Hubert Heywang – *7 rue Principale – 67140 Heiligenstein – ☎ 03 88 08 91 41 – heywang.vins@wanadoo.fr* Jean and Hubert Heywang, at the head of this family-owned 7-hectare estate, practice ecologically responsible methods such as reinforcing the vines' defences, protecting the soil and respecting local flora and fauna. They produce and market a full range of traditional Alsace wines including the village's speciality since 1742, the Klevener of Heiligenstein.

Domaine Mittnacht Frères – *27 route de Ribeauvillé – 68150 Hunawihr – ☎ 03 89 73 62 01 – mittnacht.freres@terre-net.fr - open Mon-Sat, by appointment for groups.* Marc and Christophe Mittnacht, cousins, run the family estate of 22 hectares according to ecologically responsible principles. In 2002, the estate was certified as a result of its commitment to organic farming methods. The wine is stored in stainless steel vats, tuns and barrels for one year.

Domaine Weinbach – *25 route des Vins – 68240 Kaysersberg – ☎ 03 89 47 13 21 – contact@domaineweinbach.com - open Mon-Sat 9-11.30am and 2-5pm – by appointment.* Tireless ambassadresses of Alsace, Mrs Faller and her daughters, Catherine and Laurence, maintain the highest quality standards in their 27-hectare vineyard spread over the Clos des Capucins, around the house and the Grands Crus Schlossberg, Furstentum and Mambourg. 12 hectares are devoted to biodynamic methods since 1998, while the remaining 15 others are farmed according to organic principles.

Domaine Paul Blanck – *32 Grand'Rue – 68240 Kientzheim – ☎ 03 89 72 23 56 – www.blanck.com - open Mon-Sat 9am-noon and 1.30-6pm - closed sun and public holidays.* The Blanck family, wine-growers from father to son since 1610, has lost track of the number of medals it has won over the ages. Philippe and Frédéric continue to contribute to the fine reputation of Alsace wines with their Grands Crus Schlossberg and Furstentum and their Crus Patergarten and Altenburg. Seven varieties of grape are grown on the estate.

Gérard Neumeyer – *29 rue Ettore-Bugatti – 67120 Molsheim – ☎ 03 88 38 12 45 –*

domaine.neumeyer@wanadoo.fr - open Mon-Sat 9am-noon and 2-7pm – by appointment. Gérard Neumeyer is the guardian of three generations of know-how and passion. The southeast facing vineyard enjoys maximum sunshine and is sheltered from the cold winds by the Vosges foothills. The marl-limestone conglomerate, rich in gravel, is ideally suited to the vines which are grown according to ecologically responsible principles.

Albert Boxler – *78 rue des Trois-Epis – 68230 Niedermorschwihr – ☎ 03 89 27 11 32 – open Mon-Sat 9am-noon and 2-6pm.* Mr Boxler, at the helm of this 12-hectare estate, grows and makes Riesling and Tokay-Pinot Gris wines with the help of his son Jean. Their wine-growing family is justly proud of its Grands Crus Sommerberg and Brand and its full-bodied vendanges tardives vintages.

Domaine Trimbach – *15 route de Bergheim – 68150 Ribeauvillé – ☎ 03 89 73 60 30 – contact@maison-trimbach.fr - open Mon-Fri lunchtime 9am-noon and 2-5pm – by appointment.* In the grand tradition of wine merchants who also own vineyards and make their own wine, the 27-hectare estate deals only in the very highest quality wines from which all residual sugar is banished.

Dopff and Irion – *1 cour du Château – 68340 Riquewihr – ☎ 03 89 47 92 51 – cave@dopff-irion.com - open daily 10am-6pm – by appointment.* This leading wine merchant is also at the head of an extremely well-located estate of 27 hectares, two-thirds of whose vineyards are Grands Crus. Traditional wine-growing methods including the planting of grass, severe pruning, manual harvesting and voluntarily restricted yields are applied. In 1998 the house acquired 5 hectares of the Château d'Isenbourg in the town of Rouffach.

Domaine Hugel et Fils – *3 rue de la Première Armée – 68340 Riquewihr – ☎ 03 89 47 92 15 – info@hugel.com - open Mon-Fri lunchtime 8am-noon and 2-5.30pm – by appointment.* For nearly four centuries, the Hugel family has been tending this vineyard which now covers 25 hectares. The family estate is run by Jean-Philippe, Marc and Etienne although the memory of Uncle Jean lingers still in the quality wines. Traditional harvesting and wine-making

R. Mattes / MICHELIN

methods include the absence of fertilisers, hand-picked grapes, ruthless selection of stock and voluntarily restricted yields.

René Muré – *Route des Vins – 68250 Rouffach* – ☏ *03 89 78 58 00 – rene@mure. com - open Mon-Sat 8am-7pm – by appointment.* Born into a wine-growing family whose traditions can be traced back to 1648, René Muré is at the head of a 22-hectare estate. Sylvaner, Riesling, Pinot gris, Muscat, Gewürztraminer and Pinot noir take root in a clayey-limestone soil where they are grown organically. The red wines mature in barrels for one year, while the white wines are left on the lees for between 12 to 18 months.

Le Domaine de l'Ecole, lycée viticole – *8 aux-Remparts – N83, exit Rouffach centre – 68250 Rouffach* – ☏ *03 89 78 73 16 – www.domaine-ecole-vin-rouffach. com - open Mon-Fri 9am-noon and 1.30-5pm – closed Christmas and New Year.* The wine-making school of Rouffach works 13 hectares of vineyard, 5.5 of which are Grand Cru Vorbourg, the estate's pride and joy. High quality is consistent thanks to voluntarily restricted yields. The estate's Côte-de-Rouffach, Crémant brut, *vendanges tardives* and *sélection de grains nobles* and Gewürztraminer are also worth a closer look.

Domaine Stirn – *3 rue du Château – 68240 Sigolsheim* – ☏ *03 89 47 30 58 – domains@free.fr - open daily 1.30-6.30pm – by appointment on Sun.* A family affair for six generations now, this estate is proud of its rich wine heritage. Little by little, the estate's vineyards have been spread out over several towns in a desire to grow a wide variety of vines on an equally distinctive selection of terroirs ranging from the granite soil of Brand (Turckheim) and Schlossberg (Kientzheim), the marl-limestone conglomerate of Marckrain (Bennwihr) and Mambourg (Sigolsheim) and the clayey-limestone of Sonnenglanz (Beblenheim). In 1999, Fabien and his wife Odile renewed a tradition interrupted for twenty years and began making wine on the estate again, they also modernised and improved the cellar. Today the vineyard employs ecologically responsible methods and the grapes are selected and hand-picked almost one by one. After fermentation, the wine is left on the lees in ancient oak casks.

Domaine Pierre Sparr et Fils – *2 rue de la 1ère-Armée Française – 68240 Sigolsheim* – ☏ *03 89 78 24 22 – vins-sparr@alsace-wines.com - open Mon-Sat 8am-noon and 2-6.30pm.* Alsace's most prestigious vineyard during the Lower Middle Ages, Sigolsheim seemed to slip from grace in the 19C. Of late however, largely due to the efforts of the Sparr family, it has returned to favour. The estate, which owns some 34 hectares and farms 150 hectares, is run by the ninth generation of the family which is equally determined to uphold ancestral traditions and implement state-of-the-art technology.

Seppi Landmann – *20 rue de la Vallée – 68570 Soultzmatt* – ☏ *03 89 47 09 33 – contact@seppi-landmann.fr - open 8.30am-noon and 1.30-6pm – by appointment.*

One cannot mistake the enthusiasm and passion of Seppi Landmann as he joyfully welcomes you to his estate. The south, southeast and southwest facing vines are planted over 9 hectares of the legendary "noble valley". The estate is almost exclusively organic, although the label does not say so. Wines are stored in stainless steel vats from six months. Young and vintage wines are available for tasting and if you're curious about finding an equivalent to German "*Eiswein*", ask your jovial host to tell you about his *vendanges tardives*, harvested and made using the same techniques.

Domaine Zind-Humbrecht – *4 route de Colmar – 68230 Turckheim* – ☏ *03 89 27 02 05.* This estate covers 14.9 hectares of land, 39.7 of which is covered in vines, spread over the five towns of Thann, Hunawihr, Gueberschwihr, Wintzenheim and Turckheim. A deep respect for the local terroir combined with a desire to uphold wine-making traditions characterises the approach of this reputable estate.

Domaine Barmès-Buecher – *30 rue Sainte-Gertrude – 68920 Wettolsheim* – ☏ *03 89 80 62 92 – open Mon-Sat 9am-noon and 2-7pm – by appointment.* Since 1985, Geneviève and François Barmès have been running this family estate, born out of the marriage between two well-established wine-growing families, Barmès and Buecher, according to biodynamic methods. The vines are an average of 30 years old and grow on the slopes of Wettolsheim and the surrounding villages of Leinerthal, Herrenweg and Kruelt. The clayey-marl-limestone conglomerate and excellent aspect ensure that the vines thrive.

FESTIVALS

Andlau – Wine festival on 1st weekend of August.

Colmar – Wine fair from 2nd Friday of August.

Eguisheim – Wine-growers festival on 4th weekend of August.

Guebwiller – Wine festival in May.

Heiligenstein – Klevener festival on weekend of August 15.

Marlenheim – Harvest festival on 3rd Sunday of October.

Mittlebergheim – Wine festival on last weekend in July.

Molsheim – Grape festival on 2nd weekend in October.

Obernai – Wine festival on weekend of August 15. Harvest festival on 3rd Sunday of October.

Ribeauvillé – Wine festival on last but one weekend in July. Fiddlers' festival 1st Sunday in September.

Rouffach – Organic bread, wine and cheese festival weekend of Ascension Day.

Scherwiller – "Craft and Riesling" fair on 3rd weekend of August. "Tasting trail" on 1st Sunday of September.

Soultzmatt – Night of Grands Crus Zinnkoepflé on 1st Saturday of August.

Turckheim – Festival of wine of Brand on 1st weekend of August.

Place d'Unterlinden, which literally means "square under the lime trees", in half. The **Musée d'Unterlinden★★★** is housed in a former Dominican convent founded in the 13C. Its 13C **cloisters★** built out of pink sandstone from the Vosges, are lined with rooms devoted to Rhenish art (primitive Rhine painters: Holbein the Elder, Cranach the Elder, Gaspard Isenmann and Martin Schongauer). The museum's pride and joy is however the world-famous **Issenheim altarpiece★★★** which can be found in the chapel next to works by Schongauer and members of his school (24-panel **altarpiece depicting the Passion★★**). The Issenheim altarpiece was painted by Matthias Grünewald from 1500-15 for St Anthony's Convent of Issenheim, an order specialised in the care of those suffering from what was known as "St Anthony's Fire": poisoning by an ergot fungus found in rye which causes hallucinations similar to those experienced with LSD. The altarpiece was exhibited in the church according to a complicated calendar, whereby the statues of the central panel were only visible on St Anthony's Day. The realistic detail, expressionist style, and a vivid use of light and colour make it an undisputed masterpiece of the period. *Open May-Oct 9am-6pm; Nov-Apr daily except Tue 9am-noon and 2-5pm. Closed 1 Jan, 1 May, 1 Nov and 25 Dec. 7€ with audioguide (children under 12: no charge, 12-17: 5€). ☎ 03 89 20 15 50. www.musee-unterlinden.com*

Finally, make sure you have time to explore **Little Venice★**, a neighbourhood bordered by the Colmar and Lauch canals. It is home to several districts including the Tanners' district, whose tall narrow timber-framed houses have lofts where the skins were dried.

FROM COLMAR TO THANN

59km. Michelin Local Map 315, G-I 8-10. See itinerary **3** *on map p. 79. Leave Colmar on the D 417.*

Wettolsheim

This small town claims the honour of being the birthplace of Alsatian wine. Wine-growing was introduced here in Roman times, later spreading to the rest of the region. The 13C Hagueneck castle stands 2km to the west of the town. The Steingrubler Grand Cru, also to the west, enjoys an excellent southwest aspect and a sandy, gravelly soil ideally suited to Riesling and Gewürztraminer. The biodynamic **Barmès-Buecher wine estate** produces wines noted for their body and subtlety *(see Shopping Guide)*.

Eguisheim★

A wine-growing Mecca, Eguisheim boasts Alsace's largest **cooperative cellar** *(see Shopping Guide)*.

The Eichberg and Pfersigberg Grands Crus produce Rieslings, Gewürztraminers and Pinots gris. The **Charles Baur Domaine** and **Léon Beyer firm** both offer a fine selection *(see Shopping Guide)*.

Surrounded by vineyards, Eguisheim is round in shape, spiralling out in concentric circles around a 13C octagonal castle. Even though its three famous towers which used to serve as sundials for the workers toiling in the plain below are now definitively in ruins, the town's lanes and old houses around **Grand'Rue** and a **walk around the ramparts★** offer a charming picture.

⚐ You can also embark on a **wine trail**, complete with guided tour and tasting, *(1hr 30min to 2hr). From mid-Jun to mid-Sep: Sat 3.30pm (Aug: Tue and Sat 3.30pm); rest of the year, by appointment with the wine-growers, listed with the tourist office.*

Husseren-les-Châteaux

At 390m, the village of Husseren is the highest point of the Wine Road and commands a splendid view. The ruins of the three castles of Eguisheim loom over the village and the Five Castle Route *(see Stepping Back in Time)* starts from Husseren. The **Kuentz-Bas Domaine**, one of the best known in the region, is open to the public *(admission charge)*. The wine-tasting cellar is decorated with numerous old tools and objects used in cellars and vineyards. *14 route des Vins, 68420 Husseren-les-Châteaux, ☎ 03 89 49 30 24, info@kuentz-bas.fr. Open Apr-Nov Mon-Sat 9am-noon and 1-6pm (5pm Fri).*

Voetlingshoffen

The church possesses an altar from the Capuchin Convent of Colmar. The reputation of the village's excellent Muscat is in part due to the presence of the Hatschbourg Grand Cru.

Obermorschwihr

Dominated by its half-timbered belfry, this traditional village produces Muscat and Pinot Noir wines.

Hattstatt

The origins of the old, formerly fortified town can be traced back over many centuries. The church (first half of the 11C) possesses a 15C wall and a stone altar from the same period. Note the lovely Renaissance calvary on the left in the nave. The handsome 16C town hall is flanked by old houses. Hattstatt produces part of the Hatschbourg Grand Cru suited to Gewürztraminer, Pinot Gris and Riesling.

Gueberschwihr

Camped on a vine-covered hillside, this village is proud of its magnificent three-storey Romanesque belfry. Next to the church are some Merovingian tombstones. The Goldert Grand Cru, the same golden colour of the vines, is renowned for the quality of its Pinot Gris, Gewürztraminer and Muscat, as is borne out by the Clos St-Imer wines produced by the **Ernest Burn estate** *(see Shopping Guide)*.

Pfaffenheim

Many original old wine-growers' houses are still visible in this wine-growing village, whose origins go back to the end of the 9C. The 13C apse decorated with floral motifs of the **church** is well worth a look.

Pfaffenheim shares the Steinert Grand Cru with the town of Westhalten. Its Gewürztraminer, Pinot gris and Riesling are reputed to age particularly well. The **Pierre Frick biodynamic estate** produces full-bodied wines *(see Shopping Guide)*.

Rouffach★

The historic town of Rouffach is famed throughout France for its annual fair of organic produce. The town is also well known among all those interested in taking up wine-growing as a profession for its wine-producing school which has its own vineyard. The **René Muré estate** (Clos St-Landelin) offers a particularly fine selection of wines *(see Shopping Guide)*.

The structure of **Eglise Notre-Dame de l'Assomption** dates from the 12C and 13C, but the north and south towers, unfinished due to the 1870 war, are 19C. The **Tour des Sorcières** (Witches' Tower, 13C and 15C) is machicolated and crowned with a four-sided roof complete with stork's nest. Up until the 18C, it was used to imprison women accused of witchcraft. On the same square as the Witches' Tower are the Gothic Maison de l'Oeuvre Notre-Dame and the old town hall whose Renaissance façade is surmounted by a twin gable.

Westhalten

At the start of the Vallée noble, this village surrounded by orchards and vineyards, is proud of its two fountains and a number of ancient houses. The vineyards extend over the slopes of the Grands Crus Zinnkoeplfé, Vorbourg and Steinert particularly suited to Gewürztraminer, Pinot Gris and Riesling wines.

Soultzmatt

On the banks of the Ohmbach and at the foot of the upper section of the Zinnkoepflé Grand Cru, the highest of Alsace (420m), since the 13C Soultzmatt has tempered its passion for wine with the production of mineral water, sold today under the Lizbeth brand. The Nessel mineral spring is recommended for those with liver disorders, an interesting complement to the Wine Road! Wagenbourg Castle dominates the landscape. Seppi Landmann's estate provides an excellent opportunity for wine tasting *(see Shopping Guide)*.

Guebwiller★

Since the Middle Ages, wine has been the town's main source of income, with the brief exception of the 19C when the Schlumberger Empire and its textile mills provided employment for the whole town. Guebwiller boasts four Grands Crus: Kitterlé, Kessler, Saering and Spiegel, which produce Riesling, Gewürztraminer, Muscat and Pinot gris wines. The handsome **Neoclassical collegiate church of Notre-Dame★** was built from 1760 to 1785; the rich **interior decoration★★** is strongly Baroque in style. **Eglise St-Léger★** is a fine example of the Late Romanesque Rhenish style.

The five floors of **Florival Museum★**, located in an 18C residence, are devoted to collections of minerals and objects which depict the town's wine-growing, craft and industrial past. However its pride and joy is a substantial collection of works by **Théodore Deck** (1823-91) a ceramicist who succeeded in recreating the gorgeous deep turquoise blue glazing known as "bleu de Deck". ♿ *Open daily except Tue 2-6pm, Sat-Sun and public holidays 10am-noon and 2-6pm. Closed 1 Jan and 25 Dec. 4€. ☎ 03 89 74 22 89.*

Soultz-Haut-Rhin

Soultz, a town of mineral springs and storks nesting in chimney stacks, is home to some lovely old houses such as that of the current tourist office (1575). Take a walk along the ramparts past the "witches' tower" and pause at **Eglise St-Maurice** to admire its colourful 15C wooden low-relief, Silbermann organ (1750) and immense mural.

The former headquarters of the Knights of the Order of Malta is now home to the **Nef aux Jouets** (Toy Museum) with exhibits from around the world ranging from the simplest to the most sophisticated. ♿ *Open Apr-Dec daily except Tue 2-6pm. Closed 1 Jan, 25 and 31 Dec. 4.60€ (children 2-6: 1.50€). ☎ 03 89 74 30 92*

On the road out of Soultz, the **Cave vinicole du Vieil-Armand** centralises the wine production of 150 hectares of vineyards belonging to 130 wine-growers. It produces two Grands Crus: Ollwiller, from Wuenheim and Rangen from Thann. The basement is devoted to a Wine Museum with a collection of tools and utensils used by wine-growers and makers in former times. *Open Mon-Sat 8am-noon and 2-6pm, Sun and public holidays 10am-noon and 2-6pm.* ☎ *03 89 76 73 75.*

Thann★

Thann is the last stage of the Alsace Wine Road, ending in a blaze of glory with the Rangen Grand Cru.

🚶 The vineyards can be reached by Chemin Montaigne and Rue du Vignoble: open to walkers only – restricted access during harvest time *(late Sep to late Oct)*; by Rue du Vignoble: bicycle path and path through the vines to Chemin Montaigne; by Rue du Kattenbachy: at the rear of the small valley to the right at the start of Chemin Montaigne.

The **collegiate Gothic church of St-Thiébaut★** (14C-early 16C) illustrates the transition towards the Late Gothic style. A stunning **doorway★★** adds interest to the west front. Inside notice the pentagonal chapel and polychrome wooden statue of the wine-growers' Virgin, sculpted around 1510. It is well worth taking a closer look at the 51 15C oak **stalls★★**, reworked with even more fantasy in the 19C. The foliage, gnomes and comic characters impress by their lifelike features and masterful execution.

From the bridge across the Thur, admire the view of the 15C **Tour aux Sorcières** (Witches' Tower), crowned by an onion-shaped dome which is all that remains of the former fortifications.

🚶 Finally those with energy to spare, can walk *(1hr)* up to the ruined castle of Engelbourg, whose keep collapsed leaving part of the lower wall intact around an empty centre overlooking the plain. Local folklore has dubbed this unusual shaped ruin the **"witch's eye"**.

Stepping Back in Time

Château du Haut-Koenigsbourg★★

10km W of Sélestat on the D 159. Open Jun-Aug 9.30am-6.30pm (last admission 30min before closing time); Apr-May and Sep 9.30am-5.30pm; Mar and Oct 9.45am-5pm; Nov-Feb 9.45am-noon and 1-5pm. Closed 1 Jan, 1 May and 25 Dec. 7€, no admission charge 1st Sun of the month (Oct-Mar). ☎ *03 88 82 50 60.*

The sight of this immense fortress, 300m long and perched at a height of almost 800m, rising out of the early morning mist is truly unforgettable. No wonder, then, that Jean Renoir chose it as the location for the prison camp in his anti-war masterpiece, *La Grande Illusion*, filmed in 1937. Built by the Hohenstaufens in the 12C, it fell into the hands of highway robbers for a time before being claimed back by the Hapsburgs in the 15C. It was then abandoned for several centuries, subjected to pillaging and fire, until the town of Sélestat finally gave it to Kaiser Wilhelm II, a great lover of romantic castles, who had it restored by architect Bodo Ebhardt. After visiting the various buildings, enjoy the panoramic **view★★** over all the wine, corn and salt routes to Lorraine through Alsace.

Route des Cinq Châteaux (Five Castle Route)★

🚶 *17km tour starting from Husseren-les-Châteaux followed by a 2hr walk there and back. Take the road out of Husseren and bear right onto the signposted "Cinq Châteaux" forest road. 1km further on, park your car (car park) and walk to the "three keeps" of Eguisheim (5min climb).* Weckmund, Wahlenbourg and Dagsbourg are the names of the three red sandstone **keeps of Eguisheim** perched on the hilltop. After the demise of the Eguisheim family, the three castles became the property of the bishops of Strasbourg in 1230.

From here you can either walk (1hr) to the castle of Hohlandsbourg, or return to your car, and carry on the Five Castle Route. On your left, 6km beyond the keeps of Eguisheim rises the imposing **castle of Hohlandsbourg** built from 1279. Unlike its sandstone neighbours, this castle is built out of granite like the peak on which it stands. Destroyed during the Thirty Years War, it was rebuilt and adapted to artillery warfare, which explains the numerous holes for firearms. The local towns have decided to turn it into a "historic and cultural centre" recreating a medieval garden and staging shows of knightly pageantry. It is also home to an inn. *Open Jul-Aug: guided tours (45min) 10am-7pm; Jun and early Sep to mid-Oct 2-6pm, Sun and public holidays 11am-6pm; mid-Apr to late May and mid-Oct to late Nov Sat 2-6pm, Sun and public holidays 11am-6pm. 4€, couples: 5.50€ (8-16 year olds: 1.50€, children under 8: no charge). Admission charges differ during shows.* ☎ *03 89 30 10 20.*

The **keep of Pflixbourg** can be reached on foot along a path 2km further on, to the left. The Ribeaupierre family acquired the keep, the former residence of the representative of the Holy Roman Emperor in Alsace, in the 15C. A vaulted water tank stands next to the keep. Splendid view of the Fecht Valley to the west and the plain of Alsace to the east.

Outdoor Activities in the Vosges

Flying
Ecole de Parapente Grand Vol (paragliding school) – *18km SW of Andlau on the D 425. Niedermatten farm, 67220 Breitenbach,* ☎ *03 88 57 11 42, info@grandvol.com School open Apr-Nov Sat-Sun; the paragliding site is open all year round.* Qualified instructors run courses and train beginners in the basics of paragliding. Special beginner's course. Paragliding can be practised from age 14 upwards.

Skiing over the Field of Fire
Stade de neige du Champ du Feu – *12km eastbound of Andlau on the D 425. Le Hohwald,* ☎ *03 88 97 35 05.* In the heart of the medium altitude Vosges mountains, between 900 and 1 100m, is an immense plateau suited to cross-country skiing and snowshoe hiking. The resort also boasts 17 ski-lifts. Certified French School of Skiing centre.

Breathtaking mountain views
Grand Ballon★★★ – *30km SW of Guebwiller on the D 430 and the D 431 from Markstein.* 🚶 *Leave your car at the hotel and take the path to the left (30min walk there and back).* The Grand Ballon or the Ballon de Guebwiller is the highest point of the Vosges at 1 424m. As you would expect, it commands a stunning **view★★★** of the southern Vosges mountains, the Black Forest and in fine weather as far as the Jura and the Alps. Don't forget your binoculars.

Petit Ballon★★ – *16km NW of Guebwiller on the D 430; at Lautenbach head north on the forest road to the Pass of Boenlesgrab and then onto the Petit Ballon.* 🚶 *From the Kahler Wasen farmhouse-restaurant, 1hr 15min walk there and back.* Altitude 1 267m. A view of the plain of Alsace, the hills of Kaiserstuhl and the Black Forest to the east, to the south is the Grand Ballon range while to the west and north lies the Fecht Valley.

Life in Alsace

Ecomusée d'Alsace ★★
12km N of Mulhouse on the D 430. Open Jul-Aug 9.30am-7pm; Mar-Jun and Sep 10am-6pm; early Oct to mid-Nov 10am-5pm; mid-Nov to mid-Dec, Sun only; Christmas holidays, daily. Closed early Jan to mid-Feb. 14.50€ (children: 9€). ☎ *03 89 74 44 74. www.ecomusee-alsace.com*

This open-air museum has been created on almost 20 hectares of land. You can take as much or as little time as you wish, but it would be a pity to spend less than half a day. Most of the events and shows depicting life and traditions in Alsace are held in the evenings in summertime. The wish to preserve the rich regional heritage was at the origin of this open-air museum devoted to Alsace. The tour invites you to step inside 70 peasant homes, grouped by region, offering an insight into 19C and 20C society. The museum calls upon all five senses: taste the bread baked in old ovens, touch the warm flanks of the shire horses and the potter's cold clay and witness first-hand the know-how and lifestyles of yesteryear. Nature is of course an integral facet of the museum with an apple orchard devoted to ancient varieties, a bee-hive and farmyard animals. Finally the presence of Alsace's emblematic storks nesting on the weathered roofs remind visitors that Alsace is their natural habitat.

The colourful façade of an Alsatian house in the open-air museum.

R. Mattes/MICHELIN

2

Beaujolais

Beaujolais, which owes its name to its historical capital, Beaujeu, conjures up an image of good meals, good wine and good friends. It is a relatively diverse geological region and has in fact only been planted extensively with vines since recent times. However, it holds a special place in the hearts of many Frenchmen and women because its wines, red for the most part, are so synonymous with the friendly atmosphere of the unpretentious bistros and cafés that abound in every town and village in the land. The fortunes of the vines, grown here since Roman times, have varied from flourishing in the Middle Ages, to almost ignored in the 17C, followed in the 18C by a genuine revival when Lyon, known as the "siphon of Beaujolais", ceased to be France's sole market and Beaujolais wines began to be shipped as far as Paris. The market expanded still further as the road and rail networks evolved and vine-growing become a mono culture in the region. But the region's great discovery was Beaujolais nouveau. No sooner bottled than sold! Since the 1950s, from mid-November, Paris, France and then the whole world have been inundated by this delightfully uncomplicated, easy-to-drink wine. After a period of relative commercial "madness", however, the market has wisely preferred to focus on genuinely authentic Beaujolais wines which express the full subtlety of the Beaujolais terroir. Beaujolais wines are best discovered on site, in the welcoming cellars of tiny villages nestling in a landscape of hills dotted with clumps of dark Douglas pine trees.

The terroir
Michelin Local Map no 327 – Saône-et-Loire (71) and Rhône (69)
Surface area: 23 000 hectares stretching from Mâcon in the north to the Azergues valley in the south.
Production: 1.4 million hectolitres per year.
The region's vineyards are composed of two main types of soil: "gore", a sort of clay created by decomposing granite to the north, and sedimentary limestone or clayey-limestone soils in the centre and south. Granite rock can also be found in the upper Azergues valley. The wines made from grapes grown at over 250m are lighter than their low altitude counterparts.

The wines
The region has three appellations, **Beaujolais**, **Beaujolais-Villages** and ten AOC village wines: **Morgon**, **Saint-Amour**, **Chénas**, **Brouilly**, **Côte-de-Brouilly**, **Juliénas**, **Moulin-à-Vent**, **Régnié**, **Chiroubles** and **Fleurie**.
Practically only one grape variety is grown, Gamay noir, which thrives on the sunny hills producing light, fruity wines. Chardonnay is also grown, producing a little less than 10 000 hectolitres/year of white Beaujolais.

"River Beaujolais"
"Lyon is fed by three rivers: the Rhône, the Saône and... Beaujolais." This quote of dubious origins could have been written by René Falet or Antoine Blondin who were so instrumental in developing the prosperity of wine-growing in Beaujolais.

The vineyards of Beaujolais.

Directory

WHERE TO EAT

AROUND BEAUJEU

Auberge Vigneronne – Le Bourg – 69430 Régnié-Durette – 5km south of Beaujeu on the D 78 – ☎ 04 74 04 35 95 – closed Tue evening from Oct to Apr and Mon - 10/23€. Near the church, the lovely stone façade of this traditional restaurant also hides a tasting cellar. Two welcoming Beaujolais-style dining rooms, one of which has an open fireplace, and summer terrace.

Anne de Beaujeu – 28 rue de la République – 69430 Beaujeu – ☎ 04 74 04 87 58 – closed 12 days early Aug and from 20 Dec to 20 Jan, Sun evening, Tue midday and Mon - 19/48€. This hotel-restaurant, located in a handsome 19C mansion surrounded by parkland, is a tribute to the most famous member of the Beaujeu family, regent of France. Wall hangings, frescoes of lavish dinners, paintings and antique furniture set the scene for the interior decoration. Sophisticated cuisine.

Mont-Brouilly – Au Pont des Samsons – 69430 Quincié-en-Beaujolais – 5.5km southeast of Beaujeu on the D 37 – ☎ 04 74 04 33 73 – closed 28 Jan to 24 Feb, 22 to 30 Dec, Mon except evenings from Apr-Oct and Sun evening from Oct-May. - 19/54€. The owners of this pleasant restaurant at the foot of Mount Brouilly invite guests to discover the delights of traditional dishes cooked with local produce and accompanied by a fine wine list. The spacious dining room commands a peaceful view of the flowered garden dotted with a few wine-growing tools.

AROUND BELLEVILLE

Beaujolais – 40 rue du Maréchal-Foch – 69220 Belleville – ☎ 04 74 66 05 31 – closed 13-16 Apr, 4-26 Aug, 22-29 Dec, Sun evening, Tue evening and Wed - - 15.80/43€. The culinary and decorative choices of this restaurant combine into a vibrant ode to Beaujolais: recipes and wine list, deeply anchored in local traditions, enhanced by a dining room whose local flavour and roots are equally present in the bare stone and timbers, rustic furniture and country objects.

L'Ange Couronné – 18 rue de la République – 69220 Belleville – closed 3-25 Jan, 3-11 Oct, Sun evening, Tue lunchtime and Mon – ☎ 04 74 66 42 00 - 16/34€. On the main street of a former stronghold that is now a thriving wine-growing centre, a light contemporary dining room where you can tuck into reliable traditional dishes. The bedrooms, set around a winter garden, are equally sober and tasteful.

Christian Mabeau – 69460 Odenas – ☎ 04 74 03 41 79 – closed 2-12 Jan, 30 Aug to 12 Sep, Sun evening and Mon except public holidays - 25.50/53.50€. This small family restaurant in the heart of the village of Odenas lays a few tables on the terrace overlooking the vineyards as soon

as the weather permits. A pleasant dining room where traditional recipes enhanced by local flavours are served in addition to a fine choice of regional wines.

AROUND ST-AMOUR

Restaurant Le Morgon – Haut-Morgon – 69910 Villié-Morgon – 4.5km S of Fleurie on the D 68 – ☎ 04 74 69 16 03 – closed 15 Dec to 20 Jan, public holidays, Tue evening from 20 Jan to 1 Apr, Sun evening and Wed - 13/31€. The village of Villié-Morgon, in a landscape of vineyards, is an essential halting-point for all lovers of good wine. The Morgon Restaurant in the heart of this tiny town is the ideal choice for all those who are eager to combine fine vintages with tasty Beaujolais recipes.

Auberge des Vignerons – 69840 Emeringes – 6.5km NW of Fleurie on the D 32 – ☎ 04 74 04 45 72 – closed 1-7 Jan, 23-30 Jun, Wed from Dec-Feb, Mon evening and Tue - 21/39€. Off the beaten track, this village is home to a restaurant whose tasty traditional cooking is a well-kept local secret. The bay windows of the wainscoted dining room offer a lovely view over the Beaujolais vineyards as you tuck into delicious dishes where premium fresh produce takes pride of place.

Les Platanes de Chénas – Les Deschamps – 69840 Chénas – 3.5km NE of Fleurie on the D 68 – ☎ 03 85 36 79 80 – closed in Feb, Tue and Wed except during Jul-Aug - 22/58€. This converted farmhouse is located not far from the small village of Chénas whose main source of income is wine-growing. In summer, meals are served mainly on the terrace overlooking row upon row of carefully tended vines. Beautifully prepared dishes ranging from regional recipes to more contemporary-inspired concoctions served with local wines.

Table de Chaintré – 71570 Chaintré – 4km northeast of St-Amour-Bellevue on the D 186 – ☎ 03 85 32 90 95 – closed 6-21 Aug, 24 Dec to 8 Jan, Sun evening, Mon and Tue - 32€ lunchtime. In the heart of the Pouilly vineyards, this welcoming house is where Lucie Aubrac, famous resistance fighter, was born and bred. Guests sit down in a comfortable contemporary-style dining room to enjoy a set daily menu and choose from an excellent wine list.

Chez Jean Pierre – 71570 Saint-Amour-Bellevue – ☎ 03 85 37 41 26 – closed 22 Dec - 10 Jan, Sun evening, Wed evening and Thu - 17/40€. The terrace and dining room of this attractive stone-built house provide a warm setting in which to savour the creative cooking of chef Alain Develay: wild mallard served with wild mushrooms, pikeperch in a pastry case, etc. Of course no meal would be complete without a glass of AOC St-Amour.

Le Coq à Juliénas – Place du Marché – 69840 Juliénas – 3km SW of St-Amour-Bellevue on the D 17E – ☎ 04 74 04 41 98 – closed Jan, Dec and Wed - 22.50€.

The boisterous strutting and cock-a-doodle-dos of the cockerel echo throughout the tasteful décor of this handsome country bistro. Here in the heart of the Beaujolais region, the cockerel however has a serious rival in the local wines and the excellent choice of regional vintages. Tasty country cooking.

⊖⊖**Chez la Rose** – *Place du Marché – 69840 Juliénas – 3km SW of St-Amour-Bellevue on the D 17E – ☎ 04 74 04 41 20 – closed 8-28 Feb, 13-17 Dec, Tue, Thu, Fri and Mon out of season – ⊭ - 26/48€.* Your taste-buds will begin to tingle as you approach the pleasant restaurant Chez la Rose in the heart of Beaujolais' vineyards whose rich soil and climate produce full-bodied robust wines which age particularly well. Carefully prepared regional dishes served in a country-style dining room or on a flower-decked terrace.

⊖⊖⊜**Restaurant Le Cep** – *Place de l'Eglise – 69820 Fleurie – ☎ 04 74 04 10 77 – closed Dec, Jan, Sun and Mon except public holidays – ⊭ - 35/60€.* Chantal Chagny, the owner of this proud embassy of the Beaujolais region, gave up luxury to devote herself wholeheartedly to her passion – cooking whose local flavour is strong. Local wine-growers and passing epicureans rub shoulders in this welcoming inn as they savour the lady of the house's appetising dishes.

IN VILLEFRANCHE-SUR-SAONE

⊖⊖**Juliénas** – *236 rue Anse – 69400 Villefranche-sur-Saône – ☎ 04 74 09 16 55 – closed Sun except public holidays - ⊭ - 20/53€.* This delightful bistro-style country restaurant will not empty your wallet as you tuck into a plate loaded high with inventive recipes which masterfully combine modern and traditional flavours. The wine list does full justice to the region's many delights.

WHERE TO STAY

AROUND BEAUJEU

⊖**Domaine des Quarante Ecus** – *Les Vergers – 69430 Lantignié – 3.5km E of Beaujeu on the D 78 – ☎ 04 74 04 85 80 – bnesme@wanadoo.fr - open daily – ⊭ – 5rm: 48€.* This wine-growing estate offers a few rooms furnished in a mixture of old and new pieces and decorated with reproductions of works by Van Gogh. All command views over the vineyards or the garden and orchards. Breakfast is served in a lovely countrified room. Visit to the cellar and tasting of wines produced on the estate.

⊖**Chambre d'Hôte Mr and Mrs Bonnot** – *Le Bourg – 69430 Les Ardillats – 5km NW of Beaujeu on the D 37 – ☎ 04 74 04 80 20 – closed Jan – ⊭ – 5rm: 42€ – meals: 16€.* On the edge of the village, the stone façade and wooden shutters of this restored farmhouse immediately catch the eye. Colourfully decorated rooms with bare beams, each of which is named after a fruit: raspberry, pineapple, plum and mandarin. Tasty home cooking and as much Beaujolais as you can drink.

⊖⊖**Domaine de Romarand** – *69430 Quincié-en-Beaujolais – 5.5km SE of Beaujeu on the D 37 – ☎ 04 74 04 34 49 – closed Christmas and New Year – ⊭ – 3rm: 56€.* This lovely stone-built property overlooking a rockery garden and acres of vineyards belongs to a couple of wine-growers. The modern, comfortable rooms all command pleasant views. Homemade jams and pastries take pride of place on the plentiful breakfast table.

⊖⊖**Chambre d'hôte Gérard Lagneau** – *Huire - 69430 Quincié-en-Beaujolais – 5.5km SE of Beaujeu on the D 37 – ☎ 04 74 69 02 70 – jealagneau@wanadoo.fr - open all year – ⊭ – 4rm: 57€.* This delightful stone-built house, nestled in the hamlet of Huire, is the property of a friendly wine-growing family who make it a point of honour to make sure you feel at home with them. Simple but faultlessly kept rooms. Breakfast is served in rustic, timbered room. Tasting of local wines in the 16C cellar.

AROUND FLEURIE

⊖⊖**Chambre d'hôte les Pasquiers** – *Les Pasquiers – 71570 Romanèche-Thorins – 2.5km SE of Fleurie on the D 119E – ☎ 04 74 69 86 33 – ⊭ – open all year round – bookings only – 4rm: 80€ – meals: 25€.* An immense walled garden surrounds this handsome Second Empire property many of whose original fittings and fixtures are still visible: carpets, library, grand piano in the sitting room, etc. The rooms in the main wing are furnished with lovely 19C antiques, while those in the outhouse are more "contemporary" in flavour.

⊖⊖**Chambre d'Hôte Domaine de la Grosse Pierre** – *69115 Chiroubles – on the D 119 towards Chiroubles – ☎ 04 74 69 12 17 – apassot@terre-net.fr - closed Dec and Jan – 5rm: 45/55€.* An ideal choice for a prolonged stay in the heart of Beaujolais, this handsome manor surrounded by vineyards offers a handful of tastefully, if simply decorated rooms. Wine tasting in a vaulted cellar.

⊖⊖⊜**Les Maritonnes** – *71570 Romanèche-Thorins – 3.5km E of Fleurie – ☎ 03 85 35 51 70 – contact@maritonnes. com - closed 22 Dec to 20 Jan – ℙ – 20rm: 90/130€ – ⊡ 10€ – restaurant: 23/70€.* This splendid property covered in Virginia creeper stands in the heart of well-tended

J. Damase / MICHELIN

parkland, offering spacious bright rooms. The restaurant serves traditional dishes served with the famous local wine: Moulin-à-Vent. A bistro area offers a simpler choice of menu.

AROUND ST-AMOUR
⌨⌨**Hôtel Les Vignes** – *Route de St-Amour – 69840 Juliénas – 3km SW of St-Amour-Bellevue on the D 17E – ☎ 04 74 04 43 70 – hoteldesvignes@wandoo.fr - closed 7-22 Feb, 21-28 Dec, Sun from Dec-Mar – 22rm: 42/67€ – ⟲ 10€.* On the road out of Juliénas, this hotel built on a hillside and surrounded by vineyards, offers colourful, renovated practical rooms. The Beaujolais-inspired breakfast, offers a choice of local cooked meats, is served in a sunny room and is more than worth a special mention. Friendly staff.

AROUND VILLEFRANCHE-SUR-SAONE
⌨⌨**Saint-Romain** – *Route de Graves – 69480 Anse – 7.5km NE of Charnay on the D 70 – ☎ 04 74 60 24 46 – closed 28 Nov to 9 Dec, Sun evening from early Nov to late Apr – ⊠ – 24rm: 55€ – ⟲ 7€ – restaurant 19/46€.* You could not do better than spend a night or two in this old stone farmhouse in the heart of Beaujolais where the only sounds that disturb the peace and quiet are those of birdsong and the wind in the leaves. The somewhat old-fashioned interior decoration of the rooms is fully compensated by their immaculate cleanliness and care. Tasty meals prepared with fresh produce in the restaurant.

⌨⌨⌨**La Ferme du Poulet** – *180 rue Georges-Mangin – 69400 Villefranche-sur-Saône – ☎ 04 74 62 19 07 – la.ferme. du.poulet@wanadoo.fr - closed 5-20 Aug, 23 Dec to 2 Jan, Sun evening and Mon*

– ⊠ – 10rm: 80€ - 10€ – restaurant 34€. A haven of greenery and charm, this fortified 17C farmhouse has been lovingly restored and is carefully protected from the bustle of the town by a wall. The spacious practical rooms boast excellent bedding. Pleasant dining room with old beams, in which colourful, carefully prepared meals are served.

GOURMET SHOPPING
Moulin à Huile – *29 rue des Echarmeaux – 69430 Beaujeu – ☎ 04 74 69 28 06 – jm-montegottero@wanadoo.fr – Mon-Sat 8.30-noon and 2.30-7pm – closed 1-6 Jan, Sun and public holidays.* In his parent's former ironmonger's shop, Jean-Marc Montegottero has set up an oil press to press oil traditionally. The old stone mill forgotten in a corner has come back into use and is once again working at full capacity. Argan, hazelnut and pine nut oil tastings after a visit of the workshop.

Yves Maringue – *269 rue Nationale - 69400 Villefranche-sur-Saône – ☎ 04 74 68 33 98 – Mon-Sat 7.30am-1pm and 2-7.30pm.* The tiny shop of this master of charcuterie, rewarded countless times for his homecured ham and saucisson, seems to overflow with mouth-watering terrines, pork pies, magnificent hams and hosts of other delicacies. The pastry-delicatessen shop a few yards away also belongs to Mr Maringue.

MARKETS
Anse – Friday morning
Beaujeu – Wednesday morning
Belleville – Tuesday morning
Juliénas – Monday morning
Villefranche – Monday morning and Sun morning.

It was during the Second World War, when Paris' journalists had fled Paris for Lyon, that the media became acquainted with Beaujolais, over a glass of red wine at a café counter in the early morning. The tradition has remained and the "pot Beaujolais", a thick-bottomed glass bottle, remains the ideal companion to hearty regional dishes such as *gras-double*.

Beaujolais Wine Road

See itineraries 1 *and* 2 *on the map on p. 101; itinerary* 3 *is a suggested tour of Beaujolais, but not along the wine route.*

FROM VILLEFRANCHE-SUR-SAONE TO ST-AMOUR-BELLEVUE
98km. Michelin Local Map n°327, G-H 1-3. See itinerary 1 *on map p. 101.*
A sea of green vineyards spreads out like ripples over the slopes of the Beaujolais hills down to the Saône valley. The vines are as much a part of the regional landscape as they are of the local way of life. The region lives to the rhythm of the wine-growing calendar and the precious nectar flows through the economic backbone of the entire area.

Villefranche-sur-Saône
The town owes a great deal to Guichard IV of Beaujeu who made it the capital of Beaujolais, endowing it with a charter and countless privileges. It is above all famed for its seemingly never-ending Rue Nationale which is a perfect snapshot of the town's unusual urban architecture.
Rue Nationale is lined on either side with old houses, built and transformed between the 15C and 18C. They have relatively narrow façades, because of a tax imposed on the width of the house façades in 1260 to make up for the exemption from taxes and other privileges granted the town in its charter.

At n°523, the spiral staircase, mullion windows and shell-shaped niche with elegant statue of **Hôtel Mignot de Bussy** form a delightful Renaissance picture. **Auberge de la Coupe d'Or**, at n°528, was the oldest inn in Villlefranche (14C), but was transformed in the 17C.

Eglise Notre-Dame-des-Marais owes its existence to a legend according to which a statue of the Virgin Mary, found in the marshes by peasants and transported to Eglise Ste-Madeleine, was mysteriously found again in the marshes. The inhabitants of Villefranche eagerly set about building a chapel to mark the spot. All that remains of the original 13C structure is a small Romanesque belfry (13C) above the chancel. The church has been substantially reworked over the ages: the central tower is 15C, the magnificent Late Gothic façade was a gift from Pierre II de Bourbon and Anne de Beaujeu in the 16C and the spire was rebuilt in 1862. Notice the gargoyles on the north façade one of which depicts lust.

Leave Villefranche on the D 504. Take a right onto the D 19 and then a left onto the D 44.

Montmelas-Saint-Sorlin

The feudal **castle** *(not open to the public)*, restored by Dupasquier, a pupil of Viollet-le-Duc, lies to the north. Perched in solitary splendour on a rocky outcrop, its high crenellated battlements, towers and keep cannot fail to impress.

From Montmelas, continue to the pass of St-Bonnet. From the pass, a trail leads to the Signal de St-Bonnet (30min walk there and back).

Signal de Saint-Bonnet

The panorama from the east end of the chapel unfolds to reveal Montmelas in the foreground, set against the hills and vineyards of Beaujolais, and in the distance the Saône valley; to the southwest lie the mountains of the Lyonnais and Tarare regions.

Young *(from 4 years old)* and old may enjoy romping through the acrobatic adventure course created in the trees of the **Au fil des arbres park**. *Open Jul-Aug, 10am-7pm; May-Jun Wed 2-7pm, Sat-Sun 10am-7pm; Mar, Apr, Sep, Oct Sat-Sun and school holidays, 1-7pm; Nov, school holidays 1-6pm. Closed Dec-Feb. 20€ (children: from 5€ to 16€). ☎ 06 73 38 12 82. From the pass, take the D 20 on the right.*

Saint-Julien

This delightful wine-growing village is the birthplace of **Dr Claude Bernard** (1813-78). A house bought by the French scientist amid vineyards bears the following inscription: "I live on the hillside overlooking the Dombes...". It now houses a museum created under the aegis of the Fondation Mérieux of Lyon, devoted to the life and works of Claude Bernard. Walk through the garden past the vineyards and you will reach the place where he was born at the rear of the property. *Open early Apr to late Sep, daily except Mon and Tue, 10am-noon and 2-6pm; early Oct to late Feb, daily except Mon and Tue, 10am-noon and 2-5pm. 5€. ☎ 04 74 67 51 44. www.fond-merieux.org*

Take the D 19 to Salles.

Salles-Arbuissonnas-en-Beaujolais

Salles-Arbuissonnas-en-Beaujolais is still home to a few buildings of a **priory** founded in the 10C by the monks of Cluny. A collection of souvenirs and objets d'art are exhibited in the 15C **chapter house** *(reached through the garden and the cloisters to the right of the church). Guided tours (30min) by prior arrangement with Miss Alliès. 2€. ☎ 04 74 67 51 50.*

To the right of the church, a small Late Gothic door leads into the Romanesque **cloisters;** all of which remains is an elegant arcaded gallery.

The locality produces Beaujolais-Villages.

From Salles, take the D 35, then the D 49E to the right.

Vaux-en-Beaujolais

This wine-growing village clinging to the slopes of the Beaujolais mountains inspired Gabriel Chevallier (1895-1969) to write his ribald satire of village life, *Clochemerle*.

The "**official urinal**" is a tongue-in-cheek reference to the famous novel as is the **Caveau de Clochermerle**. The superb 17C cellar, inaugurated in 1956 by Gabriel Chevallier in person, is decorated with humorous frescoes and drawings in tribute to his novel. Wine-tastings take place in a wholly immoderate spirit but wheelbarrow rides home are free of charge! The cellar is also where the ceremonies of the picturesque Confrèrerie des Gosiers Secs (Brotherhood of Parched Throats) are held at the feast of Saint Vincent. *69460 Vaux-en-Beaujolais, ☎ 04 74 03 26 58. Open daily 10.30am-noon, 3-7.30pm. Closed Christmas and New Year.*

The D 49E cuts through Le Perréon and the D 62 continues to Odenas.

Odenas

This Brouilly AOC village boasts several castles including that of **La Chaize** built in 1674 by Mansart for the nephew of Père La Chaize, Louis XIV's confessor. The

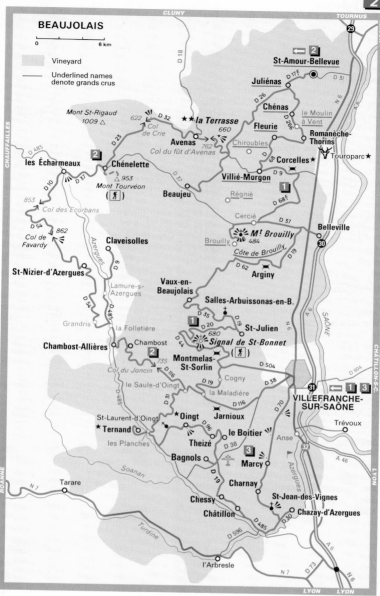

French-style garden was designed by Le Nôtre and the 18C wine vat is a listed monument. *Open Mon-Fri, 8.30am-noon and 2-5pm (3.30pm Fri), Sat by appointment.* ☎ 04 74 03 41 05.

Château Thivin is an excellent choice for wine purchases *(see Shopping Guide)*. *Continue on to Charentay.*

Charentay

This welcoming village, which produces Brouilly and Côtes-de-Brouilly AOC wines, possesses two points of interest: **Château d'Arginy**, on the Belleville road, and **Bellemère tower**. The now ruined castle, shrouded in mystery, is said to have housed the treasure of the Knights Templar entrusted for the safe keeping of Count Guichard de Beaujeu, nephew of Jacques de Molay, Grand Master of the Order. All that remains of the Templars' era is a large redbrick tower, known as the Tower of Eight Beatitudes or the Tower of Alchemy. The other tower, which rises like a lighthouse over the vines, was built by a mother-in-law who wanted to keep a discreet watch on her son-in-law's philandering ways.

The cellar of **Château du Grand Vernay** is the perfect place to find out more about these tales of yesteryear over a glass of Beaujolais. *69220 Charentay,* ☎ *04 74 03 46 20. Open daily 10am-7pm, by appointment preferably.*
Continue on the D 68, then take the D 19 on the left and D 37 to the right to Belleville.

Belleville

This old fortified town situated on the crossroads of the main routes north to south and east to west is now a thriving wine-producing and industrial centre. The 12C **church** was once part of an abbey built by the lords of Beaujeu. The square belfry dates from the 13C. A handsome Romanesque door leads into the Gothic nave. Inside, notice the naïve-style carving of the capitals, representing the Seven Deadly Sins. The **Hôtel-Dieu**, built in the 18C to replace an older hospital, was in use for the care of the sick until 1991. The three large rooms are divided into characteristic white-curtained alcoves, and are connected to the chapel through finely wrought iron gates. The dispensary houses a collection of 17C and 18C porcelain. *Open Jul-Aug, guided tours (1hr) Wed-Sun, 10am-4pm; Apr-Jun and Sep-Nov, guided tours (1hr) Wed-Sun at 3pm. 5€ (children 5-10: 3€).* ☎ *04 74 69 65 85.*
For wine purchases you could not do better than the **Ferraud et Fils estate** *(see Shopping Guide). Continue westbound on the D 37.* You will go past Château de Bel-Air, now a wine-producing school. The **Capvignes** tourist centre offers wine discovery courses including learning how to recognise aromas and an illustration of the different wine-growing professions. *Château de Bel-Air, Route de Beaujeu,* ☎ *04 74 66 45 97. Open daily, except Tue, 10am-noon and 2-6pm.*

Saint-Lager

The territory of this wine-growing locality dominated by Mont Brouilly is dotted with opulent properties tucked in among the rows of vines. The 19C **Château des Ravatys** belongs to the Pasteur Institute and the benefits of its produce are used to fund medical research. The park and cellars are open to visits. Sales of Brouilly and Côtes-de-Brouilly. *Open Mon-Fri 8.30am-noon and 2-6pm, Sat by appointment. Visits by appointment.* ☎ *04 74 66 80 35.*
⚑ An 8.5km-**walk** starts out from Saint-Lager cellar and loops round Mont Brouilly to return to the starting point.
⚑ The neighbouring village of **Cercié** leads to the **Voie verte du Beaujolais** (Beaujolais Green Belt), an 11km-trail laid out down an old railway line, for walkers and cyclists.
Alternatively, continue on the D 37 to Beaujeu, the capital of Beaujolais.

Beaujeu

Surrounded by hillsides carpeted in vines, the motto of the historic former capital of Beaujolais, whose low-lying houses line a narrow street, roughly translates as "Fair game to all who venture within".
Les Sources de Beaujolais is a wine centre-cum-museum whose original, modern displays provide a historic excursion into the wine-growing world of Beaujolais. After reviewing the illustrious past of the town of Beaujeu, the "well room" depicts the torture of the traitor Ganelon by distinctly unsympathetic craftsmen. However the museum's most unusual exhibit is without doubt a full-scale replica of a **barge** whose bridge visitors walk over. Regional produce on sale. *Enter through the Maison du pays, opposite the church.* ♿ *Open Jul-Aug, 10am-12.30pm and 2-7pm (last admission 6pm); Mar, Wed-Sun 10am-noon and 2-6pm; Apr-Jun, Sep-Dec, 10am-noon and 2-6pm (last admission 5pm). Closed Tue, 1 Jan, 25 Dec. 5€.* ☎ *04 74 69 20 56. www.beaujeu.com*

The **Musée des Traditions Populaires Marius-Audin** is also well worth a visit; a section is devoted to the cultivation of vines. *Guided tours possible by appointment. Closed Dec-Feb. 2€.* ☎ *04 74 69 22 88. www.beaujeu.com*

The **Beaujolais-villages Caveau** is located in the cellar of the museum *(see Shopping Guide).*

Back on the road to Cercié, turn right onto the D 43, left onto the D 43E and left again onto the Côte de Brouilly Route 100m further on.

Mont Brouilly

These hilly slopes are where the fruity fragrant wine of Côtes-de-Brouilly is produced. Côtes-de-Brouilly and Brouilly are both produced in the

The art of wine-making...

towns of St-Lager, **Quincié** *(see Cave Beaujolaise and Domaine Joubert in Shopping Guide)*, Charentay, Odenas, Cercié and St-Etienne-la-Varenne. Brouilly with 1 300 hectares, is one of the largest AOCs of Beaujolais, while Côtes-de-Brouilly only covers some 300 hectares.

From the esplanade at the top of the mound, admire the **view★** over the vineyards, the Beaujolais hills, the Saône plain and the Dombes region. The **chapel** at the summit (altitude 484m) is a place of pilgrimage for wine-growers. Devoted to the Vierge-aux-Raisins (Virgin Mary of Grapes), it was built in the 19C to protect the vines from mildew.

Return to Cercié and on the way out of the village, bear left onto the D 68E towards the historic town of Corcelles. From there, turn left onto the D 9.

Château de Corcelles★

♿ *Open Mar-Nov, 10am-noon and 2.30-6.30pm; Dec-Feb, 10am-noon and 2.30-5.30pm. Closed Sun and public holidays. No admission charge.* ☏ *04 74 66 00 24.*

This stronghold was originally built in the 15C to defend the border between Burgundy and Beaujolais, but transformation work carried out in the 16C has left it looking more like a manor house. The inner courtyard features Renaissance arcades and a well adorned with 15C wrought-iron work, and the chapel boasts some remarkable Gothic woodwork. The Château de Corcelles ranks among Beaujolais' most famous wine-growing estates. Its huge 17C **wine vat** is one of the most beautiful you will see in the region.

Return onto the D 9 to the right.

The road passes through some of the most prestigious vineyards of Beaujolais commanding fine views of the Saône valley. Each village has a wine cooperative or cellar where you can taste these excellent wines.

Villié-Morgon

The Morgon AOC owes its name to the small hamlet of the same name, but it is perhaps by visiting one of the 250 wine-growers of Villié-Morgon that you will discover the real meaning of the wine-word "morgonner". Morgon wines are said to "morgonne" when they express earthy, animal scents unlike those of any other wine. The Côte du Puy is the most well-known of the AOC. The **Domaine Calot** and **Domaine de Roche St-Jean** are both to be recommended *(see Shopping Guide)*. The **Morgon** firm, located in the 18C château de Fontcrenne situated in a lovely park, can be relied on to make visitors feel at home. *69910 Villié-Morgon,* ☏ *04 74 04 20 99.*

▣ Several well-signposted **walking trails** leave from the centre of the village and up through the hilly vineyards.

From Villié-Morgon, head north on the D 68 which skirts the village of Chiroubles.

Chiroubles

Chiroubles is without doubt the most floral of Beaujolais wines, renowned for its subtle fragrance of violets and peonies. The altitude (400m) of the vineyards is most probably the reason for this delicate bouquet. The local hero, whose statue adorns the village square, is Victor Puillat who saved the vines from phylloxera by grafting American rootstock onto French stock.

The landscape can be savoured to its utmost from the terrace of a superb view-point which unfolds to take in the vineyards of 10 Beaujolais wines as you walk up a panoramic path *(signposted)*.

The friendly staff of the **Maison des Vignerons**, a local cooperative, are happy to advise visitors about its fine selection of wines; if you prefer buying direct from the estate, we recommend the **Coteau de Bel-Air** and **Domaine Raousset** *(see Shopping Guide)*.

Fleurie

A Virgin Mary, erected in 1875 to protect the vine from phylloxera, dominates the village. Fleurie wines are reputed for their flavour of fresh grapes and fruity bouquet, to which the equally well-known Fleurie andouillette sausage is an ideal accompaniment. In addition to the get-ahead cooperative cellar of the **Producteurs des Grands Vins de Fleurie**, one of the most substantial in the region, **Domaine Chante-Terre** also produces good quality wines *(see Shopping Guide)*.

From Fleurie, take the D 32 eastbound, then the D 186 to the left.

Romanèche-Thorins

This thriving market town in the heart of Beaujolais-Villages is the annual meeting-point for Beaujolais nouveau lovers who come here to see the tanks leave Georges Duboeuf's store-house, where the vast majority of early wines from most of the region's cooperative cellars are grouped together and sold.

Romanèche-Thorins shares the Moulin-à-Vent AOC, Beaujolais' oldest appellation, whose reputation for distinctive robust wines produced from manganese-rich soils dates back to the 18C, with the locality of Chénas.

Around 1830, Beaujolais' vines were decimated by the pyralis worm, leaving the wine-growers helpless. **Benoit Raclet**, who owned vineyards in Romanèche, noticed that a vine growing along the side of his house, near to where the household's waste water was emptied, was totally unaffected by the scourge. He decided to water all his stock with hot water at 90°C in February to kill the worm's eggs, thereby saving his vines, despite his neighbours' scepticism. In the end, however, they also finally decided to adopt the technique. A festival is held each year in his honour in the last weekend of October. His **house** is also open to the public with a variety of souvenirs and tools on display. *Guided tours by appointment 2 weeks in advance. Closed Nov-Mar. No admission charge.* ☎ 03 85 35 51 37.

The **Hameau en Beaujolais★**, developed by Georges Duboeuf in a former railway station, offers visitors the chance to take an amusing and educational tour of a history of Beaujolais' vineyards and the different wine professions. *Open Apr-Oct, 9am-6pm; Jan-Mar and Nov-Dec, 10am-5pm. Closed 2 weeks in Jan (check beforehand), 25 Dec. 11.50€ (children: 6.10€).* ☎ 03 85 35 22 22. *www.hameauenbeaujolais.com*
Wine can be bought from the **Château du Moulin à Vent** and **Château des Jacques** *(see Shopping Guide).*

Touroparc Zoo and Amusement Park★

At the crossroads of Maison-Blanche on the N 6, take the D 466E St-Romain-des-Iles road. ♿ *Open Mar-Oct, 10am-7pm (Jun-Aug, aquatic park 1.30-5.30pm); Nov-Feb 1.30-5.30pm (rides closed). 14.50€.* ☎ 03 85 35 51 53. *www.touroparc.com*
🐾 Trees and parkland dotted with ochre-coloured buildings form the setting of this breeding and acclimatisation centre whose 10 hectares are home to birds and animals from five continents, most of whom roam free, with the exception of the big cats. Rides, play area, small aerial monorail train, picnic area with bars.
Take the D 266 through the hamlet of Moulin-à-Vent back onto the D 68.

Chénas

A restored windmill on top of a hill greets visitors arriving in the village with the offer of a glass of good wine.
Chénas, with only 280 hectares of land, is one of Beaujolais' smallest AOCs. It produces an elegant relatively light wine for the most part, with the exception of the produce from the granite slopes below Pic Rémont.
The cellar of **Château de Chénas**, housed in a lovely 19C edifice, produces 45% of this village AOC and makes visitors more than welcome; the **Domaine La Rochelle** is also an excellent choice for wine purchases *(see Shopping Guide).*
🚶 There is a pleasant walk out of the historic town up to the **Cabane des Chasseurs** (hunting lodge) affording a fine view over the vineyards *(orientation table).*

Juliénas

This village, whose name is said to be linked with that of Julius Cesar, is home to the 600 hectares of Juliénas AOC which produce Beaujolais' strongest wines, many of which age very well. They can be tasted in the **Cellier de la Vieille Eglise**, where Bacchanalian revels have somewhat astoundingly replaced the customary pious images. ♿ *Open Jun-Sep, 9.45am-noon and 2.30-6.30pm; Oct-May, daily except Tue 9.45am-noon and 2.30-6.30pm. No admission charge.* ☎ 04 74 04 42 98.
Both the **Matray** and the **Guy Voluet estates** can be recommended for purchases *(see Shopping Guide).*
🚶 Stretch your legs along an amusing 2km-**signposted walk** through the vines, past the old church and cooperative cellar.
On the way out of the village, on the D 137, notice the lovely arcaded façade of the 16-17C **Maison de la Dîme** (tithe house).
Head towards St-Amour-Bellevue.

Saint-Amour-Bellevue

This locality of Saône-et-Loire, at the northernmost tip of Beaujolais, produces more or less consistent red wines depending on whether they come from vines growing on granite or silt-laden soils. A number of terroirs with picturesque names such as Heaven or Madness can be found in the AOC. The area also produces white Saint-Véran and Mâcon wines *(see Burgundy).*

THE LAND OF GOLDEN STONE★★

59km. Michelin Local Map n°327, G-H, 3-4. See itinerary **3** *on map, p. 101.*
The "land of golden stone" in the south of Beaujolais owes its name to the limestone houses which turn a beautiful ochre hue as they catch the rays of the setting sun. It is an endearing region which offers visitors a picture of aristocratic graceful landscapes strewn with splendid abodes and medieval villages guarded by rows of well-tended vines. The omnipresent vineyards produce Beaujolais and Beaujolais-Villages AOC wines which, while they might lack the subtlety of their counterparts from northern Beaujolais, are nonetheless fully representative of the mild climate and generous soil of this golden land.
Leave Villefranche on the D 70 and turn left onto the D 39. This attractive **ridge-top road★** commands vistas over the Saône valley.

Anse

The town, at the confluent of the Azergues and the Saône, was a major halting-place in Gallo-Roman times. **Château de Tours** is home to a splendid late-2C mosaic depicting river traffic at the time. *Open Sat, 3.30pm. 2€. ☎ 04 74 60 26 16 (Pierres Dorées tourist office).*

Anse also has a pleasant water-sports centre at Colombier. The Pierres Dorées tourist office can recommend a number of walking and cycling trails around the area.

Return onto the D 70 to the left.

Marcy

On the outskirts of this town *(access by a minor road signposted "Tour Chappe")* stands a telegraph **tower** built by Claude Chappe in 1799, whose semaphore mechanism with moveable arms (restored) was used to transmit visual messages up until 1850. *Open Mar-Oct, Sun 2.30-6pm; Nov, Sun 2.30-5pm. 1.50€. ☎ 04 74 67 02 21.*

From the foot of the tower, the view encompasses the Saône valley, the Dombes region, the Monts du Lyonnais and Beaujolais hills.

Charnay

The remains of the fortifications of a 12C feudal castle can still be seen in this small country town at the summit of a hill. In the square, lined with limestone 15C and 16C houses, stands a **church**, which contains a beautiful Gothic statue of Saint Christopher (12C) in polychrome stone. It is worth climbing to the top of the church tower to enjoy the panoramic view. *Open mid-May to late Oct, 10am-12.30pm and 3-6pm.*

Higher up, an impressive 17C castle, called La Mansarde, is now the town hall.

Your visit would not be complete without tasting the wines of **Domaine des Terres Dorées** *(see Shopping Guide).*

To the south of Charnay, take the narrow road to St-Jean-des-Vignes.

Saint-Jean-des-Vignes

The tiny high-perched church amidst a riot of flowers in summer commands a fine view of the Lyon region.

The **Pierres Folles Museum** was founded to reflect the presence of important geological sites in the region. A section is given over to the history of the planet as revealed by the composition of the sub-soil. Displays, paintings and films illustrate the slow evolution of life on earth; discover the aquarium of live nautiluses (cephalopod molluscs) and the hologram of a "flight of the pterosaurs". The remainder of the museum is devoted to displays on the local countryside and its industrial and tourist activities. *Open Mar-Nov, daily except Mon morning, 9am-12.30pm and 2-6pm, Sat-Sun and public holidays, 2.30-6pm (last admission 30min before closing time). Guided tours by appointment. 5€. ☎ 04 78 43 69 20. www.espace-pierres-folles.asso.fr*

Return to the D 30 towards Chazay-d'Azergues.

Chazay-d'Azergues

A belfry and a few 15C and 16C houses continue to add character to this fortified town overlooking the Azergues. The 15C castle *(not open to the public)* was formerly the abode of the abbeys of Ainay.

Take the D 30 to Lozanne and the D 485 to Châtillon.

Châtillon

A 12C-13C fortress looms over this village, protecting the mouth of the Azergues valley. **Chapelle St-Barthélemy** *(steep walk up the hill signposted to the left of the parish church)*, extended in the 15C, originally stood within the walls of the fortress. Inside the chapel are paintings by Lavergen and H. Flandrin. *Open mid-Apr to late Oct, Sun and public holidays 2.30-6pm. No admission charge. ☎ 04 78 43 92 66.*

The Esplanade du Vingtain, further down, commands a fine view of the town.

Take the D 485 lined with red slag heaps.

Chessy

The Late Gothic church contains a handsome 16C font and a statue of Saint Martha slaying a dragon. In earlier times, the locality was the site of a major copper seam belonging to Jacques Coeur. The ore obtained was known as "Chessylite", a variety of azurite with a beautiful blue colour, greatly prized by collectors.

Take the D 19 to Bagnols.

Bagnols

A Watercolour Festival is held every year during the last weekend of July in this village whose 15C château has been turned into a château-hotel. Built at the same time, the **church** possesses a beautiful pendant keystone. Pretty 15C-16C houses with porches adorn the village square.

Head back onto the D 19 to the left. Stop at the hamlet of Le Boîtier.

Shopping Guide

INFORMATION

Union interprofessionnelle du Beaujolais – *210 bd Vermorel – 69661 Villefranche-sur-Saône –* ☎ *04 74 02 22 10 – www. beaujolais.com*

USEFUL TIPS

Almost half of Beaujolais wine-growers continue to practice the "métayage" (tenant farmer) system. Although it has disappeared from almost all the other wine-growing areas, this practice subsists in Beaujolais because many of the vineyards belong to owners who live in Lyon or further afield. A métayer is responsible for the upkeep of the vines, their cultivation and wine-making, in exchange for which, depending on the contract, he receives between half and two-thirds of the benefits of each crop. Cooperative cellars bottle approximately 30% of the region's production.

Beaujolais nouveau – Once a year on the third Thursday of November the entire wine-growing fraternity of Beaujolais frantically prepares dispatches of Beaujolais nouveau wine to the four corners of the earth. This uncomplicated wine, bottled less than three months after the harvest, has always represented a good deal for wine-growers who are able to quickly sell part of their stock. Recently, however, Beaujolais nouveau wines have suffered from a certain degree of disinterest on the part of consumers who are on the lookout for more distinctive wines.

OVERVIEW

WINE CHARACTERISTICS

The majority of Beaujolais wines are red, characterised by a deep ruby-red robe and the scent of soft red fruit and liquorice. Despite a healthy wine tang, the tannins are essentially silky.

STORAGE

Beaujolais wines can be kept for three to five years, sometimes longer in the case of good vintages. As they mature, they take on game and woody notes and "pinotent" as Burgundies do.

PRICES

The exceptional weather conditions of the summer of 2003 gave rise to the production of very good quality Beaujolais. This vintage is definitely worth looking out for particularly as prices remain stable.

Beaujolais – 3 to 5€
Beaujolais-villages and other AOC – 5 to 9€

BUYING

WINE MERCHANTS AND COOPERATIVES

Caveau des Beaujolais-villages – *Place de l'Hôtel-de-Ville – 69430 Beaujeu –* ☎ *04 74 04 81 18 – May-Nov 10.30am-1pm and 2-7.30pm – closed 3 weeks in Jan.* This "bacchanalian temple" devoted to Beaujolais-Villages is located in the vaulted cellars of the town hall. A statue of Saint Vincent, patron saint of wine-growers and a wax effigy of Anne de Beaujeu watch over wine tastings of Beaujolais-Villages, white Beaujolais-Villages and Hospices de Beaujeu Beaujolais-Villages.

Cave des Vignerons de Bully – *La Martinière – 69210 Bully –* ☎ *04 74 01 27 77 – cavedebully@wanadoo.fr - by appointment.* With an annual production of 43 000 hectolitres, half of which is Beaujolais nouveau, the Vignerons de Bully cooperative created in 1959 is the top producer of Beaujolais wine. Its 280 wine-growers cultivate 720 hectares in the south of Beaujolais.

Cave du Château de Chénas – *La Bruyère – 69840 Chénas –* ☎ *04 74 04 48 19 – cave.chenas@wanadoo.fr - Mon-Sat 8am-noon and 2-6pm, Sun and public holidays 2.30-7pm.* The sumptuous Château de Chénas plays host to this association of wine-growers created in 1934 with a total of 275 members at the present time. The 280-hectare estate produces several AOC wines, including Moulin-à-Vent and Chénas, in its superb 17C vaulted cellars.

La Maison des Vignerons – *Le Bourg – 69115 Chiroubles –* ☎ *04 74 69 14 94 – la maisondesvignerons@wanadoo.fr - summer: Mon-Fri 10am-12.30pm and 2.30-6.30pm; Sat-Sun 10am-12.30pm and 2.30-7pm; rest of the year: Mon-Fri 10am-12.30pm and 2-6pm; Sat-Sun 10am-12.30pm and 2-6.30pm – closed Christmas and New Year.* Tucked away in the tiny village of Chiroubles, this firm has 65 members who supply it with the produce of a hundred or so hectares from the AOC towns of Chiroubles, Fleurie, Morgon, Régnié and Beaujolais-Villages.

Cave des Producteurs des Grands Vins de Fleurie – *Le Bourg – 69820 Fleurie –* ☎ *04 74 04 11 70 – www.cavefleurie. com - Mon-Sat 9am-noon and 2-7pm, Sun 9am-noon and 2-7.30pm.* Created in 1927, this cooperative is the oldest in Beaujolais. It bottles one-third of the production of Fleurie, produces a range of "Cuvées Terroirs" (Chapelle des Bois, Garants, etc) and is proud of two exceptional and distinctive wines, Cardinal Bienfaiteur and Présidente Marguerite.

Cave Beaujolais de Quincié – *Le Bourg – 69430 Quincié-en-Beaujolais –* ☎ *04 74 04 34 11 – cavedequincie@terre-net.fr - Mon-Fri 8.30am-noon and 2-6.30pm, Sat 9am-noon and 2-6pm, Sun 3-6pm.* The different AOC Beaujolais-Villages, Régnié, Brouilly, etc wines of this wine cooperative established in 1928, with their exceptional fruity floral bouquets, regularly wins prizes and medals. A state-of-the-art sales and tasting room presents the cellar's wine selection in ideal conditions.

La Maison des Beaujolais – *441 avenue de l'Europe – 69220 St-Jean-d'Ardières – ☎ 04 74 66 16 46 – www. lamaisondesbeaujolais.com - daily noon-9pm, summer daily noon-10pm – closed Christmas holidays and New Year.* The sign outside leaves one in no doubt that the establishment is devoted body and soul to Beaujolais wine. Equipped with a tasting room, shop and restaurant, it provides an ideal introduction to the manifold delights of this wine-growing region.

ESTATES

Domaine P. Ferraud et Fils – *31 rue Maréchal-Foch – 69220 Belleville – ☎ 04 74 06 47 60 – ferraud@ferraud. com - Mon-Fri 8am-noon and 2-6pm by appointment.* This long-established wine merchant was founded in 1882 by the Ferraud family to whom it still belongs. Two Ferraud brothers, Jean-Michel and Yves-Dominique, have been in charge of business since 1986 and 1982 respectively. The house works exclusively with six estates from which it buys wine in bulk which is then aged in its own oak barrels and cellars. The Ferraud estate also produces a number of AOC Mâcon: Mâcon-Villages, Mâcon-Fuissé, Pouilly-Fuissé, Pouilly-Vinzelles and Saint-Véran.

Château des Granges – *Flacieu – 69620 Le Breuil – ☎ 04 74 71 83 01 – info@chateaudesgranges.com - daily by appointment.* The château has been a family-run wine estate since the 17C and its vines are the oldest of Le Breuil. The property covers over 100 hectares, 22 of which are vineyards. Just to the northwest of Lyon, the unbroken vineyard produces primarily red wines, in addition to a small proportion of rosé and white wines. Planted in clayey-limestone, pebbly and silicious soils, the four great classic vine stocks of Burgundy grow here: Gamay (90%), Pinot noir (4%), Chardonnay (4%) and Aligoté (2%). Harvests are carried out by hand and time-honoured traditions continue to play a major role in the wine-making process such as ageing in wooden barrels according to Beaujolais tradition.

Domaine Bernard Santé – *Route de Juliénas – 71570 La Chapelle-de-Guinchay – ☎ 03 85 33 82 81 – bernardsante@terre-net.fr - by appointment.* A family affair for four generations, this estate covers 9 hectares. Harvests continue to take place by hand. The estate's three wines come from a variety of plots of land and soils, but are all made from a single vine variety: Gamay.

Domaine des Terres Dorées – *69380 Charnay – ☎ 04 78 47 93 45 – Mon-Fri 9am-noon and 2-6pm by appointment.* Jean-Paul Brun has been in charge of the 22-hectare vineyard since 1979, cultivating Pinot noir, Gamay and Chardonnay in a clayey-limestone soil. This wine-grower, reputed for his commitment to ancient techniques, does not add yeast to the wine-making process and chaptalisation is banished from a proportion of his production. The wines are fermented in concrete tanks and aged in oak barrels for six to ten months.

Domaine La Rochelle – *69840 Chénas – ☎ 04 74 66 62 05 – Mon-Fri by appointment.* The estate is part of a large 48-hectare property handed down from generation to generation for over four centuries. Owned by the Sparre family since 1874, the 21-hectare estate is planted with Gamay noir vines which grow on south and east facing hills. The 45-year-old (on average) vines take root in granite soils with traces of manganese. The hand-picked grapes are made into wine using traditional "grillage" techniques. The wines are then aged in oak barrels and stainless steel vats.

Domaine Coteau de Bel-Air – *69116 Chiroubles – ☎ 04 74 04 23 77 – by appointment.* In 1969, Jean-Marie Appert took over the reins of this family property which dates back to 1750. 5.4 hectares of Gamay vines grow half-way up the east-facing hillside, in ghorr and decomposing primary granite soils. After a slow carbonic maceration process (between fifteen and twenty days), the wines are aged in oak barrels for five to eight months.

S. Sauvignier / MICHELIN

Château de Raousset – *69115 Chiroubles – ☎ 04 74 69 17 28 – chateau deraousset@wanadoo.fr - daily 8am-noon and 2-6pm – by appointment.* The estate was created by Léon Félissent in 1836. Planted in dry stony soil, the vineyards cover the AOC towns of Chiroubles, Fleurie and Morgon. His grandson, Gaston, Count of Raousset, developed the estate further and today it is run by the count's three granddaughters. Sand, granite, orthose and biotite compose the soil of the château's 23 hectares of vineyards. The grapes are hand picked and the wine-making process is carried out with whole bunches of grapes. The wines are aged in oak barrels.

Domaine de Chante-Terre – *Montgenas – 69820 Fleurie – ☎ 04 74 04 15 30 – dom.chante-terre@wanadoo.fr - 8am-noon and 2-6pm – by appointment.* Jacques is the third generation of wine-growers of this estate owned by the family since 1938. He has been running the business since 1974, with the help of his wife Florence since 1994. All the wines come from vines planted on the south- and southeast-facing hillsides of Montgenas. A single variety of vine, Gamay, is harvested by hand and the traditional wine-making process is carried out in epoxy vats.

Domaine Guy Voluet – *69840 Juliénas – ☎ 04 74 04 45 67 – domaine. guyvoluet@free.fr - daily by appointment.* Guy Voluet took over the family-owned estate handed down from father to son for four generations in 1983. The 7.5 hectares of Gamay vines are planted in clayey-limestone with traces of granite soil on south southeast facing hillsides. The grapes are hand-picked, the wine-making process is traditional and the wines are aged in enamel vats.

Domaine Matray – *69840 Juliénas – ☎ 04 74 04 45 57 – domain.matray@wanadoo.fr - daily by appointment.* The estate has belonged to the same family since it was created in the 1900s. Since 1988, it has been in the hands of the fifth generation, in the person of Lilian Matray and his wife, Sandrine. The 10.5-hectare vineyard is made up of Gamay and Chardonnay varieties spread over several localities. Every aspect of the wine-making process from pruning to picking is done by hand on this traditional estate.

Domaine du Tracot – *69430 Lantignié – ☎ 04 74 04 87 51 – j.p-dubost@wanadoo.fr - daily 8am-6pm – by appointment.* In the Dubost family since 1902. Henri Dubost has implemented a number of renovation works and improved the quality of the stock. In 2000, his son Jean-Paul built a new vaulted cellar with stainless steel vats. The vineyard is now comprised of 11 hectares of Beaujolais-Villages, 3.5 hectares of Régnié and 1 hectare of Brouilly. In 2000, a parcel of AOC Morgon and in 2001 a Chardonnay section for white Beaujolais-Villages were added to the estate.

Château Thivin – *69460 Odenas – ☎ 04 74 03 47 53 – geoffray@chateau-thivin.com - Mon-Sat 9am-noon and 2-7pm.* In 1877, Zaccharie Geoffray bought Château Thivin, which had no more than 2 hectares of vines at the time, in an auction. Claude and Evelyne Geoffray, also the owners of the Manoir du Pavé at Saint-Lager, took over the running of the business in 1987. At present, 15 hectares are devoted to AOC Côte-de-Brouilly, 6 hectares to Brouilly, 1 hectare to Beaujolais and 4 to Beaujolais-Villages.

Domaine Joubert – *La Roche – 69430 Quincié-en-Beaujolais – ☎ 04 74 69 05 83 – Mon-Sat – by appointment.* For three generations, the Joubert family has been running this splendid wine estate

endeavouring all the while to show respect for the terroir and tradition. The 10-hectare vineyard is planted entirely with Gamay and worked according to ecologically responsible principles. The grapes are hand picked and the wine is aged in wood or concrete vats, barrels and casks.

Château du Moulin à Vent – *Le Moulin à Vent – 71570 Romanèche-Thorins – 3.5km east of Fleurie – ☎ 03 85 35 50 68 – chateaudumoulinavent@wanadoo.fr - Mon-Fri 9am-noon and 2-6pm, Sat-Sun and public holidays by prior request – closed early Aug to mid-Aug.* This estate is home to one of Beaujolais' most famous sites of production. Deep purple in colour, full-bodied, spicy and generous, Moulin-à-Vent wines are powerful and elegant; and they age well. Wine tasting in the château, old vintages available.

Château des Jacques – *Les Jacques - 71570 Romanèche-Thorins – ☎ 03 85 35 51 64 – jacques@wanadoo.fr - Mon-Fri 8.30am-noon and 1.30-4.30pm by appointment.* The Château des Jacques vineyard covers 36 hectares, mainly of Gamay but also some Chardonnay. The harvest is by hand throughout the estate and the grapes are left on the bunch during the wine-making process, including very long maceration times. The wine is aged in oak barrels from eleven to twelve months.

Domaine Calot – *42 rue de la Pompe – 69910 Villié-Morgon – ☎ 04 74 04 20 55 – Mon-Sat 8am-noon and 2-7pm – by appointment.* A family-owned estate since the early 20C, it is today in the hands of François and Jean Calot, who created an SCEA in 1983. Planted by their father Georges in the 1950s, the vineyard now covers 12 hectares of east, south and southeast facing decomposing granite soil. Since 1985 it has been cultivated according to ecologically responsible principles. All the wines are made from Gamay grapes which are hand picked.

Domaine de Roche St-Jean – *69910 Villié-Morgon – ☎ 04 74 04 23 92 – daily 8am-noon and 2-7pm – by appointment Sat-Sun.* In the heart of the AOC Morgon, this estate has been run by the Mathon family for five generations. It covers 13.5 hectares and faces south and southeast. The vines are planted on a schistose and granite soil.

FESTIVALS

The arrival of Beaujolais nouveau is celebrated practically everywhere.

Belleville – Beaujolais nouveau kegs are tapped in the town hall cellar on 3rd Wednesday of November at midnight.

Juliénas – Wine Festival, 2nd or 3rd weekend of November.

Pommiers – Beaujolais nouveau pressing, 3rd Thursday of November.

Tarare – Beaujolais nouveau Festival, 3rd Thursday of November.

Le Boîtier

On the road leading out of the hamlet, on the right, is the Clos de la Platière once the home of Madame Roland, a famous French revolutionary.

Theizé

Car park on the right-hand side of the road. Take the road uphill to the right of the village square.

The pleasant village of Theizé, which is typical of the "land of golden stone", is home to two castles: Rapetour in the lower part of the village and Rochebonne in the upper part. The **Chapelle de Rochebonne**, with a Late Gothic chancel, is used for concerts and temporary art exhibitions. *Open Jul-Aug, daily except Tue, 3-7pm; May-Jun and early Sep to mid-Oct, Sat-Sun and public holidays 3-7pm. 3€.* ☎ 04 74 71 16 10.

The **Château de Rochebonne** features a Classical façade with a triangular pediment flanked by two towers. Exhibitions are held indoors where a handsome spiral staircase can still be seen. On the ground-floor is a wine centre poetically called "**Les Fiancés de l'automne**" (Autumnal Engagement) devoted to wine production in Beaujolais. *Open Jul-Aug, daily except Tue, 2-6pm; May-Jun and Sep to Oct, Sat-Sun and public holidays 2-6pm. 3€.* ☎ 04 74 71 16 10.

The 13C stronghold of **Château de Rapetour** still boasts its original Gothic arched doorway, watchtowers, corbelled artillery holes and towers. Admire the arcades of the inner Renaissance courtyard adorned with lovely carved heads.

Oingt★

All that remains of the once mighty fortress of Oingt is Nizy gate which leads into the village, whose charm is enhanced by pedestrian lanes, a 16C communal house and countless art and craft workshops (ceramics, weaving, etc). The streets lined with handsome houses lead to the church, a former chapel of the 14C castle.

The view from the top of the **tower** over the Monts du Lyonnais and Beaujolais hills and of the Azergues Valley is quite stunning. *Open Jul-Aug, daily except Sat-Sun 2-7pm; Apr-Jun and Sep, Sat-Sun and public holidays 3-7pm. Guided tours (45min) possible by appointment. 1.30€.* ☎ 04 74 71 21 24.

Saint-Laurent-d'Oingt

In addition to its unusual church with porch, this peaceful village also possesses a **cooperative,** whose cellar commands a fine view of the sector. *69620 St-Laurent-d'Oingt,* ☎ *04 74 71 20 51. Cellar: Sun and public holidays, 2-6pm; shop Mon-Fri 8am-noon and 2-6pm.*

Coming in on the D 485, turn right.

Ternand★

Former bastion of the archbishops of Lyon, Ternand retains some of its fortifications: the keep and rampart walk afford fine views of the Monts de Tarare and Azergues Valley.

The Carolingian capitals of the chancel and mural paintings of the same period in the crypt make the **church** worth a visit. *Guided tours by appointment, enquire at the town hall.* ☎ 04 74 71 33 43.

Another site of interest is the substantial **collection of wine-growing tools** accumulated by Jean-Jacques Paire, a Beaujolais producer from Ronzié. ☎ 04 74 71 35 72.

Make a U-turn, go through the town of Les Planches and continue on the D 31. This **route★★** *over the Saule-d'Oingt Pass, is extremely picturesque with lovely old farmhouses overlooking fields and meadows dotted all over the hillside. On the way down from Saule-d'Oingt to Villefranche, the horizon embraces the Valley of the Saône. At La Maladière, turn right towards Jarnioux.*

Jarnioux

The six-towered **castle** built in the 15C and 17C includes a particularly lovely Renaissance portion. Traces of the former drawbridge are visible in the majestic entrance providing access to two successive courtyards. *Open early Jul to mid-Jul and mid-Aug to late Sep, guided tours (45min) Mon, Wed, Fri 2-6pm and Tue and Thu 9am-noon, last admission 1hr before closing time). Closed Sat-Sun and public holidays. 4€.* ☎ 04 74 03 80 85.

Take the D 116 towards Villefranche.

Liergues

Mecca of wine-making, Liergues also possesses a church whose Gothic chancel is adorned with naïve wood and stone carvings as well as a profusion of medieval paintings.

Return to Villefranche on the D 38.

Le Bordelais

The Bordeaux Region

It is said that the Romans introduced the vine to Aquitaine, although the wine produced at that time was of poor quality: laced with honey and enhanced with spices, it bore no resemblance to the "agreeable" and "open" wines that mature in Bordeaux's cellars today. The vine still reigns supreme in the countryside around the city. The region is a sea of green, dotted with a splash of colour from the occasional rosebush, its vineyards covering the hillsides and extending right up to the edge of forests and towns. The eight itineraries listed below will provide a wonderful insight into this delightful region, from the most famous châteaux to tiny villages dedicated to the production of some of the world's finest wines.

Terroir

Michelin Local Map 335 – Gironde (Département 33).
Area: 120 000ha in the Gironde *département* alone.
Production: 6.5 million hectolitres (650 million litres), representing 13% of total French *Appellation d'Origine Contrôlée* (AOC) production.
The climate here is temperate-oceanic, characterised by relatively mild winters, wet springs, hot summers and sunny autumns.
Between the Garonne and the Dordogne (Côtes de Bordeaux and Entre-Deux-Mers), the soil is either a mix of clay and limestone or clay and gravel. On the left banks of the Garonne and Gironde, gravel predominates, offering natural drainage for the vineyards. On the right bank of the Dordogne, the soil is clay or limestone (Blayais) or sand and gravel (Libournais).

Wines

The region can be divided into six main production areas:
Right bank of the Garonne – AOC Premières-Côtes-de-Bordeaux, Côtes-de-Bordeaux-Saint-Macaire, Cadillac, Loupiac and Sainte-Croix-du-Mont.
Entre-Deux-Mers – AOC Entre-Deux-Mers, Sainte-Foy-Bordeaux, Entre-Deux-Mers Haut-Benauge and Graves-de-Vayres.
Left bank of the Garonne – AOC Graves, Pessac-Léognan, Graves-Supérieures, Sauternes, Barsac and Cérons.
Libournais – AOC Fronsac, Canon-Fronsac, Pomerol, Lalande-de-Pomerol, Saint-Émilion, Saint-Émilion Grand Cru, Montagne-Saint-Émilion, Puisseguin-Saint-Émilion, Saint-Georges-Saint-Émilion, Lussac-Saint-Émilion, Côtes-de-Francs and Côtes-de-Castillon.
Blayais and Bourgeais – AOC Côtes-de-Bourg, Blaye, Côtes-de-Blaye and Premières Côtes-de-Blaye.
Médoc – AOC Médoc, Haut-Médoc, Moulis, Listrac, Saint-Estèphe, Pauillac, Saint-Julien and Margaux.
Bordeaux wines are blended using the following main grape varieties:
Reds and rosés: Cabernet Franc, Cabernet Sauvignon, Merlot, Malbec and Petit Verdot.
Whites: Sauvignon, Semillon, Muscadelle and Ugni Blanc.

Harvesting by hand around Saint-Émilion.

Useful tips

The Bordeaux region does not have the reputation for being particularly friendly and hospitable towards visitors. The wine has long been able to "sell itself" and some producers still seem to feel that customers should feel honoured to be allowed to purchase their Grands Crus. Things are changing, however, with many châteaux developing better facilities in which to receive visitors and potential buyers, although don't expect to be offered the chance of tasting the very best Grands Crus, the price of which has gone through the roof. As a rule, you're likely to receive a warmer welcome in the region's cooperatives and smaller estates.

Background

History of the Bordeaux vineyards – Although in evidence since the Roman conquest, the region's vineyards only really developed from the 4C onwards. During the 300 years of English domination, from the 12C to the 14C, the reputation of Bordeaux's wines spread overseas. Though the *clairets* (pale reds) then enjoyed in Northern Europe had little in common with what we would nowadays call a claret, they ensured the prosperity of a region which, from the Renaissance onwards, was of great commercial interest to Hanseatic merchants from the Netherlands and Germany. In fact, it could be said that Bordeaux owes its success as much to these durable links as it does to its soil and climate, for it was these same traders who established a system based on merchants, estate owners and brokers which is still in place today – the first sold the wine, the second produced it, and the third acted as an intermediary between the first two.

The 18C was Bordeaux's Golden Age, with the creation of Crus (growths) – areas marked out around the main villages, and châteaux – which were built from the profits of a burgeoning industry. A "cork aristocracy" subsequently developed which, in the absence of its own heraldry, would acquire its titles under the Second Empire thanks to the famous classification of 1855, which saw hereditary privilege handed down to the châteaux rather than through lineage.

A victim, like other areas, of phylloxera and natural disasters, the Bordeaux wine area has survived with a certain flair, and even arrogance, judging by the current prices for Grands Crus in a marketplace that others consider sluggish. Even if reform is considered necessary to face up to competition from the wines of the New World, the name Bordeaux remains synonymous with perfection.

Classification of Bordeaux wines – It was at the Paris Fair-Exhibition of 1855 that Bordeaux wines received their first classification, which was based primarily on cost. Only Médoc and Sauternes wines, as well as Château Haut-Brion in Les Graves, were included at that time; Médoc wines were divided into five categories, and the wines of Sauternes three. In 1973, classification was revised to include Château Mouton Rothschild in the list of Premiers Crus. At a later stage the Médoc also established the Crus Bourgeois category. In 1955, the wines of Saint-Émilion were also classified; this list has been subsequently revised. The wines of Les Graves have their own classification.

While they remain generally valid, wine classifications are contested on a regular basis... especially by those wine producers who do not appear in them. However, the only true classification is that of the consumer, who is able to compare the value for money that the wines are able to offer.

Right Bank of the Garonne

CÔTES-DE-BORDEAUX

105km from Bordeaux in Ste-Croix-du-Mont. Michelin Local Map 335, H-J 5-7. See tour **1** *on the map on p. 120. On this map, the loop along the D 14 and D 20 is a suggested route for those wishing to visit the church in St-Genès-de-Lombaud, which is not described here.*

The right bank of the Garonne is bordered by hills which, for a distance of some 60km, form the appellation known as **Premières-Côtes-de-Bordeaux**.

This region is particularly attractive with fine landscapes dotted with small châteaux once occupied by the artists Henri de Toulouse-Lautrec and Rosa Bonheur, and the writers François Mauriac and Anatole France.

The Premières-Côtes-de-Bordeaux appellation covers 6 400ha of clayey-limestone and clayey-gravelly soil. The area encompasses the **Cadillac AOC** appellation, known for its liquoreux whites. First and foremost, the region produces well-constituted, robust reds, dominated by Merlot which gives the wines their characteristic overall roundness and suppleness. The rosés and *clairets* (pale reds) are a particular speciality of this area, where the whites range from mellow to liquoreux.

Directory

WHERE TO EAT

AROUND BLAYE

Le Troque-Sel – *1 pl. Jeantet - 33710 Bourg - ☎ 05 57 68 30 67 - Closed Sun eve, Tue eve and Mon - 11/25.80€*. The key to the success of this restaurant is the old adage that simplicity is best. The wine list here features a wide choice of Côtes-de-Bourg and Crus from the Bordeaux region to accompany dishes such as lamprey *à la Bordelaise* and duck magret with cep mushrooms.

La Citadelle – *Pl. d'Armes - 33390 Blaye - ☎ 05 57 42 17 10 - 25€ (lunch) - 20/45€*. A wonderful location in the heart of the Citadelle de Blaye is the major selling point of this hotel-restaurant. Modern, bright dining room with large bay windows, and splendid views of the Gironde estuary from the terrace. The emphasis here is on traditional cuisine. Functional bedrooms. Swimming pool.

La Filadière – *Route de la Corniche, in Furt - 33710 Gauriac - 8km/5mi SE of Blaye along the D 669 - ☎ 05 57 64 94 05 - Closed 1-14 Dec, Tue eve from 15 Sep to 30 Jun and Wed - 14.50€ (lunch) - 21/28€*. The airy dining room is decorated in bright colours with exquisite rattan furniture. In summer, guests can enjoy the panoramic view from the Filadière's terrace. Appetising local recipes.

AROUND BORDEAUX

La Bonne Table – *17 r. Huguerie - 33000 Bordeaux - ☎ 05 56 01 11 49 - Closed 15-25 Aug and Sun eve - 9.50/26.50€*. Enticing menus dominated by fresh seafood purchased at the Arcachon fish auction are on offer in this local, somewhat sombrely decorated restaurant. It's worth knowing that the chef smokes his own salmon. If you've never tasted lamprey *à la bordelaise*, then this is the place!

Bar Cave de la Monnaie – *34 r. Porte-la-Monnaie - 33000 Bordeaux - ☎ 05 56 31 12 33 - Closed Sun - 7€ (lunch) - 12/28€*. The success of this attractive bistro is based on food that is available all day (omelettes, salads, traditional dishes, plus an evening menu), wines from the southwest, wines from the bottle and barrel, sensible prices and a warm, relaxed atmosphere.

Chez Mémère – *11 r. de la Devise - 33000 Bordeaux - ☎ 05 56 81 88 20 - 12.30/30€*. Rediscover the atmosphere and recipes from yesteryear within the walls of this building dating from the 16C. The menu includes local stews (*garbure landaise*), lamb from Pauillac, beef from Bazas, fresh squid with Espelette chilli peppers, and other recipes from the southwest. The cellar has a strong showing of wines from the region.

L'Olivier du Clavel – *44 r. Charles-Domercq - 33000 Bordeaux - ☎ 05 57 95 09 50 - Closed Aug, 2-10 Jan, Sat lunchtime, Sun and Mon - 19€ (lunch) - 16€*. The chef here uses different appellations of oil from far and wide to produce cuisine inspired by seasonal produce and the Mediterranean. Neo-bistro decor in Provençal tones.

Tupina – *6 r. Porte-la-Monnaie - 33000 Bordeaux - ☎ 05 56 91 56 37 - 32€ (lunch) - 16€*. A country-style atmosphere and thoughtful decor are the hallmarks of this restaurant which has been visited by President Chirac. Dishes from the southwest roasted over an open fire or prepared on the stove according to time-honoured traditions. Impressive wine list, plus a superb collection of Armagnacs and Cognacs.

Le Bistro du Musée – *3 pl. Pey-Berland - 33000 Bordeaux - ☎ 05 56 52 99 69 - Closed for a fortnight at Christmas, 3 weeks in Aug and Sun - 14.90€ (lunch) - 21.90/28€*. It's easy to take an instant liking to this bistro with its attractive dark green wood frontage and elegant interior with exposed brick walls, oak flooring, moleskin benches and a decor embellished with tools from the wine trade. Cuisine from the southwest accompanied by a comprehensive Bordeaux wine list.

Le Cohé – *8 av. Roger-Cohé - 33600 Pessac - ☎ 05 56 45 73 72 - Closed 4-29 Aug, Sun eve and Mon - 18/54€*. An old house with a pleasant white stone façade, hushed, contemporary interior and clean, elegant layout. Cuisine with a modern edge, with an emphasis on fish and seafood.

Auberge la Forêt – *Route de la Forêt - 33370 Salleboeuf - 10km N of Créon along the D 671 - ☎ 05 56 21 25 49 - Closed Sun eve, Mon and Tue - 19/34€*. Spacious, rustic-style dining room occupying a house in a residential suburb. Pleasant veranda opening onto an attractive garden for alfresco dining in the summer months. Appetising traditional cuisine at reasonable prices.

Gravelier – *114 cours de Verdun - 33000 Bordeaux - ☎ 05 56 48 17 15 - Closed 31 Jul-30 Aug, Sat and Sun - 20€ (lunch) - 25/32€*. Run by Yves Gravelier and his wife in the Les Chartrons district, this restaurant has garnered a reputation for its inventive, contemporary cuisine based on high-quality, rigorously sourced products. New, trendy decor enhanced by refined furnishings and contrasting colours.

La Cape – *Allée Morlette - 33150 Cenon - 6km E of Bordeaux along the A 630 ring road - ☎ 05 57 80 24 25 - Closed 1-23 Aug, Christmas holidays, Sat-Sun and public hols - 28€*. This discreet house is home to two contemporary, brightly coloured dining rooms, in addition to a pleasant garden-terrace. Attractive, inventive cuisine (including pan-fried fillet of cod and Iberian loin of pork, smoked roulé of lamb with black cherry confiture etc), plus an interesting local wine list.

AROUND LANGON

Cyril – *62 cours Fossés - 33210 Langon - ☎ 05 56 76 25 66 - 10€ (lunch) - 18/38€*. This restaurant takes its name from the chef, who divides his time between the kitchen and local markets, where he sources the very best products to create unpretentious yet high-quality traditional dishes. A warm welcome from Karine in the freshly revamped dining room. Excellent value for money.

⊖⊖ **L'Abricotier** – *2 r. François-Bergoeing - 33490 St-Macaire - 3km N of Langon along the N 113 - ☎ 05 56 76 83 63 - Closed 12 Nov-12 Dec, Tue eve and Mon - 18/36€.* Set back slightly from the N 113, "The Apricot Tree" offers guests the choice of its smart, modern dining rooms or, on sunny days, a terrace in the shade of mulberry trees. In the kitchen, the culinary focus is on simple yet good quality local dishes, washed down perhaps with a bottle from the judicious wine list.

⊖⊖ **Le Cap** – *12 r. Gemin - 33210 Preignac - 8km NE of Sauternes along the D 125, then the D 8 - ☎ 05 56 63 27 38 - Closed 3-10 Feb, 24 Mar- 9 Apr, 15 Sep-8 Oct, Mon from Jun to mid-Sep and Sun eve - 19.80/33€.* The charming dining room (with seating for just 20 guests) and the fine terrace of this venerable building on the banks of the Garonne are popular with both professional and amateur sailors who come here to enjoy contemporary cuisine, including dishes that include river fish.

⊖⊖ **Le Saprien** – *R. Principale - 33210 Sauternes - ☎ 05 56 76 60 87 - Closed 1-26 Dec, Feb school holidays, Sun eve and Mon - 23/35€.* Choose between the elegant dining room, veranda or terrace with pleasant views of the vineyards. The excellent sweet wine produced locally takes centre-stage here with dishes such as Terrine in Sauternes jelly, Parfait Glacé au Sauternes, plus the obligatory fine cellar!

⊖⊖⊖ **Claude Darroze** – *95 cours Général Leclerc - 33210 Langon - ☎ 05 56 63 00 48 - Closed 21 Oct-10 Nov, 6-28 Jan, Sun eve and Mon lunchtime from Nov-Jun - 38/68€.* An old-style dining room and plane tree-shaded terrace provide the backdrop for delicious classic cuisine (Gironde lamprey in Bordeaux wine, warm duck foie gras with caramelised apples etc) and a comprehensive Bordeaux-dominated wine list. A traditional address for serious gourmets.

AROUND LIBOURNE

⊖⊖ **Chez Servais** – *14 pl. Decazes - 33500 Libourne - ☎ 05 57 51 83 97 - Closed 12-25 Aug, Sun eve and Mon - 15.50€ (lunch).* Behind the engaging façade of this small stone house is a charming dining room attractively laid-out with flower-decked tables, cane chairs and tasteful furniture. Popular with locals who flock here to enjoy a choice of enticing traditional menus.

⊖⊖ **Méhul Gourmand** – *1 Barrail-de-Tourenne - 33240 St-Germain-de-la-Rivière - 8km NW of Libourne along the D 670 - ☎ 05 57 84 44 50 - Closed Sun eve and Mon - 15.50/19€.* Under the same roof as the local tourist office (Maison du Pays Fronsadais), this restaurant enjoys pleasant views over a neighbouring small lake. The traditional dishes prepared by the chef, a former pupil of Alain Passard, are accompanied by a lively selection of wines from small vineyards.

⊖⊖ **Le Bord d'Eau** – *4 Poinsonnet - 33126 Fronsac - 2km W of Libourne along the D 670 - ☎ 05 57 51 99 91 - Closed Feb school holidays, Sep, Nov, Wed eve, Sun eve and Mon - 19/46€.* Built on piles on the banks of the Dordogne, this restaurant enjoys panoramic views of Libourne and the bell tower of the Église St-Jean-Baptiste. A profusion of plants, with sparkling colours enhanced by the silvery reflections from the water. An almost Impressionist setting in which to savour enticing traditional cuisine.

S. Sauvignier / MICHELIN

⊖⊖ **Le Villagosia** – *12 r. de la République - 33141 Villegouge - 12km N of Libourne along the D 128 - ☎ 05 57 84 40 50 - Closed 24 Dec-2 Jan, Fri lunchtime and Sun eve - Reservation recommended - 11.50€ (lunch) - 20/27€.* Opened a couple of years ago in a small village surrounded by vineyards in the hills to the north of Libourne, this restaurant has already built up a loyal following. Fresh decor, bright tones and good-quality cuisine.

⊖⊖ **Le Vieux Presbytère** – *Pl. de l'Église - 33570 Montagne - 4km SW of Lussac along the D 122 - ☎ 05 57 74 65 33 - ⊭ - 22/35€.* This restaurant occupies a former presbytery next to a Romanesque chapel. Meals are served in the rustic-style dining room or on the attractive terrace in season. Traditional cuisine complemented by a selection of Crus.

AROUND MARGAUX

⊖ **Le Lion d'Or** – *Pl. de la République - 33460 Arcins - 6km NW of Margaux along the D 2 - ☎ 05 56 58 96 79 - Closed Jul, 24 Dec-1 Jan, Sun, Mon and public hols - Reservation required - 11€.* This old coaching inn has been converted into a modern gastronomic staging post with an unpretentious atmosphere which, like its owner-chef, is full of character! The slate board on the side of the road highlights the daily menu for avid regulars who flock here for copious, well-prepared local cuisine.

Le St-Julien – *11 r. St-Julien - 33250 St-Julien-Beychevelle - 4km S of Pauillac along the D 2 -* ☎ *05 56 59 63 87 - 16€ (lunch) - 28/61€.* The village's former bakery, dating from 1850, has been converted into this pleasant restaurant with exposed stonework and wooden beams. The owner, a native of Pauillac, serves up a successful interpretation of regional cuisine, complemented by a fine selection of wines from the Bordelais.

Auberge des Vignerons – *28 av. Soulac - 33480 Listrac-Médoc -* ☎ *05 56 58 08 68 - Closed Feb school holidays, Sat lunchtime, Sun eve and Mon from Oct-May - 17/28€.* The dining room in this auberge, standing next to the Maison des Vins de Listrac-Médoc, occupies a former wine cellar. Enjoy pleasant views of the vineyards of this famous appellation from the terrace. Traditional cuisine, plus a cellar resolutely based on the quality wines of Listrac!

Ferme-Auberge Château Guittot-Fellonneau – *33460 Macau - 6km SE of Margaux along the D 2 and then the D 209 -* ☎ *05 57 88 47 81 - Closed Feb school holidays and 16 Aug-5 Sep - 18/37€.* Fine wining and dining is guaranteed on this wine-producing estate in the Médoc. Indulge in the typical fare of the southwest on a shady terrace overlooking the vines, with dishes such as rillettes, confits, foie gras etc, all prepared on the property by the owner.

Auberge de Savoie – *1 pl. Trémoille - 33460 Margaux -* ☎ *05 57 88 31 76 - Closed Feb school holidays, Christmas and Sun eve - 15€ (lunch) - 21/39€.* A friendly welcome is assured in this attractive 19C stone inn next to the tourist office. Meals are served in two pleasant and colourfully decorated dining rooms and, in fine weather, on the attractive terrace. Enticing cuisine prepared on a coal-fired stove. Impressive Bordeaux wine list.

AROUND SAUVETERRE-DE-GUYENNE

Les Fontaines – *8 r. Verdun - 33190 La Réole - 14km S of Sauveterre-de-Guyenne along the D 670 -* ☎ *05 56 61 15 25 - Closed 23 Feb-1 Mar, 17 Nov-1 Dec, Wed eve in low season, Sun eve and Mon - 15/42.70€.* This large bourgeois building adjoins a delightful wooded garden. Two dining rooms which have retained their original elegant feel, plus a terrace for summer dining. Delicious traditional cuisine at prices that remain digestible!

Le Flore – *1 Petit-Champ-du-Bourg - 33540 Coirac - 7.5km W of Sauveterre-de-Guyenne along the D 671, then the D 228 beyond St-Brice -* ☎ *05 56 71 57 47 - Closed Wed eve, Sun eve and Mon - 16€ (lunch) - 21/34€.* Creative, high-quality cuisine prepared by an up-and-coming chef is served in the flower-decked dining room of this small house. Easy-going yet professional service from the chef's wife, who will guide you effortlessly through the enticing menu.

Le Belvédère – *1 côte de la Tourbeille - 33890 Juillac - 22km NE of Sauveterre-de-Guyenne along the D 672, then the D 15 -* ☎ *05 57 47 40 33 - Closed Oct, Tue eve and Wed, except at lunchtime in Jul-Aug - 18€ (lunch) - 25/56€.* The restaurant's pleasant terrace overlooks a meander in the Dordogne and the surrounding area. In winter, a more "mountain-style" intimacy reigns in the small, wood-panelled dining room. Traditional cuisine based on a varied range of local products.

Auberge Saint-Jean – *8 av. du Pont - 33420 St-Jean-de-Blaignac - 17km N of Sauveterre-de-Guyenne along the D 670 -* ☎ *05 57 74 95 50 - Closed 5-9 Jan, 15 Nov-12 Dec, Tue eve and Wed - 50/90€.* Generous regional cuisine mixed with a dash of inventiveness, with dishes such as foie gras with tobacco, turbot and langoustine *pot au feu*, lamb with lavender sauce etc. Enjoy an unbeatable view of the Dordogne from the veranda of this former coaching inn.

AROUND ST-ANDRÉ-DE-CUBZAC

Coq Sauvage – *in Cavernes - 33450 St-Loubès - 15km S of St-André-de-Cubzac along the D 911, then the D 242 -* ☎ *05 56 20 41 04 - Closed 1-29 Aug, 24 Dec-9 Jan, Sat and Sun - 29/45€.* The Dordogne flows past this house in a small village in the Entre-Deux-Mers area. In winter, the regional fare on offer here is served in the attractively rustic dining room, and in summer on a flower-decked patio. Quiet bedrooms.

Auberge de la Vieille Chapelle – *33240 Lugon-et-l'Île-du-Carnay - 8km SE of St-André-de-Cubzac along the D 670 -* ☎ *05 57 84 48 65 - Closed 15 Sep-15 Oct, 5-21Jan, Sun eve, Tue and Wed - 17€ (lunch) - 33/56€.* This amazing restored chapel in the Fronsac area appears incongruously between the vineyards and the river. The warm stone and wood decor provides a pleasant atmosphere in which to enjoy regional dishes washed down by wines from the estate.

IN ST-ÉMILION

Le Bouchon – *1 pl. du Marché - 33330 St-Émilion -* ☎ *05 57 24 62 81 - Closed Nov-Feb - 17€ (lunch) - 14.48/28.20€.* One of the most pleasant of several restaurants on the place du Marché, the hub of St-Émilion life. The dining room, repainted in yellow and blue tones, is adorned with black and white photos. Refined traditional cuisine accompanied by a lively choice of wines.

Auberge du Château Cros Figeac – *33330 St-Émilion - 3km W of St-Émilion on the D 243 -* ☎ *05 57 24 76 32 - Closed 9-22 Aug, 20 Feb-6 Mar, Sun eve, Tue eve and Mon - 15/30€.* Housed in one of the Château Cros Figeac's old wine cellars, the vast dining room is crowned by a timber roof and embellished with a chimney, where meats are grilled above the embers of burning vine shoots. The attractive outdoor terrace, with its views of the vineyard, comes into its own in spring and summer.

⊖ L'Envers du Décor – *11 r. du Clocher - 33330 St-Émilion - ☎ 05 57 74 48 31 - Closed 22 Dec-9 Jan - 15/30€.* This wine bar adjoining the collegiate church serves seasonal dishes in a dining room where the style is a fusion of wood, old stone and aluminium. Quiet, relaxing terrace adorned with flowers and fig trees. A choice of high-quality wines is also on sale for consumption off the premises.

⊖⊜ Le Tertre – *R. du Tertre-de-la-Tente - 33330 St-Émilion - ☎ 05 57 74 46 33 - Closed 5 Jan-11 Feb, 12 Nov-18 Dec, Tue from Oct-Apr and Wed - 18€ (lunch) - 24/65€.* The elegant dining room, with its seafood tank and cellar dug into the rock containing a number of prestigious vintages, is sure to whet your appetite. Enticing contemporary cuisine with a definite Gascon influence.

⊖⊜ Clos du Roy – *12 r. Petite-Fontaine - 33330 St-Émilion - ☎ 05 57 74 41 55 - 20€ (lunch) - 26/42€.* This white stone house away from the main tourist track has several pleasant dining rooms combining the rustic and contemporary. Appetising modern cuisine in a relaxed setting.

Where to Stay

⊖ Gîtes Bacchus – *21 cours de l'Intendance - 33000 Bordeaux - ☎ 05 56 81 54 23 - gites-de-france-gironde@wanadoo.fr - ⊟ - 35€.* The Gîte Bacchus label, created in 1996 by the Gîtes de France de Gironde, is awarded to accommodation run by wine producers on their own properties. Guests are given a personalised introduction to the region's wine industry, with a presentation of the main grape varieties, access to wine cellar, tastings etc.

AROUND BLAYE

⊖ Chambre d'hôte Château du Pontet – *25 le Pontet Nord-Est - 33390 Eyrans - 9km NE of Blaye along the D 937 - ☎ 05 57 64 71 07 - ⊟ - Reservation required - 5 rms: 35/76€ - ⊑ 5€ - Meals: 16/45€.* This château is quite simply a delight. Housed in the former stables, the modern bedrooms are all equipped with brand-new bathrooms and all overlook the swimming pool. Excellent leisure facilities, including cycling, billiards and table tennis.

⊖⊜⊜ Closerie des Vignes – *Village Arnaud - 33710 St-Ciers-de-Canesse - 10km SE of Blaye along the D 669, then the D 250 - ☎ 05 57 64 81 90 - la-closerie-desvignes@wanadoo.fr - Apr-Oct - ⊇ - 9 rms: 76/80€ - ⊑ 8.50€ - Restaurant 21/31€.* This modern house is surrounded by the vineyards of Blaye. Spacious bedrooms with stylishly modern furniture, and a panelled dining room looking onto the vineyards and garden. The culinary emphasis here is on simple, traditional cuisine.

⊖⊜⊜ Villa Prémayac – *13 r. Prémayac - 33390 Blaye - ☎ 05 57 42 27 39 - ⊟ - 5 rms: 85€.* This charming 18C villa at the foot of the citadel has a handful of pleasant rooms individually furnished with antiques, pleasant colours and elegant fabrics. The owner, a former golf coach, organises breaks which combine the region's fairways and vineyards.

AROUND BORDEAUX

⊖⊜ Hôtel des 4 Soeurs – *6 cours du 30-Juillet - 33000 Bordeaux - ☎ 05 57 81 19 20 - 4soeurs@mailcity.com - 34 rms: 60/90€ - ⊑ 8€.* This longstanding hotel, frequented in the past by the composer Richard Wagner and the writer John Dos Passos, enjoys an excellent location in the heart of the city. Now restored, the bedrooms are bright and air-conditioned, with good soundproofing and attractively painted furnishings.

⊖⊜ Châlet Lyrique – *169 cours Gén.-de-Gaulle - 33170 Gradignan - 3.5km S of Pessac - ☎ 05 56 89 11 59 - info@chaletlyrique.fr - ⊇ - 44 rms: 63/86€ - ⊑ 9€ - Restaurant 29/36€.* Two buildings with contrasting styles add a certain cachet to this hotel. Rooms of varying size with differing levels of comfort – the renovated bedrooms are perhaps preferable. The restaurant, housed in the former village café, has lost none of its local atmosphere.

Chambres d'hôte at the Château Le Foulon.

⊖⊜⊜ Continental – *10 r. Montesquieu - 33000 Bordeaux - ☎ 05 56 52 66 00 - Closed 25 Dec-3 Jan - ⊟ - 51 rms: 95€ - ⊑ 7€.* This 18C mansion fronts a semi-pedestrian shopping street in Bordeaux's old quarter. The entrance hall and breakfast room have retained their original charm. The bedrooms have a little less personality, but are comfortable and refurbished on a regular basis. Attractive small lounge.

AROUND LANGON

⊖ Chambre d'hôte Chassagnol – *33410 Ste-Croix-du-Mont - 12km S of Cadillac along the D 10 - ☎ 05 56 62 00 58 - ⊟ - 3 rms: 34/53€.* This large 19C house at the heart of the Ste-Croix-du-Mont vineyards is a popular choice with wine aficionados.

Spacious bedrooms furnished with antique furniture, plus a garden and terrace with the added attraction of a barbecue.

⊜⊜ Chambre d'hôte Château du Broustaret – *33410 Rions - 4km NW of Cadillac along the D 10 - ☎ 05 56 62 96 97 - broustaret@libertysurf.com - Closed Nov-Easter - ⊯ - 5 rms: 45/50€.* The tradition of hospitality has been maintained for a quarter of a century at this wine property at the heart of the Premières-Côtes-de-Bordeaux appellation. Woods and meadows surround the house, in which the guest rooms are simply furnished yet comfortable. A peaceful retreat from which to explore the region's vineyards.

⊜⊜⊜ Relais du Château d'Arche – *Rte de Bommes - 33210 Sauternes - ☎ 05 56 76 67 67 - ▯ - 9 rms: 120/160€ - ⊒ 10€.* This fine 17C country house dominating the village stands at the heart of the vineyards of the Château d'Arche, an estate famous for its Sauternes Grand Cru. The luxurious bedrooms enjoy the benefits of peace and tranquillity, plus views across the vineyards.

⊜⊜⊜ Sources de Caudalie – *Chemin de Smith-Haut-Lafitte - 33650 Martillac - 15km NW of Podensac along the N 113 - ☎ 05 57 83 83 83 - sources@sources-caudalie.com - ▯ - 43 rms: 215/450€ - ⊒ 20€.* This complex, which includes a vinotherapy clinic, provides guests with a luxurious setting amid the vineyards in which to relax and recharge the batteries. Several types of luxury accommodation are on offer, including La Grange au Bateau, Le Comptoir des Indes and La Bastide des Grands Crus. Contemporary à la carte choices and an impressive wine list in the Grand'Vigne, an 18C orangery.

AROUND LIBOURNE

⊜⊜ Henri IV – *Pl. du 8-Mai-1945 - 33230 Coutras - 15km N of Lussac along the D 17 - ☎ 05 57 49 34 34 - hotel-henriIV. gironde@wanadoo.fr - Open all year - ⊯ - 14 rms: 49/51€ - ⊒ 7€.* This 19C mansion opposite the railway station is fronted by a garden-courtyard. Solid pine furniture in the somewhat basic yet well-maintained bedrooms – those on the top floor are air-conditioned and attic in style. Efficient double-glazing and double windows to combat noise from passing trains.

IN MARGAUX

⊜ Chambre d'hôte Château Cap Léon Veyrin – *33480 Listrac-Médoc - 4km from Listrac along the D 5E2 - ☎ 05 56 58 07 28 - capleonveyrin@aol.com - Closed Christmas to New Year's Day - ⊯ - 5 rms: 39/44€.* The same family has run this attractive property at the heart of a 20ha estate since 1810. All the Louis XV-style bedrooms are equipped with impressive bathrooms. Delightful breakfast room opening onto the wine storehouse.

⊜ Chambre d'hôte Domaine de Carrat – *Route de Ste-Hélène - 33480 Castelnau-de-Médoc - 5km S of Listrac along the*

N 215 - ☎ 05 56 58 24 80 - Closed Christmas - ⊯ - 4 rms: 45/57€. This red-shuttered house surrounded by a pine forest and leafy woodland once served as the stables for the neighbouring château. Friendly and attentive owners and bedrooms offering good levels of comfort. On arrival, you will pass under the splendid stone entrance used in former times by horse-drawn vehicles.

⊜⊜ France et Angleterre – *3 quai Albert-Pichon - 33250 Pauillac - ☎ 05 56 59 01 20 - hotel-de-france-et-angleterre@wanadoo.fr - Closed 19 Dec-15 Jan - 29 rms: 56/83€ - ⊒ 9€ - Restaurant 18/37€.* A 19C building along the waterfront with functional yet tastefully renovated bedrooms, with those on the main façade enjoying pleasant views of the Gironde estuary. Traditional and local cuisine, including Pauillac lamb, served in the modern dining room and veranda.

⊜⊜ Chambre d'hôte Château Le Foulon – *Rte de St-Raphaël - 33480 Castelnau-de-Médoc - 5km S of Listrac-Médoc along the N 215 - ☎ 05 56 58 20 18 - Closed 15 Dec-2 Jan - ⊯ - 4 rms: 70/95€.* This château dating from 1840 is the perfect base from which to discover the Grands Crus of the Médoc. The four bedrooms, all furnished with antiques, have retained their original sense of space, with views of the park, lake and resident swans. An apartment with a fully-equipped kitchen is also available here.

⊜⊜⊜ Le Pavillon de Margaux – *3 r. Georges-Mandel - 33460 Margaux - ☎ 05 57 88 77 54 - Open all year - ⊯ - 14 rms: 81/110€ - ⊒ 10€ - Restaurant 12/51€.* It's hard to imagine that this delightful 19C building on the edge of Margaux's vineyards was once the local school. Inside, each bedroom is named after and decorated in the style of a Médoc château. Those in the most recent wing are on the smaller side. Outstanding wine cellar.

AROUND SAUVETERRE-DE-GUYENNE

⊜ Chambre d'hôte La Lézardière – *Boimier-Gabouriaud - 33540 St-Martin-de-Lerm - 8km SE of Sauveterre-de-Guyenne along the D 670, D 230, then the D 129 - ☎ 05 56 71 30 12 - lalezardiere@free.fr - Closed Jan-Feb - ⊯ - 6 rms: 45/60€ - Meals 20€.* The half a dozen rooms on the first floor of this 17C farm overlooking the Dropt valley have been attractively converted with a focus on colour. Evening meals in the upper barn. A lounge containing documentation on wine and the region is located behind the old livestock feeding troughs. Swimming pool, plus a large gîte.

⊜ Chambre d'hôte Le Manoir de James – *Rte de Ste-Colombe - 33580 St-Ferme - 13km E of Sauveterre-de-Guyenne along the D 230, then the D 126 - ☎ 05 56 61 69 75 - midubois2@wanadoo.fr - Closed 15 Dec-15 Jan - ⊯ - 3 rms: 50/65€.* Around a hundred years ago, impressive towers crowned by pepperpot roofs endowed this 17C manor house with a noble air. The

warm welcome, verdant setting, bedrooms with fireplaces, vast entrance embellished with Gironde tiles, and swimming pool all play their part in ensuring a pleasant stay.

Chambre d'hôte Domaine de la Charmaie – 33190 St-Sève - 12km S of Sauveterre-de-Guyenne along the D 670, then the D 129 - ☎ 05 56 61 10 72 - lacharmaie@hotmail.com - 3 rms: 60/92€ - Meals 23€. This 17C mansion is tucked away in a verdant setting. Bedrooms with a harmonious decor of pastel shades, elegant fabrics and furniture showing the patina of age, and attractive bathrooms. The one suite is housed in a separate small farmhouse.

AROUND ST-ÉMILION

Château Meylet – La Gomerie - 33330 St-Émilion - ☎ 05 57 24 68 85 - Open all year - 4 rms: 52/58€. This typical Gironde-style château dating from 1789 stands at the heart of a small wine-producing estate. Just a handful of rooms with a rustic feel, parquet flooring and attractive 18C furnishings, a couple of which look onto the surrounding vineyards, while the others enjoy views of the garden, with its impressive catalpa tree. Breakfast is served under the arbour during the summer months.

Palais Cardinal – Pl. 11-Novembre-1918 - 33330 St-Émilion - ☎ 05 57 24 72 39 - hotel@palais-cardinal. com - Open Apr-Nov - 26 rms: 60/146€ - 11€ - Restaurant 22.50/36€. As the name suggests, this hotel occupies part of the residence of a 14C cardinal. The bedrooms in the more modern wing are spacious and elegant. Pleasant small garden and swimming pool. In the classically furnished restaurant, the cuisine is traditional with Saint-Émilion wines from the family property.

Château Monlot Capet – 33330 St-Hippolyte - 3km SE of St-Émilion along the D 245 - ☎ 05 57 74 49 47 - Open all year - 6 rms: 65/115€. This "château" is the archetype of the many bourgeois residences in the region. Bedrooms with period furniture, paintings and old photos, each named after a particular grape variety: Merlot, Cabernet, Sauvignon etc. Attractive breakfast room with viticultural decor. Tree-shaded garden for the summer months.

Logis des Remparts – 18 r. Guadet - 33330 St-Émilion - ☎ 05 57 24 70 43 - logis-des-remparts@wanadoo.fr - Closed 15 Dec-31 Jan - **P** - 17 rms: 85/150€ - 12€. This building, dating from the 17C, has a pleasant, meticulously maintained private terrace, as well as a garden facing onto the local vineyards. Comfortably furnished bedrooms, plus a breakfast veranda.

Hostellerie de Plaisance – Pl. du Clocher - 33330 St-Émilion - ☎ 05 57 55 07 55 - hostellerie.plaisance@wanadoo.fr - Closed 1 Jan-12 Feb - 18 rms: 120/336€ - 15€ - Restaurant 45/80€. Treat yourself to a short break in this elegant 14C white stone hotel located at the heart of the town's medieval quarter. Cosy bedrooms

furnished with a personal touch. Delicious contemporary cuisine in the elegant dining room, with a superb Saint-Émilion wine list.

GOURMET SHOPPING

Baillardran – 55 cours de l'Intendance - 33000 Bordeaux - ☎ 05 56 52 92 64 - Open 9am-8pm. This attractive boutique decked out in marble, mirrors and gilding sells just three products: macaroons, nougatine and the famous canelé. Originally created in the 16C but popular as ever, this Bordeaux speciality is a caramelised cake flavoured with vanilla and rum which takes the shape of the mould it is baked in.

Pierre Oteiza – 77 r. Condillac - 33000 Bordeaux - ☎ 05 56 52 38 76 - oteiza. aldudes @wanadoo.fr - Open Tue-Sat, 10am-2pm and 3.45-6.45pm. Closed 2 weeks in Aug. This temple of Basque gastronomy is overflowing with hams, sausages, and jars and tins of preserves. Its owner offers his customers the very best of the region's products from the renowned piperade to the famous Les Alludes leg of pork, which is rubbed in pepper and is prepared on the premises.

Recette des Anciennes Religieuses - Mme Blanchez – R. Guadet - 33330 St-Émilion - ☎ 05 57 24 72 33 - Mon-Sat, 8am-12.30pm and 3-7pm; Sun, 9am-12.30pm and 3-7pm. Closed late Jan-early Feb and 11 Nov-first Sun in Dec. Archives confirm the existence of macaroons in Saint-Émilion as early as 1620. Following an eventful history, the recipe finally came into the hands of the Passama family in 1930. Made from eggs, sugar and almonds, these delicious cakes are still made in this shop according to traditional methods.

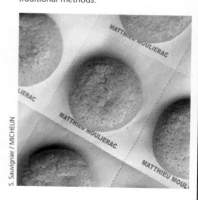

S. Sauvignier / MICHELIN

MARKETS

Bordeaux – Marché des Capucins, every morning except Tue; Marché du Colbert, along the Garonne, Sun morning; Marché St-Michel, Sat morning; organic market every Thu morning along the river opposite the Esplanade des Quinconces.

Libourne – Sun, Tue and Fri mornings.

Pauillac – Sat morning; Fri evening market in summer.

Sauveterre-de-Guyenne – Wed morning.

Bordeaux★★★

The capital of the wine industry is graced by long avenues and attractive townhouses adorned with sculpted vines. For centuries a centre of trade, Bordeaux is a vibrant, diverse city which continues to evolve: recent projects include the new tramway system, the modernisation of the river area and the development of the north bank of the river.

More than 5 000 buildings dating from the 18C can be seen in the **old town★★**, situated between the Les Chartrons and St-Michel quarters.

Place de la Bourse and Fontaine des Trois-Grâces.

The immense **esplanade des Quinconces** (126 000m²) takes its name from the quincuncial arrangement of its trees. On the esplanade, note the striking **monument aux Girondins** with its two magnificent bronze **fountains★**.

At the end of place de la Comédie, the recently restored **Grand Théâtre★★**, built by the architect Victor Louis between 1773 and 1780, is considered to be one of the most beautiful theatres in France.

The attractive **place de la Bourse★★**, overlooking the banks of the river was laid out between 1730 and 1755. The square is bordered by the Palais de la Bourse to the north and the old Hôtel des Fermes, which houses the Musée National des Douanes, to the south.

On **place du Parlement★** the façades are adorned with mascarons carved into grotesque heads or representing vine branches and wine barrels. The buildings date from the time of Louis XV.

The 11C-15C **Cathédrale St-André★** is the most impressive church in Bordeaux. Its main features of architectural interest are the attractive 13C **Porte Royale★**, with its impressive sculptures, and a fine Gothic nave and **chancel★**. *Open 9-11.30am and 2.30-5.30pm; first Sun of month, 2.30-5.30pm.*

The **Tour Pey-Berland★**, built in the 15C by the archbishop of the same name, has always stood separately from the rest of the cathedral. There is a wonderful panoramic **view★★** from the top of the tower.

Open Jun-Sep: 10am-6pm; Oct-May: daily except Mon, 10am-12.30pm and 2-5.30pm. Accessible via the stairs only (231 steps). Closed 1 Jan, 1 May and 25 Dec. 4.60€. ☎ 05 56 81 26 25.

Follow cours Pasteur. Housed in the old university, the **Musée d'Aquitaine★★** retraces the life of the people of Aquitaine from prehistoric times to the present day, with scenes illustrating traditional settlements and farming.

20 cours Pasteur. ♿ *Open daily except Mon and public hols, 11am-6pm. 4€, no charge first Sun of month. ☎ 05 56 01 51 00. www.mairie-bordeaux.fr*

Turn left into cours Victor-Hugo. Note on your left the Porte de la **Grosse Cloche★**, all that remains of a 15C bell tower that once stood here.

Continue along cours Victor-Hugo and turn right into rue des Faures. Construction of the **Basilique St-Michel★** began in 1350 and lasted two centuries. This imposing building is dominated by the late-15C **Tour St-Michel** (114m), the highest bell tower in southern France. *Open Jun-Sep, 2-7pm. 2.50€. www.bordeaux-tourisme.com*

Take the bus back along the river to esplanade des Quinconces.

Les Chartrons district, once the centre of the wine trade, lies to the north of place des Quinconces. Start your visit here on **cours Xavier-Arnozan**, where prestigious Bordeaux wine merchants have their offices.

The **Musée d'Art Contemporain★** *(7 rue Ferrère)* is housed in the old **Lainé warehouse★★**, which was once used to store exotic produce. Its permanent collection illustrates artistic trends from the 1960s to the present day. ♿ *Open daily except Mon and public hols, 11am-6pm; Wed, 11am-8pm. 5.50€, no charge first Sun of month. ☎ 05 56 00 81 50.*

The merchant's house at 41 rue Borie, built around 1720, now houses the **Musée des Chartrons**, dedicated to the different trades of the wine industry. *Open daily except Sun and Mon, 10.30am-12.30pm and 2-5pm. Closed Jan and public hols. 5€. ☎ 05 57 87 50 60. www.musee-des-chartrons.com*

A good place to finish this wine-themed tour is at **Vinorama**. This waxwork museum displays 13 different scenes illustrating the history of Bordeaux wine. *12 cours du Médoc. Open Jun-Aug: daily except Mon, 10am-noon and 2-6.30pm, Sun and public hols, 2-6.30pm (last admission 30min before closing); Sep-May: daily except Sun, Mon and public hols, 10am-noon and 2-6.30pm. 5.40€.* ☎ 05 56 39 39 20.

Leave Bordeaux to the southeast along the D 113, then follow the D 10 along the River Garonne.

Quinsac

This wine-producing village, situated on the edge of the city limits, has a **cave coopérative** which specialises in pale reds or *clairets (see Shopping Guide)*.

Continue along the D 10 to Langoiran.

It is worth stopping at **Cambes** to admire the Romanesque church of St-Martin. In the same village, the attractive **Château Puy-Bardens**, flanked by two towers, produces a quality red wine *(see Shopping Guide)*.

On the **Tabanac** hills overlooking the River Garonne stands the Château de Plassan, a unique example of Palladian architecture in the Bordeaux region.

Langoiran

A private association looks after the upkeep of the charming 13C **castle** in Langoiran. Surrounded by ramparts, a large house in the castle grounds is home to the wine storehouses of a local estate. There is a splendid **view**★ of the Garonne valley from the esplanade. *Open Jul-Aug: 10am-12.30pm and 2-8pm; Sep-Jun: 2-6pm, Sun, 10am-12.30pm and 2-6pm. Closed 1 Jan and 25 Dec. 3€.* ☎ 05 56 67 12 00.

East of Langoiran, the **Capian** area boasts some of the most beautiful châteaux in the *premières côtes* region. The **Château du Grand-Mouëys** (bed and breakfast) has one of the largest estates in this appellation and produces wines *(see Shopping Guide)*.

The attractive Château de Ramondon, with its four delightful towers, is home to a vineyard that was the property of the kings of England until 1453.

Rions

Enter this small fortified village through the Porte du Lhyan, a 14C gateway which has retained its original defensive appearance. Rions is a pleasant place for a stroll, with attractive old houses and a market hall dating from the 18C. In the village, stop at the *cercle* – this is the name for village bistros in this part of the Gironde – to taste the sweet white wine produced by the owner.

Before arriving in Cadillac, the road passes through the village of **Béguey**, home to the beautiful **Château Reynon**. This château produces a number of very good red and Cadillac liquoreux white wines under the aegis of Denis Dubourdieu, a renowned oenologist and the owner of the estate *(see Shopping Guide)*.

Cadillac

This bastide, founded in 1280, gave its name to **Cadillac wine**, a small appellation of liquoreux white wine that ages extremely well. The village is home to several excellent wine estates, including the **Château Cayla** *(see Shopping Guide)*.

Antoine de **Lamothe-Cadillac**, lord of the town (or more probably someone who simply borrowed the town's name), founded Detroit, which became the capital of the motor industry; the famous saloon car was created in his honour.

The **Château des Ducs d'Épernon** was built between 1598 and 1620. Of particular interest here are the eight richly decorated monumental fireplaces. *Open Jun-Sep: 10am-6pm; Oct-May: daily except Mon, 10am-12.30pm and 2-5.30pm. Closed 1 Jan, 1 May and 25 Dec. 4.60€ (under 18s: no charge), no charge first Sun of month (Oct-May).* ☎ 05 56 62 69 58.

At the southern exit to the town, the **Maison des Vins des Premières-Côtes-de-Bordeaux et de Cadillac** sells wine from most of the region's wine producers.

Loupiac

The Loupiac *appellation d'origine contrôlée* area extends over these hills, which are famous for their fine liquoreux white wines; the **Château Mayne du Cros** is particularly reputed for its excellent wines *(see Shopping Guide)*. The town already existed in Roman times, as vestiges of a **Gallo-Roman villa** in the Château le Portail Rouge testify; note the beautiful mosaics in the baths. *Guided tours, daily in summer; in winter, Sun and by prior arrangement. 2€.* Contact the Château le Portail Rouge, ☎ 05 56 62 93 82.

Continue to Verdelais along the D 117.

Verdelais

Notre-Dame de Verdelais **basilica**, which is said to protect the afflicted, is dedicated to the Virgin Mary. Rebuilt in the 17C, its walls are almost entirely covered with **ex-votos**.

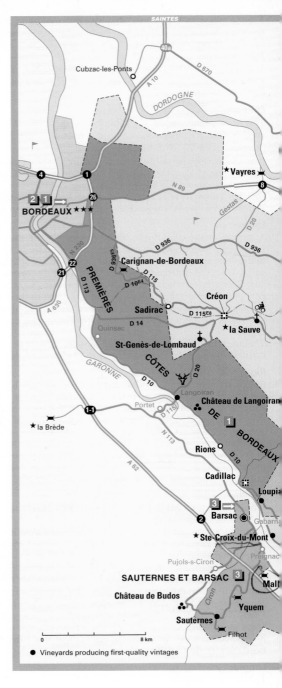

Vineyards producing first-quality vintages

In the peaceful cemetery to the right of the basilica lies the painter **Henri de Toulouse-Lautrec-Monfa** (1864-1901). His simple tombstone can be seen at the end of the central pathway, on the left-hand side.

Continue 3km northeast along the D 19.

Château de Malromé★

Open Jul-Aug: guided tours (1hr), 10.30am-12.30pm and 2.30-5.30pm; May-Jun and Sep: daily except Mon and Tue, 3-5pm; Apr and Oct: Wed, Sat-Sun and public hols, 2.30-4.30pm; Feb-Mar and Nov-Dec: Sun, 2.30-4.30pm. Closed 1 Jan. 5€. ☎ 05 56 76 44 92. www.malrome.com

Built in the 14C and enlarged in the 16C and 19C, this château was home to Toulouse-Lautrec, who spent the last few years of his life here with his mother,

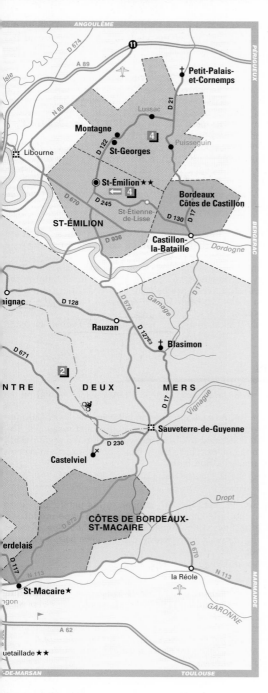

Countess Adèle de Toulouse-Lautrec. The famous painter died at the age of 37. The château comprises four buildings arranged around a courtyard: the seigniorial dwelling, the staff quarters, the wine storehouse and the stables. Toulouse-Lautrec is portrayed on the château's wine labels.

Rejoin the D 19 and head south to St-Macaire.

Domaine de Malagar ✓

&. *Open Jun-Sep: guided tours (30min), 10am-12.30pm and 2-6pm; Oct-May: daily except Mon, 2-5pm, Sat-Sun and public hols, 10am-12.30pm and 2-6pm. Closed Tue, 1 May and 22 Dec-1 Jan. 5.50€. ☎ 05 57 98 17 17. www.malagar.asso.fr*

Overlooking the St-Maixant valley, this estate was once the holiday home of the writer **François Mauriac** (1883-1970). A museum in one of the storehouses is dedicated to his life and work. A walk through the beautiful gardens leads to the stone terrace where Mauriac used to enjoy the view of his vineyards and the Landes in the distance.

Saint-Macaire★

This delightful medieval town overlooks the River Garonne. The **Côtes-de-Bordeaux-St-Macaire** appellation, which covers the area to the southeast of the *premières-côtes*, is little used. The **Maison du Pays de St-Macaire** sells local wines and organises wine-tastings, as well as providing information on walks through the vineyards. *Open Apr-Sep: Tue-Sat, 10am-12.30pm and 2-6pm, Sun, 10am-12.30pm and 2-7pm; Oct-Mar: 10am-noon and 2-6pm.* ☎ *05 56 63 32 14.*

The **walls** of the town, which have retained three old gates, date back to the 12C. Also of interest is **Église St-Sauveur** (13C-14C) which overlooks the valley; note the 14C **wall paintings★** in the transept crossing and on the vault of the eastern apse. There is a view of the River Garonne from the terrace.

Cross the Garonne on the N 113 and continue along this road to Sainte-Croix-du-Mont.

Sainte-Croix-du-Mont★

This hilltop village has given its name to liquoreux AOC white wines, which are very fruity and less heady than Sauternes; the **Château La Rame** estate enjoys a particularly good reputation *(see Shopping Guide).*

From the terrace of the Château de Tastes *(now the town hall)*, there is a fine **view★** south to the Pyrenees from the viewing table. At the end of the hill, admire the Romanesque door of the **church. Caves★** can be seen below, dug out from a bed of fossilised oysters; one of these has been converted into a picturesque **wine-tasting cellar**. *Open early-Apr to mid-Oct, daily except Wed, 2.30-7pm; Sat-Sun and public hols, 10.30am-1pm and 2.30-7.30pm. Tour free, charge for tasting.* ☎ *05 56 62 01 54.*

Entre-Deux-Mers

115km starting from Bordeaux. Michelin Local Map 335, H-M 5-7. See tour 2 *on the map on p. 120.*

The rolling green hills of the Entre-Deux-Mers region between the River Garonne and River Dordogne are covered with vineyards, small copses and meadows. The **Entre-Deux-Mers** AOC label is granted to dry white wines from the region made predominantly from Sauvignon grapes. These fruity wines are an excellent accompaniment for oysters from the Arcachon basin.

Leave Bordeaux to the E along the D 936 and turn right onto the D 936^{E5}.

Carignan-de-Bordeaux

The **Ginestet wine company**, founded in 1897, is open to the public, providing visitors with information on the little-known wine growing and wine production professions. *Open Jun-Sep: guided tours (1hr 15min) at 10am, 2pm and 4pm, Sat-Sun by prior arrangement; Oct-May: by prior arrangement. Closed public hols. No charge.* ☎ *05 56 68 81 82. www.ginestet.fr*

Head SE along the D 10^{E4}, then turn onto the D 115.

Sadirac

Housed in an old workshop, the **Maison de la Poterie-Musée de la Céramique Sadiracaise** displays ceramics dating from the 14C-18C. ⚹ *Open daily except Sun, Mon and public hols, 2-5pm. 1€.* ☎ *05 56 30 60 03.*

Also of interest in the village is the fascinating Ferme-Parc "Oh! Légumes oubliés", a farm which promotes rare plant and vegetable varieties. ⚹ *Open mid-Apr to early-Nov, 2-6pm. 7€ (children: 5.50€).* ☎ *05 56 30 62 00. www.ohlegumesoublies.com*

Follow the D 115^{E8} and the D 671 to Créon.

Créon

Centred on an attractive 14C arcaded square, this old English bastide village holds a lively market every Wednesday morning. Créon was the first village in the Gironde to be awarded the "Station Vélo" (Cycling Resort) label; a large number of bicycles are available for hire in the old railway station. An attractive 16km cycle route, "Les Vignes du Seigneur", can be followed through the vineyards. *"La gare", bd Victor-Hugo, 33670 Créon,* ☎ *05 57 34 30 95, www.creonstationvelos.free.fr For further information, contact the Entre-Deux-Mers tourist office,* ☎ *05 56 61 82 73.*

La Sauve★

The **old Abbaye de la Sauve-Majeure★**, founded by the Benedictines in 1079, was once a powerful landowning estate. It became a prison in 1793, and was subsequently used as a quarry before being completely abandoned. The abbey is a good example of the transition from the Romanesque to Gothic architectural styles. Note the magnificent **capitals★** on top of the columns in the right bay of the chancel. Remains of the 13C cloister, chapter house and refectory can be seen to the right of the abbey building. *Open Jun-Sep, 10am-6pm; Oct-May, daily except Mon, 10.30am-1pm and 2.30-5.30pm. Closed 1 Jan, 1 May and 25 Dec. 4.60€.* ☎ *05 56 23 01 55.*

The **Maison de l'Entre-Deux-Mers**, housed in the abbey's old tithing barn, provides information on local wines, which can be tasted and purchased here at estate prices *(see Shopping Guide).*

Continue along the D 671. At St-Brice, turn right and follow the D 123 and D 230.

Église de Castelviel

The main feature of interest in this church is the superb Saintonge-style **Romanesque doorway★**. Note the rich carving on the capitals and arches, which makes this one of the most beautiful architectural monuments in the Gironde.

Sauveterre-de-Guyenne

This typical bastide, built by Edward I in 1281, finally became French in 1451, having previously changed hands between the French and English on no less than 10 occasions. The village has retained its four fortified gates and a large, attractive arcaded square, which comes to life every Tuesday on market day. Around fifty regional wines can be tasted and purchased in the **Maison du Sauveterrois**, which also provides information on walks in the area *(see Shopping Guide).*

Head E along the D 230. This circuit is not shown on the map on p. 120-121.

Castelmoron-d'Albret

The smallest *commune* in France (3.5ha) stands on a rocky outcrop surrounded by fortifications. About 60 people live in this charming village.

Continue along the D 230, then turn immediately left onto the D 139.

Abbaye de Saint-Ferme

Open mid-Jun to mid-Sep: daily except Tue, 10am-noon and 2-7pm, Sun, 2-7pm; early-Apr to mid-June and mid to late-Sep: daily except Sun and Mon, 9am-noon and 2-6pm; Oct-Mar: Tue-Fri, 9am-noon and 2-6pm. Closed first Sun of month. 3.05€. ☎ *05 56 61 69 92.*

This Benedictine abbey was founded in the 11C, on the route to Santiago de Compostela in northern Spain. The courtroom, scriptorium and a museum of old tools are open to the public.

Continue N to Pellegrue along the D 16 and D 672.

Pellegrue

Two attractive Romanesque churches can be seen in this old bastide town. Several wine estates, such as the medieval Château de Lugagnac, are dotted around the vineyards amid rolling scenery that is perfect for walkers. 🚶 *Contact the tourist office for information on walks.* ☎ *05 56 61 37 80.*

Continue along the D 670.

Les Lèves-et-Thoumeyragues

This small wine-producing town, situated in the **Sainte-Foy-Bordeaux** appellation, is home to **Univitis**, one of the largest cooperatives in the Bordeaux region *(see Shopping Guide).* Note the gabled bell tower, typical of the area.

Continue to Ste-Foy-la-Grande along the D 670.

Sainte-Foy-la-Grande

One of the most colourful markets in France is held in this 13C bastide every Saturday. Once a Protestant stronghold, Sainte-Foy is proud to be the birthplace of several famous citizens, including the surgeon Paul Broca, the art critic Elie Faure, and the geographers and anarchy theorists, Élie and Élysée Reclus, all of whom were Protestants. Note the splendid medieval house in rue de la République, whose façade is decorated with strange wooden carvings.

Leave Sainte-Foy-la-Grande to the south along the D 670, then turn right onto the D 130^{E7} to Eynesse.

The picturesque road which runs along the River Dordogne passes through the villages of **Eynesse** and **Pessac-sur-Dordogne**, where the Protestant churches are found in the centre of the town, and the Roman Catholic church on the outskirts.

Gensac

This hilltop village, with its splendid viewpoint from "Calvin's throne" on the old ramparts, overlooks the Durèze valley. The efficient **tourist office** is able to provide information on a wide range of walks in the area and also sells local wine at estate prices, although it does not offer tastings. ☎ *05 57 47 46 67.*

Continue W to Pujols along the D 18.

Pujols

A lovely view of the countryside can be admired from the remains of the old feudal castle, now the town hall. The area produces good dry Bordeaux whites.

Head southwest to Blasimon along the D 17. Before entering the village, note the **Moulin de Labarthe**, an interesting example of a fortified medieval mill.

Blasimon

Hidden at the bottom of a valley is an old Benedictine **abbey**, now in ruins. Admire the Romanesque and Gothic features in its 12C-13C church.

🏃 A visit to the vineyards of Jean-François Dufaget provides a good introduction to wine-making, offering visitors the chance to follow the **Butte de Cazevert wine route**, which finishes with a tour of the storehouses and a tasting. *33540 Blasimon, ☎ 05 57 84 57 03 or 06 81 79 12 99. Open by prior arrangement from the first weekend in May to the first weekend in Oct. 2€.*

Rauzan

The **Château des Duras**, built in the late 13C, has retained its magnificent keep (30m). Also worthy of note is the late-15C tower decorated with striking rib vaulting. *Open Jul-Aug: 10am-noon and 3-7pm; at other times, daily except Mon, 10am-noon and 2-5pm. 3€. Contact the tourist office for further information. ☎ 05 57 84 03 88.*

The **Grotte Célestine** is worth visiting for its varied **concretions** and stunning rock formations. Visitors can walk the 250m through 5-15cm of water to admire these fascinating natural features. *Guided tours (45min), daily except Mon, 10am-noon and 2-4pm (daily in Jul-Aug); last tour at 5pm, mid-Jun to mid-Sep. 6.50€ (under 14s: 5€; minimum height requirement: 1.20m). ☎ 05 57 84 08 69. Reservations required. 14°C in the cave; bring a sweater, all other equipment (helmet and boots) is provided.*

The Union des Producteurs de Rauzan is one of the largest wine cooperatives in France (see Shopping Guide).

Return to Bordeaux along the D 128 towards Daignac, then take the D 936.

Left Bank of the Garonne

On the left bank of the Garonne and the outskirts of Bordeaux, the Graves wine-producing area is the only one in France to bear a geological name. Cultivated for grape production since the Middle Ages, these well-drained gravelly hills were created by the erosion of the Pyrenees. The best soil is found in the northern section of Graves, which was granted the **Pessac-Léognan** AOC in 1987; this appellation covers 1 360 ha and is known for its excellent red and white wines. The southern Graves, which extends over 3 600 ha as far as Langon, comprises the Barsac and Sauternes appellations *(see tour ③)*. The smaller **Graves-Supérieures** AOC area produces sweet white wines. For a list of châteaux which do not require a reservation, contact the **Maison des Vins de Graves** in Podensac *(see Shopping Guide)*.

THE GRAVES VINEYARDS

57km. Michelin Local Map 335, H-I 6-7.

Head SW out of Bordeaux along the N 250, following signs to "Pessac Centre".

Pessac

Less than 4km from the centre of Bordeaux, **Château Haut-Brion** is nowadays completely surrounded by suburbs. This Premier Cru wine was first listed in 1855. With its vineyards covering an area of 43ha, the château produces an interesting wine which is known not only for its fine aromas, but also for its unusually shaped bottle *(see Shopping Guide)*. Another renowned estate in the area is **Château Pape-Clément**, which during the Middle Ages belonged to Bishop Bertrand de Got, later to become Pope Clement V. The 19C neo-Gothic château is particularly imposing.

Rejoin the ring-road heading towards Toulouse. Leave the ring-road at exit 18 and take the D 651 to Léognan.

Léognan

This village on the edge of a forest is home to an impressive number of wine châteaux, many of which are signposted from the village centre.

It is well worth visiting the **Domaine de Chevalier** with its ultra-modern wine cellars and excellent wines – the estate's white is particularly renowned. At the **Château Carbonnieux** an interesting historical anecdote relates how "Carbonnieux water" sent to the Sultan of Constantinople in the 18C was in fact an excellent white wine produced by local monks. Quality remains an important priority for the estate today. *For more information on these estates, see the Shopping Guide.*

Château La Louvière is a beautiful late-18C château designed by the architect François Lhote, which became a listed building in 1991. It is particularly renowned for its Graves and Pessac-Léognan wines. *149 av. de Cadaujac, 338* *05 56 64 75 87, lalouviere@andrelurton.com Open by prior arrangem* *9am-noon and 2-5pm.*

Visitors interested in exploring the vineyards by bicycle should **Maison du Vélo** for information on bike hire and themed routes. *du Lac Bleu, 33850 Léognan,* *05 56 64 81 56.*

Head southeast along the D 109 to Martillac.

Martillac

Known both for its wine and its lily of the valley, this village has an attractive **Romanesque church** with storiated capitals. Of particular interest here is the aptly-named **Domaine de la Solitude**, a 16C-18C convent which is also a wine estate. *33650 Martillac,* *05 56 72 74 74. Visits by prior arrangement.*

Château Smith-Haut-Lafitte is home to a wine estate and a vinotherapy centre, Les Sources de Caudalie. The spa offers an interesting range of treatments, combining the virtues of iron- and fluorine-rich mineral water with grape extracts, grapeseed oil, wine yeast, red wine extracts and tannins, all of which help to moisturise and tone the skin. The unusual anti-ageing and slimming treatments include a "barrel bath" and "Merlot wrap". The "discovery" package of four treatments costs 135€. *Chemin de Smith-Haut-Lafitte, 33650 Bordeaux-Martillac,* *05 57 83 83 83. www.sources-caudalie.com*

Good places to stock up on wine include **Château Latour-Martillac** and **Château de Rochemorin**, where Montesquieu once lived and where the wines are lively and full-bodied *(see Shopping Guide).*

Follow the D 109 south to La Brède.

The road now enters the Graves du Sud region, a vast wine-producing area once home to Montesquieu, where the vineyards stretch between the River Garonne and the Landes forests of the Gironde.

Château de La Brède★

Jul-Sep: guided tours (30min), daily except Tue, 2-6.30pm; early-Oct to mid-Nov: Sat-Sun and public hols, 2-5.30pm; Apr-Jun: Sat-Sun and public hols, 2-6pm. 6€.

The austere silhouette of this château is reflected in its moat, giving the impression of a fortified island in the middle of a lake. This Gothic-style château, which is reached by a wide avenue, dates from the 12C-15C and has hardly changed since it was inhabited by the famous writer Montesquieu. The tour starts at the moat, which is crossed by small bridges linking two old fortified structures. These lead to the vestibule, where a collection of Montesquieu's travelling trunks are on display. On the first floor is the 5 000-book library and

MONTESQUIEU

In 1689, Charles de Segondat, the future Baron de Labrède et de Montesquieu, was born at the château; as a sign of humility, he was held at his baptismal font by a beggar. Montesquieu later became President of the Parliament of Bordeaux (despite considering himself a mediocre magistrate), but preferred the peace of the countryside to the town and was often found at his La Brède property: "It is the most beautiful rural scenery that I know." At the château, he would take care of his business correspondence (he sold much of his wine to England), walk in his vineyards and visit his storehouses. Of an even and easy-going temperament, Montesquieu, like Montaigne, found his intellectual work relaxing: "Study has been for me the main antidote to life's problems – I have never had a worry that could not be cured by an hour's reading."

Montesquieu's simple **room**, furnished exactly as it would have been during the writer's residence. The château has beautiful landscaped gardens.

An 11km walk, known as **Les 8 Châteaux de Pessac-Léognan**, can be followed through the Pessac-Léognan appellation. *For further information, contact La Brède tourist office.* *05 56 78 47 72, www.graves-montesquieu.com*

Head east along the D 108, then turn right onto the N 113.

Portets

The lofty silhouette of the 18C **Château de Portets** dominates this village on the banks of the Garonne. Shad and lamprey caught in the river here are ideal accompaniments for the good local wines produced by **Château Rahoul** and other estates in the area *(see Shopping Guide).*

Château de Mongenan is an attractive country house (1736) with a botanical garden inspired by Jean-Jacques Rousseau. A museum dedicated to the 18C and a reconstruction of a Masonic temple stand to the side of the château. *Open Easter to late-Sep, guided tours (1hr), 2-7pm; mid-Feb to Easter and Oct-Dec, Sat-Sun, 2-6pm. 6€.* *05 56 67 18 11.*

The **Musée de la Vigne et du Vin** at the **Château Lagueloup** displays an interesting collection of equipment found in the wine storehouses here, which were designed as a factory in the late 19C. *Open 10am-6pm. Free guided tours; wine-tasting with commentary, 5€.* *05 56 67 13 90. "Petit-déjeuner gourmand" Sat, call ahead of time for information.*

Head southeast to Podensac along the N 113.

nsac

is large village is the home of **Lillet**, a wine-based aperitif flavoured with herbs nd quinine. The distillery, which has a collection of Art Deco vats and labels, is open to the public. *Open mid-Jun to mid-Sep, 9am-6.30pm; mid-Sep to mid-Jun, Mon-Fri, 9.30am-5pm. No charge.* ☎ *05 56 27 41 41, www.lillet.com*

The **Maison des Vins de Graves** (on the right as you leave Podensac) is home to 300 different wines from the Graves region. It has tourist information and a list of châteaux that can be visited without a reservation *(see Shopping Guide)*.

Château de Chantegrive produces one of the best wines in this area.

Follow the N 113 to Cérons.

Cérons

This small village has given its name to a tiny appellation of liquoreux white wines, which covers an area of less than 100ha. Excellent examples of this fine wine are found at the **Grand Enclos du Château de Cérons** *(see Shopping Guide)*.

Head S along the N 113 to Barsac.

SAUTERNES AND BARSAC

30km starting from Barsac. Michelin Local Map 335, I-J 7. See tour **3** *on the map on p. 120.*

The Sauternes and Barsac vineyards are located in the lower Ciron valley, near the confluence of the Ciron with the Garonne. The AOC **Barsac** wines are also entitled to use the **Sauternes** appellation and have the same qualities. The grapes for both wines are not picked when ripe, but are allowed to undergo the process of "noble rot" or *botrytis cinerea*, which is caused by the damp rising from the River Ciron. It is the enzymes in this mould that concentrate the sugars in the grape. When ready, the "preserved" grapes are picked one by one and then pressed.

Barsac

The 16C-17C **church** is an example of the survival of the Gothic style during the Classical period.

Altogether Barsac is home to a dozen châteaux whose architectural styles are as elegant as their wines; **Château Climens** and **Château Coutet** are of particular interest *(see Shopping Guide)*.

Château Nairac (17C-18C) is an attractive example of the Classical style, both in terms of its architecture and its wine. *33720 Barsac,* ☎ *05 56 27 16 16. Visits by prior arrangement.*

Barsac and Sauternes wines can be tasted and purchased at the **Maison du Vin de Barsac** *(see Shopping Guide)*.

Pujols-sur-Ciron

The 16C and 19C houses are protected by ramparts with corner towers, giving the village the appearance of a fortress in the middle of the vineyards.

Cru Barréjats produces Sauternes wines using only purely natural concentration methods *(see Shopping Guide)*.

Budos

Ruins of an early-14C **feudal castle** can be seen in Budos, just outside the Sauternes area. The path to the castle passes through a gatehouse crowned by a square tower, leading to the castle esplanade. In front of the west façade admire the thickness of the curtain wall and its towers.

Sauternes

Visitors are assured of a warm welcome at the **Maison du Sauternes**. The mysteries of the Sauternes production process are explained here and some 70 wines are available for tasting (with the exception of Château-d'Yquem, which is still available for purchase). All wines are on sale at estate prices *(see Shopping Guide)*.

To the south, **Château Filhot**, which produces a Premier Grand Cru Classé, is an attractive 17C building that was rebuilt in the 19C. The château has lovely gardens. ☎ *05 56 76 61 09. By prior arrangement.*

The legendary Château d'Yquem.

A. Cascaigne/MICHELIN

Northwest of Sauternes, the village of Bommes is home to the prestigious **Château La Tour Blanche**, which now houses a wine school. The château, given to the state in 1909 by the philanthropic financier Daniel Iffla, otherwise known as Osiris, produces a Premier Cru Classé. ☎ *05 57 98 02 73. By prior arrangement.*

Château d'Yquem

33210 Sauternes, ☎ 05 57 98 07 07, info@yquem.fr. Open Mon-Fri, tours of the cellars at 2pm and 3.30pm, by prior arrangement. Closed Aug and between Christmas and New Year.

The wines produced by this prestigious château enjoyed a fine reputation as early as the 16C; they were subsequently much appreciated by Thomas Jefferson. The château *(not open to the public)*, dates from the 15C and 17C.

Château de Malle

Open Apr-Oct: guided tours (30min) by prior arrangement (mornings) 10am-noon and 2-6pm. 7€. ☎ 05 56 62 36 86. www.chateau-de-malle.fr

The estate is accessed via a splendid entrance gate adorned with wrought ironwork. The attractive ensemble formed by the château and the terraced Italian-style summer gardens was designed in the 17C. The interior houses a 17C **collection of trompe l'oeil silhouettes**, unique in France.

Take the D 8E4 to Preignac. The road passes the famous **Château Bastor-Lamontagne**, one of the jewels in the crown of the Sauternes wine-producing area *(see Shopping Guide). Return to Barsac along the N 113.*

The Libournais

The River Dordogne widens to the west of Libourne, joining the Garonne at Bec d'Ambès. On the right bank of the river lie the gentle rolling hills of the Fronsadais vineyards. East of Libourne, the renowned wine-producing areas of Pomerol and St-Émilion stand in the heart of a region with a rich historical past.

THE SAINT-ÉMILION AREA

52km, starting from St-Émilion. Michelin Local Map 335, K5. See tour 4 on the map on p. 120.

St-Émilion, the most beautiful wine-producing village in the Bordeaux region, is listed as a UNESCO World Heritage Site. This attractive village of limestone houses and red-tiled roofs is set amid gently rolling hills carpeted with vines, and is entirely dedicated to wine. It is partly as a result of the mineral-rich soil that the vines here produce such high-quality wines, and partly as a result of the slow ageing process which takes place in old quarries now used as wine cellars.

The St-Émilion vineyards cover an area of 5 400ha, extending across nine *communes*. Other "satellite" appellations, such as Montagne, Puisseguin, Lussac and St-Georges, cover an area of just under 4 000ha.

The two appellations of **Saint-Émilion** and **Saint-Émilion-Grand-Cru** were classified in 1955. In theory, there is no geographical difference between the two labels, although in practice most of the Grand Cru wines are produced from the vineyards situated on the plateau or on the hills.

JURADE AND JURATS

The famous red wines of St-Émilion were known in the Middle Ages as "honorary" wines because they were often presented in homage to sovereigns and other important personalities. During this period, the municipal council was responsible for checking the quality of the wine: today, the *jurade*, re-formed in 1948, continues this function.

Every year in spring *(3rd Sun in Jun)*, the *jurats*, dressed in their silk hoods and scarlet robes trimmed with ermine fur, attend mass before proceeding to the collegiate church cloisters, where they carry out the induction of new members. At the end of the afternoon, they proclaim their judgement of the new wine from the top of the Tour du Roi.

In autumn *(3rd Sun in Sep)*, the *jurats* announce the *bans des vendanges* (vintage banns) from the same tower.

Saint-Émilion★★

Excellent views of the village and surrounding area can be enjoyed from the top of the church bell tower or from the Tour du Roi. Local specialities here include St-Émilion **macaroons**, a delicious biscuit made from almonds, sugar and egg whites.

Start your tour of the village with the monuments in the **Place du Marché** *(guided tours only: tickets from the tourist office)*. Of particular interest is the underground **monolithic church★** built from "a single stone" between the late 8C and 12C, the

S. Sauvignier/MICHELIN

St-Émilion and its famous vineyards.

largest of its kind in Europe. The interior is striking for its wide aisles carved into the rock and for the regular cut of its vaults and quadrangular pillars.

The cave of the **St-Émilion hermitage** was built in the form of a cross by the hermit Émilion. Legend says that women hoping to have a child should sit on Émilion's chair, which is carved into the rock.

The **Chapelle de La Trinité** was built in the 13C by Benedictine monks. Converted into a cooperage, the building has retained some attractive **Gothic frescoes**, hidden for many years under a layer of soot. A series of **catacombs** – underground galleries originally used as a necropolis – can be seen in the next section of the rock. The hole visible in the central cupola was originally used to lower the bodies into the catacombs.

The **collegiate church** above the place du Marché is a huge building with a Romanesque nave and Gothic chancel. Entrance to the church is through a magnificent doorway dating from the 14C. Of particular interest in the chancel are the imaginatively carved characters adorning the 15C **choir stalls**. The 14C **cloisters**, refectory and monks' dormitory, all of which have been restored, form the "Doyenné", which now houses the local tourist office.

Climb the 187 steps of the **monolithic church bell tower** for a fine **view** of the village. *Open Jul-Aug: 9.30am-8pm; mid to late-June and early to mid-Sep: 9.30am-7pm; mid-Sep to late-Oct and early-Apr to mid-Jun: 9.30am-12.30pm and 1.45-6.30pm; Nov-Mar: 9.30am-12.30pm and 1.45-6pm. 1€.* ☎ *05 57 55 28 28.*

East of the place du Marché, near the town walls, stands the **Cloître des Cordeliers★**. Built in the 14C, these romantic cloisters comprise a series of Romanesque arches supported by small columns. The nave of the old church leads to **cellars** dug from the rock at a depth of 20m, which are home to the sparkling Crémant-de-Bordeaux wine. *For further information, call* ☎ *05 57 74 49 31.*

To the south, the rectangular keep of the **castle** (32m), known as the **Tour du Roi**, stands alone on a rocky base, providing a splendid **view★** of the town and surrounding area from its summit. It is from this tower that the *jurade* proclaim their judgement of the new wine in spring and the vintage banns in autumn. *Open Jun-Aug: 10.30am-12.45pm and 2.15-8.30pm; Sep-May: 10.30am-12.45pm and 2.15-6.45pm. Access to the top of the tower: 1€.* ☎ *05 57 24 61 07.*

The **Maison du Vin de St-Émilion** offers an introduction to the local wine industry. The centre provides visitors with a guide to the estates, a video shows the vineyards and organises wine tastings in summer. Wines from 225 châteaux for sale.

Also worth a visit is the **Union des Producteurs de St-Émilion** cooperative, where visitors are guaranteed a warm welcome *(see Shopping Guide)*.

There is no fixed route for touring the **St-Émilion wine estates**, unless you decide to join the **Train des Grands Vignobles** tour which visits the Grands Crus châteaux and includes a commentary and wine-tasting. *Château Rochebelle,* ☎ *05 57 51 30 71, www.visite-saint-emilion.com Open 10.30am-12.30pm and 2-6.30pm. Allow 30-35min. Closed 15 Oct-Easter, except school holidays. 5€ (children: 4€).*

Château Franc-Mayne is a delightful château typical of the Gironde style. Home to a 16C coaching inn and magnificent underground galleries, the château also offers bed and breakfast accommodation. *33330 St-Émilion,* ☎ *05 57 24 62 61, www. chateau-francmayne.com Tours at 9.30am, 11am, 2.30pm, 4pm and 5.30pm, by prior arrangement. Admission charge.*

The attractive fountain adorning one of the walls of **Château Cadet-Bon** recalls an episode related by Homer, in which Dionysos is captured by pirates. As the god took out his flute and began to play, the pirates' boat filled with wine, capsizing the pirates who were transformed into dolphins. The fountain has become the emblem of this château. *1 Le Cadet, 33330 St-Émilion, ☎ 05 57 74 43 20, loriene@cadet-bon. com Open by prior arrangement.*

Château La Gaffelière is situated on the site of an old Gallo-Roman villa. A mosaic from the villa representing a vine bearing fruit testifies to the presence of a vineyard here since the 4C. *BP 65, 33330 St-Émilion, ☎ 05 57 24 72 15, chateau-la-gaffeliere@chateau-la-gaffeliere.com Open Mon-Fri (daily from Jun-Aug), 8am-noon and 2-6pm (5pm Fri). By prior arrangement.*

Visitors can purchase wine *(see Shopping Guide)* at **Château Angélus** and **Château Figeac**.

Leave St-Émilion via the Porte Bourgeoise and head north along the D 122.

Saint-Georges

The **Saint-Georges-Saint-Émilion** AOC is a small appellation, covering an area of 170ha. Just before you come into the village of St-Georges on the road from St-Émilion, note the **Château St-Georges** on the right. This beautiful Louis XVI-style building was designed by Victor Louis, the architect of the Grand Théâtre in Bordeaux. The small 11C Romanesque church's bell tower stands 23m high.

Montagne

The **Montagne-St-Émilion** appellation is the largest of the St-Émilion "satellite" vineyards, covering an area of 1 560ha. These wines are endowed with less bouquet than the wines of St-Émilion, but age well. The **Maison des Vins** provides a good introduction to the four "satellite" appellations and has approximately 250 different wines for sale. Also worth a visit is the **Groupe des Producteurs de Montagne**, which gives a good general introduction to the appellation.

Château Montaiguillon enjoys an excellent hilltop location offering stunning views of the surrounding countryside. *33570 Montagne, ☎ 05 57 74 62 34, www. montaiguillon.com Free tours by prior arrangement.*

In the village of Montagne, note the Romanesque **church** topped with a square tower. From the terrace, enjoy the lovely views.

The nearby **Écomusée du Libournais** provides a full introduction to the Libournais wine-producing area. *Open mid-Jun to mid-Sep: 10am-noon and 2-6pm; early-Apr to mid-Jun and mid-Sep to mid-Nov: Sat-Sun, public and school hols, 10am-noon and 2-6pm. Closed mid-Nov to late-Mar. 5.10€ (children: 2.20€). ☎ 05 57 74 56 89.*

Continue along the D 122 to Lussac.

Lussac

Lussac has given its name to an appellation covering an area of 1 430ha. Respected producers in the area include **Châteaux La Claymore** and the **Union des Producteurs**, an umbrella organisation for 140 wine producers offering quality wines *(see Shopping Guide). Open Mon-Sat, 8.30am-12.30pm and 2.30-6.30pm; Sat in Jul-Aug, 9am-6.30pm. ☎ 05 57 55 50 40.*

Follow the D 122 for 2km, then turn left onto the D 21 and continue along this road for 4.5km.

Petit-Palais-et-Cornemps

Surrounded by a cemetery, the **Église St-Pierre** dates from the late 12C. It has a delightful Romanesque **façade★** whose delicately carved style is typical of the Saintonge and is heavily influenced by Moorish architecture.

Return to the D 21 to Puisseguin.

Puisseguin

The Puisseguin-Saint-Émilion appellation covers an area of 746ha. Now a hotel-restaurant, **Château de Roques** is also a winery with a large underground wine cellar beneath the château. *33570 Puisseguin, ☎ 05 57 74 69 56. Open 9am-5.30pm. Guided tour and wine-tasting (admission charge).*

Take the D 17 to Castillon-la-Bataille. The road now enters the **Côtes-de-Castillon** appellation (2 945ha), which produces well-structured and generally fruity red wines. The vineyards lie mainly on the hills to the north of Castillon-la-Bataille. Shortly after Puisseguin, a scenic road (D 123E7) leads to **Saint-Philippe-d'Aiguilhe**. There is a pleasant spot at Candeleyre for a picnic.

Continue along the D 17.

Castillon-la-Bataille

Castillon overlooks the right bank of the Dordogne. In 1453, the English troops commanded by General Talbot suffered a heavy defeat here, marking the end of English domination in Aquitaine. Every summer, the re-enactment of the battle with a cast of 600 provides a dramatic spectacle. *For information, contact Château Castegens, 33350 Castillon-la-Bataille, ☎ 05 57 40 14 53 (open daily, 8am-noon and 2-6pm). From mid-Jul to mid-Aug: show at 10.30pm.*

The **Maison des Vins des Côtes de Castillon** *(see Shopping Guide)* has a choice of 54 wines on sale at estate prices. It also offers wine tastings and every summer organises tours of the châteaux which take place before the re-enactment of the battle. *Book in advance; meet at the Maison des Vins at 5pm.*

POMEROL AND FRONSAC

30km from Libourne to St-André-de-Cubzac. Michelin Local Map 335, H-J 5.

Libourne

At the confluence of the River Dordogne and River Isle, Libourne's prosperity has long been linked to wine. Interest in the wine trade was revived in the early 20C by families from the Corrèze, many of whom are still active in the industry.

Place Abel-Surchamp is lined with houses from the 16C and 19C. The **Tour du Grand-Port**, on quai des Salinières, was once part of the town's fortifications. Quai du Priourat, to the left of the bridge on the town side, is home to several wine merchants, including Maison Moueix, owner of the world-famous Petrus.

Leave Libourne to the NE along the N 89.

Pomerol

Covering an area of only 800ha, **Pomerol** has an excellent reputation. This region has few grand châteaux, but many famous wines. The Petrus estate, which produces one of the best – and one of the most expensive – wines in the world, looks more like a bourgeois house than a château. Pomerol wines owe their delicacy and bouquet to the complex soil of pebbles, gravel, sand and clay. The dominant grape variety used is Merlot, which gives the wines a fruity quality. These wines are pleasant to drink when young, but also lay down well. To discover this appellation which borders the St-Émilion, contact the **Château La Fleur de Plince**, the smallest Pomerol estate, with an area of just 28ha. The friendly owner, Monsieur Choukroun, will be happy to introduce you to his estate and provide information on the local area. *Le Grand Moulinet, 33500 Pomerol, ☎ 05 57 74 15 26.*

The **church** at Pomerol dates mainly from the 19C, although it once was part of a commandery of the Knights Hospitaller of St John of Jerusalem.

To the northeast of the appellation, the 17C **Château de Salles** is the only real château in the area. Built on one level, with two wings, the château served as a model for the 18C country houses of the Bordeaux region. On the road towards St-Émilion, the elegant late-18C **Château de Beauregard** served as a model for an identical copy built by the Guggenheim family on Long Island in New York. *33500 Pomerol, ☎ 05 57 51 13 36, beauregard@chateau-beauregard.com Open by prior arrangement, Mon-Fri, 9.30am-noon and 2.30-5.30pm.*

Head N on the D 245 for 2.5km.

Lalande-de-Pomerol

Surrounding the village of Lalande-de-Pomerol, whose 12C **church** was built by the Knights Hospitaller of St John, the vineyards of Lalande-de-Pomerol cover a larger area than those of Pomerol. The Lalande wines are fleshy, robust and well-structured. Château de Viaud is one of the top producers in the appellation.

Return towards Libourne along the D 910, then turn right onto the D 670.

Fronsac

The Fronsac vineyards, west of Libourne, extend for 816ha across six *communes*. The robust red wines produced here will lay down well. Wines from Fronsac and St-Michel-de-Fronsac are permitted to use the **Canon-Fronsac** name.

The Romanesque and Gothic **Église St-Martin** is thought to have been founded by Charlemagne. The **Maison des Vins** here has a selection of 70 wines for sale at estate prices, including several old vintages. **Château Les Trois Croix** and **Château Grand-Renouil** are particularly noted for their quality.

Château de La Rivière (16C-19C) was restored by Viollet-le-Duc and owes its charm to its eclectic style. This is the largest wine estate in the appellation, with 3ha of underground cellars. *33126 La Rivière, ☎ 05 57 55 56 56. Open Jun-Sep, daily except Sun morning, 9am-noon and 2-5pm.*

As you continue along D 670, stop at **Saint-Michel-de-Fronsac** to admire its attractive Romanesque church (12C-13C), then again at **Château Cassagne Haut-Canon** to taste some of the excellent wines produced here. In **Cadillac-en-Fronsadais**, the **Château Branda**, a restored fortified farm dating from the 13C, now houses an exhibition centre dedicated to art and wine, as well as a medieval garden. The centre sells wines and Armagnac produced on the estate.

Open Easter to early-Nov: 10am-6pm; early-Nov to Easter: Sun and public hols, 2-6pm. Closed 1 May and 25 Dec. 6€. ☎ 05 57 94 09 37. www.chateau-branda.com Continue to St-André-de-Cubzac.

Saint-André-de-Cubzac

A dolphin dancing in the centre of a roundabout in Saint-André-de-Cubzac carries a small red cap in its mouth as a reminder that Jacques Cousteau was born here. The fortified 13C-14C Romanesque church has arrow-slits in the towers.

North of the town, the imposing **Château du Bouilh**, surrounded by its vineyards, was designed by Victor Louis. *Open Jul-Oct: guided tours (1hr) by prior arrangement (at least 1 week in advance), Thu, Sat-Sun and public hols, 2.30-7pm. 5€.* ☎ *05 57 43 01 45 or 05 57 43 06 59.*

The Bourgeais and Blayais regions

32km starting from Bourg. Michelin Local Map 335, H-I 4.

The limestone hills on the right bank of the Gironde offer a combination of undulating landscapes and rustic charm, characterised by small family-owned wine estates and thriving rural traditions, rather than grand châteaux and Crus Classés.

Covering an area of 3 800ha, the **Côtes-de-Bourg** appellation produces well-structured reds which lay down well, as well as a few dry whites, renowned for their fruity and rounded characteristics.

Bourg ✓

The steep narrow streets of this small hilltop town situated on the banks of the Dordogne are perfect for a leisurely stroll. Shaded by old elm and lime trees, the **Terrasse du District** has lovely views of the siena-coloured rooftops of the lower town; in the distance, the Dordogne and Garonne meet at Bec d'Ambès to form the Gironde *(viewing table)*. The lower town and port at the foot of the limestone cliff are also worth exploring. The 18C **Château de la Citadelle** is surrounded by formal French-style gardens and a terrace with a view. The château now houses the **Musée Hippomobile "Au temps des calèches"**, with a collection of 40 carriages dating from the 19C. *Open Jun-Aug: 10am-1pm and 2-7pm; Mar-May and Sep-Oct: Sat-Sun and public hols, 10am-1pm and 2-7pm, weekdays by prior arrangement. Closed 1 May. 4.50€.* ☎ *05 57 68 23 57.*

The **Maison des Côtes-de-Bourg**, housed in an attractive vaulted cellar, has a large choice of wines on sale to the public *(see Shopping Guide)*.

The **Château de la Grave**, restored in Louis-XIII style, is worth a visit for its fine setting, as well as for its good quality wines *(bed and breakfast available)*. *33710 Bourg,* ☎ *05 57 68 41 49. Open by prior arrangement.*

Before continuing to Blaye, stop in Pain de Sucre, at the foot of the cliff, where the **Maison Brouette** produces Crémant-de-Bordeaux sparkling wine. *Pain de Sucre, 33710 Bourg,* ☎ *05 57 68 42 09. Open Jul-Aug: 8am-noon and 2-6.30pm; Sep-Jun: Mon-Thu, 8am-noon and 2-6pm (5pm Fri).*

Head east along the D 669.

Grottes de Pair-non-Pair

Open mid-Jun to mid-Sep: guided tours (45min, last admission 1hr before closing), 10am-5.30pm; mid-Sep to mid-Jun, 10am-11.30am and 2.30-4.30pm. Closed 1 Jan, 1 May and 25 Dec. 2.50€, no charge first Sun of month, (Oct-May). Reservation recommended in high season. ☎ *05 57 68 33 40.*

The name Pair-non-Pair is said to come from a village lost by a nobleman in a gambling game. These caves cut into the limestone rock house Aurignacian engravings of horses, mammoth, ibex and bison from the Palaeolithic Era (20 000-25 000 BC), including a fine example of a horse with its head turned.

Head north along the D 133.

Tauriac

Tauriac, situated in the heart of the appellation, is home to several renowned wine producers. The vibrant **Cave Viticole de Bourg-Tauriac** always has a friendly welcome for visitors, offering a large selection of quality wines.

Return to Bourg and continue west along the D 669.

The scenic road follows the estuary, offering splendid views of the Gironde and Bec d'Ambès. The Château de Tayac and Château d'Eyquem along this road produce respected wines and enjoy fine locations with panoramic views.

Bayon

The Romanesque church in Bayon is renowned for its fine seven-sided apse. Also of interest is the **Château Falfas**, an attractive 17C manor house which produces excellent wines. *33710 Bayon,* ☎ *05 57 64 80 41. Open by prior arrangement, Mon-Fri, 9am-noon and 2-6pm.*

Return to the Gironde and continue towards Blaye.

The road now passes through a series of small hamlets, many of which have dwellings built into the cliff face. Square fishing nets known as *carrelets* hang on winches above the river, by huts built on piles over the water.

At Roque de Thau, turn right onto the D 250. At **Villeneuve**, *stop to admire* **Château de Mendoce**, *a fine 15C manor house with four corner towers. The château is open for tastings of its excellent Côtes-de-Bourg, which take place in a large, imposing tasting room. 33710 Villeneuve, ☎ 05 57 68 34 95, www.mendoce.com Open by prior arrangement, 9am-noon and 2-6pm.*

Return to the D 669.

Plassac

The remains of three **Gallo-Roman villas** dating from the 1C-5C AD have been found behind the church in this village. A museum provides information on the history of the villas and exhibits displays of the artefacts excavated here. *Unaccompanied visit of the museum, guided tours of the villa (30min). Open May-Sep: 9am-noon and 2-7pm; Apr and Oct: 9am-noon and 2-6pm. 3€. ☎ 05 57 42 84 80.*

Château Mondésir-Gazin produces an excellent red wine *(see Shopping Guide).*

Blaye

The Blaye region produces reds and dry whites in an area of approximately 6 000ha, which includes the **Côtes-de-Blaye**, **Blaye** and **Premières-Côtes-de-Blaye** appellations. The red wines are robust and fruity and can be laid down for between five to ten years; the whites are fruity and rounded. The **Maison du Vin** has a selection of 270 wines from the appellation, including a number of different vintages *(see Shopping Guide).*

The **citadel★**, originally built to protect Bordeaux from the English fleet, was completed by Vauban in 1689. This is now almost a small village in its own right, and is very busy in season. Excellent **views** can be enjoyed from the **Tour des Rondes**, **Tour de l'Aiguillette** and the esplanade on place d'Armes. The **Manutention** was built in 1677 to house the prison; it now houses interesting **exhibitions** on the ecosystem of the estuary, a **Musée de la Boulangerie**, and a **Musée Archéologique**. *Open Apr-Oct, 1.30-7pm. 2.80€. ☎ 05 57 42 80 96. www. estuairegironde.net*

A **cycle path** from Blaye to Étauliers runs for 13km through the vineyards. *Leaving Blaye, head east along the D 937.*

Cars

Cars is home to several interesting wine estates. The **Cave Coopérative du Blayais** offers a varied cross-section of wines from the area *(see Shopping Guide).* The **Château Bel Air La Royère** situated beyond Cars produces wines from the Malbec grape.

The Médoc

130km, starting from Bordeaux. Local Michelin Map 335, F-H 3-5. See tour on the map p. 133.

Leave Bordeaux to the NW along the N 215, then turn right onto the D 2 at Eysines. Visitors leaving from the Parc des Expositions should follow the D 209.

The Médoc peninsula is wedged between the Gironde estuary and the Atlantic Ocean. Its name is synonymous with good wine, although almost 80% of the region is covered with forest. Water is an ever-present influence in the region, which has a mild climate and is well watered by rain coming in from the Atlantic. As a result, the Médoc vineyards would have produced little good-quality wine had the locals not planted their vines at a much greater density than usual – 10 000 vines per hectare instead of the 4 000 that is typical of other areas. This dense planting of vines produces good wines even in poor soil. The other secret of the Médoc is the genius of local wine producers, who are highly skilled in blending different grape varieties and who have perfected the art of maturing wine in oak barrels.

The terroir comprises mainly gravelly hills, which slope towards the Gironde. Although the entire 16 000ha area is entitled to use the **Médoc** appellation, only the vineyards to the north do so. The closest part of the region to Bordeaux is the Haut-Médoc, a vast appellation of 4 200ha, which includes the six village Crus of Margaux, Moulis, Listrac, Saint-Julien, Pauillac and St-Estèphe.

The first village you come to in the **Haut-Médoc** AOC upon leaving Bordeaux along the D 2 is **Blanquefort**, home to the supposedly haunted ruins of an 11C-15C castle which once belonged to the mysterious Black Prince.

At Blanquefort, leave the D 2 and join the D 210. This road runs parallel to and east of the D 2.

More and more vineyards appear after **Parempuyre**. Here the splendid **Château Clément-Pichon**, typical in style of the "neo" architecture of the 19C, produces an excellent Cru Bourgeois. *30 av. du Château-Pichon, 33290 Parempuyre, ☎ 05 56 35 23 79. Open Mon-Fri by prior arrangement.*

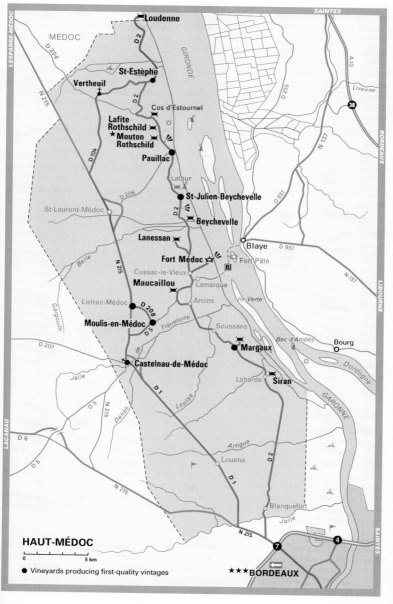

Ludon-Médoc

Just before Ludon-Médoc, note the elegant **Château d'Agassac**, an old 12C fort transformed into a Renaissance château. The château produces an excellent *cru bourgeois. 15 r. du Château-d'Agassac, 33290 Ludon-Médoc,* ☎ *05 57 88 15 47, contact. agassac.com Open Oct-May by prior arrangement, Mon-Fri, 9.30am-12.30pm and 1.30-4.30pm. No prior booking required from Jun-Sep, Tue-Sat, 10am-6.30pm.*

The main buidling of note in the town is the prestigious 18C **Château La Lagune**, producers of a Troisiéme Cru Classé *(see Shopping Guide).*

Macau

The port area in this small town renowned for its artichokes is lined with open-air cafés where people come from Bordeaux to sample shad, lamprey or eels, depending on the season. The delicious small prawns fished in the estuary and served with aniseed are available all year round. **Château Cambon La Pelouse** is one of the best value-for-money wine estates in the whole of the Haut-Médoc *(see Shopping Guide).*

Return to the D 2.

HAUT-MÉDOC

0   5 km

● Vineyards producing first-quality vintages

★★★**BORDEAUX**

Labarde

The **Margaux** appellation, covering an area of 1 400ha and producing some of the finest wines in the Médoc, begins at Labarde. These wines contain a high percentage of Merlot, resulting in strong tannins and a mellow flavour. The appellation is home to 19 Crus Classés.

The 40ha **Château Siran** is a 17C Directoire-style country house, which produces Cru Bourgeois wines. In addition to the barrel-filled storehouse, the château also contains a collection of engravings by Rubens, Vélasquez, Boucher and Daumier, as well as an excellent collection of Vieillard faïence. ♿ *Guided tours (30min), 10.15am-6pm. Last admission 30min before closing. Closed 1 Jan and 25 Dec. No charge.* ☎ *05 57 88 34 04. www.chateausiran.com*

The beautiful 18C **Château Dauzac** produces an excellent wine *(see Shopping Guide)*. Another jewel of the region is **Château Giscours**, an attractive Second Empire building which organises horse-drawn carriage rides and horse riding treks through the vineyards. *10 rte de Giscours, 33460 Labarde,* ☎ *05 57 97 09 09, www.chateau-giscours.fr Three trips in the morning from 10am; three trips in the afternoon from 2.30pm. Open by prior arrangement.*

Margaux

The **Maison du Vin de Margaux** sells around 50 wines at estate prices, but does not offer tastings *(see Shopping Guide)*.

One of the top names in the Bordeaux region, **Château Margaux** covers an area of 85ha and produces Premier Grand Cru classé wines. The harmoniously proportioned château, built in 1802, is open to the public, allowing access to the wine storehouses, the vinification facilities and a collection of old bottles. The informal landscaped gardens provide a striking contrast to the rather severe style of the buildings. *Guided tours (1hr 30min) by prior arrangement (two weeks in advance), Mon-Fri, 10am-noon and 2-4pm. Château Margaux, Bureau des Visites, 33460 Margaux. Closed Aug and during the grape harvest. No charge.* ☎ *05 57 88 83 83. www.chateau-margaux.com*

Continue along the D 2 and turn left onto the D 5 before Lamarque.

Château Maucaillou

♿ *Open May-Sep: guided tours (1hr 30min) hourly, by prior arrangement, 10am-5pm; Oct-Apr: tours at 10am, 11am, 2pm, 3pm and 4pm. Closed 1 Jan. 6.90€ (under 12s: no charge).* ☎ *05 56 58 02 58.*

This estate offers tours of its wine storehouses and its **Musée des Arts et Métiers de la Vigne et du Vin**, which provides an interesting overview of traditional and contemporary wine production methods used at Maucaillou.

Lamarque

A small ferry links Lamarque with Blaye on the opposite bank of the Gironde, making it possible to explore the Blayais region from here. Near the castle down by the port, a number of pleasant open-air cafés serve seafood caught in the estuary.

Turn right at Cussac-le-Vieux.

Fort Médoc

Open Jul to mid-Sep: 9am-12.30pm and 1pm-7pm; Apr-Jun and mid-Sep to Oct: 10am-12.30pm and 1pm-7pm; Nov-Mar: daily except Mon, 10am-12.30pm and 1pm-5pm. 2.20€ (under 12s: no charge). ☎ *05 56 58 91 30.*

This fort was built by Vauban in 1689, along with the citadel at Blaye on the other side of the estuary, to protect the approach to Bordeaux from the English fleet. A gate adorned with Louis XIV's coat of arms leads to a courtyard, where the main structural features of the fort are indicated.

Pass through Cussac and on towards Pauillac, turning left onto the road that leads to Château Lanessan.

Château Lanessan

♿ *Guided tours (1hr), 9.30am-noon and 2-6pm; Sat-Sun and public hols, 9.30am-noon and 2-5pm. Closed 1 Jan and 25 Dec. 5.50€ (children: no charge).* ☎ *05 56 58 94 80. www.lanessan.com*

Situated on a hill surrounded by a 400ha estate, Château Lanessan was built in 1878 in a mix of Dutch and Spanish Renaissance styles. The property offers a tour of its wine storehouses, which concludes with a tasting. The **Musée du Cheval**, housed in the outbuildings, exhibits an interesting collection of horse-drawn carriages dating from 1900.

Beychevelle

Grouped around the small towns of Beychevelle and Saint-Julien-Beychevelle, the **Saint-Julien** appellation comprises 11 Crus Classés produced from just 909ha. The fine wines produced here are full-bodied and are sometimes described as combining the qualities of Margaux and Pauillac wines. The name Beychevelle (from the French *baisse-voile*, meaning "lower the sails") is said to come from the salute that ships were required to give when passing the **Château Beychevelle** in the 17C. This charming white country house, rebuilt in 1757 and extended in the late 19C, has an attractive pediment sculpted with garlands and palm leaves. The château and its vineyards, classified as a Quatrième Grand Cru, belong to an insurance company. The château also produces L'Amiral de Beychevelle wine, which is of excellent quality and much more affordably priced than the Grand Cru. *Open Jul-Aug: guided tours (1hr), daily except Sun and public hols, 10-11.45am and 1.30-5pm; Sep-Jun: Mon-Fri, 10am-11.45am and 1.30-5pm. Closed Christmas and public hols. No charge.* ☎ *05 56 73 20 70. www.beychevelle.com*

Beyond Beychevelle there are lovely views of the Gironde estuary.

Saint-Julien-Beychevelle

Château Ducru-Beaucaillou, a fine Directory-style country house, produces a Second Cru Classé. This wine compares favourably with the higher-rated Premiers Crus, highlighting the full expression of the Cabernet Sauvignon grape.

Saint-Lambert

Château Pichon-Longueville-Baron, a 19C building flanked by small romantic towers, also produces a Second Grand Cru *(see Shopping Guide)*.

Pauillac

Pauillac is situated halfway between Bordeaux and the Pointe de Grave and has an attractive marina. The town and its surrounding area are above all renowned for their Grands Crus with 17 Classified Crus, including three Premiers Crus: Mouton-Rothschild, Lafite-Rothschild and Margaux. The 1 200ha of the **Pauillac** appellation cover an area of well-drained gravelly hills, which provide the ideal conditions for the Cabernet Sauvignon grape. Pauillac wines are robust, strong in colour and full-bodied. As they age, they develop an extraordinary bouquet, making them the perfect accompaniment to red meat.

The **Maison des Vins et du Tourisme** provides a wealth of information on the local vineyards and surrounding area, as well as on sporting activities available in the region. 🛈 Pauillac is the starting point for **6 circuits** (5-21km) which can be followed on foot or by bicycle. *For further information, contact the Maison du Tourisme, La Verrerie, 33250 Pauillac,* ☎ *05 56 59 03 08. www.pauillac-medoc.com*

The **Cave Coopérative Larose** offers a fine selection of Pauillac and Haut-Médoc wines. **Château Pichon-Longueville-Comtesse-de-Lalande** is home to a small museum of glass and wine-related exhibits. The château produces an excellent Second Cru Classé and enjoys a fine view of the Gironde estuary from its terrace. *33250 Pauillac,* ☎ *05 56 59 19 40, pichon@pichon-lalande.com. Open by prior arrangement, Mon-Fri (and Sat from May to mid-Sep), 9-11.30am and 2-4pm. No charge.*

Château Mouton Rothschild★

Open Apr-Oct: guided tours (1hr-1hr 30min), 9.15-11am and 2-4pm, Sat-Sun and public hols, 9.30-11am and 2-3.30pm; Nov-Mar: daily except Sat-Sun and public hols, 9.30-11am and 2-4pm. Closed 1 May and 25 Dec-1 Jan. 5€. ☎ *05 56 73 21 29. www.bpdr.com*
One of the Médoc's most famous châteaux stands in the heart of the vineyards surrounding Pauillac. The wine produced here was classified as a Premier Cru in 1973 as a result of the relentless efforts of Baron Philippe de Rothschild, who has made his wine a work of art, symbolised by the labels designed every year by a renowned artist. In addition to the **wine storehouses★**, the château houses the **Musée du Vin dans l'Art★★** displaying a collection of wine-related art from different periods, with a large section dedicated to contemporary trends.

Château Lafite Rothschild

Guided tours (45min), Mon-Fri, at 9am, 10.30am, 2pm and 3.30pm. Closed Aug-Oct and public hols. No charge. Reservations one week in advance (low season) and two weeks in advance (high season) via Château Lafite Rothschild, rte des Châteaux, D 2, 33250 Pauillac, ☎ *05 56 73 18 18. www.lafite.com*
The circular storehouse at the home of the finest and most discreet of the Grands Crus was designed by the Catalan architect Ricardo Bofill. The château stands on a terrace planted with beautiful cedar trees and enclosed by a Louis XIV balustrade; since the time of the Second Empire (1868) it has belonged to the English branch of the Rothschild family.

Saint-Estèphe

The small town of St-Estèphe, dominated by its unusual church of Romanesque origin with a Baroque interior, is situated on a hillock in the centre of a sea of vineyards. From the port, there is a fine view of the Gironde.
St-Estèphe, the northernmost of the Médoc appellations, covers an area of 1 300ha and produces wines which are robust, but which acquire a fine quality as they age. The area includes five Crus Classés.

Beyond Château Lafite-Rothschild, to the right of the D 2 on the road from Pauillac, stands the Eastern silhouette of the Indian pagodas belonging to the **Château Cos-d'Estournel**. The founder of Château Cos-d'Estournel, who exported his wine as

Shopping Guide

INFORMATION

Conseil Interprofessionnel du Vin de Bordeaux – *1 cours du 30-Juillet - 33000 Bordeaux - ☎ 05 56 00 22 66 - www.vinsbordeaux.fr - Mon-Fri, 9am-5pm - Closed Sat-Sun and public hols.*

OVERVIEW

CHARACTERISTICS

Red wines – The colour of Bordeaux's reds ranges from crimson to ruby to deep purple. On the nose, they express hints of dark fruits (blackcurrants and blackberries), and occasionally of green peppers when young, with those wines which have matured in barrels developing aromas of roasted coffee and vanilla. Upon ageing, further complexity develops with the appearance of hints of undergrowth, truffles, leather and smoke. On the palate, Bordeaux's reds are tannic when young, but soften with age, at the same time retaining their fleshy character.

Dry white wines – Clear with green tints when young, and straw-coloured to light gold upon ageing. Aromas of citrus and exotic fruit, boxwood and mint in their infancy, and crystallised fruits and the peel of citrus fruit upon ageing.

Sweet white wines – Pale yellow when young, to caramel when very mature. Exotic fruits, pear and pineapple on the nose, evolving towards underlying aromas of grilled almonds, crystallised citrus fruit and wild strawberries. Silky in the mouth with a touch of acidity.

Rosés and clairets – From bright pink rose petals to bright crimson. Fruity on the nose, with hints of red fruits and fruit drops. Pleasantly acidic.

STORAGE

Red wines – A good Bordeaux should age well in the bottle for at least five years. The best wines can continue ageing for fifty years and more.

Dry white wines – Most dry whites should be drunk within five years, although Graves whites can age for up to twenty years.

Sweet white wines – 10 to 100 years.

PRICES

Bordeaux, Bordeaux Supérieurs, Entre-Deux-Mers – 3 to 11€.

Graves, Premières-Côtes-de-Blaye, Premières-Côtes-de-Bordeaux, Côtes-de-Bourg, Côtes-de-Castillon, Médoc, Haut-Médoc – 5 to 15€.

Fronsac, Canon-Fronsac, Lalande-de-Pomerol – 8 to 23€.

Pessac-Léognan – 12 to 30€.

Pomerol, Pauillac, St-Julien – From 15€.

St-Émilion and satellites, Loupiac, Cadillac, Ste-Croix-du-Mont – 8 to 15€.

St-Émilion Grand Cru, St-Estèphe – From 11€.

Margaux, Moulis, Sauternes – From 11€.

Classified growths (Crus) from all appellations – From 30€.

BUYING

MAISONS DES VINS

Maisons des Vins have the advantage of being able to offer a good choice of wines from their appellation at the same price as those purchased directly from the estate. They are also a valuable source of information on their particular wine area.

Maison du Vin de Barsac – *Pl. de l'Église - 33720 Barsac - ☎ 05 56 27 15 44 - www.maisondebarsac.fr - Jan-Apr: Tue-Sun, 10am-12.30pm and 2.30-6pm; May-Dec: daily, 10am-12.30pm and 2-7pm.*

Maison du Vin de Blaye – *12 cours Vauban - 33390 Blaye - ☎ 05 57 42 91 19 - www.boutique-vin-blaye.com*

Maison du Vin de Bordeaux – *3 cours du 30-Juillet - 33075 Bordeaux Cedex - ☎ 05 56 00 22 88 - Mon-Fri, 9am-5pm.*

Maison du Vin des Côtes de Bourg – *1 pl. de l'Éperon - 33710 Bourg - ☎ 05 57 68 22 28 - www.cotes-de-bourg.com - mid-Jun to mid-Sep: 10am-1pm and 3-7pm; 15 Sep-15 Jun: Mon-Sat, 9.30am-12.30pm (Sat, 10.30am-12.30pm) and 2-6pm.*

Maison des Vins des Premières Côtes de Bordeaux et Cadillac – *D 10 - rte de Pangon - 33410 Cadillac - ☎ 05 57 98 19 20.*

Maison des Vins des Côtes de Castillon – *6 allée de la République - 33350 Castillon-la-Bataille - ☎ 05 57 40 00 88 - Jul-Aug: Mon-Sat, 9am-1pm and 2-6pm, Sun, 9am-1pm; Sep-Jun: Mon-Sat, 8.30am-1pm and 2-5.30pm.*

Maison des Vins de Fronsac – *Rue du Tertre - 33126 Fronsac - ☎ 05 57 51 80 51 - Open mid-Jun to mid-Sep: Mon-Sat, 10.30am-7pm; mid-Sep to mid-Jun: Mon-Sat, 10.30am-noon and 2-6pm.*

Maison du Vin de Listrac – *36 av. de Soulac - 33480 Listrac-Médoc - ☎ 05 56 58 09 56 - Jul to mid-Sep: Mon, 1pm-7pm, Tue-Sun, 10am-12.30pm and 1.30-7pm; Apr-Jun and mid-Sep to Nov: Mon-Sat, 10am-noon and 2-6pm (7pm, Sat); Dec-Mar: Mon, Tue, Thu and Fri, 10am-noon and 2-5pm - Closed Wed, mid-Sep to Apr.*

Maison du Vin de Moulis – *1137 Le Bourg - 33480 Moulis-en-Médoc - ☎ 05 56 58 32 74 - Jul-Aug: Thu-Sat, 8am-12.30pm and 2-6pm.*

Maison du Vin de Margaux – *Place de la Trémoille - 33460 Margaux - ☎ 05 57 88 70 82 - Jun-Sep: 10am-12.30pm and 2-7pm; Apr and Oct: Mon-Sat, 10am-12.30pm and 2-6pm; Jan-Mar: Tue-Fri, 10am-noon and 2-6pm; Nov-Dec: 10am-noon and 2-6pm.*

Maison des Vins de l'Union des Satellites de Saint-Émilion – *Le Bourg - 33570 Montagne - ☎ 05 57 74 60 13 - www.montagnesaintemilion.com - May-Oct: Mon-Fri, 9am-12.30pm and 2-7pm; Nov-Apr: Mon-Fri, 9am-12.30pm and 2-6pm.*

Maison des Vins de Ste-Foy-Bordeaux – *Rte de Bergerac - 33220 Pineuilh - ☎ 05 57 46 31 71 - www.saintefoy-bordeaux.com*

La Maison des Graves – *61 cours du Mar.-Foch - 33720 Podensac - ☎ 05 56 27 09 25 - Mon-Fri, 9.30am-6.30pm, Sat-Sun and public hols, 10.30am-6.30pm; Nov-Apr: Mon-Fri, 9.30am-6.30pm.*

Maison du Vin de St-Émilion – *Place Pierre-Meyrat - 33330 St-Émilion - ☎ 05 57 55 50 55 - 9.30am-12.30pm and 2-6.30pm; Aug: 9.30am-7pm - Closed 25 Dec and 1 Jan.*

Maison du Sauternes – *14 place de la Mairie - 33210 Sauternes - ☎ 05 56 76 69 83 - Mon-Fri, 9am-7pm, Sat-Sun, 10am-7pm.*

Maison de l'Entre-Deux-Mers – *4 r. de l'Abbaye - 33670 La Sauve - ☎ 05 57 34 32 12 - www.vins-entre-deux-mers.com - Jun-Sep: 10am-1pm and 2-6pm; Oct-May: Mon-Fri, 10am-12.30pm and 1.30-5.30pm.*

Maison du Sauveterrois – *2 r. St-Romain - 33540 Sauveterre-de-Guyenne - ☎ 05 56 71 53 45 - mid-Sep to early-Jun: Mon-Sat, 9am-noon and 2-6pm; early-Jun to mid-Sep: 9am-noon and 2-7pm.*

COOPERATIVES

Cave Coopérative du Blayais – *9 Le Piquet - 33390 Cars - ☎ 05 57 42 13 15 - Mon-Sat, 9am-noon and 2-6pm.* This cooperative sells a number of interesting estate wines.

Univitis – *1 r. du Gén.-de-Gaulle - 33220 Les Lèves-et-Thoumeyran - ☎ 05 57 56 02 02 - Jul-Aug: 9am-12.30pm and 2.30-7pm; Sep-Dec and Mar-Jun: Tue-Sat. 9.30am-12.30pm and 3-7pm; Jan-Feb: 9.30am-12.30pm and 3-6pm.* The Bordeaux region's largest cooperative offers its customers a fine range of wines from various estates that have been vinified separately.

Cave de Listrac-Médoc – *21 av. de Soulac - 33480 Listrac-Médoc - ☎ 05 56 58 03 19 - grandlistrac@cave-listrac-medoc. com.* Created in 1935 by a handful of wine producers from the local area, this cooperative has 58 current members covering a total vineyard area of 170ha. Operations here include wine-making in stainless steel vats, ageing in oak barrels for three châteaux, a cuvée Prestige, and the marketing of the appellation's wines. The cooperative's annual production is 8 000hl of Listrac-Médoc wines and 1 000hl of Moulis.

Union des Producteurs – *33570 Lussac - ☎ 05 57 55 50 40 - Jul-Aug: Sat, 9am-6.30pm; Mon-Sat, 8.30am-12.30pm and 2.30-6.30pm.* A grouping of 140 winemakers producing a range of quality wines.

Groupe des Producteurs de Montagne – *La Tour Mont d'Or - 33570 Montagne - ☎ 05 57 74 62 15 - Mon-Fri, 9am-noon and 2-6pm; Sat, 9am-noon.* This group of producers offers a good overview of the Montagne-St-Émilion appellation.

Cave Coopérative Larose – *44 r. du Mar.-Joffre - 33250 Pauillac - ☎ 05 56 59 26 00 - Tue-Fri, 8am-noon and 2-6pm; Mon and Sat, 9am-noon and 2-6pm.* A good choice of wines from Pauillac and the Haut-Médoc.

Cave Coopérative – *89 Pranzac - 33360 Quinsac - ☎ 05 56 20 86 09 - Mon-Sat, 8am-noon and 2-6pm; Sun and public hols,* 8am-noon and 3-6pm. Production here includes clairet, an intense rosé or pale red obtained following a brief maceration.

Union des Producteurs de Rauzan – *1 Aiguilley - 33420 Rauzan - ☎ 05 57 84 13 22 - Mon-Sat, 9am-12.30pm and 2-6pm; open Sun in Jul-Aug.* One of the largest cooperative wineries in France with an annual production of 135 000hl. Around thirty reasonably priced wines on sale.

Union des Producteurs de St-Émilion – *In the lower section of St-Émilion, near the railway line - ☎ 05 57 24 70 71 - www. uniondeproducteurs-saint-emilion.com - Mon-Fri, 8am-noon (8.30am, Sat) and 2-6pm (6.30pm, Jul-Aug).* This cooperative produces some sixty estate wines here. Warm, friendly welcome and service from the wine producers themselves.

Cave Marquis de St-Estèphe – *Leyssac - 33180 St-Estèphe - ☎ 05 56 73 35 30 - Mon-Fri, 8.30am-12.15pm and 2-6pm; Sat, 10am-noon and 2-5pm.* The Cave Marquis brings together a number of local winemakers producing a selection of good quality wines.

Cave Coopérative La Paroisse – *33180 St-Seurin-de-Cadourne - ☎ 05 56 59 31 28 - Jun-Aug: Mon-Sat, 8.30am-12.30pm and 2- 6pm; Sep-May: closed Fri at 5pm and on Sat afternoon.* This cooperative is renowned for its excellent-value Haut-Médocs.

Cave Viticole de Bourg-Tauriac – *3 av. des Côtes-de-Bourg - 33710 Tauriac - ☎ 05 57 94 07 07 - 9am-12.30pm and 1.30-6pm.* An extensive choice of quality wines.

S. Sauvignier / MICHELIN

ESTATES

Château Coutet – *33720 Barsac - ☎ 05 56 27 15 46 - chateaucoutet@aol. com - Open by prior arrangement, Mon-Fri, 10am-noon and 3-6pm.* This estate extends across 38.5ha of uninterrupted vineyards planted with Semillon, Sauvignon and Muscadelle vines with an average age of 35 years. Harvesting here is manual. In addition to the Coutet estate in Barsac, classified as a Grand Cru, which they have run since 1977, Philippe and Dominique Baly also own several hectares of Graves, where they produce the Château Marc Haut-Laville.

Château Climens – *33720 Barsac -* ☎ *05 56 27 15 33 - contact@chateau-climens.fr - Open by prior arrangement, Mon-Fri, 9am-noon and 2-5pm.* Owned by Lucien Lurton since 1971, the château has been managed by his daughter, Bérénice, since 1992. Located in the commune of Barsac, the vineyard covers 30ha of red sand and pebbles on a limestone base. A single grape variety, Semillon, is grown here. Traditional wine production methods, with limited yields, and fermentation and ageing in barrels.

Château Reynon – *21 rte de Cardan - 33410 Béguey -* ☎ *05 56 62 96 51 - reynon@gofornet.com - Open by prior arrangement, Mon-Fri, 9am-12.30pm and 2-5pm. Closed 8-20 Aug.* Denis Dubourdieu, an agricultural engineer and professor of oenology in Bordeaux, has been particularly innovative in white wine production methods and has put this into practice at Reynon. Planted on gravelly and limestone soil, his vineyards extend across 36ha and are planted with a mixture of Merlot, Cabernet Sauvignon, Semillon and Sauvignon.

Château Cayla – *Rions - 33410 Cadillac -* ☎ *05 56 62 15 40.* The vineyards of Château Cayla cover 20ha, of which 6ha are dedicated to the production of Cadillac and 14ha to Premières-Côtes-de-Bordeaux. A mix of Merlot, Cabernet Sauvignon and Semillon, the estate's vines are cultivated in line with sustainable methods. Harvesting for the estate's Cadillac production is manual, with vinification in thermoregulated stainless steel vats and oak barrels. The reds are matured in the barrel for a period of six months.

Château Puy Bardens – *33880 Cambes -* ☎ *05 56 21 31 14 - chateaupuybardens@wanadoo.fr - Open by prior arrangement, Mon-Fri, 10am-noon and 2-4.30pm.* In 1986, Yves Lamiable took over the running of this family business, where the 20ha of vineyards are cultivated according to sustainable methods. Harvesting of the older vines is by hand, with mechanical picking for the newer varieties. Vinification in thermoregulated stainless steel vats with ageing in barrels for eleven to fifteen months depending on the cuvée.

Château du Grand-Mouëys – *242 rte de Créon - 33550 Capian -* ☎ *05 57 97 04 44 - cavif.gm@ifrance.com - Open by prior arrangement, Mon-Fri, 9am-noon and 2-5pm.* Since the purchase of the château by the Bömers family in 1989, siginificant investment has been made in the restructuring of the vineyard and in the construction of the barrel storehouse. Today, a total of 80ha are under vine, planted with Merlot, Cabernet Sauvignon, Cabernet Franc, Sauvignon, Semillon and to a lesser extent Muscadelle, with cultivation in line with sustainable methods.

Château Carignan – *33360 Carignan-de-Bordeaux -* ☎ *05 56 21 21 30 - tt@chateaucarignan.com - Open by prior arrangement, Mon-Fri, 8am-noon and 2-6pm.* Purchased in 1981 by Philippe Pieraerts, the vineyard covers 150ha, 65 of which are under production. Merlot, Cabernet Sauvignon and Cabernet Franc grape varieties on clayey-limestone and gravelly soil. Manual harvesting, followed by de-stemming, vinification in thermoregulated vats and maturing in the barrel.

Château Bel Air La Royère – *Les Ricards - 33390 Cars -* ☎ *05 57 42 91 34.* Following their vine-growing studies, Xavier and Corinne Loriaud bought this forty-year-old estate with 4.5ha of vines in 1992, since when they have placed huge importance on producing wines of excellent quality. Manual harvesting, followed by vinification in concrete and stainless steel vats, with strict adherence to traditional methods and respect for the soil at every stage of production. Maturing in barrels for up to eighteen months.

SCEA du Grand Enclos du Château de Cérons – *12 place du Gén.-de-Gaulle - 33720 Cérons -* ☎ *05 56 27 01 53.* Taken over in April 2000 by Giorgio Cavanna, owner of the Catello di Ama, in Tuscany, this estate covers 10ha, in addition to a further 15ha on the Plateau de Podensac. Manual thinning-out of vines every year, with harvesting still by hand. The renovated and enlarged wine storehouse combines tradition and modernity. Although historically the Grand Enclos du Château de Cérons has always focused more on the production of whites, in recent times, and in line with the potential of the soil, the area planted with red grape varieties has significantly increased.

Château Les Trois Croix – *33126 Fronsac -* ☎ *05 57 84 32 09 - Open by prior arrangement, Mon-Fri, 8am-noon and 2-6pm.* This property bought by the family of Patrick Léon in 1995 covers 15.2ha. The estate's Merlot and Cabernet Franc vines are planted in clayey-limestone and molasses-based soil. Harvesting is by hand with rigorous sorting of the grapes, followed by vinification in thermoregulated concrete vats and maturing in barrels.

Château Grand-Renouil – *Les Chais du Port - 33126 Fronsac -* ☎ *05 57 51 29 57 - Open by prior arrangement, Mon-Sat, 8am-noon and 2-6pm.* Michel Ponty runs two estates extending over 11ha in Canon-Fronsac: Château Grand-Renouil and Château du Pavillon. He cares passionately for his wines, which are refined and not "overloaded" with wood.

S. Sauvignier / MICHELIN

3

Château Dauzac – *33460 Labarde - ☎ 05 57 88 32 10 - Open by prior arrangement, Mon-Fri, 9am-noon and 2-5.30pm.* Since 1988, Château Dauzac has been owned by the MAIF insurance company. In 1992, the job of running the estate was handed to André Lurton, whose expertise is renowned in the wine industry. 45ha of vineyards on deep gravelly soil, 58% of which is planted with Cabernet Sauvignon, 37% with Merlot and 5% with Cabernet Franc. With an average age of 20 years and planted with a density of 10 000 plants per hectare, the vines are double-guyot pruned with debudding and manual harvesting. Vinification is in thermoregulated stainless steel vats, followed by twelve months' ageing in barrels, 50-80% of which are new.

Château de Viaud – *33500 Lalande-de-Pomerol - ☎ 05 57 51 17 86 - chateaudeviaud@9online.fr - Open by prior arrangement, Mon-Fri, 9am-noon and 1pm-5pm.* This château extending across 20ha was bought-out in 1986. Three years later the estate was renovated, with new equipment brought in and a climate-controlled winestore built. Manual harvesting and sorting is followed by a traditional vinification process. The wines are then matured in oak barrels for a period of twelve months.

Domaine de Chevalier – *Chemin de Mignoy - 33850 Léognan - ☎ 05 56 64 16 16 - olivierbernard@domainedechevalier.com - Open by prior arrangement, Mon-Fri, 8am-noon and 2-6pm.* The Bernard family, fine Bordeaux wine and brandy merchants, acquired Domaine de Chevalier in 1983. Over the past two decades, Olivier Bernard has perpetuated the spirit of balanced production and a quest for perfection on this estate covering 34ha (4ha devoted to whites, 30ha to reds) with a mix of Cabernet Sauvignon, Semillon, Merlot and Cabernet Franc vines. Planted on black sandy soil and fine white gravel, they have an average age of twenty-five years. Traditional vinification, followed by maturing in the barrel for twenty-one months.

Château Carbonnieux – *33850 Léognan - ☎ 05 57 96 56 20 - chateau.carbonnieux @wanadoo.fr - Open by prior arrangement, Mon-Fri, 8am-11am and 2-5pm.* Bought by Marc Perrin in 1956, the property is now run by his son, Antony. The vineyard, extending across 45ha, produces both reds and whites, and is planted with Cabernet Sauvignon, Merlot, Cabernet Franc, Cot, Malbec, Petit Verdot, Semillon and Muscadelle. Traditional growing methods, with manual harvesting. Three-week vinification in stainless steel vats, followed by a ten-month maturing process in the barrel for the estate whites, and eighteen months for its reds.

Château Fourcas Dupré – *Le Fourcas - 33480 Listrac-Médoc - ☎ 05 56 58 01 07 - chateau-fourcas-dupre@wanadoo.fr* The Pagès family left Tunisia in the early 60s to settle in the Médoc. Since 1985, Patrice Pagès has overseen this family business acquired by his father Guy in 1971. The estate's vineyards are planted on Pyrenean

gravel and extend across an unbroken area covering 46ha, with 44% dedicated to Cabernet Sauvignon, the same area to Merlot, 10% to Cabernet Franc, 2% to Petit Verdot, and a planting density of 8 500 vines per hectare. Over the past few years, the vinification area has been completely renovated, including the installation of a high-performance thermoregulation system.

Château Mayne du Cros – *94 rte de St-Macaire - 33410 Loupiac - ☎ 05 56 62 99 31 - contact@chateauducros.com - Open 8am-noon and 2-6pm - by prior arrangement on Sat-Sun.* Michel Boyer also owns the Château du Gros (Bordeaux and Loupiac). Château Mayne du Cros is located in an undulating lansdsape on a limestone subsoil. In terms of red production, 50% of the vineyard is under Cabernet Franc, 40% Cabernet Sauvignon and 10% Merlot. For whites, the percentages are 50% Semillon, 40% Sauvignon and 10% Muscadelle. The vinification process here is monitored with great care.

Château La Lagune – *81 av. de l'Europe - 33290 Ludon-Médoc - ☎ 05 57 88 82 77 - lalagune@club-internet.fr - Open by prior arrangement, Mon-Thu, 9am-11am and 2-5pm.* The château changed hands several times prior to September 2001, when Thierry Budin took over as managing director of the La Lagune group and Ayala-Montebello champagne house. Patrick Moulin has overall responsibility for the local management of this 80ha estate planted with Cabernet Sauvignon, Cabernet Franc, Merlot and Petit Verdot on sandy gravel soil. The new vinification area was put into operation for the 2004 harvest.

Château La Claymore – *La Claymore - 33570 Lussac - ☎ 05 57 74 67 48 - laclaymore@aol.com - Mon-Fri, 8am-noon and 2-5pm, preferably by prior arrangement.* Significant improvements have been undertaken at this château following its acquisition by François Linard in 2000. These have included the construction of a maturing cellar, and the installation of a thermoregulation system in the vinification winery. Planted on ferruginous soil, the property's 32ha are mainly planted with Merlot (80%), with smaller areas of Cabernet Sauvignon and Cabernet Franc. The growing process is traditional with strict control of yields. The estate's wines are matured in oak barrels.

Château Cambon La Pelouse – *5 chemin de Canteloup - 33460 Macau - ☎ 05 57 88 40 32 - Open by prior arrangement, Mon-Fri, 9am-noon and 2-6pm.* This château, incorporating 60ha of vineyards, was bought by Annick and Jean-Pierre Marie in 1996. The estate was completely replanted in 1975, bringing together the properties of Château Cambon La Pelouse and the neighbouring Château Trois Moulins. The maturing process is monitored by daily sampling and enhanced by regular analyses. On the day of harvesting, the grapes are picked and brought to the wine storehouse, where a careful selection process is carried out on the sorting table.

Château Latour-Martillac – *Chemin de La Tour - 33650 Martillac -* ☎ *05 57 97 71 11 - latour-martillac@domaineskressmann. com.* Alfred Kressmann, a Bordeaux wine merchant, bought this estate in 1929. In 1940, his son Jean took over the running of the estate, developing it to its current size. Following the complete renovation of the wine storehouses in 1989, his two youngest sons, Tristan and Loïc, are perpetuating the family tradition. Traditional vinification and hand-picking. Reds account for the majority of production.

Château de Rochemorin – *33650 Martillac -* ☎ *05 57 25 58 58 - Andre. Lurton@wanadoo.fr - Open by prior arrangement, Mon-Fri, 9am-12.30pm and 1.30-6pm.* The owner of five estates (La Louvière, Couhins-Lurton, Coucheroy, Cruzeau and Rochemorin in Pessac-Léognan), André Lurton is a name to be reckoned with in the appellation. He has completely restructured this 110ha vineyard which he acquired in 1973. 3ha are planted with Sauvignon and Semillon for the estate's whites, and 87ha of Cabernet Sauvignon and Merlot for its reds. In 2004 a wine storehouse with a surface area of 4 000m² was built, and was operational in time for the harvest of the same year.

Château Chasse-Spleen – *2558 Grand-Poujeaux-Sud - 33480 Moulis-en-Médoc -* ☎ *05 56 58 02 37 - infos@chasse-spleen. com - Open Mon-Thu, 8am-noon and 2-5pm and Fri, 8am-noon, by prior arrangement (except Jul-Aug).* Madame Castaing gave the château its name in the 19C. A century later, another exceptional woman, Bernadette Villars, reinforced the prestige of this Grand Cru, and now it is the turn of her daughter, Céline, who is running this 83ha estate with great enthusiasm. Harvesting by hand, traditional growing methods, maturing in barrels for eighteen months, and bottling on the estate ensure the quality and traditions of this renowned château.

Château Pichon-Longueville-Baron – *Rte des Châteaux - BP 112 - St-Lambert - 33250 Pauillac -* ☎ *05 56 73 17 17 - accueil@pichonlongueville.com - Open by prior arrangement, 9am-12.30pm and 2-6.30pm.* The château standing today was built by Raoul de Pichon-Longueville in 1851. In 1988, following its acquisition by Axa-Millésimes, the property was completely restored and an architectural competition was organised for the construction of the wine production facilities. The 73ha of vineyards are comprised of Cabernet Sauvignon (60%), Merlot (35%), Cabernet Franc (4%) and Petit Verdot (1%). Picking by hand with maturing in oak barrels, 70% of which are new.

Château Les Carmes - Haut-Brion – *197 av. Jean-Cordier - 33600 Pessac -* ☎ *05 56 93 23 40 - chateau@les-carmeshaut-brion.com.* This 4.6ha estate is located on the Plateau de Haut-Brion. The vines, an amalgam of Merlot, Cabernet Franc and Cabernet Sauvignon, are planted on gravelly, sandy and clayey soil. Manual harvesting, followed by traditional vinification, malolactic fermentation and barrel ageing.

Château Pape-Clément – *216 av. du Dr-Nancel-Penard - 33600 Pessac -* ☎ *05 57 26 38 38 - chateau@pape-clement.com - Open by prior arrangement, Mon-Fri, 8.30am-noon and 2-5.30pm.* 32.5ha of this 36ha estate in Pessac are currently under production. The majority of the vineyard is devoted to Cabernet Sauvignon and Merlot, with smaller areas set aside for Sauvignon (2ha), Semillon and Muscadelle. The wines are matured in new barrels made from French oak.

Château Mondésir-Gazin – *10 Le Sablon - 33390 Plassac -* ☎ *05 57 42 29 80.* Marc Pasquet, a winemaker of Breton origin, moved to Plassac in 1990. Mondésir-Gazin's 14ha of vineyards are planted with Merlot, Malbec and Cabernet Sauvignon vines with an average age of 30 years. Hand-picking, followed by a highly rigorous sorting process. Vinification in stainless steel vats, with maturing in the barrel.

Château de Chantegrive – *Rte de St-Michel-de-Rieuffret - 33720 Podensac -* ☎ *05 56 27 17 38 - courrier@chateaucha ntegrive.com - Mon-Sat, 8.30am-5.30pm - No reservation required.* Following the redistribution of land by Henri and Françoise Levêque, the vineyard now covers around 100ha. In thirty years, the estate has seen the introduction of the best traditional equipment to enhance growing methods and the winemaking process, as well as the latest techniques to improve vinification, including the installation of fifteen vats, a temperature regulation system and automatic cap punching equipment. The estate also has an impressive bottling facility, with a capacity of 500 000 bottles. In 2003, Françoise and Henri Levêque also acquired Château d'Anice, on the route de Cérons, in Podensac, which they are currently operating on a rental basis.

Château Rahoul – *4 rte du Courneau - 33640 Portets -* ☎ *05 57 97 73 33 - chateau-rahoul@alain-thienot.fr - Open by prior arrangement, Mon-Sat, 10am-5pm.* Alain Thiénot, a Champagne merchant, owns several châteaux in the Bordelais, including this one with 20ha devoted to red Graves and 5ha to whites. Harvesting by hand followed by traditional vinification. The reds are matured for eighteen months in barrels, a third of which are new. The whites are also aged in the barrel, albeit for a shorter period (eight months).

Château Bastor-Lamontagne – *33210 Preignac -* ☎ *05 56 63 27 66 - bastorlamontagne@dial.oleane.com - Open by prior arrangement, Mon-Fri, 8.30am-12.30pm and 2-6pm.* The château's vineyards extend across 58ha of silico-gravelly soil, 52ha of which are on uninterrupted land. Harvesting is by hand and yields are low. The estate's wines are aged in stave-wood oak barrels for a period of between fifteen and eighteen months.

Cru Barréjats – *Clos de Gensac - 28 rte Illats, à Budos - 33210 Pujols-sur-Ciron -*

☏ 05 56 76 69 06 - mireille.daret@free.fr
This 5ha vineyard is owned by Mireille Daret, a former doctor who retrained in viticulture, and Philippe Andurand. The three grape varieties grown here on clayey-limestone soil are Semillon, Sauvignon and Muscadelle. Located between the Garonne and the Ciron, the vines are subject to conditions that are particularly favourable to the development of *botrytis cinerea*. Wines are aged in new oak barrels for many months prior to bottling.

Château Thieuley – 33670 La Sauve - ☏ 05 56 23 00 01 - *Open by prior arrangement, Mon-Fri, 8.30am-noon and 1.30-5.30pm*. Extending across 80ha of vineyards on three hills at an altitude of 100m, Château Thieuley has been owned by the Courselle family since 1950 and run by Francis Courselle since 1972. This traditionally dry-white producing estate decided to expand into red production in 1972; fourteen years later, in another innovative breakthrough for the area, it started to produce white wines aged in new barrels.

Château Angélus – 33330 St-Émilion - ☏ 05 57 24 71 39 - chateauangelus@chateau-angelus.com - *Open by prior arrangement, Mon-Fri, 9am-noon and 2-5pm*. This estate has remained in the hands of the same family for seven generations. Through the unstinting efforts of Hubert de Boüard de Laforest and his cousin, Jean-Bernard Grenié, the estate was awarded Premier Grand Cru status in 1996. Today, the vineyard covers 23.4ha of uninterrupted land on soil that varies from clayey-limestone to sandy-limestone, planted with Merlot, Cabernet Franc and Cabernet Sauvignon, all of which are harvested by hand. The fermentation cellar was replaced in 2001.

Château Figeac – 33330 St-Émilion - ☏ 05 57 24 72 26 - chateaufigeac@chateau-figeac.com - *Open by prior arrangement, Mon-Fri (except public hols and in Aug), 9am-noon*. Thierry and Marie-France Manoncourt are ably supported in the running of this 40ha property by their daughter Laure d'Aramon and their son-in-law Éric. The château produces a Saint-Émilion Premier Grand Cru classé.

Château Haut-Marbuzet – 33180 St-Estèphe - ☏ 05 56 59 30 54 - sfduboscq@minitel.net. When Hervé Duboscq bought this 7ha Cru property on a life annuity in 1952 he had no experience of the wine industry. Ten years later he was joined by his son Henry, who is now in charge of operations at this 58ha estate, planted with 40% Merlot, 10% Cabernet Franc and 50% Cabernet Sauvignon, and now one of the appellation's most respected names. Every vine is harvested by hand, with a preference for overmaturing and complete destemming. The wines are then aged in barrels.

Château Ducru-Beaucaillou – 33250 St-Julien-Beychevelle - ☏ 05 56 73 16 73 - *Open Mon-Fri by prior arrangement*. This estate, spread across 55ha of low-lying pebbly hills, has belonged to the Borie family since 1929. Three grape varieties are grown here: Cabernet Sauvignon, Merlot and Cabernet Franc. The maturing process takes place in oak barrels.

Château Cassagne-Haut-Canon – 33126 St-Michel-de-Fronsac - ☏ 05 57 51 63 98 - jjdubois@club-internet.fr. Members of the "Expression Fronsac" association, Jean-Jacques Dubois and his wife Zita run this property with a combination of ambition, painstaking care, great passion and an innovative approach that includes vinifying selected parcels of vineyard to enhance complexity. Situated at the heart of the low-lying Fronsac hills, this 14ha estate overlooks the Dordogne valley from its altitude of 76m. Three grape varieties are grown here: Merlot, Cabernet Sauvignon and Cabernet Franc.

Château Sociando-Mallet – 33180 St-Seurin-de-Cadourne - ☏ 05 56 73 38 80 - scea-jean-gautreau@wanadoo.fr - *Open by prior arrangement, Mon-Thu, 9am-noon and 2-5pm and Fri, 9am-noon*. Jean Gautreau fell in love with this château superbly situated alongside the Gironde, and created a Cru wine whose quality has earned it international acclaim. 72ha of vines on land that is pebbly in nature, with a clayey-limestone subsoil, and planted with Cabernet Sauvignon, Cabernet Franc and Merlot with an average age of 25 years. Wines are aged in oak barrels, 70% to 90% of which are new, for a period of between twelve and fifteen months.

S. Sauvignier / MICHELIN

Château Cos-d'Estournel.

Château La Rame – 33410 Ste-Croix-du-Mont - ☏ 05 56 62 01 50 - dgm@wanadoo.fr - *Open by prior arrangement, Mon-Fri, 9am-noon and 2-6pm*. On the south-facing slopes of a hill overlooking the Garonne, this 20ha vineyard descends down to the river. Since taking over his parents' estate, with his children, in 1985, Yves Armand has continually strived to perpetuate traditional methods including leaf-thinning, manual harvesting and moderate yields.

Remember that, to buy wine directly from a Bordeaux château, it is usually necessary to book a visit. Take advantage of appellation open days, generally in May, October and November (see "Sales, Fairs and Markets") far as India, had the château built in the 19C in memory of his overseas expeditions. This well-established château also produces a very good Second Cru, "Les pagodes de Cos". *33180 St-Estèphe, ☎ 05 56 73 15 50. By prior arrangement.*

Not far from here, in the hamlet of **Marbuzet**, **Château Haut-Marbuzet** produces a Cru Bourgeois worthy of a Cru Classé; a good place to purchase this wine is at the **Marquis de St-Estèphe** wine cellar in **Leyssac** *(see Shopping Guide).*

The estate of **Château Montrose** stands on a hill overlooking the Gironde. The château, its storehouses, vinification buildings and winegrowers' houses all form a small village, the streets of which are named after the successive owners of the estate. *33180 St-Estèphe, ☎ 05 56 59 30 12. Open by prior arrangement, Mon-Fri, 9-11.30am and 2-4.30pm.*

Saint-Seurin-de-Cadourne

The area beyond St-Estèphe is part of the Haut-Médoc appellation. Several quality Crus Bourgeois are produced around the village of Saint-Seurin-de-Cadourne. Estates worthy of particular note here include **Château Sociando-Mallet** and the **Cave Coopérative La Paroisse** *(see Shopping Guide).*

The **Château de Verdus** has a splendid dovecote (14C-17C) and a small museum dedicated to the history of the Médoc; wine tasting. *Domaine Dailledouze Père et Fils, Bardis, 33180 St-Seurin-de-Cadourne, ☎ 05 56 73 17 31. Open Jun-Sep: Mon-Sat, 9.30am-noon and 2-6pm, Sun, 3-6pm; Oct-May: open afternoons only.*

2km before St-Izans-de-Médoc, turn right onto a small road.

Château Loudenne

Open May-Oct: 9am-7pm; Nov-Apr: by prior arrangement. 5€. ☎ 05 56 73 17 80. www.lafragette.com

Château Loudenne is a delightful pink-hued 17C country house with a terrace that opens onto its **landscaped gardens**. The wine storehouses are home to a **museum** dedicated to wine. Tastings are available here.

Return to St-Seurin, turn right towards Pez, then follow the D 104E3 to Vertheuil. Continue along the D 104, then rejoin the N 115. Continue as far as Listrac.

Listrac-Médoc

Moulis and **Listrac**, two neighbouring village appellations, are the only wine-producing areas that do not skirt the Gironde estuary. They are characterised by a complex mix of soils that includes clay, limestone, gravel and pebbles.

Listrac produces wines that are more robust, and sometimes rustic; however, the tendency to replace Cabernet Sauvignon with Merlot is resulting in wines that are more rounded.

Standing at an altitude of 46m, the village is the highest point in the Médoc. Its most impressive architectural feature is its 12C church. The **Maison du Vin de Listrac** sells all the appellation's wines at estate prices. Good buys can also be found at the **Cave de Listrac-Médoc**. The **Château Fourcas-Dupré** is one of the appellation's most renowned estates *(see Shopping Guide).*

Moulis-en-Médoc

Moulis, the smallest appellation in the Médoc, produces some very fine wines, and even though Crus Classés are not represented in Moulis, Crus Bourgeois of a similar quality are produced here.

In Grand-Poujeaux, the **Maison du Vin de Moulis** sells the appellation's wines as well as offering visitors the opportunity to enjoy a 12km walk through the surrounding vineyards. In the same area, the etymology of the interestingly named and famous Cru Bourgeois, **Château Chasse-Spleen**, continues to provoke discussion, some believing that it owes its name to Baudelaire, others to Lord Byron.

The nearby **Château Poujeaux**, an exceptional Grand Cru Bourgeois, is comparable with many Crus Classés in terms of the quality of its wines. The château's extensive barrel cellar is open to visitors. *33480 Moulis-en-Médoc, ☎ 05 56 58 02 96, poujeaux@chateaupoujeaux.com Mon-Fri (and Sat, Jun-Sep), 9am-noon and 2-5.30pm; Oct-Mar: by prior arrangement.*

Follow the D 1 to return to Bordeaux.

Along the Coast

Lacanau-Océan

55km NW of Bordeaux along the D 6. The resort of Lacanau-Océan stands at the foot of sand dunes carpeted in maritime pines, making it the ideal base from which to explore the surrounding «lèdes» (sandy valleys swathed in forest) and the 20km of glorious beaches. More active visitors can take advantage of the 120km of coastal cycle routes which dissect the pine forest. The area is also renowned for its surfing, with a choice of popular areas such as the plage Centrale, Nord,

Sud and Super Sud, all of which are subject to the frequent displacement of sand dunes. Golfers are also well catered for with three local clubs, including one 18-hole course. Another activity centre popular with the whole family is the **Forêt des Accromaniaques**, an adventure park with elevated trails built through the forest, along with rope bridges and "Himalayan" walkways. *Rte du Baganais, 33680 Lacanau-Océan,* ☎ *05 56 03 91 00. Closed 1 week in the spring, 1 week in the autumn (outside of school holidays) and 15 Nov-1 Apr.*

The 8km-long **Lac de Lacanau**★, covering 2 000ha, is popular with fishing enthusiasts with abundant stocks of pike, eel and perch, as well as offering sailing, windsurfing (particularly at Le Moutchic), water skiing, canoeing and kayaking, and the opportunity to rent boats, dinghies and pedalos.

Hourtin⌂

26km W of Pauillac along the D 205. At the northern tip of the "lakes and canals route", this popular lakeside resort has developed into a popular base for pleasure craft following the development of the 500-berth Hourtin-Port.

Hourtin has been awarded a "Kid's Resort" *(Station Kid)* label because of the wide choice of children's activities on offer here.

Soulac-sur-Mer⌂

40km NW of Vertheuil along the N 215. On the Médoc coast, Soulac is relatively well protected from the Atlantic swell by a deep offshore bank, although the four beaches here are still supervised by lifeguards. In common with every resort along this coastline, Soulac is the ideal base for all water sports enthusiasts, as well as those who enjoy land-based activities such as hiking, cycling and fitness trails. The main beach is accessible via a dedicated cycle route from the town's Amélie district.

The resort's pine trees provide welcome shade on a hot summer's day.

Around the Bassin d'Arcachon

Cap-Ferret⌂

71km to the SW of Bordeaux along the D 106. This thin strip of land between the Atlantic and the Bassin d'Archachon runs for approximately 20km. Cap-Ferret is a popular holiday destination with plentiful options including cycling through the pine forests, swimming in the calm waters of the *bassin* or the surf of the Atlantic, sampling the delicious local oysters in open-air restaurants, or visiting oyster farms.

Parc Ornithologique du Teich★

&. *Jul-Aug: 10am-8pm; mid-Apr to late-Jun and early to mid-Sep: 10am-7pm; mid-Sep to mid-Apr: 10am-6pm. 6.40€ (children: 4.60€).* ☎ *05 56 22 80 93. www.parc-ornithologique-du-teich.com*

This 120ha nature reserve is located in the Eyre delta, which flows into the Bassin d'Arcachon. It is incredibly luxuriant in vegetation, particularly in summer, and is a popular stop on the migration route of several species of birds, which can be viewed as you explore the four themed parks within the reserve. Walking shoes or boots and binoculars are recommended.

Dune du Pilat★★

Access via the D 218 to the S of Pilat-Plage. Leave your car in the car park (pay parking). To reach the top, climb up the side of the sand dune (the ascent is relatively difficult) or climb the steps (only in use during the summer season). Climbing or hiking footwear advisable; the sand can also be very hot, so care is recommended.

This bulbous mass of sand is the highest dune in Europe. Currently measuring 2.7km in length, 500m in width and 107m high, it swells in size every year in line with the effects of the wind and ocean currents. Its western slope descends at a gentle angle down to the sea, whereas its eastern side plunges steeply down towards a huge forest of pine trees. A visit here is an invigorating experience and should not to be missed.

La Bourgogne

Burgundy

Nowhere in the world is the idea of "terroir" more prized and understood than in Burgundy. Here, more than anywhere else, centuries of observation and experience have made it possible to adapt the grape varieties to the various soils and climatic conditions, so that each village, estate or plot can produce a unique, inimitable wine. Indeed, the word "climate" has a special sense in Burgundy, where it is used to refer to a wine-growing area producing a particular wine. However, this geographical diversity would be useless without the human factor and in particular the contribution of the monks of Cîteaux and Cluny abbeys, who pioneered the great adventure of Burgundy wine. The modern-day wine region, between the Auxerrois and Mâconnais areas, represents only a tiny part of historic Burgundy, once as mighty a dukedom as any in France. Its ancient but still fruitful legacy is a relationship between nature and culture. Burgundy's diversity lies in its vineyards within their walled-in plots, in the neatly cultivated slopes of the hillside estates, but also in charming villages, their bell towers capped with colourful glazed tiles, in castles combining military austerity with rich ornamentation, and in cellars where the fruit of human labour is left to mature beneath the earth.

Terroirs

Michelin Local Maps 319 and 320 – Yonne (89), Côte-d'Or (21) and Saône-et-Loire (71).
Area: 26 500ha (5% of the total wine-growing land in France), extending from north to south over 160km.
Production: about 1.5 million hl (180 million bottles) in five wine-growing regions, the Chablis, Auxerre, Tonnerre and Vézelay areas in the Yonne *département;* the Côte de Nuits and Hautes-Côtes de Nuits between Dijon and Corgoloin in the Côte-d'Or *département;* the Côte de Beaune and Hautes-Côtes de Beaune between Beaune and Les Maranges astride the Côte-d'Or and Saône-et-Loire *départments;* the Côte Chalonnaise and Mâconnais in Saône-et-Loire.
The vineyards, backing on to the eastern foothills of the Massif Central and the Burgundy plateaux, extend over the slopes of the Jurassic escarpments, at an altitude varying from 80m to 350m. The semi-continental climate features oceanic influences. Winters are cold, summers temperate and sunny. Rainfall is most abundant in springtime.

Grape varieties

Burgundy features a remarkable ampelographic unity, with the almost exclusive dominance of two grape varieties: Pinot Noir for red wines and Chardonnay for white wines. Also present are Gamay, Sauvignon and minor grape varieties such as Sacy, Aligoté and Melon for white wines, César for the reds and Pinot-Beurot for some rosé wines.
Mention of the grape variety linked with a regional appellation is allowed, but on AOC Villages and Premier Cru labels the name of the appellation alone is allowed.

Clos de Vougeot, a Burgundian jewel set in the heart of its vineyard.

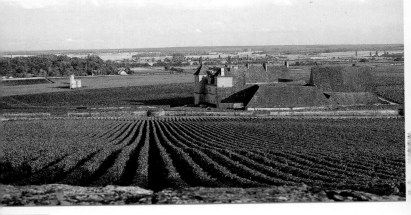

Appellations

In Burgundy, there are four grades of appellation:

23 regional appellations: Bourgogne, Bourgogne-Passetoutgrain, Mâcon-Villages, Bourgogne-Vézelay etc.

44 local appellations: Beaune, Chablis, Nuits-St-Georges, St-Romain etc.

33 Grands Crus: Corton, Musigny, Montrachet, Romanée-Conti, Clos-de-Vougeot, Clos-de-Tart etc.

570 *climats* (vineyards) classified as Premiers Crus: Les Ruchottes, La Renarde, Les Genevrières, Les Caillerets, Les Perrières etc.

Background

In its methods and standards, Burgundy has always been something of a world apart, even reckoning its parcels of ground not in hectares but by the *ouvrée* (about 0.04ha). Historically, this was defined as the area a man with a pick could work in a day. A small unit of measurement also makes it easier to determine the geological diversity of the soils which depends in part on the gradient of the slope, and the amount of sunshine, wind and frost it receives. There are, for instance, 59 soil types in the Côte de Nuits area alone.

This extremely precise information about each plot of ground has enabled Burgundian wine growers to give a name to each **climat** or **vineyard**. These names are often picturesque and their origin varies. It can be based on botany: Les Genevrières, Blanches Fleurs, Clos des Chênes, La Truffière; on zoology: Grenouilles, Clos des Mouches, Dent de Chien, Aux Perdrix, La Levrière, Les Corbeaux; on climate: Clos Tonnerre, Les Brouillards, Bel Air, Côte Rôtie, Les Embrasées, Vigne du Soleil; on geology: Sur les Grèves, Les Terres Blanches, Les Perrières, Les Gravières. Some names are drawn from an anecdote or a fanciful idea: La Pucelle, Les Amoureuses, Bâtard, Paradis, Maladière, Clos l'Évêque, Les Demoiselles, Les Joyeuses, Chevalier, Les Procès, L'Homme Mort, Redrescul, Tonton Marcel, Vide Bourse...

The Yonne Valley Wine Road

THE AUXERROIS, CHABLIS AND TONNERRE VINEYARDS

About 60km. Michelin Local Map 319, D4, E5, G4, H4.

Joigny

Joigny is a picturesque little town clinging to the slopes of the Côte Saint-Jacques, on the edge of the forest of Othe; its steep streets, lined with half-timbered old houses and Renaissance monuments, plunge down towards the River Yonne.

Joigny was, for a long time, an important wine-growing centre and its inhabitants were referred to as "maillotins", after the mallets they used to make their wine barrels. Today, the Côte-Saint-Jacques vineyards are being slowly revived thanks to the care of a handful of enthusiastic wine growers and to the promotion made by the renowned chef **Michel Lorain** *(see Directory, Where to Stay, Around Auxerre: Hôtel La Côte St-Jacques).*

On top of the Côte Saint-Jacques★

1.5km north along D 20. The road, climbing in hairpin bends, reaches Croix de Guémard where a path on the right runs across the vineyards. Fine view over Joigny and the Yonne Valley.

Leave Joigny southwest along D 67.

Pressoir de Champvallon

Closed while work is in progress. Re-opening likely in 2006.

Located inside a monumental cellar, in the heart of the village, this winepress boasting a 12C pendulum mechanism is still in working order.

Drive south along D 367, then D 955. Take the first road left after the motorway bridge.

Musée rural des Arts populaires de Laduz★

Jul-Aug, 10am-12.30pm, 2.30-6.30pm; Apr-Jun and Sep-Oct, Wed, Sat-Sun and public hols, 2-5pm; Nov-Mar, Wed, 2-5pm. Guided tours (2hr 30min) available on request. 6€ (children 6-14: 3€).

This folk museum, situated at the southeast entrance to the village, recalls rural working life before 1914.

Drive 20km along D 31 to Auxerre.

Directory

WHERE TO EAT

AROUND AUXERRE

Au Vrai Chablis – *6 pl. Gén.-de-Gaulle - 89800 Chablis - ☎ 03 86 42 11 43 – closed Jan, Tue and Wed evenings - ✗ - 13.50/28.80€.* Once a prison, this 16C building now houses a convivial restaurant mainly devoted to regional specialities. Chablis chitterling sausage, Chablis-style ham, ham seasoned with parsley and, of course, eggs in red-wine sauce are available to gourmets year-round. Tables in the square outside in summer.

Le Saint Père – *2 av. Georges-Pompidou - 89700 Tonnerre - ☎ 03 86 55 12 84 – closed 29 Dec to 20 Jan, Sun evening and Wed – 14/40€.* The menu of this small Tonnerre restaurant does credit to local products. Joint of beef gratinéed with Époisses cheese, Chablis-style ham or pork cheek braised in red wine delight gourmets sitting comfortably in the pleasant dining room decorated with a fine collection of coffee grinders.

Le Bistrot des Grands Crus – *8 r. Jules-Rathier - 89800 Chablis - ☎ 03 86 42 19 41 – Closed 20 Dec to 20 Jan - ✗ - 20€.* There is a choice of appetising regional dishes on the menu of this restaurant where one eats in cramped conditions in the dining room or outside in summer. Try a small dish of Burgundy snails, eggs cooked in Pinot Noir sauce or chitterling sausage flavoured with Chablis!

Le Moulin de la Coudre – *2 r. Gravottes - 89290 Venoy - ☎ 03 86 40 23 79 – closed 6-29 Jan, Sun evening and Mon - 20/48€.* This 19C mill nestling in pastoral surroundings is a real haven of peace only a few minutes' drive from Auxerre. Sitting outside under the trees or in the comfortable dining room, you will be able to enjoy to the full the tasty cuisine which combines tradition with regional trends.

La P'tite Beursaude – *55 r. Joubert - 89000 Auxerre - ☎ 03 86 51 10 21 - 21€.* The regional-sounding name, the plain, convivial country-style dining room, the staff dressed in local costume and copious dishes based on regional cuisine: it's Burgundy in miniature!

Le Bourgogne – *15 r. de Preuilly - 89000 Auxerre - ☎ 03 86 51 57 50 – closed between Ascension and Whitsun, 7-31 Aug, 23 Dec to 2 Jan, Thu evening, Sun and Mon - ✗ - 25€.* This establishment can boast a lovely paved terrace bedecked with flowers which welcomes gourmets in summer. When it is raining or chilly, guests take shelter in the small rustic-looking dining room where they enjoy regional dishes varying according to the availability of fresh produce.

Hostellerie des Clos – *18 r. Jules-Rathier - 89800 Chablis - ☎ 03 86 42 10 63 – closed 22 Dec to 16 Jan - 35/73€.* This former hospital, which has retained a 14C chapel, used to own many vineyards. The attractive vaulted cellar, with some thirty Chablis on the wine list, pays tribute to this wine-growing past. Pleasant restaurant looking out on a patio, copious dishes and extensive wine list. Well-furnished rooms.

AROUND BEAUNE

Auberge des Vignes – *N 74 - 21190 Volnay – 3.5km N of Meursault along D 23 and D 973 – ☎ 03 80 22 24 48 – closed 3 Feb to 3 Mar, 29 Nov to 9 Dec, Sun and Wed evenings and Mon - 15/33€.* Appreciated by kings, red Volnay wine has had a long, illustrious history. If you wish to be introduced to its subtle bouquet while enjoying eggs in red-wine sauce, braised knuckle of beef or a thick steak of Charolais beef, go to this restaurant with its veranda overlooking the vineyards.

Le Relais de la Diligence – *R. de la Gare - 21190 Meursault - ☎ 03 80 21 21 32 – closed 9 Dec to 21 Jan, Tue evening and Wed in low season - 15/35€.* This imposing stone building houses dining rooms opening onto the vineyards. Vine leaves undulating in the wind form an appropriate setting for the regional cuisine which includes Burgundy snails, poached eggs, frogs' legs in cream or ham in wine sauce.

S. Sauvignier / MICHELIN

La Bouzerotte – *21200 Bouze-lès-Beaune - ☎ 03 80 26 01 37 – closed 1-9 Sep, 22 Dec to 20 Jan, Mon and Tue - 15/38€.* The menus of this restaurant, featuring an unassuming rustic setting, combine regional specialities with trendy dishes: it is possible to enjoy a traditional coq au vin as well as fillet of ling in lime sauce, or pancetta served with confit of pork cheek seasoned with lemon and clove.

Aux Vignes Rouges – *45 r. Maufoux - 21200 Beaune - ☎ 03 80 24 71 28 – closed Tue - 17/30.20€.* Unusual setting: the kitchen forms an integral part of the dining room and the chef works in full view of the guests who can follow step by step the preparation of cream of chicory soup and red-wine sauce, or watch eggs being poached and coq au vin stewing in a casserole dish.

La Cuverie – 5 r. Chanoine-Donin - 21420 Savigny-lès-Beaune - ☎ 03 80 21 50 03 – closed 20 Dec to 20 Jan, Tue and Wed - 17/37€. Here in the heart of the Savigny vineyards, everything points to the terroir: the name refers to the place where wine is fermented. The spacious dining room is furnished in Burgundy style and the cuisine is based on regional produce: try snails in their shell or stewed, ham seasoned with parsley or Charolais beef.

La Ciboulette – 69 r. de Lorraine - 21200 Beaune - ☎ 03 80 24 70 72 – closed 2-25 Feb, 2-18 Aug, Mon and Tue - 18/24€. This small, convivial establishment offers its guests a typical Burgundian cuisine. The concise menu concentrates on sure-fire regional favourites such as Burgundy-style pork cheek fillet, ham seasoned with parsley or thick steak of Charolais beef with Époisses cheese. This limited choice enables the chef to take even more care over each dish.

Ma Cuisine – Passage Ste-Hélène - 21200 Beaune - ☎ 03 80 22 30 22 – closed Aug, Christmas hols, Wed and Sat-Sun - 18€. No-one who has eaten here would deny that the contemporary cuisine is delicious, but the real strong point of this restaurant is its wine list, headed by Burgundy wines and including a wealth of Crus from every region, each one a famous wine. In addition, the storehouse retails its stock.

Le Verger – 21 rte de Seurre - 21200 Beaune - ☎ 03 80 24 28 05 – closed 31 Jan to 4 Mar, Mon and Wed lunchtime, and Tue - 20/43€. The chef's special blend of flavours is enhanced by a selection of wines from local wine growers: poached eggs in red-wine sauce together with stewed snails and a garlic emulsion, pikeperch with a spicy poached pear and stuffed duck breast with an herb salad sprinkled with parmesan.

Le Fleury – 16 pl. Fleury - 21200 Beaune - ☎ 03 80 22 35 50 – closed 5-19 Jan and Thu Oct-May – 19.80€ lunch - 26/49€. Paintings hanging on soft-toned walls, dishes of slow-cooked bœuf bourguignon by a chef trained at Guy Savoy's in Paris: this restaurant, overlooking a lively square in Old Beaune, delights both the eyes and the taste buds of its guests. Appetising menus inspired by the terroir.

AROUND CHALON-SUR-SAÔNE

Le Bourgogne – 28 r. de Strasbourg - 71100 Chalon-sur-Saône - ☎ 03 85 48 89 18 – closed 4-19 Jul, 25-30 Dec, Sun evening and Mon – 14.50/45€. In a charming setting - of the sort you only ever find in fine old buildings - you are sure to enjoy regional dishes (snails, eggs in red-wine sauce or tournedos of Charolais beef) as well as a few trendier ones such as red mullet bavarois, brochette of spicy scallops or duck breast with caramelized peaches.

Le Petit Comptoir d'à Côté – 32 av. Jean-Jaurès - 71100 Chalon-sur-Saône - ☎ 03 85 90 80 52 – closed Sat lunchtime and Sun - 15/20€. Local and passing guests of this discreet restaurant located on the ground floor of Hôtel St-Georges are offered the choice between two set menus and a rich selection of dishes. Traditional dishes change regularly according to the availability of fresh produce and are quoted at reasonable prices.

Chez Jules – 11 r. de Strasbourg - 71100 Chalon-sur-Saône - ☎ 03 85 48 08 34 – closed Feb school hols, 1-20 Aug, Sat lunchtime and Sun - 15.50/30€. The three set menus of this Chalon restaurant offer a fine range of appetising traditional dishes extended by tempting suggestions of the day. Particular mention should be made of the selection of no fewer than fifteen mouth-watering desserts … Thank you Jules!

Le Bistrot – 31 r. de Strasbourg - 71100 Chalon-sur-Saône - ☎ 03 85 93 22 01 – closed Sat-Sun - 16€ lunch - 21/26€. Entirely remodelled in the original spirit - woodwork, lights, posters and enamelled plaques - the retro decor of this bistro now comes across as very stylish. In the kitchen, the owner prepares bistro-style dishes combining traditional and regional influences. In the dining room, his wife extends a particularly convivial welcome to her guests.

Le Vendangerot – 6 pl. Ste-Marie - 71150 Rully - 5.5km S of Chagny along D 981 and D 581 - ☎ 03 85 87 20 09 – closed 2-15 Jan, 15 Feb to 10 Mar, Wed except evening Jul-Sep, and Tue - 17/42€. This house, bedecked with geraniums, awaits you in the heart of a real wine-growing village. In the dining room, decorated with a collection of old photographs on the theme of wine growing, you will discover the chef's tasty Burgundian dishes, successfully blending local produce with Rully wines.

Le Chassagne – 2 imp. Des Chenevottes - 21190 Chassagne-Montrachet - 4.5km NW of Chagny along D 62D and D 113A - ☎ 03 80 21 94 94 – closed 25 Jul to 10 Aug, 19 Dec to 12 Jan, Sun and Wed evenings, and Mon - 18/58€. Wild turbot glazed with orange peel candied with ginger, truffle salad served with artichoke chips, veal cooked with citrus fruit…All these delicacies, enhanced by a very fine selection of Chassagne-Montrachet wines, offer you a glimpse of gourmet paradise!

Le Terroir – Pl. du Jet-d'Eau - 21590 Santenay - 5km W of Chagny along D 62 and D 113 - ☎ 03 80 20 63 47 – closed 10 Dec to 10 Jan, Wed evening Nov-Mar, Sun evening and Thu except 20 Jul to 20 Aug - 19/38€. This stone house nestling in a peaceful village, situated at the end of the prestigious "Grands Crus road", has two comfortable dining rooms where guests enjoy a tasty cuisine combining tradition and regional flavours. The essential finishing touch to this feast of the palate comes from the cellar well stocked with local Crus.

AROUND DIJON

Ma Bourgogne – 1 av. Paul-Doumer - 21000 Dijon - ☎ 03 80 65 48 06 – closed 1-25 Aug, Sun evening and Sat - 19/29€.

The chef of this restaurant deliberately limits the number of his guests in order to be able to control everything from A to Z himself and to prepare regional dishes which justify the good name of the house. His wife and his daughter welcome and serve their guests with a smile in the simple, well-kept dining room.

⊜⊜ **Les Deux Fontaines** – *16 pl. de la République - 21000 Dijon - ☎ 03 80 60 86 45 – closed 1-11 Jan, 3 weeks in Aug, Sat and Mon - 23/46€.* The menu of this attractive bistro begins with a tribute to the owner's grandmother, a true *cordon bleu*. The decor of the dining room, housed in a former warehouse, brings about a nostalgic feeling. As for the dishes, drawn from recipes of the past, they are brought up to date through the use of spices and flavours from around the world.

⊜⊜ **Le Chambolle Musigny** – *28 r. Basse - 21220 Chambolle-Musigny - 5.5km S of Gevrey-Chambertin - ☎ 03 80 62 86 26 – closed 1-16 Jul, 19 Dec to 20 Jan, Sun evening Dec-Apr, Wed and Thu - 24/35€.* A friendly greeting welcomes you to this small dining room where you can enjoy dishes inspired by the terroir. Eggs in red-wine sauce, Burgundy snails, coq au vin and boeuf bourguignon are cooked slowly, with the greatest care by the chef who will advise you to wash it down with a Chambolle-Musigny as tradition requires.

⊜⊜ **La Toute Petite Auberge** – *N 74 – 3.5km S of Nuits-St-Georges along N 74 - 21700 Vosne-Romanée - ☎ 03 80 61 02 03 – closed Feb, Tue evening and Wed - 24/40€.* The regional and traditional dishes served in both dining rooms or on the terrace overlooking the small park and the vineyards are truly delicious. Burgundy-style crispy beef cheek, for instance, reveals subtle flavours enhanced by a rich red-wine sauce.

⊜⊜ **Chez Guy** – *3 pl. de la Mairie - 21220 Gevrey-Chambertin - ☎ 03 80 58 51 51 – closed Wed - 25/29€.* Ham seasoned with parsley, pastilla of snails, Burgundy-style beef cheek, blackcurrant cake or gingerbread ice cream are on the menu and the wine list includes the best Crus: you are in one of the most famous wine-growing villages of the Côte, and in the perfect place to make the most of it.

⊜⊜ **Le Bistrot des Halles** – *10 r. Bannelier - 21000 Dijon - ☎ 03 80 49 94 15 – closed Sun and Mon - 16€ lunch - 26/35€.* The 1900-style bistro faces the covered market. Among the must-try specialities, choose the pie, the snails or the unusual Dijon-style cod in mustard cream. On the other hand, the description of some specialities might arouse your curiosity: their roast duck with pineapple and gingerbread springs to mind...

AROUND MÂCON

⊜ **Le Charollais** – *71 r. Rambuteau - 71000 Mâcon - ☎ 03 85 38 36 23 – closed 8-23 Aug, Sun and Thu evenings, and Mon - 13/30€.* The chef of this restaurant prepares traditional dishes which pay tribute to the fine Charolais breed. Fixed-price menus and à-la-carte dishes (game in season) are served by the amiable lady of the house in two rustic dining rooms (including one reserved for non-smokers) which are plain but convivial.

⊜⊜ **Au P'tit Pierre** – *10 r. Gambetta - 71000 Mâcon - ☎ 03 85 39 48 84 – closed 25 Jul to 15 Aug, Tue evening, Wed Sep-Jun, Mon lunchtime and Sun Jul-Aug - 16/29€.* P'tit Pierre can be proud of its initials which could stand for Pleasant, a fitting description of its bright, colourful bistro-style decor, or for Pleasure, or for Patrick, the chef, who trained in a prestigious Michelin-starred restaurant in Mâcon and now devises his imaginative and well-prepared dishes here.

⊜⊜ **Pouilly Fuissé** – *Le Bourg - 71960 Fuissé - 9.5km from Mâcon along D 17, D 54 and D 172 - ☎ 03 85 35 60 68 – closed 2-26 Jan, 2 Jul to 6 Aug, Sun, Mon and Tue evenings, and Wed - 17/38€.* This establishment named after the famous local Cru is bound to favour regional wines. Served by the glass or the bottle, they go perfectly well with the good-value, tasty cuisine which combines traditional and typically Burgundian dishes: chitterling sausage with Époisses cheese and vacherin flavoured with Burgundy marc.

⊜⊜ **Le Terminus** – *21 av. Gambetta - 71700 Tournus - ☎ 03 85 51 05 54 – closed 2 weeks in Jan, 3 weeks in Nov and Wed - 19/47€.* Spacious dining room and shaded terrace where you will feel perfectly at ease to enjoy the tasty traditional dishes prepared by the chef, including Provence-style fresh frogs' legs, Bresse chicken with morels and fillet of Charolais beef with béarnaise sauce. Refurbished rooms.

⊜⊜ **Aux Terrasses** – *18 av. du 23-Janvier - 71700 Tournus - ☎ 03 85 51 01 74 – closed 2 Jan to 2 Feb, 6-14 Jun, 1-22 Nov, Sun evening, Tue lunchtime and Mon - 20€ lunch - 25/54€.* It is unthinkable to go through Tournus without tasting Michel Carette's delicious, classical cuisine: hot mallard pie, Bresse chicken braised in Chardonnay wine or pikeperch with ham from Morvan, which you wash down with a Cru selected from the inspiring wine list. Attractive dining rooms. Friendly welcome.

IN VÉZELAY

⊜ **Les Aquarelles** – *6 ruelle des Grands-Prés, in Fontette - 89450 Vézelay - ☎ 03 86 33 34 35 – closed 12 Nov to 5 Dec, 26 Dec to 12 Mar, Mon and Tue Nov-Dec - 15/25€.* Former farmhouse located in a peaceful hamlet, where you will be welcomed as among friends. The rooms are small yet fresh and well kept. Table d'hôte offering simple meals prepared with regional produce and served on two large farm tables. Tasting of the wines produced on the estate.

WHERE TO STAY

AROUND AUXERRE

⊜ **Chambre d'hôte M. et Mme Piedallu** – *5 av. de la Gare - 89160 Lézinnes - 11km SE of Tonnerre along D 905 - ☎ 03 86 75*

4

68 23 - ✉ - *3 rooms: 35/43€*. This new house built in traditional style is full of charm. The garret rooms are nevertheless spacious and decorated with antique furniture. The veranda of the dining room offers a pleasant breakfast setting. There is a small drawing room for those who wish to read or rest.

⊜ **Chambre d'hôte Domaine Borgnat Le Colombier** – *1 r. de l'Église - 89290 Escolives-Ste-Camille – 9.5km S of Auxerre along D 239 - ☎ 03 86 53 35 28 - domaineborgnat@wanadoo.fr - 5 rooms: 40/50€ - meal 23/35€*. This magnificent 17C fortified farmhouse is the headquarters of a fine wine-growing estate. You will have a choice between guesthouse rooms and the self-catering cottage housed in the dovecot. Meals introduce guests to the wines produced by the estate; these can also be tasted when visiting the superb cellars.

⊜⊟ **Le Calounier** – *5 r. de la Fontaine - hameau de Arton - 89310 Môlay - 8km N of Noyers along D 86 and a minor road - ☎ 03 86 82 67 81 - ✉ - 5 rooms: 51/56€ - meal 23€*. Everything is aimed at seducing you in this splendidly restored Burgundian farmhouse; its name in local dialect is also that of the walnut trees planted around the estate. The half-British, half-regional decoration of the rooms located in the two wings is very attractive. The cuisine is based on products of the terroir.

⊜⊟ **Chambre d'hôte Château de Ribourdin** – *89240 Chevannes - 7km SW of Auxerre along N 151, D 1 and a minor road - ☎ 03 86 41 23 16 - ✉ - 5 rooms: 51/70€*. This splendid, small 16C castle and its dovecot, standing beneath the village, in the middle of a wheat field, look very elegant. The former 18C barn houses the bedrooms, each one named after a local castle, and the breakfast room adorned with a fireplace.

⊜⊟ **Rive Gauche** – *R. Port-au-Bois - 89300 Joigny - ☎ 03 86 91 46 66 - clorain@dial.oleane.com - 🅿 - 42 rooms: 60/105€ - ☲ 8€ - meal 28/35€*. Contemporary building erected on the west bank of the River Yonne. Fairly spacious, refurbished rooms with a sensible layout. Pleasant park with ornamental pond and helipad. The contemporary dining room-veranda and the terrace both look out towards the river.

⊜⊟ **Parc des Maréchaux** – *6 av. Foch - 89000 Auxerre - ☎ 03 86 51 43 77 - contact@hotel-parcmarechaux.com - 🅿 - 25 rooms: 70/110€ - ☲ 12€*. This Napoleon III residence houses lovely cosy bedrooms with Empire-style furniture and a view of the park planted with one-hundred-year-old trees (fine swimming pool).

⊜⊟⊟ **Hôtel La Côte St-Jacques** – *14 fbg de Paris - 89300 Joigny - ☎ 03 86 62 09 70 - lorain@relaischateaux.com – closed 3 Jan to 3 Feb - 🅿 - 27 rooms: 135/330€ - ☲ 27€ - meal 140/160€*. A luxury hotel overlooking the River Yonne, so far from everything… and so close to perfection. There's also a private boat for river cruising and a shop. The splendid inventive cuisine and a profusion of Grands Crus are the strong points of this leading gastronomic establishment.

AROUND BEAUNE

⊜⊟ **Hôtel du Parc** – *13 r. du Golf - 21200 Levernois - 5km SE of Beaune via rte de Verdun-sur-le-Doubs, then D 970 and D 111ᴸ - ☎ 03 80 24 63 00 - hotel. le.parc@wanadoo.fr - closed 28 Nov to 27 Jan - 🅿 - 25 rooms: 48/87€ - ☲ 6.50€*. An attractive courtyard bedecked with flowers separates the two buildings which make up the hotel. The façades are decorated with Virginia creeper; the rooms contain antique furniture, retro lights and colourful draperies which create a warm atmosphere. The park situated at the back ensures peace and quiet. Attentive family-style service.

⊜⊟ **Grillon** – *21 r. Seurre - 21200 Beaune - ☎ 03 80 22 44 25 - joel.grillon@wanadoo. fr – closed Feb - 🅿 - 18 rooms: 52/65€ - ☲ 7€*. This elegant pink house with almond-green shutters, nestling inside an enclosed garden, contains fresh-looking rooms partly furnished with items found in antique shops. Lounge-bar in the vaulted cellar and flower-decked terrace where breakfast is served in fine weather.

⊜⊟ **Domaine du Moulin aux Moines** – *Auxey-Duresses - 21190 Meursault - ☎ 03 80 21 60 79 - 6 rooms: 65/75€ - ☲ 6€*. This fine residence set in the middle of a vineyard once belonged to Cluny Abbey. The spacious, tastefully decorated rooms are full of charm. Those located in the mill are particularly attractive. Wine-tasting cellar for sampling the wines produced by the estate and small wine-growing museum (handsome winepress).

⊜⊟ **La Villa Fleurie** – *19 pl. Colbert - 21200 Beaune - ☎ 03 80 22 66 00 - la.villa. fleurie@wanadoo.fr – closed Jan - 🅿 - 10 rooms: 67/77€ - ☲ 8€*. The branches of a fragrant wisteria intertwine on the railings of this small 1900-style villa which has three kinds of rooms: contemporary, bourgeois-style or family-style, the latter – two maisonettes – located on the top floor. Attractive, slightly British-looking breakfast room and a small garden-terrace.

Cabalus B & B in Vézelay.

S. Sauvignier / MICHELIN

AROUND CHALON

⊖⊕ **Chambre d'hôte Au Temps d'Autrefois** – *Pl. Monge - 21340 Nolay - 14km NW of Chagny along N 6, D 33 and D 973 -* ☎ *03 80 21 76 37 -* 🖅 *- 4 rooms: 50/60€.* A charming old-world atmosphere pervades this lovely 14C timber-framed house standing in a small square adorned by a fountain. The interior is very welcoming, with its share of exposed beams, antique furniture and red-brick floor tiles, and the rooms are attractive and quiet. Breakfast is served on the terrace in summer.

AROUND DIJON

⊖ **Chambre d'hôte Les Brugères** – *7 r. Jean-Jaurès - 21160 Couchey - 10km S of Dijon via N 74 and D 122D -* ☎ *03 80 52 13 05 – closed Dec-Mar - 4 rooms: 40/60€.* If you wish to talk about wine and taste it, this charming 17C wine grower's home is the perfect place for you. Attractively decorated bedrooms featuring exposed beams and pieces of antique furniture. Pleasant breakfast room. The cellar is open to visitors who are invited to taste the wine.

⊖⊕ **La Musarde** – *7 r. des Riottes - 21121 Hauteville-lès-Dijon -* ☎ *03 80 56 22 82 - hotel.rest.lamusarde@wanadoo. fr – closed 20 Dec to 10 Jan; restaurant closed Sun evening and Mon -* 🅿 *- 12 rooms: 54/61€ -* ⊐ *8€ - meal 17/64€.* The terrace of this hotel is very pleasantly shaded in fine weather by cypress, hazelnut and oak trees mingling their foliage, and the peaceful village all around adds to the appeal of the place. The rooms, plainly furnished in rustic style, look out on the quiet garden.

⊖⊕ **La Bonbonnière** – *24 r. des Orfèvres - 21240 Talant - 5km NW of Dijon along D 107A -* ☎ *03 80 57 31 95 - labonbonniere@wanadoo.fr -* 🅿 *- 20 rooms: 65/90€ -* ⊐ *8€.* Private house turned into a hotel in a lovely village overlooking Lake Kir. The interior decor lives up to the name of the establishment: period furniture and pastel colours add a slight "bijou" touch to the place. Spacious, quiet bedrooms, bourgeois-style sitting rooms and convivial breakfast room.

⊖⊕ **Les Grands Crus** – *R. de Lavaux - 21220 Gevrey-Chambertin -* ☎ *03 80 34 34 15 - hotel.lesgrandsCrus@ipac.fr – closed 1 Dec to 28 Feb -* 🅿 *- 24 rooms: 70/80€ -* ⊐ *10€.* Treat yourself to a break here, in the heart of wine country: the old village, celebrated by so many writers – one of them, Gaston Roupnel, even tried his hand at wine growing – is understandably popular with wine lovers. The hotel rooms, in either bourgeois or rustic style, offer fine views of the vineyards.

⊖⊕⊕ **La Gentilhommière** – *Rte de Meuilley -* ☎ *03 80 61 12 06 - contact@lagentilhommiere.fr – closed mid-Dec to early Feb -* 🅿 *- 31 rooms: 85/250€ -* ⊐ *12.50€.* This 16C hunting lodge, with its regional-style roof, contains comfortable, distinctive rooms and suites. Some of these look out on the 13ha park through which flows a good trout river, the Meuzin. Expect contemporary dishes on the menu but a healthy respect for age on the wine list: a fine selection of Burgundy wines includes some noble old vintages.

AROUND MÂCON

⊖ **Chambre d'hôte Château de Salornay** – *71870 Hurigny - 6km W of Mâcon along D 82 and a minor road -* ☎ *03 85 34 25 73 -* 🖅 *- 4 rooms and 2 self-catering cottages: 35/52€.* This castle, dating from the 11C and 15C, looks very elegant with its handsome towers and thick walls crowned by a watch path. The spacious rooms, one of them in the keep, contain antique furniture and look out on the surroundings fields. Two distinctive, self-catering cottages are also available.

⊖ **Chambre d'hôte Manoir de Champvent** – *Lieu-dit Champvent - 71700 Chardonnay - 11km SW of Tournus via D 56 and D 463 -* ☎ *03 85 40 50 23 – closed Nov-Feb -* 🖅 *- 5 rooms: 40/55€.* The outbuildings of this handsome yellow-stone manor contain several rooms decorated with antique furniture, still-lifes and abstract paintings. There is a large meadow where children can let off steam and a lovely courtyard bedecked with flowers. Shows (plays, concerts, humour etc) and exhibitions are regularly staged in the theatre.

⊖⊕ **Chambre d'hôte Le Château d'Escolles** – *71960 Verzé - 2km N of La Roche-Vineuse along D 85 -* ☎ *03 85 33 44 52 - 4 rooms: 55/70€.* You will be given a friendly welcome in this outbuilding of a 17C castle, located on the edge of a 5ha park. The garret rooms are cosy: thick wall-to-wall carpet, exposed beams, antique furniture… Breakfast features a selection of homemade jams and fresh fruit juice. Charming terrace.

AROUND VÉZELAY

⊖ **Cabalus, l'Ancienne Hôtellerie de l'Abbaye** – *R. St-Pierre - 89450 Vézelay -* ☎ *03 86 33 20 66 - contact@cabalus. com – closed Mon in low season and Tue - 4 rooms: 38/54€ -* ⊐ *8,80€ - 15€.* The former hostel of Vézelay Abbey is an unusual place to stay, owing to its exceptional situation only 100m from the basilica and to its magical atmosphere. The very spacious, comfortable rooms are decorated with originality. Copious breakfasts are enhanced by the enchanting setting of the terrace.

⊖⊕ **Chambre d'hôte La Palombière** – *Pl. du Champ-de-Foire - 89450 Vézelay -* ☎ *03 86 33 28 50 - lapalombièrehost@wanadoo.fr – closed Jan to mid-Feb and Mon in low season - 10 rooms: 55/78€ -* ⊐ *9€.* This 18C residence covered with Virginia creeper has a lot of character. The spacious, plush rooms, with en-suite "retro" bathrooms, tastefully combine Louis XIII, Louis XV and Empire styles. Breakfast, featuring homemade jams, is served on the veranda.

Garden full of flowers.

Hôtel Crispol – Rte d'Avallon, à Fontette - 89450 Vézelay - 5km E of Vézelay along D 957 - ☎ 03 86 33 26 25 - crispol@wanadoo.fr – closed 10 Jan to end of Feb, Tue lunchtime and Mon - 🅿 - 12 rooms: 71/115€ - ☐ 10€ - 21/48€. This stone building, located in a hamlet of the Vézelay area, features rooms decorated in contemporary style and brightened up by the artist-owner's works. You will appreciate the peace and quiet of the garden, in spite of the hairpin bend in the road at that very spot. Elegant restaurant looking out towards Vézelay hill.

GOURMET SHOPPING

Au Fin Palais – 3 pl. St-Nicolas, off quai de la Marine - 89000 Auxerre - ☎ 03 86 51 14 03 - aufinpalais@9online.fr – daily, 9.30am-7.30pm – closed 15-30 Mar. This shop sells renowned specialities of Burgundian gastronomy, bought from the best local producers: terrine from Morvan, streaky salted pork with lentils, boeuf bourguignon, gingerbread, nonnettes (small iced gingerbread), croquets (dry crispy biscuit with almonds), various kinds of jam, mustard and vinegar… and the famous snails. A small space is set aside for wines and spirits.

Amuse-Bouche – 7 pl. Carnot - 21200 Beaune - ☎ 03 80 25 06 62 – Tue-Sat, 10am-1pm, 2-7pm, Sun, 10am-1pm; closed Feb school hols. This shop specialises in rare delicacies: morels, truffles, caviar and prestigious wines are prominently displayed on the shelves, among Espelette pimentos, smoked hams, various kinds of olive oil and homemade dishes like boeuf bourguignon, coq au vin.

Au Cep Gourmand – 15 r. Auxerroise - 89800 Chablis - ☎ 03 86 18 97 83 – Tue-Sat, 9am-1pm, 2.30-6.30pm, Sun, 9am-1pm; Jun-Sep, daily, 9am-6.30pm; closed Jan. This shop stocks many products manufactured by local cottage industries intended for the palate and the table. You will find, among others, terrines, foie gras, chitterling sausages, biscuits, a selection of local wines and some fresh produce as well as a selection of tableware and gifts.

Légendes Gourmandes – 4 pl. St-Vincent - 71100 Chalon-sur-Saône - ☎ 03 85 48 05 64 – Tue-Sat, 9.30am-12.30pm, 2.30-7pm, Sun, 9.30am-12.30pm. Mesdames Lotz and Sotty offer their clients a real gastronomic tour of France: from Provence to Brittany via Lorraine or Burgundy of course, they have selected all kinds of products for the quality of their taste: vinegars, terrines, fruit drinks, caramels, sardines, spirits etc.

Auger – 61 r. de la Liberté - 21000 Dijon - ☎ 03 80 30 26 28 – Mon, 10am-12pm, 2-7pm, Tue, 9am-12pm, 2-7pm, Wed-Sun, 9am-7pm. Orange-flavoured gingerbread brought fame to this establishment taken over in 1974 by the renowned Dijon company, Mulot et Petitjean. The shop offers a great variety of local products, including nonnettes, gingerbreads, gimblettes, blackcurrant liqueur, Fallot mustard, wines, confectionery, jams and biscuits.

Ph. Gajic / MICHELIN

L'Escargotière de Marsannay-le-Bois – 9 rte d'Épagny - 21380 Marsannay-le-Bois - ☎ 03 80 35 76 15 - sylvainmansuy@wanadoo.fr – daily, 10am-8pm. Tours of the snail farm, from the breeding stage to the final product, are regularly organised. In the shop, you will find snails prepared according to the traditional Burgundian recipe, others cooked in white wine with fresh vegetables, empty shells ready to be filled and ready-cooked specialities.

MARKETS

Joigny – Wed and Sat mornings, pl. du Marché.

Auxerre – Tue and Fri mornings, l'Arquebuse market. Sun morning, Ste-Geneviève market.

Chablis – Sun morning, in the town centre.

Tonnerre – Sat morning, pl. de la Gare.

Dijon – Tue, Fri and Sat mornings, in the town centre.

Nuits-St-Georges – Fri morning, covered market.

Beaune – Wed and Sat mornings.

Buxy – Thu morning, in the town centre.

Tournus – Sat morning, in the town centre.

Châlon-sur-Saône – Wed morning, pl. de l'Hôtel-de-Ville.

Mercurey – Sat morning, in the town centre.

Mâcon – Sat morning, esplanade Lamartine.

Auxerre★★

The cathedral and old houses of the capital of Lower Burgundy proudly rise in terraces above the River Yonne. The town used to be renowned for its wine, but the vineyards have disappeared with the exception of Clos de la Chaînette, a 3ha estate belonging to... the psychiatric hospital. Its production is shared between the employees of the establishment, who are only entitled to 12 bottles a year.

The fine Gothic **Cathédrale St-Étienne★★** was built over a period of nearly four hundred years, from 1215 to 1525. It is therefore a blend of Gothic and Renaissance features. The interior boasts a splendid array of 13C **stained-glass windows★★**. The **Romanesque crypt★** is adorned with medieval frescoes. Do take a look at the Treasury before leaving! *7.30am-6pm. Treasury and crypt, Easter to All Saints', Mon-Sat, 9am-6pm, Sun, 2-6pm; the rest of the year, daily except Sun, 10am-5pm.* ☎ *03 86 52 23 29.*

To reach the abbey of St-Germain, walk along the north side of the cathedral and down rue Cochois. The famous **Abbaye St-Germain★★**, founded in the 6C by Queen Clotilda, the wife of Clovis, was a centre of learning which attracted many saints including St Patrick. Inside the **abbey church**, the most interesting part is the **crypt★★**. This underground church contains **frescoes★** dating from 850. The **Musée St-Germain**, located in the conventual buildings, houses an **archaeological museum**. *Jun-Sep, guided tours of the crypt (45min, last admission 1hr before closing), 10am-6.30pm; Oct-May, 10am-12pm, 2-6pm. Closed Tue, 1 Jan, 1 and 8 May, 1 and 11 Nov, 25 Dec. 4.20€ (children under 16, 1st Sun of the month: no charge), 5.80€ ("passeport été" discount card). ☎ 03 86 18 05 50.*

In order to penetrate deep into the Auxerre vineyards, follow the scenic D 362 to Augy rather than N 6, then cross the River Yonne towards Vaux. The **Vaux** vineyard, stretching along the Yonne, was revived some twenty years ago.

Drive 4.5km south along the river to Escolives-Ste-Camille.

Escolives-Sainte-Camille

The charming Romanesque **church** has an 11C crypt where the relics of St Camille were once kept. At the northern end of the village, excavations are in progress to explore the **remains** of a Gallo-Roman village and public baths (1C to 3C) and a Merovingian cemetery. A 2C fresco discovered on the site testifies to the long-standing presence of vineyards in the region. *Apr-Oct, guided tours, 10 and 11am, 2-7pm; Nov-Mar, by prior appointment. Closed 1 Jan, 1 May, 1 and 11 Nov, 25 Dec. No charge. ☎ 03 86 53 34 79 or 03 86 53 39 09.*

Coulanges-la-Vineuse

The very name of this hilltop village suggests an ancient wine-growing tradition. The vineyard, extending over 135ha, produces **Bourgogne-Coulanges-la-Vineuse** wines: soft, light reds, fruity whites and good rosés.

In addition to its display of old wine-growing implements, the **Musée de la Vigne et du Vin** houses a winepress of the kind used in medieval times. *55 bis r. André-Vildieu, 89580 Coulanges-la-Vineuse. Guided tours (1hr) on request, ☎ 03 86 42 20 59 (town hall) or 03 86 42 54 48 (museum), daily except Sun and Wed, 2-6pm. 3.50€.*

Follow D 85 to Vincelottes, then D 362 towards Auxerre until you reach Bailly (3.5km).

Vincelles and **Vincelottes** are ancient moorings for river boats loading wine bound for Paris. On the way to Auxerre, one comes across the hillside Caves de Bailly. These underground quarries, which used to supply Paris with building stones, were turned in 1972 into storehouses covering 3ha where members of the wine growers' cooperative stock bottles of Crémant-de-Bourgogne. *Guided tour of the rooms decorated with sculptures, introduction to the making of Crémant and wine tasting to finish. Apr-Oct, guided tours and wine-tasting (1hr) 2.30-5pm; Nov-Mar, Sat-Sun and public hols 4-5pm. 4€. ☎ 03 86 53 77 77.*

Return to Vincelottes then drive 2.5km along D 38 to Irancy.

Irancy

This village, lying in a dale planted with cherry trees, produces **Irancy** AOC wines that are the most renowned red wines yielded by the Auxerre vineyards. They are made partly from an original grape type, César, believed to have been imported by Roman legions. Palotte and Côte du Moustier are the best Irancy vineyards.

Local wine growers are very friendly. Among others, pay a visit to **Anita and Jean-Pierre Colinot** *(see Shopping Guide)*. Conducted with the leisurely hospitality the occasion demands, the introductions to wine are worth allowing time for: you're more likely to be pressed to stay longer than hurried out of the door...

Continue along D 38 towards St-Cyr-les-Colons and turn left onto a minor road climbing towards St-Bris.

Saint-Bris-le-Vineux

One of the most charming villages of the Yonne region gave its name to the **Saint-Bris** AOC which only produces white wines from Sauvignon grapes. Built over an amazing network of vaulted cellars, Saint-Bris boasts fine old houses and a 13C Gothic church. The main sight is the **Baphomet**, a strange sculpture representing the horned head of a man surrounded by angels, which is believed to have been a symbol of the Knights-Templars.

The **Maison du vignoble auxerrois** offers an excellent selection of wines (see Shopping Guide). **Ghislaine and Jean-Hugues Goisot** invite you to a wine-tasting

The village of St-Bris-le-Vineux and its vineyards.

tour of their medieval cellars. *30 r. Bienvenu-Martin, 89530 St-Bris-le-Vineux, ☎ 03 86 53 35 15. Mon-Sat 8am-12pm, 2-6.30pm. By appointment.*
Follow D 62 towards Chablis.

Chitry

This pleasant village boasts an imposing 14C fortified church. The terroir is famous for its white Burgundy wines.
Drive on for 4km along D 62 towards Chablis. Shortly before reaching Courgis, there is a picnic area with a viewpoint offering a fine panorama of the vineyards.

Courgis

Although situated within the Chablis Appellation, this village, with its network of narrow streets, also produces red Burgundy wines. Every Sunday before Assumption Day, a pilgrimage is staged here to celebrate the "holy thorn" from Christ's crown, kept in the church.
A minor road runs south to Préhy.

Préhy

The **Domaine Jean-Marc Brocard** organises one-day tours of the vineyards. The wine-tasting room is located at the foot of Ste-Claire Church, in the middle of the vineyards. *3 rte de Chablis, 89800 Préhy, ☎ 03 86 41 49 00, info@brocard.fr Mon-Sat, 9.30am-7pm. By appointment. Admission charge.*
Drive to Chablis along D 2.

Chablis

This opulent village, entirely devoted to the reputation of its white wines, has retained a few old houses, monuments and shops which testify to the wealth derived from the "golden liquid". Although less famous than its wines, the chitterling sausages of Chablis are considered to be among the best anywhere.
The **William Fèvre** and **Vincent Dauvissat** estates together with the **Château Long-Depaquit** are among the most famous estates. You can also visit **La Chablisienne** cooperative, founded in 1923, which produces a quarter of the Chablis Appellation and has a monopoly on Château Grenouille (see Shopping Guide).
At the **Domaine Laroche**, you will be able to visit the Obédiencerie, a noble family residence dating from the 9C and 16C; the cellars house a 13C winepress and a small crypt which, between 877 and 887, contained the relics of St Martin. *10 r. Auxerroise, 89800 Chablis, ☎ 03 86 42 89 28, www.michellaroche.com By appointment. Apr-Dec, Mon-Sat, 10am-12.30pm, 2-6.30pm, Sun, 10.30am-1pm, 3-6pm ; Jan-Mar, Mon-Sat, 10am-12pm, 2-6pm. Closed 25 Dec and 1 Jan. Admission charge.*

Villages of the Chablis region

Nineteen villages are entitled to the **Chablis** Appellation. We suggest visiting some of the most charming of them before going on to Tonnerre.
Beine – *6km W of Chablis along D 965.* The high spire of the Église Notre-Dame (12C-16C) towers above the village. A 15ha artificial lake was created on municipal land to supply water to the sprinklers used in the vineyards against spring frost.
Maligny – *7km N of Chablis along D 91.* This small hillside village boasts one of the finest terroirs of the Chablis Appellation. Here, you will find many pleasant local estates, such as the **Jean Durup Père et Fils** estate (see Shopping Guide).
Béru – *11km E of Chablis along D 45 and D 98.* The old fortified village is overlooked by a vast castle with 12C, 15C and 17C features.

Noyers-sur-Serein★★

26 km SE of Chablis along D 961 and D 956. Tucked inside a meander of the Serein and enclosed by ramparts, Noyers (pronounced noyère) is a small, delightful medieval town; its old timber-framed or stone houses all have cellars opening directly on to the street, a reminder that this was wine country before the phylloxera crisis.

Place de l'Hôtel-de-Ville is surrounded by lovely half-timbered houses, dating from the 14C and 15C and by arcaded houses. The triangular **place du Marché-au-Blé** is lined with old houses. From there, walk through an archway and along the picturesque **rue du Poids-du-Roy**. The street leads, via a covered passage, to the tiny **place de la Petite-Étape-aux-Vins**, framed by half-timbered houses, some of them adorned with sculptures. Turn left onto the main street, **rue de la Petite-Étape-aux-Vins**, also lined with old houses, which leads to place du Grenier-à-Sel. The **Église Notre-Dame** is a vast late-15C church featuring gargoyles, a Renaissance west front and a square tower.

Return to Chablis then drive on to Tonnerre, 18km E via D 965.

Tonnerre

This small city backing on to a hill and surrounded by vineyards lies on the banks of the Canal de Bourgogne and the Armançon. The once flourishing vineyards covered over 1 000ha at the end of the 19C. Having practically disappeared during the 1970s, they have now found a new lease of life and cover about 150ha in the localities of Tonnerre, Épineuil, Danemoine, Molosmes and Vaulichère. Roughly equal quantities of white, red and rosé wines are produced from traditional grape types.

When in Tonnerre, go and see the **Fosse Dionne★**. This circular basin, filled with blue-green water, was used as a wash-house. It is fed by a spring emerging out of the rocks at the centre of the pool, its flow varying according to rainfall.

The **Église St-Pierre** stands on a terrace affording a fine view of the town and its surroundings. With the exception of the 14C chancel and the 15C square tower, the church was rebuilt in 1556 following a major fire.

The **old hospital★**, erected between 1293 and 1295 by Marguerite de Bourgogne, the widow of Charles d'Anjou, king of Naples and Sicily and brother of Saint Louis, has survived intact, with its impressive roof covering an area of 4 500m². Every Easter weekend, the great hall (90m long, 18m wide) is the venue of the local wine fair, Les Vinées tonnerroises. The hospital church, opening off the end of the hall, contains a 15C **Entombment★**. *Apr-Oct, Mon-Sat, 9am-12pm, 2-6pm, Sun and public hols 10-11.30am, 2-4.30pm; Nov-Mar, daily except Sun 9-11.30am, 2-5.30pm. Closed 1 May. 3.50€.* ☎ *03 86 55 14 48.*

From Tonnerre, follow D 188 across the Armançon.

Épineuil

The village gave its name to the Épineuil Appellation which includes 80ha of hillside grapevines planted on steep slopes combining marl and clay soils. Easily spotted are the *cabottes*, small stone sheds used for storing tools. Pinot Noir, the dominant variety, produces light reds and full-bodied rosés. The Côte du Grisey vineyards produce generous wines. Among the producers, try the **Domaine de l'Abbaye du Petit Quincy** located on the site of a former abbey.

Drive on to Molosmes, 5km NE via a steep minor road to Vaulichères, then along D 202.

The tiny village of **Molosmes**, nestling among hills, is surrounded by Chardonnay terroirs.

Return to Tonnerre along D 202.

VEZELAY AND THE SURROUNDING VINEYARDS

Michelin Local Map 319, F7.

The hillsides surrounding Vézelay have always been planted with grape vines and the wines they produced were once much appreciated by pilgrims. However, successive crises had almost wiped out the vineyards when a handful of indomitable wine growers decided to revive them. Marc Meneau, the famous restaurant owner, and the small local cooperative were the main driving force behind this revival. Red and white Burgundy is produced today, but the **Bourgogne-Vézelay** Appellation is reserved for white wine made from the Melon grape variety, also used for Muscadet.

Vézelay★★

Situated on the borders of Morvan, Vézelay extends over the slopes and top of a hill towering above the Cure Valley. Such was the spiritual influence of Vézelay, a main stop on the way to Santiago de Compostela, that many writers settled in the town.

From place du Champ-de-Foire, at the lower end of the town, walk along the promenade des Fossés, following the line of the old ramparts, to the château terrace, behind the basilica. Return by Grande-Rue lined with shops established in old houses with carved doors and mullioned windows.

The monastery founded in the 9C was dedicated in 1050 to Mary Magdalene whose relics it retained. The miracles that happened drew a great number of pilgrims and the church was extended until 1215. However, the discovery of other relics created misgivings. There were fewer pilgrimages, and the fairs and markets lost much of their importance. The old abbey church became a parish church in 1791 and was elevated to a **basilica★★★** in 1920.

The **west front** was reconstructed by Viollet-le-Duc in the 19C. The upper part forms a tympanum framing the statues of Christ Crowned, surrounded by the Virgin Mary, Mary Magdalene and two angels. The **narthex or pre-nave** is roofed with Romanesque arches and vaulting. Pilgrims used to pray in silence before stepping into the sanctuary... and into the light. There is a marvellous perspective along the full length of the nave and chancel, radiant with light. Visitors should take time to examine the sculptures on the doorways dating from the second quarter of the 12C. Those of the tympanum of the **central doorway★★★** show Christ Enthroned surrounded by His Apostles. Crowding all around them are the converts received by St Peter and St Paul.

The Romanesque **nave** was rebuilt between 1120 and 1135 after a terrible fire. It is noteworthy for its impressive size – 62m long – the different hues of the limestone used and its brightness. The **capitals★★★** in particular are worth a closer look.

There is no wine road but you will get a good idea of the local production when you visit the small **Henry de Vézelay** cooperative and the **Domaine Marc Meneau** (see Shopping Guide).

In the town itself, the **Caves du Pèlerin** stock wines produced by all the cooperatives of the Yonne region and offer guided tours of medieval cellars laid out on 3 levels. 32 r. St-Étienne, 89450 Vézelay, ☎ 03 86 33 30 84. Mid-Mar to Dec. Admission charge.

The Côtes Road

The Côte de Nuits and Côte de Beaune stretch from Dijon to Santenay, over a distance of 65km. Every signpost announces legendary names: Nuits-Saint-Georges, Vosne-Romanée, Vougeot, Aloxe-Corton, Puligny-Montrachet... These hillside villages are at the very heart of an exceptional region which produces, within a restricted area, some of the rarest and most precious wines in the world.

TERROIRS OF THE CÔTE DE NUITS

Michelin Local Map 320, J-K 5-7. See itinerary **1** *on the map p. 158.*

The **Côte de Nuits** extends from Fixin to Corgoloin, almost exclusively producing great red wines. The most famous Crus are, from north to south: Chambertin, Musigny, Clos-Vougeot and Romanée-Conti. Very rich and full-bodied, these wines take eight to ten years to acquire superlative qualities of body and bouquet.

The road, sometimes known as the "Champs-Élysées of Burgundy", runs at the foot of vine-covered hills and through opulent towns and villages with evocative names. To the south, on the western slopes of the Côte, the **Hautes-Côtes-de-Nuits** vineyards produce less complex wines.

Dijon★★★

The former capital of the dukes of Burgundy is a museum town with a prestigious past and well-preserved architectural heritage. A major university, intensive cultural activity and numerous shops bring a continuous flow to the city and enliven the streets running through the conservation area. Lovers of Burgundy wine will find Dijon the ideal starting point of the Grands Crus road.

The old district around the Palais des Ducs et des États de Bourgogne is full of character. As you stroll along the streets, often pedestrianised, you will come across handsome stone mansions and numerous half-timbered houses dating from the 15C and 16C. **Rue des Forges★** is one of the busiest streets in town. Lined with several 13C-15C mansions, it starts from **place François-Rude** in the centre of the pedestrian zone, overlooked by the statue of the "Bareuzai", a wine grower clad only in verdigris and looked upon as the local guiding spirit. He is busy grape-treading, but the product of his work only flows during the wine festivals.

Musée des Beaux-Arts★★ – *May-Oct, 9.30am-6pm ; Nov-Apr, 10am-5pm. Closed Tue, 1 Jan, 1 May, 25 Dec. 3.40€, no charge on Sun.* ☎ *03 80 74 52 09.*

If you have too little time to make a thorough visit of Dijon, we advise you to give priority to this huge fine arts museum housed in the **Palais des Ducs et des États de Bourgogne★★**. Created in 1799, the museum is famous above all for its **Salle des Gardes★★★**, which contains art treasures from the Chartreuse de Champmol (see below), the necropolis of the dukes of Valois. The prize exhibit is the **tomb of Philip the Bold★★★**. Several Flemish artists worked successively on this masterpiece from

1385 to 1410. The recumbent figure is watched over by 41 extremely realistic statuettes. You will also be able to admire the **tomb of John the Fearless and Margaret of Bavaria★★★**, carved between 1443 and 1470, and marvel at the richly carved decoration of two wooden altarpieces: the **Crucifixion altarpiece★★★** and the **altarpiece of the Saints and Martyrs★★★**. In the centre, note an **altarpiece of the Passion★★**, carved in an Antwerp workshop at the beginning of the 16C.

Musée archéologique★ – *Daily except Tue, 9am-6pm. Closed 1 Jan, 1 and 8 May, 14 Jul, 1 and 11 Nov, 25 Dec. 2 .20€, no charge on Sun.* ☎ *03 80 30 88 54.*

Gevrey-Chambertin: the castle.

In the basement, two early-11C Romanesque rooms contain a collection of Gallo-Roman sculptures. In the former chapter house, the **goddess Sequan★★** sits enthroned in her boat; this bronze statuette was found during the excavation of the sanctuary of the source of the River Seine. In the former monks' cells there is a rich display of prehistoric remains including, in particular, a **solid-gold bracelet** found in **La Rochepot** (9C BC) and the **Blanot Treasure★**, a group of objects from the late Bronze Age including a belt, leggings, a necklace and a bracelet.

Musée de la Vie bourguignonne★ – *R. Ste-Anne.* ♿ *May-Sep, 9am-6pm; Oct-Apr, 9am-12pm, 2-6pm. Guided tours (1hr) available Sun, 3 and 4pm. Closed Tue, 1 Jan, 1 and 8 May, 14 Jul, 1 and 11 Nov, 25 Dec. 2.80€, no charge on Sun. (ticket combined with the Musée d'Art sacré).* ☎ *03 80 44 12 69.*

This museum, housed in the cloisters of the Bernardines' monastery built around 1680, illustrates local history through regional and urban ethnographic collections brought to life by imaginative displays. Nearby, the **Musée d'Art sacré** contains Catholic liturgical objects from the 13C to the 19C.

Chartreuse de Champmol★ – *1 bd Chanoine-Kir. Follow signposts marked "Puits de Moïse". 10am-6pm. Apply to the tourist office,* ☎ *03 80 44 11 40.*

Wanting a burial place of royal standing, Philip the Bold founded this Carthusian monastery in 1383. All that remains today are the **chapel doorway★** and the **Puits de Moïse★★**: six large statues of Moses and the prophets (14C-15C) leaning back against a hexagonal pillar.

Musée Amora – *W via quai Nicolas-Rolin. Guided tours mid-May to mid-Sep, daily except Sun and public hols at 3 and 4pm; mid-Sep to mid-May, Wed and Sat at 3 and 4pm; the rest of the year, apply to the tourist office.* ☎ *03 80 44 11 41.*

Add a tang of originality to your stay in Dijon by visiting this museum, created by the world's leading mustard manufacturer, which recounts the history of this staple product and its origins.

Leave Dijon via the appropriately named "route des Grands Crus" (D 122).

Chenôve

Located in the old village, the **Cuverie des ducs de Bourgogne** (winery of the dukes of Burgundy) contains two magnificent 13C winepresses. ♿ *Jul-Sep, 2-7pm; the rest of the year, on request (3 weeks in advance). No charge.* ☎ *03 80 51 55 00.*

Marsannay-la-Côte

The terroir of the **Marsannay** AOC is famous for its rosé wines obtained after a short maceration of Pinot Noir grapes. The **Domaine Bart** and the **Château de Marsannay** both offer wine tasting in a pleasant setting *(see Shopping Guide)*.

A small museum of local heritage is housed in the tourist office building which is the starting point of several 🔢 **hiking trails** leading to the municipal forest and across the vineyards.

Fixin

The vineyards of the **Fixin** AOC only spread over some 100ha which produce very fine wines with a deep bouquet. The most famous of these are Clos-du-Chapitre, Clos-de-la-Perrière and Les Arvelets.

The **Philippe Naddef** estate, which produces fine wines, also offers three guest-house rooms *(see Shopping Guide)*.

The village commemorates Napoleon through a monument erected by the sculptor Rude at the request of a former soldier of the Imperial Guard and through a museum located in Parc Noisot.

Brochon

Situated on the edge of the Côte de Nuits, Brochon produces excellent wines. The **château** was built in 1900 by the poet Stephen Liégard. The title of one of his works, honoured by the French Academy in 1887, was destined to a brilliant future: its author had just coined the phrase "Côte d'Azur".

Gevrey-Chambertin

Situated at the opening of a gorge, Combe de Lavaux, the town is framed by hillside vineyards. **Chambertin**, which comes from the two vineyards of Chambertin-Clos-de-Bèze and Chambertin, is the most famous of the Côte-de-Nuits great wines. The area producing it only covers 28ha whereas the **Gevrey-Chambertin** AOC covers almost 500ha. It is possible to compare the two wines at the **Domaine Trapet Père et Fils** *(see the shopping guide)*.

In the upper part of the village stands the square-towered **château** erected in the 10C by the lords of Vergy and given to the monks of Cluny in the 11C. The great tower has retained its watchroom and bowmen's room. Vintage wines are stored in the vaulted cellars. The vineyards of the château produce, among others, the Charmes-Chambertin Grand Cru and Lavaux-St-Jacques Premier Cru. *Guided tours (1hr) on request (the day before), Mar-Nov, 11am-12pm, 2-6pm; Dec-Feb, 11am-12pm, 2-5pm. Closed 25 Dec. 5€. ☎ 03 80 34 36 77.*

Morey-Saint-Denis

Situated in the heart of the Côte de Nuits, the east-facing vineyards include five prestigious Grands Crus: Clos-des-Lambrays, Clos-de-Tart, part of Bonnes Mares, Clos-St-Denis and Clos-de-la-Roche. **Morey-Saint-Denis** AOC wines combine richness and subtlety and the Grands Crus can be aged for fifteen to twenty years. The **Domaine Louis Remy** is worth a visit *(see Shopping Guide)*.

Follow N 74 south.

Vougeot

The terroir which produces the highly valued Clos de Vougeot wines was owned by the abbey of Cîteaux from the 12C to the Revolution. The vineyard of **Clos de Vougeot** covers 50ha divided between 70 wine growers. Its fame outshines the small **Vougeot** appellation, yet the **Christian Clerget estate** produces an excellent white wine *(see Shopping Guide)*.

Surrounded by vineyards, the **Château du Clos de Vougeot★** is visible from afar. Completed during the Renaissance, it was restored in the 19C. The visit includes the 12C Grand Cellier where the ceremonies of the Order of the Tastevin are held, the 12C *cuverie* containing four huge winepresses, the 16C kitchen and the monks' dormitory with its spectacular 14C roof structure.

There is a 15min slide show about the Brotherhood of the Knights of the Tastevin. ♿ *Apr-Sep, guided tours (45min), 9am-6.30pm, Sat 9am-5pm; Oct-Mar, 9-11.30am, 2-5.30pm (Sat 5pm). Closed 1 Jan, 24-25 and 31 Dec. 3.40€. ☎ 03 80 62 86 09.*

Drive W along D 122H.

THE KNIGHTS OF THE TASTEVIN

The Brotherhood of the Knights of the Tastevin has owned the Château du Clos de Vougeot since 1944. In 1934, a small group of Burgundians met in a cellar of Nuits-St-Georges and, in order to fight against the wine slump, they decided to form a society whose aim was to promote "the wines of France in general and, in particular, those of Burgundy". The brotherhood was founded and its renown grew so fast that it soon spread throughout Europe and America. Every year, several chapter meetings of the order, famous the world over, are held in the Great Cellar of the Château du Clos de Vougeot. Five hundred guests take part in these **"disnées"** (banquets), at the end of which the Grand Master and the Grand Chancellor, surrounded by high dignitaries of the brotherhood, initiate new knights according to a rite strictly established in pseudo-Latin and inspired by Molière's *Malade Imaginaire*.

Chambolle-Musigny

Yet another highly prestigious name! Here, the terroirs have evocative titles such as Les Amoureuses, Les Groseilles or Les Charmes and produce extremely subtle wines bearing the **Chambolle-Musigny** and **Musigny** AOC. The latter, located above the Clos de Vougeot is synonymous with excellence. The **Amiot-Servelle estate** is worth a visit *(see Shopping Guide)*.

Continue W along D 122H, then turn left onto D 116.

Reulle-Vergy

This village has a 12C church and an unusual little town hall built on top of a wash house. Opposite the town hall, a barn houses the **Musée des Arts et Traditions des Hautes-Côtes**, illustrating work in the vineyards, archaeology, local flora and fauna as well as daily life in the 19C. *Mar-Dec, daily except Mon and Tue, 10am-1pm, 2-6pm. Make a prior appointment with Mme Griuot. 1.50€. ☎ 03 80 61 41 98.*

Drive SE through Curtil-Vergy and Villars-Fontaine to Vosne-Romanée on a peaceful road running along the edge of Mantua Forest.

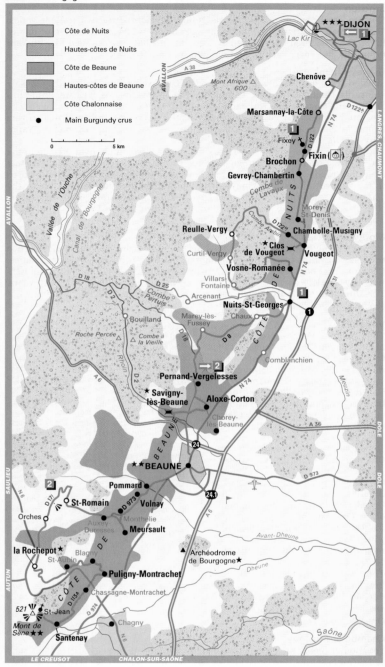

	Côte de Nuits
	Hautes-côtes de Nuits
	Côte de Beaune
	Hautes-côtes de Beaune
	Côte Chalonnaise
●	Main Burgundy crus

Vosne-Romanée

The **Vosne-Romanée** AOC is only represented by rich, subtle and delicate red wines. Among the vineyards which make up the appellation, those of **La Romanée-Conti**, La Tâche and Richebourg produce some of the best, and most expensive, wines in the world. To seal Vosne-Romanée's reputation as a connoisseur's paradise, the surrounding woods are known to supply good Burgundy truffles *(Tuber incinatum)*.

In addition to its wines, the estate of **Armelle and Bernard Rion** sells tinned truffles all year round. *8 r. Nationale, 21700 Vosne-Romanée, ☎ 03 80 61 05 31, rionab@wanadoo.fr. Mon-Sat, 8am-7pm. By appointment.*

Nuits-Saint-Georges

The attractive "capital" of the Côte is proud of its **Nuits-Saint-Georges** AOC and of its Cru Saint-Georges established as early as AD 1000. Its wines owe much of their reputation to the dynamic wine merchants settled in the town. Blackcurrant is its other treasure. If you wish to learn all about the small black berry, visit the **Cassisium**, where a museum display, an audio-visual presentation, a guided tour of the production and a free tasting are available. *R. des Frères-Montgolfier,* ☎ *03 80 62 49 70, www.cassisium.com Apr to end of Nov, tour (1hr 30min), 10am-1pm, 2-7pm; end of Nov to end of Mar, Tue-Sat, 10.30am-1pm, 2-5.30pm. Closed Sun and Mon Dec-Mar. 6€.*

Offering a more family-style atmosphere, the **Ferme Fruitrouge** makes red-berry jams and other delicacies from its own production. *Hameau de Concoeur, 21700 Nuits-St-Georges,* ☎ *03 80 62 36 25, fruitrouge@wanadoo.fr Mon, Thu-Sun, 9am-12pm, 2-7pm, Wed, 2-7pm.*

The **Chantal Lescure estate** opens its cellars dating from the 11C and 18C to the public *(admission charge).* The oldest part, located beneath the Black Tower, is the remains of the fortifications of Nuits-St-Georges. *34 r. Thurot, 21700 Nuits-St-Georges,* ☎ *03 80 61 16 79, contact@domaine-lescure.com. Mon-Fri, 8am-12pm, 2-5pm, Sat-Sun by appointment.*

If you are interested in archaeology, visit the museum. The vaulted cellars of an old wine business house archaeological collections from the Gallo-Roman site at Les Bolards, as well as Merovingian funerary objects and jewellery. One room is devoted to the artist Jean François (1906-80), a native of Burgundy whose paintings depict work in the vineyards and wine making. *May-Oct, daily except Tue, 10am-12pm, 2-6pm. 2.10€.* ☎ *03 80 62 01 37.*

Beyond Nuits-St-Georges, the itinerary follows D 8, going through **Chaux** and **Marey-lès-Fussey**, in the Hautes-Côtes de Nuits vineyards. As you leave Marey-lès-Fussey, you may want to stop at the very pleasant picnic area. Note the blackcurrant and raspberry fields on either side of the road.

Drive to Pernand-Vergelesses situated 5km S via D 18.

FROM REDS TO WHITES ALONG THE CÔTE DE BEAUNE

Michelin Local Map 320, I-J 7-8. See itinerary **2** *on the map on p. 158.*

Unlike the Côte de Nuits, the Côte de Beaune, extending from Aloxe-Corton to Santenay, includes great white-wine terroirs. Beaune, which boasts architectural treasures, is, in a way, the Mecca of wine connoisseurs.

Pernand-Vergelesses

"Pernand je bois, verre je laisse": the French word-play, meaning literally "I drink Pernand but leave the glass", could stand as the unofficial motto of this charming wine-growing village. Nestling inside a combe cut through the Côte, it has retained its authentic appearance. The **Pernand-Vergelesses** AOC produced here includes good-value-for-money red and white wines such as those of the **Rapet Père et Fils estate** *(see Shopping Guide).*

Aloxe-Corton

Located at the foot of the "Corton mountain", the **Aloxe-Corton** (pronounced 'alosse') appellation produces mostly red wines, but it is less renowned than the **Corton** and **Corton-Charlemagne** terroirs. Corton produces intense, slow-developing reds and Corton-Charlemagne some of the greatest white Burgundy wines. The **Château de Corton-André**, roofed with polychrome Burgundian tiles, is one of the most photographed buildings in Burgundy. The estate produces top-quality wines which can be bought on the premises and tasted in a fine 14C vaulted cellar. *21420 Aloxe-Corton,* ☎ *03 80 26 44 25, www.pierre-andre.com Apr-Oct, daily 10am-12.30pm, 2.30-6pm; Nov-Mar, Thu-Mon, 10am-12.30pm, 2.30-6pm. Closed 1 Jan and 25 Dec.*

Aloxe-Corton is situated near the villages of Chorey and Ladoix-Serrigny which include part of the Corton and Corton-Charlemagne terroirs. Their red wines are supple and their whites are light. The **Edmond Cornu et Fils** estate, in Ladoix-Serrigny, and the **Tollot-Beaut et Fils** estate *(see Shopping Guide)* will both welcome you and offer good advice.

Savigny-lès-Beaune

Tucked away in its valley, Savigny comprises the largest wine-growing area of the Côte-d'Or, covering over 600ha. The light and fruity red wines of the **Savigny** Appellation are best drunk rather young. White wines are lively, becoming rounder after two or three years in the bottle. They are available at the **Simon Bize et Fils** estate *(see Shopping Guide).*

Pay a visit to the **Château-musée★** which houses amazing collections. At the entrance stands the 17C "small château" adapted to include an area for tasting and buying wines as well as an exhibition...of Abarth racing cars (uphill and endurance races). The second floor is devoted to motorbikes, with a display of more than 500 items from all countries, from the most prestigious makes to short-lived ones. *Apr-Oct, 9am-6.30pm; Nov-Mar, 9am-12pm, 2-5.30pm. Closed first fortnight in Jan. 7€. ☎ 03 80 21 55 03. www. chateau-savigny.com*

Beaune★★

A prestigious wine town, Beaune is also an incomparable artistic city. Its Hôtel-Dieu, its museums, its Église Notre-Dame, its ring of ramparts with bastions housing the most important cellars, its gardens, its old houses all combine to make it the jewel of Burgundy. The **Beaune** AOC produces very subtle red and white wines. The most famous Crus are Les Grèves, Les Bressandes and Le Clos-du-Roy.

Place de la Halle marks the town centre. The beautiful roof of the Hôtel-Dieu dominates the area. The square and neighbouring streets are lined with shops selling regional specialities: wines and spirits, of course, but also confectionery.

Hôtel-Dieu★★★ – ἓ *End of Mar to mid-Nov, 9am-6.30pm; the rest of the year, 9-11.30am, 2-5.30pm. 5.40€. ☎ 03 80 24 45 00. www.hospices-de-beaune.tm.fr*

The Hôtel-Dieu, a marvel of Burgundian-Flemish art, was founded in 1443 by Nicolas Rolin, Philip the Good's chancellor. It was used as a general hospital until 1971. You have to enter the **main courtyard** to appreciate the extent of the buildings: with their roofs of multi-coloured glazed tiles, they form a group which looks more like "a dwelling fit for a prince than a hospital for the poor". The old well, with its wrought-iron well-head, adds the finishing touch to this now familiar picture. The **Grand'salle** or **Chambre des Pauvres★★★** has retained a magnificent polychrome timber roof in the shape of an upturned keel; the ends of the long tie-beams disappear into the gaping mouths of sea monsters. The way the beds are lined up, with their testers, hangings and bedclothes in matching red and white colours, is impressive. At the end of the room stands a moving, larger than life-size, polychrome wooden statue (1.76m seated) of ***Christ bound★*** (15C). The **Salle du Polyptyque** contains Roger Van der Weyden's famous rendering of the **Last Judgement★★★**, a masterpiece of Flemish art made between 1445 and 1448, which depicts Christ presiding over the Last Judgement above St Michael who is weighing the souls. The **kitchen** *(commentary and "son et lumière" show every 15min)* and the **pharmacy** can also be visited.

Musée du Vin de Bourgogne★ – *Apr-Nov, 9.30am-6pm; Dec-Mar, daily except Tue, 9.30am-5pm. Closed 1 Jan and 25 Dec. 5.40€. ☎ 03 80 22 08 19.*

The inner courtyard of this wine museum recalls a charming theatre setting. The 14C cellar contains an impressive collection of presses and vats. On the first floor, a large room, decorated with two Aubusson tapestries, is the headquarters of the "Ambassade des Vins de France" (Embassy of French wines). The history of Burgundian vineyards and of wine growing is related on the ground floor. Also on display is a 16C polychrome stone statue of the **Virgin Mary with grapes** (Notre-Dame-de-Beaune).

Collégiale Notre-Dame★ – This collegiate church, begun around 1120, is a fine example of Burgundian Romanesque art. Beyond the wide 14C porch, one enters the lofty nave flanked by narrow aisles. Numerous sculptures in 15C and 16C Burgundian style adorn the chapels. Behind the high altar, there is a magnificent set of **tapestries★★** depicting the Life of the Virgin Mary, which mark the transition from medieval to Renaissance art.

Leave Beaune S along D 973.

Pommard

Pommard takes its name from an ancient temple dedicated to Pomona, the goddess of fruits and gardens. Red wines of the **Pommard** AOC, which are "firm, deeply coloured, bold and age well", were much enjoyed by by Renaissance poet Pierre de Ronsard, kings Henri IV and Louis XV, and Victor Hugo. Premiers Crus such as Les Épenots, Les Vaumuriens and Les Rugiens are very much sought after. The **Château de Pommard** is a fine 18C building surrounded by a park, once the home of the mathematician Gaspard Monge (1746-1818); the **Clos des Éperneaux** estate is also one of the reliable producers of this appellation *(see Shopping Guide).*

Volnay

Its wines, exclusively red, have a delicate bouquet and silky taste and are often described as "feminine". It is said that Louis XI was very partial to them. The **Volnay** Appellation includes no fewer than 34 Premiers Crus, among them Les Caillerets, Les Santenots and les Champans. There is a fine view of the vineyards

CEREMONIAL

Every year, the medieval market is the venue of the famous sale of wines from the Hospices de Beaune vineyards, under the patronage of a celebrity. Experts listen for the bids called out by the auctioneer, the bids lasting only as long as it takes for two small candles to burn, hence the name of "sale by candlelight". The proceeds of what has been called "the greatest charity auction in the world" are used for charitable works, for the modernisation of medical facilities and for the maintenance of the Hôtel-Dieu.

from the esplanade below the small 14C church. The village is very attractive with its picturesquely named streets, such as rue d'Amour, rue de l'Abreuvoir or rue de la Piture. The **Domaine de Montille** is one of the many cellars waiting to welcome you *(see the shopping guide)*.

Meursault

This prosperous little town, dominated by a beautiful Gothic spire, owes its name to a gap separating the Côte de Meursault and the Côte de Beaune, known as the "Rat's Leap", in Latin *Muris Saltus*; hence the name of the inhabitants: the Murisaltiens.

Although red **Meursault** wines are made, the appellation is devoted to top-quality white wines with characteristic hazelnut and ripe-grape aromas, which can age for as long as fifteen years. The most renowned vineyards are Les Perrières, Les Genevrières and Les Charmes.

The **Château de Meursault** is the largest estate of the appellation. It boasts a fine 17C building, later remodelled, with extensive, much older cellars *(see Shopping Guide)*.

Drive 6.5km NW to St-Romain via Monthélie and Auxey-Duresses.

Monthélie and **Auxey-Duresses** are not among the best known appellations despite their undeniable quality. They mainly produce red wines, which are robust and improve with age. White wines are fairly subtle and similar to Meursaults.

In **Auxey-Duresses**, the **Piguet-Girardin** and **Vincent Prunier** estates are worth a visit *(see Shopping Guide)*.

Saint-Romain

This locality is made up of two distinct villages. St-Romain-le-Haut is perched on a limestone spur surrounded by a semicircle of cliffs, with the ruins of its 12C-13C castle on the southern edge *(archaeological site; 200m-long visitor trail)*. Right at the top stands the beautifully restored 15C church. The town hall, located lower down, in St-Romain-le-Bas, houses a permanent **exhibition** about local archaeology and traditions. *Aug, 3-6pm; Jul and first two weeks in Sep, daily except Sat-Sun 3-6pm. Guided tours (1hr) available. No charge.* ☎ *03 80 21 28 50.*

Red and white wines of the **St-Romain Appellation** are reputed to be closed when young but to age very well. They are generally good value for money. **Alain Gras** is one of the most reliable estates of the appellation *(see Shopping Guide)*.

Drive towards La Rochepot along D 171. Just before **Orches**, a village set in a rocky site, the road offers a fine **view★** of St-Romain, Auxey, Meursault and the Saône Valley (spring surrounded by Gallo-Roman steles). *Beyond Orches, drive 4km further S.*

Château de la Rochepot★

Jul-Aug, guided tours (1hr) 10am-6pm; Apr-Jun and Sep, 10-11.30am, 2-5.30pm (4.30pm in Oct); Sun at 11.30am, visit-lecture (30min) outside the château, by appointment. Closed Tue. Admission charge. ☎ *03 80 21 71 37. www.larochepot.com*

The castle rises above the woods, on top of Nolay peak, like a fairy-tale apparition. The original building dates from the 13C but was remodelled in the 15C. The tour includes the guardroom and its weaponry, the kitchen with its monumental stove, the richly furnished dining room, the former chapel and the watch path.

Drive to Nolay along D 973. Make the most of your visit to **Nolay** by getting acquainted with the Hautes-Côtes de Beaune wines.

On leaving Nolay, follow D 33 towards St-Aubin.

Saint-Aubin

The vineyards surrounding this pretty village, dominated by a belfry shaped like a sugar loaf, produce excellent slow-developing white wines under the **Saint-Aubin** AOC, on fine terroirs such as the picturesque Murgers des Dents de Chien *climat*. St-Aubin also makes delicate, fruity red wines.

The **Henri Prudhon et Fils, Hubert Lamy** and **Patrick Miolane** estates are a credit to the appellation *(see Shopping Guide)*.

Leave St-Aubin towards Puligny-Montrachet, then take the minor road running through Blagny.

Come in early autumn, when it's harvest time.

B. Kaufmann / MICHELIN

In the hamlet of **Gamay**, which boasts a "castle" immortalised by the artist Utrillo, a steep minor road, offering a lovely panoramic view of the vineyards, leads to the hamlet of **Blagny**, a small red-wine enclave in an area given over to great white wines.

Puligny-Montrachet

This is the world capital of great dry white wines. They seem to draw their richness from the pebbly limestone soils which are better at releasing the heat of the sun than any other in Burgundy. Their intense bouquet is very rich and their colour almost green. The rare red wines of the appellation are very subtle. The Puligny terroir is shared between prestigious Grands Crus with legendary names: **Montrachet**, Bâtard-Montrachet, Chevalier-Montrachet and Bienvenue-Bâtard-Montrachet. On the heights surrounding the village of Puligny, a small road runs between the high walls protecting these jewels. If you wish to buy, visit the **Louis Carillon et Fils** estate *(see Shopping Guide)*.

Situated 3km south, the village of **Chassagne-Montrachet** has given its name to the **Chassagne-Montrachet** appellation which also produces great white wines such as the Criots-Bâtard-Montrachet Cru.

Santenay

Surrounded by cliffs, Santenay spreads its three districts among vast vineyards which, together with its lithia water and casino, have made its reputation. Isolated at the foot of the cliffs, the small **Église St-Jean** boasts a 13C nave.

Santenay wines are mainly red and characterised by their great diversity due to the variety of geological elements making up the soils of the appellation. The excellent whites respond well to the wood flavour of oak barrels. Of all the Santenay wines, those from the estates of **Françoise et Denis Clair** and **Anne-Marie et Jean-Marc Vincent** are among the best value for money *(see Shopping Guide)*.

In spite of its numerous alterations, the **Château de Santenay** (also known as the castle of Philip the Bold, the first duke of Burgundy) looks handsome with its roof of multicoloured tiles. The château and the estate belong to the Crédit agricole which use them for seminars. *1 r. du Château, 21590 Santenay, ☏ 03 80 20 61 87, www.chateau-de-santenay.com Sales and wine tasting, Mon-Fri, 8.30am-12pm, 1.30-5.30pm.*

The Côte Chalonnaise

70km from Chagny to Montagny. Michelin Local Map 320, I 8-9.
Situated north of the Saône-et-Loire, the Côte chalonnaise stretches east of D 981 over some 30km, across land where the vineyards alternate with the pastures of Charolais cattle. The Côte chalonnaise appellation applies to red and white wines produced within an area which also includes the village appellations of Bouzeron, Rully, Mercurey and Givry, picturesque little towns in the heart of a region still marked by strong rural traditions.

Chagny

This peaceful city lying along the Canal de Bourgogne is a famous gourmet stop-over, boasting the renowned Lamelloise restaurant.

Follow D 974 W. The road runs through **Remigny**, where you can enjoy a flight over the vineyards in a hot-air balloon. *71150 Remigny, ☏ 03 85 87 12 30. www.air-escargot.com*

Les Maranges

This small wine-growing "republic" comprises 3 picturesque hamlets, **Dezize-lès-Maranges, Sampigny-lès-Maranges and Cheilly-lès-Maranges**, rising like islands above a sea of vines. The **Maranges** AOC mostly includes red wines, which are both fruity and robust, and a few very subtle white wines.

Return to Chagny then follow D 219 S towards Bouzeron.

Bouzeron

The 12C church of this quiet village, entirely given over to wine growing, has a nave paved with funerary steles. The grape variety grown here is Aligoté, a white grape which flourishes on local ferruginous clay soils and produces floral white wines, at their best when drunk young. The **Chanzy** estate is worth a visit *(see Shopping Guide)*.

Continue S until you reach Rully. From Bouzeron to Rully, a minor road climbs up the hillside then runs down on the other side of the hill through a gap in the forest.

Rully

The Rully AOC produces twice as much white wine as red wine. The whites are "friands" (with a good fruity balance), best drunk within three to four years. The reds are light and fruity. Rully is a large prosperous village dominated by its castle, a fortress erected round a 12C keep with interesting features of military architecture. Stroll through the beautiful English-style park and try the wines of the estate. *71150 Rully, ☎ 03 85 98 12 12. Mon-Thu, 9am-12pm, 1.30-6pm, Fri, 9am-12pm. By appointment.*

Leave Rully S and follow the small road running just beneath the castle. For some 5km, it is lined with low stone walls intended to protect the vineyards then, as it comes to a bend, it offers a beautiful view of the vineyards and of Mercurey.

Mercurey

Mercurey is the largest and best known of the village appellations of the Côte chalonnaise. The red and white wines produced here are at their best within a few years and reasonably priced. The **Michel Juillot estate** is worth a visit *(see Shopping Guide)*. The **Château de Chamirey**, a fine 17C edifice, has a cellar classified as a historic monument and produces wines matured in oak barrels.

71640 Mercurey, ☎ 03 85 98 12 12, rodet@rodet.com Mon-Thu, 9am-12pm, 1.30-6pm, Fri 9am-12pm. Admission charge.

Drive east along D 978 to Chalon-sur-Saône.

Chalon-sur-Saône

Situated in the heart of the Côte chalonnaise vineyards, Chalon is the economic capital of a region sharing its activities between industry, arable farming and stockbreeding. Its fairs and carnival are very popular. Wine can be bought at the **Maison des vins de la côte chalonnaise** *(see Shopping Guide)*.

Some of the houses in the old town, particularly in the St-Vincent district, boast fine half-timbered façades. The **Cathédrale St-Vincent** is not uniform in appearance but has features dating from the 11C to the 19C. The chapel is lit through a beautiful stained-glass window depicting "the woman with the twelve stars" of the Apocalypse, a symbol which inspired the European flag.

Roseraie St-Nicolas★ – *4km S from the banks of the Saône, via the bridges across the Saône islands then left along rue Julien-Leneveu.* ⓕ *5km rambling trail starting from the St-Nicolas leisure park: 1hr 30min though the rose garden.*

The flowerbeds of this prestigious rose garden (including some 25 000 rose bushes) are scattered over huge expanses of lawn.

Musée Denon★ – *Daily except Tue 9.30am-12pm, 2-5.30pm. Closed public hols. 3.10€, Wed and 1st Sun in the month, no charge. ☎ 03 85 94 74 41.*

Housed in an 18C annexe of the former Ursulines convent, this museum is named after one of the town's illustrious citizens, Vivant Denon, an engraver and a painter, who drew up a list of Egypt's antique monuments during Napoleon's campaign there. The museum displays works by Bassano and Caravaggio as well as fine 17C Dutch paintings. The *Portrait of a Black Man* by Géricault is one of the museum's prize exhibits.

Musée Nicéphore-Niépce★★ – *Jul-Aug, 10am-12.30pm, 1.30-6pm ; the rest of the year, 9.30-11.45am, 2-5.45pm. Closed public hols. 3.10€, Wed and 1st Sun in the month, no charge. ☎ 03 85 48 41 98. www.museeniepce.com*

This museum, supported by the Kodak factory in Chalon, is dedicated to the pioneer of photography, Nicéphore Niépce (1765-1833), a native of Chalon. Housed in the Hôtel des Messageries, the museum exhibits a rich collection of pictures and vintage equipment illustrating the discovery and evolution of photography.

Leave Chalon-sur-Saône along D 69 towards Givry, 8km E.

Givry

The **Givry** AOC produces red and white wines which Henri IV drank every day. They are similar to Mercurey wines. If you need convincing, go and taste the wines made on the estate of **Guillemette and Xavier Besson** *(see Shopping Guide)*.

Givry looks like a small 18C city with its town hall housed inside a monumental gatehouse dating from 1771, its fountains and its **church** surmounted by cupolas. The **Halle ronde**, a former corn exchange was built in the early 19C.

Leave Givry W along D 170. The road runs through several wine-growing villages, **Jambles, Moroges** and **Bissey-sous-Cruchaud**, where there are many pleasant cellars. If you feel like enjoying an overall view of the vineyards, stop in Moroges and treat yourself to a hot-air balloon flight; 3-hour flights at the start and close of the day are available from **Bourgogne-montgolfières**, *71390 Moroges, ☎ 03 85 47 99 85, www.eole71.com*

D 125 leads S from Bissey to Buxy.

Buxy

This large village on the border of the Mâconnais has an important cooperative, the **Cave des Vignerons de Buxy** *(see Shopping Guide)*.

The small **Musée du Vigneron** illustrates work in the vineyard and in the cellar over a period of a year. Display of old implements. *In the village centre. Jul-Aug, Tue-Thu, 2-6pm. ☎ 03 85 92 00 16.*

Drive 2km W along D 977.

Montagny-lès-Buxy

The small **Montagny** appellation, exclusively devoted to white wines, surrounds a picturesque village clinging to a hillside above Buxy. The character of the wines is similar to white Mâcon wines for their fruity qualities and to Chablis for their aromas.

Not far from the village, there is a fine viewpoint with a statue of the Virgin Mary and a picnic area.

White Wines of the Mâconnais

93km from Tournus to Mâcon. Michelin Local Map 320, I-J 10-12. See round tour **1** *on the map on p. 165; round tour* **2** *is a suggested itinerary meant to explore other aspects of the Mâconnais than its vineyards.*

Although its wines are, in theory, entitled to the **Bourgogne** appellation, the Mâconnais differs from the Côtes area in several aspects: a geological homogeneity featuring a high proportion of limestone and red clay, a higher production-to-area ratio, the use of Gamay grapes for red wines and the predominance of white wines. It is a fine hilly region fashioned by man over thousands of years, lending itself to rambling and dominated by the high rocky spurs of Vergisson and Solutré.

Tournus

This transition town between "oc" and "oïl" country (southern and northern France) is worth a visit for its provincial character, its fine restaurants and its splendid Romanesque abbey.

The buildings of the church and abbey of St-Philibert (10C-13C) are closely linked to the history of Tournus. The **Église abbatiale St-Philibert★★** boasts a remarkably high nave and lovely 12C mosaics discovered in 2000, which illustrate work in the fields. The **crypt★** – access is on the left of the chancel – dates from the late 10C. Its height (3.50m) is exceptional. The 12C fresco decorating the vaulting of the south chapel is the best preserved of all.

The **Musée bourguignon**, housed within the former precinct of the abbey, recreates scenes from rural daily life in the past, with the help of wax figures dressed in regional costume. *End of Mar to beginning of Nov, daily except Mon, 10am-1pm, 2-5pm. 2.30€. ☏ 03 85 51 29 68.*

You can buy local wines at the **Cave des Vignerons de Mancey** *(see Shopping Guide).*

Leave Tournus SW along D 14. Driving through a dale, you will come to the village of **Ozenay**, *with its small 13C castle and rustic 12C church. Beyond Ozenay, the road runs over the Brancion pass on its way to Brancion.*

Brancion★

Cars are not allowed in town. Use the parking area provided outside the walls.

The old feudal market town of Brancion is perched on a spur overlooking two deep ravines, forming one of the strikingly picturesque settings of the region.

Once through the portcullised gateway set in the 14C ramparts, visitors discover the imposing ruins of the fortress, narrow streets lined with medieval houses, the 15C covered market and the church standing proudly at the end of the spur.

The feudal castle dates back to the early 10C. Remodelled in the 14C by Philip the Bold, it was ruined by the Catholic League in 1594. The keep and a few rooms have been restored. From the top platform (87 steps, viewing table), there is a fine **view★** of the village and its hilly surroundings. *Mid-Mar to mid-Nov, 9am-7pm. 3.50€. ☏ 03 85 51 11 41. www.brancion.fr*

The **Église St-Pierre** is a squat 12C church built in the Cistercian Romanesque style, surmounted by a square bell tower. Inside there are 14C frescoes and many tombstones. The church terrace affords a panoramic view of the valley.

Leave Brancion towards Tournus then turn right on D 161.

Cruzille

This wine-growing village, which produces red and white Mâcon-Cruzille wines (**Mâcon-Villages** AOC), boasts an unusual wash house looking like an antique temple. The **Musée de l'Outillage artisanal rural et bourguignon** contains an amazing collection of several thousand old implements used by 32 different trades. It is housed in an estate pioneering organic wine growing. *Domaine des Vignes du Maynes, ☏ 03 85 33 20 15, www.vignes-du-maynes.com*

Continue on D 161 to Bissy-la-Mâconnaise and turn left on D 82.

Lugny

Nestling amid green scenery along the "Mâconnais Wine Road", Lugny produces an excellent white wine. The **Cave de Lugny** is one of the largest wine cooperatives in France *(see Shopping Guide).*

Return to Bissy then head south.

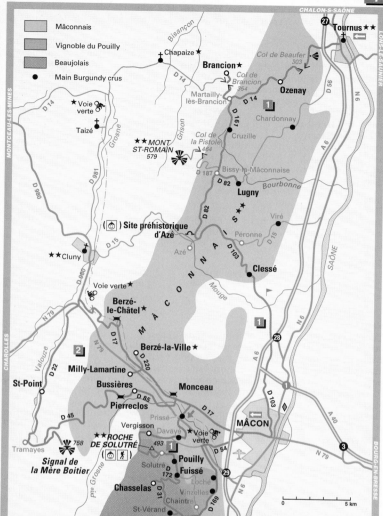

Azé

Azé produces mostly light white wines, such as those on sale at the **Domaine de la Garenne** *(see Shopping Guide)*.

However, Azé is known mainly for its **prehistoric site**. The **museum** displays numerous items found during the course of the excavations. An arboretum precedes the entrance to the **caves**. The first of these, 208m long, served as a refuge for cave bears (300 000-year-old bones), prehistoric men, Gallo-Romans etc. An underground river, which can be followed over a distance of 800m, flows through another cave. *Apr-Sep, guided tours (1hr 30min), 10am-12pm, 2-7pm; Oct, Sun, 10am-12pm, 2-7pm. 5.50€ (children: 4€).* ☎ *03 85 33 32 23.*

Leave Azé E along D 15 then turn right on D 103.

Clessé

This wine-growing village has a late 11C **church** with a small yet elegant bell tower and a spire covered with glazed tiles.

Situated in the heart of one of the best white-wine terroirs in the Mâconnais, Clessé forms, together with neighbouring Viré, the **Viré-Clessé** Appellation which offers excellent value for money. You will be amazed at the quality of the wines produced by the **Domaine de la Bongran** *(see Shopping Guide).*

Continue S along D 103 to Mâcon.

Mâcon

Spread between the Saône and the Mâconnais hillsides planted with vines, the town looks almost southern with its roofs covered with round tiles. Every year in May, Mâcon hosts one of the most important French wine competitions (Concours des vins de France). The **Maison des vins** is a good place to buy wine and a reliable source of information about local wines, in particular the **Mâcon** AOC *(see Shopping Guide).*

Housed in a former 17C convent, the **Musée des Ursulines★** contains sections on archaeology, regional ethnography, painting and ceramics. A prehistory section displays finds from the excavations at Solutré and other regional sites. The first floor is devoted to local crafts and traditions. The second floor exhibits 17C and 18C furniture, ceramics and paintings. *10am-12pm, 2-6pm, Sun and public hols, 2-6pm. Closed Mon, 1 Jan, 1 May, 14 Jul, 1 Nov, 25 Dec. 2.50€.* ☏ *03 85 39 90 38.*

Inside the **Hôtel-Dieu**, the Louis XV **dispensary★** has retained a fine collection of glazed earthenware. In addition to the wood panelling, the woodwork of the windows, blending perfectly with the general decor, is remarkable. Note the frescoes in the chapel. ﴾ *Jun-Sep, daily except Mon, 2-6pm; Oct-May, apply to the Musée des Ursulines. Closed 14 Jul. 1.60€.* ☏ *03 85 39 90 38.*

Leave Mâcon W along D 17 then turn left towards Prissé.

Prissé

This village produces Mâcon-Prissé white wine (Mâcon-Villages AOC). The **Groupement des producteurs de Prissé-Soligny-Verzé** is one of the most important cooperatives in the region *(see the Shopping Guide).*

From Prissé, head S along D 209 which passes under N 79.

Davayé

This pleasant wine-growing village boasts a 12C Romanesque church and two 17C castles. Many wine growers from all over the region attended its wine-growing school.

D 177 runs W to Vergisson.

Vergisson

Tucked between the rocks of Solutré and Vergisson, this village, with its typical ochre-coloured stone houses, is included in the Pouilly-Fuissé Appellation. The **Barraud estate** is worth a visit *(see Shopping Guide).*

Just like Solutré, it is a prehistoric site where remains of Neanderthal men have been excavated. A 3m-high menhir towers above the vines. ⚑ A **footpath**, to the right along the road to Pierreclos, leads to the summit of the rock of Vergisson.

Donkey rides along the paths running through the vineyards, at the foot of the rock of Vergisson, are organised by **Ânes et Sentiers**. *Roger Lassarat, 71960 Vergisson,* ☏ *03 85 35 84 28.*

Drive W to Solutré.

Roche de Solutré★★

This true emblem of southern Mâconnais, on the borders of Beaujolais and in the heart of the Pouilly-Fuissé vineyards, can be seen from miles away between Bourg-en-Bresse and Mâcon. The superb limestone escarpment, with its slender outline and sphinx's profile, is one of the major prehistoric sites in France.

Before reaching the Solutré cemetery, take the second road on the left to the parking area. Follow the yellow markings, 45min on foot there and back. ⚑ A path leads to Crot-du-Charnier (where the museum is situated) then to the top of the rock of Solutré (alt 493m) affording a panoramic view of the Saône Valley, the Bresse, the Jura and, on a clear day, the Alps.

The Roche de Solutré, looking like the "Sphinx with its claws clutching the vines"

The **Musée départemental de Préhistoire**, buried at the foot of the rock, is devoted to the prehistoric archaeology of southern Mâconnais, horses and hunting in the Solutré area during the Upper Palaeolithic Age and Solutrean man in the European context. ♧ *Apr-Sep, 10am-6pm; Feb-Mar and Oct-Nov, daily except Tue, 10am-12pm, 2-5pm. Closed Dec-Jan, 1 May. 3.50€, 1ˢᵗ Sun of the month, no charge.* ☏ *03 85 35 85 24.*

Pouilly

This hamlet gives its name to various white Crus of the Mâconnais region: Pouilly-Fuissé, Pouilly-Loché, Pouilly-Vinzelles.

Beyond the village, the vineyards spread over the gentle curves of the hillsides. **Fuissé** *(1.5km S of Pouilly)* shares with Pouilly the renown of **Pouilly-Fuissé**, the greatest white wine produced in the Mâconnais, although its quality varies a lot from one estate to the next. The **Château de Fuissé** is one of the reliable producers *(see Shopping Guide)*.

From Fuissé, drive W along D 172.

Chasselas

This village, dominated by an outcrop of grey rock showing through the heath, is situated on the borders of Beaujolais. The local vineyards produce well-known dessert grapes.

Leave Chasselas SE along D 31.

Saint-Vérand

Nobody really knows why St-Vérand lost its "d" on becoming the **St-Véran** AOC, producing lively, dry white wines such as can be bought at the **Domaine de l'Ermite de St-Véran** *(see Shopping Guide)*. The hilltop village looks picturesque with its Romanesque church and its large wine growers' houses.

Drive east to Vinzelles via Chânes along D 169.

Vinzelles

The main point of interest in this village on the outskirts of Mâcon is its **Cave des Grands Crus Blancs** bringing together wine growers from Vinzelles and Loché; The **Domaine de la Soufrandière** is also worth a visit *(see Shopping Guide)*.

Return to Mâcon via N 6.

Legendary Abbeys

Since Burgundy is one of the birthplaces of monasticism, you might think it appropriate to visit a number of legendary abbeys.

Ancienne abbaye de Cluny★★

26km NW of Mâcon along D 17, then N 79 and D 980. May-Aug, 9.30am-6.30pm; Sep-Apr, 9.30am-12pm, 1.30-5pm. Closed 1 Jan, 1 May, 1 and 11 Nov, 25 Dec. 6.10€, ticket combined with the Musée d'Art et d'Archéologie (children: no charge). ☏ *03 85 59 15 93 or 03 85 59 82 04.*

The name of Cluny evokes the monastic order which exercised an immense influence on Western Christendom during the Middle Ages. For 200 years, the Benedictine abbey, founded in 910 by Guillaume of Aquitaine, was tremendously prosperous, as testified by the huge abbey church completed under Peter the Venerable, abbot from 1122 to 1156.

However, the monks' luxurious way of life was strongly condemned by St Bernard. The foundation of the austere Cistercian order and the Hundred Years War followed by the Wars of Religion progressively reduced the influence of the abbey which was finally closed in 1790. In 1793, the local authorities ordered the tombs to be demolished and sold as building material. From then until the Restoration, the abbey was turned into a quarry and its stones used for various buildings throughout the region. All that was left standing in 1823 was what we see today, including the ruins of the Église St-Pierre-et-St-Paul. The church comprised a narthex, five naves, two transepts, five belfries, two towers, 301 windows; it was furnished with 225 stalls and the painted vaulting of the apse rested on a marble colonnade.

Housed in the former abbey palace, an elegant 15C residence, the **Musée d'Art et d'Archéologie★** contains the remains of the abbey found during excavations. There are models in the entrance hall and, upstairs, an audio-visual reconstruction *(16min)* of Cluny III by means of computer-generated images giving a realistic idea of the size of the abbey church.

Shopping Guide

INFORMATION

Bureau interprofessionnel des vins de Bourgogne (BIVB) – *12 bd Bretonnière - BP 150 - 21024 Beaune Cedex -* ☎ *03 80 25 04 80 - www.bivb.com* The BIVB provides extensive information and publishes several brochures about wines, including an *Annuaire des caves de Bourgogne* listing the localities and the names of the various estates, cooperatives and merchant-producers.

USEFUL TIP

"From vineyards to cellars" – Over 250 wine-growing estates, producers, merchants and cooperatives signed the Charter entitled "De vignes en caves", guaranteeing a quality welcome in the vineyards of Burgundy.
A sign at the entrance to their property identifies them and a free guide available from various tourist organisations and wine centres gives their location.

OVERVIEW

CHARACTERISTICS

Burgundy wines are referred to by the name of their appellation. This includes the name of the village appellation, of the Cru, the locality, the vineyard and, of course the name of the wine grower. Crémants-de-Bourgogne wines have no Cru or village name.

Auxerrois and Tonnerrois – White wines are light and tangy with aromas of flower and honey. Red wines are not very tannic, relatively clear, with fine red-berry flavours. Irancy wines are more structured and age well.

Chablis – These white wines are floral when young; the best of them acquire aromas of honey, roasts and dry fruit when very old.

Côte-de-nuits – These red wines are famous for being both robust and subtle. Their quality and characteristics vary considerably according to the village appellations, the Crus and the vineyards. White wines are fat with a lingering flavour.

Côte-de-beaune – Great white wines, round and generous, becoming very rich with age. Red wines are generally full-bodied and always very aromatic.

Côte chalonnaise – Fairly light red and white wines, best drunk within three to four years.

Mâconnais – White wines made from Chardonnay, fairly unpretentious (except for the more complex Pouilly-Fuissé), for drinking young. The same thing applies to the reds made from Gamay. Those made from Pinot Noir are entitled to the Burgundy Appellation.

STORAGE

White wines – They age well owing to their acid content. Most can easily be kept for 3 to 5 years and the richest even much longer.

Red wines – The best bottles can be kept for 20 years and more. Maturing red and white wines in casks is common practice in Burgundy. Most of the time casks are made of French oak: this gives young wines vanilla or roast aromas, which fade with ageing.

PRICE

The price range of Burgundies is very wide.

Regional Bourgognes, Aligotés de Bouzeron, Bourgognes Grand Ordinaire and Bourgogne-Passetoutgrain – 3 to 11€.

Bourgognes Hautes-Côtes-de-Nuits, Hautes-Côtes-de-Beaune, ordinary Chablis and Crémants-de-Bourgogne – rarely more than 8€.

Chablis – 5 to 10€; **Chablis Premier Cru**: 8 to 12€, sometimes over 20€; **Chablis Grand Cru**: 20 to 30€.

Côte-de-nuits – 20 to 50€, sometimes more for the most sought-after appellations.

Small village appellations such as Ladoix and Pernand-Vergelesses – less than 15€.

Côte-de-beaune – 11 to 30€ for Beaune and Côte de Beaune wines as well as for Pommard, Volnay and Meursault.

Auxey-Duresses, Saint-Romain, Saint-Aubin, Maranges and Santenay – 8 to 15€.

Chassagne-Montrachet and Puligny-Montrachet white wines – 15 to 30€.

Grands Crus from Montrachet and subsidiary appellations – over 70€.

Rully, Mercurey and Givry wines – around 8€.

Côte chalonnaise and Mâcon – 5 to 8€.

BUYING

WINE MERCHANTS

Les Agapes – *13 r. Preuilly - 89000 Auxerre -* ☎ *03 86 52 15 22.* In this shop named Best independent wine merchant 2003, you will discover many fine wines, in bulk and bottled, as well as spirits and objects for your cellar…

La Cave des Cordeliers – *6 r. de l'Hôtel-Dieu - 21200 Beaune -* ☎ *03 80 25 08 85 – Oct-Mar, daily 10.30am-12pm, 2-6pm; Apr-Sep: daily 9.30am-7pm – closed 25 Dec, 1 Jan.* The former Couvent des Cordeliers in Beaune (1243) houses this cellar which you can visit before tasting a few Grands Crus from Burgundy. The firm stocks 80 different wines, among them some Côte-de-Beaune, Côte-de-Nuits and wines from the Hospices de Beaune vineyards. There is also a choice of regional products.

Marché aux Vins – *2 r. Nicolas-Rolin - 21200 Beaune -* ☎ *03 80 25 08 20 - www.marcheauxvins.com – showroom, mid-Jun to end of Aug, daily 9.30am-7pm; Sep to mid-Jun, 9.30-12pm, 2-6.30pm. Tour of the cellar, mid-Jun to mid-Sep, daily 9.30am-5.30pm; Sep to mid-Jun, 9.30-11.30am, 2-5.30pm – closed 25-26 Dec, 1-2 Jan.* This wine market situated opposite the famous Hospices is housed in part of the former Eglise des Cordeliers (13C-14C). The wine-tasting tour (13 Crus from Burgundy) starts with the cellars and moves on to the chapels. Visit of the old-vintage storehouse on request. The tour ends in the shop.

Le Cellier de l'Abbaye – *13 r. Municipale - 71250 Cluny - ☎ 03 85 59 04 00 - www. cellier-abbaye.com – Tue-Sat, 9.30am-12.30pm, 2.30-7.30pm, Sun 10am-12.30pm. Open Mon 14 Jul to 15 Aug – closed Feb.* It is better to go into this historic and prestigious cellar through the entrance on rue du 11-Août-1944. A superb stone-vaulted corridor leads to the shop furnished with wooden racks, shelves loaded with bottles and a few casks. Over 300 local wines are sold here at prices set by the estates, but you will also find whiskies, brandies and liqueurs.

Nicot Yves – *48 r. Jean-Jacques-Rousseau - 21000 Dijon - ☎ 03 80 73 29 88 - nicotvins@infonie.fr – Mon-Fri, 8am-12.30pm, 3-8pm, Sat 8am-8pm, Sun 8am-12.30pm.* Mr Nicot has a real passion for wine. That is the reason why he founded this business in 1985. Four years later, he opened a wine school where he gives courses in wine tasting and oenology. Fine selection of Burgundies.

Les Caves de Saint-Valérien – *58 r. du Dr-Privey - 71700 Tournus - ☎ 03 85 51 78 74 - Tue-Sat, 9am-12.30pm, 2.30-7.30pm, Sun 9am-12.30pm; Easter to end of Sep, daily 9am-12.30pm, 2.30-7.30pm.* In his cellar, where he stocks over 1 000 different wines, Mr Bayet, who loves his terroir and specialises in Grands Crus from Burgundy, gives pride of place to wines from the Mâconnais such as Pouilly-Fuissé, Saint-Véran or Mâcon-Solutré, yet he also favours Côte chalonnaise and Côte de Beaune wines.

COOPERATIVES AND WINE CENTRES

Cave des Vignerons de Buxy – *Les Vignes-de-la-Croix - 71390 Buxy - ☎ 03 85 92 03 03 – 9am-12pm, 2-6pm – by appointment.* This cooperative makes Bourgogne-Côte-chalonnaise, Montagny and Mercurey wines.

La Chablisienne – *8 bd Pasteur - 89800 Chablis - ☎ 03 86 42 89 89 - www. chablisienne.com – 9am-12pm, 2-6pm – closed 1 Jan, 25 Dec.* This cooperative has around 300 wine growers as members; they represent a quarter of the Chablis vineyards and produce the 6 Grands Crus of the appellation: Bougros, Blanchot, Les Clos, Les Preuses, Valmur, Vaudésir and Grenouille. The wine-tasting room is the ideal place to discover the range of Premiers Crus and Petits Chablis.

Maison des vins de la côte chalonnaise – *2 prom. Ste-Marie - 71100 Chalon-sur-Saône - ☎ 03 85 41 64 00 – Mon-Sat, 9am-7pm – closed public hols.* This renowned centre, run by an association of wine growers of the Côte chalonnaise, only sells regional wines at prices set by the estates. Givry, Montagny, Rully or Mercurey, have all been selected through blind tasting…This in itself tells you that you're dealing with real professionals. Glasses and decanters for sale.

Cave coopérative de Lugny – *R. des Charmes - 71260 Lugny - ☎ 03 85 33 22 85 - www.cave-lugny.com – Mon-Sat, 8.30am-12.30pm, 1.30-7pm (Oct-Mar, 6pm) – closed Sun and public hols.* This cooperative produces all the Mâconnais Crus, which can be tasted in the convivial cellar.

Maison des vins – *484 av. de Lattre-de-Tassigny - 71000 Mâcon - ☎ 03 85 22 91 11 - www.maison-des-vins.com – daily 11.30am-6.30pm – closed 1 Jan, 1 May, 25 Dec.* Showroom, bookshop, boutique, wine tastings conducted by professionals…The Maison des vins de Mâcon is really worth a visit. In addition, its restaurant offers some regional specialities (fish in white wine, chicken in cream sauce, coq au vin) served with selected Crus from the Mâconnais.

B. Kaufmann/MICHELIN

Groupement de producteurs de Prissé-Sologny-Verzé – *Les Grandes Vignes - 71960 Prissé - ☎ 03 85 37 88 06 - cave. prisse@wanadoo.fr – 9am-12.30pm, 1.30-6.30pm.* This association of wine growers from Prissé-Sologny-Verzé is the result of the merger of three cooperatives. It includes 500 members and covers 1 000ha of vineyards. It is today the second most important cooperative in Burgundy and holds an ISO 9002 certificate.

Maison du vignoble auxerrois – *14 rte de Champs - 89530 St-Bris-le-Vineux - ☎ 03 86 53 66 76 - maison.du.vignoble. auxerrois@wanadoo.fr – Mon-Tue and Thu-Fri, 9am-12pm, 3-7pm, Sat, 9am-12.30pm, 2.30-7pm, Sun, 2.30-6.30pm – closed Jan-Feb.* Centre run by an association of wine-growing unions of the Grand Auxerrois region. Wine tastings (sometimes thematic) and sale of 25 Crus selected by the wine growers themselves in an attempt to show the best of their know-how. There are also guided tours of the vineyards.

Cave Henry de Vézelay – *89450 St-Pèresous-Vézelay - ☎ 03 86 33 29 62 – Mon-Fri, 8am-12pm, 2-6pm, Sat-Sun, 10am-12.30pm, 2.30-6pm – closed 1 Jan, 25 Dec – BIVD Welcome Charter.* The cooperative has brought together 12 wine growers and 46ha of vineyards producing a good Bourgogne-Vézelay and a Melon-de-Bourgogne.

Cave des Vignerons de Mancey – *N 6 - 71700 Tournus - ☎ 03 85 51 00 83 - bdvv@wanadoo.fr – daily 8am-12pm, 2-6pm.* This cooperative is the showroom of an association of 80 wine growers tending 140ha of vineyards. Their wines are varied but never fail in quality. Among the better ones are Les Essentielles, a fine range including a Mâcon-Villages, a Mâcon-Mancey and a Bourgogne-Pinot Noir (all three remarkable), Crémants and Aligotés.

Cave des Grands Crus Blancs – *Rte des Allemands - 71680 Vinzelles - ☎ 03 85 27 05 70.* This popular cooperative offers the whole range of white wines produced in the Mâconnais at very reasonable prices.

ESTATES

SCE Piguet-Girardin – *R. du Meix - 21190 Auxey-Duresses - ☎ 03 80 21 60 26.* The vineyards cover 12ha, spread across seven villages of the Côte de Beaune. Harvesting by hand is followed by traditional vinification. Lightly crushed, the Pinot Noir grapes are left to macerate in tanks for ten days. Red wines are then matured in new casks and in vats. Chardonnay and Aligoté grapes pass into a pneumatic press before undergoing vinification in barrels and in tanks at low temperatures.

Domaine Vincent Prunier – *Rte de Beaune - 21190 Auxey-Duresses - ☎ 03 80 21 27 77 – Mon-Sat, 8am-12pm, 1.30-6.30pm, Sun, 8-11am – by appointment.* Created in 1988, the estate now comprises 12ha of vineyards located on the prestigious hillsides of Auxey-Duresses, Meursault, Puligny and Chassagne. After vinification, the vintage is traditionally matured in oak casks.

Domaine de la Garenne – *Rte de Péronne - 71260 Azé - ☎ 04 74 55 06 08.* Marcel Périnet – voted Best Sommelier of France in 1978 – and Michel Renoud-Grappin, both former executives of the Georges-Blanc firm, combined their passion for wine growing in 1987. Exclusively planted with Chardonnay, their 4.3ha vineyard is tended by traditional methods. Burgundy wine spends nine months in casks whereas Mâcon wine is matured in tanks and left on the lees for nine months.

Domaine Chanzy – *1 r. de la Fontaine - 71150 Bouzeron - ☎ 03 85 87 23 69 - Daniel.Chanzy@wanadoo.fr – Mon-Fri, 8am-12pm, 2-6pm, Sat-Sun, by appointment.* This long-neglected estate was taken over by Catherine and Daniel Bouzeron in 1974 and extended five years later. Today, it is managed according to the most up-to-date methods. The vineyard spreads over 40ha, planted with Aligoté, Chardonnay and Pinot Noir varieties. It includes seven appellations in the three Côtes areas: Côte de Beaune, Côte de Nuits and Côte Chalonnaise. Wines are matured in oak casks, a third of them new.

Domaine William Fèvre – *21 av. d'Oberwesel - 89800 Chablis - ☎ 03 86 98 98 98 - france@williamfevre.com - ☎ 03 86 42 12 06 – daily except Wed, by appointment.* The Henriot family has owned the estate since 1998. With its 16ha of Grand Cru land, the vineyard boasts one of the most prestigious ranges of Chablis Grands Crus. Every effort is made to produce quality wines: harvesting by hand, careful sorting of the grapes, maturing in casks and stainless-steel tanks for ten to fifteen months depending on the vintage.

EARL Vincent Dauvissat – *8 r. Émile-Zola - 89800 Chablis - ☎ 03 86 42 11 58.* Robert Dauvissat marketed his 1931 vintage on his own. Today, his grandson Vincent runs the estate covering 11ha, including 3ha of Grand Cru. It has always been the owners' policy to prefer a small production to large yields. Most wines are matured in oak casks.

Château Long-Depaquit – *45 r. Auxerroise - 89800 Chablis - ☎ 03 86 42 11 13 - chateau-longdepaquit@wanadoo.fr – Mon-Sat, 9am-12.30pm, 1.30-6pm – closed 24 Dec to 2 Jan, 1 May, 1 Nov.* This vast wine-growing estate which, until the Revolution, was owned by the Cistercian abbey of Pontigny, produces Chablis AOC Premier and Grand Cru wines, matured in oak casks. The wine made from grapes grown on the plot of La Moutonne is considered to be the "eighth Chablis Grand Cru". Wine-tasting cellar.

Domaines Jean Durup Père et Fils – *4 Grande-Rue - Maligny - 89800 Chablis - ☎ 03 86 47 44 49 - info@durup-chablis.com – Mon-Fri, 9am-12pm, 2-6pm.* Jean Durup, a Paris lawyer, who comes from a long line of wine growers from Chablis, heads one of the two wine growers' unions; his son Jean-Paul ensures continuity in running the estate covering 180ha. Vinification and maturing methods are still traditional. The wines are left in stainless-steel tanks for a minimum of five to six months depending on the appellation.

S. Sauvignier/MICHELIN

Domaine Amiot-Servelle – *21220 Chambolle-Musigny - ☎ 03 80 62 80 39 - domaine@amiot-servelle.com – Mon-Sat, by appointment.* Intent on providing quality, Christian Amiot manages his vineyard by ecologically responsible methods. Yields are limited and harvesting is done by hand with careful sorting of the grapes. Traditional vinification (temperature control, remontage, pigeage) takes place in open wooden vats. The wines are then matured in oak casks.

Domaine Tollot-Beaut et Fils – *R. Alexandre-Tollot - 21200 Chorey-lès-Beaune - ☎ 03 80 22 16 54 - tollot. beaut@wanadoo.fr – Mon-Fri, 9am-12pm, 2-6pm, by appointment.* This vast family estate has loyal customers, particularly in the catering business. The vineyards cover

4

24ha spread over the municipalities of Beaune, Savigny-lès-Beaune, Aloxe-Corton and Chorey-lès-Beaune. The estate produces several Grands Crus under the Corton-Bressandes, Corton-Charlemagne and Corton appellations as well as some Premiers Crus: Aloxe-Corton Les Vercots and Les Fournières; Beaune Grèves and Clos du Roi; Savigny Les Lavières and Champ Chevrey.

Domaine de la Bongran – 71260 Clessé - ☎ 03 85 36 94 03 - contact@bongran. com. Jean Thévenet believes in methods that respect nature: weeding by machine instead of chemicals, harvesting by hand, slow fermentation without adding yeasts etc. His Mâcon-Villages wine is thus made according to the true ancestral tradition of Burgundy.

Domaine de l'abbaye du Petit Quincy – R. du Clos-de-Quincy - 89700 Épineuil - ☎ 03 86 55 32 51 – daily, 10am-12.30pm, 2.30-6pm – closed Sun from Jan to Mar. In this 13C building owned by the monks of the Cistercian abbey of Quincy, Dominique Gruhier produces quality wines: Bourgogne Épineuil made with grapes from a recently recreated vineyard, Chablis and Crémant-de-Bourgogne. Ask someone to show you the interesting wine press.

Château de Fuissé – 71960 Fuissé - ☎ 03 85 35 61 44 or 03 85 27 05 90 - www.chateau-fuisse.com – Mon-Fri, 8.30-12pm, 1.30-5.30pm (Fri 4.30pm), Sat-Sun and public hols by prior appointment – closed 1 week in Aug, 1 week at Christmas, Sat-Sun. Elegant building flanked by a 15C tower standing opposite two bottle-shaped yew trees, in the middle of a 30ha estate. Visit of the cellar and opportunity to taste the Pouilly-Fuissé originating from renowned terroirs, some of which are the exclusive property of the estate (Le Clos, Les Combettes, Les Brûlés).

Domaine Philippe Naddef – 30 rte des Grands-Crus - 21220 Fixin - ☎ 03 80 51 45 99 - domaine.phil.naddef@wanadoo. fr – Mon-Sat, 9am-12pm, 2-7pm – by appointment. In 1983, Philippe Naddef took over 2.5ha of Gevrey-Chambertin, forming part of the family estate originally created by his grandfather. Since then, the estate has spread to the Fixin and Marsannay terroirs to cover 5ha, 4ha of Pinot Noir and the rest of Chardonnay. He manages to produce 11 wines on such a small area, including two Gevrey-Chambertin Premiers Crus, Les Cazetiers and Les Champeaux, and a Mazis-Chambertin Grand Cru. In keeping with tradition, the wines are matured in oak casks stored in a 17C cellar. The wood comes from the finest French forests.

Domaine Trapet Père et Fils – 53 rte de Beaune - 21220 Gevrey-Chambertin - ☎ 03 80 34 30 40 - message@domainetrapet.com – Mon-Fri, 9-11am, 2-5pm – by appointment. The vineyard extends over 12ha: Chambertin, Chapelle-Chambertin and Latricières-Chambertin Grands Crus, and two Gevrey Premiers Crus, Clos-Prieur and Petite-Chapelle. On this estate having used bio-dynamic methods since 1998, harvesting is done by hand. For these wine growers who value traditional wine growing, it is very important to respect the terroir. Red wines are matured for up to twenty months in oak casks.

Domaine Guillemette et Xavier Besson – 9 r. des Bois-Chevaux - 71640 Givry - ☎ 03 85 44 42 44. Family-owned since 1938, Guillemette and Xavier Besson's vineyards cover some 7ha planted with Pinot Noir and Chardonnay, including several plots of Givry Premier Cru (Les Grands Prétans, Le Petit Prétan) and of Beaune Premier Cru (Champs Pimont). Harvesting is done by hand and vinification is traditional with full de-stalking, temperature control, etc. The wines are then left to mature in oak casks.

Domaine Anita, Jean-Pierre et Stéphanie Colinot – 1 r. des Chariats - 89290 Irancy - ☎ 03 86 42 33 25 – Mon-Sat, 8.30am-6.30pm, Sun 9.30am-12pm. Jean-Pierre Colinot, his wife and his daughter make their wines according to ancestral methods used in Burgundy. They make six vintages of Irancy wine: Palotte, Côte du Moutier, Les Mazelots, Les Cailles, Les Bessys and Vieilles Vignes. Wine tasting and tour of the 17C cellars.

Domaine Edmond Cornu et Fils – Le Meix Gobillon - r. du Bief - 21550 Ladoix-Serrigny - ☎ 03 80 26 40 79 – Mon-Sat, 9am-12pm, 3-6pm – by appointment. Extending over 14ha spread within a 3km radius, this family-owned estate with its various buildings stands inside a walled perimeter. Harvesting is done by hand. The grapes are then fermented in tanks and matured in casks. The estate produces Aloxe-Corton and Ladoix Premiers Crus, and a Corton Grand Cru.

Domaine Bart – 23 r. Moreau - 21160 Marsannay-la-Côte - ☎ 03 80 51 49 76 – Mon-Fri 8am-12pm, 2-7pm – by appointment. The estate spreads over 20.5ha, including 3.5ha of rented land, as a result of the merger between Jean Bart's estate and part of Joseph Clair-Dau's (Madame Bart's father) estate. Two of their children, Odile and Martin, joined them in 1982 and a company was set up in 1987. Martin is in charge of vinification and maturing while Odile deals with the marketing of the wines. The estate has a wide range of appellations, including the Marsannay AOC in red, white and rosé wines. It also produces a Fixin-Villages and a Fixin Premier Cru, Les Hervelets.

Château de Marsannay – Rte des Grands-Crus - 21160 Marsannay-la-Côte - ☎ 03 80 51 71 11 - château.marsannay@kriter.com – Apr-Oct, daily, 10am-12pm, 2-6.30pm – closed 24 Dec to 17 Jan and Sun Nov-Mar. The Château de Marsannay estate owns a 38ha vineyard. A tour of the old cellar and of the storehouses stocked with casks and bottles (around 300 000) ends with a wine tasting in the shop selling wines produced by the estate. A showroom illustrates the history of the Marsannay tournament (1443).

Domaine Michel Juillot – 59 Grande-Rue - BP 10 - 71640 Mercurey - ☎ 03 85 98 99 89 - infos@domaine-michel-juillot.fr

– daily 9am-7pm – by appointment. Laurent Juillot took over from his father Michel in 2002, after having worked with him for nearly fifteen years. With his wife Carine, he now works 30ha, including 3ha in the Aloxe-Corton Appellation. The vineyard is cultivated by ecologically responsible methods, harvesting is done by hand and the wines are matured in casks: twelve months for the whites, fifteen to eighteen months for the reds.

Château de Meursault *– R. du Moulin-Foulot - 21190 Meursault -* ☎ *03 80 26 22 75 - mitanchey.chateau.meursault@kriter. com – daily 9.30am-12pm, 2.30-6pm.* Bought by André Boisseaux in 1973 from the count of Moucheron, the 60ha estate is now run by his son Jacques with the help of Jean-Claude Mitanchey, the manager. The vineyard is planted with Pinot Noir and Chardonnay. Their constant preoccupation is to limit the yields and maintain the quality of the grapes. Following a careful sorting of the grapes, the black variety is slightly crushed, fermented and transferred into casks. White wines are either fermented in tanks or in casks.

Domaine Louis Remy *– 1 pl. du Monument - 21200 Morey-Saint-Denis -* ☎ *03 80 34 34 08.* Founded in 1821 by the Riembault-Rodier family, the estate was taken over by their descendants, the Remy family. Mrs Louis Remy and her daughter Chantal Remy-Rosier are now running the estate: 3ha planted with Pinot Noir. Harvesting is done by hand, yields are low and vinification is traditional. Before being bottled unfiltered, the wines are matured in oak casks for twenty-two months. The estate produces a Chambolle-Musigny Premier Cru.

Domaine Rapet Père et Fils *– 21420 Pernand-Vergelesses -* ☎ *03 80 21 59 94 – Mon-Sat, by appointment.* This 18ha estate (6ha for the reds, 12ha for the whites) spreads across the municipalities of Pernand-Vergelesses, Aloxe-Corton, Savigny and Beaune. It is run by Roland Rapet and his son Vincent. The vineyard, planted with Pinot Noir and Chardonnay, is cultivated by ecologically responsible methods. Long considered as a white-wine specialist, the estate in fact makes a fine range of red wines as well. The Rapets have always made a point of respecting the terroir and the specificity of the appellations.

Domaine du Clos des Épeneaux *– Pl. de l'Église - 21630 Pommard -* ☎ *03 80 24 70 50 - contact@domaine-des-epeneaux. com.* Limited to 5ha for its exclusive Pommard Premier Cru, Clos des Éperneaux, the estate was extended by the purchase of the Volnay Premier Cru Frémiets, of a plot of red Auxey-Duresses Premier Cru, and of a few acres of Bourgogne-Villages. It has remained a family-owned vineyard covering 7.5ha, and its production is entirely organically grown.

SCEA Louis Carillon et Fils *– 1 impasse Drouhin - 21190 Puligny-Montrachet -* ☎ *03 80 21 30 34.* The Carillon family works a 12ha vineyard planted with Chardonnay for white wines and Pinot Noir for red wines. Harvesting is done by hand and vinification is traditional. Matured in oak casks for a year, the wines spend an additional six months in stainless-steel tanks before being bottled.

Domaine Hubert Lamy *– Le Paradis - 21190 St-Aubin -* ☎ *03 80 21 32 55 – by appointment.* Successive generations of the Lamy family have been wine growers in Saint-Aubin since 1640. The 17ha estate, planted with Pinot Noir for red wines and Chardonnay for white wines, is now run by Olivier Lamy, Hubert's son. He cultivates the vineyard by ecologically responsible methods and harvesting is done by hand. The wines are matured in oak casks and small barrels in modern cellars extended in 2003. The estate produces eight Saint-Aubin Premiers Crus.

Henri Prudhon et Fils *– 32 r. des Perrières - 21190 St-Aubin -* ☎ *03 80 21 36 70 – Mon-Sat, by appointment.* The estate owns around 14ha within the "sacred triangle" formed by Saint-Aubin, Chassagne and Puligny-Montrachet and produces equal quantities of white and red wines. The steep hillsides, consisting of ancient geological strata of limestone and clay, enjoy a splendid aspect with plenty of sunshine; they are planted with noble Burgundy varieties: Chardonnay for white wines and Pinot Noir for red wines.

Domaine Patrick Miolane *– 21190 St-Aubin -* ☎ *03 80 21 31 94 – Mon-Sat, 9am-12pm, 2-6pm, Sun 9am-12pm – by appointment.* Patrick Miolane took over the family estate in 1987. Today it covers 9ha spread across the villages of Saint-Aubin, Puligny-Montrachet and Chassagne-Montrachet. Chardonnay and Pinot Noir grape varieties, planted in clayey limestone soil, face south-east. The Chardonnay vines are 15 years old and the Pinot Noir vines are 25 years old. The wines are matured in oak casks.

Domaine Alain Gras *– 21190 St-Romain-le-Haut -* ☎ *03 80 21 27 83.* Since the 1997 vintage, Alain Gras has been working nearly 12ha of vines. He loves his work, which he calls "meticulous and classical", and he uses traditional methods: harvesting done by hand, limited yields, pneumatic pressing, temperature control.

Domaine de l'Ermite de St-Véran *– Les Truges, rte de Pruzilly - 71570 St-Vérand -* ☎ *03 85 36 51 09.* This wine-growing estate, created in 1978, spreads over 12ha. White grape varieties are planted in clayey limestone soil and red varieties in sandy soil mixed with silica and granite. Traditional growing methods are used and harvesting is done by hand. The wines are then made in epoxy-resin vats, enamelled vats and oak vats. The estate also produces three Beaulolais wines, a Beaujolais-Villages, a Juliénas and a Saint-Amour.

Domaine Françoise et Denis Clair *– 14 r. de la Chapelle - 21590 Santenay -* ☎ *03 80 20 61 96 – daily 8am-12pm, 2-6pm – by appointment.* Having run a family estate for ten years, Françoise and

Denis Clair decided in 1987 to create their own estate over an area of 5ha. Today, the vineyard covers 11ha; 80% of the production is sold to private and loyal customers.

Domaine Anne-Marie et Jean-Marc Vincent – *3 r. Ste-Agathe - 21590 Santenay - ☎ 03 80 20 67 37*. This family-owned estate covers 5ha mostly devoted to the Santenay Premier Cru and Auxey-Duresses-Villages appellations. Wine-growing methods are environment-friendly: ploughing, grassing. The vines are pruned back short and strict disbudding is applied. The wines are matured in oak casks and bottled almost unfiltered.

Simon Bize et Fils – *12 r. Chanoine-Donin - 21420 Savigny-lès-Beaune - ☎ 03 80 21 50 57 - domaine.BIZE@wanadoo.fr – Mon-Fri, 9am-12pm, 3-6pm – by appointment*. The vineyards of this domaine cover 22ha, spread across the villages of Savigny-lès-Beaune, Aloxe-Corton and Pernand-Vergelesses. The estate also owns a plot of Latricières-Chambertin Grand Cru. Anxious to respect Burgundian traditions, Patrick Bize leaves his wines to mature in oak casks for a minimum of one year.

Domaine Barraud – *Le Bourg - 71960 Vergisson - ☎ 03 85 35 84 25 – Mon-Fri, 9am-12pm, 2-6pm – by appointment*. This family estate, extending over 7ha of clayey limestone soil, offers a wide range of Crus, the finest of them being the Pouilly-Fuissé Les Crays Vieilles Vignes.

Domaine Marc Meneau – *R. du Moulin-à-Vent - 89450 Vézelay - ☎ 03 86 33 39 11 - by appointment*. The 16ha of vines planted by the famous chef at the foot of the basilica produce an excellent Bourgogne-Vézelay made from Chardonnay grapes. If you feel like treating yourself, his restaurant L'Espérance (which is also a hotel), awarded two Michelin stars, will welcome you in St-Père-sous-Vézelay.

Domaine de la Soufrandière – Bret Brothers – *La Soufrandière - 71680 Vinzelles - ☎ 03 85 35 67 72 - lasoufra ndiere@libertysurf.fr* In 1947, Jules Bret, a professor of medicine, bought 1ha of Pouilly-Vinzelles Les Quarts AOC vines. After extending the vineyard, Jules left it in the care of his son in 1969. In 1998, La Soufrandière pulled out of the cooperative and welcomed Jean-Guillaume and Jean-Philippe, two of Jules's three grandchildren. Today, the vineyard covers 4.5ha planted with Chardonnay. Wine growing is done both by modern and traditional methods: the land is worked by machines, yields are limited, bio-dynamic methods are tested, harvesting is done by hand using small crates. Since 2001, grapes grown at La Soufrandière have been sold to Bret Brothers which markets Pouilly-Vinzelles, Pouilly-Vinzelles Les Longeays and Les Quarts.

Domaine de Montille – *R. du Pied-de-la-Vallée - 21190 Volnay - ☎ 03 80 21 62 67 – by appointment*. The vineyard of the estate extends over 8ha across the villages of Volnay, Pommard and Puligny-Montrachet. Organic wine growing and harvesting by hand: the soil and the vines are worked by traditional methods. The grapes are fermented in wooden vats, with a minimum of interference and maturing takes place in oak casks.

Domaine Christian Clerget – *21640 Vougeot - ☎ 03 80 62 87 37*. This 6ha estate produces a wide range of Grands Crus and Premiers Crus. Harvesting, pruning and disbudding are done by hand. Vinification takes place in enamelled tanks and in concrete tanks, inside the cellar built in 1999. The wines are then matured in oak casks for eighteen months. A laboratory has been installed in the estate, where ecologically responsible wine-growing methods are being developed.

A. Cassaigne / MICHELIN

WINE FESTIVALS

In Burgundy, the feast of St Vincent is celebrated in a different village every year. It takes place during the weekend nearest to 22 January. On this occasion, wine brotherhoods parade with pomp and ceremony on their way to the church where the saint's blessing is sought for the future harvest. The village then welcomes wine growers and tourists to extensive libations; becoming more and more popular and accompanied by varied entertainment. A contribution of around 6€ is required to take part in the tasting.

Beaune, Meursault, Clos de Vougeot – "Les Trois Glorieuses": auction sale of wines from the Hospices de Beaune vineyards, 3rd weekend in Nov.

Chablis – Wine festival, 4th weekend in Nov.

Nuits-St-Georges – Sale of wines from the Hospices de Nuits-St-Georges estate, last weekend in Mar. Fête du vin bourru (Festival of rough wine), last weekend Oct.

Throughout the Burgundy vineyards – Music festival of the Grands Crus of Burgundy, Jul-Sep, in various wine-growing villages.

St-Bris-le-Vineux – Fête des peintres de vignes en caves (Festival of painting from vineyards to cellars), 3rd weekend in Jul. Wine festival in the Auxerrois, the weekend before 11 Nov.

Abbaye de Pontigny★

17km NE of Auxerre via N 77.

Pontigny abbey, founded in 1114, has preserved its huge church intact, thus bearing witness to the Cistercian spiritual and artistic influence. The abbey buildings are occupied by an important "professional retraining centre".

The **church★**, of impressive proportions (108m long inside – 117m including the porch – and 52m wide at the transept) and almost as large as Notre-Dame Cathedral in Paris, is the largest Cistercian church in France. It is quite unadorned both outside and inside, in conformity with the Cistercian rule. The late-12C chancel has 11 radiating chapels. At the end of the chancel, an 18C shrine contains the relics of St Edmund. The imposing **stalls★**, the transept railing and the organ case date from the end of the 17C. The elaborately decorated organ loft, the chancel parclose and the altar date from the end of the 18C, when there were very few monks left.

Abbaye de Cîteaux

23km S of Dijon along D 996. Under the great driving force of St Bernard, who joined the community in 1112 three years before becoming abbot of Clairvaux, this off-shoot of Cluny spread its influence throughout the world.

There is very little left of this important centre of Western culture: all that remains are the ruins of the former library, with its facing of enamelled bricks, dating from the 15C. There is also a handsome 18C building, at present inhabited by the monks who make the excellent Cîteaux cheese, a perfect companion for the regional wines. ☎ *03 80 61 35 34, monastere@citeaux-abbaye.com Tue-Sat, Summer, 10am-12pm, 2-7pm, winter, 10am-12pm, 3-5pm; Sun, 11.45am-12.30pm, 2-6.30pm.*

Gourmet Delights

"On the Burgundy truffle and wine trail" (Yonne)

The Loisirs-Accueil service of the Yonne *département* offers you a wide choice of themed courses to enjoy what you like, without having to organise anything. From mid-September to mid-December, Saturday mornings are devoted to Burgundy truffles (lecture, demonstration, tasting) with Jean-Luc Barnabet, the chef of a starred restaurant in Auxerre, and a truffle producer.

Service Loisirs-Accueil Yonne, 1-2 quai de la République, 89000 Auxerre, ☎ *03 86 72 92 10, www.tourisme-yonne.com*

Visit Bourgogne (Saône-et-Loire)

18km W of Chalon-sur-Saône along D 978. M Carpentier, r. Ouches, 71510 Charrecey, ☎ *03 85 45 38 97, fax 03 85 45 38 98.* Cookery courses in the Beaune vineyards (half a day), bike tours (7 nights), themed tours.

The ABC of haute cuisine (Yonne)

Hôtel La Côte St-Jacques, 14 fbg de Paris, BP 197, 89304 Joigny Cedex, ☎ *03 86 62 09 70, www.cotesaintjacques.com* Jean-Michel Lorain, from La Côte Saint-Jacques, shares his gastronomic experience and introduces his guests to contemporary cuisine. Apply for details about the package, the programme and the calendar.

The Yonne Valley train

Av. de la Gare, 89460 Bazarnes, ☎ *03 86 42 25 51 or answerphone 03 86 94 64 14. End of Jun to end of Aug (1hr), information and reservations at Cravant Station. 7.62€ (children: 4.57€).* Discover the region's cultural and gastronomic heritage aboard the Auxerre-Avallon rail car.

Water Adventures

Canoë-kayak down the Cure

Club Canoë-kayak – *Gérard Valdiviesso, r. de la Guinguette, 89460 Cravant,* ☎ *03 86 42 20 31. Introduction: Sat, 2-5pm.* The club hires the equipment and organises the transport for a day trip (or longer) down the magnificent Cure Valley, from the Malassis dam to the Sermizelles dam; also down the Yonne Valley.

Ab Loisirs – *R. du Camping, 89450 St-Père-sous-Vézelay,* ☎ *03 86 33 38 38, www. abloisirs.com. 9.30am-6.30pm. Closed 25 Dec and 1 Jan.* This leisure park offers a trip down the Cure from Malassis to Sermizelles (4hr, 18km), an adventure trail with swinging footbridges, rope ladders, high-wire slides and Nepal bridges in Pierre-Perthuis *(from 8 years upwards, open Sat-Sun, public and school hols)*, and rafting in the Morvan region *(starting 20km S of St-Père)*.

Along the Canal de Bourgogne

Over 950km of canals, now almost free of commercial transport, are waiting for leisure-cruising enthusiasts. Mostly built from the 17C onwards, these canals, together with navigable rivers (the Yonne, the Saône and the Seille), provide an exceptional network for those who wish to discover the real soul of Burgundy, become familiar with its landscapes, experience the pace of country life, enjoy fishing and bike trips and meet the locals.

Hiring a house-boat with a capacity for 4 to 12 people enables visitors to get a different perspective of the sites encountered along the canals. Several formulas are available: for a day, a weekend or a week. Rates vary according to the period, the size and degree of comfort of the boat. No licence is required (the control lever only moves to two positions), but the helmsman gets a theoretical and practical lesson before the start of the cruise. To pilot such a boat, all one needs to do is to observe the speed limits, be careful and heed the advice of the hirer, particularly when passing through locks and mooring. The main starting points are Auxerre, Digoin, Joigny, St-Jean-de-Losne, Tournus.

Centrale de réservation Bateaux de Bourgogne – *1-2 quai de la République, 89000 Auxerre,* ☎ *03 86 72 92 10.* Some 12 hirers and 25 boarding points.

Game fishing in the River Saône

Mâcon Pêche au gros – *4 r. de la Liberté, 71000 Mâcon,* ☎ *03 85 39 07 50.*
This association offers you the opportunity of being introduced to catfish fishing in the Saône. Michel, a fishing guide, explains all you need to know to track down this river giant which can be over 2.50m long. All the necessary fishing tackle and a specially equipped boat are at your disposal. Meals are taken on location. Three-hour introduction or trips lasting one day or more, suitable for everyone.

Keeping Fit

The "Green Trail"

This 44km trail between Givry and Cluny follows the route of a former railway line linking the Mâconnais and Chalonnais regions. Mostly tarmacked, it is reserved for pedestrians, in-line skaters and cyclists; there is a special track for horses between Massily and Cluny. The *Guide de la Voie verte* is available free from the Comité départemental de tourisme. It lists all the stops, the accommodation on offer, the restaurants and the cycle-hire companies. *Kits Voie verte* are also available for bikers: they enable them to follow the green trail one way only and to return to their starting point between Dijon and Mâcon by loading their bike on to a bus or a train. *On sale in SNCF stations, valid for 1 to 6 persons. N°7 bus line between Chalon and Mâcon, 6 buses daily. TER from Dijon, Nuits-Saint-Georges, Beaune, Chagny, Chalon, Tournus, Mâcon, some fifteen trains daily. 7.50€ to 21€.*

Cycling across the vineyards of the Auxerre and Chablis regions

This round trip of about 80km across hilly countryside will take someone with trained muscles one weekend to complete, starting from Auxerre. The route runs through Coulanges-la-Vineuse, Irancy, St-Bris-le-Bineux, Chablis, Ligny-le-Châtel, Pontigny and Appoigny. *Information from the Comité départemental du tourisme de l'Yonne, 1-2 quai de la République, 89000 Auxerre,* ☎ *03 86 72 92 00, www.trouisme-yonne.com*

Auxerre-Vézelay

Every spring, this classic itinerary draws some two to three thousand bikers who cover in a single day all or part of the 60km separating the two cities, along a route lined with vineyards and cherry trees. There is also a night version.
Information on *www.clubalpin.com/yonnenievre*

Champagne

Champagne, a wine that has fascinated and intrigued ever since its creation, has been called the "nectar of gods" and the "wine of kings". Henri IV, impatient with the Spanish ambassador's recitation of his master's lordly titles, interrupted him with the words, "Tell his Majesty the King of Spain, Castille and Aragon that Henri, lord of Ay and Gonesse, is master of the greatest vineyards in the world...". Often imitated but never equalled, this legendary wine, born out of the meeting between the terroir, the know-how of wine-growers and the marketing genius of wine merchants, has become the epitome of French sophistication throughout the world. Given its international reputation, one can perhaps forgive those who have forgotten that the only true Champagne is wine grown and made in the Champagne region. Its champions are quick to remind us that "real" Champagne can only be made from a blend of Chardonnay, Pinot Noir and Pinot Meunier grapes grown on a mixture of Champagne terroirs. The vineyards of Champagne are spread over five French départements, although the vast majority can be found on the hillsides of the Marne and the Aube. These sunny slopes bring strength and aroma to the wine which in turn brings prosperity to the entire region. Despite periods of hardship, France's Champagne vineyards are today more prosperous than ever and a trip to Reims, Épernay and the Aisne and the Marne valleys will provide visitors with an insight into the intricacies of this complex world, quite unlike that of any other wine-growing region. Like the subtle, even secret nuances of the wine itself, the region's art de vivre and the skills of its wine-makers are best discovered at a leisurely pace.

The terroir

Michelin Local Map 306 and 313 – Marne (51), Aisne (02) and Aube (10).
Surface area: a little over 30 000 hectares and an Appellation d'Origine Contrôlée of 32 000 hectares, three-quarters of which lies in the departments of the Marne and the Aube, with a few forays into the Aisne, Seine-et-Marne and Haute-Marne.
Production: some 2.3 million hectolitres yearly.
In the Marne, the vineyards are located mainly on the hillsides around the Montagne de Reims, in the Marne Valley and in the area around Epernay on the Côte des Blancs. The latter comprises an area in its own right in the south of the *département* around Sézanne.
In the Aisne, the vineyards dominate the valley of the Marne from Charly to Dormans.
In the Aube, the wine-growing area stretches from the densely-planted Côte des Bars around Bar-sur-Seine, to the more dispersed area around Bar-sur-Aube, all predominantly on a base of chalky marl. It also includes the sector around Les Riceys to the south.
In the Marne, the soil is mainly chalky and clayey-limestone. The climate is on the border of the oceanic and semi-continental zones. Harsh winters and springs are attenuated by the humidity of dense forests which raises the temperature. The summers and autumns are temperate and very sunny.

The vineyards of the Côte des Blancs in the early morning mist.

C. Sauvignier/MICHELIN

The wines

Champagne has three appellations d'origine contrôlée.

Champagne AOC – Champagne is defined as a sparkling wine made from grapes from the region of Champagne which are pressed and made into wine using the Champagne method, described later in this chapter. Only wines from grapes grown in Champagne appellations are entitled to the name. The different varieties of vines used are Chardonnay, which adds floral, refreshing notes, Pinot Noir, pressed without maceration, which provides the white juice that brings body and substance, and Pinot Meunier, a cousin of the Pinot Noir, used for its full-bodied yet supple notes.

Coteaux-Champenois AOC – These are non-sparkling red and white wines made according to traditional methods. The white wines are made from Chardonnay and the red and rosé wines from Pinot Noir and Pinot Meunier.

Rosé-des-Riceys AOC – The only Champagne AOC village which makes rosé wines from Pinot Noir grapes which are macerated for a very short period.

A sparkle in the eye

"Champagne", wrote Louis XV's mistress, Madame de Pompadour, "is the only wine which leaves a woman beautiful after drinking it. It gives brilliance to the eyes without flushing the cheek." Wines from other countries have attempted for many years to usurp the name, but the Champagne watchdog body (CIVC) finally won a legal battle which forced other producers of sparkling wines to abandon the word "Champagne".

Background

The mysteries behind Champagne making – The first stage consists in hand picking and carefully sorting and selecting the bunches of grapes so that the grapes' black skin does not leave any trace of colour. The grapes are then pressed according to very strict regulations. No more than 4 000kg of grapes may be pressed at one time and the juice collected must not exceed 2 050 litres.

The must, or juice, collected is left to ferment in vats, generally through the winter, before being blended in the spring. If the wine is to become a vintage Champagne, it can only be made from grapes harvested in the same year. The still wine is then drawn into thick glass bottles and selected yeasts and sugar are added. As a result a second fermentation takes place and the sugar is transformed into alcohol or carbonised into gas, which when uncorked, creates foam.

The bubbles take about two months to develop, after which time the bottles are stored in dark cellars for at least fifteen months for non-vintages and three years for vintage wines. At this point, the bottles are placed upside down on racks where they are rotated either manually or automatically, in order to progressively move the deposit that has formed down to the neck of the bottle.

The *dégorgement* process then takes place. The bottles are placed in a refrigerated solution which freezes the deposit and thereby facilitates its expulsion when the cap is removed. The bottle is then topped up with a "liqueur d'expédition", a blend of old wine and a dose of sugar depending on the taste wanted (demi-sec, sec, extra dry, brut, extra brut and brut zero). It is then corked, wired, labelled and ready for shipping.

Different sorts of Champagnes – Champagne is a blend of wines from a variety of vines, terroirs and often years. It is this distinctive combination that enables each brand to develop its own distinctive character and style.

A **blanc de blancs** is a Champagne made only from white Chardonnay grapes.

A **blanc de Noirs** contains only black Pinot Noir and Pinot Meunier grapes.

A **Rosé Champagne** is made by adding a measure of red Coteaux-Champenois before the bottle fermentation stage.

A **vintage Champagne** is a blend of wines from different plots of land and/or different varieties of grapes, all of which are harvested in the same year. Wines of several years which are blended together are sometimes referred to as "brut sans année". The terms "cuvée prestige" or "cuvée spéciale" refer to Champagnes which are often vintage and made from the best wines of the year.

Champagne Wine Routes

The roads around Reims, Epernay, Troyes or Château-Thierry lead the traveller from huge cellars to tiny museums and from opulent Champagne firms to lush hillsides covered in vineyards.

Discover how each variety of vine, Chardonnay, Pinot Noir and Pinot Meunier, is blended together before partaking in the ritual tasting: it would be a crime to refuse!

Directory

WHERE TO EAT

AROUND BAR-SUR-AUBE

⊖⊜ **La Toque Baralbine** – *18 Rue Nationale – 10200 Bar-sur-Aube – ☎ 03 25 27 20 34 – closed 5-25 Jan, Sun evening and Mon - 17/45€.* The chef of the Toque Baralbine bends over backwards to make sure you will fall in love with his restaurant: plush welcoming dining room, round tables, elegant fabrics and regional-inspired decorative style. An attractive setting to taste up-to-date dishes with a delicious local flavour.

⊖⊜ **Le Cellier des Moines** – *Rue du Général-Vouillemont – 10200 Bar-sur-Aube – ☎ 03 25 27 08 01 – closed Tue midday and evenings except for Fri and Sat - 19/28€.* This 12C storeroom was the headquarters of the Baralbin wine-growers during their fight to retain their Champagne AOC status. Over the centuries, the vaulted ceilings have witnessed many events, including the wine-growers' revolt in 1912, as the graffiti shows. Appetising traditional fare served by staff in local costume.

⊖⊜ **Hostellerie de la Chaumière** – *81 Rue Nationale – 10200 Arsonval – ☎ 03 25 27 91 02 – closed 10 Dec to 20 Jan, Sun evening out of season and Mon - 18/50€.* Countless delights await visitors behind the appealing bare stone façade of this hostelry: delightful garden to the rear, pleasant summer terrace, half-timbered dining room with contemporary furnishings, lovingly prepared dishes and rooms in the former stables.

⊖⊜ **Auberge de la Montagne** – *17 Rue Argentolles – 52330 Colombey-les-Deux-Eglises – ☎ 03 25 01 51 69 – closed 17 Jan to 2 Feb, 8-16 Mar, 13-21 Sep, 20-29 Dec, Mon and Tue - 26/52€.* A peaceful inn, just outside the village which rose to fame as the home of Charles de Gaulle. Traditional creative cooking made from fresh market produce, against a décor of bare stone walls and exposed beams. The rooms overlooking the Champagne countryside are perfect for a weekend getaway.

AROUND BAR-SUR-SEINE

⊖ **Le Commerce** – *30 Place de la République – 10110 Bar-sur-Seine – ☎ 03 25 29 86 36 – closed 21-29 Aug, Fri except evenings during Jul-Aug and Sun - 12/33€.* The tiny Aube capital of Champagne houses this deliciously simple inn run by a determined and enthusiastic owner-couple. Seated in the dining room with bare beams and a fireplace, guests are treated to traditional recipes full of regional flavour.

⊖ **Le Magny** – *38 Rue du Général-Leclerc – 10340 Les Riceys – ☎ 03 25 29 38 39 – closed Sep-Mar, Sun evening, Tue evening out of season and Wed, 12/39€.* The restoration of this country inn surrounded by a garden is faultless. A comfortable dining room is the backdrop for tasty traditional dishes and excellent local AOC wines: Rosé-des-Riceys, Coteaux-champenois and Champagne. Quiet rooms. Swimming pool.

IN CHATEAU-THIERRY

⊖⊜ **L'Estoril** – *1 Place des Granges – 02400 Château-Thierry – ☎ 03 23 83 64 16 - 19/36€.* Brightly coloured sponge-painted walls and *azulejos* tiles set the scene for this small restaurant in a little square whose Portuguese inspiration is equally noticeable in the culinary menu. Fish and seafood dishes rub shoulders with Portuguese specialities and traditional fare, to the delight of discerning palates.

⊖⊜ **Auberge Jean de la Fontaine** – *10 rue des Filoirs – ☎ 02400 Château-Thierry – ☎ 03 23 83 63 89 - 25-58€.* All the paintings on wood in the small dining room illustrate the fables of La Fontaine. The chef's impeccable traditional recipes are as appreciated by a steadfast core of regular customers as by passing travellers lucky enough to stop here. To do full justice to the meal, make sure you leave room for some cheese.

AROUND EPERNAY

⊖ **La Cave à Champagne** – *16 Rue Gambetta – 51200 Epernay – ☎ 03 26 55 50 70 – closed Tue evening and Mon - 14.50/28€.* In a neighbourhood rich in restaurants, the Cave à Champagne stands out from the competition thanks to a trump card: its very reasonably priced wine list. This is the perfect opportunity to treat yourself to Champagne throughout the entire meal, served in a dining room decorated with a collection of bottles of this precious nectar.

⊖⊜ **Les Cépages** – *16 Rue de la Fauvette – 51200 Epernay – ☎ 03 26 55 16 93 – closed 26 Feb to 11 Mar, 12-30 Jul, 25-30 Dec, Wed evening, Sun evening and Thu - 17/65€.* As the name of this establishment, formerly a wine institute, suggests, its wine list offers an excellent choice of Champagnes. The meals display a decidedly modern flavour. Exhibitions of works by local artists.

⊖⊜ **Le Théâtre** – *8 place Mendès-France – 51200 Epernay – ☎ 03 26 58 88 19 – 21/40€.* This handsome early 20C building is home to an attractive dining room where efficient staff masterfully maintain a pleasant muted atmosphere. A refreshing up-to-date interpretation of a classical French repertoire.

⊖⊜ **La Table de Kobus** – *3 Rue du Dr-Rousseau – 51200 Epernay – ☎ 03 26 51 53 53 – closed 1-9 Jan, 19-26 Apr, 1-19 Aug, 24-31 Dec, Sun evening, Thu evening and Mon - 24/33€.* Decorated in a turn-of-the-19C style, this bistro provides the ideal setting to break open a bottle of Champagne, even one from your own cellar, at no extra cost! So do as the locals do, and enjoy the appetising bistro cuisine rustled up by a chef whose culinary talents leave nothing to be desired.

Le Caveau – *Rue de la Coopérative – 51480 Curnières – 5km NW of Epernay on the D 301 –* ☎ *03 26 54 83 23 – closed Sun evening, Tue evening and Wed – 16/50€.* As you venture into this establishment you will first pass through a small room decorated on a vine theme, before a long corridor takes you into a magnificent vaulted dining room carved out of the local chalk. Immaculate table layouts. Regional specialities.

Auberge de la Chaussée – *La Chaussée de Damery – 51480 Vauciennes – 6km W of Epernay on the N 3 –* ☎ *03 26 58 40 66 – closed 1 week in Feb, Sun evening and Fri – lunch 10.50€ - 18.50/45€.* Lovers of traditional French cuisine will be enchanted by this well-located inn by the side of the main road. An unaffected setting with black and white floor tiles. Clean simple accommodation.

Le Mesnil – *2 Rue Pasteur – 51190 Le Mesnil-sur-Oger – 16km E of Epernay on the D 3 and D 40 –* ☎ *03 26 57 95 57 –19/64€.* It would be a crime to pass through this delightful wine-growing town without tasting the hospitality of the Jaillant husband and wife team. Claude supervises the kitchen while Yvette is in charge of the dining room. The result is sophisticated classical dishes served with a smile, all to the accompaniment of a fine wine list.

Au Bateau Lavoir – *3 Rue Port-au-Bois – 51480 Damery – 5km W of Epernay on the D 22 and N 13 –* ☎ *03 26 58 40 88 – closed 1 week in Feb, Aug and Mon – lunch 10.60€ – 20/32€.* This pretty flower-decked house is admirably situated on the banks of the Marne in the birthplace of a famous French actress, Adrienne Lecouvreur. Tasty traditional fare served in an attractive modern dining room with huge bay windows.

La Maison du Vigneron – *N 51 – 51160 St-Imoges – 8km N of Epernay on the N 51 –* ☎ *03 26 52 88 00 – closed Sun evening and Wed – 22/48€.* This vast regional-style building is hidden away in the forest between Reims and Epernay. The exterior is a haven of greenery – there's a pleasant summer terrace – and comfort abounds within. On the kitchen side, generous classical dishes perfectly set off by a good selection of local wines to tantalise the taste buds of the most discerning palate.

Auberge St-Vincent – *1 Rue St-Vincent – 51150 Ambonnay – 20km E of Epernay on the D 201, D 1 and D 37 –* ☎ *03 26 57 01 98 – closed Feb holidays, 18 Aug to 1 Sep, Sun evening and Mon – 27/70€.* This smart regional-style inn is located in the heart of the village surrounded by acres of vineyards and forest. A pleasing flower-decked façade leads into a light dining room complete with fireplace and ancient cooking utensils. Tasty traditional fare prepared by a chef who favours local produce. Renovated rooms.

La Table Sourdet – *6 Rue du Dr-Moret – 51700 Dormans – 20km NW of Epernay on the N 3 –* ☎ *03 26 58 20 27 – closed 1-15 Jul and Fri – 33/45€.* La Table Sourdet has been run by the same family for six generations. A plush bourgeois interior decoration provides the backdrop to appetising classical recipes. At lunchtime La Petite Table veranda serves simple meals at low prices.

AROUND REIMS

Le Vergeur – *32-34 Place du Forum – 51100 Reims –* ☎ *03 26 47 56 87 – closed Sun – 12/28€.* This welcoming bistro stands next to the Vergeur Museum, a former mansion now home to a museum devoted to the history of Reims. Its pleasant interior decoration, a combination of zinc and painted wood, is further enhanced by art exhibitions. Classical fare. Pleasant terrace in fine weather.

S. Sauvignier/MICHELIN

Univers – *41 Boulevard Foch – 51100 Reims –* ☎ *03 26 88 68 08 - 15/28€.* The dining room of the Univers Hotel provides an elegant, muted setting, which is perfectly suited to the menu inspired by classical recipes. Excellent value-for-money. The cosy sitting room-bar is ideal for a relaxed after-dinner drink.

Brasserie Le Boulingrin – *48 Rue Mars – 51100 Reims –* ☎ *03 26 40 96 22 – closed Sun - 16/23€.* Home to Le Boulingrin since 1925, this brasserie is a favourite with the town locals who appreciate its Art Deco style and Bacchanalian-inspired frescoes of grape harvests. Tuck into appetising bistro-style dishes or treat yourself to a platter from the well-stocked oyster bar.

Le Jamin – *18 Boulevard Jamin – 51100 Reims –* ☎ *03 26 07 37 30 – 18/27.50€.* Mr Milon, a trained chef, is the enthusiastic owner of this small neighbourhood restaurant. Guests are served faultless traditional dishes in an attractive country-style dining room. The daily suggestions, chalked up on the traditional slate, offer excellent value-for-money.

Vonelly-Gambetta – *13 Rue Gambetta – 51100 Reims –* ☎ *03 26 47 22 00 – 18/45€.* Just a few steps from the magnificent cathedral of Reims, a comfortable 1970s-style dining room and a pleasant summer terrace in the rear await you. Sit down and enjoy the refreshingly up-to-date culinary delights rustled up by Eric Arnaud. Make sure you take a look at the wine list which features a fine selection of Champagnes.

😋😋 **La Table Anna** – *6 Rue Gambetta – 51100 Reims – ☎ 03 26 89 12 12 – lunch 12€ - 19/32€.* Champagne takes pride of place in the window of this establishment next to the Music School. Some of the paintings on the walls inside are the work of the owner, an artist in his spare time. His creative talent can also be appreciated in the delicious traditional dishes made with fresh market produce.

😋😋 **Continental** – *95 Place Drouet-d'Erlon – 51100 Reims – ☎ 03 26 47 01 47 – 20.40/50.50€.* The inhabitants of Reims have long favoured this attractive bourgeois establishment along a pedestrian square in the heart of the city. Faultless, personalised service and equally impeccable traditional cuisine.

😋😋 **Au Chant des Galipes** – *2 Rue Chanzy – 51380 Chanzy – ☎ 03 26 97 91 40 – lunch – 13€ – 20.50/41€.* This wine-grower's house has been converted into an inn with two contemporary-style dining rooms and an appealing courtyard-terrace. The up-to-date menu with a distinctly regional preference is full of delightful surprises, thanks in particular to the subtle use of Champagne, both on the plate and in the glass.

😋😋 **La Vigneraie** – *14 Rue de Thillois – 51100 Reims – ☎ 03 26 88 67 27 – 20.40/50.50€.* Drouet-d'Erlon Square, complete with night-clubs, theatres and cinemas, is the city's liveliest neighbourhood. La Vigneraie, the proud owner of a splendid collection of carafes, lies just off the square. Classic tasty cuisine. Good wine list. Excellent value for money.

😋😋 **Café du Palais** – *14 Place Myron-Herrick – 51100 Reims – ☎ 03 26 47 52 54 – closed Sun, public holidays, 1-15 Aug – 25€.* Founded in 1930, this cheerful café stands next to the law courts. The inhabitants of Reims appreciate its simple unfussy cuisine and dining room decorated with red hangings under the original glass roof. Copious salads, assorted cold meats, menu of the day and homemade pastries. Reasonably priced Champagne by the glass.

😋😋 **Le Millénaire** – *4 Rue Bertin – 51100 Reims – ☎ 03 26 08 25 62 – 25/66€.* Two minutes from Place Royale, this spacious modern dining room is decorated with exhibitions of local art work; private lounges up in the mezzanine. Up-to-date menu oozing with creative inspiration to tantalise the taste buds of gourmets from far and near.

😋😋 **Au Petit Comptoir** – *17 Rue de Mars – 51100 Reims – ☎ 03 26 40 58 58 – 26/39€.* This trendy bistro is greatly in vogue with the locals who adore its unabashed contemporary spirit and the creative culinary talents of Patrice Maillot. The kitchen is in full view of the dining room. The well-stocked wine list boasts 170 names.

AROUND THE LACS DE L'AUBE

😋 **Le Renoir** – *1 Place de la Mairie – 10360 Essoyes – 17km SE of Bar-sur-Seine on the N 71 and D 67 – ☎ 03 25 29 60 42 – closed evenings – lunch 11€ – 15€.* The shaded terrace of this unassuming riverside restaurant is an invitation to sit down and relax. The set menu of the day is as simple as it is reasonably priced. An unfussy relaxed atmosphere reigns in what also doubles as the village café.

S. Sauvignier/MICHELIN

😋 **Le Vieux Logis** – *1 Rue de Piney – 10220 Brevonnes – ☎ 03 25 46 30 17 – logisbrevonnes@wanadoo.fr – closed 1-24 Mar, Sun and Mon out of season – 13-34€.* A family atmosphere reigns throughout this old abode from the country-style furniture and old souvenirs and knick-knacks to the deliciously old-fashioned fabrics. The kitchen is equally traditional in flavour.

😋😋 **Auberge du Lac au Vieux Pressoir** – *5 Rue du 28-Août-1944 – 10140 Mesnil-St-Père – ☎ 03 25 41 27 16 – auberge.lac. p.gublin@wanadoo.fr – closed 12-30 Nov, Sun evenings from Oct to 15 Mar and Mon midday – lunch 20€ - 31/60€.* A delightful half-timbered house on the outskirts of a village in the vicinity of the forêt d'Orient. Regionally flavoured cuisine served in a dining room with bare beams or a flower-decked terrace. Attractive patio-bar under a glass roof. Comfortable rooms.

Where to Stay

AROUND BAR-SUR- AUBE

😋😋 **Le St-Nicolas** – *2 Rue du Général-de-Gaulle – 10200 Bar-sur-Aube – ☎ 03 25 27 08 65 – le.saintnicolas@tiscali.fr – 27rms: 60/65€ - ⬜ 8€.* Three appealing houses whose main wing dates from the 18C and two other wings overlooking the swimming pool, make up this town centre establishment. The rooms, all renovated, have practical painted wooden furnishings. Delightful breakfast area. Sauna available.

AROUND BAR-SUR-SEINE

😋 **Chambre d'hôte Capitainerie de St-Vallier** – *Rue du Pont – 10110 Bourguignons - 3km N of Bar-sur-Seine by the N 71 – ☎ 03 25 29 84 43 – closed 1 Jan to 15 Apr – ⌿ 4rms: 35/54€.* The owner of this former lock keeper's house is a great art lover who enjoys entertaining fellow artists and organises regular art exhibitions and concerts. The personalised rooms overlooking the Seine and the trees and flowers of the well-cared for garden will soon make you forget the nearby road.

☞ **Chambre d'hôte Le Prieuré** – *1 Place de l'Eglise – 10260 Fouchères – 10km NW of Bar-sur-Seine by the N 71 – ☎ 03 25 40 98 09 – ⊅ 5rms: 38/48€*. The 11C towers and Renaissance wings undoubtedly add character to this former priory now a working farm. The loving restoration work cannot be faulted. The quiet spacious rooms are furnished in a regional style and two possess a fireplace. Breakfasts have a distinctly Quebec flavour.

☞ **Chambre d'hôte Ferme de la Gloire Dieu** – *10250 Courteron – 10km E of Riceys on the D 70 and N 71 – ☎ 03 25 38 21 77 – closed 1 Jan to 15 Feb – ⊅ 3rms: 30/36€*. This immense 16C fortified farmhouse is located in a dip of a valley. Attractive well-kept rooms with lovely bare stone walls. The table d'hôte, piled high with home-made terrines, cooked meats and home-raised poultry, will satisfy even the fussiest of palates. Warm welcome and low prices.

☞ **Le Val Moret** – *10110 Magnant – 9km NE of Bar-sur-Seine near the motorway interchange – ☎ 03 25 29 85 12 – contact@le-val-moret.com – ▣ – 42rms: 40/70€ - ☕ 7€ – restaurant 15/45€*. This large modern flower-decked building has a definite motel style. The simple practical rooms are all on the ground floor and are well soundproofed. Good value-for-money. Traditional unpretentious cuisine.

AROUND CHATEAU-THIERRY

☞ **Chambre d'hôte La Grange du Moulin** – *15 Rue du Moulin – 02810 Bussiares – 13km W of Château-Thierry by the N 3 and D 9 – ☎ 03 23 70 92 60 – closed Dec – ⊅ – 4rms: 30/40€ – meals 16€*. This distinctive ivy-covered house offers comfortable, beautifully renovated rooms and an appealing dining room complete with exposed beams and antique furniture. The small garden is delightful in summer.

☞ **Chambre d'hôte M et Mme Leclère** – *1 Rue de Launay – 02330 Connigis – 12km east of Château-Thierry by the N 3 and D 4 – ☎ 03 23 71 90 51 – closed 24 Dec to 1 Jan – 5rms: 34/48€ – meals 15€*. The 16C castle of Connigis is located in an immense park surrounded by vineyards. The estate makes its own Champagne which guests are invited to taste before dinner. A country style prevails indoors. The table is laden high with home-made produce and as much wine as you can drink.

AROUND EPERNAY

☞ **Hôtel Saint-Pierre** – *14 Avenue P-Chandon – 51200 Epernay – ☎ 03 26 54 40 80 – closed Feb – 15rms: 21/36€ - ☕ 5.50€*. An unpretentious hotel in a quiet neighbourhood, just outside the town centre, which offers simple comfortable rooms at low prices. Friendly family staff.

☞ **Chambre d'hôte M. et Mme Tarlant** – *Rue de la Coopérative – 51480 OEuilly – 13km W of Epernay by the N 3 (Dormans road) – ☎ 03 26 58 30 60 – closed Dec to Mar – 4rms: 38/48€*. Take advantage of your stay with a real wine-grower to find out more about how Champagne is made, and taste your host's own wine. The ground-floor rooms of this unpretentious house are wonderfully spacious and all afford a relaxing view of the surrounding vineyards. Courteous welcome and family ambience.

☞ **Chambre d'hôte Les Botterets** – *5-7 Rue du Fort – 51190 Oger – 13km S of Epernay by the D 10 – ☎ 03 26 57 94 78 – closed around Christmas-New Year – ⊅ - 6rms: 40/44€*. The house and former wine-making premises of this property have been turned into chambres d'hôte. Although the interior decoration is sometimes felt to be rather lacking in character, the friendly authentic welcome and characteristic wine-growing atmosphere nonetheless endear the establishment to travellers.

☞ **Chambre d'hôte La Boursaultière** – *44 Rue de la Duchesse-d'Uzès – 51480 Boursault – 9km W of Epernay by the N 3 and the D 222 – ☎ 03 26 54 47 76 – closed around Feb – ⊅ – 2rms: 43/58€*. This appealing house built out of local stone extends a faultless welcome to guests who are treated to delightful rooms hung with medieval- or Renaissance-style printed fabrics. The luxurious bathrooms boast beautiful Italian glazed tiles and the paved courtyard is a riot of lush green plants.

☞☞ **Les Berceaux** – *13 Rue des Berceaux – 51200 Epernay – ☎ 03 26 55 28 84 – les. berceaux@wanadoo.fr – 29rms: 66/75€ - ☕ 11€ – restaurant 28/61€*. Guests to this hundred-year-old flower-decked house are assured of a warm welcome. Ask for one of the tastefully renovated rooms. The elegant restaurant offers tasty classic dishes served with AOC Champagne and Coteaux-champenois wines. Wine by the glass and simpler fare in the Wine Bar.

☞☞ **La Famille Guy Charbaut** – *12 Rue du Pont – 51160 Mareuil-sur-Ay – 8km E of Epernay on the D 1 – ☎ 03 26 52 60 59 – 6rms: 53/61€ – meals 37€*. Wine-growers from father to son since 1930, the Charbaut family bends over backwards to make guests feel welcome in their attractive 19C home, taking them on tours of the cellars and organising tasting sessions of their best Champagnes. Antique furniture in the bedrooms. Meals are served in a magnificent old storeroom.

☞☞ **Chambre d'hôte Château du Ru Jacquier** – *51700 Igny-Comblizi – 7km SE of Dormans by the D 18 – ☎ 03 26 57 10 84 – closed mid-Nov to mid-Feb – 11rms: 60/120€ - ☕ 7€ – meals 28/40€*. A host of surprises awaits you in the immense parkland surrounding this 18C château, which is home to an unusual collection of exotic animals including kangaroos and llamas. The rooms, in the main wing or in the out buildings, all display the same faultless good taste. Handsome dining room. Countless leisure activities on site.

⊖⊜⊜ **Chambre d'hôte Manoir de Montflambert** – *51160 Mutigny – 7km NE of Epernay on the D 201 –* ☎ *03 26 52 33 21 – manoir-de-montflambert@wanadoo. fr – 6rms: 82/102€ -* ☑ *4€.* This former 17C hunting lodge on the edge of a wood commands a splendid view of the Marne and the vineyards. The price is more than compensated for by the manor's lovely woodwork, impressive staircase up to the rooms, quiet ambience and rich past – its walls are said to have witnessed the romance between Henry IV and the Countess of Montflambert.

AROUND REIMS

⊖ **Ardenn Hôtel** – *6 Rue Caqué – 51100 Reims –* ☎ *03 26 47 42 38 – closed Dec to early Jan – 14rms: 31/54€ -* ☑ *5.50€.* Behind a pretty brick façade, this establishment offers a quiet location not far from the town centre, impeccably well-kept premises, tastefully decorated rooms and ever-smiling staff. In short, a sound, affordable choice.

⊖ **Chambre d'hôte Lapie** – *1 Rue Jeanne-d'Arc – 51360 Val-de-Vesle – 21km SE of Reims by the N 44 and D 326 on the left –* ☎ *03 26 03 92 88 – closed 15 Dec to 15 Jan –* ⊯ *- 5rms: 37/47€.* Five bedrooms stylishly decorated in pastel colours have been fitted out in the main wing of this farmstead in the heart of the village: a happy blend of old and new. The pleasant ground-floor dining room is ideal for breakfasts.

⊖ **Chambre d'hôte Ferme du Grand Clos** – *Rue Jonquery – 51170 Ville-en-Tardenois – 17km SW of Reims by the D 980 –* ☎ *03 26 61 83 78 – closed late Dec to early Mar –* ⊯ *- 4rms: 40/50€.* The fully renovated large rooms of this former stone-built farmhouse all have a small sitting room area. The warm welcome and low prices make it a popular choice for "pilgrims" along the Champagne Wine Road.

⊖ **Chambre d'hôte Delong** – *24 Rue des Tilleuls – 51390 St-Euphraise-et-Clarizet – 16km SW of Reims by the D 980 and D 206 –* ☎ *03 26 46 20 86 – jdscom@wanadoo.fr – 4rms: 49/56€.* In the heart of a wine-growing estate, this former cowshed has been beautifully converted: lovely old stone walls and exposed timbers in the rooms which also have attractive bathrooms. The estate organises visits to the cellars, the wine press and Champagne tasting.

⊖⊜ **Reflets Bleus** – *12 Rue G.-Voisin – 51100 Reims –* ☎ *03 26 82 59 79 – info@ lesrefletsbleus.com –* 🅿 *- closed 18-25 Apr, 9-22 Aug – 41rms: 47/52€ -* ☑ *7€ – meals 19/26€.* Several pavilions, most of which are a fair distance from the main road, offer small garden-level rooms, some of which have been renovated. Meals are served in a traditional-style restaurant with bare timbers.

⊖⊜ **Grand Hôtel du Nord** – *75 Place Drouet-d'Erlon – 51100 Reims –* ☎ *03 26 47 39 03 – grandhoteldunord-reims@wanadoo.fr – closed Christmas holidays – 50rms: 49/59€ -* ☑ *6€.* The stately façade of this building, characteristic of the 1920s, overlooks a lively pedestrian square. Most of the rooms have been renovated; the quietest are those to the rear. Countless restaurants and leisure activities in the vicinity.

⊖⊜ **Hôtel La Cathédrale** – *20 Rue Libergier – 51100 Reims –* ☎ *03 26 47 28 46 - 17rms: 49.50/62€ -* ☑ *6.50€.* Notre-Dame Cathedral rises majestically at the far end of the street where this smart establishment is located. The pretty rooms with cosy inviting beds are bright and comfortable. Tasteful old engravings adorn the walls of the breakfast room. Warm welcome, faultless upkeep.

⊖⊜ **Crystal** – *86 Place Drouet-d'Erlon – 51100 Reims –* ☎ *03 26 88 44 44 – hotelcrystal@wanadoo.fr – 31rms: 50/67€ -* ☑ *7.50€.* An amazing haven of greenery and tranquillity right in the heart of town and yet protected from the busy town bustle is what this 1920s house offers tired travellers. All the rooms have been treated to a fresh coat of paint and excellent bedding. In summer, breakfast is served in a charming flower-decked garden-courtyard lined with trees.

⊖⊜ **Hôtel Continental** – *93 Place Drouet-d'Erlon – 51100 Reims –* ☎ *03 26 40 39 35 – grand-hotel-continental@wanadoo.fr – closed 21 Dec to 7 Jan – 50rms: 55/150€ -* ☑ *10.50€.* The smart late-19C façade of this hotel overlooks a pedestrian square which is the liveliest spot in town. Renovated rooms in a variety of styles reached by a magnificent staircase; avoid the rooms overlooking Boulevard du Général-Leclerc for maximum peace and quiet. Elegant Belle Epoque reception rooms.

⊖⊜ **Hôtel du Cheval Blanc** – *51400 Sept-Saulx – 18km SE of Reims by the N 44 and the D 37 –* ☎ *03 26 03 90 27 – cheval. blanc-sept-saulx@wanadoo.fr – closed Feb, Tue and Wed from Oct to Mar –* 🅿 *– 26rms: 58/132€ -* ☑ *9€ – restaurant 29/86€.* Peace and quiet guaranteed in this former coaching inn off the main roads. Attractive rooms overlooking a well-tended garden on the banks of a branch of the Vesle. Plush comfortable dining room and flower-decked courtyard which doubles as a dining terrace in summer. Tennis and mini-golf.

⊖⊜ **Hôtel Porte Mars** – *2 Place de la République – 51100 Reims –* ☎ *03 26 40 28 35 – hotel.porte-mars@wanadoo.fr – 24rms: 65/96€ -* ☑ *9€.* A charming place to have a cup of tea by the fireplace of the cosy sitting room, or a drink before dinner in the sophisticated bar. The comfortable personalised rooms are all excellently soundproofed. Copious breakfasts served in an attractive conservatory decorated with old photos and mirrors.

Univers – *41 Boulevard Foch – 51100 Reims – 03 26 88 68 08 – hotel-univers@ebc.net – 42rms: 74/80€ - 9.50€ – restaurant 15/28€.* This Art Deco inspired establishment stands alongside a tree-lined boulevard. Comfortable well soundproofed bedrooms all equipped with wireless internet access. Elegant wood panelling adds character to the renovated restaurant.

Assiette Champenoise – *40 Avenue Paul-Vaillant-Couturier, Tinqueux – 51100 Reims – 03 26 84 64 64 – assiette.champenoise@wanadoo.fr – P - 55rms: 125/245€ - 14€ – restaurant 55/84€.* An immaculate park provides the setting for this elegant mansion to which an extra wing has been recently added with attractive renovated rooms; some have a private sitting room. The classic beautifully prepared cuisine is served in a huge dining room dotted with columns.

AROUND THE LACS D'AUBE

La Bergeotte – *6 Rue de Dienville – 10220 Brevonnes – 03 25 46 31 44 – - 3rms: 26/37€ – meals 15€.* The warm friendly welcome awaiting you in this pretty farmhouse, entirely rebuilt in 1940, is exceptional. The tastefully decorated rooms are beautifully cared for. Small kitchen available for use by guests, who also have the run of the large, peaceful garden in summer.

Chambre d'hôte Mme Jeanne – Les Colombages Champenois – *33 Rue du Haut – 10270 Laubressel – 7km NW of Lusigny-sur-Barse by N 19 and D 186 - 03 25 80 27 37 – - 6rms: 27/40€.* Two charming half-timbered houses typical of the Champagne region are home to cosy rooms with exposed beams. It is a pleasure to sit down in front of the open fire or relax on the terrace overlooking the meadows as you tuck into the tasty farm produce. Gîte accommodation nearby.

Gourmet Shopping

Deléans – *20 Rue Cérès – 51100 Reims – 03 26 47 56 35 – vincent.frodefond@worldonline.fr* Everything is home-made and of superb quality in this delicious chocolate shop. Hundred-year-old carvings and mouldings frame the window displays, piled high with mouth-watering delicacies such as the ginger and orange flavoured Péché au diable, cognac cherry Nelusko and the Perle de Champagne, made with vintage liqueur.

Fossier – *25 Cours Langlet – 51100 Reims – 03 26 47 59 84.* Founded in 1756, the Fossier biscuit shop and factory has long been an institution in Reims. It is the last place still to produce the legendary half-crumbly, half-crunchy pink biscuits. If you're not comfortable with the idea of dipping a biscuit into your glass of Champagne without making an awful mess, make a beeline for this shop to learn the proper etiquette of eating these sophisticated biscuits.

La Petite Friande – *15 Cours Jean-Baptiste-Langlet – 51100 Reims – 03 26 47 50 44.* It was in this institution of Reims founded in 1832 that the mythical dark chocolate Bouchon au marc de Champagne was first invented in 1951. It was also here that the Bulle made with vintage Champagne was created in 1987. Nowadays such inventions rank high in "France's national heritage list of delicacies".

S. Sauvignier/MICHELIN

Markets

AISNE

Charly-sur-Marne – *Thursday morning.*

Château-Thierry – *Friday morning, Place de la Mairie.*

Nogent-l'Artaud – *Sunday morning.*

MARNE

Avize – *Thursday morning.*

Ay – *Friday morning, Place Henri-Martin.*

Dormans – *Saturday morning.*

Epernay – *Thursday and Saturday morning, Place Hugues-Plomb.*

Reims – *Monday morning, Avenue de Laon; Tuesday morning, Place and Rue St-Maurice; Wednesday, Place du Boulingrin; Thursday, Boulevard Cartelet; Friday morning, Boulevard Wilson; Saturday morning, Place du Boulingrin; Sunday morning, Avenue Jean-Jaurès.*

AUBE

Bar-sur-Aube – *Saturday morning.*

Bar-sur-Seine – *Friday morning.*

Essoyes – *Tuesday morning.*

Les Riceys – *Thursday morning.*

REIMS AND THE MONTAGNE DE REIMS

100km. Michelin Local Map 306, F-G 7-8. See itinerary **1** *on the map on p. 186-187.*
The Montagne de Reims refers to a promontory south of Reims which rises to an altitude of 287m. The picturesque massif is covered with forests and its north and southeast slopes are planted with vineyards. The entire sector now makes up the Regional Nature Park of the Montagne de Reims.

Reims★★★

If you can't decide between Champagne tasting or Gothic art, Reims is just the place for you, offering the unforgettable prospect of a visit to the cathedral and the Palais du Tau combined with the chance to venture into the cellars of some of the world's most prestigious Champagne firms.

Cathédrale Notre-Dame★★★ – *Open early May to early Sep, 9.30am-6.30pm; early Sep to early May, 9.30am-12.30pm and 2-5.30pm. Guided tours by appointment. Closed Mon, 1 Jan, 1 May, 1-11 Nov, 25 Dec; 6.10€, no charge 1st Sun of the month (between Oct-Mar). Enquire at the Palais du Tau,* ☎ *03 26 47 81 79.*

Reims Cathedral, a gem of Gothic art, has witnessed great moments in French history: it was on this site that Clovis, king of the Franks, was anointed and where Charles VII was crowned in the presence of Joan of Arc. But the succession of cathedrals which have stood here have endured a troubled past, culminating in the heavy German bombardment of 1914. The first cathedral to be built here was erected by Saint Nicaise in 401, very probably on the site of a Gallo-Roman temple of worship. This was replaced in the 9C by a larger edifice, destroyed by a fire in 1210. At this point, Archbishop Aubry de Humbert decided to rebuild in Gothic style, taking the great cathedrals of Paris, Soissons and Chartres as his models. The first stone was laid in 1211, but the towers were not completed until the late 15C due to a fire which delayed building. A long restoration programme carried out during the 19C had just been completed when the First World War broke out. On 19 September 1914, heavy shelling set fire to the timber framework, causing the bells and the lead of the stained glass to melt and the stone to split. The walls held up, however, and at the end of the war a new restoration programme was launched, partly financed by the Rockefeller Foundation.

The **exterior** of the cathedral was originally decorated by some 2 300 statues, but most of these are now copies. The **façade**, composed of three doorways, is reminiscent of Notre-Dame in Paris. The central doorway is devoted to the Virgin and depicts several periods of her life.

Inside the **nave** is three storeys high. The oldest capitals are decorated with carvings of acanthus leaves, monsters and two wine-growers carrying a basket of grapes *(6th pillar in the nave on the right)*. The 13C **stained-glass windows★★** suffered considerable damage; those of the apse are still intact. The great 13C rose-window, dedicated to the Virgin, is a masterpiece of Gothic art.

Palais du Tau★★ – *2 Place du Cardinal-Luçon. Open early May to early Sep, daily except Mon, 9.30am-6.30pm; rest of the year, daily except Mon, 9.30am-12.30pm and 2-5.30pm. Closed 1 Jan, 1 May, 1-11 Nov, 25 Dec. 6.10€, (children under 17: no charge).* ☎ *03 26 47 81 79.*

The former palace of the archbishops of Reims, first built in 1138, was reworked in the 15C in a Late Gothic style and towards 1670 in a Classical style. Listed on the Unesco World Heritage List, it is now home to the cathedral treasure and to many of the original statues from the cathedral's façade.

Basilique St-Remi★★ – *Place Saint-Remi.* The oldest church in Reims. In 533, Saint Remi was buried in a small chapel dedicated to Saint Christopher. Shortly after a basilica was erected on the site and in the second half of the 8C a group of Benedictine monks moved in and founded the Abbaye de Saint-Remi.

Work on the present building began c 1007 and the church was formally consecrated by Pope Leo IX in October 1049. The building was remodelled in the 12C, 15C, 16C and 17C. Many archbishops of Reims and the first kings of France are buried here; the Holy Phial used during the Royal coronations was also kept here. Behind the altar, Saint Remi's grave, rebuilt in 1847, has retained its 17C statues representing St Remi, Clovis and 12 peers who took part in the coronation.

Chapelle Foujita★ – *33 Rue du Champ-de-Mars. Open May-Oct, daily except Wed, 2-6pm. Closed 1 Jan, 1 May, 14 Jul, 1-11 Nov, 25 Dec. 3€ (1 month pass with access to the Fine Arts Museum, Musée-Abbaye de St-Remi, Musée de l'ancien college des Jésuites, Musée de la Reddition, the planetarium and the Chapel), no charge 1st Sun of each month.* ☎ *03 26 40 06 96, www.reims.fr*

Donations by the Champagne firm Mumm led to the construction of this chapel, designed and decorated in a primitive Christian style by Léonard Foujita (1886-1968): Foujita, a Japanese painter who belonged to the early-20C school of art known as the Ecole de Paris, was aged 80 at the time. Inaugurated in 1966, the chapel commemorates the mystical inspiration felt by the Japanese painter in the Basilique St-Remi, leading him to convert to Christianity and be baptised in Reims Cathedral.

Champagne cellars of Reims★★

Allow between a half and a full day. Also consult our Shopping Guide.

The world-famous Champagne cellars of Reims are located in the Champ de Mars district and along the limestone slopes of St-Nicaise hill, riddled with 250km of galleries, known as *crayères,* which date from the Gallo-Roman period. The depth and extent of the galleries make them ideal Champagne cellars.

Pommery – *5 Place du Général-Gouraud. Open Easter to mid-Nov, guided tour (1hr) 9.30am-7pm, mid-Nov to Easter, 10am-6pm. Closed Christmas holidays. 7.50€ (children under 12: no charge). ☎ 03 26 61 62 56, www.pommery.com*

Founded in 1836 by Narcisse Gréno and Louis-Alexandre Pommery, the firm was expanded by the latter's widow who inaugurated Brut Champagne and had the present buildings erected in 1878. She also linked the 120 Gallo-Roman *crayères* by 18km of galleries. Pommery now belongs to the Vranken group. The tour enables visitors to discover the different stages of Champagne-making through galleries decorated with 19C sculptures and to see a 75 000-litre tun by Emile Gallé.

Taittinger – *9 Place St-Nicaise. Open mid-Mar to mid-Nov, guided tour (1hr) 9.30am-12.30pm and 2-4.30pm, rest of the year, daily except Sat-Sun and public holidays, 9.30am-noon and 2-4.30pm. Closed 1 Jan and 25 Dec. 7€. ☎ 03 26 85 84 33*

In 1734 the Fourneaux family of wine merchants from Reims began producing sparkling wines. In 1932, Pierre Taittinger took over the management of the firm which was renamed after him. Today the Taittinger vineyards extend over 250 hectares and the firm owns 6 grape-harvesting centres on the Montagne de Reims, the Château de la Marquetterie in Pierry and the Hôtel des Comtes de Champagne in Reims in addition to superb cellars. Visitors are taken on a fascinating tour of the cellars where 15 million bottles are stored in the cool Gallo-Roman galleries and in the crypts of the former 13C Abbaye St-Nicaise, destroyed during the Revolution.

Veuve Clicquot-Ponsardin – *1 Place des Droits-de-l'Homme. Open Apr-Oct, guided tour and tasting (1hr 30min) daily except Sun; Nov-Mar, daily except Sat-Sun. 7€ (children free). By appointment: ☎ 03 26 89 53 90, www.veuve-clicquot.fr*

The firm founded in 1772 by Philippe Clicquot was considerably expanded by his son and later by his son's widow, whose maiden name was Ponsardin, thus explaining the firm's present name. The "Grande Dame" of Champagne, after whom a special cuvée was named, was responsible for many initiatives including *remuage* (art of blending) in 1816. Today, Veuve Clicquot-Ponsardin, which owns 265 hectares of vineyards and exports three quarters of its production, is owned by the LVMH group. The cellars are located in Gallo-Roman *crayères.*

Ruinart – *4 Rue des Crayères. Guided tours (1hr) by appointment, contact the visits and receptions department. From 10€/person depending on the programme. ☎ 03 26 77 51 21, www.ruinart.com*

Founded in 1729 by the nephew of the monk Dom Thierry Ruinart, who was a great friend of Dom Pérignon, this Champagne firm prospered during the Restoration period and again after 1949, having gone through years of decline during the two world wars. Today Ruinart, which belongs to the Moët-Henessy group, specialises in high quality Champagne. Its Gallo-Roman galleries on three levels are particularly interesting.

Piper-Heidsieck – *51 Boulevard Henry-Vasnier. Open 9.30am-12.30pm and 2-6pm (last admission 1hr before closing time). Closed Jan-Feb, 25 Dec. 7€. ☎ 03 26 84 43 44, www.piper-hiedsieck.com*

The firm, founded in 1785 by Florens-Louis Heidsieck, now belongs to the Rémy Cointreau group. The various stages of Champagne-making are explained by means of an audio-visual presentation, after which visitors can tour the 16km of underground cellars in a gondola car.

Mumm – *34 Rue du Champ-de-Mars. Open Mar-Oct, guided tour (1hr 15min) 9-11am and 2-5pm; Nov-Feb 9-11am and 2-5pm (by appointment), Sat-Sun and public holidays 2-5pm. Closed 1 Jan, 25 Dec. 7.50€. ☎ 03 26 49 59 70, www.mumm.com*

After its creation in 1827, this firm prospered throughout the 19C in Europe and the United States. Today it belongs to the Anglo-Spanish group Allied Domecq and owns 218 hectares. Its 25km-long cellars are open to the public.

Leave Reims by the N 51 as far as Montchenot, then take the D 26 towards Villers-Allerand. The D 26 skirts the northern flank of the Montagne de Reims, winding its way past the vineyards and villages of Champagne.

Rilly-la-Montagne

Countless wine-growers and merchants have brought prosperity to this well-off village. One excellent address among many is **Domaine Daniel Dumont** *(see Shopping Guide).*

From the D 26, at the top of the hill to the right, you can see a contemporary sculpture by Bernard Pages in celebration of the Earth and in tribute to works by Gaston Bachelard.

Mailly-Champagne

The name of Mailly is inextricably linked with that of its cooperative cellar located in elegant modern buildings which produce excellent Champagnes under the brand of **Mailly Grand Cru** *(see Shopping Guide).*

Carrière pédagogique de Mailly-Champagne – *The geological specimens discovery path is open all year. Departure from the village hall of Mailly-Champagne. Visitors who do not wish to go on a guided tour are advised to purchase the "Carrière péda-gogique de Mailly-Champagne" guide (7€) from the reserve's offices in Pourcy. Guided tours are organised by the Montage de Reims regional nature reserve (5.50€): contact the reserve's offices for the programme.* ☎ *03 26 59 44 44*

A journey back in time! 1km beyond Mailly-Champagne there is an interesting *carrière géologique* (geological quarry) showing a complete cross-section of the Tertiary formations of the eastern Paris Basin, taking you back millions of years to a time when the sea was not so far away!

Verzenay

This wine-growing village of renown is dominated by a windmill to the west and by the somewhat unusual sight of a lighthouse in the midst of the vineyards. This unexpected monument is the work of Joseph Goulet who had it built in

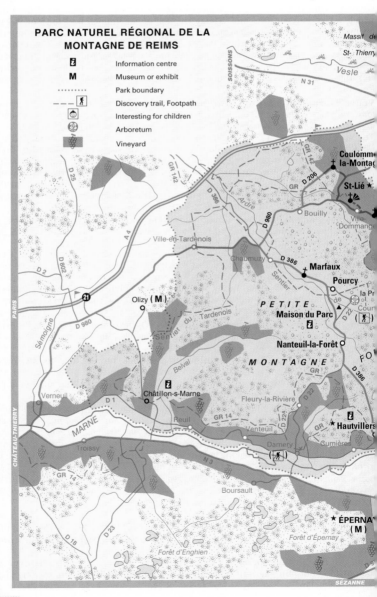

1909 in order to promote his Champagne firm. Originally an outdoor café with swings and a croquet lawn, it was used by the English in 1940 as an anti-aircraft machine gun post. After being superbly restored, it is now home to the **Musée de la Vigne★**, which is reached by a hanging bridge. Inside visitors are invited to get better acquainted with Champagne: its land, climate, vineyards, history and production secrets. ᕗ *Open daily except Mon 10am-6pm, Sat-Sun and public holidays 10am-6.30pm (last admission 1hr before closing time). Closed early Jan-Feb and 25 Dec. 5€.* ☎ *03 26 07 87 87.*

Verzy

This ancient wine-growing village prospered under the protection of the Benedictine abbey of St-Basle founded in the 7C by the archbishop of Reims, Saint Nivard, and destroyed in 1792. It is still home to a number of reputable wine estates such as that of **Etienne Lefevre**. Under the buildings of this 19C property are amazing pointed vaulted cellars at a depth of 15m. A collection of old wine-growing tools and presses is on display including a press which dates from the 18C. Tasting and sales after the visit. *30 Rue de Villiers, 51380 Verzy.* ☎ *03 26 97 96 99, www. champagne-etienne-lefevre.com. Open Mon-Sat, 9am-noon and 2-7pm. Closed 25 Dec, Easter and a fortnight in Aug.*

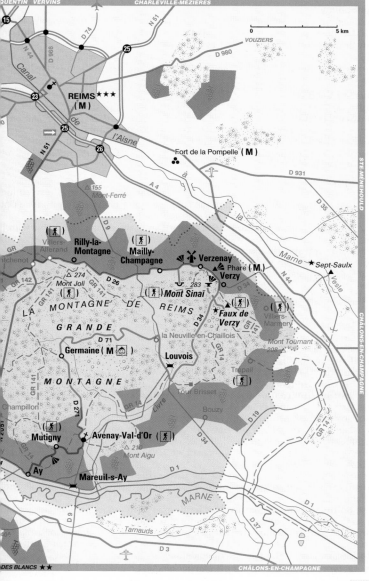

However the main claim to fame of this area are the **Faux de Verzy★**. In Verzy take the D 34 towards Louvois. On reaching the plateau, take the second left towards the Parking des Pins, follow the path over a distance of about 500m. Verzy Forest is home to a thousand specimens of a very rare species, Faux (from the Latin *fagus*, meaning birch). These twisted, stunted birches are the result of a genetic phenomenon, probably reinforced by natural layering, of which there are only two other examples in Europe. *Guided tours are organised by the Montagne de Reims nature reserve park depending on the time of year. 5.50€. Visitors are advised to purchase Les Faux de Verzy brochure (6.86€). Enquiries and brochure from the reserve offices. Open all year round. ☎ 03 26 59 44 44.*

Return onto the D 34 towards Louvois.

Château de Louvois

Not open to the public. Erected by Mansart for Louis XIV's minister, the château became the property of Louis XV's daughters. This splendid residence, surrounded by a park designed by Le Nôtre, was for the most part demolished between 1805 and 1812. The present castle consists of a pavilion partly rebuilt in the 19C.

From Louvois, the road continues towards **Bouzy** *(5km SE on the D 34)*, reputed for its subtle Coteaux-champenois red wines; tasting at **Maison Brice** *(see Shopping Guide)*. This portion of vines, for some unknown reason, was untouched by phylloxera and has kept up one or two traditional aspects of the 19C vineyard.

Ambonnay

Although it also produces red wines, this area is far better known for its Champagnes, particularly those produced by the **Egly-Ouriet**, **Serge Pierlot** and **Soutiran-Pelletier** firms *(see Shopping Guide)*.

Back in Louvois, return to the D 9 and head N as far as Neuville-en-Chaillois, then turn left onto the D 71 through the forest via Germaine (see "Back to Grass Roots" at the end of this chapter).

Avenay-Val-d'Or

Eglise St-Trésain, 13C and 16C, has a fine Late Gothic west front.

A **discovery trail** starting from the station *(brochure available from the Maison du Parc in Pourcy)* enables visitors to discover a rural community.

Avenay produces vintages made from Chardonnay and Pinot Noir varieties.

Opposite Avenay station, take the D 201, and immediately after the railway line, take the small road uphill to Mutigny.

Mutigny

Surrounded by vineyards and forest, this village stands on an outcrop at an altitude of 240m. There is a fine view from the simple country church of Ay and the Côte des Blancs to the right and over Châlons and the plain to the left.

A 2.2km *(round trip)* **wine-growers' trail** starts from the village; it is dotted with 12 signposts which inform the walker about the Champagne vineyards and how the vines are cultivated from season to season. *From mid-Apr to early Nov, daily except Mon at 9.30am, 2pm and 4.30pm, Tue 2pm and 4.30pm, Sat-Sun by appointment. 7.50€ (children under 12: no charge). ☎ 03 26 52 31 37. www.mutigny-en-Champagne. com*

The road down to Ay affords some fine views of Epernay and the Côte des Blancs.

Ay

This ancient city, well known in Gallo-Roman times and well liked by several French kings including Good King Henri (IV), lies in a secluded spot at the foot of a hill among famous vineyards. **Eglise St-Brice** possesses a Late Gothic doorway and on Rue St-Vincent, the visitor will see a lovely timber-framed house called the **Pressoir Henri IV**.

The **Institut International des vins de Champagne** (Villa Bissinger) is situated in a former 19C manor house. Equipped with a documentation centre, it is devoted to research into Champagne and offers visitors the chance to discover the wines of Champagne through a presentation of the vines and a tasting session with commentary. *15 Rue Jeanson, 51160 Ay. ☎ 03 26 55 78 78, www.villabissinger. com Open Apr-Oct, 1st Sat of the month at 2.30pm, tasting and commentary of 4 Champagnes, 23€.*

At n°69 Rue Jules-Blondeau stands the **Gosset firm** whose founder was listed as a wine-grower in the city's records of 1584, making it the oldest firm in the whole Champagne region *(see Shopping Guide)*.

The **Bollinger firm** *(see Shopping Guide)*, despite an international reputation which rests in part on the James Bond films, remains a family affair committed to upholding ancestral traditions. It possesses one of the last remaining cooperages in Champagne, as well as a portion of "Vieilles Vignes Françaises", which is ungrafted stock that survived the phylloxera epidemic.

In Ay, turn left on the D 1 towards Mareuil-sur-Ay.

Mareuil-sur-Ay

The château was erected in the 18C for J.-B. de Dommangeville whose daughter fell in love with the poet André Chénier. The estate was bought in 1830 by the Duke of Montebello who created his own brand of Champagne.

Founded in 1818, the **Billecart-Salmon** family firm, known for its pink Champagne, is the proud possessor of vats which combine state-of-the-art technology with traditional methods. Take a stroll round the formal garden à la française and enjoy the sweet-scented roses. *40 Rue Carnot, 51160 Mareuil-sur-Ay.* ☎ *03 26 52 60 22, billecart@Champagne-billecart.fr Open Mon-Thu 9.30-11.30am and 2.30-5.30pm. By appointment. Admission charge.*

The Clos des Goisses vintage is the pride and joy of the **Philipponat estate** *(see Shopping Guide).*

Return to Ay and continue towards Dizy, then turn onto the N 2051 towards Champillon.

Between Dizy and Champillon, the road rises to command a good view of the vineyards, the Marne Valley and Epernay.

Hautvilliers★

It is in this attractive village in the heart of Champagne that the famous 17C monk Dom Pérignon is said to have invented the art of blending wines to produce sparkling champagne. He was in charge of the cellars of the Benedictine abbey of Saint-Pierre in Hautvilliers for 47 years. Although he may not have "discovered" Champagne, his contribution to the transformation from non-sparkling into sparkling wines was essential. Dom Pérignon's knowledge of winemaking was extensive and his discoveries include the benefits of blending grapes from different terroirs into "vintages", the quick, successive pressing of black grapes to produce a perfectly clear white

Hautvilliers Abbey.

S. Sauvignier/MICHELIN

juice, the use of the first thick glass bottles and corks to contain the bubbles, and the digging of chalk cellars to enable the wine to age at a constant temperature. In 1715 he was laid to rest in the abbey church of St-Sindulphe, where his black marble tombstone can be seen at the foot of the high altar to the left. A vast chandelier (1950) made up of four wheels from winepresses hangs over the high altar.

Founded in 650 by Saint Nivard, nephew of King Dagobert, the **abbey of Saint-Pierre** now belongs to the Moët et Chandon firm.

Leave Hautvilliers on the D 386, then turn right on the D 1 as far as Reuil (14km).

Reuil

In Reuil, park your car and go for a ride round town in a horse-drawn carriage. **Calèche Evasion** offers a variety of themed excursions from a short ride to a full-day trip around the surrounding hillsides and vineyards. "Calèche et terroir", a combination of ride and tasting, "Calèche et danse" for music lovers or "Calèche et champagne" to discover the cellars – there is something for everyone! *From mid-Apr to mid-Oct, several options are available: ride 8€, ride and riverside Champagne tasting 11€, day trip with Champagne lunch, visits (museums and cellars) and cruise 22€. Call* ☎ *03 26 55 68 19 for reservations.*

Take a U-turn and return on the D 1, then turn left on the D 22 (14km). Head for Venteuil, then Nanteuil-la-Forêt.

Nanteuil-la-Forêt

This village, tucked away in a narrow pastoral vale surrounded by forest, once possessed a Templar's priory. Today's visitors come here to admire the plants in the **Centre botanique de la Presle** (botanic gardens). A couple of nursery-owners organise exhibitions in the garden which has a fine collection of spirea, willow and a dozen or so species of rose, including the Marne rose. *Carrefour de la Presle. Open daily except Sun 2-6pm, Sat, 9am-noon and 2-6pm. Closed public holidays (except for some Sun afternoons, enquire beforehand). 4€.* ☎ *03 26 59 43 39.*

Continue on the D 386 northbound, via Pourcy, home to the Maison du Parc of the Montagne de Reims regional nature reserve (see "Back to Grass Roots" at the end of this chapter).

Marfaux

The **church** boasts fine capitals carved with acanthus foliage and small charac
ters.

Beyond Chaumuzy, turn right on D 980, then, as you reach Bouilly, turn left on D 20
towards Coulomnes-la-Montagne.

Coulomnes-la-Montagne

In this flower-decked village, there is a fine Romanesque **church** whose belfr
has just one opening. Note the foliage decoration of the capitals in the transep
and chancel.

Turn right to rejoin the D 980 via Pargny-les-Reims, 1.5km further on, turn left towar
Saint-Lié.

Chapelle St-Lié★

This chapel, dating from the 12C, 13C and 16C, stands on a mound near Ville
Dommange, at the centre of a copse which was probably a holy grove i
Roman-Gallo times. Dedicated to a 5C hermit, the chapel is surrounded by it
cemetery. There is an extended **view★** of Ville-Dommange, the Côte d'Ile-de
France, Reims and its cathedral, the plain as far as the St-Thierry massif and th
Tardenois region.

Sacy

Eglise St-Remi has a late 11C east end and a 12C tower. Admire the view ove
Reims from the adjoining cemetery.

Return to Reims via Bézannes (9km).

THE CÔTE DES BLANCS★★

28km from Epernay to Mont Aimé. Michelin Local Map 306, F-G 8-9. See itinerary
on map p. 194-195.

From Epernay to Vertus, the north-south facing Côte des Blancs lies on the edg
of the Plateau de Brie. It owes its name to its white-grape vineyards consistin
almost exclusively of Chardonnay vines. This elegant variety of grapes is used t
produce prestigious vintages and blanc de blancs, as Champagnes made exclus
vely from white grapes are known. The majority of the great Champagne firm
own vineyards and wine-making facilities in this area.

This itinerary, which runs half-way up the slopes, offers splendid views of th
vineyards and the immense Châlons plain below.

Epernay★

Although both claim the title of capital of Champagne, Epernay, which is hom
to prestigious firms such as Moët et Chandon and Mercier to name but a few
may have a slight edge over Reims. Avenue de Champagne in the east of town i
lined with Champagne firms of international repute some of which date back t
the 18C. The avenue runs above a limestone cliff riddled with miles of gallerie
whose temperature remains constant (9-11°C) all year round. Some of the cellar
are open to the public.

Moët et Chandon – *18 Avenue de Champagne. Open early Mar to mid-Nov, guide*
tours (1hr) 9.30-11.30am and 2-4.30pm; mid-Nov to early Mar, daily except Sat-Su
and public holidays, 7.50€. ☎ *03 26 51 20 20, www.moet.com*

The leading Champagne firm in terms of volume, the firm owes its name t
Claude Moët, who founded the house in 1743 and to his grandson's son-inlaw
Pierre Gabriel Chandon, whose name was added later. The brand now belong
to LVMH (Louis Vuitton Moët-Hennessy) which has done much to promote th
image of French luxury goods in general and Champagne in particular: its famou
brands include Veuve Clicquot, Dom Pérignon, Mercier and Ruinart.

Mercier – *73 Avenue de Champagne. Car park and reception opposite the firm. Ope*
mid-Mar to late Nov, guided tours (45min) 9.30-11.30am and 2-4.30pm; Dec to mi
Mar, daily except Tue and Wed, 9.30-11.30am and 2-4.30pm. Enquire about closir
periods. 6€. ☎ *03 26 51 22 22.*

Eugène Mercier created his firm in 1858 and had 18km of galleries dug. To ce
ebrate the World Exhibition of 1889 he asked a sculptor, Navlet, from Châlons, t
decorate a huge tun with a capacity of 215 000 bottles which were placed on a ca
drawn by 24 oxen with 18 horses to help the uphill sections and taken to Pari
This exceptional convoy took twenty days to travel from Epernay to Paris: som
bridges had to be reinforced and walls demolished along the way. The 34-to
barrel is now displayed in the main reception hall.

De Castellane – *54 Rue de Verdun. Open Apr-Dec, guided tours (45min) 10am-noc*
and 2-6pm, (last admission 45min before closing time). 6.50€ (children: 5€). ☎ *03 2*
51 19 11.

The tower, built in 1900 by Marius Toudoire, architect of the Gare de Lyon railwa
station in Paris, was formerly a water tower and is now an exhibition area. It
devoted to the history of the Castellane family – including the famous art collect

Boni de Castellane who married the American millionairess Anna Gould. The **museum** is devoted to the evolution of the Champagne-making process, illustrated by models.

Musée municipal – *Closed for renovation.*

The city museum is housed in the former Château Perrier, a copy of a castle in the Louis XIII style built in the mid-19C by a wine merchant. Two rooms are devoted to the life and work of a wine-grower. Collection of Champagne bottles and labels.

Leave Epernay on D 951 to the SW.

Pierry

The town of Pierry is justly proud of its handsome 18C **château**, whose reception rooms, small apartment, wine-press museum and cellars are open to the public. Visitors to the property are offered a glass of Champagne at the end of the visit. *Open daily except Mon and Sun, 9am-noon and 2-6pm. Guided tours with tasting session (1hr 30min) by appointment. 8€. ☎ 03 26 54 02 87.*

The **Domaine Henri Mandois** cellars, dating from the 18C, are located beneath the church of Pierry. *66 Rue du Général-de-Gaulle, BP 9, 51530 Pierry, ☎ 03 26 54 03 18, info@Champagne-mandois.fr Mon-Sat, 10am-noon and 2-5pm. By appointment.*

The **Vollereaux firm** can also be recommended *(see Shopping Guide).*

Those with a sweet tooth shouldn't miss the **Chocolaterie Thibaut**, where you will be able to see the firm's speciality made in front of your eyes: Champagne cork-shaped chocolates filled with Champagne spirits. Free tour and tasting. *ZA de Pierry, Pôle d'activités St-Julien, 51530 Pierry, ☎ 03 26 51 58 04. Mon-Sat 9am-noon and 2-7pm. Tours 9-11.30am and 2-6.30pm. No visits during the fortnight before Christmas and the fortnight before Easter. Closed last week of Jan and public holidays.*

Take the D 40 to Cuis, overlooked by a Romanesque church, and continue on the D 10 to Cramant.

Cramant

Cramant lies in a pleasant setting and is the capital of Chardonnay vines. At the entrance to the village stands an enormous bottle (a rheoboam, equivalent to 6 bottles) over 8.6m high and 7.9m round at its base. **Lilbert Fils** and **Bonnaire** both have a fine selection of local wines *(see Shopping Guide).*

Avize

The church dates from the 12C but the transept and chancel are 15C. After a stroll round the town, walk out to the west for extended views of the whole area, or stop at the house of **Marie-Hélène Waris-Larmandier**, wine-grower, painter and potter, specialised in the decoration of Champagne bottles. *608 Rempart du Nord, 51100 Avize, ☎ 03 26 57 79 05. By appointment only.*

Known for its wine, Avize also runs a school for future Champagne wine-growers. The Champagnes of **Jacques Selosse** and **Agrapart et Fils** are among the best-known of this prestigious locality *(see Shopping Guide).*

The **Corbon** firm offers visitors the chance to get better acquainted with the subtleties of Champagne through a choice of two tasting courses: the first focuses on which foods go best with Champagne, while the second teaches the rudiments of tasting. The theory is accompanied by a series of practical tests and trials. Children can also join in the fun and games and learn to distinguish the aromas and flavours of a variety of different fruits. If at all possible, it is best to get together a small group of around six like-minded friends, because Messrs Corbons' long experience in the area has convinced them that working with such groups is far more pleasant and effective all round. *541 Avenue Jean-Jaurès, 51100 Avize. ☎ 03 26 57 55 43. www.Champagne-corbon.com By appointment only. Closed late Dec to late Jan.*

Oger

Despite its wealth of picturesque fountains, wash-houses and weather-vanes, Oger is far more than just a pretty flower-decked village, even if it is ranked among the Most beautiful villages of France! It is also the regional capital of marriage thanks to its highly unusual **Museum** devoted to "Love and Champagne"! Wedding traditions between 1820 and 1920 are illustrated through a series of surprising objects including an interesting collection of bride's mementoes under glass covers. The museum also houses a fine collection of 19C Champagne labels, bottles and tools which retrace the history of Champagne making. Tasting at the end of the visit. *Open Apr-Nov, 9.30am-noon and 2-6pm, Sun 9.30-11am and 3-6pm; Dec-Mar, by appointment. 6€. ☎ 03 26 57 50 89.*

The **Milan** firm, founded in 1864 and renowned for its *blancs de blancs*, organises guided tours of its presses, storehouses and cellars, followed by a tasting session. Friendly atmosphere guaranteed! *6 rue d'Avize, 51190 Oger, ☎ 03 26 57 50 09, www.Champagne-milan.com Open Oct-May, 10am-noon and 2-5pm; Jun-Sep 10am-pm. Closed Jan.*

Le Mesnil-sur-Oger

This widely-spread wine-growing village possesses a peaceful shaded close in its centre inside of which is a Romanesque church with a Renaissance doorway.

The wine-growing and producing Launois family has created an interesting **Musée de la Vigne et du Vin★**. In addition to an impressive collection of 17C, 18C and 19C presses, the museum also boasts countless pumps, corking and other wine-making machinery. The high point of the visit is the entrance to the secret tasting cellar, followed by a ride round the vineyards on board a small train. *Guided tours (1hr 30min) by appointment, 10am-3pm; Sun and public holidays 10.30am. Closed 1 Jan, Easter, 25 Dec. 6€. ☎ 03 26 57 50 15. www.champagne-launois.fr*

The **Domaine Pierre Moncuit** has a fine (and rare) selection of vintage Champagnes. The **Domaine Philippe Gonet** can also be recommended *(see Shopping Guide).*

A small road winds its way across the vineyards to Vertus.

Vertus

Vertus, at the foot of the Côte des Blancs and devoted body and soul to vines (450 hectares of vineyards), affords the picture of a tiny town whose twisting lanes are dotted with pretty squares and countless springs and fountains. **Eglise St-Martin** (11C and 12C), built over four crypts and restored after the Second World War, has preserved its lovely pointed vaulting and a 16C Pietà.

Treat yourself to a visit to the **Veuve Fourny et Fils** and the **Duval Leroy** firms *(see Shopping Guide).*

On the way down to **Bergères-lès-Vertus** with its small Romanesque country church, the road affords pleasant views of the surrounding countryside.

South of Bergères-lès-Vertus, turn right onto the road leading to Mont Aimé.

Mont Aimé

Once part of the Ile-de-France cliff, this isolated hill reaches 237m. Inhabited since prehistoric times, it was fortified successively by the Gauls, the Romans and the Counts of Champagne who built a feudal castle, known as the White Queen; its ruins are today scattered among the greenery.

A viewpoint (viewing table) offers an extended view of the Côte des Blancs to the north of the plain of Châlons to the east.

VALLÉE DE LA MARNE

You can choose between two possible round tours, one out of Epernay and one out of Château-Thierry.

The villages in this valley lined with vineyards and dotted with forests are spread out on either bank of the Marne river. The Pinot Meunier variety reigns supreme over the area producing fruity, lively characterful Champagne.

Round tour from Epernay

63km. Michelin Local Map 306, E-F 8. See itinerary 3 on the map p. 194-195. Leave Epernay westbound on the N 3 and turn right towards Mardeuil, then cross over the Marne and continue alongside the river to Cumières.

Cumières

Located beneath a cirque of vineyards, this riverside town is reputed for its red Coteaux-champenois wines and those produced by René Geoffroy, together with an excellent Champagne, all to be recommended *(see Shopping Guide).*

Cumières is the starting point for boat trips on board the Champagne Vallée which take you past vineyards and through locks. *Cruises (1hr 30min) on the Marne. Send bookings to Croisi-Champagne, BP 22, 51480 Cumières, ☎ 03 26 54 49 51. www champagneetcroisiere.com*

Damery

Damery offers fine walks along the banks of the River Marne at the foot of vineyards. In former times, horse-drawn barges used to stop alongside its embankments. The 12C-13C **church** possesses a *Virgin and Child* by Watteau (18C).

The main wing of the **A.R. Lenoble wine estate** with its vaulted 18C cellars and wooden presses is a fine example of regional architectural styles. *35 Rue Paul-Douce, 51480 Damery, ☎ 03 26 58 42 60, contact@champagne-lenoble.com Open Mon-Fri, 8.30am-12.30pm and 1-5pm. By appointment.*

Another worthwhile address is that of the **Domaine Louis Casters** *(see Shopping Guide).*

Turn right towards Fleury-la-Rivière.

Fleury-la-Rivière

The **wine cooperative** is decorated with a huge 500m² **fresco** by an artist from Moselle, Greg Gawra. The fresco depicts the history of Champagne, work in the vineyards and wineries and the era from phylloxera up until the present day. Little by little this work of art is being transferred indoors where it will be better pro

tected from the weather. *Guided tours (45min) by appointment except Mon morning and Wed, 8.30am-12.30pm and 2-5.15pm, Sat 9am-12.30pm and 2-6pm, Sun and public holidays by appointment. Closed 24 Dec to 2 Jan, 1 May. 4€. ☎ 03 26 58 42 53.*
The D 324 winds in and out of the vineyards.
At Cuchery, bear left towards Châtillon-sur-Marne.

Châtillon-sur-Marne

Camped on a vine-covered hill overlooking the Marne, this ancient fortified town stands at an altitude of 148m at the mouth of the vale of Cuchery.
Leave your car in the car park; take Rue de l'Eglise then turn right into Rue Berthe-Symonet. The 33m-high statue of Pope Urban II was erected in 1887 on a mound formerly crowned by the castle keep, in homage to this local boy who instigated the first crusades. It is made from eighty blocks of granite which were brought all the way from Brittany by ox-cart. Inside, a staircase leads up the arm of the statue. *Open May-Sep, 11am-5pm, Mar-Apr, Sat-Sun 11am-5pm. 1.50€. ☎ 03 26 58 32 86.*
Enjoy the view from the nearby viewing table over the 22 villages in the valley and the vineyards.
Head west on the D 1 towards Vandières.

Vandières

Whether the town's name comes from *vinum dare* ("give wine") or from *vendemiare* ("to harvest the grapes"), its close relationship with wine is clear to see. An 18C château stands in the middle of a park at the top of the village. The 11C church has a beautiful porch. Admire the views over the valley framed by hills to the south.

Verneuil

The small 12C-13C church, carefully restored, stands on the banks of the Sémoinge, a tributary of the Marne.
Continue towards Vincelles then Dormans.

Dormans

A park, lined in trees, including a beautiful sequoia near the Chinese bridge, is the setting for the **castle** which houses temporary exhibitions, receptions and the tourist office. The **Mémorial des Victoires de la Marne**, a memorial chapel dedicated to the battles of the Marne, stands to the rear of the park on a spot chosen by Maréchal Foch. *Open Apr-Oct, daily except Tue, 2.30-6.30pm. No admission charge. ☎ 03 26 57 77 87.*
The **Moulin d'en Haut**, a former communal mill, houses an old mill wheel, in addition to a collection of rural tools related to wine-growing and making over the ages. *Open Jun-Aug, 11am-6pm, Sat 2.30-6pm, Sun and public holidays, 3-6pm, May and Sep-Oct, 2.30-6pm, Sun and public holidays, 3-6pm. Closed Mon. 4€. ☎ 03 26 58 85 16.*
Continue on the N 3 as far as Port-à-Binson, from where you will be able to see Châtillon, dominated by the statue of Pope Urban II. Take the N 3 to ŒEuilly.

Œuilly

This ancient fortified hillside town is home to several museums. The **Maison Champenoise** (1642) features a typical wine-grower's house of the late 19C. The **Musée de la Goutte**, devoted to the brandy of the same name, possesses the village's old alembic (1850) and an exhibition about the 1911 riots which took place in Champagne, and another about cooperage techniques. The **1900 village school**

Frescoes from the wine-growing cooperative of Fleury-la-Rivière.

still has its original desks, stove, blackboard and even a dunce's hat! *Open Apr-Oct, guided tours (1hr 15min) daily except Tue, 2-6pm; Nov-Mar, daily except Tue, 2-5pm. Closed Christmas holidays, 1 May. 5.50€ (children: 2.50€). ☎ 03 26 57 10 30.*

Take D 222 towards Boursault.

Château de Boursault

Built in 1848 by architect Arveuf for the legendary widow Veuve Clicquot, this sprawling Renaissance-inspired edifice boasts no less than 365 openings. It was the venue of magnificent receptions organised by Madame Clicquot. The estate produces wonderfully subtle blanc de blancs Champagnes.

Continue on towards Vauciennes and the D 22 to the Marne, then the N 3 back to Epernay.

The road commands fine views of the Marne valley, the village of Damery and the Montagne de Reims.

ROUND TOUR FROM CHATEAU-THIERRY

60km. Michelin Local Map 306, B-D 8-9. See itinerary **3** *on the map below.*

The Aisne vineyards which follow the River Marne from Crouttes to Trélou, near Dormans, belong to the Champagne wine-growing region.

Château-Thierry

Although it is located in the Aisne, Château-Thierry is genuine Champagne territory both by its origins and by its vineyards. It is built on the slopes of an isolated hill crowned by an old 14C **castle**, which has become a favourite walking spot with fine views of the Marne valley.

Walking down from the Tour Bouillon on the hilltop, you will go past the **birth-place** of the world-famous fable writer, **Jean de la Fontaine**. 🖰 The small reception rooms furnished in the style of the era display magnificent editions of the author's *Fables* and *Tales*, including volumes illustrated by Oudry (1755) and Gustave Doré (1868). There is also a collection of unusual objects decorated with scenes from the *Fables. Open Apr-Sep, daily except Tue, 9am-noon and 2-6pm; Oct-Mar, daily except Tue, 10am-noon and 2-5pm. Closed 1 Jan, 1 May, 1 Nov and 25 Dec. 5€. ☎ 03 23 69 05 60.*

A visit to the **cellars of the Pannier firm** located in 13C stone quarries makes a fine finish to your tour of the town; audiovisual display and guided tours of the Champagne-making process. *23 Rue Roger-Catillon, to the west of the town.* ♿ *Guided tours (1hr) by appointment. Daily except Sun and public holidays, 9am-noon and 2-6.30pm, 5€, ☎ 03 23 69 51 33. www.champagnepannier.com*

Leave Château-Thierry westbound on Avenue J. Lefebvre, then take the D 969.

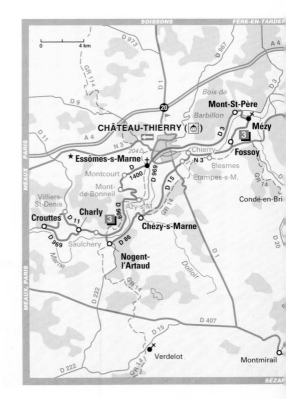

Essômes-sur-Marne

The **interior** of **Eglise St-Ferréol★**, founded in 1090, is characteristic of Decorated Gothic architecture. The 38 stalls of the chancel are Renaissance in style. *Open Sat 10am-noon and 2-5pm. Guided tours possible by appointment, enquire at the town hall (except Jul-Aug).* ☎ 03 23 83 08 31.
From Essômes, make for Montcourt then bear left onto the D 1400.
The road runs through vineyards, offering an interesting panorama of a meander of the Marne between Mont-de-Bonneil and Azy, with the wooded Brie region in the distance.
At Azy, rejoin the D 969 and continue past the built-up suburbs of Saulchery, to Charly.

Charly-sur-Marne

This is the most important wine-growing centre of the Aisne *département*. It is impossible to miss the statue of Emile Morlot, mayor and member of parliament, to whom the Aisne owes its current status of AOC Champagne.
Take the D 11 towards Villiers-Saint-Denis, then the D 842 to Crouttes. On the way, admire the sweeping views to the south of the meanders of the Marne.

Crouttes

This wine-growing village owes its name to its cellars dug out of the rock (from the Latin *cryptae*). Park your car in the Place de la Mairie and walk up the hill to the picturesque church.
From Crouttes, return to Charly on the D 969 and cross the river. Once on the other side, take the D 86 to Nogent-l'Artaud.

Nogent-l'Artaud

All that remains today of the former abbey of the Poor Clares Order, founded in the 13C by Blanche d'Artois, Queen of Navarre, can be seen in the Convent district near the school.
*Take the D 86. The picturesque road which looks down over the Marne takes you past hillsides covered in vines. It passes through **Chézy-sur-Marne**, a delightful village popular with painters and tourists, offering fine walks along the banks of the Dolloir.*
Take the D 15. The road runs under the D 1 to Etampes-sur-Marne and joins the N 3 in Chierry. Between Chierry and Blesmes, the road commands a fine panorama of the valley. 1.5km beyond Blesmes, turn left onto a minor road.

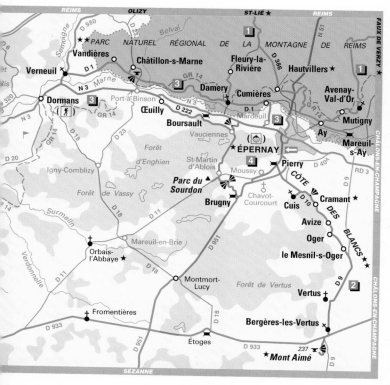

Fossoy

The Déhu firm, run by the seventh generation of a wine-growing family, welcomes tourists along the Champagne wine road. They have created a small **Musée de la Vigne et du Vin** (Le Varocien) in former stables. In addition to explanations of the three grape varieties, visitors can see tools and machinery used in former times by wine-growers. Note the refractometer dating from 1863 used to measure alcohol content. ♿ *Guided tours (30min) by appointment, contact Mr Déhu,. 3 Rue Saint-Georges, 02650 Fossoy. Closed Sun and public holidays. 4€. ☎ 03 23 71 90 47. Continue along the minor road as far as Mézy (Gothic church), then cross the Marne to take a left on the D 3 and along the north bank.*

Mont-Saint-Père

The 1 000 or so paintings by Léon Lhermitte (1844-1925), born in Mont-Saint-Père, were inspired by rural life and landscapes. He painted *The Harvesters' Wages*, which Van Gogh so admired (and which now hangs in the Musée d'Orsay in Paris) in the fortified farmhouse, Rue Chailly in Fossoy, on the south bank of the Marne.

The D 3 skirts the wood of Barbillon, before rejoining Château-Thierry.

ROUND TOUR SOUTH OF EPERNAY

28km. Michelin Local Map 306, F8. See itinerary **4** *on the map p. 194-195. Leave Epernay on the D 51.*

The road follows the Cubry Valley with vineyards on both sides of the river. As you come to Moussy, look left towards the church of Chavot (13C) perched on a peak. At Moussy, the place known as la Loge-Pinard commands a fine view of the Cubry Valley and Epernay framed by hills.

1km beyond Vaudancourt, turn right onto the D 951.

Château de Brugny

The castle overlooks the Cubry Valley. Built in the 16C, it was remodelled in the 18C. The square stone keep, flanked by round brick-built bartizans, is particularly attractive.

At the crossroads, turn right onto the D 36 towards St-Martin-d'Ablois.

Admire the splendid **views★** of the glacial Sourdon cirque with the church of Chavot to the right, Moussy in the centre and Epernay Forest on the left.

Turn left onto the D 11 to Mareuil-en-Brie.

Parc du Sourdon

Open Apr-Oct, 9am-7pm. No admission charge.

The Sourdon takes its source under a pile of rocks then flows through the park planted with fine trees and forms a series of rock pools where trout flourish.

Drive back to the D 22, then turn left. The road runs through Epernay Forest (private property) and the village of Vauciennes, then reaches the N 3. Turn right towards Epernay.

THE COTE DES BARS

Although traditionally looked down on by the wine-growers from the Marne region, the Champagne vineyards of the Aube *département* have gradually managed to forge a name and a reputation for themselves; they now produce one-quarter of the output of Champagne. On the borders of Burgundy, the Aube is the kingdom of Pinot Noir. The tiny parcels of vineyards are dotted around a landscape of forest, and also on the outskirts of Bar-sur-Seine and Bar-sur-Aube whose high slopes are home to mountain flowers. Vines also grow on the mound of Montgeux near Troyes, the surroundings of Villenauxe-la-Grande in the south and the regions of Les Riceys closer to Burgundy.

Le Barséquanais

56km from Bar-sur-Seine. Michelin Local Map 313, G-H 5-6.

Since the Roman Empire, vines have been grown on the hillsides of the Aube. The Barséquanais vineyards today represent the largest portion of the Côte des Bars wine-growing region of 7 000 hectares.

Bar-sur-Seine

The River Seine runs through this small town, nestling at the foot of the hillside. Admire the timber-framed 16C and 17C houses along Grande-Rue, which bear witness to the town's prosperous past.

Église St-Etienne, built between 1505 and 1616, is a fine mixture of Late Gothic and Renaissance. **Inside★** an interesting set of grisaille stained-glass windows are typical of the local 16C school. *Visits by appointment, contact the tourist office.* ☎ *03 25 29 94 43, or the presbytery,* ☎ *03 25 29 82 01.*

Cross over the square and turn left into Cour de la Mironne then through a covered passageway. Note the fine stone house along **Rue de la République**, on the left. Opposite is the largest house in Bar, formerly the town's casino. To the right, the Passage de la Poste is lined with half-timbered houses with carved beams. At n°17, you can identify Saint Roch and his dog in a small alcove of the Renaissance house on the corner.

Turn right into Avenue Paul-Portier. On the corner you will see the oldest house of Bar-sur-Seine, the 15C **Maison de l'Apothicaire**. On the way at the end of Rue Lagesse is **Maison du Charron**, so called because of its wheel-shaped timber frame.

Turn into Rue des Fossés, built on the site of old graveyards, then turn right into **Rue de la Résistance**. At n°**118**, admire the Corinthian-inspired pilasters of the Chapelle de la Passion, founded in the 12C. At n°**135** of **Grande-Rue**, behind the porch, a stone staircase *(173 steps)* up the hill leads to the former castle of the counts of Bar, all of which that now remains is the **Clock** or Lion Tower, rebuilt in 1948.

A fine selection of Champagnes and Rosé-des-Riceys wines can be found at **Veuve A. Devaux** *(see Shopping Guide)*.

Leave Bar-sur-Seine southbound on the N 71 and head for Celles-sur-Ource by the D 67.

Celles-sur-Ource

This welcoming village is home to forty or so wine-growers.

A **wine trail** *(11km, 3hr 30min)* winds its way through the vineyards commanding fine views of the valleys of the Ource and the Seine. *The town hall will be able to provide you with a folding map,* ☎ 03 23 38 52 68.

During the grape harvest, the **Marcel Vezien et Fils** firm organises afternoon beginners' courses in grape picking and pressing by appointment. After a hot afternoon's work, your efforts will be rewarded by a bottle of Champagne. *68 Grande-Rue, 10110 Celles-sur-Ource,* ☎ *03 25 38 50 22, www.champagne-vezien.com Open Mon-Fri 10am-5pm, Sat-Sun, by appointment. Closed 15 Aug to 2 Sep and Sun afternoons. Head for Landreville by the D 67.*

Landreville

In the winding lanes of this delightful market town are a remarkable set of 12C to 16C edifices including a castle, roadside cross, chapel and church; inside the latter is an altarpiece by Bouchardon.

René Jolly makes a splendid rosé Champagne; after a tour of the 18C cellars, don't miss the firm's museum which unveils the secrets of Champagne-making. *10 Rue de la Gare, 10110 Landreville,* ☎ *03 25 38 50 91. Open Mon-Sat, 10am-4pm. Closed public holidays.*

Continue on the D 67 as far as Essoyes.

Essoyes

Auguste Renoir (1841-1919) bought a house in Essoyes, his wife's birthplace, in 1865, and for 25 years the family spent all their summers here. Many of his paintings depict the surrounding countryside and his studio is open to the public. A collection of photos, documents and personal belongings is on display and every summer the Renoir Association invites a different artist to display their work in the gallery upstairs. *7 Rue Extra. Open late Mar to early Nov, 2-6.30pm. 2€,* ☎ *03 25 38 56 28.*

Continue your pilgrimage to the **cemetery**. The busts by Guino remind visitors that Auguste Renoir is buried here in the company of his wife and their three sons, Pierre, actor, Jean, film director and Claude, ceramicist.

Under a lovely glass-roof, the former stables of the château have been turned into a **Maison de la Vigne**, which explains how Champagne is made, from the planting of the vine stock to the bottling. Space is also devoted to the daily life of wine-growers, including their revolt in the early 20C, when the vines, destroyed by phylloxera in 1865, were gradually replanted but the Aube wine-growers encountered opposition on the part of Marne wine-growers regarding their right to AOC status. This struggle culminated in 1911 in the wine-growers' revolt led by Gaston Checq prompting the government to despatch some 3 000 men to Bar-sur-Seine on May 3 to put down the revolt. The men and women of Aube finally obtained satisfaction on July 22 1927 with one

ROSÉ-DES-RICEYS

It really is a privilege to drink Rosé-des-Riceys! The geographic location of the vineyards and the particularly strict regulations mean that wine-growers are not able to make it every year. It is made exclusively from Pinot Noir grapes grown on the steepest and sunniest slopes of Les Riceys. The grape harvest takes place only in dry weather and only the highest quality grapes are picked.

The wine-making process is complex and the slow maceration period is followed by a fast fermentation period, further speeded up by a special light pressing of some of the grapes. This stage is the most delicate of the entire process, requiring the utmost vigilance on the part of the wine-growers. They must judge the exact point at which the wine takes on the distinctive Rosé-des-Riceys taste: a delicate bouquet of wild flowers, violets and hazelnuts.

concession: they had to replace Gamay by other varieties (Pinot and Chardonnay) authorised for Champagne. *Place de la Mairie. Open Jul-Aug, 2.30-6.30pm; rest of the year by appointment. 2.50€. ☎ 03 25 29 64 64.*

Take the D 79 southbound then take a sharp right onto the D 117 through the forest and then bear right onto the D 17.

Mussy-sur-Seine

Former residence of the bishops of Langres, this town has retained its 15C and 16C houses, including an old salt storehouse.

It is difficult not to be impressed by the dimensions of the huge late 13C **Eglise St-Pierre-ès-Liens**. In the baptismal chapel, a 2m-high sculpture of Saint John the Baptist dates from the 14C; it was the work of craftsmen whose reputation was known throughout the Aube and Burgundy. *Enquire at the tourist office, ☎ 03 25 38 42 08.*

Continue heading SW on the D 17.

After passing through the forest, the road reaches the vine-covered hillsides of Les Riceys countryside. On the way down, it is possible to make out three hamlets, each of which is dominated by a Renaissance church.

Les Riceys

On the border with Burgundy, this unusual village is made up of three hamlets dotted along the banks of the River Laignes. It boasts no less than three listed churches, six chapels and seven wash houses! However its main claim to fame is its delicious Pinot Noir rosé wine, considered to be one of the best in France.

The lovely 16C **Eglise St-Pierre-ès-Liens** (in Riceys-Bas) possesses a richly carved porch. The oldest section dates back to the 13C and inside, two carved wooden altarpieces adorn the Chapelles de la Passion on the north and south sides. *Open 9am-noon and 1-5pm; by appointment with the tourist office, ☎ 03 25 29 15 38.*

Vineyards around Les Riceys.

Eglise St-Vincent (in Riceys-Haut) is unusually made up of two churches, joined together by extending the transept of the second church. On the square, note the imposing timber frame (18C) of the **Halle au Vin**, where the annual Grand Jeudi fair is held.

The **Morel**, **Gallimard**, **Morize** and **Coquet** firms are among the best known producers *(see Shopping Guide)*.

From Les Riceys, head north on the D 452 to Polisy, then take the D 207 via **Polisot**, a village surrounded by vineyards and woods.

Rejoin Bar-sur-Seine by the N 71.

The Baralbin region

70km from Bar-sur-Aube. Michelin Local Map n°313, I4.

More spread out than those of the Barséquanais, the vineyards around Bar-sur-Aube stretch over the best-facing hillsides of the region as far as the *département* of Haute-Marne.

Bar-sur-Aube

Since the era of the counts of Champagne, Bar-sur-Aube has been a thriving wine centre and its medieval fairs were major events. They were among the six annual Champagne events which drew visitors from all over Europe. The Foire aux Bulles in early September perpetuates the tradition and it is the ideal moment to taste the Champagne of Bar-sur-Aube, whose vineyards cover the town's surrounding hillsides.

The town is surrounded by boulevards, laid out on the site of the former ramparts, and has retained many fine old houses (16C and 18C).

Eglise St-Pierre★ (12C) was built on the site of a sanctuary, the floor of which remains; visitors may notice that the entrance to the nave is, unusually, down eight steps. The high altar was originally in Clairvaux Abbey and the organ in Remiremont Abbey. Some fifty tombstones mark the graves of local lords and wealthy merchants.

At n°16 and 18 of **Rue d'Aube** is the post office, an 18C edifice with beautiful wrought-iron balconies. **Eglise St-Maclou** is not open to the public; it was the former chapel of the counts of Bar's castle, destroyed in the late 16C. The 12C belfry was the castle keep.

Rue Nationale is the town's main street. At n°14 note the deconsecrated **Chapelle St-Jean** (11C-12C). The former town house of the monks of Clairvaux, the **Cellier des Moines** has retained a fine cellar covered with 12C ribbed vaulting, now a restaurant. It was used as the wine-growers' headquarters during their rebellion in 1912 which cemented the Bar region's right to the name Champagne.

Leave Bar-sur-Aube southbound on the D 4. 3km further on, turn left, in a bend, onto a steep lane and park your car.

Chapelle Sainte-Germaine

The footpath leads up to a pilgrimage chapel dedicated to Saint Germaine, a virgin martyred by the Vandals in 407. Walk beyond the chapel and around the house to reach the viewing table which offers **glimpses** of Bar-sur-Aube, the valley, Colombey-les-Deux-Eglises and its cross of Lorraine, as well as the Dhuits and Clairvaux forests.

Those more energetic might prefer to walk along the "Côte d'Aube" path *(10km, 2hr 30min)* up the hill from Bar-sur-Aube and through the vineyards. *Enquire at the tourist office.*

Rejoin the D 4 and continue for 6km to Meurville.

Meurville

This village is home to several Champagne producers. A fine view of the village can be had from the picnic area known as Quatre-Napoléon.

Continue northbound on the D 44 as far as Spoy. **Spoy** is a delightful flower-decked village which possesses a recently restored Roman bridge.

Return to Meurville and take the D 4 to Bligny.

Château de Bligny

Open Jun-Aug, Mon-Sat, 10.30am-6.30pm. 3€, ☎ 03 25 27 40 11.

This château is one of the rare châteaux to have given its name to a Champagne. The 18C edifice built by the marquis of Dampierre was transformed during the 19C and restoration work in 1999 has restored the painted ceilings and lovely neo-Gothic glass roofs. The visit includes a tour of the château, the cellar and a tasting session.

Rejoin the D 4 via Meurville, then turn right onto the D 44 towards Urville.

Urville

The wine-growing village of Urville is home to a number of traditional old houses and to the family-run firm of **Drappier**, who were official suppliers of Champagne to General de Gaulle and who continue to supply the Elysées palace today. The firm is renowned for several prestigious vintages and its 12C vaulted cellars built by the monks of Clairvaux are open to the public. This Champagne-producing firm is the only one in the world to use a single bottle throughout the entire process. *Grande-Rue, 10200 Urville, ☎ 03 25 27 40 15, www.champagne-drappier.com Open Mon-Sat by appointment. Closed public holidays.*

Continue on the D 44, then turn right onto the D 70 to Champignol-lez-Mondeville.

Champignol-lez-Mondeville

This peaceful village has a 12C chapel with an unusual wooden door and an 18C church which possesses a Baroque altarpiece and staffs from brotherhoods of wine-growers. The **Dumont** establishment has a fine selection of local wines.

Rejoin Barroville NE on the D 70.

Barroville

Champagne is the main attraction of Barroville, but the town's wine-growers also make excellent red Coteaux-Champenois wines.

Head eastbound on the D 170 then take the D 396 left.

Bayel

Founded by a Venetian master glassworker, Jean-Baptiste Mazzolay who was granted a letter of patent by Louis XIV, the **Royal crystal-works of Champagne** is famous the world over. Since its foundation in 1666, its kilns have never been extinguished and glass-blowers and cutters continue to uphold ancient traditions. A mixture of sand, lime, soda and lead heated for 12 hours to a temperature of 1 450°C produces a kind of paste which is ready to be shaped by blowing or casting; all the items are handmade. ♿ *Guided tours (1hr30min) daily except Sun 9.30am, 11am, Sat by appointment. Closed mid-Jul to mid-Aug, public holidays, 25 Dec-1 Jan. 5.30€ (combined ticket for the crystal-works and Ecomusée: 7.60€). ☎ 03 25 92 42 68.*

The **Ecomusée du Cristal** is housed in three small workers' cottages *(entrance through the tourist office)*. A series of models offers an insight into the origins of crystal, its various components, the manufacturing process and the different methods used to decorate glass such as guilloche and engraving. A 15-minute video about the crystal-works and the town of Bayel and the surrounding area

Shopping Guide

INFORMATION

Comité interprofessionnelle des vins de Champagne – *5 rue Henri-Martin – 51204 Epernay* – ☎ *03 26 55 19 79* – *www.champagne.fr*

Syndicat général des vignerons de la Champagne – *44 Avenue Jean-Jaurès – 51205 Epernay* – ☎ *03 26 55 19 79* – *www.champagnesdevignerons.com*

USEFUL TIPS

Les carnets des Champagnes – Published by the Comité Interprofessionnelle des vins de Champagne, these guides of around twenty pages each (in French) initiate the reader into the world of Champagne. Wine hints, tips and characteristics, food and wine, and the ins and outs of Champagne etiquette are all covered.

OVERVIEW

CHARACTERISTICS

Champagne is generally light gold or rosé in colour. The streams of bubbles in the glass should be lasting and the wine should be sparkling with a slight head of froth but without being aggressive. The range of aromas varies greatly from fresh brioche bread and white flowers to ripe grapes and soft red fruit.

In terms of taste, Champagnes can be brut, sec or demi-sec depending on the quantity of sugar added. The Coteaux-Champenois are still red wines with a beautiful deep, rich, robe and a distinctive bouquet of raspberry and cherry notes.

The deep pink Rosé-des-Riceys are still, rosé wines, which are fruity and intense with a hint of bitterness.

STORAGE

Champagne, once it has been bottled, and whether it be a vintage wine or not, is rarely kept for more than five years.

Coteaux-Champenois and Rosé-des-Riceys can be kept for between five to eight years.

PRICES

Despite the fact that the last three years have been far from exceptional, particularly 2003 when many wine-growers had to acidify the wines, 2004 was the best year ever for Champagne sales worldwide. Rumour has it that there might even be a shortage of Champagne and that the authorities could be considering extending the boundaries of the appellation d'origine contrôlée.

As a result a short-term drop in prices is highly unlikely and Champagne, the wine of celebrations and special events, remains expensive.

Wine-growers Champagne – Average of between 11€ and 15€.

Vintage Champagne – Between 15€ and 30€.

Grande cuvée prestige Champagne – Between 50€ and 100€.

BUYING

WINE MERCHANTS

Confrérie la St-Vincent de Rizaucourt et Argentolles – *Cellier St-Vincent – Musée de la Vigne – 52330 Colombey-les-Deux-Eglises* – ☎ *03 25 02 58 05* – Open Apr-Nov, Sat-Sun and public holidays 11am-noon and 2-6pm (8pm in summer). It is not very surprising to find that an oenological brotherhood has chosen to name itself after Saint Vincent, who is the patron saint of wine-growers; his saint's day is in late January, at a time when the vines require the least care. The establishment, which is also home to a small wine museum (2.60€ per person) sells locally produced Champagnes.

La Cave d'Erlon – *40 Place d'Erlon – 51100 Reims* – ☎ *03 26 47 44 44* – *caverderlon. vinexport @wanadoo.fr* This treasure trove boasts over fifty brands of Champagne, thirty or so of which are from the top Champagne firms, some five hundred different whiskies and over 1 200 wines and spirits. The establishment also has another shop in Rue Courmeaux and a third boutique behind the cathedral.

H. Champollion / MICHELIN

Les Delices Champenoises – *2 Rue Rockefeller – 51100 Reims* – ☎ *03 26 47 35 25* – *lesdeliceschampenoises@franc egourmande.fr* Not a single Grand Cru Champagne is missing from the roll call in this cellar, which is barely two minutes from the cathedral. Row upon row of Veuve Clicquot, Pommery, Perrier-Jouët, Taittinger, Jacquart, Bollinger and Mumm, to name but a few, stand smartly to attention, alongside wine from Bouzy, pink Champagne biscuits, Reims mustard and chocolates stuffed with marc de Champagne.

Mumm – *29 Rue du Champ-de-Mars – 51100 Reims* - ☎ *03 26 49 59 70* – *loilier@mumm.fr* Mumm Cordon Rouge, light, sparkling Mumm Cramant and Mumm demi-sec… This prestigious Champagne firm founded in 1827 produces no less than seven varieties of its own Champagne brand which can be found in its store not far from the Chapelle Foujita.

GROUPS OF CHAMPAGNE-PRODUCERS

Champagne Clément – *Rue St-Antoine – 10200 Colombé-le-Sec – ☎ 03 25 92 50 70 – www.champagne-charles-clement. fr - Open mid-Jun to Aug, Mon-Sat, 8am-noon and 1.30-5.30pm, Sun 10am-noon and 2-6pm; rest of the year, Mon-Sat, 8am-noon and 1.30-5.30pm, (Fri 4.30pm) – tours of the cellars: 10am, last afternoon visit at 3.30pm.* This wine cooperative is a happy mix of old and new with pneumatic and traditional presses. Excellent selection of rosé Champagnes and still Coteaux-Champenois wines. Many of the wines and Champagnes on sale have won medals.

Mailly Grand Cru – *28 Rue de la Libération – 51500 Mailly-Champagne - ☎ 03 26 49 41 10 – contact@champagne-mailly.com - Open Mon-Sat (daily in summer), 9am-noon and 2-6pm.* In 1923 six wine-growers joined forces to press their grapes, make wine and sell their produce together. Six years later, their ranks had risen to 20 and they founded the Société des producteurs de Mailly-Champagne. The firm, which now has 77 members who cultivate some 70 hectares of vineyards, is a particularly get-ahead enterprise which combines traditions, state-of-the-art technology and a permanent quest for excellence.

WINE ESTATES

Serge Pierlot – *10 Rue St-Vincent – 6.5km SE of Louvois on the D 34 and D 19 – 51150 Ambonnay - ☎ 03 26 57 01 11 – Champagne-serge-pierlot@wanadoo.fr - Open Mon-Fri, 9am-noon and 2.30-6.30pm, Sat 9am-noon and 2.30-6pm, Sun 9am-noon-Closed Jan, late Aug to early Sep.* The south- and southeast facing Côte d'Ambonnay-Bouzy is renowned for its AOC Champagnes and red Coteaux-Champenois. Stop at Agnès and Serge Pierlot's wine-growing estate and taste their wines after visiting their small museum complete with an 18C press and old vine and wine-making tools.

Soutiran-Pelletier – *12 Rue St-Vincent – 6.5km SE of Louvois on the D 34 and D 19 –51150 Ambonnay - ☎ 03 26 57 07 87 – www.soutiran.com - tasting Mon-Sat 8am-noon and 2-6pm; visits by appointment only – closed Sat from Dec to Easter.* The heir to five generations of wine-growing know-how, Alain Soutiran is far from a beginner in the blending department and his AOC white Champagnes and red Coteaux-Champenois enjoy an excellent reputation. The visit includes a tour of the estate's presses, vats and cellars, all of which are accompanied by explanations and a tasting session at the end.

Egly-Ouriet – *9-15 Rue de Trépail – 51150 Ambonnay - ☎ 03 26 57 00 70 – Daily 9am-1pm and 2-6pm.* Charles Egly founded his Champagne firm in 1936; today it is run by his son Michel and his grandson is in charge of the 9 hectares of vineyards, all of which are Grand Cru class. The Egly family also produces red Ambonnay wines. The estate continues to employ traditional agricultural methods and the vines are tended and pruned extremely carefully, optimising the quality of the grapes. The vineyards are cultivated using ecologically responsible methods and the soil is regularly ploughed and aired.

Agrapart et Fils – *57 Avenue Jean-Jaurès – 51190 Avize - ☎ 03 26 57 51 38 – Champagne.agrapart@wanadoo.fr - Mon-Sat, 9am-1pm and 2-5pm.* It was in 1894 that Arthur Agrapart created this estate in Avize, now run by his heirs Fabrice and Pascal Agrapart. Together the two men work 9.5 hectares of vineyard spread over Avize (Côte des Blancs Grands Crus), Oger, Cramant and Oiry. The chalky soil is ideally suited to Chardonnay. The vineyards are still regularly ploughed (mechanical weeding) to ensure constant microbic life and enable the roots to draw rich mineral elements from deep down in the ground. The grapes are harvested manually and selectively depending on the health and maturity of each plot of land.

Jacques Selosse – *22 Rue Ernest-Vallé –51190 Avize - ☎ 03 26 57 53 56 – a.selosse@wanadoo.fr - Mon-Sat by appointment.* Anselme Selosse, Jacques' son, has been running this 7-hectare vineyard since 1980. He produces between 45 000 and 48 000 bottles yearly. Regularly renewed oak barrels and casks ensure that the wines develop and are able to breathe and mature fully.

Champagne Gosset – *69 Rue Jules-Blondeau – BP 7 – 51160 Ay - ☎ 03 26 56 99 56 – info@champagne-gosset.com - Mon-Fri 9-11am and 2-5pm.* Since it was founded by Pierre Gosset in 1584 up until today, this firm has been in existence for over four centuries. One of the objectives of Béatrice Cointreau, the current manager of the firm, is to obtain recognition for Champagne's status as a fine wine full-stop rather than just a wine for special occasions. She has taken up this challenge with as much determination as her illustrious predecessors, ever faithful to the firm's motto: "Do it well, very well".

Bollinger – *16 Rue Jules-Lobet – 51160 Ay - ☎ 03 26 53 33 66 – contact@champagne-bollinger.fr - wine merchant: BLD France, 193 Rue de Bercy – 75012 Paris – 01 53 02 44 44 – Mon-Fri 10am-3pm.* The great-great-grandson of the founder and company director since 1994, Ghislain de Montgolfier has been with the firm since 1992. With 160 hectares of excellently located Champagne vineyards, Bollinger is one of the rare Champagne firms to produce 70% of its own grapes; the remainder is purchased from a few carefully selected growers. The Bollinger style is founded on a blend of Pinot Noir aromas which rise to perfection in the Premier Cru and Grand Cru Champagnes of Ay, Bouzy and Verzenay.

Veuve A. Devaux – *Domaine de Villeneuve – 10110 Bar-sur-Seine - ☎ 03 25 38 30 65 – info@champagne-devaux.fr - Mon-Fri 9am-noon and 1.30-6pm.* Founded in 1846 in Epernay by two brothers, Auguste and Jules Devaux, the firm was taken over by Mrs Augusta Devaux, widow. The latter's influence on the firm was so great that the establishment continues to bear her name today. Since 1967 the brand has been the property of the Union auboise des producteurs de vins de Champagne.

Brice – *3 Rue Yvonnet – 50110 Bouzy - ☎ 03 26 52 06 60 – Champagnebrice@wanadoo.fr - daily 9am- 6pm.* This 7-hectare estate of vineyards has belonged to the same family since the 17C. Today Jean-Paul Brice is proud of his production which includes four Grands Crus from Bouzy, Ay, Cramant and Verzenay (brut). The vines are grown and the wine made according to traditional methods.

Champagne Dumont – *Route de Champagne – 10200 Champignol-lez-Mondeville - ☎ 03 25 27 45 95.* This family of wine-growers has owned and worked the vineyard for over two centuries. Staunch champions of the merits of traditional methods, it has recently managed to introduce new technology to maintain its rank in the profession. Tours are organised of the wine-making premises (presses, vats, etc) with Champagne tasting.

Champagne R. et L. Legras – *10 Rue des Partelaines – 51530 Chouilly - ☎ 03 26 54 50 79 - contact@legras.fr - Mon-Fri 8.30am-noon and 2-4.30pm by appointment.* The firm of R. and L. Legras possesses 14 hectares of vineyards, 10 of which are under contract for the supply of noble varieties of vines. In the heart of the exclusive Côte des Blancs region, the estate also enjoys a south-facing aspect. Philippe Legras is specialised in old vintage Champagnes which he nurtures carefully in his cellars. The stainless steel vats are equipped with a thermo-regulation system.

Breton Fils – *12 Rue Courte-Pilate – 15km S of Epernay by the N 951 and D 943 – 51270 Congy - ☎ 03 26 59 31 03 – contact@champagne-breton-fils.fr - 9am-noon and 2-5.30pm – closed 3rd Sun in May, 25 Dec and 1 Jan.* The firm has been cultivating 17 hectares of vineyards under the brand name of Breton Fils for over half a century. Johann, the current guardian of the family savoir-faire, enjoys taking visitors round his estate and into the cellars dug out of chalk where over 450 000 bottles are laid down to age.

Lilbert Fils – *223 Rue du Moutier – BP 14 – 51530 Cramant - ☎ 03 26 57 50 16 – info@champagne-lilbert.com - Mon-Sat, 10am-noon and 2-6pm.* Specialised in the production of white Champagne for which he has received countless medals and awards, Georges Lilbert has even gone so far as to forego rosé Champagne completely. Born into a family of wine-growers from father to son since 1746, Georges upholds ancient traditions and the bottles are still turned by hand on traditional racks and the *dégorgement* process is also carried out according to ancestral customs.

Bonnaire – *120 Rue d'Epernay – 51530 Cramant - ☎ 03 26 57 50 85 – info@champagne-bonnaire.com - daily 8.30-11.30am and 2-4.30pm.* The same family of wine-growers and producers has been at the helm of this house created in 1932 for three generations. Today, the firm of Champagne Bonnaire works 22 hectares of vineyards, the majority of which is classed in the Grand Cru or Premier Cru categories.

Champagne René Geoffroy – *150 Rue du Bois-des-Jots – 51480 Cumières - ☎ 03 26 55 32 31 – info@champagne-geoffroy.com - Mon-Sat 9am-noon and 2-6pm.* This Champagne firm has been handed down from generation to generation since the 17C. René Geoffroy and his son Jean-Baptiste, both dedicated and enthusiastic wine-growers, supervise every step of the wine-making process of each of their wines, leaving nothing to chance. This attention to detail can be felt in every aspect of the production process from the vine stock to the thick heavy glass bottles. Their 13-hectare estate is planted with Pinot Noir, Pinot Meunier and Chardonnay, all according to ecologically responsible methods. The grapes are harvested by hand and subjected to a stringent selection process. The wine is fermented mainly in small oak tuns.

Louis Casters – *26 Rue Pasteur – 51480 Damery - ☎ 03 26 58 43 02 – Mon-Sat 10am-noon and 2-6pm.* The ten-hectare vineyards of this estate are spread over the communes of Damery, Vauciennes, Reuil, Binson-Orquigny and Villers-sous-Châtillon. In 1985, this traditional family-run affair took on the status of néogociant-manipulant (buyer and blender). Since then, it has been buying grapes from a further 25 hectares of carefully selected vineyards.

Champagne Moët et Chandon – *20 Avenue de Champagne – 51200 Epernay - ☎ 03 26 51 20 20 – 9.30-11.45am and 2-4.45pm – closed Sat-Sun from 12 Nov to 31 Mar.* According to the firm's PR department, "a cork of Moët et Chandon Champagne pops open very two seconds around the world". This family-run affair has always been a champion of the historical and cultural traditions and prestige of Champagne throughout the world. Since 1987, the name of this exclusive firm is associated with that of the flagship of luxury goods, Louis Vuitton Moët-Hennessy.

Champagne Richardot – *38 Rue René-Quinton – 10110 Loches-sur-Ource - ☎ 03 25 29 71 20 – Champagne.richardot@wanadoo.fr - Mon-Fri 9-11.30am and 2-6pm, Sat-Sun by appointment only, closed Christmas to New Year.* The superb vaulted cellars of the Richardot firm are adorned with a collection of old wine-grower's tools and utensils. The view over the vineyards as you sip a glass of Champagne in the pleasant tasting room is well worth the visit.

Beaumont des Crayères – *64 Rue de la Liberté – 51530 Mardeuil - ☎ 03 26 55 29 40 – Mon-Fri 9am-noon and 1.30-6pm, Sat 10am-noon and 2-5pm, closed 25 Dec and Easter.* The Beaumont firm, whose reputation for outstanding wines is a secret to no one, was awarded the Grand Prix d'Excellence by the French Union of Oenologists in 2004. Among other exhibits, its museum devoted to Champagne boasts the largest bottle of Champagne in the world. Tasting, sales and guided tours of the cellars.

Philipponnat – *13 Rue du Pont – Domaine Clos des Goisses – 51160 Mareuil-sur-Ay -*

5

☎ 03 26 56 93 00 – info@champagnephilip
ponnat.com - Mon-Fri 9am-noon and 2-5pm.
Established in Champagne since the early
16C, the Philipponnat family has earned its
living from the making and selling of fine
wines for centuries. Today the firm run by
Charles Philipponnat is located in Mareuil-
sur-Ay in the heart of the Champagne
region; it offers a selection of wines, made
primarily from Pinot Noir grapes.

Pierre Moncuit – *11 Rue Persaut-Maheu
– 51190 Le Mesnil-sur-Oger - ☎ 03 26 57
52 65 –Mon-Sat 10.30am-noon and 2-
3.30pm.* Yves and Nicole Moncuit, who have
taken over from their parents, are now at
the head of a vineyard which rose to fame at
the inauguration of the Universal Exhibition
of 1889. Yves is in charge of the sales side
of the business and customer relations,
while his sister Nicole devotes herself to
running the 19 hectares of vineyards planted
exclusively with Chardonnay. The estate has
retained a vine over 80 years old which is at
the origin of the "Nicole Moncuit – Vieille
Vigne" prestigious Champagne.

Philippe Gonet – *Rue de la Brèche-d'Oger –
BP 18 – 51190 Le Mesnil-sur-Oger - ☎ 03 26
57 53 47 – info@champagne-philippe-gonet.
com - Mon-Fri 8am-noon and 2-6pm.* Philippe
Gonet's family owns Grand Crus plots of
vineyards in Le Mesnil-sur-Oger and a total of
19 hectares, spread over a variety of communes,
enabling Philippe to blend high quality
Champagnes. He is the seventh generation
of the family to take over the business. The
Champagne is stored for at least three years in
the family's traditional Champagne cellars.

Launois Père et Fils – *2 Avenue Eugène-
Guillaume – 11km S of Epernay by the D 40
and D 10 - 51190 Le Mesnil-sur-Oger -
☎ 03 26 57 50 15 – www.champagne-launois.
fr - Mon-Fri 8am-noon and 2-6pm, Sat-Sun
10am-1pm and 3-5pm – closed 25 Dec, 1 Jan
and Easter.* This négociant-manipulant (buyer
and blender) firm founded in 1872 has its
own museum devoted to vines and wine. The
tour ends with a tasting session of the firm's
own brand. Gourmet meals and "days" – in
particular during the harvest period – are also
organised. Bookings essential.

Champagne Vollereaux – *48 Rue Léon-
Bourgois – BP 4 – 51530 Pierry - ☎ 03 26 54
03 05 – Champagne.vollereauxsa@wanadoo.
fr - Mon-Sat 10.30am-noon and 3-6pm,
Sun by appointment.* The Vollereaux wine-
growing family, established in Pierry and
Moussy since 1805, owns 40 hectares of
vineyards spread throughout the Champagne
AOC, although most of it is on the hills
around Epernay. The three traditional
varieties of vines are cultivated according to
ecologically responsible methods; the harvests
are by hand. Fermented in modern vats, the
Champagne is then stored for four years in
the estate's own cellars.

Piper-Heidsieck – *51 Boulevard Henry-Vasnier
– 51100 Reims - ☎ 03 26 84 43 44 – Mar-
Dec, 9-11.45am and 2-5.15pm.* Florens-Louis
Heidsieck, son of a Lutheran pastor, founded
his Champagne firm in 1785. His success was
swift and he was granted the privilege of

presenting Queen Marie-Antoinette with
a wine made specially in her honour. On
his death, his nephew Christian Heidsieck
took over the company with a partner Henri-
Guillaume Piper. The outstanding salesmanship
of the latter propelled Heidsieck Champagne
into the international arena and the brand
acquired its current name of Piper-Heidsieck. In
1989 the house was purchased by the Rémy-
Martin group, now the Rémy-Cointreau group.
Its Champagnes are blended from a variety of
different wines.

Domaine Pommery – *5 Place du Général-
Gouraud - BP 1049 – 51689 Reims Cedex
2 - ☎ 03 26 61 62 63 – info@pommery.
fr - 10am-6pm (5pm from mid-Nov to
Easter).* Every year, the head of the Pommery
wine cellars endeavours to ensure that the
year's vintage will be representative of the
distinctive, elegant Pommery style initiated
by Madame Pommery over a century ago.
In April 2002, the Vranken group, founded
by Paul-François Vranken, and owner of
Heidsieck & Co Monopole, acquired the
Pommery firm of Champagne.

Champagne Taittinger – *9 Place St-Nicaise
– 51100 Reims - ☎ 03 26 85 84 33 – Mon-Fri
9.30am-1pm and 2-5.30pm.* Founded in the
early 1930s by Pierre Taittinger, since 1960
the firm has been run by his son, Claude. With
property in all the major Champagne-producing
regions (Epernay, Montagne de Reims
and Essoyes), the vineyards are located on
hillsides and worked according to ecologically
responsible methods. Its 270 hectares are
planted with Chardonnay (40%), Pinot Noir
(45%) and Pinot Meunier (15%). The Taittinger
firm also purchases high-quality produce from a
selection of the best Champagne vineyards. The
firm's cellars store some 19 500 000 bottles.
In addition to vineyards in France, Taittinger
also owns 70 hectares of vines in the Carneros
region of California.

Daniel Dumont – *11 Rue Gambetta
– 51100 Rilly-la-Montagne - ☎ 03 26 03
40 67 – daily 8am-noon and 1.30-6pm.*
Daniel Dumont planted his vineyard in
1962 and in 1970 he began to sell a few
hundred bottles under his own brand. Today
his three children, Alain, Jean-Michel and
Marie-Claire all work on the estate with him.
Their vineyards cover some 10 hectares of
Premiers Crus, planted with Chardonnay
(40%), Pinot Noir (40%) and Pinot Meunier

Ph. Gajic / MICHELIN

(20%). The presses and the storehouse have both been modernised in keeping with Champagne traditions dear to the hearts of wine-growers. The wine is bottled and aged (between four and seven years) in the estate's cellars. Annual production ranges between 75 000 and 90 000 bottles.

Morel Père et Fils – *93 Rue du Général-de-Gaulle – 10340 Les Riceys - ☎ 03 25 29 10 88 – morel.pereetfils@wanadoo.fr – Mon-Sat 9am-noon and 2-6pm.* A descendant of a family of owner-wine-growers from Les Riceys, Pascal Morel took over the family business in 1974. The property is planted with Pinot Noir (90%) and Chardonnay (10%). The vines enjoy a very favourable south-southeast facing aspect. In keeping with traditions, Pascal Morel continues to make his Rosé-des-Riceys from old plots of his 7 hectares of vineyards according to ecologically responsible methods. The wine is fermented in stainless steel vats.

Gallimard Père et Fils – *18-20 Rue Gaston-Cheq – Le Magny – BP 23 – 10340 Les Riceys - ☎ 03 25 29 32 44 – Mon-Fri 9am-noon and 2-5.30pm.* The Gallimards have been making Champagne since 1930, when wine-growers Jules and Ernest Gallimard decided to try their hand at blending for the first time. Today, the family business is managed by Didier who runs the 10 hectares of vineyards in Les Riceys. The vines, aged between 3 and 40 years old, are comprised of Pinot Noir (90%) and Chardonnay (10%) and cultivated according to ecologically responsible methods. The wine is fermented in thermo-regulated enamelled steel vats.

Champagne Coquet – *10 Route de Gyé-sur-Seine – 10340 Les Riceys - ☎ 03 25 29 33 83 – Mon-Sat 9am-noon and 2-5.30pm by appointment.* At the southernmost tip of the Côte des Bars, the commune of Les Riceys is the only one in France with three AOCs: Champagne, Coteaux-Champenois and Rosé-des-Riceys. A dozen or so buyer-blenders, among them Christian Coquet, share the privilege of owning these highly profitable vineyards.

Champagne Morize Père et Fils – *122 Rue du Général-de-Gaulle – 10340 Les Riceys - ☎ 03 25 29 30 02 – www.champagne. morize.com - Mon-Sat 9-11am and 2.30-6pm – closed public holidays.* The cellars which date from the 12C are as welcoming as they are attractive. After the ritual tour of the property in the company of the owner, you can choose between sipping a glass of Champagne at the stone bar or taking a seat for a gourmet meal. Whatever you decide, you will be spoilt for choice by the estate's 100 000 bottles of sparkling nectar.

Veuve Olivier et Fils – *10 Route de Dormans – 2.5km west of Dormans on the D 6 – 02850 Trélou-sur-Marne – ☎ 03 23 70 24 01 – Champagne.veuve.Olivier@cder. fr - Mon-Fri 9am-noon and 2-5pm, Sat 9am-noon, afternoons by appointment – closed Aug and public holidays.* This admirably situated estate commands a splendid panoramic view of the Marne valley. A video and guided tour of the premises includes a look at the traditional press and an explanation of how Champagne is made. Tasting and sales on the estate.

Duval-Leroy – *69 Avenue de Bammenthal – BP 37 – 51330 Vertus - ☎ 03 26 52 10 75 – Champagne @duval-leroy.com - Mon-Fri 9-11.30am and 2-4.30pm.* Located right in the heart of the prestigious Côte des Bars since 1859, this establishment now owns and cultivates over 170 hectares of vineyards which provide it with one-quarter of its needs in grapes. Since 1991, Carol Duval-Leroy has made a name for herself in the exclusive circle of women Champagne blenders. Her dynamic, get-ahead outlook and that of her team have played a fundamental role in turning this family affair into a highly successful enterprise.

Veuve Fourny et Fils – *5 Rue du Mesnil – Domaine du Clos du Faubourg-Notre-Dame – 51330 Vertus - ☎ 03 26 52 16 30 – info@champagne-veuve-fourny.com - Mon-Sat 9am-noon and 2-6pm.* Four generations of the Fourny family have been running this Premier Cru class vineyard in Vertus according to ecologically responsible methods. All the Champagnes are blended from reserve wines kept in barrels. In the 1950s, the grandfather-father team who founded the firm produced a highly distinctive vintage matured in oak barrels from three varieties of vine. Roger Fourny's sons, Emmanuel (an oenologist) and Charles-Henry, found a few of these old bottles and have managed to recreate this vintage blend, naming it "R" in tribute to their father.

FESTIVALS

Ay – Fête Henri IV, first Sat-Sun of July in even years. The festival lasts two days, the first is devoted to visits to the cellars and tasting. The second day is given over to a parade of some 2 000 people, 40 horses and 15 carriages and carts, all in honour of Good King Henry.

Vignoble Châtillonais – Festibulles (festival of bubbles) on 3rd Sat-Sun of July.

Epernay – Grand Cochelet des Vendanges – last day of the grape harvest, includes a huge wine-growers' meal.

One of the Marne towns – Festival of Saint Vincent de Champagne, Sunday after 22 January.

Les Riceys – Walking festival, 1 May. Sign up with the tourist office.

One of the towns of the Massif of St-Thierry – Traditional-style grape harvesting, 3rd Sat-Sun of Oct, odd years.

S. Sauvignier/MICHELIN

takes a closer look at some of the work by the factory's master craftsmen. *2 Rue Belle-Verrière. Open early Apr to mid-Oct, 9.15am-1pm and 2-6pm, Sun 2-6pm; mid-Oct to late Mar, daily except Sun, 9.15am-1pm and 2-6pm. Closed 1 May, 1 Nov, 25 Dec-1 Jan. 3.80€ (combined ticket for the crystal-works and ecomusée: 7.60€). ☎ 03 25 92 42 68.*

Leave Bayel NE on the D 47 and head for Rouvres-les-Vignes via Lignol-le-Château. At Rouvres, take a left onto the D 74.

After driving through the forest, the attractive sight of hillsides carpeted in vineyards once again comes into view from Rouvres-les-Vignes. This area is the oldest section of the Baralbin vineyards, originally planted by monks in the High Middle Ages.

Colombé-le-Sec

Despite its name (Colombé the Dry), this picturesque flower-decked village was the site of an immense storehouse where the monks of Clairvaux used to keep their wine in the 12C. The **Clément** brand, made up of several producers, continues to uphold the monks' traditions *(see Shopping Guide)*. **Bernard Breuzon** offers a tour with commentary explaining the various stages of Champagne making, finishing with a tasting of the firm's Colombine vintage Champagne. *Rue St-Antoine, 10200 Colombé-le-Sec, ☎ 03 25 27 02 06, breuzon@ wanadoo.fr*

The village has retained an interesting octagonal wash-house thought to date back to the 12C and a number of fountains. Although remodelled in the 16C, the church still has a Romanesque lintel, decorated with a Greek cross surrounded by an Easter lamb and a wolf.

Rejoin Bar-sur-Aube on the D 13.

Treats for the Children

Nigloland★

At Dolancourt, 9km NW of Bar-sur-Aube on the N 19. Open from mid-Jul to mid-Aug, 10am-7pm; early Apr to early May and mid-Jun to mid-Jul, 10am-6pm (Sun 7pm); early May to mid-Jun, daily except Wed 10am-6pm, Sun 10am-7pm; Sep, Sat-Sun 10am-6pm; Oct and Nov half-term, Sun 10.30am-5.30pm. 16€ (children under 12: 14.50€, children under 1m: no charge). ☎ 03 25 27 94 52. www.nigloland.fr

ⓘ This leisure park in a green setting traversed by River Landion, the fourth largest in France, offers some fifteen attractions for young and old alike. Discover the park aboard a small train or along the meandering enchanted river. Those who prefer more thrills should head for the Gold Mine Train, the Canadian River Ride and the Space Shuttle, while the Bat Roller Coaster hurtles up and down steep slopes at almost 100kph. Don't miss the Niglo Show (electronic automata) staged in the theatre of the Canadian village. A balloon ride provides a splendid bird's eye view of the park.

Parc de vision animalier

At Lac d'Orient, 34km W of Bar-sur-Aube on the N 19 and D 79, the park is on the D 43 between Mesnil-St-Père and the Maison du parc. Open from Jul to Aug, daily except Thu and Fri from 5pm to nightfall; Apr-Jun and Sep, Sat-Sun and public holidays from 5pm to nightfall; Oct-Mar, Sun and public holidays (1ˢᵗ and 3ʳᵈ Sun of the month) from 2pm to nightfall. No admission charge. ☎ 03 25 43 38 88.

ⓘ Located on the peninsula of Luxembourg-Piney (89 hectares), wild boars, deer and roe-deer roam free in three separate enclosures surrounded by woods and meadows. This wildlife observation area has a number of high viewing points; the boar are easiest to see because they are active day and night. The deer and roe-deer are nocturnal animals, however, so you will have to come early in the morning or late at night and wait very patiently and quietly to catch sight of them. Don't forget your binoculars.

Back to Grass Roots

Created in 1976, the **Regional Nature Park of the Montagne de Reims** covers an area of 50 000 hectares between the towns of Reims, Epernay and Châlons-en-Champagne. The forest, consisting mainly of deciduous trees such as oaks, beech and chestnut trees, covers 20 000 hectares, more than a third of the park.

🚶 Numerous footpaths and hiking trails thread their way through the park, including the GR 14 and its offshoots such as the 141 and 142. Discovery trails have been created on the banks of the canal which runs alongside the Marne: 41

information panels on the stretch between Condé-sur-Marne and Damery, provide walkers with insights into the local flora, fauna, know-how and traditions. Picnic areas abound, as do viewpoints such as those in Ville-Domange, Hautvilliers, Dizy, Verzy and Châtillon-sur-Marne.

Pourcy
21km SW of Reims on the D 980 and the D 386 to the left.

Maison du parc – *Chemin de Nanteuil, 51480 Pourcy,* ☎ *03 26 59 44 44, www. parc-montagnedereims.fr Open Apr-Oct, 2.30-6.30pm; Nov-Mar, daily except Sat-Sun and public holidays, 8.30am-noon and 1.30-6pm. Closed 1 Jan, 25 Dec. No admission charge.*

Anyone even the tiniest bit interested in the nature park of the Montagne de Reims really should stop at the Maison du parc. Offering documentation about the wildlife and the region, calendar of events and excursions, exhibitions, guides and maps, the Maison du parc is a treasure-trove of information. Make sure you pick up a copy of the Journal du parc, with a list of everything going on in the region.

Verger conservatoire – *Access via the Maison du parc.* Some species of fruit trees are threatened with extinction in Champagne by the existence of other more dominant varieties. The Maison du parc set up this orchard to protect rare species such as the Montmorency de Sauvigny cherry, the Rousselet pear or the Imperial plum of Boursault, to name only a few of the 25 protected species.

Musée de la vie rurale at Germaine
24km S of Reims on the N 51, then take a left onto the D 71.

Maison du bûcheron – *Route du Pré-Michaux. Open from late Mar to mid-Nov, Sun and public holidays 2.30-6.30pm. 1.83€ (children: no charge).* ☎ *03 26 59 44 44 www. parc-montagnedereims.fr*

This appealing small museum is devoted to different aspects of forestry (marking, clearing, cutting, felling, carrying) and its corresponding trades and professions. Documents, tools and photographs illustrate each aspect. Nearby is a nature trail through the forest.

Musée de la Basse-Cour – *Temporarily closed.* ☎ *03 26 55 48 78.*

Petrol-fuelled hatching incubators, tools to clean pigeon houses, drinking troughs and instruments to turn cock fowls into capons (!): the sheer variety gives an idea of the unusual character of this museum. The objective is to provide a broad overview of farmyard tools since the 19C with a selection of animals to boot, including some of the region's rarest specimens.

Parc nature de Sept-Saulx★
22km SE of Reims on the N 44, towards Châlons-en-Champagne. Open Jun-Aug, 10am-6.30pm, Sun and public holidays, 10am-10pm; Mar-May and Sep-Oct, 10am-6.30pm. 7€ (children: 4€). ☎ *03 26 03 24 91.*

Situated to the east of the Montagne de Reims regional park, this nature reserve is well-located two minutes from La Vesle and devoted to the theme of water. Venture into the heart of a **peat bog** through a succession of low wooden bridges over running water. Unusual walking trails, planted with weeping willows and reeds, are dotted with explanatory panels and hosts of visual and tactile interactive games. A visit with commentary provides even more insight into this fascinating eco-system. The park is divided up into **themes**: bamboo island invites walkers to relax and "chill out", flower island is designed to awaken your sense of smell while duck island will teach you more about the local fauna.

Leisure Activities on the Lacs de l'Aube

Lac d'Orient: sailing and swimming
14km E of Troyes on the N 19.

Created in 1966, the artificial Lac d'Orient covers 2 500 hectares set in a superb landscape of forests, the peace and quiet of which are disturbed only by the flight of thousands of migratory birds (bird sanctuary to the northeast) and the multicoloured sails of yachts, catamarans, windsurfers and little sailing dinghies. The spot is ideal for a quiet doze in the sun after a dip in the water, because in addition to a marina, three sandy beaches (lifeguards on duty from Jul-Aug) have been created in Géraudot, Lusigny-sur-Barse and not far from the harbour-master's office in Port-Mesnil.

Le Bateau Ivre – *Departures from Lusigny, cruise with commentary and cruise with meal on Lac d'Orient aboard Le Bateau Ivre. From mid-Mar to mid-Sep, cruise (1hr) 9am-7pm, cruise with meal 11am-2pm and 6.30-8.30pm by appointment. Cruise 5€ (children: 3€), meal 26€ (children: 15€).* ☎ *03 25 41 20 72. www.la-mangeoire.fr*

CNA Voile Ecole française de voile – *Plage de Mesnil-St-Père,* ☎ *03 25 41 24 37. www.cnavoile.com Open Mar-Oct, daily 9am-6pm; Jul-Aug, daily 9am-7pm.*

This sailing centre rents out equipment and offers half-day windsurfing, catamaran and kayak courses.

Lac du Temple: fishing and canoeing
30km E of Troyes on the D 960.

Lac du Temple, smaller than Lac d'Orient with 1 800 hectares, has since 1990 been a favourite haunt of the region's anglers and canoeists. However walkers also appreciate the lake's peace and quiet.

Anglers will be interested to know that although fishing is authorised in all three lakes, Lac du Temple remains the best choice and that some impressive catches have been recorded here in recent times!

Lac Amance: motor water sports
34km E of Troyes on the D 960.

The smallest of the Aube lakes, with 490 hectares, Lac Amance is nonetheless the largest artificial lake in Europe reserved for motor water sports such as speedboat and motor-boat racing. It is prized by enthusiasts who appreciate the space and the splendid woodland landscape. Near the harbour-master's office in Port-Dienville, you will find information relating to rentals or courses.

Ski nautique club de l'Aube (SNCA) – *10500 Dienville,* ☎ *03 25 92 25 66 or 85. Open Jul-Aug, 9am-7pm; May-Jun and Sep, Sat-Sun and public holidays by appointment. Water skiing.*

CSB Marine – *10500 Dienville,* ☎ *03 25 92 94 17. Open early Apr to early Oct, daily. Boat and jet-ski rentals.*

Swimmers are also welcome in the cove of Arcot on 2 hectares of sandy beach *(lifeguards on duty from Jul-Aug)* to the south of the small residential area of Port-Dienville. It is also possible to rent small boats without a licence to tour the lake and picnic on the Ile aux Carpes and the Ile aux Oiseaux.

Mesnil-St-Père water-sports centre on Lac d'Orient.

S. Sauvignier / MICHELIN

Le Vignoble de Cognac

The Cognac Vineyards

Cognac owes its very existence to the River Charente. Had this peaceful little waterway not been navigable between Angoulême and the sea, cognac would have had a much harder time conquering the rest of the world. Over the years the Charentes region's brandy has become such a household name that its producers have to do battle on every front to bring it back into the fold of protected appellations. Its fascinating history can be read like an open book on the green banks of the River Charente, along the 80km stretch between Saintes and Angoulême. The massive stores that you will see have been blackened over time by mould that thrives on what is known as the "Angels' Share", caused by the natural evaporation of the spirit while it is maturing in the cask. You will also see splendid Romanesque churches and quiet little towns with red tile roofs. Throughout Charentes, with its characteristic "art de vivre", the gentle pace of life will enable you to savour the region's subtle blends of nature and culture.

Terroir

Michelin Local Map 327 – Charente (16) and Charente-Maritime (17).

Surface area: the vineyards cover 77 871ha divided into six districts, each with its own distinctive quality: Grande Champagne (13 343ha), Petite Champagne (15 813ha), Borderies (4 015ha), Fins Bois (32 451ha), Bons Bois (10 600ha) and Bois Ordinaires (1 649 ha).

Production: 452 000hl. Given the limit currently in force, only part of the grape harvest can be distilled.

The climate is oceanic and temperate, with relatively mild winters, temperate to hot summers, rain in the spring and quite a lot of sunshine in the autumn. The soil is chalky, or part clay, part lime, with the best growing areas located on the chalkiest soil.

Wines and spirits

The Cognac vineyards are almost exclusively made up of white grape varieties. Ugni Blanc (or St-Émilion des Charentes) is the most widespread, followed by Folle Blanche and Colombard. These varieties produce light acidic white wine suitable for distilling.

Over the past few years, new grape varieties have been introduced to make the Charentes region's local wines (vins de pays) – Chardonnay and Sauvignon for the whites, and Merlot and Cabernet for the reds and rosés.

The fortified wine Pineau des Charentes is made exclusively with a red or white grape juice base that derives its alcohol content from the addition of cognac that has been aged for at least a year.

Travel tips

If you are driving through the Cognac area in summer, make the most of the picnic sites laid out on the banks of the Charente. It's an absolute delight to stop and enjoy the shade in peaceful surroundings. And you won't have any trouble stocking up on delicious products in the local markets.

The Fins Bois vineyards.

M. Thierry/MICHELIN

Directory

WHERE TO EAT

⊜ **Taverne du Coq d'Or** – Pl. François-ler - 16100 Cognac - ☎ 05 45 82 02 56 – 12.80/38.30€. The mosaic cockerel on the sign proudly welcomes clients who come to the restaurant (founded in 1908) for the calf's head in gribiche sauce (vinaigrette, chopped boiled eggs, gherkins, capers and herbs) or the veal chops with ceps and Pineau des Charentes gravy. Strictly Limousin beef and beautifully fresh ingredients contribute to the place's popularity. Recently renovated art deco setting.

⊜⊜ **Le Bistrot Galant** – 28 r. St-Michel - 17100 Saintes - ☎ 05 46 93 08 51 – closed Sun except lunch on public holidays, and Mon – 15.10/30.50€. The chef Patrick Aumon creates temptingly inventive dishes with market-fresh produce that you can try in one of the bright dining rooms. How about a grenadier fish dish in pastry with stuffed artichokes or the conserve of quail salad with vegetables in balsamic vinegar?

⊜⊜ **La Ciboulette** – 36 r. Pérat - 17100 Saintes - ☎ 05 46 74 07 36 - closed Sat lunch and Sun - 19/63€. Country-style dining room decorated with paintings by a local artist, where you can treat yourself to hearty meals cooked by Jean-Yves Homo. A culinary trip through the region's specialities awaits you, with dishes such as Saintonge mouclade (mussels), fricassée de jaud (cockerel) with cognac, and conserve of duck à la charentaise.

⊜⊜ **La Boîte à Sel** – 68 av. Victor-Hugo - 16100 Cognac – on the road to Angoulême - ☎ 05 45 32 07 68 - closed 23 Dec to 8 Jan, and Mon – 12€ lunch - 20/53€. This former grocery store in a shopping street close to place François-Ier has preserved picturesque details like the shelves lined with bottles, a small old-fashioned counter, and a wooden floor covered with rugs. Air-conditioned dining room serving local, traditional cuisine.

⊜⊜ **Le Saintonge** – Rte de Royan, at Complexe Stes-Végas - 17100 Saintes - ☎ 05 46 97 00 00 - closed on Sun and Mon evenings - 21/41€. The 1970s-style decor and neat layout set the scene for Guy Gireau's classical fare. You can try crayfish tempura, choice meat à la plancha, salmon and mussel blanquette, boned quail with truffle sauce, and other delicacies. Bon appétit!

⊜⊜ **La Table du Bois** – R. de Royan - 17100 Saintes - ☎ 05 46 93 50 99 – 24€. This chic bistro will enable you to enjoy a privileged setting and Mickaël Gallas's delicious cuisine for very little. On offer are mussels in Chardonnay with tandoori spices, roast veal with thyme, and grilled hake with orange sauce. Fine choice of AOC wines.

⊜⊜ **Château** – 15 pl. du Château - 16200 Jarnac - ☎ 05 45 81 07 17 - closed 17 to 31 Jan, 9 to 31 Aug, Sun, Tue and Wed evenings, and Mon - 17.50€ lunch - 26/39€ This town house covered in attractive Virginia creeper gives onto the square where the castle once stood. Inside, the dining room is bright and stylish and serves personalised traditional cuisine with flavours from Charentes: La Rochelle fish soup, and venison cutlets with blueberries and pepper sauce.

WHERE TO STAY

⊝ **Hôtel Avenue** – 114 av. Gambetta - 17100 Saintes - ☎ 05 46 74 05 91 - contact@hoteldelavenue.com - closed 24 Dec to 3 Jan - 🅿 - 15 rooms: 34/50€ - ⌷ 6.30€. The rooms in this 1970s hotel in the Abbaye aux Dames district are relatively peaceful because they all face away from the street. They are gradually being renovated and given warm, personalised touches. Attractive breakfast room.

⊝ **Chambre d'hôte Anne et Dominique Trouvé** – 5 r. de l'Église - 17810 St-Georges-des-Coteaux - 9km northwest of Saintes heading for Rochefort on N 137 then D 127 - ☎ 05 46 92 96 66 - adtrouve@yahoo.fr - closed 15 Nov to 28 Mar - ⧉ - 4 rooms: 39/47€. A stay in this 18C Charentes farmhouse set in a large garden is a must. The stables and hayloft have been converted into a huge space combining sitting room, library and billiards room. The bedrooms with regional furnishings are all named after famous authors.

⊝ **Hôtel Résidence** – 25 av. Victor-Hugo - 16100 Cognac - ☎ 05 45 36 62 40 - laresidence@free.fr - closed 20 Dec to 3 Jan - 18 rooms: 40/45€ - ⌷ 8€. The hotel's sober façade with its exposed stones provides a contrast with the colour scheme inside. Sitting room in shades of green and garnet, modern breakfast room in pink and fuchsia, and functional rooms in brightly coloured prints. Warm welcome.

⊝⊝ **Messageries** – R. des Messageries - 17100 Saintes - ☎ 05 46 93 64 99 - info@hotel-des-messageries.com - closed 19 Dec to 7 Jan - 33 rooms: 52/80€ - ⌷ 7€. Ideally located in the heart of the old town, this former stagecoach inn built around a courtyard dates from 1792. It is bathed in a quiet atmosphere and gives onto a peaceful alleyway. Country-style rooms. Convenient garage.

⊝⊝ **Valois** – 35 r. du 14-Juillet – 16100 Cognac – ☎ 05 45 36 83 00 – hotel.levalois@wanadoo.fr - closed 24 Dec to 2 Jan – 🅿 - 45 rooms: 61/69€ - ⌷ 7.50€. This recently built hotel stands in a good position a stone's throw from the storehouses, right in the centre of town. Spacious rooms with functional furniture, a pleasantly redecorated bar-lounge in the lobby, and a sauna and gym for guests.

Background

Cognac is a spirit or *eau-de-vie* that is made by distilling white wine from grapes grown in the Charentes region. The distilling process takes place until the end of March and is completed in two stages, both of which involve heating. The first yields a liquid known as *brouillis,* a light spirit containing around 30% alcohol. The second consists in distilling the *brouillis* to obtain a colourless spirit with a maximum strength of 72%. This is then stocked in oak casks where it takes on its characteristic colour and matures slowly, gradually losing its strength. To be fit for sale, cognac has to mature for at least thirty months and have a minimum strength of 40%. As it takes a long time to reach this strength, producers are allowed to add distilled water. The same goes for the colour, which can be modified by adding an infusion of oak shavings or caramel. The secret of a good cognac lies in the blending of different growths and vintages.

Along the Charente

Itinerary of around 85km. Michelin Local Map 324, G-H-I 5, J-K 6.

The River Charente, dotted with locks, bridges and ferries winds its way between Saintes and Angoulême, telling the story of the flat-bottomed *gabares.* These were barges that travelled up-river carrying salt and spices and then headed back down to the sea, laden with liquid gold.

Saintes★★

With its plane trees and white houses with tiled roofs, Saintes has a southern look about it. The town has so much in the way of historic and artisitic heritage that it is difficult to know where to begin. Take the time to stroll through the **old town★**, which abounds in remarkable sights. **Cathédrale St-Pierre** was built on the site of a Romanesque church, of which only a dome remains. The cathedral dates in the main from the 15C. The original spire has been replaced by a lead dome. The Flamboyant doorway within the porch at the foot of the tower is adorned with fine carvings.

The **Présidial** (*r. Victor-Hugo, set back at the far end of the garden*), a mansion built in 1605, now houses the **Musée des Beaux-Arts★**, mainly devoted to painting from the 15C to the 18C. One of the rooms contains 14C-19C ceramics from Saintonge province. *May-Sep: daily except Mon 1.30-6pm; Oct-Apr: daily except Mon 1.30-5pm. Closed 1 May. 1.50€ (children under 18: no charge), no charge Wed and Sun. ☎ 05 46 93 03 94. www.saintes.fr*

To reach the 11C **Église St-Eutrope**, head west through the old town. The church was an important stop on the pilgrim route to Santiago de Compostela. The only remaining parts of the original building are the transept and the Romanesque chancel, with magnificent historiated **capitals**. The plan of the **crypt★** is identical to that of the church above it. Follow the signs from the church to the amphitheatre, or **Arènes★** (*access via rue St-Eutrope and rue Lacurie*). This was built in the early 1C AD and is one of the oldest amphitheatres in the Roman world. It could hold 20 000 spectators. *June-Sep: 10am-8pm; Oct-Apr: 10am-5pm, Sun 1.30-5pm. 1€. Guided tours (1hr 30min) from late June to third Fri in Sep: Mon-Sat 11am and 4.30pm, ☎ 05 46 97 73 85.*

Standing on the opposite bank of the Charente is the **Arc de Germanicus★**, with twin arcades, erected in the year AD 19. It was a votive – not a triumphal – arch. Behind it, the **Musée Archéologique** houses an interesting Roman lapidiary collection and the metal remains of a **ceremonial chariot★** (late 1C AD). *June-Sep: 10am-6pm, Sun 1.30-6pm; Oct-May: 10am-5pm, Sun 1.30-5pm. Closed 1 Jan, 1 May, 25 Dec, 1.50€, no charge Sun and Wed, ☎ 05 46 74 20 97. www.ville-saintes.fr*

A few hundred yards east, you come to the large **Abbaye aux Dames**, which was consecrated in 1047. It was placed in the hands of Benedictine nuns who were entrusted with the education of young daughters of the nobility. The Abbey Church, **Église Abbatiale★** is in the local Saintonge Romanesque style and is surrounded by convent buildings. The main **doorway** is adorned with fine sculptures. Note the historiated capitals (knights and monsters). Inside, thirteen tapestries illustrate the book of Genesis. *Apr-Sep: 10am-7pm; Oct-Mar: daily except Mon (from Nov) 1-6pm. Closed 25 Dec-1 Jan, 3€, (under 16s: no charge). ☎ 05 46 97 48 48. Possibility of guided tours (1hr 30min) from late June to third Fri in Sep, Tourist office ☎ 05 46 74 23 82.*

Head SW out of Saintes along D 128. You leave Saintes by driving alongside the quays on the left bank of the Charente, passing a row of fine mansions belonging to wine merchants. The buildings gradually give way to pastureland and then you reach the vineyards around **Courcoury**, where tall houses flanked by storehouses indicate that this is wine-making country. From April to the end of October, you can take the ferry across to **Chaniers** to see the pretty Romanesque

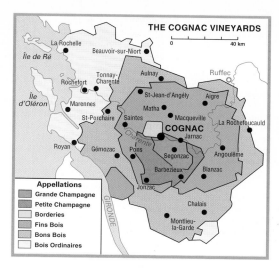

THE COGNAC VINEYARDS

church. Alternatively, you could continue on D 128, then turn left towards Beillan, and once you've crossed the Charente, bear right on D 24 heading towards Cognac.

Dompierre-sur-Charente

The stores lining the Charente testify to a long-standing wine-making tradition. The chain ferry to the opposite bank is the last of its kind operating in France. At **Domaine de Flaville**, which you reach along a narrow road, there is an excellent choice of Pineau des Charentes, cognac and vins de pays, including a worthwhile Chardonnay Moelleux. *GAEC Bureau, 302 rte du Pineau, 17610 Dompierre-sur-Charente, ☎ 05 46 91 00 45. From mid-June to mid-Sep: 8.30am-7.30pm; from mid-Sep to mid-June: Mon-Sat 8.30am-7pm, Sun 8.30am-12.30pm.*

The picturesque road between Dompierre and Cognac runs alongside the shady banks of the Charente.

Cognac★

In Cognac, probably the best known French town in the world, the colour black is omnipresent. You can see it on the buildings darkened by *torula compniacensis,* a mould that thrives on the alcohol fumes released through the natural evaporation known as the "Angels' Share". The stores and cellars themselves, where the precious nectar matures away from the light, are also black. The only thing darker, in fact, is the long film-noir shadow of the annual Festival du Film Policier, which screens a selection of the year's best and most sinister thrillers.

The steep streets of old Cognac run up between the quays and the Church of St-Léger. Access to the town was once through the 15C gateway, **Porte St-Jacques**, which leads on to **rue Grande** and the old quarter. Rue Grande, originally the main street in Cognac is lined with 15C houses with timber fronts. Rue Saulnier, on the other hand, is Renaissance in style. Its name recalls one of the traditional activities of Cognac – the salt trade. It has retained its irregular cobblestone surface and its handsome 16C and 17C houses. Also of interest are **rue du Palais**, **rue Henri-Germain**, and **rue Magdeleine** with its Maison de la Salamandre.

For a good introduction to Cognac and the surrounding area, you would do well to visit the **Centre d'Accueil du Visiteur**, recently set up in an old wine merchant's premises. There's a model of the countryside, as well as interactive terminals and an excellent audio-visual show. *Pl. de la Salle-Verte. Jul-Aug: 9.30am-6.30pm; Apr-June and Sep-Oct: daily except Mon 9.30am-6.30pm; Mar and Nov: daily except Sun and Mon 1.30-6pm. No charge. ☎ 05 45 36 03 65.*

The **Musée des Arts du Cognac**, the only one of its kind in France, has recently been set up near the quays along the Charente. It is dedicated to cognac and its history, focusing on the economic role of the brandy through a description of the trades and techniques associated with it: wine-growing, distilling, glass-making, cooperage, corks and labelling. You can see extracts of famous films in which cognac is featured. *Pl. de la Salle-Verte. May-Sep: 10am-6pm; Mar-Apr and Oct: daily except Mon 11am-noon, 1.30-6pm; Nov, Feb: daily except Mon 2-5.30pm. Closed 1 Jan, 1 Nov, 25 Dec. 4.50€. ☎ 05 45 32 07 25. www.ville-cognac.fr*

The cognac trading companies or **Maisons de Cognac★** stretch out along the riverside quays, near the port and in the suburbs. They are open to the public.

Camus – *Guided tours (45min) June-Sep: daily except Sun 10am-5pm; Oct-Apr by prior arrangement, daily except Sat-Sun. Closed public holidays. 5€ (children: no charge). ☎ 05 45 32 72 96.*

The tour offered by this cognac trading company, founded in 1863, concentrates on the history of cognac, its distillation, ageing and blending. Visitors can see the cooper's shop and wine stores *(chais)* before watching the bottling process.

Otard – *In the castle. Guided tours (1hr, last admission 1hr before closing), Jul-Aug: 10am-7pm; Apr-June and Sep-Oct: 10am-noon, 2-6pm; Nov-Dec: daily except Sat-Sun and public holidays 10am-noon, 2-6pm. Closed Jan-Mar, 1 May, 1 and 11 Nov, 25 Dec. 5€ (12-18 year olds: 2.50€). ☎ 05 45 36 88 86. www.otard.com*
This 15C and 16C château recalls the memory of the Valois family and François I, who was born here. It was sequestrated by the Republicans during the Revolution before being bought in 1795 by Baron Otard, who was from Charentes and of Norwegian and Scottish extraction. During the tour you can see some of the old castle rooms, such as the Helmet Room or Salle au Casque, where Richard the Lionheart married his son Philip to Amélie de Cognac. The room contains a magnificent chimney-piece. The tour ends with a visit to the wine stores and a tasting.

Hennessy – ♿ *Guided tours (1hr 15min) June-Sep: 10am-6pm (last admission); Mar-May and Oct-Dec: 10am-5pm. Closed 1 May. 6€ (under 16s: no charge). ☎ 05 45 35 72 68. www.hennessy.com*
Richard Hennessy, a former captain of Louis XV's Irish Brigade, settled in Cognac in 1760. In 1765 he founded a trading company that was to prove very prosperous. The stores of the company are located on both banks of the River Charente, which you cross by boat. One of the buildings displays the three symbols of cognac: copper (for the still), oak (for the casks) and glass (for the bottles). In the wine stores the various stages of brandy making are explained with the help of special effects involving sounds and smells.

Martell – *Apr-Oct: guided tours (1hr) Mon-Fri 9.30am-5pm, Sat-Sun and public holidays 11am-5pm. 4€. ☎ 05 45 36 34 98. www.visitez-martell.com*
Jean Martell, a native of Jersey, settled in 1715. The tour includes the semi-automated bottling process, and the stores and cellars where the brandy is left to age. In the blending room, brandies of different origins are mixed. Some of the blends, such as the Cordon Bleu, are famous worldwide. Rooms in the house of the founder recreate the life and work of an entrepreneur in the early 18C.

Rémy Martin – *4km south-west on D 732. Head towards Pons, then turn left onto D 47 towards Merpins. Apr-Oct, admission fee. It is advisable to book. ☎ 05 45 35 76 66.*
This firm, founded in 1724, makes its cognac exclusively from the elite Grande Champagne and Petite Champagne wines. A small train takes visitors on a tour of the plant, going through the cooper's shop, part of the vineyard and various cellars and stores used for ageing.

Prince Hubert de Polignac – *4km SE on N 141. Head for Angoulême and leave at the first exit; drive under the main road and follow signs for ZA. Shop open Mon-Fri. ☎ 05 45 82 51 72. www.polignac.fr*
This cooperative for local growers in the Charentes region was founded in 1949. A tour can be made of the different facilities in Pavillon du Laubaret.
Head E for Jarnac via St-Brice (D 157). The narrow road follows the winding course of the Charente. Near the magnificent 16C **Logis de Garde-Épée**, a dolmen comes into view. Not far from there in the middle of a field stands a very fine church, **Église de Châtre**★. It was the abbey church of a convent destroyed during the Wars of Religion. Note the festoons on the main doorway and the beautifully carved motifs.

Bourg-Charente

Bourg-Charente stands on the left bank of the Charente, looking over the spot where the river branches out into several arms, forming low islands covered in meadows. The façade of the **church** in the Saintonge Romanesque style consists of three levels, with a triangular pediment at the top. Note the Latin Cross plan of the church, and the three domes on pendentives. Inside, on the left wall of the nave, there is a 13C fresco of the Adoration of the Magi. The **château** standing on a rise on the other side of the Charente dates from the time of Henri IV.
Visitors are warmly welcomed to **Domaine de la Grange du Bois**, which produces a good Pineau des Charentes aged in casks for ten years. *SCEA Cartais-Lamaure, 16200 Bourg-Charente, ☎ 05 45 81 10 17. 10am-7pm, by prior arrangement.*

Jarnac

The native town of the former President of France, François Mitterrand, whose family ran a vinegar factory, has changed so little over the years that it could easily provide a backdrop to a 1930s-style film. Visitors can go on a **boat trip** aboard the *Chabot*, between Jarnac and Bourg-Charente, for a commentary on the history of the Salt and Cognac Route. *Departure from Jarnac bridge. Jul-Aug: departures at 11am, 3pm, 4.30pm and 6pm; Apr-June: irregular times. It is advisable to book. ☎ 05 45 82 09 35.*

Shopping guide

INFORMATION

Bureau National Interprofessionnel du Cognac (BNIC) – *23 allées du Champs-de-Mars - BP 18 - 16101 Cognac Cedex -* ☎ *05 45 35 60 00 - www.cognac.fr*

Comité National du Pineau-des-Charentes – *112 av. Victor-Hugo - 16100 Cognac -* ☎ *05 45 32 09 27 - www.pineau.fr*

OVERVIEW

CHARACTERISTICS

Cognac – Before a cognac can be sold it has to be at least two and a half years old, counting from 1 October of the year the grapes were harvested. It is the age of the youngest *eau-de-vie* in the blend that determines the age of the cognac. What cognac labels mean:

VSOP (Very Special Old Pale) or ★★★: The youngest *eau-de-vie* is at least four and a half years old.

VSOP Reserve: The youngest *eau-de-vie* is between four and six years old.

Napoléon, XO, Hors d'âge: The youngest *eau-de-vie* is at least six and a half years old.

The term "*fine*" is allowed for *eaux-de-vie* made with a wine that has AOC (*Appellation d'origine contrôlée*) status, such as Grande Champagne.

Pineau des Charentes – The fortified wines bearing this label are liqueurs, or *mistelles*, obtained by mixing fresh (unfermented) grape juice with cognac. They may be white or rosé, young or old.

Vins de pays – The Charentes region's *vins de pays* are white, red or rosé. They should be drunk young. The whites go well with seafood.

PRICES

Cognac – From 15€.
Pineau des Charentes – 8€ to 15€.
Vins de pays – From 3€.

A Charantais still.

© Atelier Marton / HENNESSY

You can also find out about the origin of the cooperage industry in Charentes by going on an 'oak tour', **Circuit du chêne** *(2hr 30min)*, during which you will meet a woodcutter. *From mid-June to mid-Sep: Mon-Thu at 2pm, departure from the Tourist office.* ☎ *05 45 81 09 30 or 05 45 80 98 91.*

The former **Abbey Church** dates from the 11C and has a square tower. In the 13C crypt the remains of wall paintings can be seen. The sober-looking **Protestant Church** was built in 1820 and is open to the public in summer.

The **Donation François-Mitterrand** museum, known as the Orangerie Cultural Centre is housed in a former brandy store on the banks of the Charente. The exhibition contains some of the works of art presented to François Mitterrand by people from all over the world during his 14-year presidency. On the way out, peruse the *Livre d'Or*, where visitors leave their comments. The President is buried in Grands-Maisons cemetery to the west of Jarnac. *Jul-Aug: 10am-noon, 2-6pm; Sep-Oct and Feb-June: daily except Mon and Tue 2-6pm. Closed Nov, Dec and 1 May. 3.50€.* ☎ *05 45 81 38 88.*

Maison Courvoisier is set up in a former warehouse that has been attractively refurbished. The museum proposes an interesting tour through the blending workshop, which resembles a perfumery. Stills and barrels are on display to explain how cognac is produced. You are then greeted by the heady fumes of the evaporating "Angels' Share" as you enter the fine reconstructed *chai* or wine store. *Pl. du Château.* ♿ *Guided tours (45min) June-Aug: 11am-7pm; May and Sep: daily except Sat 11am-7pm. Closed 1 May. 3€ (children under 17: no charge).* ☎ *05 45 35 56 16.*

As you go into **Maison Louis Royer** you pass through a hall with beautiful inlaid work, which leads into the *Espace Voyage*. This exhibition presents the production of cognac and its exportation throughout the world. The tour then continues through the stores where the ageing is carried out. *Quai de la Charmille.* ♿ *July-Aug: daily except Mon and Tue 10am-noon, 2-5pm, Sat 10am-noon, 2-6pm, Sun 2-6pm. No charge.* ☎ *05 45 81 02 72.*

Leave Jarnac heading E along D 22 to Bassac.

Abbaye de Bassac

♿ *From mid-June to the Journée du Patrimoine in Sep, guided tours (45min) daily except Mon: 3-7pm. 2€ (no charge 15 Aug). Mid-Sep to mid-June daily except Mon, guided tours, no charge: 3-6pm.* ☎ *05 45 81 94 22. www.abbayedebassac.com*

Bassac Abbey was abandoned at the time of the Revolution and returned to religious life in 1947 by the Missionary Brothers of St Theresa of the Infant Jesus. During the Revolution, an anonymous patriot inscribed the following words of

Robespierre on the façade of the 15C Romanesque-style **church★**: *"The people of France recognise the Supreme Being and the immortality of the soul."* Inside, the single nave testifies to the far-reaching influence of the Angevin Gothic style. On the right, the statue of St Nicholas (probably 13C) has worn feet, rubbed smooth by girls hoping to find a husband.

Continue along D 22.

Châteauneuf-sur-Charente

The church, **Église St-Pierre** has a façade in the Saintonge style. The doorway with intricate carvings of foliage, animals and figures on its mouldings is flanked by two blind arches. The upper level of the façade, separated from the lower by a cornice supported by carved modillions (amusing figures of people), is pierced by a bay with a statue of an Apostle on either side. On the left, there is an equestrian statue of Emperor Constantine (with the head missing).

Drive to Angoulême along D 699.

Angoulême and Comic Strips

Angoulême is pleasant to explore on foot, with its maze of narrow streets, its beautiful old buildings and wonderful views from the ramparts. It is also fun in late January when the place goes wild during the Comic Strip *(Bande Dessinée)* Festival. The whole town bears the mark of the festival, from the paintings on the walls to the plaques of street names shaped like comic strip speech bubbles.

Painted walls

The largest concentrations of painted walls can be seen between the town hall and place St-Martial (pedestrian street), and between place du Champs-de-Mars and the railway station. *Check out the tour suggested by the Tourist office.*

Centre National de la Bande Dessinée et de l'Image (CNBDI)★

Go down from the upper town (known as the plateau) by bus or on foot, taking the path that leads off from Tour Ladent. Entrance: r. de Bordeaux. Access is also possible via some steps leading from av. de Cognac. ⎇ *July-Aug: Mon-Fri 10am-7pm, Sat-Sun 2-7pm; rest of the year: Tue-Fri 10am-6pm, Sat-Sun 2-6pm. Closed 1 Jan, 1 May, 25 Dec. 5€ (children 7-18: 2.50€).* ☎ *05 45 38 65 65.*

The centre pays homage to great comic strip authors including the Swiss Töpffer, Christophe (*La Famille Fenouillard,* 1889), Pinchon (*Bécassine,* 1905), Forton (*Les Pieds Nickelés,* 1908), and Alain St-Ogan (*Zig et Puce,* 1925), as well as the Belgians Hergé (*Tintin,* 1929) and Franquin (*Gaston Lagaffe,* 1957), the Americans Raymond (*Flash Gordon,* 1934) and Schulz (*Peanuts,* 1950), and the French Goscinny and Uderzo (*Astérix,* 1959), Gotlib, Bretécher, Reiser, Bourgeon, Wolinski, Loustal, Bilal, Baudoin, Tardi and more.

Musée du Papier "Le Nil"

Opposite the CNBDI. ⎇ *July-Sep: daily except Sun and Mon 12-6.30pm; Jan-Jun; daily except Mon 2-6pm. Closed public holidays. No charge.* ☎ *05 45 92 73 43.*

The former Bardou-Le Nil paper mill, which specialised in the manufacture of cigarette papers, operated here until 1970. It has since been converted into a museum on the papermaking industry, where you can learn about a tradition that grew up in Angoulême thanks to the purity of its river water. In the 17C, the town counted almost 100 mills that supplied Holland with watermarked paper. An exhibition called *Imaginaires d'usines* describes the different stages in the industrial manufacture of paper and cardboard. The raw material – first rags, then wood and waste paper – is turned into a paste and subsequently into a continuous sheet by a machine invented by Louis-Nicolas Robert in 1799. Once dried, the sheet undergoes many other treatments before the final product is obtained. The exhibition on the history of papermaking and related industries is on the upper floor.

Cathédrale St-Pierre★

This dates from the 12C. It was partially destroyed by the Calvinists in 1562, and restored in 1634, followed by a more complete restoration started by the architect Abadie in 1866.

The sculptures on the **façade★★** form an impressively lively tableau carved in the Poitiers style. More than 70 characters, statues and bas-reliefs illustrate the Last Judgement. The ensemble is presided over by a Christ in Majesty, surrounded by the symbols of the Evangelists, and angels and saints set in medallions. Note also the archivolts and friezes above and around the side doors with their finely carved foliage, animals and figures. On the lintel of the first blind doorway, on the right, are strange scenes of combat based on episodes from the medieval epic *La Chanson de Roland* (Song of Roland).

La Corse

Corsica

The "Island of Beauty", as the French call it, is a mountain rising out of the deep blue sea, where vineyards have been part of the scenery since the Phoenicians settled here thousands of years ago. However, wine growing only developed relatively recently, when mechanised vineyards were established on gravelly slopes, along sun-drenched ravines and on arid soils where vines have a hard time trying to yield their best. There are vineyards right around the coast, so that a wine tour is a perfect opportunity for a complete tour of Corsica. From one end of the island to the other, one encounters enthusiastic wine growers, proud of producing quality wines which are only one of the fascinating charms of this jewel of the Mediterranean.

Terroir

Michelin Local Map 345 – Corse-du-Sud (2B) and Haute-Corse (2A).
Area: about 3 200ha spread all round the island.
Production: about 115 000hl, including 45% rosés, 40% reds, 10% whites and 5% Muscat-du-Cap-Corse. In this Mediterranean climate, expect hot, dry summers, temperate springs and autumns and cold winters in the mountains. The effects of the sun are tempered by altitude and the influence of the sea. The soil varies, featuring a predominance of schist in the north, granite in the south and west, limestone in the Patrimonio area and clayey sand along the east coast.

Wines

Corsican wines bear the effects of the sun, characterised by a rather high alcohol content. They are made from traditional grape varieties: Vermentino for the whites, Nieluccio and Sciaccarello for the reds and rosés. Many continental grape varieties are used to make the *Vins de Pays de l'Île-de-Beauté:* Chardonnay, Pinot Noir, Cinsault, Grenache.
AOC – Corse AOC over most of the island except in the Patrimonio and Ajaccio terroirs: Corse-Cap-Corse and Muscat-du-Cap-Corse, Corse-Calvi, Corse-Sartène, Corse-Figari, Corse-Porto-Vecchio, Ajaccio, Patrimonio.
Vins de Pays – Vins de Pays de l'Île-de-Beauté, produced all over the island.

Useful tip

Corsican wine growers will be only too pleased to welcome you in springtime (May or June), or in autumn (September-October), when the island is free of its usual hordes of tourists and weather conditions are ideal for wine tasting.

Corsican Wine Routes

THE BALAGNE VINEYARDS

63km starting from Calvi. Michelin Local map 345, B-C 4. See round tour ☐1 on p. 218.
A tour of the Balagne vineyards offers a good opportunity of discovering splendid mountainous landscapes between Lumio and Belgodère, with vines clinging to the screes. This is where **Corse-Calvi AOC** and Vins de Pays are produced.

The Patrimonio vineyards, among the most famous in Corsica.

G. Magnin / MICHELIN

WHERE TO EAT

A Mandria – *Rte de Ghisonaccia, pont de Solenzara - 20145 Solenzara -* ☎ *04 95 57 41 95 – closed Jan, Sun evening and Mon in low season -* 🍴 *- 20€.* This converted sheep barn offers a choice of mouth-watering Corsican dishes, carefully prepared, including a good selection of meat grilled on a wood fire. Other strong points are the reasonable prices including a set menu which is very good value for money, and a terrace shaded by a climbing vine.

La Table du Marché – *Pl. du Marché - 20200 Bastia -* ☎ *04 95 31 64 25 – closed Sun - 22€ lunch - 21/39€.* This convivial restaurant offers a cosy setting and an impeccable cuisine exclusively prepared from fresh produce. Fish with garlic mayonnaise, traditional Corsican charcuterie or tripe Bastia-style are among the tasty dishes served on the terrace in fine weather.

L'Antigu – *51 r. Borgo - 20137 Porto-Vecchio -* ☎ *04 95 70 39 33 – closed Jan to mid-Feb, Sun lunchtime early Apr to early Nov and Mon - 21/40€.* Here you will be able to enjoy the superb view and the tasty cuisine at the same time. The rooftop terrace affords a magnificent panorama of the gulf of Porto-Vecchio and the copious, well-prepared regional dishes, served with care, are a delight to the palate!

Le Guaïtella – *10 hameau de Guaïtella - 20200 Ville-di-Pietrabugno -* ☎ *04 95 34 20 51 – closed lunchtime - 24€.* Perched on the heights overlooking Bastia, the Guaïtela offers a spectacular view of the town and the harbour. Making good use of carefully chosen ingredients, the dishes are well prepared but never over-elaborate: try fillet of beef and slice of foie gras with chestnut flavouring, or a swordfish steak with capers. Young clientele, convivial atmosphere.

La Corniche – *Castagneto - 20200 San-Martino-di-Lota -* ☎ *04 95 31 40 98 – closed 1 Jan to 15 Feb, Tue lunchtime and Mon - 25/45€.* Don't hesitate to "climb up" to this establishment and sit at a table under the old plane trees shading the terrace. You will enjoy tasty traditional dishes while admiring an unforgettable panorama: the village of San Martino and its surroundings plunging into the sea.

Le 20123 – *2 r. du Roi-de-Rome - 20000 Ajaccio -* ☎ *04 95 21 50 05 – closed mid-Jan to mid-Feb, lunchtime and Mon -* 🍴 *- reservations required - 26€.* The owner, a native of the lower valley of the Taravo, attempted to recreate the atmosphere of his village (square and fountain, traditional dining room, sheep-barn-mezzanine) in the centre of old Ajaccio. No need to say that the food served in such a picturesque decor is 100% Corsican!

U Licettu – *Plaine-de-Cuttoli - 20167 Mezzavia - 15km NE of Ajaccio along the Bastia road, then the Cuttoli road (D 1) and the Bastelicaccia road -* ☎ *04 95 25 61 57 – closed Jan, Sun evening and Mon except Jul-Aug - reservations required - 34€.* What a pleasant surprise it is to find this lovely villa isolated in the middle of the maquis and to sit down and enjoy generous Corsican dishes! A terrace, a garden full of flowers and a large fireplace where meat is roasted: nothing is missing right down to the warm welcome. One gourmet menu only, drinks included.

WHERE TO STAY

Domaine de Croccano – *Rte de Granace - 20100 Sartène – 3.5km NE of Sartène along D 148 -* ☎ *04 95 77 11 37 – closed Dec - 4 rooms: 46/68€ - meal 25€.* This comfortable granite house, rising above cork oaks and olive trees, offers rooms looking like cosy cocoons (fine stone walls, tiled floors). The owners, who love horses, take their guests on riding tours through the Corsican maquis. Very friendly welcome.

Chambre d'hôte Piaggiola – *20166 Porticcio - 13km SE of Agosta beach along D 255A (towards Pietrosella) then right onto D 255 -* ☎ *04 95 24 23 79 – closed end of Jan to 15 Apr -* 🍴 *- 6 rooms: 62€ - meal 20€.* A warm welcome, great hospitality, a cuisine favouring local produce and huge rooms… these are the strong points which appeal to the guests at this large guest house nestling in the centre of a magnificent estate. And all this is only a few minutes from the finest beaches on the island!

Chambre d'hôte Château Cagninacci – *20200 San-Martino-di-Lota - 8km NW of Bastia along D 80 (towards Cap-Corse) then onto D 131 in Pietranera -* ☎ *06 78 29 03 94 – closed Oct to 14 May -* 🍴 *- 4 rooms: 66/95€.* Clinging to the mountain slopes, this 17C Capucines monastery, remodelled in the 19C in the style of a Tuscan residence, has been tastefully restored and offers spacious, traditionally furnished rooms and modern, spotlessly kept bathrooms. It is extremely quiet and the panorama is superb.

Casa Musicale – *20220 Pigna -* ☎ *04 95 61 77 31 - info@casa-musicale.org – closed Jan - 7 rooms: 66/93€ -* 🍴 *6€ - meal 34/46€.* This extremely charming old house, only accessible on foot along the flower-decked lanes of the superb hilltop village, offers rooms adorned with frescoes, with a view of the sea or the mountains. The olive-oil pressing shed has been turned into a restaurant; in addition, there are an idyllic terrace and a concert room.

GOURMET SHOPPING

U San Petrone – *Pl. de l'Ancienne-Poste - 20217 St-Florent -* ☎ *04 95 37 10 95 – Tue-Sun, 9am-noon, 3-7pm, Mon in Jul-Aug - closed mid-Sep to Easter.* Mr Rinaldi, who is both a farmer and a pork butcher, can tell you all about the lonzu, coppa and hams he has dealt with. As for other products (cheeses, liqueurs, wines), he calls on craftsmen who, like him, use good local produce.

Calvi★

Proudly established round a luminous bay, against a background of often snow-covered mountains, Calvi is one of the most beautiful Corsican sites. The ochre-coloured walls of the **Citadel★★** tower above the lower town. A walk along the watch path offers fine **views★**. The **fortifications★** were erected by the Genoese at the end of the 15C. The 13C **Église St-Jean-Baptiste**, overlooking the place d'Armes, was rebuilt in 1570 after being severely damaged by the explosion of a powder magazine. The **seafront★**, with its cafés and restaurants along the quayside lined with palm trees, offers an ever lively spectacle.

Leave Calvi via N 197 towards Île-Rousse.

Lumio★

Rising like an amphitheatre above its large Baroque church flanked by a lofty openwork campanile, this opulent market town of the Balagne region stands amid olive trees and orchards, offering panoramic views of the gulf of Calvi. The long winding street offers a pleasant stroll. As far as wine is concerned, the **Clos Culombu** is worth a visit *(see Shopping Guide)*.

Sant'Ambroggio Marina⚓

The Sant'Ambroggio marina offers all the facilities yachtsmen look for. The site has retained its natural setting with a fine sand beach set inside the curve of the bay.

Turn right onto the narrow D 313, then right again onto D 151 towards Pigna.

Corbara's convent

After 2km, take the minor road on the left (statue of St Dominic). The entrance to the convent is in the centre of the main façade. Cloister and church: Jul-Aug, guided tours at 3, 4 and 5pm; the rest of the year, guided tours available at 3pm on request. In summer, visitors can also visit the church by themselves. ☎ 04 95 60 06 73.

This former orphanage, founded in 1430 at the foot of Monte Sant'Angelo and turned into a convent in 1456, was ruined during the Revolution then rebuilt and extended by the Dominicans from 1857 onwards. The conventual church, dating from 1735, overlooks the bay of Algajola, the lower Balagne region and the village of Pigna.

Pigna★

Lined with carefully restored houses bedecked with flowers, the cobbled or stepped winding streets and the paved village square all convey an impression of authenticity. Since the end of the 1960s, Pigna has become a symbol of the revival of traditional crafts and music. Various Corsican crafts are promoted in the **Casa di l'artigiani**. *Jul-Aug, Mon-Sat, 9.45am-8.30pm, Sun 10am-1pm, 3.30-8pm; Apr-Jun and Sep-Oct, daily except Sun 10.30am-12.30pm, 2.30-6.30pm. ☎ 04 95 61 75 55.*

Turn left onto the mountain road separating the Regino and Algajola basins and leading to the mountain village of Sant'Antonino.

Sant'Antonino★★

Like an eyrie towering some 500m above the last slopes of the Balagne, the village offers a harmonious maze of narrow cobbled streets and vaulted passages. Following its successful restoration, it has become a popular tourist sight and a centre for the revival of Corsican crafts. As you walk clockwise round the village, you will be able to admire the remarkable panorama encompassing the Regino Valley, the undulating Balagne region between Belgodère and Lumio, the high snow-covered mountains, Algajola bay and the sea.

Return to D 151 then turn left onto D 71.

Feliceto

This village, surrounded with orchards, overlooks the Regino Valley where excellent wines, such as those of the **Clos Reginu e Prove** *(see Shopping Guide)*, are produced. Below stands the Baroque church with its dome and tiered tower.

Turn back and, at the crossroads, continue along D 71 towards Lumio.

Cateri

Nestling among olive trees, Cateri rises above the Algajola basin. Walk to the end of the village through narrow cobbled streets linked by vaulted passages and lined by lofty granite houses occupied by various craftsmen.

Lavatoggio

From the platform in front of the church or from the terrace of Le Belvédère restaurant (100m further), the **view★** extends over the fine beach of Algajola, the coast and the foothills of the Balagne, west of the crest-line separating them from the Regino basin. The village was once famous for the quality of its springs.

Drive to Lumio, then to Calvi along N 197.

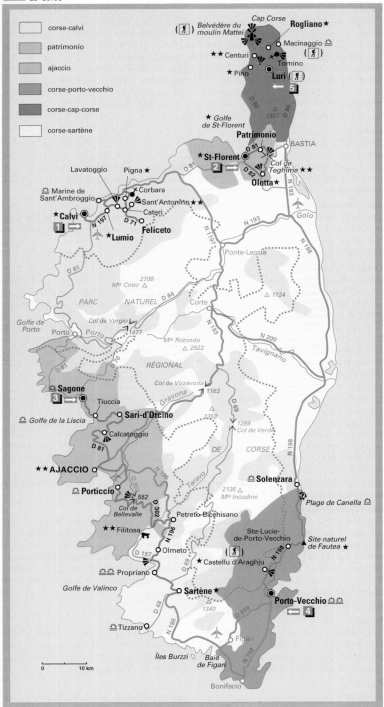

THE PATRIMONIO VINEYARDS

60km. Michelin Local Map 345, E-F 3-47. See round tour 2 *on the map p. 218.*

The **Patrimonio AOC** vineyards surrounding the gulf of St-Florent owe their reputation to their red wines grown on an enclave of limestone soil barely covering an area of 400ha. Their success is also due to the talent of the wine growers who were the first to go in for quality. A tour of the area will enable you to discover not only fine wines but also splendid landscapes and mountain villages which seem to defy time.

Saint-Florent★

Set inside a beautiful **gulf★**, St-Florent is a seaside resort and a marina lined with colourful houses, dominated by the fortifications of its citadel. The nearest vineyard is that of the **Domaine Gentile** in the Olzo locality *(see Shopping Guide)*. The old town surrounds the church and its belfry overlooking the harbour protected by a long pier. **Place des Portes**, surrounded by outdoor cafés, is the real centre of the city. Built on a promontory by the Genoese, the **citadel** founded in 1439 towers above the town and the harbour. The **former Cathédrale du Nebbio★★ (Église Santa-Maria-Assunta)** is one of the most significant examples of religious architecture in Corsica. Built in the Pisan Romanesque style, it was probably completed around 1140. *Access: 1km along the narrow street starting opposite the war memorial and heading towards Poggio-d'Oletta. Apply to the tourist office,* ☎ *04 95 37 06 04.*

Leave St-Florent S along D 82. The **Nebbio** is an area of vineyards, olive groves, orchards and pastures, crisscrossed by drystone walls, very appropriately named the "golden conch". The region has many small friendly villages, built on high ground like so many observatories.

Oletta★

The tall white, ochre and pink houses of Oletta rise in terraces up the green slopes of a hill. The pleasant **view★** encompasses the gulf of St-Florent and the Nebbio. The surrounding area is famous for its cheese made from ewe's milk; this cheese goes very well with the rich wines produced in the neighbouring village of **Poggio-d'Oletta** where the **Domaine Leccia** is among the top ten producers of Patrimonio wine *(see Shopping Guide)*.

Rejoin D 38 and turn right. The road offers extended **views★** over the next 9km. The **Teghime pass★★**, situated at an altitude of 536m, is often swept by the violent *libecciu* wind blowing from the west. The **panorama★★** embraces the gulf of St-Florent, the Nebbio, Bastia and the eastern plain.

At the pass, turn left onto D 81 towards Patrimonio.

Patrimonio

The houses and large church of Patrimonio are scattered over fertile hillsides covered with orchards and vineyards. Patrimonio wine has, for a long time, been classified as one of the best Corsican Crus. The Domaine **Antoine Arena** *(see Shopping Guide)* is one of many prominent estates in the area. Most wine growers also produce Muscat-du-Cap-Corse.

The **Église St-Martin★** (16C and 19C) forms one of Corsica's most famous tourist pictures. The limestone menhir-statue of the **Nativu★**, standing next to the war memorial, is protected by wire fencing. This 2.29m-high statue features prominent shoulders and ears, a protruding chin and a mysterious engraving on the torso.

Return to St-Florent along D 81.

THE AJACCIO AND SARTÈNE VINEYARDS

150km starting from Sagone. Michelin Local Map 345, B-C 7-10. See itinerary 3 *on the map opposite.*

Alongside Napoleon, Ajaccio takes pride in its small vineyard, hardly more than 20ha of **Ajaccio AOC** covering the hillsides overlooking the gulfs of Ajaccio and Sagone.

Sagone⌂

Sagone offers a large beach, a marina and facilities for the practice of various water sports (sailing and diving schools). The **Genoese tower**, to the west of the town, stands guard over the cove of Sagone and the harbour.

Tiuccia

This small seaside resort lies inside the **gulf of La Liscia⌂**; it is overlooked by the ruins of Capraja castle.

Turn left onto D 601.

Sari-d'Orcino

This is an area of terraced olive groves and orchards of orange and lemon trees, as well as vineyards which wine-growers have worked hard to keep going.

Head S along D 101.

Calcatoggio

This large hamlet and its fruit gardens overhang the gulf of Sagone and the inland area. Fine **view★**.

Turn left onto D 81.

Ajaccio★★

In the **old town★**, which corresponds to the ancient Genoese city, the 200m long pier of the citadel offers an excellent **view★** of the seafront. The 2-year-old Napoleon was christened in the Renaissance **cathedral** in July 1771. Rue Bonaparte leads to place du Maréchal-Foch, the very hub of daily life in Ajaccio. The Quatre-Lions fountain is surmounted by the statue of **Bonaparte Premier**

Consul. The town hall houses the **Salon napoléonien★**, an exhibition room displaying mementoes of the Emperor and his family.   *Mid-Jun to mid-Sep, Mon-Fri, 9-11.45am, 2-5.45pm; mid-Sep to mid-June, Mon-Fri, 9-11.45am, 2-4.45pm. Closed public hols. 2.30€ (children under 15: no charge).* ☎ *04 95 51 52 53.*

Rue du Cardinal-Fesch (U Borgu), a long, bustling shopping street, runs through the former "Borgo". The **Musée Fesch★★** houses the most important collection of **Italian painting★★★** in France apart from the Louvre collection.   *Jul-Aug, Mon 1.30-6pm, Tue-Fri 9am-6.30pm (Fri late night, 9pm-midnight), Sat-Sun and public hols 10.30am-6pm; Apr-Jun and Sep, Mon 1-5.15pm, Tue-Sun, 9.15am-12.15pm, 2.15-5.15pm; Oct-Mar, Tue-Sat, 9.15am-12.15pm, 2.15-5.15pm. 5.35€ (children under 15: no charge).* ☎ *04 95 21 48 17. www.musee-fesch.com*

Leave Ajaccio along N 193 and follow N 196 towards Sartène. At the intersection of N 196 and D 302, in a place called Pisciatello, you will find the **Clos Capitoro** *(see Shopping Guide). Turn back and turn left onto D 55 towards Porticcio.*

Porticcio≘

The tourist trade of this seaside resort, ideally situated opposite Ajaccio, is developing fast. Sand beaches, numerous hotels and restaurants, a thalassotherapy centre and residential complexes attract many holidaymakers. From the extremity of the headland, the view extends over the Ajaccio roadstead and Sanguinaires islands, recalling Alphonse Daudet's atmospheric tale of the Sanguinaires lighthouse.

On leaving Porticcio, the road skirts the long stretch of **Agosta beach**. *Turn left onto D 255A. At the end of the road, the* **Bellevalle pass** *offers a fine view of the gulf and the alluvial plain of La Gravona.*

Turn right onto D 302. On the way, stop in **Pila-Canale** *where the* **Domaine Alain Courrèges** *is worth a visit (see Shopping Guide). 7km further on, turn left onto D 757.*

Petreto-Bicchisano

Situated at an important intersection, this village actually consists of two villages: Bicchisano, the lower one, along N 196 and Petreto, the upper one, along D 420. Bicchisano spreads its massive granite houses on both sides of the road.

Drive S along N 196.

Olmeto

The fine granite houses of this large village rise in tiers up the steep south-facing slope of the Punta di Buturettu (alt 870m). The ruins of the **Castello della Rocca** crown the isolated hill which stands opposite the village, to the east.

N 196 runs down towards Propriano, offering fine **glimpses★** of the gulf of Valinco and the plain of Baracci planted with olive trees.

Propriano≘≘

Sheltering deep inside the gulf of Valinco with its calm, clear waters, this small harbour is today a busy tourist centre and a seaside resort sought after for its water sports facilities and numerous beaches of fine sand.

Sartène★

The **Corse-Sartène Appellation** covers a relatively wide area extending from the shores of the gulf of Propriano to the back country around Sartène. These are the sunniest vineyards on the island. Some ten producers get good results. This is the case, in particular, of the **Domaine Saparale** *(see Shopping Guide).*

Sartène still has a lot of character with its old austere houses and its traditions. Place de la Libération, with its cafés and its market, is the liveliest part of town.

THE PORTO-VECCHIO VINEYARDS

46km from Porto-Vecchio to Solenzara. Michelin Local Map 345, E-F 8-10. See itinerary 4 *on the map p. 218.*

The **Corse-Porto-Vecchio AOC** is scattered around the town of the same name; it is the smallest Corsican appellation. Made from grape varieties grown on steep granite screes, sometimes overhanging the sea, these wines are generally extremely subtle.

Porto-Vecchio≘≘

Built deep inside a vast gulf with an indented coastline, Porto-Vecchio is a thriving seaside resort and the third largest town in Corsica. Some of the finest Corsican beaches nestle along the coast nearby.

The cours Napoléon cuts across the old town and, on either side of it, there is a maze of narrow streets, vaulted passages and flights of steps. Outdoor cafés liven up the shaded place de la République in the city centre. The former Genoese **fortifications** have retained their bastions and bartizans towering above the seafront.

Leave Porto-Vecchio N along D 368 towards L'Ospédale; 4km further on, turn right onto D 759 towards Araggio.

Shopping Guide

INFORMATION

Comité intersyndical des vins de Corse
– 7 bd du Gén.-de-Gaulle - 20200 Bastia -
☎ 04 95 32 91 32 - www.vinsdecorse.com

OVERVIEW

CHARACTERISTICS

Red wines – Wines with a fairly high alcohol content, full-bodied and rich. Their colour varies from deep garnet red to dark purple. Typical aromas include stewed fruit, prune, developing into hints of chocolate, spices and game.

Rosé wines – Fairly rich colour with orange highlights at times. Their aromas point to red berries, citrus fruit and spices.

White wines – Generally bright, well-structured, with aromas of citrus fruit, white fruit and honey.

Muscat-du-cap-corse – These wines are generous, silky, with fine aromas of candied citron, honey and spices.

STORAGE

Reds – Great red wines: 10 years and more. Other wines: 5 years at least.

Rosés – Best drunk young.

Whites – Good-quality wines: within 5 years. Other wines: within 2 years.

PRICE

Between 3 and 8€. The Patrimonio AOC wines are generally sold between 8 and 15€.

BUYING

Clos Reginu e Prove – *Domaine Maestracci - leaving Feliceto on the way to Muro, follow D 215 towards Santa-Reparata - 20225 Feliceto - ☎ 04 95 61 72 11 - www.closreginu-eprove.com - Summer, Mon-Sat, 9am-noon, 2-7.30pm; low season, Wed-Sat, 9am-noon, 2-5pm.*

Planted on a glacial moraine, the vineyard of this estate, situated in the Reginu Valley, produces two excellent vintages (matured for three years in wooden vats and casks). You will be able to taste them on the premises after a tour of Michel Raoust's cellars.

Domaine Leccia – *20232 Poggio-d'Oletta - ☎ 04 95 37 11 35 - leccia.y@mic.fr – Mon-Sat, 9am-noon, 3-6pm – by appointment.* Yves Leccia manages a 22ha vineyard. The vines (Nielluccio, Vermentino and Muscat à Petits Grains) are espaliered and pruned "en cordon de Royat" – trained horizontally. Following the restructuring of the vineyard and the building of the new storehouse, the estate now produces two new vintages, white E. Croce and red Petra Bianca.

Clos Culombu – *Chemin San-Petru - 1.5km from Lumio on the way to Calvi; follow the road on the left leading to the cemetery - 20260 Lumio - ☎ 04 95 60 70 68 - daily 9am-noon, 3-7pm.* Prestige and tradition are the watchwords of this estate and, what's more, they are the names of the two red and white vintages produced here. The growing success of his wines is encouraging for Étienne Suzzoni who makes

it a point of honour to grow his vines by ecologically responsible methods as much as possible.

Domaine Pieretti – *Santa-Severa - intersection of D 80 and D 180 - 20228 Luri - ☎ 04 95 35 01 03 – Jun-Sep, daily, 10am-1pm, 4.30-8.30pm; low season, by prior appointment.* The fifth generation of Pierettis today manages the 9ha vineyard (Nielluccio, Vermentino) of the family estate, situated by the sea. You will be given the opportunity to taste some delicious crus such as the famous Muscats or Corse-Coteaux-du-Cap-Corse appellation.

Antoine Arena – *Morta-Majo - at the southern entrance to the village - 20253 Patrimonio - ☎ 04 95 37 08 27 - by appointment.* In his small 11ha estate, Mr Arena only works for connoisseurs and enthusiasts. It is for them that he makes very high-quality, entirely natural wines such as the Muscat-du-Cap-Corse, the Patrimonio (100% Vermentino and 100% Nielluccio) or the "Bianco Gentile" (a grape variety which he has revived).

Domaine Alain Courrèges – *Les Cyclamens – A Cantina - 20123 Cognocoli-Monticchi - ☎ 04 95 24 35 54 – Mon-Sat, 8.30am-noon, 3.30-7pm, public hols by appointment.* Alain Courrèges's estate, extending over 27ha, produces an excellent Ajaccio AOC, awarded a prize at the Concours Général. Tour of the cellar, wine tasting and sale on the premises. An outlet called A Cantina is open along the Porticcio seafront.

Clos Capitoro – *Rte de Sartène - Pisciatella, intersection N 196/D 302 - 20166 Porticcio - ☎ 04 95 25 19 61 - www.clos-capitoro.com – Mon-Sat 8am-noon, 2-6pm – closed public hols.* Owned by the Bianchetti family since 1856, the Clos Capitoro produces Ajaccio AOC wines and fortified wines used as aperitifs (made from Grenache grapes) and dessert wines (Les Malvoisies: sweet wines also served with foie gras and white meat). Tour of the cellar, wine tasting and sale.

Domaine de Torraccia – *N 198 - Lecci - 20137 Porto-Vecchio - ☎ 04 95 71 43 50 – Mon-Sat, 8am-noon, 2-6pm – closed public hols.* Mr Imbert manages his 43ha vineyard by traditional methods and continuous attention. The result? Red, rosé and white Corse-Porto-Vecchio AOC wines, now renowned, which you will discover in his estate situated between the sea and the mountains. The domaine also produces home-made olive oil.

Clos Nicrosi – *20247 Rogliano - ☎ 04 95 35 41 17.* In 1959, the Clos Nicrosi vineyard was entirely recreated at the foot of the village of Rogliano by Toussaint and Paul Luigi. Today, it is managed by Paul's son Jean-Noël. Renowned for its white wine and its Muscat, the estate uses the *passerillage* method: packed in wooden trays, the grapes are left out in the sun in order to concentrate the natural sugar content and the aromas.

Domaine Gentile – *Olzo - 20217 St-Florent - ☎ 04 95 37 01 54 or 04 95 37 20 20 - domaine.gentile@wanadoo.fr – Mon-Fri, 8am-noon, 2-6pm.* Dominique Gentile created this estate in 1970 and since then he has gone into partnership with Jean-Paul Gentile, an oenologist. Today, the vineyard extends over 30ha, on clayey limestone hillsides. In addition to the red, rosé and white Patrimonio wines, the estate produces Muscat (Vendemia d'Oru) and a small quantity of Rappu, a sweet wine made from four grape varieties harvested when overripe: Muscat à Petits Grains, Nielluccio, Malvoisie and Grenache.

Domaine Saparale – *5 cours Bonaparte – 20100 Sartène - ☎ 06 11 89 26 69 - p.ferinelli@libertysurf.fr* The 20ha Domaine Saparale spreads over granitic sand. Grape varieties planted on its south-eastern hillsides include Sciacarello, Vermentino and Nielluccio. White and rosé wines are vinified by direct pressing with thermo-regulated fermentation in stainless-steel tanks. The wines are then matured on fine lees and bottled early. In the case of red wines, harvesting is done by hand, followed by treading and stalking. The Cuvée Casteddu, a special vintage, comprises red, rosé and white wines.

Domaine de Solenzara – *20145 Solenzara - ☎ 04 95 57 89 69 – Jun-Sep, daily, 9am-noon, 4.30-7pm; Oct-May, Tue-Sat, 9am-noon.* This 16ha vineyard is the only one in Solenzara to be classified as Corse-Porto-Vecchio AOC. It produces white, rosé and red wines from traditional grape varieties (Nielluccio, Sciacarello, Vermentino…).

Castellu d'Araghju★

As you enter the hamlet, leave the car in the parking area on the right (walking shoes recommended). The path leading to the site starts in the hamlet (signposting). ⏱ 1hr there and back. Built on a rocky spur and looking like a crow's nest above the gulf of Porto-Vecchio, the Castellu (fortress) d'Araghju is a typical large Torrean buildings. The **view★★** extends over the coastal plain and the gulf.

At the end of D 759, turn left onto N 198. In order to break the journey, you could stop in **Lecci** and try the wines produced by the **Domaine de Torraccia**.

Site naturel de Fautea★

The **Genoese tower** *(lit at night by solar panels)* marks the northern limit of the two coves which are one of the sites protected by the Conservatoire du littoral, the coastline protection authority. Fautea beach, covered with fine sand, is sheltered by two rocky points. The site is close to the Cerbicale nature reserve and it is possible to see black **shags** *(marangone in Corsican)* flying low over the sea then diving in to catch their food.

Solenzara⌓

This seaside resort separates the rocky **Côte des Nacres** in the south from the flat northern coast. It offers the facilities of its marina and combines pleasures derived from the sea and from the nearby mountains. It is also appreciated for its local wine, such as that produced by the **Domaine de Solenzara**.

THE CAP CORSE VINEYARDS

53km starting from Luri. Michelin Local Map 345, F2. See round tour ⑤ on the map p. 218.

One of the island's oldest vineyards, renowned for its Muscat fortified wines, is located at the northern extremity of Cap Corse. Traditional **Corse-Cap-Corse Appellation** wines are also produced here. It is a magnificent wind-swept region, affording some of the most beautiful landscapes in Corsica.

Poster of the Luri wine fair, attended by many Corsican wine growers.

Luri

This locality is split into several hamlets spread across a green valley, sheltered from the wind. The **Domaine Pieretti** produces a good-quality Muscat *(see Shopping Guide)*.

Follow D 180 W towards Pino. A half-ruined watchtower, dating from the Middle Ages and known as the **Tour de Sénèque**, stands in a remote **site★**, on one of the peaks of Monte Rottu (alt 564m).

On reaching the Ste-Lucie pass, take the road starting near the chapel. It leads to a parking area. 🚶 1hr 15min on foot there and back along a steep path beginning at the southwestern extremity of the platform. In clear weather, the **view★** extends as far as the islands of Elba and Capraia and the Italian coast.

Pino★

The houses, Genoese towers, church and numerous funerary chapels of this charming village rise in tiers up the mountain slopes amid luxuriant vegetation. *Continue N along D 80.* **Morsiglia** slopes down in terraces to the sea. The main hamlet, surrounded by tall cliffs, is guarded by large square towers. The road narrows and offers a spectacular bird's-eye view of the indented coastline. The slopes form green undulations dotted with holly and white rock roses.

Centuri★★

This is one of the most charming villages of the Cap Corse area; D 35 leads down to the **seaside area★★** which forms a pleasant resort.
Beyond Centuri on the left, a minor road leads to the lovely village of **Cannelle★**, with its traffic-free, flower-decked alleyways.
A little further on, it is possible to take a short walk starting from the **Mattei mill** viewpoint. 🚶 *30min on foot there and back.* From the pass *(parking area)*, follow the path on the right which climbs to the old mill rising above the maquis at an altitude of 404m. Restored by Mattei, who produce the famous Cap Corse Mattei aperitif, this old windmill became the symbol of the modern trade name. It offers a vast **panorama★★** extending from the island of La Giraglia in the north to the Centuri cove and the rocky coast in the west.

Rogliano★

The locality of Rogliano, inhabited since Roman times, comprises seven hamlets perched on several rocky spurs. Rogliano spreads its towers, churches and tall old houses in tiers inside a green hollow sheltered by Monte Poggio. The **Clos Nicrosi** produces Muscat and Coteaux-du-Cap-Corse wines *(see Shopping Guide).*
Leave D 80 before Macinaggio and turn left onto D 353.

Tomino

From the square in front of the church, the **view★★** plunges down to the bay and the port of Macinaggio, extending far towards the islands of Finocchiarola and Capraia. The inhabitants of Tomino share the running of the vineyards with their neighbours in Rogliano.

Macinaggio⚓

This seaside resort has mooring facilities for 600 boats in its modern marina. Genoese towers are dotted along the splendid **Sentier des Douaniers★** (customs officers' path) which starts from the beach and skirts the protected coastline. 🚶 *About 3hr on foot from Macinaggio to Barcaggio – 45min as far as Santa Maria Chapel. This hike is not difficult in any way. The itinerary is practicable year-round but it is most pleasant in spring and autumn. Inquire beforehand about weather conditions,* ☎ *08 36 68 02 20. Wear walking shoes and take water with you.*

Underwater Adventures

Corsican shores are famous for their abundant and varied underwater flora and fauna. Wearing only a mask and snorkel, it is possible to get a clear view to a depth of 15m. The best spots are the gulf of Valinco, the Tizzano area, the bay of Figari, the islands of Burzzi as far as Porto-Vecchio and the Centuri area in the Cap Corse peninsula. If you wish to practise scuba-diving, contact the **Comité corse de la Fédération française de sports sous-marin**, *BP 12, 20145 Solenzara,* ☎ *04 95 57 48 31, fax 04 95 57 48 32. www.plongee-corse.org.* It has the list of diving clubs and provides information about local regulations.

A Short Walk in the Neolithic

Site archéologique de Filitosa★★

17km NW of Propriano along N 196, D 157 and D 57. Early Apr to mid-Oct, 8am to dusk. Preferably in the middle of the day when there is enough daylight to study the sculptures and engravings. Information in four languages. 5€. ☎ *04 95 74 00 91.*
The invaluable remains on this site offer a summary of early Corsican history from the Neolithic period (6000-2000 BC) to Roman times.
Among the 70 menhir-statues which have been excavated, Filitosa V is the largest and the most heavily armed: on one side, it appears with a long sword and a slanted dagger in its sheath; on the other side, one can see details of anatomy and clothing.

Jura

Secluded, even secretive, the Jura wine-growing area has a resilient, unique identity, characterised by wines with mysterious-sounding names – *vin de paille, vin jaune, vin d'Arbois* – produced from grape varieties that are found nowhere else. The area stretches north-south for some 100km, backing on to the Revermont, a limestone plateau formed by the foothills of the Jura as they descend towards the eastern edge of the Bresse plain. Everywhere you will come across enthusiastic wine-growers, proud of their identity and ready to extend a warm welcome. The region's Comté cheeses, freshwater fish and smoked pork make it a gastronome's paradise. But, if you want to stretch your legs, the Jura also offers countless opportunities for walking, in both vineyard and forest. With the saltworks of Arc-et-Senans, Arbois, Poligny and Lons-le-Saunier, the region is also possessed of a historical and architectural heritage which is second to none.

The terroir
Michelin Local Map 321 – Jura (39).
Area: approximately 1 800ha – equivalent to a mere 2% of the Bordeaux wine-growing area – located at altitudes of between 250 and 400m, spread over 81 *communes* (local authority areas).
Production: approximately 78 400 hl.
The soils consist mainly of clays and marls, with extensive limestone areas in the southern sector. The region has a continental climate with cold winters, relatively little rainfall, plenty of sunshine and temperate-to-hot summers.

The wines
Côtes-du-Jura – From north of Arbois to south of Lons-le-Saunier. White wines made from Chardonnay and Savagnin grapes, the latter being virtually unique to the Jura region and reds (Pinot Noir, Poulsard and Trousseau).
Arbois – Whites (Chardonnay and Savagnin) and reds (Pinot Noir, Poulsard and Trousseau). **Arbois-pupillin** is a local name for certain reds and rosés.
Château-Chalon – North of Lons-le-Saunier, an area which produces exclusively *vin jaune*, made from the Savagnin grape.
L'Étoile – Southwest of Château-Chalon, where they make only traditional whites, *vins jaunes* and *crémants* (sparkling wines, less effervescent than champagne) from Chardonnay (90%), Poulsard and Savagnin.

Background

Vin jaune, vin de paille, crémant and macvin – As well as being known by their appellation of origin, Jura wines are also described in terms of the way they are made. The unique **vin jaune**, a white wine made exclusively from the Savagnin grape, is left to age for six years and three months in 228l containers, without topping-up. In other words, the wine is left to slowly evaporate. In contact with the air, a film of yeast – the "veil" – forms on the surface of the wine. This protects it from oxidisation and fosters development of the wine's characteristic flavours, which range from fresh walnut via "petroly" aromas to

Vineyards on the slopes below Château-Chalon.

Directory

WHERE TO EAT

AROUND ARBOIS

☻ **Le Caveau d'Arbois** – *3 route de Besançon - 39600 Arbois -* ☏ *03 84 6610 70 – closed Sun evening and Mon - 15/29€.* This restaurant's menu is a good introduction to the culinary wealth of the Franche-Comté region: jésus de Morteau à la cancoillotte chaude (a sausage and cheese dish), coq au vin jaune with morel mushrooms, trout in a Savagnin wine sauce, poached eggs au Trousseau, chicken breasts in a Poulsard sauce, regional cheeseboard etc.

☻ **Auberge Le Grapiot** – *R. Bagier - 39600 Pupillin - 3km S of Arbois on the D 246 -* ☏ *03 84 37 49 44 – closed Mon – advance booking recommended - 14/30€.* In the heart of a wine-growing village, this friendly little inn is characteristic of the local style of architecture. Seated by the large fireplace in the dining room, you can enjoy typical regional dishes.

☻☻ **La Balance Mets et Vins** – *R. de Courcelles - 39600 Arbois -* ☏ *03 84 37 45 00 – closed 30 Jun to 7 Jul, 12 Dec to 28 Jan, Sun evenings, Tue evenings and Wed, except public hols - 20/38€.* The patron presides over his casseroles on an old stove in full view of his diners. His recipes are often matched with wines from the Franche-Comté region, some on offer at very affordable prices: if you're looking for an interesting local wine list, this is a good place to try. The decor is simple and there is a pleasant terrace.

☻☻☻ **Jean-Paul Jeunet** – *R. de l'Hôtel-de-Ville - 39600 Arbois -* ☏ *03 84 66 05 67 – closed Dec, Jan, Wed except evenings in Jul-Aug and Mar - 45/125€.* This establishment, located at the heart of the little town, successfully combines tradition and modernity: comfortable bedrooms in contemporary style, dining room with exposed beams and an open fireplace, and a pleasant, plant-shaded patio. A superb wine list complements the skilfully prepared local dishes.

AROUND ARC-ET-SENANS

☻ **Le Relais** – *9 pl. de l'Église – 25610 Arc-et-Senans -* ☏ *03 81 57 40 60 – closed 15 Dec to 15 Jan and Sun evenings - 11/27€.* This family-run inn near the magnificent Royal Saltworks designed by Claude-Nicolas Ledoux has a pleasant terrace at the front. If the sun refuses to shine, enjoy the chef's energising regional specialities indoors under the exposed beams of one of a series of three rustic dining rooms.

☻ **Auberge de la Lavandière** – *R. de la Lavandière - 25440 Lavans-Quingey – 12.5km SE of Courtefontaine by the D 101 to Byans-sur-Doubs then the D 13 to Quingey and on towards Lavans-Quingey -* ☏ *03 81 63 69 28 – closed 20 Dec to 4 Jan, Sat 12pm, Sun evening and Mon - 12/32€.* One feels dwarfed by this magnificent barn with its imposing wooden roof and old fireplace. In summer, you can also enjoy their sucking calf or carved ham with Comté cheese and morel mushrooms out of doors, on a large garden table set up near a wood with a charming stream.

AROUND LONS-LE-SAUNIER

☻ **Le Mirabilis** – *41 Grande-Rue - 39570 Mirebel - 15km E of Lons-le-Saunier via the D 471 -* ☏ *03 84 48 24 36 – closed 2 to 10 Jan, Mon, Tue and Wed lunchtimes out of season - 13/30€.* Well-known to local gourmets, this restaurant is tucked away in a little village in the Jura countryside. Sophie and Hugo Meyer invite you to savour their home-grown cuisine: suprême de pintade (guinea fowl) in a morel and vin jaune sauce, and baked trout flambé in vieux pontarlier, a kind of local absinthe.

☻ **Les Grottes** – *Aux Grottes – 39210 Baume-les-Messieurs - 9km NE of Lons-le-Saunier –* ☏ *03 84 48 23 15 – closed 16 Oct to 19 Mar and Mon except in Jul - Aug – reservation essential - 14/35€.* This fine early-20C pavilion and its well-shaded terrace is a good vantage point from which to view the natural wonders of Baume-les-Messieurs, in particular its waterfalls. Savour such local dishes as terrine comtoise, émincé de volaille au macvin – thinly sliced poultry in a macvin sauce – and entrecôte with morels.

☻☻ **Ferme-auberge La Grange Rouge** – *39570 Geruge - 9km SW of Lons-le-Saunier on the D 117 -* ☏ *03 84 47 00 44 – closed 25 Aug to 17 Sep – advance booking recommended - 18/21€.* This dairy farm, perched at an altitude of 500m, draws lovers of good food from all over the region, with such dishes as its duck in a cream and morel sauce, croûtes aux champignons and home-made cottage cheese. The spacious, comfortable bedrooms are enhanced by the bucolic peace and quiet of the location.

☻☻ **Les 16 Quartiers** – *Pl. de l'Église - 39210 Château-Chalon - 10km N of Lons-le-Saunier via the D 70 –* ☏ *03 84 44 68 23 – closed mid-Nov to end Mar, evenings except weekends from Mar to Jun, Mon midday and Thu evenings in Jul-Aug – 9.90€ lunch - 19/25€.* Time seems to have stood still on the shady terrace or in the semi-cave-dwelling dining room of this charming 16C house, tucked away at the heart of a little town famed for its vin jaune. Enjoy its local – or rather, medieval – cuisine, accompanied by Jura wines, which are available by the glass.

AROUND POLIGNY

☻ **Le Chalet** – *7 rte de Genève – 39800 Poligny -* ☏ *03 84 37 13 28 – closed Wed - 11/38.50€.* Local specialities are the pride of this simple, friendly restaurant: escalope polinoise, Morteau sausage with Comté cheese, or salade montagnarde with Gex blue cheese and smoked ham, all served with the best Jura wines, by the bottle, carafe or glass.

◛ **La Maison du Haut** – *Les Bordes - 6km SW of Poligny via the D 259 then a minor road -* ☎ *03 84 37 35 19 – closed 1 to 15 Oct - reservation essential - 12/20€.* In a quiet rural location, enjoy the simple pleasures of genuine local family cooking in this attractive little 18C farmhouse, which also has some plain but nevertheless pleasant bedrooms if you want to stay the night. Dormitory accommodation for ramblers. Stabling and paddock for horses.

AT SALINS-LES-BAINS

◛◛ **Les Bains** – *1 pl. des Alliés – 39110 Salins-les-Bains -* ☎ *03 84 73 07 54 – closed 1 to 16 Jan, Tue 12pm, Sun evening and Mon - 17/47.40€.* "Morillette" and "comtine" are two of the mouth-watering inventions devised by chef Maurice Marchand, who also has plenty of other tasty recipes up his sleeve. Classic cuisine is served in the country-style dining room, regional dishes in the brasserie.

◛◛ **Le Relais de Pont d'Héry** – *Rte de Champagnole - 39110 Salins-les-Bains -* ☎ *03 84 73 06 54 – closed 18 Oct to 4 Nov, 15 Feb to 3 Mar, Tue from Sep to May and Mon. 17/38€.* Behind the somewhat bland façade of this small house are two very pleasant dining rooms where appetising traditional dishes are served: try breaded quail fillets with hazelnuts, baked turbot aux herbes, noix de saint-jacques in flaky pastry with candied lemons, foie gras soufflé or gratin d'écrevisses.

WHERE TO STAY

AT ARBOIS

◛ **Hôtel Les Messageries** – *R. de Courcelles - 39600 Arbois -* ☎ *03 84 66 15 45 - hotel.lesmessageries@wanadoo.fr - closed Jan and Dec - 26 rm: 27/61€ -* ☲ *7€.* On one of the town's main streets, this old post house has an attractive ivy-clad façade. The bedrooms are gradually being refurbished. Book one of the rooms at the rear, which are quieter and have fully equipped bathrooms.

◛◛ **Annexe Le Prieuré** – *R. de l'Hôtel-de-Ville - 39600 Arbois -* ☎ *03 84 66 05 67 – closed Dec, Jan, Wed from Sep to Jun and Mar - 7 rm: 70/135€ -* ☲ *15€.* This rambling but comfortable old 17C building is the annex of the Jean-Paul Jeunet hotel-restaurant some 200m up the street. The bedrooms are stylishly furnished, some overlooking an attractive garden.

AROUND ARC-ET-SENANS

◛ **Chambre d'hôte Le Val d'Amour** – *29 rte de Salins - 39380 Ounans - 13km SW of Arc-et-Senans via the D 17E then the D 32 and D 472 -* ☎ *03 84 37 62 28 -* ⤳ *- 4 rm: 35/43€.* You will receive a friendly welcome in this quiet private house not far out of Arc-et-Senans. In fine weather, you can take your breakfast on the terrace, overlooking fields and meadows. The rooms are simple but cosy.

AROUND LONS-LE-SAUNIER

◛ **Nouvel Hôtel** – *50 r. Lecourbe – 39000 Lons-le-Saunier -* ☎ *03 84 47 20 67 - nouvel.hotel39@wanadoo.fr - closed 17 Dec to 9 Jan -* 🅿 *- 26 rm: 35/50€ -* ☲ *7€.* Superb models of French warships, made by the owner, adorn the entrance hall of this town-centre hotel. The rooms are of varying sizes, furnished in rustic style. Those on the third floor are the least spacious.

◛ **Chambre d'hôte Château de la Muyre** – *39210 Domblans - 8km W of Château-Chalon on the D 5 as far as Voiteur then D 120 to Domblans then D 57E on the left -* ☎ *03 84 44 66 49 – closed Jan and Feb -* ⤳ *- 6 rm: 30/80€ -* ☲ *10€.* Simplicity is the order of the day in this aristocratic mansion which has been in the same family for several centuries and has lent its name to a distiguished AOC wine. The rooms, from which there are fine country views, are soberly furnished, except for the vast, stylish "bridal chamber". Shared bathroom.

◛ **Chambre d'hôte Le Jardin de Misette** – *R. Honoré-Chapuis - 39140 Arlay - 12km W of Château-Chalon on the D 5 as far as Voiteur then D 120 -* ☎ *03 84 85 15 72 -jardindemisette@aol.fr -* ⤳ *- 4 rm: 46€ - meals 20€.* Former restaurateurs and authors of the recipe book Saveurs comtoises, Misette and her husband fell in love with this vigneron's property on the banks of the Seille. The bedrooms are calm and comfortable. The most agreeable is the curiously named "Chabotte" (anvil stand), in a separate little house at the bottom of the garden. Convivial atmosphere, family cooking.

◛◛ **Parenthèse** – *3000 chemin du Pin - 39570 Chille - 3km N of Lons-le-Saunier on the D 157 -* ☎ *03 84 47 55 44 - parenthese. hotel@wanadoo.fr -* 🅿 *- 34 rm: 92/134€ -* ☲ *10€ - restaurant 17.50/48€.* On the Jura wine route, this is a modern hotel with rooms offering two different levels of comfort. Most have balconies and views over the hotel's park-like garden. The restaurant produces dishes combining local ingredients and non-local ideas.

AROUND POLIGNY

◛◛ **La Ferme du Château** – *R. de la Poste - 39800 Bersaillin - 9km W of Poligny via N 83 then D 22 -* ☎ *03 84 25 91 31 – closed Jan - 9 rm: 50/60€ -* ☲ *8€ - meals 30€.* This magnificently restored 18C farmhouse has retained many of its original features, including a room with fine vaulting and pillars, which in summer is used for concerts and art exhibitions. The sober but elegant bedrooms overlook open countryside.

AT SALINS-LES-BAINS

◛◛ **Grand Hôtel des Bains** – *Pl. des Alliés - 39110 Salins-les-Bains -* ☎ *03 84 37 90 50 - hotel.bains@wanadoo.fr - closed 2 to 23 Jan -* 🅿 *- 31 rm: 54/73€ -* ☲ *7.50€.* This hotel is in a central location, on a busy street. It has direct access to the spa's fitness centre and mineral water pool. The bedrooms are functional, decorated in 1970s style. Those at the back are quieter.

GOURMET SHOPPING

Charcuterie Guyon – *5 r. de l'Hôtel-de-Ville- 39600 Arbois- ☎ 03 84 66 04 25.* Everything is wholesome and home-made chez Jean-Claude Guyon, high priest of local pork butchery: wild boar ham, ham steeped in vin jaune, sausage incorporating Comté cheese or pine honey, red deer brési (dried salted meat). A glance in the window is enough to get your taste buds working.

Hirsinger – *38 pl. de la Liberté – 39600 Arbois - ☎ 03 84 66 06 97 - www.chocolat-hirsinger.com - winter: Wed-Sun 8am-7.30pm; summer: daily 8am-7.30pm – closed Wed and Thu except public hols.* It would be an unforgivable oversight to pass through Arbois without paying a short visit to this chocolate-maker (winner of the Meilleur Ouvrier de France award, 1996), who produces a succulent range of chocolates – flavoured with mint, ginger or spices – as well as celebrated local specialities such as galets d'Arbois biscuits or Bouchons.

Au Prince d'Orange - *Éts Pelen – 1 r. St-Désiré - 39000 Lons-le-Saunier – ☎ 03 84 24 31 39 - shop: Mon-Fri 9am-12.30pm, 2pm-7pm (Sat 7.15pm), Sun 9am-12.30pm; tea room: 2.30pm-7pm.* Since 1899, the Pelen family has been spoiling the inhabitants of Lons-le-Saunier with its galets de Chalain (nougatine and praline robed in chocolate), gâteau Écureuil (praline-hazelnut butter cream on an almond-hazelnut base, all covered in marzipan) and many other delicious sweetmeats. Stylish tea room upstairs.

Fruitière de Plasne — *39800 Plasne - 5km SW of Poligny on the D 68 - ☎ 03 84 37 14 03 – 10am-12pm, 6pm-7pm – closed Tue.* As well as Comté, other local gastronomic delights, such as Tomme du Jura and Morbier, are made in this cooperative dairy. During the season, favoured individuals are invited to visit the department where Comté is made and the cellars where the cheeses are matured, followed by a tasting session.

Juraflore – *15 pl. des Déportés – 39800 Poligny - ☎ 03 84 37 13 50 – Mon-Sat 8am-12pm and 2.30pm-7pm, Sun and public hols 9am-12pm.* Over three generations, the maturing of Comté cheese has been raised to an art form by the family which owns this shop. At every stage of maturity (6, 12, 18 or 23 months), mild, medium or intensely mature and salty, it is worthy of the highest praise. Also try their Mont d'Or, Morbier and Tomme de Castelviel.

Fumé du Jura – *Hameau de Moutaine - 39110 Pont-d'Héry - 8km S of Salins-les-Bains on the D 467 - ☎ 03 84 73 02 49 – Tue-Sat 8am-7pm, Sun 9am-7pm.* Ham on the bone, dried sausages, palette (shoulder of pork), brési, tongue, sausage marinaded in vin jaune, pâtés of various kinds: these delicious delicatessen products are made exclusively with pork meat and offal from the Franche-Comté region. Some are smoked by local craftsmen, always using juniper wood. Temptations no gourmet could resist...

S. Sauvignier / MICHELIN

MARKETS

Poligny – *Monday and Friday morning, Place des Déportés.*
Lons-le-Saunier – *Thursday, Place de la Liberté.*
Arbois – Friday morning.

curry. *Vin jaune* is therefore a very dry wine and newcomers may well be surprised by its strong personality. It is aged in a special bottle, known as a *clavelin*, which contains just 62cl.

Vin de paille derives its name from the old practice of spreading the best grapes, picked at the beginning of the harvest, on beds of straw and leaving them to drip slowly as a way of concentrating the sugar content. Nowadays, this practice has been replaced by a ventilation process. A unique product, *vin de paille* is a very sweet wine with subtle currant and walnut flavours.

Crémant-du-jura is a high-quality sparkling wine, made following the traditional Champagne method. It is produced all over the region.

Macvin is a red or white liqueur wine made from fresh grape juice to which local brandy *(eau-de-vie)* has been added. It is drunk as an aperitif or dessert wine and has a subtle spicy flavour.

Fruitières – The Jura was one of the first French regions to establish cooperative wineries. Here they are referred to as "fruitières", a name borrowed from cheese-making, "fruit" being a general term for the product of human labour. The five Jura *fruitières* are those of Arbois, Pupillin, Poligny, Voiteur, and the Caveau des Byards.

The Jura Wine Route

Approximately 60km. Allow a whole day, including stops to visit places of interest. Michelin Local Map 321, E-F 4-7. See map on p. 229.

FROM ARC-ET-SENANS TO POLIGNY ①

Leaving the Arc-et-Senans saltworks, you will not see any vineyards for several kilometres, until you come to a bend in the River Loue, near Port-Lesney. There is less evidence of wine-growing around Salins-les-Bains, but there are vineyards all the way from Montigny-les-Arsures to Poligny.

Royal Saltworks at Arc-et-Senans★★

Jul-Aug: 9am-7pm; Jun and Sep: 9am-6pm; Apr-May and Oct: 9am-12pm, 2pm-6pm; Nov-Mar: 10am-12pm, 2pm-5pm. Closed 1 Jan, 25 Dec. 7€. Guided tour all the year round, by request for groups, ☎ 03 81 54 45 45. www.salineroyale.com

The former Royal Saltworks stands between the River Loue and the Forest of Chaux. A prime example of 18C industrial architecture, it is a UNESCO World Heritage Site. Here salt was produced by evaporation, boiling the brine drawn from below ground at Salins-les-Bains in immense cauldrons. The brine was conveyed to the works by gravity in wooden "saumoducs", which formed a sort of underground pipeline. The building is striking for the beauty of its geometrical arched vaults and futuristic architecture. The architect, Claude-Nicolas Ledoux, in fact designed an entire community complex, with dwellings for 250 workers and the management, workshops, and even a prison for those who stole salt, a very valuable commodity at the time. The saltworks operated until the end of the 19C, but was never very profitable. The vast amount of wood it consumed for fuel led to the virtual destruction of the Forest of Chaux. Having gone to wrack and ruin, the saltworks was used by the Vichy regime as an internment camp for gypsies. Later, after an intensive programme of work, it was restored to it former glory in 1996.

> ### CLAUDE-NICOLAS-LEDOUX (1736-1806)
>
> Inspector General of the Saltworks of Lorraine and Franche-Comté, Ledoux was a visionary architect who was influenced by Enlightenment ideas. His greatest achievement was the Arc-et-Senans Saltworks, but he was also the creative mind behind some other bold projects, as the museum devoted to him at the saltworks explains: he had a hand in the design of the pavilions of the Fermiers Généraux complex in Paris – and the rotundas of La Villette and the Parc Monceau – the Château de Bénouville in Normandy, the theatre in Besançon. In 1804, he published a treatise on architecture and its relation to the arts, the law and customs, which enlarges on his plans for an ideal settlement at Chaux.

Chemin des Gabelous (salt-tax collectors' path) d'Arc-et-Senans – ⚑

On leaving the saltworks, turn left, then right at the roundabout into the Rue des Graduations. The waymarked path begins at the camp site. 5hr 30min on foot, 2hr 30min by bicycle. This 24km path roughly follows the route of the "saumoduc" which carried brine from the salt mine at Salins to the works at Arc-et-Senans. To get to Port-Lesney, take the D 17ᴱ then the D 121 and finally the D 48ᴱ.

Port-Lesney★

The road to this pretty riverside village cuts through vineyards contained by a bend in the Loue. One of Port-Lesney's former mayors was President Edgar Faure, who played an important political role during the Fourth and Fifth Republics. On Sundays, anglers, boating enthusiasts and lovers of trout and fried fish converge on this spot. The harbour district, on the left bank of the Loue, has some fine wine merchants' houses.

⚑ From the Chapelle de Lorette, a pathway (1hr there and back) leads through undergrowth to the **Edgar-Faure viewing point**, which overlooks the village and the whole of the valley.

From Port-Lesney, take the D 48 to the hamlet of Pagnoz, then the D 472 to Salins-les-Bains.

Salins-les-Bains⚑

As its name suggests, the town owed its former prosperity to salt, an inexhaustible source of taxation under the Ancien Régime, levied in the form of the *gabelle* or salt tax. Dominated by **Fort Belin** and **Fort Saint-André**, Salins is strung out along the valley bottom of the Furieuse. The town still has fragments of its ramparts and towers. Nowadays, it is a pleasant spa, whose waters are used for treating rheumatic and gynaecological conditions *(see "Water Sports and Spas" section)*.

The impressive buildings and tall chimneys of the saltworks still stand on the banks of the Furieuse. A visit will complete your understanding of the salt-making process. Here the brine was extracted before being conveyed by "saumoduc" (a primitive pipeline) to the Royal Saltworks at Arc-et-Senans. Salt is no longer extracted from the mines, but the salt spring is still used by the spa establishment. The underground tunnels (13C), 200m long and supported by impressive medieval vau-

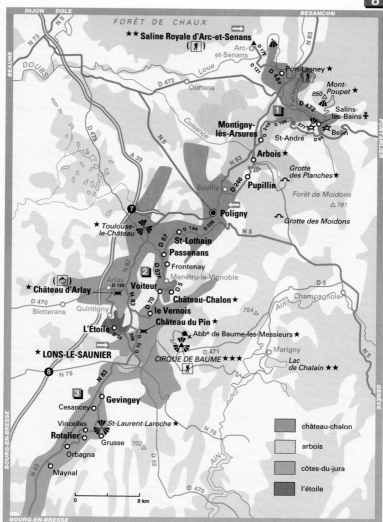

lting, are well worth a visit. *Guided tour (1hr), Jul-Aug: 10am, 11am, 12pm, 2.30pm, 3.30pm, 4.30pm, 5.30pm; from Easter hols to end Jun and beginning Sep to mid-Sep: 10am, 11am, 2.30pm, 3.30pm, 4.30pm; from beginning Mar to Easter hols and mid-Sep to end Oct: 10.30am, 2.30pm, 4pm; from beginning Nov to end Feb: weekends and school hols 10.30am, 3pm. Take something warm to wear: 12°C. Closed 1 Jan, 25 Dec. 4.20€ (children: 2.40€). ☎ 03 84 73 10 92. www.salins-les-bains.com*

Travel S from Salins on the D 472, turn right onto the D 94, then right again onto the D 271. In Marnoz, take the D 105 towards Arbois then the D 249 in the Montigny-lès-Arsures direction.

Montigny-lès-Arsures

This authentic wine-growing village, where every house has its own cellar, backs onto the Revermont. It has a fine Romanesque church. In the hamlet of Les Rosières (below the village, near the N 83), is a sign indicating the **"Vigne historique Pasteur"**, a property belonging to the Académie des Sciences. It was here that Louis Pasteur performed his first experiments on yeasts.

He demonstrated that the juice from bunches of grapes wrapped in cotton, and therefore not in contact with the atmosphere and the yeasts it contains, did not ferment, unlike the juice from grapes that had been exposed to the air. The village is situated in the Arbois appellation area and there are at least ten vignerons selling local wines. The terroir is known for red wines made from the Trousseau grape, the full character of which is expressed in the wines produced by **André and Mireille Tissot** and **Jacques Puffeney** *(see Shopping Guide)*.

The **Frédéric Lornet** winery is housed in a former 16C abbey and you can taste its wares in the old chapel. *Abbaye de la Boutière, 39600 Montigny-lès-Arsures,* ☎ *03 84 37 44 95. Daily 9am-12pm, 2-6pm. No charge.*

If weather permits, you can take advantage of a picnic area laid out on the outskirts of the village, with views of the vineyards. It is on the right, in the Arbois direction.

Drive to Arbois on the N 83.

Arbois★

Arbois derives its name from two Celtic words, Ar and Bos, meaning "fertile soil". The real capital of wine-growing in the Jura, Arbois lent its name to the region's first *appellation d'origine contrôlée* (AOC) in 1936. In the past, its wine was praised by Rabelais, Voltaire and Henry IV, who knew how to appreciate good things. However, this did not prevent Henry from besieging the town in 1595 and looting it when it fell. Arbois has a number of wine cellars and wine merchants in the Place de la Liberté area. It has a well-deserved reputation for gastronomy, with Jean-Paul Jeunet's excellent restaurant and Claude Hirsinger's chocolate. But Arbois also owes much to the great **Louis Pasteur**, who through his scientific research and advice made an important contribution to the revival of the wine-making industry after it had been devastated by phylloxera.

Take time to stroll around Arbois and absorb its rural elegance. A tour of the old walls *(map/brochure from the tourist office)* brings you to the picturesque **Gloriette Tower** and the **Pont des Capucins** over the Cuisance, a small river whose banks were formerly crowded with paper mills and tanneries. Also take a walk in the **Faubourg Faramand**, the old wine-merchants' district, where you will see, on the pavement in front of each house, the "trappon" (trap-door) giving access to the cellar below. Nowadays, Arbois is home to just a few dozen wine growers, but in the 18C there were more than a thousand of them. You will receive a warm welcome at the celebrated **Maison Henri Maire**, or the domaine **Rolet Père et Fils** *(see Shopping Guide)*.

Fruitière vinicole Château Béthanie – *2 r. des Fossés, 39600 Arbois,* ☎ *03 84 66 11 67, www.chateau-bethanie.com. Tours of the cellars: Tue-Sun (Jul-Aug) 11am, 2.30pm, 4.30pm. Closed 1 May and 25 Dec.* Founded in 1906 by 26 wine-growers overwhelmed by competition from the South of France, this *fruitière* was France's second cooperative winery. Nowadays, it is an extremely well-equipped enterprise which produces wines from approximately 200ha of vineyards and has made a name for itself with its Béthanie vintage, a pleasant white made from Savagnin and Chardonnay grapes, with a pronounced *vin jaune* character. A tour of the cellars will give you a thorough knowledge of how *vin jaune* is made, and you can taste the winery's products in a former chapel building.

Musée du Vin et de la Vigne – *Jul-Aug: 10am-12.30pm, 2pm-6pm; Mar-Jun and Sep-Oct: daily except Tue 10am-12pm, 2pm-6pm; Nov-Feb: daily except Tue 2pm-6pm. Guided tours may be possible (1hr). Closed Jan, 1 May, 25 Dec. 3.30€ (under 14s: no charge).* ☎ *03 84 66 40 45.*

A vestige of the town's ancient fortifications, the **Château Pécauld** houses the region's wine museum and institute. Outside, the work of the vigneron is introduced by a tour of small plots of different grape varieties. Inside, the history of the vineyards and the wine-growing community, past and present, is illustrated by photographs and artefacts. The visit includes an opportunity to taste some selected wines.

Arbois: vineyard and church tower.

Maison de Pasteur★ – *Jun-Sep: guided tour (30min) 9.45am, 10.45am, 11.45am and 2pm-6pm; Apr-May and beginning Oct to mid-Oct: 2.15pm, 3.15pm, 4.15pm, 5.15pm. 5.50€.* ☎ *03 84 66 11 72.*

A visit to the house where Louis Pasteur spent part of his life is a surprisingly moving experience. Standing on the bank of the Cuisance, his father's tannery was not as large as it is now, but was gradually extended and modernised by the famous scientist. The house has lost nothing of its opulent decor and the family atmosphere is faithfully preserved. Pasteur's bedroom appears to be untouched: his penholder, inkwell and blotter await him on the bureau; his trade-mark fur hat is still there. In the laboratory, you can see the instruments and apparatus he used for his experiments.

Church of St-Just★ – Beside the building is an esplanade, giving a good view of the Cuisance. The outstanding feature of this priory church (12-13C) is its bell tower, 60m high, which lords it over the town. Built in the 16C of golden-ochre coloured stone, it culminates in an onion-shaped dome housing a chime of bells. On the first Sunday in September each year, the wine-growers pay homage to the parish's patron saint, processing to the church of St Just with a giant bunch of grapes, the *Biou*, plaited from grapes from all over the commune. This time-honoured tradition is celebrated by the whole town, whose prosperity is closely bound up with the life of its vignerons.

Leave Arbois and travel S on the D 246.

Pupillin

After climbing up onto the plateau, with a fine view of the red roofs of Arbois in your rear mirror, you will reach Pupillin, a village totally devoted to wine-growing. It likes to think of itself as the "world capital" of Poulsard (or Ploussard), a grape variety which does well on the blue and red marls of the area. It produces light wines, pale in colour, whose flavours are reminiscent of cherry, and slightly smokey. Of the Arbois-Pupillin estates, those of **Pierre Overnoy** and the **Renardière** can be relied on for quality. Another good address is that of the **fruitière vinicole de Pupillin** *(see Shopping Guide)*.

Pupillin is also a centre of hazelnut growing. You will see plantations on either side of the road as you travel towards Poligny. A viewing point has been laid out on the outskirts of the village, from which you can survey some of the vineyards.

Continue on the D 246 as far as Buvilly, then turn left onto the N 83 towards Poligny.

Poligny

To the great joy of connoisseurs, Poligny successfully combines the production of excellent wines with the manufacture of Comté cheese, of which the town is the acknowledged centre. For centuries, its rich soils, at the heart of the AOC Côtes-du-Jura wine-growing area, have ensured its prosperity, and this is borne out by the town's cultural heritage.

Poligny's main place of interest is the very unusual **Caveau des Jacobins**. A former 13C church, deconsecrated at the time of the Revolution, it passed into public ownership and was purchased by the local vignerons for use as a winery. This marriage between Christ and Bacchus seems to have worked well, as the winery now sells some excellent *vins jaunes*, together with a whole range of high-quality Côtes-du-Jura wines. *R. Nicolas-Appert, 39800 Poligny,* ☎ *03 84 37 01 37, www.caveaudesjacobins.com Mon-Fri, 9.30am-12pm, 2-6.30pm, Sat 9.30am-12pm, Sun 10am-12pm; Jul-Aug: daily 9.30am-12pm, 2pm-6.30pm. Closed 25 Dec and 1 Jan.*

In the town itself, you will find several well-regarded wine merchants', such as the **Xavier Reverchon** and **Benoît Badoz** establishments *(see Shopping Guide)*.

After wine, cheese: be sure to visit the **Maison du comté**, which also houses the Comté trade association, for an explanation of the various operations involved in cheese-making, from collecting the milk to maturing of the finished cheese. It will certainly stimulate your appetite. ♿ *Jul-Aug: 10am-11.30am, 2pm-6pm; school hols: 2pm-5pm; other times: except weekends 2pm-5pm. Closed Mon, 1 Jan, 1 May, 14 Jul, 15 Aug, 25 Dec. 4€ (children 6-16: 2.50€).* ☎ *03 84 37 23 51.*

You should still have time to see the **Collegiate Church of St-Hippolyte**. Under the porch, the dividing pillar of the doorway supports a 15C polychrome sculpture of the Virgin Mary. Above the doorway is a bas-relief depicting the quartering of St Hippolytus. In the right-hand doorway, a 15C Pietà stands on a console. Inside, there is a remarkable wooden **calvary cross**, on the rood beam dominating the entrance to the choir, and a fine collection of statues of the 15C Burgundian school.

Ramparts ramble – *roughly 2hr. Map from the tourist office.* This walk through the old parts of Poligny follows the line of the ancient ramparts, with the keep of Saint-Laurent and the tower of the Sergenterie still in good shape. You can climb up to the site of the former Château de Grimont for a good view over the town.

FROM POLIGNY TO LONS-LE-SAUNIER 2

After Poligny, our itinerary follows minor roads along the Revermont corniche, where in many places the vineyards cling to very steep slopes.

From Poligny, take the D 259 S, then the D 194 for about 8km.

Saint-Lothain

Huddled at the foot of its hill, this village, named after a local saint, is dominated by vineyards interspersed with meadows and pinewoods. The village boasts some imposing vignerons' houses and an interesting little church in the late-Romanesque style peculiar to the Franche-Comté region. On the outskirts of the village, on the right-hand side of the Passenans road, is a well-laid-out picnic site.

Continue for 3km on the D 57, until you come to Passenans.

Passenans

This pretty village has some solid stone houses with steep-pitched roofs and crow-step gables. In a relaxed atmosphere, you can investigate the excellent crémants and Côtes-du-Jura wines of the **Grand Frères estate**, on the outskirts of the village *(see Shopping Guide)*.

Then climb the narrow road to the site of **Frontenay**, where an avenue of ancient lime trees leads to a 15C church surrounded by a cemetery. **The château**, further up, was a stronghold of the counts of Frontenay, standing guard over the salt route. Its 14C keep survives. At the entrance to the château, about 1km up the road from the church, you will find a display panel showing the routes of several country walks.

From Passenans, you can make a detour via **Toulouse-le-Château**, and return on the N 83. Drive up to the **viewing point★**, at the summit of which stands a church in the local 15C style, near the ruins of the former castle, and enjoy a magnificent view over the Revermont and the Bresse plain.

Take the D 57E1 to Menétru-le-Vignoble then the D5, climbing all the way to Château-Chalon.

Château-Chalon★

A former stronghold, solidly anchored on its rocky escarpment, this splendid village reigns over a small but prestigious terroir. The Château-Chalon appellation, which covers a mere 50ha spread over the communes of Menétru-le-Vignoble, Nevy-sur-Seille, Voiteur and Domblans, in fact only applies to *vin jaune*. It is an untypical terroir of marly soils, whose sun-drenched slopes are clothed in vines. Another contributing factor is the wide temperature range of its dry, well-ventilated cellars, where this "solid gold" wine matures slowly, apparently benefiting from the vagaries of wind and weather.

The **Berthet-Bondet winery**, housed in a fine 16C mansion in the upper part of the village is reckoned to be one of the most representative of this appellation. The **Jean-Claude Crédoz estate** also has a good reputation *(see Shopping Guide)*.

It would be wrong to focus exclusively on the village's precious vintage: everywhere there are reminders of the historical importance of a site that was fortified as early as Gallo-Roman times, even before the building of its castle and Benedictine abbey (7C). The flower-bedecked **streets** have plenty of character, featuring multistorey vignerons' houses, some of which have flights of steps up to them and outside access to the cellars below.

To find out how well *vin jaune* complements Comté cheese, pay a visit to the **fromagerie Vagne**. Housed in the cellars of the former abbey building, this *fructerie* sells cheeses which have been matured for up to two years. A guided tour reveals all the mysteries of this famous cheese. *R. St-Jean, 39210 Château-Chalon, ☎ 03 84 44 92 25. Guided tour with cheese-tasting from mid-Jun to mid-Sep: 2.30pm-6.30pm; from mid-Sep to mid-Jun: Wed, Fri, Sat, Sun and public hols 2.30pm, 3.30pm. Shop: 11am-12.30pm, 2pm-7pm.*

Leave Château-Chalon on the D 5.

Voiteur

The fruitière vinicole is the chief place of interest in this little market town located in the plain below Château-Chalon, where several roads meet. The cooperative has some fifty members, who own 75ha of vineyards, 13ha of which qualify for the Château-Chalon appellation. The blue marls of the surrounding terroirs are well suited to Savagnin, while the Chardonnay grape does better on limestone scree. *Route de Nevy, 39210 Voiteur, ☎ 03 84 85 21 29, www.fruitiere-vinicole-voiteur. fr Mon-Sat 8.30am-12pm, 1.30pm-6pm (7pm in Jul-Aug), Sun and public hols 10am-12pm, 2pm-7pm.*

Take the D 70 S towards Vernois.

Le Vernois

This tiny village is something of a Mecca for lovers of Jura wines, as it has so many estates producing high-quality wines. Like many others, **Baud Père et Fils** *(see Shopping Guide)*, are the descendants of a long line of growers who have made the best of their Chardonnay and Savagnin vines, *cépages* which are completely at home here on the clayey-limestone and blue-marl soils.

For a better idea of local wine production, make a stop at the **Caveau des Byards**. This is France's smallest wine cooperative with just 15 members, almost half of whom belong to the same family. They produce mainly Côtes-du-Jura whites from Chardonnay grapes, wines which keep well *(see Shopping Guide)*.

On leaving Vernois, turn right in the direction of Plainoiseau, then travel back N on the N 83 towards Arlay.

Château d'Arlay★

It is wise to make an appointment to visit the winery. Mid-Jun to mid-Sep: guided tour of the château (30min), free access to the park and garden 2pm-6.30pm. 8.40€ or 6.10€ depending on whether or not you visit the mansion (children: 6.40€ or 4.60€). ☏ *03 84 44 41 94. www.arlay.com*

On the banks of the Seille, in the heart of a highly regarded wine-growing area, this village is still associated with the knightly deeds of the powerful Arlay family from Chalon. The medieval fortress was abandoned in the 17C and replaced in the 18C with an impressive country mansion. It has a fine collection of furniture in the Restoration style. Note particularly the library and doll's house.

In the **park**, a pleasant path climbs the hill to the ruins of the medieval fortress. Along the route you will encounter driveways lined with lime trees and decorative features – a grotto, an open-air theatre and extensive lawns – and enjoy fine views over the Bresse plain, the Revermont and the château's own vineyards. The ruins of the fortress provide a romantic setting for the **Jurafaune** collection of birds of prey. The staff give demonstrations, which are always impressive and much enjoyed by children.

The Laguiche family, who own the estate, were originally from Burgundy. This is no doubt why 45% of the 30ha of **vineyards** are planted with Pinot Noir, something quite exceptional in the Jura. As well as his black-cherry flavoured reds, Alain de Laguiche, who manages the estate, produces a very pleasant *"rosé corail"* and a particularly fine red macvin *(see Shopping Guide)*.

From Arlay, drive W on the D 120 towards Bletterans, then turn immediately left and continue for 7km as far as L'Étoile, passing through Quintigny.

L'Étoile

Unusually, this village owes its name to a marine invertebrate, the five-tentacled crinoid or feather star, fossils of which are abundant in the local soil.

This is an excellent terroir for Chardonnay and Savagnin and the Étoile appellation (AOC) applies exclusively to white wines, more or less distinctively of the *vin jaune* type. One of the more picturesque wineries is that run by the Vandelle family at the **Château de L'Étoile**. The **Montbourgeau** estate also produces reliable wines *(see Shopping Guide)*.

Leave L'Étoile in a southerly direction and join the D 38. Travel N on the N 83 for about 1km, then turn right towards the Château du Pin.

Château du Pin★

Beginning Jul to end Sep: 1pm-7pm. 4€. ☏ *03 84 25 32 95.*

The château stands in a setting of meadows and vineyards. Built in the 13C by Jean de Chalon, count of Burgundy and lord of Arlay, then destroyed by Louis XI, it was reconstructed in the 15C and has been restored in recent times. From the 15C keep there are magnificent views of the surrounding countryside.

Drive to Lons-le-Saunier via the D 208, then the D 70.

Wine growers' houses in Lons-le-Saunier.

M. Paygnard / MICHELIN

Lons-le-Saunier★

The hills around the town were formerly covered in vines. Now, only the fine vignerons' houses in the Place de la Comédie bear witness to the importance of this activity, as urbanisation has gradually separated Lons-le-Saunier from its wine-growing roots.

The real heart of Lons-le-Saunier is the **Place de la Liberté**, where much of the town's activity takes place. At one end is the imposing rococo façade of the **theatre★**, whose clock grinds out two bars of the *Marseillaise* before striking the hours. Why this patriotic tune? Simply because Rouget de Lisle, the author of France's national anthem, was born in Lons: there is a statue of him on the Promenade de la Chevalerie.

The arcaded **Rue du Commerce★**, with its 146 arches dating from the second half of the 17C, is a picturesque sight. No 24, the house where Rouget was born, is now the **Musée Rouget-de-Lisle**. Little of the original furniture remains, but memorabilia and documents bear witness to the extraordinary destiny of the artist and of the Marseillaise itself. There is also a video presentation. *Mid-Jun to mid-Sep: 10am-12pm, 2pm-6pm, weekends and public hols 2pm-5pm. No charge.* ☎ 03 84 47 29 16.

Begun in 1735, the 18C **Hôtel-Dieu** has a very handsome wrought-iron gateway. Though no longer in use as a hospital, it still houses a superb **pharmacy★**, the wooden panelling of which sets off a collection of ceramic, pewter and copper pots. *End Jun to end Sep: guided tour (1hr) Tue 10am and Sat 3pm, meet in front of the iron gateway. 3€.* ☎ 03 84 24 65 01.

The **Place de la Comédie**, to the right on the way to the Rue du Puits-Salé, is lined with former wine-growers' houses. The lintels of nos 20 and 22 are decorated with pruning knives, symbols of their occupation. At the bottom of the Rue du **Puits-Salé**, in a small park, flows the mineral-water spring known as the Puits-Salé, once used by the Romans and around which the town grew up. Finally, a visit to Lons would not be complete without seeing the **Archaeological Museum**, where you are greeted by the famous plateosaurus, the fossil remains of which were found in the region. The museum is awaiting an extension to its premises so that it can properly display its fine collections, which include an exceptional outrigger canoe dating from the Bronze Age, found in the Lac de Chalain. In the meantime, it draws on its reserves to stage some fascinating temporary exhibitions. *25 r. Richebourg. Daily except Tue 10am-12pm, 2pm-6pm, weekends and public hols 2pm-5pm. Closed 1 Jan, 1 May, 25 Dec. 2€, free Wed and 1st Sun in month.* ☎ 03 84 47 12 13.

A good selection of wines from the region is available at the **Maison du vigneron** *(see Shopping Guide)*.

WINE-GROWING VILLAGES OF THE SOUTHERN REVERMONT AREA ③

The serious business of growing Côtes-du-Jura wines begins again a few kilometres south of Lons-le-Saunier, in countryside criss-crossed by winding roads.

Most of the wines produced here are white, but Pinot Noir also gives good results. Over the next 20 kilometres, along the slopes of the Sud-Revermont, stretches a string of pretty wine-growing villages nestling in verdant little valleys.

Drive S out of Lons-le-Saunier on the N 83.

Gevingey

This picturesque village was the scene of a terrible tragedy during the Second World War, recorded on a plaque on the front of the Mairie.

The mixed limestone-scree and blue-marl soils produce some good Savagnin whites, such as those grown by **Bernard Frères**; the brothers are a fount of information about the wines grown in the region *(see Shopping Guide)*.

Continue towards Cesancey.

Country lanes link the charming villages of **Cesancey**, **Grusse**, **Vincelles**, **Rotalier** and **Orbagna**, whose histories are intimately linked with wine-growing. They all have fine fountains and old wash-houses.

At Grusse, drive up to the **viewing point★** at **Saint-Laurent-Laroche** *(2.5km)* for a magnificent overview of the southern Sud-Revermont villages and the Bresse plain.

You can then continue southwards to **Maynal**, which also has a fine viewing point and an interesting church surmounted by a fortified bell tower, visible from miles around.

The wine-growing estates of this region are very small in area, but produce a wide variety of wines. Good examples are the **Domaine Labet** at **Rotalier**, for its pinots and Chardonnays, and the **Domaine Ganevat** *(see Shopping Guide)*.

A Place for Reflection

Abbey of Baume-les-Messieurs★

7km SE of Voiteur on the D 70. Mid-Jun to mid-Sep: guided tour 10am-12pm, 2pm-6pm. On request. 3€. ☎ 03 84 44 99 28. *Easter to All Saints: free access to the abbey church (except altarpiece and tomb chapel).* ☎ 03 84 44 95 45.

The abbey was founded in 890. It was self-governing from 1157 to 1186, thanks to Frederick Barabarossa, the Holy Roman Emperor, who married the heiress of the county of Burgundy, and from this time the foundation enjoyed "imperial" status. In the 16C, the humble monks were replaced by aristocratic canons, who changed the name of their establishment from Baume-les-Moines to Baume-les-Messieurs. In 1793, at the time of the Revolution, their pride was dashed when the abbey was closed down and its property auctioned off.

In the front doorway (15C) of the **church** is a sculpture of God the Father in the act of blessing and, in the niches on either side, angels blowing wind instruments. In the **Chalon Chapel** *(on the left)* and on either side of the choir, you will see a fine collection of 15C **statues in the Burgundian style**. However, the abbey's chief treasure is its magnificent early 16C **Antwerp altarpiece** *(on display during the guided tour)*, the central subject of which is Christ's Passion.

On the right, a door gives access to the former **cloister**. The monks' refectory and dormitory opened onto this courtyard, which still has its fountain. If you pass through an archway on the left, you will come to another courtyard, surrounded by buildings which housed the aristocratic canons. Then return to the former cloister and first courtyard via a vaulted passageway through the former cellars (13C).

Some Magnificent Views...

Cirque de Baume★★★
12km NE of Lons-le-Saunier via the D 471. Shortly before Crançot, turn left onto the D 471, then right to reach the Roche de Baume viewing point.

Roches de Baume viewing point★★★ – ⚐ Walk along the edge of the cliff which forms the celebrated Roches de Baume "belvedere", commonly known as the "belvédère de Crançot".

The natural amphitheatre before you is impressive and, when you come upon it suddenly, takes your breath away. Near the viewing platform furthest to the right, you will see steps cut in the rock to form the **Échelles de Crançot**, a steep pathway leading down to the bottom of the cirque *(the descent is difficult: proceed cautiously)*.

Mont-Poupet
10km N of Salins-les-Bains via the D 492. After 5.5km, turn left onto the D 273, then 1km farther on, again on the left, is a road leading to the Mont Poupet cross (car park).

⚐ From the viewing point (alt 803m; *15 min on foot there and back*), there is a magnificent **view★** (viewpoint indicator and cross) over the Salins basin and the fort of St-André; in the distance, you can see as far as Mont Blanc, the Alps and the Jura; in the opposite direction, the Bresse plain and, beyond, the mountains of Burgundy and the Beaujolais.

The Cirque de Baume.

B. Kaufmann/MICHELIN

Poupet gliding school (École de vol libre du Poupet) – *9 r. du Poupet, 39110 Saint-Thiébaud, ☎ 03 84 73 04 56. www.poupetvollibre.com First flights in two-seaters, beginners' and improvers' courses from Mar to Sep.*

Fort Saint-André
4km S of Salins-les-Bains via the D 472, the D 94 right, the D 271 right and right again.

The fort – *Jul-Aug: 10am-6pm; Apr-Jun, Sep and until mid-Oct: weekends and public hols 10am-6pm. 2€. ☎ 03 84 37 90 29 or 06 84 42 81 84.*
Built in 1674 to plans by Vauban, the fort is a fine example of 17C military architecture. At the foot of the ramparts on the right, is a viewing platform with a good **view★** over Salins.

Salins Forts Aventure – *39110 Salins-les-Bains, ☎ 03 84 73 06 79 our 06 89 71 39 44, www.salins-aventure.com. Mid-Jun to mid-Sep: 10am-7pm (last departure 5pm); mid-Sep to mid-Jun: weekends and public hols 10am-6pm.* ⚐ This adventure playground is laid out around Fort Saint-André. Play at being Tarzan, swinging through the trees-tops and climbing rock-faces. There are various routes to suit different ages and levels of fitness and daring.

INFORMATION

Comité interprofessionnel des vins du Jura (trade association) – *Château Pecauld - 39600 Arbois -* ☎ *03 84 66 26 14 - www. jura-vins.com*

OVERVIEW

CHARACTERISTICS

Jura wines are distinguished by appellation, but even more so on a varietal basis.

Chardonnay – Gives dry whites, with a floral character when young, which acquire a fine golden hue and more honeyed flavours as they age.

Savagnin – Generally produces *vin jaune* style wines, distinguished by walnut and spicy notes on ageing.

Poulsard – Gives pale-coloured reds with smokey and berry-fruit flavours.

Trousseau – Gives dark red wines, cherry-flavoured when young, gamey on ageing.

Pinot Noir – Highly coloured, with berry-fruit notes when young, acquiring a black-cherry flavour as it ages.

STORAGE

Vin jaune wines age exceptionally well, even for a century or more. *Vins de paille* also keep very well. Whites made from Savagnin will keep for up to ten years, while Chardonnays and reds can be aged for between three to five years.

PRICES

White Chardonnays, crémant-du-jura and red wines – 5 to 8€.

Whites made from Savagnin – 8 to 13€.

Vin jaune and Château-Chalon – 20 to 30€.

Vin de paille – 11 to 20€ (50 cl).

BUYING

COOPERATIVES

Maison du vigneron – *23 r. du Commerce - 39000 Lons-le-Saunier -* ☎ *03 84 24 44 60 - mbailly@cguj.fr - Tue-Sat 10am-12pm, 2pm-7pm – closed public hols.* This winery, whose entrance is opposite the house of Rouget de Lisle, represents approximately 150 growers. The diversity of Jura wine-production is expressed in a wide range of AOC wines: Côtes-du-Jura, Arbois, vin jaune, vin de paille… They also sell liqueurs and local brandies.

Fruitière vinicole de Pupillin – *39600 Pupillin -* ☎ *03 84 66 12 88 – 8am-12pm, 2pm-6pm – it may be possible to visit the cellars, if they are not too busy; open day 2nd weekend in Jun.* This cooperative, founded in 1909, has 48 members cultivating 84ha of vines in the communes of Pupillin, Buvilly, Arbois et Grozon. The winery specialises in making reds from the Poulsard grape, but also produces whites, including an interesting Margillat made from a blend of Savagnin and Chardonnay grapes grown on clay and marls, and some sound vins jaunes.

ESTATES

Domaine Rolet Père et Fils – *11 r. de l'Hôtel-de-Ville - 39600 Arbois -* ☎ *03 84 66 08 89 - www.rolet-arbois.com - 9.30am-12pm, 2pm-6.30pm – closed 25 Dec and 1 Jan.* On this 62ha estate, the second-largest in the Jura, the grapes are harvested exclusively by hand. They produce AOC Côtes-du-Jura, Etoile and Arbois wines, vins jaunes and vins de paille, white and rosé crémants, and marc (local brandy) aged in oak barrels. The firm has been awarded many medals at national agricultural fairs.

Henri Maire, Les Deux Tonneaux – *Pl. de la Liberté - 39600 Arbois -* ☎ *03 84 66 15 27 - www.henri-maire.fr - 9am-7pm but variable depending on season – closed 1 Jan.* It is hard not to be aware of the Henri Maire establishment in Arbois; the firm's advertising and its immense and tempting display windows are the measure of its standing in the region. They show films, hold wine-tastings and let you visit the winery.

Château d'Arlay - *Alain de Laguiche – Château d'Arlay - Lieu-dit du Château - 39140 Arlay -* ☎ *03 84 85 04 22 - alaindelaguiche@aol.com - Mon-Sat 9am-12pm, 2pm-6pm – Admission charge.* The Château has one of the Jura's oldest vineyards, which was already going strong in the Middle Ages. Consisting of clayey-limestone soils, its 27ha are planted with Pinot Noir, Trousseau, Poulsard, Savagnin and Chardonnay. The grapes are harvested by hand and vinified in temperature-regulated vats. The wines are matured in old barrels for at least three years.

Domaine Berthet-Bondet – *39210 Château-Chalon -* ☎ *03 84 44 60 48 - domaine.berthet.bondet@wanadoo.fr - daily 10am-12pm, 2pm-7pm.* After training as an agricultural engineer and learning in situ, Jean Berthet-Bondet set up his winery in 1985. He now has 9ha of vines, facing south and west, planted on marly soil under a surface layer of limestone scree. He grows Chardonnay and Savagnin for making white wines; Poulsard, Trousseau and Pinot Noir for the reds and rosés. After pressing and fermentation, his whites and vins jaunes are aged in oak barrels.

Domaine Jean-Claude Crédoz – *R. des Chèvres - 39210 Château-Chalon -* ☎ *03 84 44 64 91 - domjccredoz@aol.com - daily 8am-12pm, 1.30pm-8pm.* Founded by Victor Crédoz and still in the family, the estate now runs to 6ha. The property is in the throes of reorganisation and, since 2004, the vinification, cellaring and marketing operations have been performed in Château-Chalon. The wines are aged in oak barrels for several years, two as a minimum and up to seven for his vin de paille.

Château de L'Étoile – *994 r. Bouillod - 39570 L'Étoile -* ☎ *03 84 47 33 07 - info@chateau-etoile.com - daily 8am-12pm, 2pm-7pm.* Passion, conscientiousness and method are the watchwords of this estate, which was acquired by Auguste Vandelle in 1883 and has been managed on the same principles generation by generation. Its 16ha are planted with Chardonnay, Savagnin,

Poulsard and Trousseau vines. Both vineyard and buildings are situated on the slopes of Mont Muzard, the marly sub-soil of whose eastern, southern and western flanks are particularly well suited to wine-growing.

Domaine de Montbourgeau
– 53 r. de Montbourgeau - 39570 L'Étoile - ☎ 03 84 47 32 96 - domaine.montbourgeau@wanadoo.fr - Mon-Sat 9am-12pm, 2pm-7pm – by appointment. A family property purchased in 1920, the estate runs to 30ha, 9.2ha of which are planted with productive vines. The principal grape varieties are Chardonnay, Poulsard and Savagnin. The vineyard is managed on a chemically non-interventionist basis and the grapes are harvested by hand.

Bernard Frères – 15 r. Principale – 39570 Gevingey - ☎ 03 84 47 33 99 - daily. This estate has belonged to the Bernard family since 1910. Its 5ha of brown limestone and Liassic marl soils, planted with Chardonnay, Savagnin, Poulsard and Pinot Noir, are cultivated in an environmentally responsible way. The resulting wines are aged in oak barrels and stainless-steel vats, then bottled without fining or filtering.

Jacques Puffeney – Rte de Saint-Laurent - 39600 Montigny-lès-Arsures - ☎ 03 84 66 10 89 - jacques-puffeney@wanadoo.fr - Mon-Sat 9am-12pm, 2pm-6pm. A family-run business, the estate consists of 7.4ha of vineyards, planted with Savagnin, Trousseau, Chardonnay and Poulsard. The harvesting is done exclusively by hand. The musts are fermented and the wines aged in oak tuns.

Domaine André et Mireille Tissot
– Quartier Bernard - 39600 Montigny-lès-Arsures - ☎ 03 84 66 08 27 – Mon-Sat 9am-12pm, 2pm-7pm – by appointment. From 0.25ha in 1962 to 30ha in 2000, this estate has registered spectacular growth. Wanting to manage their terroir responsibly, André and Mireille Tissot have converted the whole of the vineyard to organic status. In 2000 and 2001, they produced their first vintages without using sulphur. The owners have invested in truncated wooden vats for vinifying their Pinot Noirs. Since 2004, André and Mireille have been officially retired, but their retirement is a very active one, as they continue to help their son, Stéphane, who has run the estate since 1999.

Domaine Grand Frères – R. du Savagnin - 39230 Passenans - ☎ 03 84 85 28 88 - grandfreres@wanadoo.fr - daily except weekends from 1 Jan to 31 Mar. The Grand brothers, working in partnership, have been producing wines since 1976 on a family property whose origins date back to the 17C. The grey marls of the area are particularly well suited to the Savagnin and Trousseau varieties. The vineyards, covering 22ha, are planted with Chardonnay and Savagnin, vinified separately or in a blend, to produce white wines; and with Poulsard, Trousseau and Pinot Noir for reds and rosés. The musts are processed in temperature-regulated vats, and the resulting wines are matured in wooden barrels or tuns.

Domaine Xavier Reverchon – EARL Chantemerle – 2 r. du Clos – 39800 Poligny - ☎ 03 84 37 02 58 - reverchon.vinsjura@libertysurf.fr - daily 2pm-7pm. For four generations, this family firm has been tending 6.6ha of vines: Poulsard (1.4ha), Trousseau (0.25ha) and Pinot Noir (0.75ha) for making red wines; Chardonnay (2.5ha) and Savagnin (1.7ha) for whites.

Benoit Badoz – 15 r. du Collège – 39800 Poligny - ☎ 03 84 37 11 85 - infos@badoz.fr - Mon-Sat 8am-7pm – by appointment. Wine-growers since 1659, the Badoz family manage 8ha of vines. As well as Côtes-du-Jura and macvins, the estate specialises in making vin jaune and vin de paille.

Pierre Overnoy – R. du Ploussard – 39600 Pupillin - ☎ 03 84 66 14 60 or 03 84 66 24 27 – by appointment. The wines of this unusual estate are produced as naturally as possible: hand-digging, no inputs of chemicals. The main varieties grown are Poulsard, Chardonnay and Savagnin, which draw their sustenance from the clayey-limestone soils of the area. Taken over on 1 January 2001 by Emmanuel Houillon, the estate is managed organically, without the use of sulphur. The wines are vinified in stainless-steel vats, then aged in tuns, barrels or 600-litre vessels (demi-muids).

S. Sauvignier / MICHELIN

Domaine de la Renardière – R. du Chardonnay - 39600 Pupillin - ☎ 03 84 66 25 10 - renardiere@libertysurf.fr - 9am-12pm, 1.30pm-7pm – by appointment. Laurence and Jean-Michel receive you in their vaulted cellar, where the motto is "Strive for excellence and respect tradition". The 6ha estate produces vin de paille and vin jaune. The wine-making process is traditional and the wines are matured in vats and barrels for up to eighteen months.

Domaine Ganevat – R. du Pont - La Combe - 39190 Rotalier - ☎ 03 84 25 02 69 – 10am-6pm. After ten years as winery manager at Chassagne-Montrachet, in 1998 Jean-François Ganevat took over the running of the business, which has been in the family since 1650! In addition to its traditional vins de paille and vins jaunes, the estate produces an original liqueur, Combette.

Domaine Labet – Pl. du Village – 39190 Rotalier - ☎ 03 84 25 11 13. On the Labet's property the grapes from different plots are vinified separately in consideration of the differing climatic conditions. Alain Labet believes in organic farming: no fertilisers, hand pruning, careful staking and hand-digging. His vineyard covers 10ha, and a third of his vines are more than 60 years old. The grapes are harvested manually. The Pinot Noir and Trousseau vintages are aged in new barrels, Poulsard in older ones.

Caveau des Byards – *D 70 – 39210 Le Vernois* - ☎ *03 84 25 33 52 - info@caveau-des-byards.fr - daily 9am-12pm, 2pm-6pm.* Established in 1953, this 30ha vineyard lies at the heart of the Jura massif and enjoys a fine sunny position. The varieties grown are Chardonnay, Savagnin, Poulsard, Trousseau and Pinot Noir. Wines intended for keeping are matured in oak barrels. New storage facilities were erected in 1998. The estate also produces vin de paille and vin jaune.

Domaine Baud Père et Fils – *Rte de Voiteur - 39210 Le Vernois* - ☎ *03 84 25 31 41 – Mon-Sat 8am-12pm, 2pm-6pm.* Managed by the Baud family since 1875 (when there were just 6ha of vineyards), the estate now runs to 16ha.

Wine Festivals

A wine-growing village – To celebrate the broaching of the vin jaune, the 2nd weekend in Feb. This festival rotates around the villages. For 9€, you get a taster glass and 10 tickets entitling you to try 4 vins jaunes and 6 other wines. Since 1997, this has been one of the biggest wine festivals in France. The idea is to celebrate the broaching of the latest vin jaune vintage, harvested six years and three months previously. There are various activities, opportunities to sample local dishes and a parade organised by the wine-growing guilds.

Arbois – Fête du Biou, 1st Sun in Sep. Music festival celebrating the Arbois wines, on the last weekend in July.
Traditional-style grape harvest at Château Pecauld, 2nd Sun in Sept.

Champlitte – Festival of St Vincent, 22 January.

Montigny-lès-Arsures – Fête du Trousseau, 3rd weekend in Aug, alternate years.

Pupillin – Fête du Biou, 3rd Sun in Sep.

Fête du Poulsard – 3rd weekend in Aug, alternating with the Fête du Trousseau.

Vadans – Fête du Biou, 4th Sun in Sep.

Cirque du Fer à Cheval viewing point★★
7km SE of Arbois on the D 469. 🚶 *10min there and back. Leave your car at the inn below and follow the waymarked path, which starts off to the left.*
As you come out of a small wood, the natural amphitheatre yawns before you *(safety barrier)*. From the vantage point, some 200m above the valley, there is a superb view of the Reculée des Planches, a steep-sided blind valley carved into the limestone plateau.

Venturing Underground

Grotte des Planches★
6km SE of Arbois via the D 107. By the church in Mesnay, turn right onto the D 247, which soon enters the valley bottom. At Planches-près-Arbois, after the church, you will cross a stone bridge and, immediately on your left, find a narrow metalled road which runs along the foot of the cliffs. Leave your car 600m further on (drinks kiosk). Mid-Jul to end Aug: guided tour (1hr) 10am-6pm; beginning Apr to mid-Jul and end Aug to end Oct: 10am-12pm, 2pm-5pm. Closed Mon in Oct. 5.50€ (children: 2.80€). ☎ *03 84 66 13 74.*
In this cavern, carved out at the base of the cliff under a prodigious overhang, tunnels running 250m beneath the Jura plateau illustrate the effects of water erosion. The lower tunnel, which serves as the bed of the Cuisance in the wet season, is occupied in the summer months by a string of pools formed by the eddying waters. Known as **marmites de géants** (giants' cooking pots), the water they contain is of a striking bluish colour. In an adjoining tunnel is a display showing how the cavern was formed, explored and is now managed, and how the *reculée* itself was formed. Under the overhang at the entrance to the cavern, excavations have brought to light evidence of Palaeolithic, Neolithic and Bronze Age settlement.
A visit to the Grotte des Planches in the autumn is a quite different experience from in the summer months. When it rains, part of the itinerary is flooded, but the rush and roar of the raging Cuisance is a truly awesome spectacle.

Grottes des Moidons
10km SE of Arbois by the D 469. Jul-Aug: guided tour (45min) 9.30am-5.30pm (last departure); mid-Jun to end Jun and beginning Sep to mid-Sep: 10am-12pm, 2pm-5pm; beginning Jun to mid-Jun: daily except Wed 10am-12pm, 2pm-5pm; mid-Sep to end Sep: daily except Wed: 2pm-5pm; Apr-May: daily except Wed 2pm-5pm. 5.60€ (children: 2.90€). ☎ *03 84 51 74 94.*

8

In the depths of the Moidons forest, a fascinating aspect of these caverns is their many stalactite and stalagmite formations. The visit ends with a *son et lumière* display featuring the cavern's underground pools.

Grottes d'Osselle★

16km N of Arc-et-Senans via the D 17, D 12 and D 13. Jul-Aug: guided tour (1hr 15min) 9am-7pm (last departure; Jun: 9am-6pm; Apr-May: 9am-12pm, 2pm-6pm; Sep: 9am-12pm, 2pm-5pm; Oct: 2.30pm-5pm, Sun and public hols 9am-12pm, 2pm-5pm. 5.60€ (children: 3€). ☎ 03 81 63 62 09.

These caverns are carved in a cliff dominating a meander in the River Doubs.

Discovered in the 13C, they have been regularly visited since 1504. The dry tunnels were used as a place of refuge and worship by Catholic priests during the Revolution. A clay altar is still visible. The skeleton of a cave-dwelling bear has been reconstructed from bones found under fallen rock.

Of a total of 8km of tunnels, 1 300m of long, regular stretches have been opened up for visiting, following the ridge line of the mountain. The first "halls", their mineral formations still fed by dripping water, have been dulled by the smoke from resin torches. Then, after negotiating a low passageway, you come upon white stalagmites of almost pure calcite, and others coloured by iron, copper or manganese oxides.

Water Sports and Spas

Bathing and archaeology at the Lac de Chalain★★

26km E of Lons-le-Saunier via the D 471 and the D 39. Parking is not allowed on the shores of the lake, but there are paying car parks near the beaches.

This 232ha lake is undoubtedly the most beautiful and impressive in the Jura region. Our ancestors evidently thought so too, since they established a lake-dwellers' village here in prehistoric times.

At the **leisure centre**, you can enjoy wind-surfing, canoeing, or just swimming in the lake. However, the water is not warm all the year round, and anglers also have opportunity to test their skills and patience; the lake is classed in category 2 for fishing purposes and is a paradise for pike and perch.

Chalain is not only a place to relax. It is also a **site of archaeological interest**, where you can visit the former lacustrine village. **Neolithic dwellings on piles** have been reconstructed on the shores of the lake, using Stone Age techniques. For the purposes of experimentation, they are being left to deteriorate naturally. *Access via La Pergola camp site (pay parking) at Marigny.* There are just three guided tours and one conference each year. An annual exhibition is also organised to report on the progress of the excavations. Information can be obtained from the Clairvaux-les-Lacs tourist office.

Canoeing and kayaking on the River Loue

You can take a 6hr trip down the River Loue by canoe or kayak, covering the 21km stretch between Port-Lesney and Ounans through a magnificent landscape of mountains and vineyards. The **Val d'Amour Loisirs sportifs association** also organises introductory courses to different kinds of fishing. *39380 Ounans. 27€/ pers. ☎ 03 84 37 72 04.*

Spas

Valvital Spa at Lons-Le-Saunier – *Parc des Bains, 39000 Lons-le-Saunier, ☎ 03 84 24 20 34, www.valvital.fr Mon-Thu 1pm-8pm, Fri 1pm-7pm, Sat 12pm-7pm; open mornings for treatments. Closed Nov-Mar.* This establishment uses strong (305g/l) and medium (10g/l) sodium-chloride-enriched waters in treating rheumatic conditions, child development problems and psoriasis (application for certification pending). As in most spa establishments, a fitness section is open to the general public in the afternoons.

There are many discounts available. The 7ha park surrounding the buildings is a pleasant place for a stroll.

Les Thermes de Salins – *Pl. des Alliés, 39110 Salins-les-Bains, ☎ 03 84 73 04 63, www.thermes-salins.com Mon-Sat 3pm-6.30pm, Sun 10am-11.45am, 3pm-5.30pm. Closed Jan, 1 May, 20 Jun and 15 Aug.* This centre is officially approved for specialised treatments for rheumatic, gynaecological and children's conditions. The establishment has been completely refurbished and also has residential facilities for people suffering from fatigue and stress.

Languedoc-Roussillon

Cultivated by the Iberians from 7C BC, the vines in this region are, more than anywhere else, synonymous with life. Though extended by the Romans and then by the monastic orders, the vineyards remained confined within their ancient limits until the Canal du Midi was cut in the 17C, enabling a better circulation of wines. However, it was above all the appearance of the railway in the 19C that made possible the extraordinary expansion of the vineyards. Between 1850 and 1870 production increased from 4 million to 15 million hectolitres, in what proved to be a veritable cultural and economic revolution for the region. From Carcassonne to the sea, and from Banyuls to Nîmes, a sea of vines swept over Languedoc and Roussillon, submerging plains that had until then been dedicated to cereal growing. There are many wine routes, and each one passes through landscapes full of character, where the heritage of bricks and mortar is as valuable as the region's natural riches.

Terroirs
Michelin Local Maps 339 and 344 – Gard (30), Hérault (34), Aude (11) and Pyrénées-Orientales (66).
Surface area: the vineyards of Languedoc cover 300 000ha in the Hérault, Aude and Gard *départements*; the vineyards of Roussillon cover 9 000ha in the Pyrénées-Orientales.
Production: 40% of French wines, ie around 20 million hl, 90% of which are local wines *(vins de pays)* and table wines *(vins de table)*.
The climate is Mediterranean with mild winters and hot dry summers. Precipitation is low but sometimes violent. The soils vary from one *terroir* to another: schist in Faugères, St-Chinian, the Corbières, Minervois and Roussillon; round pebbles in the Minervois, Rivesaltes and the Val d'Orbieu; limestone soils in Roussillon and the Corbières; alluvial land and granitic soils in the Coteaux du Languedoc.

Wines
The Languedoc-Roussillon region produces every kind of wine: red, white, fortified and sparkling.
Gard – AOC Clairette-de-Bellegarde (white), Coteaux-du-Languedoc (red, rosé, white). The AOC Costières-de-Nîmes (red, rosé, white) is connected to the Rhône Valley vineyards.
Hérault – AOC Clairette-du-Languedoc (white), Coteaux-du-Languedoc (red, rosé, white), Faugères (red, rosé), Minervois (red, rosé, white), Minervois-La-Livinière (red), Saint-Chinian (red, rosé), Muscat-de-Frontignan (fortified wine), Muscat-de-Lunel (fortified wine), Muscat-de-Mireval (fortified wine), Muscat-de-St-Jean-de-Minervois (fortified wine).
Aude – AOC Blanquette-de-Limoux (sparkling), Côtes-de-Cabardès (red, rosé), Crémant-de-Limoux (sparkling), Corbières (red, rosé, white), Côtes-de-la-Malepère (red, rosé), Coteaux-du-Languedoc (red, rosé, white), Fitou (red), Limoux (red, white), Minervois (red, rosé, white).

The vineyards of the Corbières.

Pyrénées-Orientales – AOC Banyuls and Banyuls Grand Cru (fortified wine), Collioure (red, rosé, white), Côtes-du-Roussillon (red, rosé, white), Côtes-du-Roussillon-Villages (red), Maury (fortified wine), Muscat-de-Rivesaltes (fortified wine), Rivesaltes (fortified wine).

There are also 55 *vins de pays* designations in Languedoc-Roussillon.

What's in a word?

"*Midi rouge*", "the red south", denotes both a political colour and a colour of wine. It dates back to the early 20C when Languedoc sent Socialist deputies – among them Léon Blum, later Prime Minister of France – to sit in the Chamber of Deputies. The wine crisis, a tradition of opposition to Paris, attachment to the Republic, the old Cathar roots, the influence of Protestantism and wine's ability to inflame passions all led to the growth of this political tendency. In fact, the wine-growing "Midi", a region of small landowners, has always been more politically rosé than red and its modern-day activism is usually more watered-down.

Background

The qualitative revolution – The phylloxera crisis, which broke out in the late 19C, was a disaster for Languedoc. In 1907, the wine-growers, reduced to penury by competition from imported Algerian wines and the "dishwater" produced by the wine merchants, finally rebelled. Led by charismatic café owner Marcelin Albert, hundreds of thousands of demonstrators clashed with the army, who mutinied out of solidarity in Narbonne. It was to take all of the Interior Minister Georges Clemenceau's skill as a tactician to restore order. Then, rather than enter into a dead-end struggle, the most astute wine-growers founded the first cooperatives but high-quality production did not emerge for another two generations. Indeed, until the 1980s, the wine-growing Midi had been content with exploiting the vines to satisfy the demand – mainly for red wine – of the toiling population. But a sudden change in drinking trends meant that a qualitative transformation became necessary, and this took the guise of a real revolution. The replacement of the traditional grape varieties by quality varieties, reduced yields, and the creation of *appellations d'origine contrôlée* formed the basis of the revival. Today, the four *départements* of the wine-growing Midi are still producing 40% of French wine. And despite the tremendous efforts made, competition from New World wines has scored a direct hit on the wines of Languedoc-Roussillon. With one of the highest rates of unemployment in France, if the wine-growing Midi loses its wine, it will lose everything. And until new activities come to bolster the regional economy, viticulture will remain both its strength and its weakness.

Les Coteaux du Languedoc

PIC ST-LOUP AND THE TERRACES OF THE HÉRAULT

115km. Michelin Local Map 339, F-I 6-7. See itinerary 1 *on the map on p. 254-255.*
North of Montpellier, the summit of Pic St-Loup rises 658m above the garrigue, facing the white mass of the Hortus plateau. The clayey limestone soils of their northern and western approaches are covered by the vineyards of the **AOC Coteaux-du-Languedoc-Pic-St-Loup**.

Montpellier★★

Bathed in a uniquely Mediterranean light, Montpellier, capital of Languedoc-Roussillon, owes much of its charm to its historical districts and superb gardens, which are delightful to explore on foot during the day, and to its theatres, cinemas and Opera, which liven up the nights. The salty air betrays the nearby presence of the sea. However, Montpellier has only a distant view of the vineyards; the city's economy has never relied on vines. Its modernity pays little heed to the scenery, as urban development gradually devours the surrounding countryside: you have to drive some distance to find traditional southern tranquillity and the song of cicadas.

Between place de la Comédie and the Peyrou Arc de Triomphe, on either side of rue Foch, lie the **historic districts★★** of Montpellier, with their narrow, winding streets, the last vestiges of the original medieval town. Lining these streets are superb 17C and 18C private mansions, or *hôtels particuliers*, with their main façades and remarkable staircases hidden from the public eye in inner courtyards. *Itinerary available from the tourist office.*

Directory

WHERE TO EAT

ITINERARIES 1 *AND* 2

⊜ **Le Pastis** – *3 r. du Terral- 34000 Montpellier* – ☎ *04 67 66 37 26 – closed 3 weeks in Aug, 1 week at Christmas, Sat lunchtime, Sun and Mon – 14/23€.* This restaurant is popular with wine connoisseurs on account of its cellar filled with wines from the Languedoc vineyards. But it appeals to all gourmets with its market-fresh dishes that delight the palate: roast sea perch with fennel, scallops and prawns, goat's cheese millefeuille, etc.

⊜⊜ **La Pomme d'Amour** – *2 bis r. Albert-Paul-Allies - 34120 Pézenas -* ☎ *04 67 98 08 40 – closed Jan, Feb, Mon evening and Tue – booking essential Jul-Aug – lunch 8€ – 15.50/21€.* This welcoming family-run restaurant occupies the ground floor of an 18C house. Old beams and bare-stone walls form the intimate decor of the dining room, which also has a little summer terrace that gives onto a cobbled street. Delicious, sun-filled recipes.

⊜⊜ **Le Jas d'Or** – *2 bd Victor-Hugo - 34110 Frontignan -* ☎ *04 67 43 07 57 – closed Tue evening and Wed in low season, Mon lunchtime, Thu lunchtime and Sat lunchtime in Jul-Aug – 18/34€.* The clientele of regulars finds this little dining room set in a former wine storehouse *(chai)* entirely to its taste. The chef, formerly an instructor at a catering and hotel school, prepares dishes using the very same recipes that he used to teach, recommending whenever possible a Muscat-de-Frontignan – of course – to go with them.

⊜⊜ **Après le Déluge** – *5 av. du Mar.-Plantavit - 34120 Pézenas -* ☎ *04 67 98 10 77 – closed from 15 Nov to 15 Dec – 19/45€.* Will you dine at Noah's Table or in Perrault's Room? This restaurant offers its patrons five different decors in which to sample the chef's recipes, taken from old books. You'll also have a unique opportunity to taste one of the Marquis de Sade's more innocent pleasures: his favourite cake! A very entertaining setting, with two flower-filled terraces. Musical evenings.

⊜⊜ **La Pastourelle** – *Chemin de la Prairie – 34380 St-Martin-de-Londres –* ☎ *04 67 55 72 78 – closed during school holidays in Feb, 15-30 Sep, Sun evening, Mon evening, Tue evening in winter, Thu lunchtime and Wed in high season – 19/45€.* La Pastourelle, below the village of Saint-Martin, is a fine place to eat, with a pleasant garden terrace and a charming dining room decorated with watercolours. The traditional cuisine suffused with southern flavours and the accompanying wine list merit your attention.

⊜⊜ **Hôtellerie de Balajan** – *41 rte de Montpellier – 34110 Frontignan -* ☎ *04 67 48 13 99 – closed from 24 Dec to 5 Jan, in Feb, Sat lunchtime, Sun evening and Mon lunchtime from 15 Oct to 15 Mar – 20/47€.* A nice place to eat on the N 112, surrounded by the vines that produce the famous Muscat-de-Frontignan. The modern-style building houses a dining room decorated with warm colours where you can enjoy traditional recipes infused with southern flavours.

⊜⊜ **Le Ban des Gourmands** – *5 pl. Carnot - 34000 Montpellier -* ☎ *04 67 65 00 85 – closed 1 week in Feb, 2 weeks in Aug, 1 week at Christmas, Sat lunchtime, Sun and Mon – 28€.* In his little restaurant on place Carnot, Jacques Delépine calls all gourmands to sample his delicious market-fresh cuisine: try roast *pelardon* goat's cheese with Cévennes onions, or perhaps an octopus stew, washed down with a glass of wine from his wonderful regional selection.

⊜⊜ **Les Bains de Montpellier** – *6 r. Richelieu - 34000 Montpellier -* ☎ *04 67 60 70 87 – closed during holidays in Feb, early Nov, Christmas, Mon lunchtime and Sun – booking advisable – lunch 20€ - 28€.* Change of scene guaranteed in this restaurant with its old "Parisian baths" setting. The terrace is shaded by palm trees and the old changing rooms have been converted into charming little glass-roofed rooms where you can enjoy appetising dishes updated to suit contemporary tastes: tomato pesto and Serrano ham and cuttlefish grilled *à la plancha.*

⊜⊜⊜ **Mimosa** – *34725 St-Guiraud – 7.5km N of Clermont-l'Hérault via the N 9, N 109 then D 130E -* ☎ *04 67 96 67 96 – closed Sun evening except Jul-Aug, lunchtime except Sun and Mon – 52/78€.* This old wine-grower's house is tucked away in the heart of the village. In its charming contemporary dining room you can sample pleasant, market-fresh Mediterranean-style cuisine, accompanied by a good choice of regional wines.

ITINERARY 3

⊜ **Au Cep d'Or** – *7 r. Viennet – 34500 Béziers -* ☎ *04 67 49 28 09 – closed 15 Nov to 10 Dec, Sun evening and Mon – 12.20/24.40€.* Family atmosphere guaranteed in this restaurant serving neat cuisine based on fresh seafood. Shellfish platter, cuttlefish *à la sétoise*, fillet of bream cooked in Provençal stock, and monkfish *bourride* (soup served with aïoli) are among the appetising suggestions on the menu.

⊜ **Café des Louis** – *3 r. de la Petite-Jérusalem – 34500 Béziers -* ☎ *04 67 49 93 13 – closed from 15 Feb to 1 Apr, Mon lunchtime and Sun – lunch 12.50€ – 14.50/18.50€.* Just a stone's throw from the cathedral, this restaurant's 12C vaulted dining room is full of colour. On the menu you'll find tasty dishes full of southern flavours, such as *gardiane de taureau* (bull stew), cuttlefish *à la toscane*, fillet of monkfish with vanilla, and a real homemade classic: *confit de canard.*

⊜⊜ **Le Val d'Héry** – *67 av. du Prés-Wilson – 34500 Béziers -* ☎ *04 67 76 56 73 – closed 15-30 Jun, Sun and Mon – 18/36€.* A pre-prandial stroll on the Plateau des Poètes, an attractive park in the centre of town, and here you are in this restaurant with its walls decorated with paintings. Don't hesitate to compliment the chef, who painted some of the pictures on display... and also perfectly masters the art of adapting recipes to suit contemporary tastes.

⊜⊜ **L'Échalote** – *In Soumartre – 34600 Faugères* - ☎ *04 67 23 18 05 – closed Mon and Tue – 25/40€.* This place is full of nice surprises: simple but pleasant decor, local cuisine updated for contemporary tastes and available in three tempting menus, an extensive wine list – made up exclusively of Languedoc wines – and a pleasant view of the countryside... Booking essential.

⊜⊜ **L'Ambassade** – *22 bd de Verdun (opposite the station) – 34500 Béziers -* ☎ *04 67 76 06 24 – closed 25 May to 15 Jun, Sun and Mon – 25/70€.* L'Ambassade is very much the talk of the town. It was entirely renovated a few years ago and boasts a beautiful contemporary interior. The restaurant is also well served by its delightful cuisine updated for contemporary tastes and a wine list that is quite simply outstanding.

ITINERARIES ④ AND ⑦

⊜⊜ **L'Estagnol** – *5 bis cours Mirabeau – 11100 Narbonne -* ☎ *04 68 65 09 27 – closed 16-24 Nov, Mon evening and Sun – 16/20€.* A lively brasserie on a small square near the covered market, with a pleasant terrace in fine weather. The locals appreciate its good traditional dishes with their regional flavour.

⊜⊜ **Cave d'Agnès** – *29 r. Gilbert-Salamo – 11510 Fitou -* ☎ *04 68 45 75 91 – closed 16 Nov-14 Mar, Thu lunchtime and Wed – booking essential – 20.50/29.50€.* Once you have experienced the relaxed atmosphere of this old barn high up in the village you will not want to leave. In addition to grilled meats prepared in front of you in the rustic dining room, the chef prepares generous regional recipes. A good Fitou makes an ideal accompaniment...

⊜⊜ **Relais Chantovent** – *34210 Minerve -* ☎ *04 68 91 14 18 – closed 18 Dec to 18 Mar, Sun evening and Mon – lunch 16€ – 22/38€.* This Cathar village stretched out on a rocky promontory is a car-free zone, so you will have to walk there. The Relais Chantovent, a pleasant inn whose terrace offers a clear view of the Gorges du Brian, serves good regional dishes with wines from the Minervois, of course.

⊜⊜ **Le Souquet's** – *Domaine de la Pierre Droite – 11430 Gruissan – 5.5km NW of Gruissan in the direction of Narbonne via the D 32 and minor road -* ☎ *04 68 49 13 23 – closed 1 Oct to 15 Apr and lunchtimes except Sat-Sun – ⊠ – 20/40€.* Fish and meats grilled over vine cuttings, which you can enjoy in the dining room of this wine-growers' *mas* (farmhouse) at the foot of La Clape mountain, or on the superb terrace with its panorama of the vineyards and bare hills. There are two *gîtes* should you wish to prolong your stay.

⊜⊜ **L'Os à Table** – *Rte de Salles-d'Aude – 11110 Coursan - 7km NE of Narbonne*

in the direction of Béziers via the N 9 - ☎ *04 68 33 55 72 – closed during holidays in Feb, 1st week of Nov holidays, Sun evening and Mon – 20/42€.* With its two modern dining rooms and its summer terrace facing a little garden, this restaurant provides a pleasant setting in which to sample the chef's flavourful cuisine, which is updated for contemporary tastes and makes use of regional produce whenever possible.

⊜⊜ **Table St-Crescent** – *Rte de Perpignan, in the Palais du Vin – 11100 Narbonne -* ☎ *04 68 41 37 37 – closed 6-20 Sep, 21 Feb to 7 Mar, Sat lunchtime, Sun evening and Mon – 30/48€.* This restaurant on the way out of town is set in an old oratory that has been converted into a *Palais du Vin* (wine palace). In addition to a beautiful vaulted dining room, it has a pleasant terrace surrounded by vines. Tasty, inventive cuisine and a wine list that pays homage to the Languedoc-Roussillon region.

D. Pazery / MICHELIN

ITINERARY ⑤

⊜ **Chez Saskia** – *R. St-Louis, in the "Cité" – 11000 Carcassonne -* ☎ *04 68 71 98 71 – closed from 1 Dec to 15 Jan – 15/31€.* Flowing lines, great luminosity and a low-key atmosphere characterise this modern-style brasserie, the Hôtel de la Cité's second restaurant... An ideal place to sample traditional, heartwarming dishes with all the flavour of Cathar country: homemade *cassoulet*, a rich casserole of haricot beans and meat, and *clafoutis* – a kind of battered fruit tart – will give you a taste of the region and spare your wallet.

⊜ **La Maison de la Blanquette** – *46 bis prom. du Tivoli – 11300 Limoux -* ☎ *04 68 31 01 63 – closed Oct and Wed – 15/31.50€.* Drinks are included in the set menus here: a good opportunity to discover or rediscover Blanquette-de-Limoux and other local wines, while sampling sparkling local recipes. Before you leave, make a detour via the well-stocked wine shop.

⊜⊜ **Chez Fred** – *31 bd Omer-Sarraut – 11000 Carcassonne -* ☎ *04 68 72 02 23 – closed 9 Feb to 2 Mar, 20 Oct to 3 Nov, Sat lunchtime, Tue evening and Wed in winter - lunch 10€ - 18/27€.* Trendy decor, shimmering colours, laid-back atmosphere and culinary theme evenings. This bistro focuses on the authentic flavours of Languedoc and Andalusia, which you can discover in the cosy dining room or on the terrace out front when the weather permits.

⊜⊜ **L'Écurie** – *43 bd Barbès - 11000 Carcassonne - ☎ 04 68 72 04 04 - closed Sun evening and Wed - 21/35€*. Pebble floor, varnished wooden stalls, gleaming brasses… These former stables built in the 18C now house a restaurant, with a delightful summer terrace set in a garden planted with trees. Well-prepared traditional dishes on the menu and, out of deference to the former occupants, there's not a horse steak in sight.

ITINERARY ⑥

⊜⊜ **Auberge de Cucugnan** – *2 pl. de la Fontaine - 11350 Cucugnan - ☎ 04 68 45 40 84 - closed from 1 Jan to 15 Mar and Wed - 16/40€*. You have to wend your way – on foot rather than by car – through a maze of narrow streets to reach this converted barn. Its authentic setting, rustic atmosphere and wine cellar full of regional wines allow you to fully appreciate the chef's generous local-traditional cuisine.

⊜⊜ **La Balade Gourmande** – *Bd Léon-Castel - RN 113 - 11200 Lézignan-Corbières - ☎ 04 68 27 22 18 - closed Mon evening, Tue evening and Wed evening – booking advisable - 20/32€*. Inside this modern pink house are two dining rooms with southern-style decor (yellow walls and Provençal fabrics). Good regional produce and traditional cuisine – if you like cassoulet, the one here is a must – served in a lively, friendly atmosphere.

ITINERARY ⑧

⊜⊜ **Les Antiquaires** – *Pl. Desprès - 66000 Perpignan - ☎ 04 68 34 06 58 - closed 1-23 Jul, Sun evening and Mon - 21/38€*. This family-run restaurant, which recently celebrated its 30th anniversary, is run by a charming couple. The lady of the house decorates the rustic yet well-appointed dining room with objects unearthed at antiques shops, while her husband offers the regulars and other patrons good traditional dishes that are always generous and well-prepared.

⊜⊜ **Al Fanal and Hôtel El Llagut** – *18 av. du Fontaulé - 66650 Banyuls-sur-Mer - ☎ 04 68 88 00 81 - 22/50€*. The dining room's maritime decor, the shaded terrace overlooking the harbour, the comings and goings of the boats, and the silvery reflections all make for a holiday atmosphere. So go with the flow and choose a Banyuls from the establishment's small selection before tucking into the chef's delicious regional dishes.

⊜⊜ **Les Trois Soeurs** – *2 r. Fontfroide - 66000 Perpignan - ☎ 04 68 51 22 33 - closed Mon evening except in summer and Sun all year round - 25€*. A restaurant with three contemporary and colourful dining rooms. *Parillada,* a kind of mixed grill, cod carpaccio, squid grilled *à la plancha, crème catalane* (custard with caramel) and other generous dishes full of southern aromas and flavours can also be sampled on the lovely terrace on the cathedral square.

⊜⊜ **La Galinette** – *23 r. Jean-Payra - 66000 Perpignan - ☎ 04 68 35 00 90 - closed from 26 Jul to 16 August, from 23 Dec to 4 Jan, Sun and Mon - lunch 12€ - 26/35€*. The tasty market-fresh cooking of this young chef-cum-boss is resolutely inspired by the Roussillon region. His wife's attentive welcome, the warm colours of the walls, the clever combination of styles, and the friendly atmosphere have quickly attracted a young and chic clientele… Definitely an up-and-coming place!

⊜⊜ **Les Clos de Paulilles** – *66660 Port-Vendres - 3km N of Banyuls via the N 114 - ☎ 04 68 98 07 58 – open in the evening from Jun to Sep and Sun lunchtime – booking essential - 32€*. At the heart of a wine-growing estate, this restaurant serves rustic cuisine, each course accompanied by a different wine from the estate. To avoid rapid intoxication, sit on the shaded terrace with its sobering fresh sea breeze!

WHERE TO STAY

ITINERARIES ① AND ②

⊜ **Chambre d'hôte M. Gener** – *34 av. Pierre-Sirven - 34530 Montagnac – 6.5km NW of Pézenas via the N 9 and N 113 - ☎ 04 67 24 03 21 – open all year round - ⊟ - 4rm: 45€*. In 1750, these buildings set around a large inner courtyard, tucked well out of sight, belonged to the mounted constabulary. Today, the former stables house spacious, quiet and well-appointed rooms. In summer, breakfast is served on the pleasant terrace upstairs.

⊜⊜ **Hôtel du Parc** – *8 r. Achille-Bège - 34000 Montpellier - ☎ 04 67 41 16 49 - open all year round - ⊟ - 19rm: 48/72€ - ⊐ 9€*. Although the grounds of this fine 18C residence have been parcelled out, its noble façade has remained intact. The well-appointed rooms have been personalised and gradually renovated with discerning taste. In summer, lunch is sometimes served on the terrace.

⊜⊜ **Le Molière** – *Pl. du 14-Juillet - 34120 Pézenas - ☎ 04 67 98 14 00 - 🅿 - 23rm: 49/99€ - ⊐ 7€*. The façade of this charming hotel in the town centre is adorned with sculptures. The comfortable, functional rooms are equipped with modern furniture, and the lounge area, in a superb patio, is decorated with attractive wall frescoes illustrating Molière's plays.

⊜⊜ **Ostalaria Cardabela** – *10 pl. de La Fontaine - 34725 St-Saturnin-de-Lucian - 10km N of Clermont-l'Hérault via the N 9, N 109, D 908, D 141 then D 130 - ☎ 04 67 88 62 62 - ostalaria.cardabela@wanadoo. fr - closed from 1 Jan to 10 Mar, from 31 Oct to 31 Dec - ⊟ - 7rm: 65/90€ - ⊐ 10€*. A discreet sign is the only indication that this delightful house is a hotel. Its recently redecorated rooms are stylish: colourful *boutis* embroidery, designer lights and Provençal furniture blend in perfectly with the attractive bare-stone walls, polished floor tiles, beams and original fireplaces.

⊖⊖ **Domaine de St-Clément** – *34980 St-Clément-de-Rivière - 10km N of Montpellier via the D 17 and D 112 - ☎ 04 67 66 70 89 - closed Dec-Feb -* 🍴 *- 5rm: 66/76€ -* ☕ *7€.* This very beautiful 18C squire's house, just 10min away from the centre of Montpellier, is a haven of peace and quiet. The huge rooms, with their antique furniture and paintings, give onto the park or swimming pool. Lovely series of lounges, pleasant library, and a patio decorated with *azulejos* tiles.

⊖⊖⊟ **Hôtel Guilhem** – *18 r. Jean-Jacques-Rousseau - 34000 Montpellier - ☎ 04 67 52 90 90 - hotel-le-guilhem@mnet.fr - 36rm: 82/135€ -* ☕ *11€.* This hotel offers both the charm of a 16C residence and the tranquillity of a location away from all the hustle and bustle, in a quiet little street in the capital of Languedoc. Moreover, the windows at the back open onto private gardens and the Faculty of Medicine. Attractive, spacious rooms.

ITINERARY ③

⊖ **Champ de Mars** – *17 r. de Metz - 34500 Béziers - ☎ 04 67 28 35 53 - closed 12-20 Feb - 10rm: 33.50/46€ -* ☕ *5€.* A small, family-run hotel in a quiet alley, near the square that every Friday hosts the town's biggest non-food market. The average-sized rooms are plainly decorated and fully equipped.

⊖ **La Bastide Vieille** – *La Bastide Vieille - 34310 Capestang - 13km W of Béziers via the D 11 - ☎ 04 67 93 46 23 - closed from 1 Nov to 1 Mar -* 🍴 *- 3rm: 51€.* Guaranteed peace and quiet in this serene, isolated country house surrounded by vines, whose venerable façade is flanked by a 12C tower. The spacious rooms in the old outbuildings are attractively decorated in Provençal style. Charming lounge-cum-library where you can read at leisure.

⊖⊖⊟ **Château de Lignan** – *34490 Lignan-sur-Orb - 7km NW of Béziers via the D 19 - ☎ 04 67 37 91 47 - chateau.lignan@wanadoo.fr -* 🅿 *- 49rm: 114/130€ -* ☕ *13€ - restaurant 39/59€.* A former bishop's residence set in a beautiful 6ha park on the banks of the River Orb. The renovated rooms are modern and well equipped. Jacuzzi, hammam, swimming pool and open-air restaurant on a terrace with a view of the estate and its age-old trees.

ITINERARIES ④ AND ⑦

⊖⊖ **Chambre d'hôte Domaine de St-Jean** – *11100 Narbonne - 10km SW of Narbonne via the N 9, N 113, D 613 then D 224 - ☎ 04 68 45 17 31 -* 🍴 *- 4rm: 45/65€.* This large wine-growers' house is ideal for those in search of authenticity and peace and quiet. The walls and furniture of its comfortable rooms are decorated with hand-painted motifs. One of the rooms has its own terrace

with a lovely view of the Massif de Fontfroide. Pleasant garden cared for by the owner-cum-nursery gardener.

⊖⊖ **La Résidence** – *6 r. du 1ᵉʳ-Mai - 11100 Narbonne - ☎ 04 68 32 19 41 - closed from 15 Jan to 15 Feb - 25rm: 68/96€ -* ☕ *8€.* This late 19C house has been popular with politicians, sportsmen and artists ever since it first opened as a hotel in the 1950s. French actor Louis de Funès notably stayed here while filming the *Petit Baigneur*. Some of the rooms overlook the Archbishops' Palace and Cathedral.

⊖⊖ **Hôtel de la Plage** – *At the beach - 11430 Gruissan - ☎ 04 68 49 00 75 - closed mid-Sep to Easter -* 🅿 *- 17rm: 55€.* From the terrace of this hotel set in a small 1960s building you can see the famous houses on stilts immortalised by Jean-Jacques Beineix's film *Betty Blue*. Bright, well-kept, but modestly furnished rooms. Friendly welcome.

⊖⊖⊟ **Relais du Val d'Orbieu** – *11200 Ornaisons - 14km west of Narbonne via the N 113 and D 24 - ☎ 04 68 27 10 27 - relais.du.val.dorbieu@wanadoo.fr - closed 5 Nov to 5 Feb and Sun evening from Nov to Mar -* 🅿 *- 20rm: 95/150€ -* ☕ *15€ - restaurant 41/55€.* This old mill set back from a secondary road and surrounded by vines offers guests a peaceful setting in which to enjoy their stay. Comfortable rooms on the same level as the flower-filled garden, a restaurant with terrace, and a nice swimming pool.

ITINERARY ⑤

⊖ **Le Mauzac** – *9 av. Camille-Bouche - 11300 Limoux - RD 118 - ☎ 04 68 31 12 77 -* 🅿 *- 21rm: 34/48€ -* ☕ *6€.* A handy place to stop on the road to Carcassonne, this hillside hotel was recently entirely renovated and offers comfortable, well-soundproofed rooms with pine furniture. The ones at the rear are best. Charming breakfast room. Warm welcome.

⊖⊖ **Chambre d'hôte Le Liet** – *11610 Pennautier - 5km NW of Carcassonne via the N 113 and D 203 - ☎ 04 68 11 19 19 - chateauleliet@francemultimedia.fr - closed Nov-Feb - 6rm and 4 gîtes: 53€. 36/68.60€.* This turreted 19C château stands in wooded grounds that boast a wide variety of flora and fauna, including peacocks, hares and pheasants. The rooms and suites with their polished decor enjoy views of this profusion of nature. Some have a balcony. Magnificent breakfast room.

⊖⊖ **Chambre d'hôte La Maison sur la Colline** – *Lieu-dit Ste-Croix - 11000 Carcassonne - 1km S of the "Cité" via the road to Ste-Croix - ☎ 04 68 47 57 94 - closed 1 Dec to 15 Feb -* 🍴 *- booking advisable in high season - 6rm: 60/85€ –27€.* Perched on a hilltop, this old restored farmhouse offers an enchanting view of the medieval *"cité"*. Its spacious rooms, furnished with objects unearthed in second-hand shops, are each decorated in a different colour: blue, yellow, beige, white… Breakfast is served at the poolside in summer.

ITINERARY [6]

⊜⊜ Chambre d'hôte La Bastide des Corbières – *17 r. de la Révolution - 11200 Boutenac – 7.5km S of Lézignan via the D 61 to Luc-sur-Orbieu - ☎ 04 68 27 20 61 - closed 15 Jan to 15 Feb, 15-30 Nov - 5rm: 65/84€ – meal 29€.*
A late 19C squire's house where modern conveniences blend in perfectly with the atmosphere of yesteryear. Cinsault, Carignan, Grenache, Syrah, Chardonnay: each of the spacious, colourful rooms, some of them with antique furniture, bears the name of a grape variety of the AOC Corbières. Large garden with swimming pool.

ITINERARY [8]

⊜⊜ Casa Païral – *Imp. des Palmiers - 66190 Collioure - ☎ 04 68 82 05 81 - contact@hotel-casa-pairal.com - closed 5 Nov to 31 Mar - 🅿 - 28rm: 68/170€ - ☐ 10€.* An old Catalan residence set in a cul-de-sac. Rather old-fashioned, but full of charm. The rooms in the main building are full of character. The others are plainer, but also quieter. In summer, you can make the most of the swimming pool and lush garden with its babbling fountain.

⊜⊜⊜ Chambre d'hôte Domaine du Mas Boluix – *Chemin du Pou-de-les-Colobres - 66000 Perpignan - 5km S of Perpignan on the road to Argelès - ☎ 04 68 08 17 70 - ⊠ - 7rm including 1 suite: 73€.* A peaceful atmosphere reigns in this 18C *mas* (farmhouse) surrounded by the vineyards of Cabestany. Its rooms, with their pristine walls and superb Catalan fabrics, each bear the name of a local artist. Far-reaching view of Roussillon. Wine-tasting and sale of wines from the estate.

GOURMET SHOPPING

Cabanel – *72 allée d'Iéna - 11000 Carcassonne - ☎ 04 68 25 02 58 - Mon-Sat 8am-12pm, 2pm-7pm.* This liqueur store has traded under the same sign since 1868. It offers a wide choice of original spirits such as Or-Kina, made with plants and spices, Micheline, believed to date back to the Middle Ages, Audoise, known as the liqueur of the Cathars, and homemade grog. A small selection of regional wines is also available.

Maison Roque – *17 Rte d'Argelès - 66190 Collioure - ☎ 04 68 82 22 30 - roque.collioure@wanadoo. fr – open every day 8am-7.30pm; tour of the workshop: Mon-Fri 8am-12pm, 2pm-5pm.* Founded in 1870, the Maison Roque perpetuates the traditional small-scale production of the famous anchovies of Collioure. The boutique is on the ground floor, but you can also go up to the first-floor workshop to see expert hands at work preparing the tasty little fish.

A. Thuillier / MICHELIN

Aux Croquants de Montpellier – *7 r. du Faubourg-du-Courreau - 34000 Montpellier - ☎ 04 67 58 67 38 - closed in Aug - Tue-Sun 7am-7pm, Mon 7am-1pm and 4pm-7pm.* This tiny shop has been catering to biscuit lovers for over a hundred years. The star product is, of course, the almond-flavoured *croquants de Montpellier*, the recipe for which dates back to 1880. Around fifteen different kinds of shortbread biscuit and some special breads and pastries are also made here.

Accent d'Oc – *56 r. Droite - 11100 Narbonne - ☎ 04 68 32 24 13 - www. accentdoc.fr - Tue-Sun 10am-12.30pm, 2.30pm-7pm; summer 10am-1pm, 3pm-7pm (open Mon afternoon 3pm-7pm) - closed 1 May.* The young owners opened this shop in celebration of the gastronomic wealth of Languedoc. Here you will find an array of products made using recipes of long ago: a surprising olive jam, sweet and sour condiments, flavoured vinegars and oils, wine jellies, milk jams etc.

The **Hôtel des Trésoriers de France** houses the **Musée Languedocien★**. It was called the Hôtel Jacques-Coeur when the king's treasurer was living there in the 15C. In the 17C it became the Hôtel des Trésoriers de France, after the resident senior magistrates in charge of administering the royal estates in Languedoc. The medieval room houses Romanesque sculptures from the abbey of Fontcaude and the cloisters of St-Guilhem-le-Désert, furniture and earthenware from the Languedoc region. The second floor is devoted to archaeological collections and folk art and traditions. *7 r. Jacques-Coeur. Jul-Aug: 3pm-5pm; rest of the year: 2pm-5pm. Closed Sun, public holidays. 5€. ☎ 04 67 52 93 03.*

The **Promenade du Peyrou★★** was created in the late 17C as a setting for a monumental statue of Louis XIV; destroyed during the Revolution, this was replaced by the present statue in 1838. The upper terrace affords a sweeping **view★** of the garrigues and Cévennes in the north, and the Mediterranean and, on a fine day,

Mont Canigou to the south. Monumental flights of steps lead to the lower terraces decorated with wrought-iron railings. The **Arc de Triomphe**, built in the late 17C, is decorated with low-relief sculptures depicting the victories of Louis XIV.

Behind the Polygone shopping centre and office complex *(starting from place de la Comédie, walk to the Antigone district via Le Polygone shopping centre)*, the **Antigone District★** is the creation of Catalan architect Ricardo Bofill. Covering the 40ha of the old polygonal army exercise ground, this vast neo-Classical project combines prefabrication techniques (the prestressed concrete has the grain and colour of stone) with rigorously harmonious design on a gigantic scale.

Lastly, take the time to visit the **Agropolis Museum★**, devoted to agriculture and food throughout the world. The presentation is as attractive as it is educational; the "Dining Table of the World" display illustrates the variety and inequality inherent in this theme. In addition, there are thematic exhibitions, a Cyber Museum, and activities for children. *6km north of the Hôpitaux-Facultés district. Access by car or by tram to St-Éloi then shuttle to Agropolis-Lavalette. Open every day except Tue 2pm-6pm. 5€ (free for children under 10).* ☎ *04 67 04 75 01. www.agropolis.fr*

Take D 986 NW out of Montpellier and, after 10km, turn right to Les Matelles.

Les Matelles

This fortified village has beautiful houses with external staircases. In the Neolithic age, nomadic herdsmen settled here; this period is illustrated in the **Musée Municipal de Préhistoire**. *From mid-Jun to mid-Sep: open every day except Tue and Fri 3pm-6pm; from mid-Sep to mid-Jun: Fri and Sun 3pm-6pm.* ☎ *04 67 84 18 68.*

Continue E along the D 17^{E3} for 3km then turn left onto the D 113^{E3}.

Saint-Jean-de-Cuculles

This tiny village has a pretty Romanesque church. A very respectable rosé Coteaux-du-Languedoc is produced here at the **Domaine Haut-Lirou**.

Carry on to St-Mathieu-de-Tréviers via the D 113E4.

Saint-Mathieu-de-Tréviers

🚶 A **walk** in the garrigue *(2hr round trip)* will take you up to the ruins of the old Château de Montferrand. Lovely view of the vineyards. Some fine wines are produced at the **Domaine Devois du Claus** *(see Shopping Guide)*.

Take the D 17 to Valflaunès.

Valflaunès

This is where most of the estates of the Coteaux-du-Languedoc-Pic-St-Loup appellation are to be found. The **Domaine de l'Hortus** remains a benchmark *(see the Shopping Guide)*.

Head SW out of Valflaunès on the D 1E9, which joins up with the D 1, then take the D 122 to Saint-Martin-de-Londres.

Saint-Martin-de-Londres★

Vines are scarcer on the southern side of the Causse de l'Hortus (Hortus limestone plateau), and give way to an austere landscape of garrigue. The word "Londres" comes from the Celtic word *lund* meaning "marsh". In the centre of the old village, the defences of the "old fort" date from the 12C; its bounds are marked by a gateway. The 11C Romanesque **church★** is delightful.

Take the D 32 towards Viols-le-Fort then turn left onto the D 113.

Village préhistorique de Cambous

The access road is rather bumpy. Leave the car in the Cambous car park and walk to the prehistoric village. Jul-Aug: open Tue-Sun 2pm-6pm; Sep-Oct: Sat-Sun and public holidays 2pm-6pm; Apr-Jun and Easter holidays: Sat-Sun and public holidays 2pm-6pm. 2.50€. ☎ *04 67 86 34 37.*

The substantial remains of stone dwellings, with 2.5m-thick drystone walls and openings forming corridors, date from 2800-2300 BC. A prehistoric house has been reconstructed.

Continue along the D 113 to Cazevieille and leave your car in the car park.

Pic Saint-Loup★

🚶 *Follow the signs to Pic St-Loup. Beware, the limestone is very slippery in wet weather. The wide stone path leads up to a calvary. From there, take a little winding footpath which climbs up to the chapel and observatory. Allow 3hr there and back.* From the summit, there is a magnificent **panorama★★** of the whole region.

Take the same road back to Cambous. Turn left onto the D 32.

Aniane

Aniane has lost all trace of the abbey founded here in the 8C by St Benedict. A stroll through the streets takes in the church of St-Jean-Baptiste-des-Pénitents, built in a mixture of architectural styles and now used to house temporary exhibitions.

The Aniane terroir is shared by the Coteaux-du-Languedoc and vins de pays. The **Mas de Daumas Gassac** produces some great regional red and white wines, with a character as atypical as their prices *(see Shopping Guide)*.

Head N on the D 32 then turn left onto the D 27. The road crosses the River Hérault by a modern bridge near the **Pont du Diable** (Devil's Bridge) which, though you might not guess so by the name, was actually built by Benedictine monks in the early 11C. View of the Hérault gorge and the bridge aqueduct that enables irrigation of the vineyards of the St-Jean-de-Fos region.

Grotte de Clamouse★★★

Jul-Aug: guided tour (1hr) 10am-7pm; rest of the year: 10am-5pm; Nov-Jan: every day except Sat 10am-5pm. 7.50€. ☎ 04 67 57 71 05. www.clamouse.com

This cave is renowned for its wealth of crystalline formations. It takes its name from the resurgent spring that cascades noisily into the Hérault after very heavy rain, hence its Occitan dialect name of *Clamosa*, the "howler".

Continue 4km along the D 4 to St-Guilhem-le-Désert.

Saint-Guilhem-le-Désert★★

This village is built around an old abbey at the mouth of untamed river gorges, where the Verdus flows into the Hérault. It owes much of the story of its origins to legend, related in the 12C *chanson de geste* by Guillaume d'Orange. It relates that Guilhem, one of Charlemagne's officers, founded the abbey after bringing back a piece of the real Cross. This relic is on display in the 11C **abbey church★** and is carried in a procession to the village square every year in May.

From the alley lined with old houses, the rich decoration of the church's **chevet★** can really be appreciated. Flanked by two apsidal chapels, it features three windows and a series of arched openings separated by slender columns with curious capitals. The whole is embellished by a frieze of cog-tooth indentations echoing that of the doorway.

Take the D 4 in the other direction to St-Jean-de-Fos.

Saint-Jean-de-Fos

This old fortified village was once a major centre of pottery production and has an interesting Romanesque church.

Continue along the D 141 to Montpeyroux.

Montpeyroux

At the foot of an old fortress in ruins, Montpeyroux has lent its name to the **AOC Coteaux-du-Languedoc-Montpeyroux**. Here full-bodied, intense red wines are produced, such as those of the renowned **Domaine d'Aupilhac** *(see Shopping Guide)*.

Take the D 9 N to Arboras.

Arboras

A splendid **panorama★** can be enjoyed from the terraces of the old castle, of which only one tower remains.

Take the D 130 SW to St-Saturnin-de-Lucian.

Saint-Saturnin-de-Lucian

The old town still has a few old houses. St-Saturnin adds its name to the **AOC Coteaux-du-Languedoc-Saint-Saturnin**. The **Cave des vins de St-Saturnin** produces very fine cuvées with the emphasis on Syrah *(see Shopping Guide)*. From the village, a little road runs up to the **Rocher des Vierges** (Virgins' Rock), a place of pilgrimage which offers an extraordinary **panorama★★**.

Head to Clermont-l'Hérault taking the D 130 and the D 141 as far as Ceyras. Then turn right onto the D 908.

Clermont-l'Hérault

Like Lodève, Clermont-l'Hérault specialised for a long time in the manufacture of military cloth. It is now an important wine-growing centre and a market for dessert grapes.

The narrow alleys climb up the hill that is crowned by the ruins of a 12C castle (beautiful view of the village and surrounding area). The fortified **Church of St-Paul★** (13C-14C) gives an impression of solidity and strength.

Villeneuvette

Jul-Aug: guided tour of the town (2hr) 3.30pm, every day except Mon and Sat-Sun 10.30am; Sep-Jun: by prior arrangement. 4€. Contact the town hall, ☎ 04 67 96 06 00.

This former royal textile factory was founded by Colbert in the 17C and has retained its architectural unity. The square, main street and approaches to the workers' houses have been recobbled as in the 17C and the houses, now with pleasant, flower-filled gardens, have been converted and restored.

After Villeneuvette turn left onto the D 15.

Cabrières

Decomposing shale and high slopes produce the quality of **Coteaux-du-Languedoc-Cabrières**, powerful wines that should be kept. The surrounding area also produces the **AOC Clairette-du-Languedoc**, a dry or smooth white wine which, upon ageing, takes on a *"rancio"* quality: a sweet, golden character and a nutty aroma. Make the most of your time in Cabrières to visit the hamlet of **Les Crozes**, entirely built of schist and set in magnificent scenery. You can also tour the old **Pioch-Farrus copper mine**, which dates back to prehistoric times. ♿ *Apr-Oct and school holidays in Feb: guided tour (45min, last departure 1hr before closing time) 10am-7pm. 7€.* ☎ *06 14 91 46 02.*

To return to Montpellier, take the D 908 to Gignac then the N 109.

WINE AND SHELLFISH ROUTE

145km. Michelin Local Map 339, F-I 7-8. See itinerary **2** *on the map on p. 254-255.*
Eaten away by urban development, the vineyards only begin to come into their own about a dozen kilometres west of Montpellier. Even further away, the shores of the Thau lagoon still have some protected areas which attract pink flamingos. Those partial to seafood will enjoy the oysters from Bouzigues and other shellfish on offer, washed down with **AOC Coteaux-du-Languedoc-Picpoul-de-Pinet**.

Leave Montpellier on the D 5 towards Lavérune then turn right onto the D 5[E].

Château de l'Engarran

34880 Lavérune, ☎ *04 67 47 00 02, lengarran@wanadoo.fr, 10am-7pm.*
Beyond the superb entrance gate stands a Louis XV style building. Only the estate's small cellar is open to the public. Here you will find a good red Coteaux-du-Languedoc-St-Georges-d'Orques.

Go back and carry on along the D 5. The Château de Lavérune is on the far west side of the village.

Château de Lavérune

Sat-Sun 3pm-6pm. 2€. ☎ *04 99 51 20 00 (town hall) or 04 99 51 20 25 (museum).*
This former residence of the bishops of Montpellier (17C-18C) stands in the middle of a park and houses works by contemporary artists.

Take the road to St-Georges-d'Orques. Before reaching the village, turn right onto the D 5[ES] *to Pignan.*

Abbey of Saint-Martin-de-Vignogoul

Mon-Fri 10am-12pm, 2pm-4pm; for a guided tour, contact the cultural association of the abbey of Vignogoul, ☎ *04 67 79 35 13.*
Not much remains of the former 11C Cistercian abbey. The 13C Gothic church stands not far from the **Domaine de la Prose**, surrounded by some of the oldest Carignan vine stock in the Languedoc region *(see Shopping Guide)*.

Pignan

This once fortified wine-growers' town is at the heart of the **Coteaux-du-Languedoc-Saint-Georges-d'Orques** appellation.

Take the D 27 NW to Murviel.

Murviel-lès-Montpellier

Some results of the excavations of the Gallo-Roman *oppidum* (fortified town) of Le Castellas are on display in the town hall. *By appointment,* ☎ *04 67 47 05 14.*
You will find out more by going to the Domaine des Belles Pierres where you can discuss archaeology over a glass of white Coteaux-du-Languedoc. *24 r. des Clauzes, 34570 Murviel-lès-Montpellier,* ☎ *04 67 47 30 43.*

Take the D 102 S to Cournonterral.

Cournonterral

In autumn each year, during the Pailhasses festival, straw-covered monsters hunt down young people dressed all in white and plunge them into a tub of wine lees. Purple, squelching fun guaranteed...

From Cournonterral, take the D 114 SE to Mireval, turning left onto the N 112.

Mireval

The village is famous for the **AOC Muscat-de-Mireval** vineyards, which grow between the Étang de Vic and the slopes of the Massif de la Gardiole. The **Domaine de la Capelle** is a fine example *(see Shopping Guide)*.

Frontignan

Frontignan lends its name to a famous, golden Muscat, whose 800ha of vineyards grow near the shores of the Étang d'Ingril. The door of the **Gothic church** (12C-14C) has a beautiful frieze of fish and boats.
The **Cave Coopérative de Frontignan** (wine cooperative, guided tour possible) produces 80% of the **Muscat-de-Frontignan** appellation. It offers several cuvées corresponding to different stages of maturity as well as some "forgotten wines", ie wines that have aged for many years in oak tuns *(see Shopping Guide)*.
The **Musée d'Histoire locale** (local history museum) houses prehistoric collections and illustrates the production of Muscat. *4 bis r. Lucien-Salette, next to the church.*

Open every day except Tue 10am-12pm, 2.30pm-6.30pm. Closed from beginning of Dec to mid-Mar. No charge. ☎ *04 67 48 50 05.*

Frontignan-Plage and Les Aresquiers

From the beach at Frontignan *(2km S)*, you can follow the narrow offshore bar to the shingle beach of Les Aresquiers, which is popular with nudists. The *guinguettes*, as the open-air cafés are called, serve *bouillabaisse* (fish stew) and sometimes have musical evenings in summer.

Return to Frontignan and take the D 2 W, then turn right onto the D 2ᴱ, which runs alongside the Thau lagoon.

Balaruc-le-Vieux

Perched on a hill overlooking the lagoon, the village still has its original circular layout. Some of the houses feature striking arched doorways.

Take the D 2 to Bouzigues, turning left onto the N 113.

Bouzigues

The evolution of shellfish farming techniques is illustrated at the **Musée de l'Étang de Thau** *(on the quay of the fishing harbour).* & *Jul-Aug: 10am-12.30pm, 2.30pm-7pm; Mar-Jun and Sep-Oct: 10am-12pm, 2pm-6pm; Nov-Feb: 10am-12pm, 2pm-5pm. Closed 1 Jan, 25 Dec. 4€.* ☎ *04 67 78 33 57.*

From the shores of the small bay in the far north of the lagoon you can see groups of pink flamingos and enjoy the view of Balaruc-le-Vieux.

Take the N 113 to Mèze.

Mèze

The port of Mèze, its narrow streets, 15C church, oysters and friendly bistros attract a large number of tourists. The **Étang de Thau** is nearby. This vast lagoon (8 000ha) stretches out along the Languedoc coast, separated from the sea by the isthmus of Onglous (Sète beach). On the north shore a few fishing villages, their huts hidden by reeds, specialise in oyster and mussel farming. Admire the rigorous geometry of the shellfish parks whose delicious produce you can sample to your heart's content, washed down with a fresh white wine from the region... a Picpoul-de-Pinet, for example.

Take the D 159 W, then turn left onto the D 51.

Marseillan

Probably founded in the 6C BC by sailors from Marseilles, Marseillan is the birthplace of **Noilly-Prat**. The Noilly-Prat **storehouses** *(near the harbour)* are open to the public. One of the distinctive stages of the production of dry vermouth is the ageing of the blend of grape varieties in the open air in 600-litre casks. *May-Sep: guided tour (1hr) 10am-11am, 2.30pm-6pm; Mar-Apr and Oct-Nov: 10am-11am, 2.30pm-4.30pm. Closed 1 May. 3.50€.* ☎ *04 67 77 75 19. www.noillyprat.com*

6km S, Marseillan-Plage boasts miles of sandy beaches.

Take the D 51 in the opposite direction then turn left onto the D 18ᴱ¹ to Pinet.

Pinet

This small village is famous for the Picpoul (or Piquepoul) grape, formerly used to make vermouths. Since vermouth is no longer in fashion, it is now used to make a pleasant white wine that is dry and fruity and goes well with shellfish.

The welcoming **Château de Pinet** makes Coteaux-du-Languedoc-Picpoul-de-Pinet wines and produces several high-quality cuvées *(see Shopping Guide)*.

The D 161ᴱ² to the NW then the D 161 will take you to Castelnau-de-Guers. Then take the D 32ᴱ⁵ N.

Oyster beds in Thau lagoon.

Pézenas★★

This little artistic town is set in the "garden of the Hérault", a fertile plain covered in vineyards. In **old Pézenas★★** you can stroll among magnificent mansions, 17C *hôtels*, inner courtyards and restored streets full of crafts and antiques shops *(a historic route leaflet is available from the tourist office)*. Pézenas has one big literary claim to fame: Molière stayed there from 1653 to 1657. Don't forget to try the delicious local speciality, *petits pâtés*, made of mutton, preserved lemon peel and curry.

Take the N 9 SW to Béziers.

Faugères and Saint-Chinian

125km. Michelin Local Map 339, C-E 7-9. See itinerary **3** *on the map on p. 254-255.*

The southwest edge of the Larzac plateau forms a mass covered in peaks reaching heights of between 600 and 700m. In the lowest parts, vines thrive on the schist that alternates with limestone scree. Vineyards are this somewhat austere region's only resource and produce red wines that are renowned for their strong character on the *terroirs* of Faugères and St-Chinian.

Béziers★

The town of Béziers, with its cathedral perched on high, drops steeply down to the plain where the long silvery corridor of the Canal du Midi snakes along, and provides some wonderful photo opportunities. It is also the capital of the Languedoc vineyards, which stretch as far as Carcassonne and Narbonne. Béziers was the hometown of Pierre-Paul Riquet, the famous creator of the Canal du Midi. The town comes alive during the annual *féria* (festival) in August and every Sunday when it comes out to support its legendary rugby team, the ASB.

In 1907 the **allées Paul-Riquet**, a broad avenue shaded by plane trees and lined with cafés and restaurants, provided the stage for the mutiny of the 17th infantry regiment which took place when the regiment – made up of wine-growers' sons – refused to shoot at the crowd of angry wine-growers.

The old **Cathédrale St-Nazaire★**, perched on a terrace above the River Orb, symbolised the might of the bishops of Béziers between 760 and 1789. The Romanesque building was damaged in 1209 during the Albigensian Crusade, and alterations were carried out on it from 1215 until the 15C. Go round the south side of the cathedral to the **cloisters** then take a flight of steps to the Jardin de l'Évêché, from which there is a lovely view of the church of St-Jude and the River Orb spanned by a 13C bridge, the Pont-Vieux.

Housed in the old St-Jacques barracks, the **Musée du Biterrois★** contains substantial collections on local archaeology, ethnology and natural history. A major part of the museum is given over to the region's Gallo-Roman heritage. The highlight of the exhibition is the *"Trésor de Béziers"*, consisting of three large chased silver platters discovered in 1983 in a vineyard on the outskirts of town. Various aspects of local economy are also illustrated (fishing, wine-growing and the construction of the Canal du Midi).

Jul-Aug: open Tue-Sun 10am-6pm; Apr-Jun and Sep-Oct: open Tue-Sun 9am-12pm, 2pm-6pm; Nov-Mar: open Tue-Sun 9am-12pm, 2pm-5pm. Closed 1 Jan, Easter Sunday, 1 May, 25 Dec. 2.35€. ☎ 04 67 28 38 78.

Take the D 14 west out of Béziers and after 15km turn left onto the D 134ᴱ¹. This is Saint-Chinian country. The **AOC St-Chinian** covers 3 200ha scattered over a vast area of schist, limestone scree, sandstone and red clay. The wines of St-Chinian, which have been enjoyed since the Middle Ages, had a reputation for being robust. With the planting of new vines and the aid of new techniques, more supple and fruity red wines can now be produced.

Abbaye de Fontcaude

Jul-Aug: 10am-7pm, Sun and public holidays 2.30pm-7pm; Jun and Sep: 10am-12pm, 2.30pm-7pm, Sun and public holidays 2.30pm-7pm; Oct-May: 10am-12pm, 2.30pm-5.30pm, Sun and public holidays 2.30pm-5.30pm. Closed Jan (except Sun pm), 25 Dec. 4€. ☎ 04 67 38 23 85.

Set on the road to Santiago de Compostela, the abbey reached the peak of its influence during the Middle Ages before being ruined. In summer, concerts are held here. A **museum** is housed in the large room where the monks illuminated manuscripts. A 12C bell foundry is still standing, as is the canons' oil mill.

At the end of the D 134ᴱ¹, turn right onto the D 134. Before reaching St-Chinian the road passes through the pretty red-stone villages of **Cazedarnes** and **Pierrerue**. *Turn left onto the D 20.*

Saint-Chinian

The entire town – its name associated throughout France with its enjoyable wines – exudes a relaxed way of life, from its little squares edged with plane trees to its pleasant cafés, which could have been taken straight from a Marcel Pagnol story. The church contains a fine Baroque organ.

You will gain good insight into the production of the AOC at the friendly **Maison des vins**, where you can taste and buy more than 150 items at the producer's price. It also offers wine-tasting courses, weekend ideas, and vineyard tours. *1 av. de la Promenade, 34360 St-Chinian, ☎ 04 67 38 11 69. www.vin-saintchinian. com 9am-12pm, 2pm-6.30pm.*

The **Domaine de la Madura** produces good wines *(see Shopping Guide)*.

Take the D 20 E then turn left onto the D 117.

This little road passes through splendid scenery where small areas of old vine stock clinging to the red earth play hide-and-seek with the garrigue, dotted with the occasional olive tree.

Berlou

Stop at the **Cave des Coteaux du Rieu**, where a fossil exhibition will give you an insight into the character of the terroir. The cooperative has also signposted four mountain-bike circuits through the vineyards. *34360 Berlou, ☎ 04 67 89 58 58. Mon-Sat 9am-12pm, 2pm-6pm, Sun 10am-1pm, 2pm-6pm.*

Continue N along the D 177. The corniche road becomes increasingly narrow and affords picture-postcard views of **Escagnès**, and of the medieval village of **Vieussan**, perched on high.

Take the D 14 S to Roquebrun. The sometimes lazy, sometimes raging River Orb runs through the valley, canoes gliding along its surface while swimmers, sunbathers and picnickers gather along its banks, which are equipped with facilities in some places (for example on the outskirts of **Ceps** and Roquebrun).

Roquebrun

Backed by a mountain cirque, the village is dominated by a medieval tower. Its exceptional climate enables it to maintain a **Mediterranean garden** containing 400 Mediterranean and exotic species. *Jul-Aug: 9am-7pm; from mid-Feb to end of Jun and from beginning of Sep to mid-Nov: 9am-12pm, 1.30pm-5.30pm. 4€. ☎ 04 67 89 55 29.*

Take the D 19 to Causses-et-Veyran. All the goodness of the excellent limestone soil of **Causses-et-Veyran** goes into Château Maurel Fonsalade, one of the musts of the AOC St-Chinian.

Take a little road E out of Causses-et-Veyran and you will join up with the D 136^{E2}, which becomes the D 136 as it cuts through the woods at Fabrègues. You are entering the terroir of the **AOC Faugères**. This appellation covers 1 870ha extending over seven communes. The vineyards spread up over steep schistose slopes and produce dark, full-bodied red wines.

Lenthéric

You can stop here for the wines of the renowned **Château des Estanilles**.

Follow the D 136^{E6}, which turns into the D 154, and you will come to **Cabrerolles** and one of the stars of the Faugères appellation, **Clos Fantine** *(see Shopping Guide)*. The D 154 forges on through wild landscape to Caussiniojouls.

Caussiniojouls

Take a walk in the **Jardin des Cistes** before heading up through the national forest of St-Michel to the radio relay station for a magnificent **view★★**.

Faugères

The town is dominated by three ancient mills that have been restored. Follow a botanical path up to enjoy the beautiful panorama. The vineyards are dotted with *capitelles*, also known as *calabelles*, old drystone huts that were once used by shepherds. An association restores them and organises walks. *Contact Faugères town hall, ☎ 04 67 90 15 79 or www.pierreseche.net*

The wines of the **Domaine Jean-Michel Alquier** await behind a magnificent 3m-long bar *(see Shopping Guide)*.

The D 909 will take you straight back to Béziers.

Le Minervois

123km. Michelin Local map 344, G-I 2-3. See itinerary **4** *on the map on p. 254-255.*
The land of Minerva, straddling the Hérault and Aude *départements*, is named after the ancient Roman goddess of War and Reason. It is a vast region, stretching out over the foothills of the Montagne Noire, between Narbonne and Carcassonne. An important centre of the austere Cathar religion in the Middle Ages, the Minervois has managed, despite the wars, to keep its wine-growing tradition intact while moving on into the modern age.

Five thousand hectares of vines are grown in the region and include three AOCs: **Minervois**, **Minervois-La-Livinière** and **Muscat-de-Saint-Jean-de-Minervois**. *Vins de pays* are also produced here.

Narbonne★★

Under the hot sun, Narbonne displays the architectural traces of its glorious past as the ancient capital of Gallia Narbonensis, the residence of the Visigoth monarchy and an archiepiscopal seat. It is now a lively Mediterranean city playing an important role as a wine-producing centre and a road and rail junction.

The **Palais des Archevêques★** (Archbishops' Palace) overlooks the lively **place de l'Hôtel-de-Ville** in the heart of the city, where a section of Roman road, the Via Domitia, was recently discovered *(visible on the square)*. Originally a modest ecclesiastical residence, the palace is now an example of religious, military and civil architecture bearing the imprint of centuries, from the 12C (Old Palace) to the 19C (town hall).

The **Donjon Gilles-Aycelin★** *(entrance on the left inside the town hall)* is a forti-fied tower, which stands on the remains of the Gallo-Roman rampart that once protected the heart of the old town. From the sentinel path on the platform *(162 steps)*, the **panorama★** stretches over Narbonne and the cathedral, the surrounding plain, and away across La Clape mountain, the Corbières and the coastal lagoons, with the Pyrenees on the horizon. *Jul-Sep: 10am-6pm; Oct-Jun: 9am-12pm, 2pm-6pm. Closed 1 Jan, 25 Dec. 2.20€. ☎ 04 68 90 30 65.*

The Palais neuf (New Palace) houses the **Archaeological Museum★★**. It undoubtedly possesses one of the finest collections of **Roman paintings★★** in France. Most come from the archaeological excavations at Clos de la Lombarde (north part of the ancient town), and were used to decorate the homes of the rich in Narbo Martius. A large collection of stone fragments evokes the institutions, daily life, religious practices and commercial activi-ties of Roman Narbonne. *Apr-Sep: 9.30am-12.15pm, 2pm-6pm; Oct-Mar: open Tue-Sun 10am-12pm, 2pm-5pm. Closed 1 Jan, 1 May, 1 and 11 Nov, 25 Dec. 5.20€ (3.70€ for 1 single museum). ☎ 04 68 90 30 54.*

The palace communicates with the **Cathédrale St-Just-et-St-Pasteur★★**, the first stone of which was laid on 3 April 1272 after being sent from Rome by Pope Clement IV, a former archbishop of the city (however, it was not completed until the 18C). The flower-filled **cloisters** (14C) on the south side of the cathedral are a haven of peace and coolness. The **interior** of the cathedral features vaulting in the chancel that is 41m high, a height exceeded only by that

The Canal de la Robine and the Pont des Marchands in Narbonne.

L. Campion/MICHELIN

in the cathedrals of Amiens (42m) and Beauvais (48m). The chapel of Ste-Marie-de-Bethléem has regained its **large Gothic altarpiece★**, discovered by chance in 1981 under a coat of stucco. See how the damned scream on their way to Hell in a cart, a terrifying sight in striking contrast with that of the chosen going up to Heaven.

Take the D 13 N out of Narbonne. At Cuxac-d'Aude, turn left onto the D 1118.

Sallèles-d'Aude

The banks of the Canal du Midi, shaded by umbrella pines, are an ideal place for a stroll or a picnic before a trip to **Amphoralis★**, the **Museum of Gallo-Roman Potters** *(access via the D 1626 NE of Sallèles-d'Aude, follow signs to "Musée des Potiers"; the road follows the canal that links the Canal du Midi and the Canal de la Robine)*. A tour of the excavation site reveals the ancient production of household ceramics, tiles and wine amphorae. The civilisation of wine, daily life and trade in the Roman Empire are illustrated here. *♿ Jul-Sep: 10am-12pm, 3pm-7pm; Oct-Jun: open Tue-Sun 2pm-6pm, Sat-Sun and public holidays 10am-12pm, 2pm-6pm. Guided tours possible by prior arrangement. Closed 1 Jan, 1 May, 25 Dec. 4€. ☎ 04 68 46 89 48.*

Continue along the D 1626 to Argeliers.

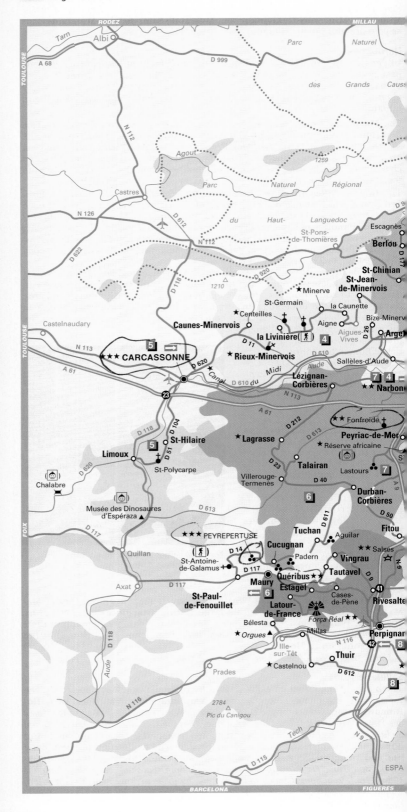

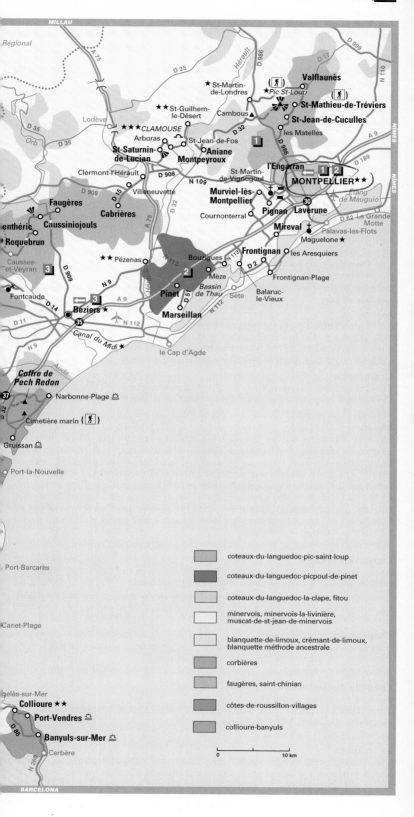

Argeliers

Les Vignerons Réunis wine cooperative continues to pay homage, in a small museum, to **Marcelin Albert**, the bistro owner from Argeliers who stirred up the crowds during the "*Gueux du Midi*" uprising in 1907. *11120 Argeliers, ☎ 04 78 46 11 14. 8.30am-12pm, 2pm-6pm.*

Take the D 426 S, then turn right onto the D 5 and continue to Cabezac. From there, turn right onto the D 26.

Bize-Minervois

This village surrounded by hills is an olive-growing centre; the oil is marketed by the **Oulibo** cooperative. Guided tours of the cooperative in summer *(no charge)*. *Hameau de Cabezac, 11120 Bize-Minervois, ☎ 04 68 41 88 88, contact@loulibo.com Winter: Mon-Fri 8am-12pm, 2pm-6pm; summer: Mon-Fri 8am-12pm, 2pm-7pm, Sat and Sun from 10am. Closed at Christmas and New Year.*

Continue along the D 26 then turn left onto the D 177.

Saint-Jean-de-Minervois

In an austere landscape of *causse* (limestone plateau) dotted with a few *capitelles*, the old twisted Muscat vines take all the goodness from the limestone scree to produce a fortified wine with a peerless bouquet. The **Coopérative du Muscat de St-Jean-de-Minervois** will give you a very warm welcome. *34360 St-Jean-de-Minervois, ☎ 04 67 38 17 97. Mon-Fri 8am-12pm, 2pm-4pm. If it is closed, there are several other sales outlets in the village.*

The **Domaine de Barroubio**, outside the village, is an excellent establishment *(see Shopping Guide)*.

Take the D 176 S and turn left onto the D 175 to get to Aigues-Vives. The D 910 will take you to Aigne.

Aigne

Vines are so much part of this attractive town that its coat of arms, on the church font, depicts a vine bearing bunches of grapes. Take a stroll around the winding streets before admiring the panorama on the road to Minerve.

Take the D 177 and D 907 to La Caunette.

La Caunette

This old fortified village still has a 13C monumental gateway. Outside the village, the Romanesque church of Notre-Dame is set amid charming scenery.

Take the D 10 to Minerve.

Minerve★

Minerve stretches out on a rocky promontory, a veritable island detached from the *causse* by the combined effects of glacial and then fluvial erosion. Dominating an arid, seemingly scorched passage crisscrossed by rugged gorges, the town occupies a very picturesque **site★★** boasting a number of rare features, such as its **natural bridges★**. Nothing remains of the proud fortress that stood atop this spur in the Middle Ages, and the echo of the Cathar tragedy caused here by Simon de Montfort is now muffled by an ocean of vineyards. In the narrow rue des Martyrs are a few crafts workshops and a number of wine-growers' shops.

Take the D 10^{EI} W out of Minerve then take the D 182 towards Cesseras.

Canyon de la Cesse

At the beginning of the Quaternary Era, the waters of the Cesse hollowed out a canyon, enlarging existing caves and making new ones.

Turn left onto the road to Cesseras, which leads down to the plain and vineyards. Go through Cesseras and turn right onto the D 168 to Siran. After 2km, turn right again.

Chapelle de Saint-Germain

This Romanesque chapel, which nestles in a grove of pine trees, is particularly interesting on account of the decoration of its apse.

Return to the D 168 and carry on towards Siran.

Chapelle de Centeilles★

North of Siran. Sun 3pm-5pm.

Surrounded by cypress trees, holm oaks and vines, this 13C chapel takes in a vast panorama. Beautiful 14C-15C **frescoes★** inside.

Take the D 168 to La Livinière.

La Livinière

This wine-growing village has lent its name to the AOC Minervois-La-Livinière, which produces red wines only, in five communes. Their powerful, fruity character sets them apart, and some fine examples are to be found at the **Domaine Piccinini** *(see Shopping Guide)*.

Take the D 168 SW.

🚶 Starting from **Félines-Minervois**, a 12km **footpath** *(3hr 30min, a̶* allows you to explore woods, *capitelles* and vineyards of the Miner *Turn back then turn right onto the D 52, before making a left turn to F̶*

Rieux-Minervois
Rieux boasts a beautiful 12C **church★** with an interior decorated with remarkable carved capitals. The **Domaine des Homs** has a good reputation *(see Shopping Guide).*

Carry on to Caunes-Minervois via the D 11, turning right onto the D 620.

Caunes-Minervois
The village is known for the red marble with grey and white veins quarried nearby and much sought after in the 18C. Two fine mansions stand round the town hall square: Hôtel Sicard (14C) with its corner mullioned window and **Hôtel d'Alibert** (16C), now a charming hotel and restaurant, which opens onto a delightful Renaissance courtyard. The abbey church of the former Benedictine abbey has retained its beautiful 11C Romanesque east end.

Outside the village, the welcoming cellar of the splendid **Château Villerambert-Julien** (16C) is a good place to stop to discover a wide range of local wines. The Château houses a small and tastefully arranged repository of wine-growers' tools. *11160 Caunes-Minervois, ☎ 04 68 78 00 01, contact@villerambert-julien.com 9am-11.30am, 1.30pm-6.30pm, Sat-Sun by appointment. No charge.*

Take the D 620 southwest to Carcassonne.

The Blanquette Trail

60km. Michelin Local Map 344, E 3-4. See itinerary ⑤ on the map on p. 254-255.
South of Carcassonne, the Limoux region remains very attached to its festive and cultural traditions. With respect to wine growing, its great originality is that it produces mainly sparkling wines under three different appellations: **Blanquette-de-Limoux**, **Crémant-de-Limoux** and **Blanquette Méthode Ancestrale**. Blanquette is made mainly with Mauzac grapes, while Crémant contains a good proportion of Chardonnay. The region also produces well-constructed red and white still wines under the **Limoux** appellation.

Carcassonne★★★
When you reach the outskirts of Carcassonne or see its outline from the motorway, prepare for a breathtaking sight. The town was renovated in the 19C by the architect Viollet-le-Duc and dominates the wine-growing plain, with the garrigue-covered mountains of the Corbières in the background.

The "Cité" of Carcassonne is the largest fortress in Europe. It consists of a fortified nucleus, the Château Comtal, and a double curtain wall: the outer ramparts, with 14 towers, separated from the inner ramparts (24 towers) by the outer bailey, or lists *(lices)*. The main entrance, the **Porte Narbonnaise**, is flanked by two massive towers which house temporary exhibitions of modern art.

The **rue Cros-Mayrevieille** leads directly to the castle, although visitors might prefer to take a less direct route through the medieval town, with its narrow, winding streets lined with many shops (crafts, souvenirs). To the right of place du Château is a large well, nearly 40m deep. Nearby, in rue St-Jean, is the **Imaginarium**. There are no collections here, but instead an interactive presentation of the Albigensian crusade: a historical show *(15min)*, a room with 13 illuminations, each with its own soundtrack, and a multimedia area. *From Easter to school holidays in early Nov, enquire about opening times. Closed 1 Jan, 25 Dec. 7€ (children: 4.75€). ☎ 04 68 47 78 78. www.art-hist.com/imaginarium*

Built in the 12C by Bernard Aton Trencavel, with its back to the Gallo-Roman fortified wall, the **Château comtal** was originally the palace of the viscounts. It was converted into a citadel after Carcassonne was made part of the royal estate in 1226. *Apr-Sep: guided tour (30min) 9.30am-6pm; Oct-Mar: 9.30am-5pm. Closed 1 Jan, 1 May, 11 Nov, 25 Dec. Admission fee payable – enquire for details. No charge 1st Sun Oct-Mar. ☎ 04 68 11 70 70. www.monum.fr*

Leave the castle and follow rue de la Porte-d'Aude on the left. The **Porte d'Aude** is the main feature of the **outer bailey**, the part between the two walls. It is reached by a fortified path from the lower town and is heavily defended on all sides. A tour of the outer bailey ends at the **Tour St-Nazaire**, a handsome square tower whose postern was only accessible up ladders. There is a viewing table at the top.

Enter the Cité through the Porte St-Nazaire. All that remains of the old **Basilique St-Nazaire★** consecrated in 1006, is the nave. The interior is a combination of Romanesque and Gothic architecture. The **stained-glass windows★★** (13C-14C) are considered the most interesting in the South of France. Remarkable **statues★★** adorn the chancel walls.

Drive S out of Carcassonne on the D 104.

Hilaire

discovery of the Blanquette's sparkle is traditionally attributed to the
Benedictine monks of St-Hilaire.
From the foot of the church apse, take the ramp to the trapezium-shaped **cloisters**
before entering the much altered Romanesque **church**. Inside, in the chapel on
the right, is the "ossuary of St Sernin", a sarcophagus believed to be the work of
the 12C Master of Cabestany, which depicts the life and martyrdom of the founder
of the church of Toulouse around the middle of the 3C.
Drive S along the D 51 to St-Polycarpe.

Saint-Polycarpe

Beneath the high altar of the **fortified church** various items from the old treasury
are on display: head reliquary (bare head) of St Polycarp, head reliquary of St
Benedict and a reliquary of the Holy Thorn, all 14C works, and fabrics from the
8C. The two side altars feature Carolingian decoration carved with knot-work and
palm leaves. On the walls and vault are the remains of 14C frescoes (restored).
Take the D 129 W.

Limoux

Limoux has gained quite a reputation for its carnival, which runs from January
to April; every Sunday, processions of masked people (the *"fécos"*) accompanied
by musicians dance through the arcades on place de la République. The town's
skyline is dominated by the distinctive outline of the Gothic spire of St Martin's
church, which overlooks the river. The lively narrow streets are still partly
enclosed within a fortified wall built in the 14C.
The large **Cave Coopérative Sieur d'Arques** (wine cooperative) is the main producer of Blanquette and Crémant-de-Limoux. Its meticulous selection procedures
result in high quality cuvées. Private tours and wine tastings with commentaries
are available by appointment. The cooperative organises an auction of white AOC
Limoux wines and devotes part of the funds raised to conservation of the local
architectural heritage. Wine appreciation and wine-tasting courses are organised.
*Av. de Carcassonne, 11300 Limoux, ☎ 04 68 74 63 00, vpc@sieurdarques.com 9am-
12pm, 2pm-7pm. No charge.*

Les Corbières

125km. Michelin Local Map 344, F-H 3-6. See itinerary [6] *on the map on p. 254-255.*
The Corbières, a mountainous region in the Aude *département* bordering on the
eastern Pyrenees, tower above the furrow of the Fenouillèdes. Here stand the
vertiginous fortresses that provided the stage for famous episodes of the Cathar
drama, surrounded by the spiny, sweet-smelling scrub known as garrigue.
The **AOC Corbières** is the biggest in the Languedoc region, covering 14 400ha.
After many years of producing table wines, the region underwent a radical transformation in the 1980s-1990s and now produces quality wines, making every effort
to bring out the individuality of its terroirs.
This drive provides an opportunity to visit several of the castles that played a part
in the Cathar epic. Be prepared for very strong winds. A hat, sturdy footwear, sun
cream and drinking water are essential. Binoculars may come in handy.

Maury

At the foot of the arid mountain pass known as the Grau de Maury, this village
has lent its name to an appellation of fortified wine, Maury, which is made from
Grenache Noir grapes growing on schist in vineyards covering 1 700ha. **Mas Amiel**
is the appellation's star estate. You can visit its open-air store of demijohns (3 000
in all), where the wine is left to age. Guided walks through the vineyards are also
possible. *66460 Maury, ☎ 04 68 29 01 02. 8am-6pm. Tours by appointment.*
You can also visit the **Vignerons de Maury** cooperative *(see Shopping Guide)*.
Take the D 117 W.

Saint-Paul-de-Fenouillet

This peaceful place was once a border town between France and Roussillon. One
of the local specialities is *biscottin*, a sort of almond biscuit.
The D 7 to Cubières follows a winding route before threading its way through the
vines. A big bend in the road reveals a view of the Canigou peak on the left.

Ermitage Saint-Antoine-de-Galamus

⬆ *Leave the car in the car park before the tunnel. 30min on foot there and back.*
The path runs down from the hermitage terrace (view of Canigou). The hermitage
building conceals the chapel in the dim depths of a natural cave.
The road enters the **Gorges de Galamus★★** and follows a very narrow corniche.
The gorge is so narrow and steep that one only gets rare glimpses of the mountain
stream gushing down below.
At Cubières, turn right onto the D 14.

Château de Peyrepertuse★★★

From the car park, follow a steep path up to the entrance (30min on foot; sturdy footwear advisable). Visitors should proceed with caution if the "cers" – a strong southwesterly wind – is blowing. Jun-Sep: 9am-8pm; Apr-May and Oct: 9am-7pm; Nov-Mar: 10am-5pm. Closed Jan. No access in stormy weather. 4€. ☎ 04 68 45 40 55. www.chateau-peyrepertuse.com

The craggy outline of the castle on its rocky spur can be seen clearly from the outskirts of Rouffiac, to the north. It is not only one of the finest examples of fortification in the Corbières, but also the biggest and probably the most evocative of the Cathar castles.

Peyrepertuse comprises two adjacent but separate castles, on the east (Peyrepertuse) and west (St-Georges) ends of the ridge, and measures 300m at its longest point.

Château de Quéribus★★

Audioguides available. Jul-Aug: 9am-8pm; Apr-Jun and Sep: 9.30am-7pm; Oct: 10am-6.30pm; Nov-Jan: 10am-5pm; Feb: 10am-5.30pm; Mar: 10am-6pm. Closed 3 weeks in Jan (excluding school holidays), 1 Jan, 25 Dec. 5€ (ticket also gives access to the Achille-Mir Theatre). ☎ 04 68 45 03 69.

This lofty castle seems to melt into the rock, looking for all the world like a thimble on a thumb. At an altitude of 729m, this sentinel watches over the plain of Roussillon, defying the winds. In 1255, it was the last Cathar fortress to be taken by the crusaders. Three successive lines of fortifications protect the two-storey polygonal keep. The high **Gothic hall★** has vaulting resting on a central pillar.

Cucugnan

Dominated by its restored mill, this village is well known for the sermon of its parish priest, a jewel of Oc folklore which was adapted into French by Alphonse Daudet. The tiny **Achille-Mir Theatre** on place du Platane hosts a theatre performance on the theme of the "Sermon du curé de Cucugnan". &

Jul-Aug: 10am-9pm; Apr-Jun and Sep: 10am-8pm; Oct: 10am-7pm; Mar: 10am-7pm; Feb: 10am-6.30pm; Nov-Dec: 10am-6pm. Closed 3 weeks in Jan (excluding school holidays), 1 Jan, 25 Dec. 5€ (ticket also gives access to the Château de Quéribus). ☎ 04 68 45 03 69.

Under the dual protection of the parish priest and the Château de Quéribus, the village of Cucugnan can quietly go about tending its vines; most of the wine is produced by the wine cooperative.

Continue along the D 14.

Padern

To reach the castle, follow the yellow-marked "sentier cathare", ⬚ 20min on foot there and back. The ruins are dangerous in places. The Château de Padern, now in ruins, was rebuilt in the 17C. Fine view of the village and the River Verdouble.

At the end of the D 14, turn left onto the D 611.

Tuchan

Tuchan is surrounded by Fitou vineyards.

Some good Muscat-de-Rivesaltes and Rivesaltes are also produced at the **Producteurs du Mont Tauch** wine cooperative. Visitors are welcomed in the converted cellar; a film recounts the vine cycle and reveals the secrets of wine-making. *11350 Tuchan, ☎ 04 68 45 41 08. Mon-Sat 11am-4pm. No charge.*

East of Tuchan, a surfaced path going through vineyards branches off the D 39 to the left and leads to Aguilar Castle.

Château d'Aguilar

10min on foot there and back from the parking area. Enter the enclosure from the SW.

Aguilar became a royal fortress in 1257. Built on top of a small rounded hill rising up from an ocean of vines, it was reinforced in the 13C on the orders of Louis IX. There is an attractive view of the vineyards in the Tuchan basin and, to the west, the ruins of Donneuve Castle.

Return to Tuchan and turn right onto the D 611 to Durban.

Durban-Corbières

The castle overlooking the village consists of a rectangular two-storey building. Durban is one of the terroirs shown to advantage by the Corbières AOC appellation.

Wine-growers' stone huts in the Corbières.

A. Thuillier/MICHELIN

Shopping Guide

INFORMATION

Conseil interprofessionnel des vins du Languedoc – *6 pl. des Jacobins - BP 221 - 11102 Narbonne Cedex -* ☎ *04 68 90 38 30 - www.languedoc-wines.com*

Maison des vins du Languedoc – *Mas de Saporta - 34970 Lattes -* ☎ *04 67 06 04 44 - www.coteaux-languedoc.com - Mon 1.30pm-5.30pm, Tue-Fri 10am-7pm, Sat 10am-1.30pm, 3.30pm-7pm.*

Syndicat des vignerons du Pic St-Loup – *Maison de la Charte - BP 18 - 34270 St-Mathieu-de-Tréviers -* ☎ *04 67 55 16 96 - www.pic-saint-loup.com*

AOC Picpoul-de-Pinet – *www.picpoul-depinet.com*

Maison des vins de St-Chinian – *1 av. de la Promenade - 34360 St-Chinian -* ☎ *04 67 38 11 69 - www.saint-chinian.com - 9am-12pm, 2pm-6.30pm.*

AOC Faugères – *www.faugeres.com*

Syndicat du cru minervois – *Château de Siran - av. du Château - 34210 Siran -* ☎ *04 68 27 80 00.*

AOC Limoux – *www.limoux-aoc.com*

Maison des terroirs en Corbières – *Le Château - 11200 Boutenac -* ☎ *04 68 27 73 00 - www.aoc-corbieres.com*

Maison des vignerons du Fitou – *RN 9 - 11480 La Palme -* ☎ *04 68 40 42 77 - www.cru-fitou.com*

Conseil interprofessionnel des vins du Roussillon – *19 av. de Grande-Bretagne - 66000 Perpignan -* ☎ *04 68 51 21 22 - www.vins-du-roussillon.com*

OVERVIEW

CHARACTERISTICS

Red wines – Crimson to deep purple when young; dark ruby to rich mahogany with age. Aromas of black or red berries, liquorice, fennel and spices during the first years. Hints of truffle, game and chocolate with age. They are generally smooth to the taste, and sometimes very tannic when young, quite quickly becoming more supple with age.

Dry white wines – Pale golden when young, more or less dark straw-coloured with age. Aromas of citrus fruit, exotic fruit, ripe grapes and pear when young, and of spices and currants with age.

Fortified wines – The Muscats have hints of lemon or menthol; Rivesaltes, Maurys and Banyuls have hints of cocoa and cherry when young, then develop aromas and flavours of grilled almonds, kirsch, honey and incense.

Rosé wines – Generally deep colours. Fruity, with hints of raspberry and redcurrant.

STORAGE

Red wines – Ageing varies greatly depending on the appellation. Most wines can be kept for at least 5 years, rarely more than 10.

Dry white wines and rosé wines – Most should be drunk within 5 years.

Fortified wines – Most Maurys, Rivesaltes and Banyuls can easily be kept for 10 to 20 years. Most Muscats should be drunk young.

PRICES

Vins de pays (local wines) – 3 to 11€.

AOC – 5 to 15€. Some Coteaux-du-Languedoc and outstanding *vins de pays* cost over 20€.

Fortified wines – 5 to 15€.

SHOPPING

WINE COOPERATIVES

Cave coopérative du Muscat-de-Frontignan – *14 av. du Muscat - 34110 Frontignan -* ☎ *04 67 48 12 26 or 04 67 48 93 20 - www.frontignan-cooperative.fr - Jun-Sep: guided tour (20min) 10am, 11am, 3.30pm, 4.30pm; shop: Jun-Sep: 9.30am-12.30pm, 3pm-7.30pm; Oct-May: 9.30am-12.30pm, 2.30pm-6.30pm - closed Christmas and New Year.*

Les Vignerons de Maury – *128 av. Jean-Jaurès - 66460 Maury -* ☎ *04 68 59 00 95 - a.majoral@vigneronsdemaury.com - 8am-12pm, 2pm-6pm - by appointment.* The Vignerons de Maury brings together 252 wine producers who run 1 454ha of the 1 755ha covered by the appellation. Every year, 6 to 7 million kilos of grapes are selected, destemmed and put into vats for fermentation. The originality of this terroir comes from the schist-marl soils that are exposed to an arid Mediterranean climate.

Les Vignobles du Rivesaltes – *1 r. de la Roussillonnaise - 66600 Rivesaltes -* ☎ *04 68 64 06 63 - vignobles.rivesaltais@wanadoo.fr - Mon-Sat 9am-12pm, 2pm-6pm - by appointment.* The Vignobles du Rivesaltais wine cooperative is made up of seven hundred small-scale wine-growers and is the result of the merger between the Salses-le-Château cooperative founded in 1927 and the Rivesaltes cooperative, which dates back to 1932. Its vineyards contain 3 000ha of vineyards spread over more than ten communes and planted with around twenty grape varieties, including Grenache Noir, Carignan, Syrah, Mourvèdre, Merlot, Maccabeu, Chardonnay, Grenache Blanc and Muscat.

Les Vins de Saint-Saturnin – *Rte Arboras - 34725 St-Saturnin-de-Lucian -* ☎ *04 67 96 61 52 - Mon-Fri 8am-12pm, 2pm-5pm - by appointment.* The 700ha of the wine cooperative's vineyards are set on the foothills of the Larzac plateau at an altitude of 300m. Carignan, Syrah, Grenache, Mourvèdre, Chenin, Marsanne and Bourboulenc are rooted in very stony clayey limestone soil. The cooperative's annual production currently stands at 3 500 000 bottles.

ESTATES

Mas de Daumas Gassac – *Daumas Gassac - 34150 Aniane -* ☎ *04 67 57 71 28 - contact@daumas-gassac.com - Mon-Sat 9.30am-12.30pm, 2pm-6.30pm.* Aimé Guibert understood the extraordinary qualitative potential of the subsoils of

Languedoc long before anyone else. His 100ha estate contains 45ha of vines grown according to traditional methods, using ploughs and "not the slightest chemical product". Although there are others hot on its heels, Daumas Gassac is still one of the best.

Domaine du Traginer – *16 av. du Puig-del-Mas - 66650 Banyuls-sur-Mer - ☎ 04 68 88 15 11 - www.traginer.com - Mon 3.30pm-7pm, Tue-Sat 10am-12.45pm and 3.30pm-7.30pm; boutique open Apr-Oct.* Jean-François Deu grows his vines according to organic methods. The soil is ploughed by a mule driven by a *traginer* ("mule driver" in Catalan), and the grapes are picked by hand. The resulting Banyuls and Collioures - which are of outstanding quality – have won several awards at the *Concours général agricole* (general agricultural competition).

Château La Voulte Gasparets – *11200 Boutenac - ☎ 04 68 27 07 86 - 9am-12pm, 2pm-6pm.* A great defender of Carignan, Patrick Reverdy runs one of the appellation's leading estates. Located on a terrace of ancient alluvium, the 60ha vineyard is planted with Grenache, Carignan, Syrah, Mourvèdre, Rolle and Maccabeu grapes. The vines are pruned into a goblet shape and the grapes picked by hand before vinification in concrete and stainless steel vats.

Clos Fantine – *La Liquière - 34480 Cabrerolles - ☎ 04 67 90 20 89.* In 1960, Jacques Andrieu restructured the vineyard, introducing an interesting policy of eco-friendly wine growing. His children, Olivier, Carole and Corinne, took up the torch in 1996 and continue to run the 22ha estate of vines planted on hillsides according to the same principles. Champions of the forgotten grape varieties, they have been marketing a cuvée made from the unfashionable Aramon grape – La Lanterne Rouge – since the harvest of 2002: no back-marker in the quality stakes! Likewise, their cuvée Valcabrières de Fantine is made from the Terret grape: uncommon, but more than just a collector's curio.

Château de Jau – *66600 Cases-de-Pène - ☎ 04 68 38 90 10 - daure@wanadoo. fr - Mon-Fri (open every day in summer) - 10am-7pm (in summer); 8am-5pm (in winter).* The Château's vineyard covers 134ha in the communes of Cases-de-Pène, Tautavel and Estagel. The vineyards planted with Syrah, Mourvèdre, Grenache, Carignan, Muscat, Vermentino, Maccabeu etc, are rooted in limestone plateaux, schistose marl and gravelly and clayey limestone soils. The vines are still grown according to traditional methods, and the grapes are picked both manually and mechanically.

SCEA Domaine de Cazal Viel – *Château Cazal Viel - Hameau Cazal Viel - 34460 Cessenon-sur-Orb - ☎ 04 67 89 63 15 - l-miquel@mnet.fr - 9am-12.30pm, 2pm-6pm - Sat-Sun by appointment.* This 85ha estate has belonged to Henri and Christiane Miquel since 1980. The vineyard covers 85ha of clayey limestone soil that is particularly well suited to viticulture. The

new barrel storehouse dates from 2003.

Domaine Jean-Michel Alquier – *34600 Faugères - ☎ 04 67 23 07 89 - jmalquier@yahoo.fr* Jean-Michel Alquier runs this 12ha estate, 11ha of which is dedicated to the production of red wine and 1ha to white wine. The Syrah, Grenache Noir, Mourvèdre, Marsanne, Grenache Blanc and Viognier grape varieties are planted in schistose soil, 80% of them on southeast facing slopes. The grapes are picked by hand, partially destemmed for traditional vinification, and fermentation times are long. The wines mature in barrels.

Domaine Ollier-Taillefer – *Rte de Gabian - 34320 Fos - ☎ 04 67 90 24 59 - by appointment.* The vineyards of this 25ha family-run estate stretch out over schistose hillsides. Grape varieties consist of Grenache, Carignan, Syrah and Mourvèdre for the production of red wines, and of Grenache Blanc, Roussanne and Rolle for the whites. Each grape variety is vinified separately and blended later. Since the 2001 harvest, the estate has been approved by eco-friendly organisation Terra Vitis, which combines *"lutte raisonnée" (see p. 25)* principles with a broader respect for the environment.

The Cellier des Templiers, at Banyuls.

L. Campion / MICHELIN

Clos de l'Anhel – *11220 Lagrasse - ☎ 04 68 43 18 12 - anhel@wanadoo.fr* The history of Clos de l'Anhel dates back to the meeting of two students, one of whom became an oenologist, the other a manager of wine-growing estates in the Corbières. In 2000, with a wealth of experience behind them, they created this estate. The 7ha vineyard, partly cultivated according to biodynamic methods, overlooks the Orbieu valley from an altitude of 220m. Half of it spreads out on shallow alluvial clayey limestone soils and the other half on soils consisting of a surface layer of gravelly, clayey limestone on top of a deeper second layer of clayey soil. The grapes are harvested by hand, vinification lasts around three weeks and 95% of maturing takes place in vats.

Château des Estanilles – *34480 Lenthéric - ☎ 04 67 90 29 25 - Mon-Fri 9.30am-5pm - by appointment.* Michel Louison left his native Savoie and in 1976 took over 20ha of abandoned vineyards in Lenthéric. In 1996 he was joined by his daughter Sophie, with whom he runs a 32ha vineyard planted on hillsides in schistose soils, applying *"lutte raisonnée" (see p. 25)* principles. Renovation work on the estate's buildings was completed in 2000, and the very modern cellar contains thermo-regulated stainless steel vats.

Domaine Piccinini – *Rte des Meulières - 34210 La Livinière - ☎ 04 68 91 44 32 - 8am-12pm, 1pm-6pm - by appointment.* Located in the Petit Causse area in the northeast of the Minervois, the vineyards of this family-run estate cover 15ha of clayey limestone soil. The vines - Syrah, Grenache, Carignan and Mourvèdre, which are on average 30 years old – benefit from maximum sunshine. The yield is controlled and the grapes picked by hand. The wines age in oak casks.

Domaine Força-Réal – *Mas de la Garrigue - 66170 Millas - ☎ 04 68 85 06 07 - info@forca-real.com* Old drought-resistant vines have taken deep root in this 40ha vineyard, and the yield is low (30 hl/ha on average). 10ha are devoted to growing olives. An underground storehouse for ageing the wines and a small wine-tasting cellar were built in 2002.

Domaine de la Capelle – *34110 Mireval - ☎ 04 67 78 15 14 - Mon-Sat 10am-7pm.* The estate has belonged to the Maraval family since 1865. The old vines, planted in very stony soils, cover 30ha. Vinification and bottling take place in storehouses in the cellar. The estate also produces red table wines.

Domaine d'Aupilhac – *28 r. du Plô - 34150 Montpeyroux - ☎ 04 67 96 61 19 - aupilhac@wanadoo.fr* The vineyard stretches out over 25ha, mainly in the locality of Aupilhac. The vines spread out on terraces below the castle of Le Castellas and benefit from a southeast facing location. Sylvain Fadat is today one of the wine-growers of Languedoc who receives the most media coverage: well-deserved success and recognition.

Château Pech-Redon – *Rte de Gruissan - 11100 Narbonne - ☎ 04 68 90 41 22 - bousquet@terre-net.fr - Mon-Sat 10am-12pm, 2pm-7pm.* At 150-180m, the Pech-Redon vineyard is the highest on the Massif de la Clape. Spreading over 41ha, it produces around 1 500hl per year in the three colours. Planted with Grenache Noir, Grenache Blanc, Syrah, Carignan, Mourvèdre, Cinsault and Bourboulenc, the vines are grown according to *"lutte raisonnée" (see p. 25)* principles and the grapes are picked exclusively by hand.

Domaine des Deux Ânes – *Rte de Sainte-Eugénie - 11440 Peyriac-de-Mer - ☎ 04 68 41 67 79 - mag-terrier@wanadoo. fr.* Travelling wine-growers Magali and Dominique have run vineyards in the Jura and the Mâconnais and Beaujolais regions. This unusual career path led these wine enthusiasts to discover the great potential of the terroirs of the Languedoc region, and in 2000 they purchased around twenty hectares on hillsides overlooking the Étangs de Bages and the sea. The vineyard benefits from a considerable amount of sunshine and little rainfall. The soils consist of soft rocks and a rather chalky red-brown earth, locally stony. These deep, ploughed soils enable the vines to resist drought. The vineyard produces mainly red wines from four grape varieties: Grenache Noir, Carignan, Mourvèdre and Syrah. The grapes are harvested by hand over a period of one month. The cellar is particularly functional, equipped with stainless steel vats, a thermoregulation system and barrels for maturing the wines. Organic farming methods were adopted in 2002.

Domaine de la Prose – *Rte de St-Georgesd'Orques - 34570 Pignan - ☎ 04 67 03 08 30 - domaine-de-la-prose@wanadoo.fr* In 1990, Patricia and Alexandre de Mortillet bought some vines surrounded by garrigue and holm oaks. They managed to regroup 30ha and plant vines in new parcels. In 1995, their son Bertrand, a young viticulture and oenology graduate, carried out his first vinification at the family's estate. In 2000, a new cellar was hollowed out of the rock.

Château de Pinet – *Vignobles Gaujal de St-Bon - 34850 Pinet - ☎ 04 68 32 16 67.* Passed down from father to son for two hundred and fifty years, the estate is now run by women: in the driving seat, Simone Arnaud-Gaujal, assisted by her pharmacist-oenologist daughter. The 50ha vineyard planted with Picpoul, Merlot, Syrah, Cabernet-Sauvignon, Grenache and Cinsault covers clayey limestone soils. The vines face south-southeast and are on average 25 to 50 years old. The Château's production is characterised by low yields.

Château de Lastours – *11490 Portel-des-Corbières - ☎ 04 68 48 29 17 - portel. chateaudelastours@wanadoo.fr* The Château has 104ha of vines planted on terraces in the middle of 600ha of garrigue. The clayey limestone soil and a sunny microclimate result in generous wines. In the context of a *Centre d'aide par le travail (CAT)*, sixty handicapped people work on the estate and run the vineyard.

Les Clos de Paulilles – *Baie de Paulilles - 66660 Port-Vendres - ☎ 04 68 38 90 10 - daure@wanadoo.fr - Mon-Sat 10am-12pm, 2pm-7pm.* This 90ha estate belonging to the

D. Pazery / MICHELIN

9

Dauré family - who also own the Château de Jau and Mas Cristine – has proved to be one of the stars of the appellation. The vineyard, which is all in one block, surrounds the listed site of Paulilles. Except for the terraced parcels, it is cultivated according to *"lutte raisonnée"(see p. 25)* principles.

Domaine des Homs – *Rte de Puichéric - 11160 Rieux-Minervois - ☎ 04 68 78 10 51 - jm.decrozals@free.fr – open every day 8am-7.30pm - by appointment.* Set at the foot of the Montagne Noire, the estate has belonged to the de Crozals family for three generations. The 20ha estate is planted with Syrah, Grenache, Mourvèdre, Carignan and Cinsault. The vines are tended in the traditional manner: trimming off some grapes and leaves to allow others to grow *(vendanges vertes)*, working the soil and harvesting by hand. Vinification involves a long fermentation time in vats and half of the production is put into Burgundy barrels.

Domaine Cazes – *4 r. Francisco-Ferrer - BP61 - 66600 Rivesaltes - ☎ 04 68 64 08 26 - info@cazes-rivesaltes.com - Mon-Sat 8am-12pm (12.30pm in summer), 2pm-6pm (7pm in summer) - by appointment.* The vineyard, created in the early 19C, now covers 160ha. Around twelve grape varieties are rooted in its clayey limestone soils and produce about fifteen wines using biodynamic methods.

Domaine La Madura – *12 r. de la Digue - 34360 St-Chinian - ☎ 04 67 38 17 85 - lamadura@wanadoo.fr* The vineyard purchased by Nadia and Cyril Bourgne in 1998 is located on the outskirts of Saint-Chinian on hillsides of clayey limestone, schist and sandstone, at altitudes of between 150 and 300m. The 14ha of vines are tended with care and in an environmentally friendly manner in order to obtain grapes that concentrate all the specific characteristics *(typicité)* and richness of their terroir. During vinification and maturing, the wine-growers focus on respecting the grapes harvested in order to bring out the elegance and complexity of this vineyard. This is reflected in blends *(assemblages)* of the estate's various terroirs and grape varieties – those southen champions Grenache, Mourvèdre, Syrah and Carignan.

Château Puech-Haut – *2250 rte de Teyran - 34160 St-Drézéry - ☎ 04 99 62 27 27 - domainesbru@wanadoo.fr - Mon-Sat - by appointment.* Located in the commune of St-Drézéry, this 100ha vineyard – 90ha of which is in production – stretches out over clayey limestone soils covered in round pebbles. The grape varieties are Syrah, Carignan, Grenache and Mourvèdre for the red wines; Roussanne, Marsanne and Grenache Blanc for the whites. Each grape variety is vinified and matured separately. The wines are then aged in oak casks and bottled on the estate.

Domaine Haut-Lirou – *34270 St-Jean-de-Cuculles - ☎ 04 67 55 38 50 - Domaine. Haut.Lirou@mnet.fr - Mon-Sat (open every day in summer).* This estate's 60ha of vines stretch out over the clayey limestone slopes of the last foothills of the Cévennes. A family-run estate for five generations, it was

entirely replanted by current owners Jean-Pierre and Maryse Rambier. The vineyard is planted with Grenache, Syrah, Mourvèdre, Cabernet-Sauvignon and Sauvignon Blanc, with a few parcels of Vieux Carignan and Cinsault, and *"lutte raisonnée" (see p. 25)* principles are applied. The grapes are harvested by hand before traditional vinification, and maceration times are long. The wines age twelve to sixteen months in the barrel.

Domaine de Barroubio – *34360 St-Jean-de-Minervois - ☎ 04 67 38 14 06 - 9am-12pm, 3pm-7pm.* A family-run estate since the 15C, the Domaine de Barroubio covers 27ha on a limestone plateau and is planted with Muscat à Petits Grains, Carignan, Syrah and Grenache. The terroir favours the production of *Vin du pays d'oc*, matured in the traditional way. The red wines are matured in barrels.

Domaine Devois du Claus – *38 impasse du Porche - 34270 St-Mathieu-de-Tréviers - ☎ 04 67 55 37 19 58) - devoisduclaus@9online.fr* The estate was created in 1998 by André Gely, son, grandson and great-grandson of wine-growers, and covers 27ha. Set at the foot of Pic St-Loup, the Cévennes foothills, the vineyard is planted on slopes with clayey limestone soils that benefit from a Mediterranean climate. Syrah, Grenache, Merlot, Carignan and Cabernet-Sauvignon are grown in the traditional way: they trim off some grapes and leaves to allow others to grow *(vendanges vertes)*, prune the vines into the old-style "goblet" form and harvest manually. Fermentation in vats lasts twenty-eight days and the wines mature for fourteen months in vats and oak casks.

Domaine Peyre Rose – *Rte de Villeveyrac - 34230 St-Pargoire - ☎ 04 67 98 75 50 - Mon-Sat - by appointment.* Marlène Soria is one of the region's recognised wine-growers. She created this 25ha estate in 1983. The grape varieties consist of Syrah, Grenache and Mourvèdre, grown using biodynamic methods. Vinification is traditional and the wines mature in barrels.

Domaine de l'Hortus – *34270 Valflaunès - ☎ 04 67 55 31 20 - domaine. hortus@wanadoo.fr - Mon-Sat 8am-12pm, 3pm-6pm - Sun by appointment.* The estate's vineyards, created in 1978, cover 55ha planted with Mourvèdre, Syrah and Grenache for the red wines; Chardonnay, Viognier, Roussanne and Sauvignon for the whites. They are rooted in clayey limestone soils. One of the two red wines is matured in oak casks for between thirteen and fifteen months, while one of the two white wines ferments in new barrels. The Orliac family runs another estate, Clos du Prieur, which covers 10ha in St-Jean-de-Buèges, at the foot of the Larzac plateau.

SCEA Domaine des Chênes – *7 r. du Mar.-Joffre - 66600 Vingrau - ☎ 04 68 29 40 21 - domainedeschenes@wanadoo. fr.* Purchased by the Razungles family in 1919, the estate was given a new lease of life in the late 1980s by Gilbert, Simone and their son Alain. The vineyard's 30ha are planted on exceptional terroirs on the steep foothills of the Hautes Corbières. The yield is intentionally limited and the grapes are picked by hand.

WALKING TOURS OF THE VINEYARDS

De vignes en caves – *Information and booking at CDT des Pyrénées-Orientales*

(tourist board) - ☎ *04 68 51 52 53.* Six days' hiking on your own or with a guide in the Côtes-du-Roussillon appellation area. Each day, you'll explore a terroir and its natural and cultural heritage and enjoy a picnic and wine tasting. Accommodation is provided by the producers. A similar itinerary is available in the Collioure and Banyuls areas.

The combination of black schist and clayey limestone soils results in high-flying cuvées such as those of **Château Haut-Gléon**. Every summer there is an exhibition of works by the young artists invited to the Château to paint on the theme of vines. *CD 611, Villesèque-des-Corbières, 11360 Durban-Corbières, ☎ 04 68 48 85 95, info@gleon-montanie.com 9am-12.30pm, 1.30pm-6pm.*

Take the D 40 W out of Durban.

Villerouge-Termenès

At the heart of the village stands the castle with its four towers (12C and 14C). It was owned by the archbishops of Narbonne and in 1321 was the scene of the burning at the stake of the last Cathar Parfait, Guillaume Bélibaste. The castle has been renovated and now houses an audiovisual exhibition on Bélibaste and on daily life in the Middle Ages. One wing of the castle houses a medieval restaurant (La Rôtisserie), which serves 13C and 14C dishes – with the same decorum – as well as hypocras, a wine flavoured with plants and spices. *Jul-Aug: 9.30am-7.30pm (last admission 1hr before closing); Apr-Jun and from beginning of Sep to mid-Oct: 10am-6pm; Feb-Mar, from mid-Oct to end of Dec: some weekends, public holidays and school holidays: 10am-5pm. Closed in Jan. 5€. ☎ 04 68 70 09 11 or 04 68 70 04 89.*

Carry on to Talairan on the D 613.

Talairan

The chapel of Notre-Dame-de-l'Aire (13C-14C), which dominates the village, contains a touching St Vincent holding two bunches of grapes. If you wish to take a look, contact Jean-Pierre Mazard at the **Domaine Serres-Mazard**; he can tell you all about the vineyards and also about the wild orchids in the region, which are a passion of his. *11220 Talairan, ☎ 04 68 44 02 22. 8am-8pm.*

Turn back and then turn right onto the D 23.

Lagrasse★

With its fragile bridges, ruined ramparts and old houses, Lagrasse is a striking sight. Set on the banks of the River Orbieu, the town serves as the setting for a famous abbey. The surrounding area constitutes one of the best terroirs of the Corbières, as illustrated in particular by **Clos de l'Anhel** *(see Shopping Guide)*.

A pleasant stroll through the narrow streets will take you past medieval houses where a number of craftsmen have set up their workshops.

The **Abbaye Ste-Marie-d'Orbieu** consists of a palace and a church with a 13C **bell-tower** that affords an attractive view from the top. The **abbot's chapel★** opens onto the courtyard of the **Palais vieux** and has some rare 14C ceramic paving with geometric motifs. On the upper floor of the Palais Vieux is the monks' dormitory with its fine timber frame. A staircase leads, via the "pre-Romanesque tower", to the cellars, store rooms and bakery are located. *Jul-Aug: 10.30am-7pm; Apr-Jun and Sep-Oct: 10.30am-12.30pm, 2pm-6.15pm; from beginning of Nov to mid-Dec and from mid-Jan to mid-Mar: 2pm-5.30pm. 2.50€. ☎ 04 68 43 15 99.*

Take the D 212 N of Lagrasse.

Lézignan-Corbières

In the undulating landscape of the Corbières, half way between Carcassonne and the sea, Lézignan is a small active town which relies on wine-growing and the wine trade. You can explore the tiny squares and alleyways around the church of St-Félix, and enjoy the shade of the promenades lined with plane trees.

The **Musée de la Vigne et du Vin** is a vine and wine museum that has been set up in an old vineyard. The main courtyard opens onto the saddle room, the stables and a winepress, and under an awning are displayed the tools of the now vanished cooper's trade. The winemaking cellar contains a large vat for treading the grapes. On the first floor, the tools used for tending the vine are displayed by season, and include swing ploughs, pruning shears, grafting knives, back-baskets, wooden tubs, funnels and branding irons. A room near the information desk is devoted to wine transport along the Canal du Midi from the 18C to the present time. The museum also offers an introduction to tastes and smells. ♿ *9am-7pm. 5.35€, no charge during the Semaine du Goût (Tasting Week). ☎ 04 68 27 07 57.*

Return to Narbonne via the N 113.

La Clape and Fitou

137km. Michelin Local Map 344, I-J 3-5. See itinerary **7** *on the map on p. 254-255.*

To the west and south of Narbonne the vines sweep down to the sea and cover the slopes overlooking the lagoons. The nearby Mediterranean tempers the heat of the sun a little, but the wines still have plenty of character. The small limestone island that forms La Clape mountain has become joined to the continent by the process of silting. This great "pile of stones", which rises to a height of 214m, is crowned by pine trees and garrigue which give way to well-ordered vineyards on the slopes down to the sea. The **AOC Coteaux-du-Languedoc-La-Clape**, which covers 625ha, produces heady red wines, fruity rosé wines and robust white wines.

The **Fitou** territory, split, unusually, into two parts, yields full-bodied wines.

Take the D 168 E out of Narbonne.

Narbonne-Plage☺

This resort stretching along the coast is typical of the traditional Languedoc seaside resorts.

The D 332 S leads to Gruissan.

Gruissan☺

Gruissan is no longer isolated in the middle of lagoons as it once was, but the very distinctive houses of fishermen and wine-growers still coil around the ruins of the castle. The houses of the **old village**, home to fishermen and salt-pan workers, are set out in concentric circles around the ruins of the Barbarossa tower.

Cimetière marin

🚶 *4km, then 30min on foot there and back. Leave Gruissan on the D 32 to Narbonne. At the crossroads beyond the tennis courts, take the road signposted to N.-D.-des-Auzils into the Massif de la Clape and keep left all the way. Leave the car in the car park (in front of the Rec d'Argent nursery) and walk up to the chapel. If you prefer, you can drive the 1.5km of forest track signposted to Les Auzils, leave the car on a piece of rough ground and continue on foot.*

All along a stony path, among the broom, umbrella pines, holm oaks and cypresses, are touching memorials and plaques to sailors lost at sea. From the **Chapel of Notre-Dame-des-Auzils** in the heart of a thicket at the top of the hill, there is an extensive view over Gruissan and La Clape mountain.

Follow the little road across the lower slopes of La Clape. On reaching the D 32, turn right towards Narbonne. At Ricardelle, take a steep, narrow little road on the right.

Coffre de Pech Redon

This marks the summit of La Clape mountain. From it, there is a scenic view over the lagoons and Narbonne. The stony soil, which looks rather inhospitable, provides a happy home for the vineyards of **Château Pech-Redon** *(see the Shopping Guide).*

Turn back and return to Narbonne on the D 32. Stay on the city's ring road until you reach the N 9 in the S. Turn left onto the D 105 passing under the motorway. The road runs alongside the Bages lagoon (Étang de Bages).

Peyriac-de-Mer

This village with its 14C fortified church stands on the shores of the little Étang du Doul, a welcome stopping place for migratory birds. The nearby **Domaine des Deux Ânes**, which uses organic farming methods, produces some interesting red wines *(see Shopping Guide).*

Réserve africaine de Sigean★

♿ *Apr-Sep: 9am-6.30pm; rest of the year: 9am-4pm. 21€ (children: 17€).* ☎ *04 68 48 20 20. www.reserveafricainesigean.fr*

📷 A paradise for pink flamingos, egrets and gulls, the wild landscape of the Sigean African Safari Park stretches for 300ha along the coast. Large areas of garrigue dotted with lagoons have been made to resemble the species' original native environment as closely as possible. Visitors who are quiet and patient enough, and equipped with a good pair of binoculars, will be rewarded with sightings of lions, zebras and antelopes.

Take the D 611^A to Portel-des-Corbières.

Portel-des-Corbières

The **Château de Lastours**, southwest of the village, is one of the Corbières' most famous wine-growing estates *(see Shopping Guide).*

A botanical path leads to the entrance of **Terra Vinea**, a former gypsum quarry converted into cellars where the wines of the cooperatives operating under the name of Caves Rocbère are left to age. Visitors can learn about the wine-growing activity in the old quarrying galleries. A Gallo-Roman villa illustrates life in ancient times. Wine-tasting at the end of the tour. ⟨ *Jun-Aug: guided tour (1hr 15min) 10.30am-6.30pm; Apr-May and Sep: 10.30am, 2.30pm-5.30pm; Oct: 2.45pm, 3.30pm and 4pm; Feb-Mar: 2.30pm, 3.15pm, 4pm, 4.45pm. Closed 1 Jan, 25 Dec. 5€ (children: 2.50€).* ☎ *04 68 48 64 90. www.terra-vinea.com*

Take the D 3 towards Sigean, and at the roundabout take the second road on the right (D 205). The road starts by winding through a rocky landscape where pines and holm oaks stand at the mercy of fierce winds. Then, before reaching Fraissé-des-Corbières, a dense host of vine plants invades the landscape, covering the red earth shared by the Fitou and Corbières appellations.

Take the D 50 to Fitou. In a heroic struggle against the wind, the vineyards, protected by cypress hedges, nestle in the most sheltered recesses of the surrounding bare mountains. Between Treilles and Fitou the landscape is sublime.

Fitou

This seaside village has given its name to an appellation which covers 2 565ha in two separate areas: Fitou Maritime and Haut Fitou. The traditional Fitou, matured in tuns, is appreciated for its *tuilé* (reddish-brown) colour and slightly oxidative character. The more fruity, new-style Fitou is very similar to Corbières.

Take the N 9 S to Perpignan.

The Roussillon Wine Route

185km. Michelin Local Map 344, G-J 5-8. See itinerary **8** *on the map on p. 254-255.*

Roussillon, united with France under Louis XIV, has for a long time reaped the benefits of its dessert wines, of which Spain was particularly fond. Proud of its Catalan identity, the region is full of charm and always reserves a warm welcome for visitors. There are three major production areas here: the **Côtes-du-Roussillon-Villages** to the north of Perpignan, **Côtes-du-Roussillon** to the south, and **Collioure** and **Banyuls** on the coast, near the border with Spain. The **Rivesaltes** and **Muscat-de-Rivesaltes** fortified wines are produced throughout Roussillon.

Perpignan★★

Both close to the sea and to the Pyrenees, Perpignan is still part of France but also very much part of Catalonia. Walks shaded by plane trees, cafés serving tapas with aperitifs, and a pace of life between siesta and busy nightlife are all part of Perpignan's appeal. Here, the architecture speaks of the past: of the counts of Roussillon and the kings of Majorca, of the Catalans and the people of Aragon, and of the French.

Le Castillet★, an emblem of Perpignan, dominates place de la Victoire with its two towers crowned with crenellations and machicolations. It houses the Casa Pairal, which is devoted to the popular arts and traditions of the Catalans.

The **place de la Loge** and the pedestrianised rue de la Loge form the lively centre of town life. In the centre, the **Loge de Mer★** housed a commercial tribunal for maritime matters in the 16C. In the arcaded courtyard of the **Hôtel de Ville★** stands a bronze by Aristide Maillol, entitled *The Mediterranean*.

The **Cathédrale St-Jean★**, begun in 1324 by Sancho, second king of Majorca, was not consecrated until 1509. The façade of bricks and pebbles is flanked by a square tower with a fine 18C wrought-iron campanile. The impressive nave rests on robust interior buttresses separating the chapels, which feature sumptuous 16C and 17C altarpieces.

Away from the town centre, on the hill of Puig del Rey, stands the **Palais des Rois de Majorque★**, a palace built during the reign of the kings of Majorca (1276-1344). Today the Queen's suite (superb ceiling painted with Catalan colours) and the Flamboyant Gothic style chapel-keep are open to the public. *Jun-Sep: 10am-6pm (last admission 30min before closing time); Oct-May: 9am-5pm. Guided tours by prior arrangement. Closed 1 Jan, 1 May, 1 Nov, 25 Dec. 4€ (children: 2€).* ☎ *04 68 34 96 26.*

To return to the world of wine, we suggest a trip to the **Comptoir des Crus**, where the terroirs of Roussillon are presented with the aid of geological samples; wine tasting in the company of the producers and a magnificent choice of wines from the region. *67 r. du Gén.-Leclerc, 66000 Perpignan,* ☎ *04 68 35 54 44. Tue-Sat 9.30am-12.30pm, 2.30-7.30pm.*

Take the D 117 N out of Perpignan.

Rivesaltes

This is one of the wine-producing capitals of Roussillon and the birthplace of Maréchal Joffre (1852-1931), a statue of whom graces the main square. The name of Rivesaltes is attached to that of Muscat, although **Muscat-de-Rivesaltes** is produced throughout the *département*. Several producers are to be found on

the beautiful avenues in the town centre. The **Vignobles du Rivesaltais** wine cooperative brings together the wine-growers of Rivesaltes and Salses-le-Château; the **Domaine Caze** is a safe bet *(see Shopping Guide)*.
Take the D 12 NW to Vingrau.

Vingrau

Tautavel Man, the oldest European human fossil, could have been called Vingrau Man since the Caune de l'Arago cave where he was discovered is closer to Vingrau than to Tautavel. A narrow hillside path leads up to the cave, but the excavation site is closed to the public.

Present-day Vingrau Man is above all a wine-grower, producing good Rivesaltes like those at the **Domaine des Chênes** *(see Shopping Guide)*.
Take the D 9 S to Tautavel.

Tautavel

The man who lived in this area 700 000 years BC has been named after the town of Tautavel. The **Centre européen de préhistoire★★** (European Centre of Prehistory) enables visitors to appreciate the wealth of this important place from the past. The rooms are equipped with interactive consoles and video screens illustrating man's place in the universe and the lifestyle of Tautavel Man. The main attraction is the reproduction of the Caune de l'Arago. ⟐ *Jul-Aug: 10am-8pm; Apr-Jun and Sep: 10am-12.30pm, 1.30pm-7pm; Jan-Mar and Oct-Dec: 10am-12.30pm, 1.30pm-5.30pm. Closed 1 Jan, 25 Dec. 7€ (children: 3.50€). ☎ 04 68 29 07 76. www. tautavel.com*

Another museum on the same theme is the **Musée de la Préhistoire européenne – Préhistorama**. Five "virtual theatres" offer visitors 3D illustrations of the daily life of Europe's first inhabitants. ⟐ *Jul-Aug: 11am-9pm; Apr-Jun and Sep: 11am- 1.30pm, 2.30pm-8pm; Jan-Mar and Oct-Dec: 11am-1.30pm, 2.30pm-6pm. 3.20€ (children 7-14: 1.60€). ☎ 04 68 29 07 76. www.tautavel.com*

Les Maîtres Vignerons de Tautavel, next to the Centre of Prehistory, will give you a very warm welcome and offers a large number of interesting cuvées. Free admission to an exhibition on the work of wine-growers through the seasons. *24 av. Jean-Badia, 66720 Tautavel, ☎ 04 68 29 12 03, vignerons.tautavel@wanadoo.fr 8am-12pm, 2pm-6pm. By appointment.*
Take the D 59 S.

Cases-de-Pène

A picturesque road joins the Agly Valley at Cases-de-Pène, a wine-growing area of which the **Château de Jau** is the star attraction *(see Shopping Guide)*. A walk up to the **Ermitage Notre-Dame-de-Pène** will reward you with a fine panorama.

Estagel

This is the birthplace of the great physicist and politician **François Arago** (1786-1853) and an important wine-growing centre that produces good Côtes-du-Roussillon-Villages.
Continue W to Latour-de-France along the D 17.

Latour-de-France

The remains of a castle stand in this one-time border village. The Macabeu grape thrives on the schist and produces remarkable Rivesaltes.
Take the D 79 and turn right onto the D 612. At the Col de la Bataille, turn right onto the D 38.

Ermitage de Força Réal

A 17C chapel stands on the summit (altitude 507m). There is a magnificent **panorama★★** over the plain, the coast from Cap Leucate to Cap Béar, the Albères mountains and Mont Canigou.
Return to the Col de la Bataille and go straight ahead. A pleasant stretch of road along the crest between the valleys of the Têt and the Agly leads to the Col and then to the **Château de Caladroy**, in the middle of a park planted with exotic trees.

Bélesta

This remarkable village perched on a rocky outcrop rising up out of the surrounding vineyards used to be a border town between the kingdoms of Aragon and France. The town has been of interest for some time to archaeologists who have found numerous prehistoric remains, including a collective grave dating from roughly 6 000 years ago (Middle Neolithic). Visitors can see a reconstruction of the archaeological site at the **Château-Musée**. *From mid-Jun to mid-Sep: 2pm-7pm; from mid-Sep to mid-Jun except Tue and Sat: 2pm-5.30pm. Closed 1 Jan, 24, 25 and 31 Dec. 4.50€. ☎ 04 68 84 55 55 or 04 68 84 51 73 (town hall).*
Take the D 21 S. The road bends back into a little valley dominated by amazing geological formations consisting of *cheminées de fées* or "fairy chimneys", columns of soft rock eroded by rain and capped with hard, erosion-resistant conglomerate; they are known as the **Orgues★** or "Organ Pipes" of **Ille-sur-Têt**. These phenomena are grouped on two sites, one of which, to the east, is accessible to the public.

In the centre stands an impressive fairy chimney known as "the Sibyl". *Jul-Aug: 9.30am-8pm; Apr-Jun and Sep: 10am-6.30pm; Feb-Mar: 10am-12.30pm, 2pm-5.30pm; school holidays: 10am-5.30pm; Oct: 10am-12.30pm, 2pm-6pm; Nov-Jan: 2pm-5pm. Last admission 45min before closing time. Closed 1 Jan, 25 Dec. 3.50€. ☎ 04 68 84 13 13. www.ille-sur-tet.com*

Drive to Ille-sur-Têt then turn left onto the D 916. You can make one last stop at **Millas**, at the **Domaine Força Réal**, from where there is an extraordinary view of the plain of Roussillon *(see Shopping Guide)*.

Take the D 612 SE then turn right onto the D 58 and cross the D 615 to go to Castelnou.

Calstelnou★

The tiny cobbled streets of this splendid fortified village are clustered around the foot of the 10C feudal **castle**, remodelled in the 19C. Several rooms are open to the public. *Jun-Sep: 10am-7pm; Feb-May: 10.30am-6pm; Oct-Dec: 11am-5pm. Closed Jan (except Sat-Sun 11am-5pm). 4.50€. ☎ 04 68 53 22 91.*

Take the D 48^E.

Thuir

Thuir is known mainly for its wine cellars, the **Caves Byrrh**. The "Cellier des Aspres" offers information on local wines and crafts in neighbouring villages. ♿ *Jul-Aug: guided tour (45min) 10am-11.45am, 2pm-6.45pm; Apr-Jun and Sep-Oct: 9am-11.45am, 2.30pm-5.45pm; Nov-Mar: by prior arrangement. Closed Sun in Apr (except Easter Sunday), Sat-Sun in Oct and 1 May. 1.60€. ☎ 04 68 53 05 42.*

Take the D 612^E.

Elne★

This little town surrounded by ramparts is the oldest in Roussillon. The superb **cloisters★★** of the **Cathédrale Ste-Eulalie-et-Ste-Julie★** testify to Elne's former splendour. Building work began on the cathedral in the 11C and was completed in the 14C-15C. The superb capitals (12C-14C) on the columns are decorated with imaginary animals, biblical figures and plants. From the east gallery, a spiral staircase rises to a terrace from which there is a fine view of the surrounding area. *Jun-Sep: 9.30am-7pm; Apr-May and Oct: 9.30am-6pm; Nov-Mar: 9.30am-12pm, 2pm-5pm. Closed 1 Jan, 1 May, 25 Dec. 4€ (children: 1.50€). ☎ 04 68 22 70 90.*

Take the N 114 to Collioure. After Argelès, the road reaches the first foothills of the Albères mountain range, from then on endlessly crossing the spurs that form headlands washed by the Mediterrean.

Collioure★★

With its fortified church next to the sea, its two little ports with their bobbing Catalan boats, its old castle, anchovies and wine, Collioure is a delight for both the eyes and the palate.

The AOC Collioure has just 480ha and covers the same area as the AOC Banyuls. Collioure Blanc recently joined the red and rosé wines. The disused church of the old Dominican monastery (13C) on the road to Port-Vendres now houses **Le Dominicain** wine cooperative. *Pl. Orphila, Port d'Avall, 66190 Collioure, ☎ 04 68 82 05 63. 8am-12pm, 2pm-6pm.*

A waymarked route through Collioure, the **Chemin du Fauvisme**, leads past some of the views painted by Henri Matisse and André Derain. Each stage – there are 20 in all – is indicated by the reproduction of the relevant painting on a panel. *Guided tours are also available (Thu); contact the tourist office or Espace Fauve. ☎ 04 68 98 07 16.*

Port-Vendres⌂

Port-Vendres grew up around a cove that offered convenient shelter for galleys, and its development as a naval port and stronghold really took off in 1679, under the influence of Louis XIV's military architect and strategist Vauban. It is today the busiest fishing port on the Roussillon coast.

As you continue along the N 114, be sure to stop off at the **Clos de Paulilles** estate, which not only produces good Banyuls and Collioures, but is also a farm inn *(see the Directory and Shopping Guide)*.

Banyuls-sur-Mer⌂

This charming town is France's most southerly seaside resort. It stretches out around a pretty bay, overlooked by terraced vineyards which produce the fortified wines of the AOC Banyuls, and also Collioure wines.

The youngest and most fruity Banyuls are called *"Rimage"*. When they have matured in tuns for at least thirty months, they become Banyuls Grand Cru. The bunches of grapes are left to macerate with an added grape spirit which causes the fermentation to stop (this is called *mutage*) and encourages the development of aromas. After being left to age for a long time in oak vats or in glass demijohns that are exposed to sunshine, Banyuls is drunk as an aperitif or with dessert. The **Domaine Traginer** is a good address *(see Shopping Guide)*.

The **Grande Cave** shows a video on the history of Banyuls and organises a guided tour of the place where the oak vats are kept, where the wines are left to age in the sun, and the cellars with their ancient casks. *Apr-Oct: guided tour (45min) 10am-7.30pm; Nov-Mar: 10am-1pm, 2.30pm-6.30pm. Closed 1 Jan, 25 Dec. Admission free.* ☎ *04 68 98 36 92. www.banyuls.com*
Take the little D 86 SW out of Banyuls. The picturesque road with its endless views of the slopes passes in front of the underground cellar of Mas Reig, set in the oldest wine-growing estate of the Banyuls terroir. The **Cellier des Templiers-Cave du Mas Reig** dates from the days of the Knights Templar (13C), whose

Banyuls matures in the sun (Cellier des Templiers).

J. Malbure/MICHELIN

feudal castle and sub-commandery (Mas Reig) are nearby. ♿ *Jul-Aug: guided tour (45min) 11am-7.30pm. No charge.* ☎ *04 68 98 36 92. www.banyuls.com*
Continue along the D 86 to Collioure. If you wish to return to Perpignan, cross the plain of Roussillon on the N 114.

Fine Buildings in Fine Settings

Abbaye de Fontfroide★★

15km SW of Narbonne, via the N 113, turning left onto the D 613, and then along a tiny little road, keeping left. The reception is located in the abbey farm, about one hundred metres below the abbey. This building, which dates back to the 13C, houses the ticket office, a bookshop, cellar and restaurant. From mid-Jul to end of Aug: guided tour (1hr 10min) 9.30am-6pm; from beginning of Apr to mid-Jul: 10am-12.15pm, 1.45pm-5.30pm; Nov-Mar: 10am-12pm, 2pm-4pm. 7.25€. ☎ *04 68 45 11 08. www.fontfroide.com*
This old Cistercian abbey lies tucked almost out of sight deep in a little valley in a peaceful setting surrounded by cypress trees. The fine flame-coloured shades of ochre and pink in the Corbières sandstone used to build the abbey enhance the serenity of the sight, particularly at sunset. Most of the abbey buildings date back to the 12C and 13C. The conventual buildings were restored in the 17C and 18C. The setting is delightful, with rose-filled courtyards and superb terraced gardens.
🚶 *Various footpaths enable visitors to walk around the abbey and fully appreciate the charms of its setting.*

Ancient cathedral of Maguelone★

16km S of Montpellier via the D 986, then along a little road heading W from Palavas-les-Flots. 9am-7pm (from mid-May to beginning of Sep: you must park in the car park and take the little train). No charge. ☎ *04 67 50 63 63. www.espace-maguelone.com*
The cathedral of Maguelone, which stands on an island surrounded by lagoons, is peaceful and charming. The vestiges of the buildings stand on a slight hill, framed by umbrella pines, cedars and eucalyptus. This Romanesque cathedral was extensively fortified, as witnessed by the high, very thick walls with their narrow asymmetric loopholes. A remarkable sculpted doorway leads into the church: on the tympanum is the figure of Christ surrounded by St Mark (represented by a lion), St Matthew (a winged man), St John (an eagle) and St Luke (a bull).

Fort de Salses★★

16km N of Perpignan on the N 9. Jun-Sep: 9.30am-7pm (last admission 1hr before closing time); Oct-May: 10am-12.15pm, 2pm-5pm. Guided tours available (for the upper parts, 45min) by prior arrangement. Closed 1 Jan, 1 May, 1 and 11 Nov, 25 Dec. 6.10€ (children under 18: no charge), no charge 1st Sun of the month (Oct-Mar). ☎ *04 68 38 60 13.*
Rising above the surrounding vineyards, this half-buried fortress is surprisingly big. Today, the weathered pink sandstone and red patina of the brickwork add a softness to its massive severity. Salses fortress, built in the 15C, is a unique example in France of Spanish medieval military architecture; it was adapted by Vauban to meet the demands of modern artillery, only for the Franco-Spanish frontier to be moved south to the Pyrenees.

Relax by the Waterside

Beaches

The sea is never very far from the vineyards in Languedoc-Roussillon. At Banyuls and Collioure, the vines tumble right down to the seashore. The beaches generally have lifeguards and offer all the services and activities related to water sports. Water quality control tests take place from June onwards.

From La Grande-Motte to Argelès-Plage, the seaside resorts of the Golfe du Lion offer miles of sandy beaches.

From Collioure to Cerbère, the sand gives way to the rocky coast of the Côte Vermeille; the beaches are smaller, but full of charm.

Cruising the Canal du Midi

The waters of the canal flow peacefully between its beautiful banks, crossing Languedoc from one end to the other through bucolic landscapes and cities full of history and interesting monuments. What better way to relax than to take a timeless, leisurely cruise along this waterway?

Cruising the Canal du Midi.

Béziers Croisières – *BP 4052, 34545 Béziers Cedex, ☎ 04 67 49 08 23. Timetable, prices and bookings by phone.* Cruises and lunch cruises on the Canal du Midi between Béziers and Poilhès.

Croisières du Midi (Luc Lines) – *35 quai des Tonneliers, BP 2, 11200 Homps, ☎ 04 68 91 33 00. From end of Mar to end of Oct. Booking required. 10€ (children: 5.50€).* Cruises with commentaries aboard traditional *gabares* (barges) on the Canal du Midi (2hr), starting from Homps.

Castel Nautique – *BP 25, port de Bram, 11150 Bram, ☎ 04 68 76 73 34, www. castelnautique.com* You don't have to hire a live-on boat to explore the Canal du Midi. This company hires out electric boats by the hour or half-day (no licence required).

In Search of Lost Languedoc

Parc de loisirs historique du château de Chalabre

25km SW of Limoux via the D 620. From Easter to end of Aug, school holidays, public holidays and long weekends: 10am-6.30pm. Closed Sat in Jul-Aug. 14€ per day (12€ for half a day 1.30pm-6.30pm), children: 7€. ☎ 04 68 69 37 85, www.chateau-chalabre. com

◉ In a Cathar-country castle the Chevaliers du Kercorb will give you a taste of medieval life with demonstrations of horseback jousts, weapons exercises and trick riding, and invite you to don a knight's cape and sword for a fun journey into the Middle Ages. Workshops (including calligraphy, mosaic and heraldry) and guided tours of the castle.

Musée des Dinosaures d'Espéraza

20km S of Limoux via the D 118. ♿ Jul-Aug: 10am-7pm (last admission 1hr before closing time); Feb-Jun: 10am-12pm, 2pm-6pm; rest of the year: by prior arrangement. Closed 1 Jan, 25 Dec. 6.50€ Jul-Aug, 4.90€ in low season. ☎ 04 68 74 26 88. www. dinosauria.org

◉ The extinction of dinosaurs at the end of the secondary era remains unexplained. Researchers are therefore keenly examining the fossilised remains discovered notably on the plateau overlooking Espéraza. Set in the old station, the museum houses a reconstruction of one of the local digs, bone fragments (mostly remoulds) and semi-fossilised eggs in showcases. The 11m-long skeleton of a dinosaur discovered in the region and related to the American species of titanosaurs has been reconstructed.

The Loire Valley

Dotting the banks of Europe's last untamed river and its tributaries is a patchwork landscape mirroring the extraordinary range of wines to be explored while meandering through the Loire Valley vineyard country. The trail will lead you to the many keeps and Renaissance châteaux, gardens and royal abbeys, wine-growing villages and historic towns in the Loire Valley, one of UNESCO's World Heritage Sites, from Sully-sur-Loire to Chalonnes.

Terroirs

Michelin Local Maps 316, 317, 318 and 323 – Nièvre (58), Cher (18), Loir-et-Cher (41), Indre (36), Indre-et-Loire (37), Maine-et-Loire (49), Loire Atlantique (44).

Vineyards cover more than 70 000ha in the Loire Valley, on a strip of land nearly 600km long. The climate is predominately temperate, ranging from semi-continental in the east to oceanic towards the west. The four main regions are the Central Loire, Touraine, Anjou-Saumur and the Pays Nantais. Yet the variety of soils and microclimates has created greatly diverse *terroirs*, reflected in the richness of their wines.

In the Central Loire, the Sancerre vineyards extend westward on chalky-clay soil, and to the east on flinty ground. The Pouilly vineyards – on the other side of the Loire in Burgundy – are planted on chalky, clay or flinty soil that is predominately Kimmeridgian marl.

In Touraine, the vines planted on the slopes of the Loire, Cher, Indre and Loir Rivers grow on a wide variety of soils ranging from *aubuis* (chalky clay on a chalky substratum) to *perruches* (flinty clay) as well as sand over clay and light gravel.

Saumur, or "white Anjou", is characterised by chalk tufa, while western Anjou, or "black Anjou", lies on the dark slate of the Massif Armoricain, like the Pays Nantais as a whole.

Wines

Centre – Sauvignon is the king of white wine grapes, used in AOC Sancerre, Coteaux-du-Giennois, Menetou-Salon, Quincy, Reuilly, and Pouilly-Fumé. Apart from Pouilly and Quincy, limited to white wines, these same AOC appellations produce reds from Pinot Noir grapes, as well as rosés. Further south, the Côtes-Roannaises and the AOVDQS Châteaumeillant (reds and rosés) are worthy of note.

Touraine – AOC Chinon, Bourgueil and Saint-Nicolas-de-Bourgueil produce red wines from Cabernet Franc – or Breton – grapes, as well as rosés. Some Chinon Blancs also come from Chenin Blanc grapes, or Pineau-de-Loire.

AOC Vouvray and Montlouis, planted with 100% Chenin Blanc, produce whites with fine bubbles (55%) and still whites (45%) ranging from dry to very sweet. Touraine has many other AOCs which often produce blends with Gamay as the dominant in reds and Sauvignon in whites, including Touraine (reds, rosés, effervescent whites), Touraine-Azay-le-Rideau (100% Chenin in the whites, predominantly Grolleau in the rosés), Touraine-Mesland, Touraine-Amboise, Touraine-Noble-Joué (*vin gris*, a pale dry rosé, made with three Pinots), Jasnières (whites made with Chenin), and Coteaux-du-Loir.

Add to that the AOC Valençay, using similar varieties to the Touraines, and the Cheverny and Cour-Cheverny (whites made with mainly Romorantin grapes) in the Sologne vineyards.

Anjou-Saumur – With their thirty AOCs, the Anjou and Saumur vineyards offer an extraordinary range of flavours. The two main varieties are Chenin Blanc for the whites and Cabernet Franc for the reds and rosés. The AOCs include Saumurs and Anjous (reds, whites, and lightly sparkling wines), Saumur-Champigny (reds), Coteaux-de-l'Aubance (whites), Coteaux-du-Layon (very sweet whites), Bonnezeaux, Quarts-de-Chaume and Chaume (very sweet whites), as well as Savennières (medium-dry or dry whites, including the famous Coulée-de-Serrant).

Pays Nantais – It mainly produces Muscadet (white) from Melon-de-Bourgogne in the AOC Muscadet-de-Sèvres-et-Maine, Muscadet-de-Coteaux-de-la-Loire and Muscadet-de-Côtes-de-Grandlieu. In addition, there are the AOVDQS Gros-Plant du Pays Nantais (white), between Nantes and the ocean, made with Folle Blanche grapes; the Coteaux-d'Ancenis (white, red and rosé) east of Nantes; and the Fiefs Vendéens (whites, reds and rosés) to the south.

Directory

WHERE TO EAT

IN AMBOISE

L'Épicerie – *46 pl. Michel-Debré – 37400 Amboise – ☎ 02 47 57 08 94 - closed 27 Oct-17 Dec, Mon and Fri - 10.50€ lunch - 18.50/35.50€.* A lovely half-timbered house in old Amboise with a friendly staff, pretty terrace overlooking the château, a pleasant – and tightly packed – dining room, and above all fine, unfussy traditional cuisine: *confit de canard*, tournedos of duck in pepper sauce and scallops *en brochette*.

IN ANCENIS

La Toile à Beurre – *82 r. St-Pierre - 44150 Ancenis - ☎ 02 40 98 89 64 - closed Sun and Wed eve, and Mon - 15/33€.* It's hard to resist Jean-Charles Baron's seasonal – and delicious – traditional dishes. No one could top his *ventrèche de thon* (tuna) with a conserve of summer vegetables, fresh asparagus with *mousseline* sauce, or veal kidneys in red wine sauce. The house, dating from 1753, has been renovated in excellent taste. Terrace in summer.

IN ANGERS

Ma Campagne – *14 Prom. de la Reculée - 49000 Angers - ☎ 02 41 48 38 06 - closed 16 Aug-8 Sep, Sun and Tue eve, Mon - 19/35€.* Weather permitting, meals are served in a comfortable dining room with a veranda, or on the peaceful terrace. Both afford views of the river. Carefully prepared traditional dishes are offered in two set menus with appetising seasonal fare.

Le Relais – *9 r. de la Gare - 49100 Angers - ☎ 02 47 57 08 94 - closed 22 Aug-13 Sep, 24 Dec-4 Jan, Sun and Mon - 19/30€.* The chef, who cooked for several famous restaurants, has invented some mouth-watering personal recipes. His partner, in charge of service, has put together a wine list with a focus on the Loire Valley. A wood-panelled bar and contemporary furniture contribute a little to the pleasant decor.

Le Lucullus – *5 r. Hoche - 49100 Angers - ☎ 02 41 87 00 44 - closed 7-22 Feb, 1-20 Aug, Sun and Mon, except public hols - 26/55€.* The reference to Roman General Lucullus, known for his refined table, sets the tone for this restaurant near the château. The menu features classical dishes - rabbit and herb stew, *joue de boeuf* (ox cheeks) stewed in red wine - interspersed with regional specialities. Good wine list.

IN BLOIS

Côté Loire – *2 pl. de la Grève - 41000 Blois - ☎ 02 54 78 07 86 - closed Sun and Mon - ⌿ - 13/19€.* An inviting 16C inn located near the banks of the Loire. The interior decor was remodelled in very good taste, and the menus of traditional cuisine (pike in butter sauce, *coq au vin*, veal in white sauce, etc) are changed every day. Cosy rooms and a terrace too.

Les Banquettes Rouges – *16 r. des Trois-Marchands - 41000 Blois - ☎ 02 54 78 74 92 - closed 1 week in Jun, Christmas hols, Sun and Mon - ⌿ - 19.50/37.50€.* This little restaurant in the centre of town offers a daily menu displayed on the window, as well as traditional seasonal dishes served à la carte such as *emincé* of duck *bavarois* with tomatoes and basil. A warm welcome goes with the colourful decor.

Au Rendez-vous des Pêcheurs – *27 r. Foix - 41000 Blois - ☎ 02 54 74 67 48 - closed 2-10 Jan, 1-23 Aug, Mon lunch and Sun except public hols - reservations advised - 24/68€.* This quiet place is an excellent restaurant where Christophe Cosme has shown what he is capable of. Enjoy the Montlouis or Chinon wine served with *sandre rôti sur peau* (baked pike-perch), *croustillant d'anguilles de Loire* (Loire eels) with figs stewed in wine sauce, or *escalope de foie gras*. A real treat!

AROUND CHINON

Le Moulin Bleu – *7 r. du Moulin-Bleu - 37140 Bourgueil - ☎ 02 47 97 73 13 - closed 29 Jun-7 Jul, end Nov - beginning. Mar, and Tue - 18/35€.* Chef Michel Breton's traditional dishes, such as *escargots de Saint-Michel* in walnut butter, pike-perch braised in red wine, or roasted squab in a walnut crust, go deliciously well with a bottle from one of the area's small winemakers. Dine out on the terrace with a panoramic view or inside the 15C mill.

L'Écho de Rabelais – *2 r. du Château - 37500 Chinon - ☎ 02 47 93 95 87 - closed 1-12 Feb, 15-30 Nov, evenings except Sat from Oct-Mar; open Tue, Wed, Sun and Mon eve in season - 19/26€.* This restaurant overlooks the prestigious Clos de L'Écho vineyard, which once belonged to the writer's family. While your eyes drink in the delightful landscape, your taste buds can savour the talented Jean-Pierre de Boissière's tasty dishes.

L'Océanic – *13 r. Rabelais - 37500 Chinon - ☎ 02 47 93 44 55 - closed 28 Jun-4 Jul, 29 Dec-26 Jan, Sun eve and Mon - 21/60€.* Only the freshest seafood is used in Patrick Descoubes' restaurant: he even indicates its provenance on the menu. So relax and enjoy his fine fish and shellfish – whether in the dining room or on the terrace in summer.

IN LE LUDE

Auberge du Port des Roches – *At Port-des-Roches - 72800 Le Lude - 2.5km E of Luché-Pringé on D 13 then D 214 - ☎ 02 43 45 44 48 - closed 28 Jan-10 Mar, Sun eve, Tue noon and Mon - 20/40€.* Whether you're dining out on the garden-terrace by the water or in the cosy dining room of this family-run inn, try the monkfish and fennel in green olive sauce or the braised guinea-fowl with *girolle* mushrooms and hazelnuts, concocted by Thierry Lessourd and served with a smile.

IN NANTES

Les Capucines – *11 r. de la Bastille - 44000 Nantes - ☎ 02 40 20 41 58 - closed 1st week Feb school hols, 30 Jul-24 Aug, Sat* noon, Mon eve and Sun - 10.60/30€. You can't miss the snazzy yellow façade of this building in a somewhat out-of-the-way neighbourhood. People come here for the good prices and the traditional cooking by a chef who sometimes ventures into more modern gastronomic territory – with equally good results. Southwestern dishes and seafood are also offered.

La Cigale – *4 pl. Graslin - 44000 Nantes - ☎ 02 51 84 94 94 - 15.20/24.80€.* This brasserie built in 1895, a historic monument, attests to the ornamental exuberance of Art Nouveau. Not only were some well-known French films shot here, it's also the place where Jacques Prévert met André Breton: the start of an important artistic friendship in the world of '20s Surrealism. This *Cigale* will charm you all day long, serving breakfast, lunch, tea, dinner or supper!

La Bouche à Oreille – *14 r. Jean-Jacques-Rousseau - 44000 Nantes - ☎ 02 40 73 00 25 - closed 5-25 Aug, Sun noon, Sun and public hols - reservations required - 12€ lunch - 16/30€.* The *bouchon lyonnais* bistro style is cultivated in this restaurant with its checked tablecloths, enamel plaques, corkscrew tails and collection of straw boaters from Beaujolais winegrowers. The dishes are typical Lyon fare – grilled *andouillette*, sausages, *quenelles de brochet* (pike), *jarret de porc* (ham hocks) – best accompanied with an everyday wine from there.

Le Café Cult' – *2 pl. du Change - 44000 Nantes - ☎ 02 40 47 18 49 - closed Sun and 2 wks in Aug - 14.50€ lunch - 16/28.50€.* Waiting for you behind the half-timbered façade of this 15C house is a warm and colourful café-restaurant where you can enjoy a salad, grilled braided *andouillette* with mustard, or a homemade rabbit terrine with Muscadet and conserved onions.

AROUND SANCERRE

Le Beauvoir – *1 av. Marx-Dormoy - 18000 Bourges - ☎ 02 48 65 42 44 - closed 23 Feb-4 Mar, 5-27 Aug and Sun eve - 16/40€.* The tempting food created by the chef here is in keeping with current tastes. The four set menus and excellent wine list will thoroughly captivate food-lovers. The setting has undergone a discreetly contemporary face-lift.

La Pomme d'Or – *Pl. de la Mairie - 18300 Sancerre - ☎ 02 48 54 13 30 - closed 25 Feb-5 Mar, All Saints' Day holidays (early November), Tue eve and Wed - reservations required - 23/42€.* The tables at this popular restaurant are often booked up for lunch. The *ris de veau* (calf sweetbread) fried in basil, pike-perch baked in white wine, and the *magret de canard* in honey sauce are all delicious and reasonably priced. Bistro-style decor features a Sancerre-inspired fresco.

Côte des Monts Damnés – *18300 Chavignol - 4km W of Sancerre on D183 - ☎ 02 48 54 01 72 - closed Feb, 22-30 Jun, Tue and Sun eve, and Wed - reservations required - 25/44€.* The famous *côte des Monts Damnés* hillside in Chavignol was thus named because its slopes were so hard

to work on. Today, it evokes the tasty regional cuisine updated by Jean-Marc Bourgeois with dishes like *foie gras poêlé* and Berry lentil ragout or *crottin* tagliatelle in nutmeg butter.

Le Prieuré – *2 rte de St-Laurent -18500 Vignoux-sur-Barangeon - 8km NW of Mehun-sur-Yèvre on N 76 - ☎ 02 48 51 58 80 - closed Tue and Wed - 25.50/64€.* This fine 19C building has been pleasantly reconverted into a hotel/restaurant with a refined decor - the perfect setting for Manuel Ribail's delicious contemporary cuisine featuring pike-perch steak baked with green Berry lentils, fried filet of beef, and roasted fresh figs.

AROUND SAUMUR

Auberge Saint-Pierre – *6 pl. St-Pierre - 49400 Saumur - ☎ 02 41 51 26 25 - closed Sun eve and Mon from Oct-May - 14/24€.* Enjoy a gastronomic break in the bistro-style setting of this 15C house (next to the église St-Pierre) with its pretty façade blending half-timbering and red brick. The traditional cuisine is very affordable: marrowbone with Guérande salt, *confit de canard*, and rib of beef.

S. Sauvignier / MICHELIN

Le Tire-Bouchon – *10 pl. de la République - 49400 Saumur - ☎ 02 41 67 35 05 - closed Tue - reservations advised - 11€ lunch - 15/30€.* The generous and tasty bistro cuisine, relaxed atmosphere and smart decor - black-and-white tiled floors, bistro furniture and *art naïf* paintings - explain the success of this little restaurant ideally located on the banks of the Loire.

Auberge Bienvenue – *104 rte de Cholet - 49700 Doué-la-Fontaine - ☎ 02 41 59 22 44 - closed Feb hols, Sun eve and Mon - 19/42€.* This pleasant inn near the zoo is decked with flowers and has a very enticing programme in store for you: a cosy dining room, shady flower-filled terrace, carefully prepared traditional cuisine including *confit* of tongue, ox cheeks and tails, and roasted saddle of hare, not to mention a fine wine list and spacious bedrooms, if you feel like staying.

Prieuré St-Lazare – *R. St-Jean-de-l'Habit - 49590 Fontevraud-l'Abbaye - ☎ 02 41 51 73 16 - closed 3 Jan - Mar 31 and 1 Nov-26 Dec - 25/55€.* The former Prieuré St-Lazare and its monks' cells are a haven of peace in the Abbaye de Fontevraud gardens, and the perfect place to refresh yourself. The restaurant is in the small cloister. The chapel is reserved for banquets. Contemporary cuisine.

AROUND TOURS

Le Petit Patrimoine – 58 r. Colbert - 37000 Tours - ☎ 02 47 66 05 81 - closed Sun noon - 12/26€. Behind the smart bistro-style façade is a cosy dining room where you can meet with friends to sample regional dishes such as country-style sausages poached in white wine, salmon stew with chopped pork in ambassadeur butter, and pike fillet in white wine.

L'Hédoniste – 16 r. Lavoisier - 37000 Tours - ☎ 02 47 05 20 40 - closed Sun and Mon except in summer - reservations advised - 11€ lunch - 16/29€. The owner of this restaurant prepares flavourful bistro fare at reasonable prices. But the wines are the real stars here – with a list of 250, mainly from the Loire Valley. Cellar-style decor and friendly welcome.

La Mère Hamard – Pl de l'Église - 37360 Semblançay - ☎ 02 47 56 62 04 - closed 18 Feb - 18 Mar, Tue noon from 15 Jun-30 Sep, Sun eve and Mon - 16/46€. Monique and Pierre Pégué will give you a warm welcome before treating you to their delicious classical cuisine with a regional accent featuring dishes like Racan squab in Szechuan pepper sauce or fried scampi in cream of artichoke sauce, accompanied by a fine wine list from the Loire Valley.

L'Atelier Gourmand – 37 r. Étienne-Marcel - 37000 Tours - ☎ 02 47 38 59 87 - closed 15 Dec-5 Jan, Sat and Mon noon, Sun - 17€. This little 15C house has a cosy, rustic dining room with exposed beams and sponge-painted walls. Food-lovers will satisfy their taste buds with tasty dishes from the classic menu. A lovely terrace is set up in the inner courtyard in summer.

Cap Sud – 88 r. Colbert - 37000 Tours - ☎ 02 47 05 24 81 - closed 1-22 Sep, 21 Dec-5 Jan, Sun and Mon - 18/39€. The refined southern French cuisine will delight your taste buds in this simple but inviting red-and-yellow decor: sauté of veal in lemon sauce, pavé de saumon (salmon steak) with lavender mousse, and rabbit in rosemary-lavender honey. You can almost hear the cicadas chirping!

Le Grand Vatel – 8 av. Brûlé - 37210 Tours - ☎ 02 47 52 70 32 - closed 1st half of Mar, Sun eve and Mon - 18/46€. Frédéric Scicluna's delicious terroir-inspired cooking – braised lettuce stuffed with pigs' feet and herbs, monkfish stew with saffron, three-coloured pike-perch pie – goes wonderfully with the fine selection of still or sparkling white Vouvray. Pleasant terrace.

L'Odéon – 10 pl. du Gén.-Leclerc - 37000 Tours - ☎ 02 47 20 12 65 - closed 2-22 Aug and Sun - 19.50/45€. This restaurant near the station is one of the oldest in town (1893). In its Art Deco dining room one can sample traditional market dishes such as duck in cider sauce, entrecôte in wine sauce, and grilled fillet of John Dory. The wide selection of Loire Valley wines completes the picture.

La Tourangelle – 47 quai Albert-Baillet - 37270 Montlouis-sur-Loire - ☎ 02 47 50 97 35 - closed 7-14 Feb, 30 Jun - 7 Jul, 15-22 Nov, Sun eve and Mon except public hols - 23.50/50€. The tasty contemporary cuisine served here – aiguillettes de canettes (duck) with mushrooms, turbot poached in liquorice, honey-roasted Touraine grouse – is prepared with fresh market ingredients and goes down very nicely with a glass of Montlouis selected from the excellent wine list.

IN VENDÔME

Auberge de la Madeleine – 6 pl. de la Madeleine - 41100 Vendôme - ☎ 02 54 77 20 79 - closed Feb, 8-17 Nov, and Wed - 14/35€. This restaurant in the centre of town is mainly noted for its pleasant terrace on the banks of the Loire, but its varied, mouth-watering traditional menu has its own appeal in dishes like scalloped bass with chorizo sausage and sweetbreads sautéed in mushrooms. Warm welcome.

S. Sauvignier / MICHELIN

SELECTED HOTELS AND GUESTHOUSES

AROUND ANGERS

Chambre d'hôte Le Grand Talon – 3 rte des Chapelles - 49800 Andard - 11km E of Angers on N 147 towards Saumur then D 4 - ☎ 02 41 80 42 85 - ☒ - 3 rms: 46/63€. An elegant 18C residence covered in Virginia creeper, with a lovely square courtyard in front. The tastefully decorated rooms are very pleasant. In sunny weather, breakfast is served under parasols in the pretty garden. There's no question about it – this is a haven of peace! Delightful welcome.

Hôtel Mail – 8 r des Ursules - 49100 Angers - ☎ 02 41 25 05 25 - hoteldumailangers@yahoo.fr - ☐ - 26 rms: 49/61€ - ☒ 7€. The walls of this former Ursuline convent will shield you from the noisy town centre close by. The cosy rooms are quite spacious and have a personal touch. Those on the top floor have sloping ceilings. In summer, breakfast is served on the terrace under the linden tree.

AROUND BLOIS

Chambre d'hôte Le Béguinage – 41700 Cours-Cheverny - ☎ 02 54 79 29 92 - closed Jan - 6 rms: 45/95€. The beautiful grounds with many trees and a pond are not the only treasures belonging to this lovely, low-roofed house covered with Virginia creeper. The rooms are spacious and elegant, with parquet or red-tiled floors, exposed beams, fireplaces and large beds. Hot-air balloon rides over the Loire can be arranged.

Chambre d'hôte La Raboullière – Chemin de Marçon - 41700 Contres - 10km S of Cheverny on D 102 and a smaller road - ☎ 02 54 79 05 14 - 5 rms: 47/60€. This pretty Sologne farmhouse was rebuilt with old materials gleaned from neighbouring farms. The richly furnished rooms have ceilings with exposed beams. Breakfast is taken by the fire in winter and in the garden in summer. Lovely walks in the surrounding countryside.

Chambre d'hôte La Villa Médicis – 1 r. Médicis, in Macé - 41000 Blois - 4km NE of Blois on N 152 towards Orléans - ☎ 02 54 74 46 38 - reservations required in winter - 6 rms: 53.36/94.52€ - meals 15.24/30.49€. This former thermal establishment built in 1852 got its name from Marie de Medici who used to take the waters at the springs on the grounds. Breakfast can be taken outside. Canoeing-kayaking, golf, riding and hiking are available nearby.

AROUND BOURGES

Chambre d'hôte Domaine de l'Ermitage – L'Ermitage - 18500 Berry-Bouy - 6km NW of Bourges on D 60 - ☎ 02 48 26 87 46 - 5 rms: 42/56€. This beautiful house, once a priory, owes its name to Jacques the hermit who lived here for a time. The adjoining paper mill is said to date from 1495. The two buildings now contain quite spacious and well-decorated rooms, which all enjoy the same quiet atmosphere. The grounds are planted with fine mature trees.

Hôtel de la Loire – 2 quai de la Loire - 18300 St-Thibault - ☎ 02 48 78 22 22 - hotel_de_la_loire@hotmail.com - closed 21 Dec - 7 Jan - 🅿 - 10 rms: 65/85€ - ☑9€. Georges Simenon, famous for his Maigret detective mysteries, was a regular guest at this hotel set on the banks of the Loire. You can sleep in the room he stayed in during the 1930s, decorated in the style of the times. The decor of the other rooms is inspired by different themes , including Africa, Provence and Regency. All rooms have modern comforts.

AROUND CHINON

La Milaudière – 5 r. St-Martin - 37500 Ligré - 8km SE of Chinon towards L'île-Bouchard on D 749 then D 29 - ☎ 02 47 98 37 53 - 6 rms: 38/60€. This 18C house built with Touraine tufa is a choice stopover in Chinon. The garret rooms are very pleasant and the ground floor room has a great deal of character with its old red-tiled floor and rustic furniture. The breakfast room has an old baker's oven.

Chambre d'hôte La Pilleterie – 8 rte de Chinon, D 16 - 37420 Huismes - 6km N of Chinon on D 16 - ☎ 02 47 95 58 07 - 4 rms: 55/60€. This estate out in the country is ideal for those in search of peace and quiet. The rustic-style rooms are very pleasant. The quietest are in a separate little house. The estate also has geese and other farm animals kept in a pen – a delight for children.

AROUND FONTEVRAUD-L'ABBAYE

Chambre d'hôte Domaine de Mestré – 49590 Fontevraud-l'Abbaye - 1km N of Fontevraud on D 947 towards Montsoreau - ☎ 02 41 51 72 32 - domaine-de-mestre@wanadoo.fr - closed 20 Dec-1 Apr - 12 rms: 40/55€ - ☑7€ - meals 24€. This farm once belonged to the royal abbey of Fontevraud. Today it contains rooms with a nice personal touch. Breakfasts and dinners – made with homemade products – are served in the former chapel. The lovely grounds and the small soap factory add to the charm of the place.

Hôtel Le Bussy – 4 r. Jeanne-d'Arc - 49730 Montsoreau - ☎ 02 41 38 11 11 - closed Dec-Feb - 🅿 - 12 rms: 43.91/54.73€ - ☑6€. The sign for this 18C house evokes the memory of Bussy d'Amboise, the Dame de Montsoreau's lover. The windows in most of the rooms – decorated with Louis-Philippe furniture – give onto the castle and the Loire. Breakfast in the troglodyte room or in the flower garden. Very friendly reception.

AROUND LANGEAIS

Chambre d'hôte La Meulière – 10 r.de la Gare - 37130 Cinq-Mars-la-Pile - 19km NW of Tours on N 152 - ☎ 02 47 96 53 63 - lameuliere.free.fr - 3 rms: 36/50€. This fine 19C home has the advantage of being located very near the station without experiencing any of its inconveniences. The colourful rooms with soundproofing and period furniture give onto a handsome staircase. Breakfast is served in a comfortable, attractive dining room. The garden is pleasant.

Chambre d'hôte Le Clos Phillipa – 10-12 r.de Pineau - 37190 Azay-le-Rideau - ☎ 02 47 45 26 49 - 5 rms: 49/81€. This large and pleasant 18C house is ideally located in the centre of town. The rooms are spacious and well laid-out, with some fine antiques. The main living room is very welcoming. The beautiful garden is next to the grounds of the château. Regional wine-tastings.

Chambre d'hôte La Butte de l'Épine – 37340 Continvoir 2km E of Gizeux on D 15 - ☎ 02 47 96 62 25 - 3 rms: 52/57€. This charming house was inspired by 16C and 17C styles and reconstructed from old building materials. The breakfast/living room has furniture from different periods as well as a large fireplace. The impeccable rooms are like bijou apartments. The grounds are full of flowers.

IN LE LUDE

Chambre d'hôte Mme Pean – 5 Grande-Rue - 72800 Le Lude - ☎ 02 43 94 63 36 - closed Oct-Mar - 3 rms: 40/50€. You'd never know there was such a heavenly garden on the other side of the imposing wall surrounding this lovely 17C house. The spacious rooms, all on the 1st floor, have period-styled furniture. A hearty breakfast and a warm welcome are guaranteed.

IN MONTLOUIS-SUR-LOIRE

Château de la Bourdaisière – *25 r. de la Bourdaisière - 37270 Montlouis-sur-Loire - 18km N of Chenonceaux on D 40 - ☎ 02 47 45 16 31 - chateaulabourdaisiere. com - closed 12 Jan-9 Feb - 🅿 - 20 rms: 115/230€ - 🍽13€. If you're tempted by the château life, this Renaissance-style house among the vineyards is made for you. Rooms with a personal touch – often with period furniture – give onto the vast grounds planted with cedars and sequoias. The vegetable garden is worth having a look at.*

AROUND MONTRICHARD

Le Moulin de la Renne – *11 rte de Vierzon - 41140 Thésée - between Montrichard and Noyers-sur-Cher, on D 176, along the Renne - ☎ 02 54 71 41 56 - contact@moulindelarenne.com - closed mid-Jan to mid-Mar, Sun eve, Tue noon in season and Mon - 🅿 - 15 rms: 26/51€ - 🍽 8€ - restaurant 16/39€.* An old mill surrounded by a shady garden with the Renne running through it. The rooms have all been refurbished in a simple style, and the dining room has been brightened up with cheery colours. The lounge has a fireplace and an aquarium. Children's toys and a terrace overlooking the mill race complete the picture.

Background

The discovery of the remains of a stone wine press near Azay-le-Rideau attests to the existence of vineyards in the Loire Valley as far back as Roman times. St Martin probably planted the first vines on the Vouvray slopes in the 4C. Monks and princes further expanded the vineyards. When the Comte d'Anjou took the English throne in 1154, as Henry II Plantagenet, he started the tradition of serving Anjou wines at Court. It was the white *moelleux* wines that made the reputation of the Anjou vintages, and their reputation was still high in the 15C, when Good King René of Provence was proud to say: "Of all the wines in my cellar – Anjou, Lorraine and Provence – the first are the best." The presence of the Loire River, an ideal mode of transport, played a crucial role in developing exports to Northern Europe. Demand from Dutch merchants, particularly in the 16C, fuelled the expansion of viticulture in Sèvre-et-Maine, Layon, Saumurois and Vouvray. At about the same time, laws were passed requiring wine merchants to obtain their stock over twenty leagues (around 80km) from the capital, which spurred wine-growing around Blois and Orléans, in the Cher Valley and in Sologne. The Loire Valley vineyards suffered during the French Revolution, and during the terrible, counter-revolutionary Vendée wars which followed, nor were they spared in the phylloxera crisis of the late 19C. In spite of these problems, striving for high quality has been a major objective of Loire Valley winemakers ever since.

Central Loire Wine Route

140km from Sancerre to Reuilly (Cher). Michelin Local map 318, M-O 8, J-L 9. See itinerary 1 *on the map on p. 280-281.*

Sancerre★

Sancerre, perched above a sea of vineyards, takes in the Loire Valley and Nivernais towards the east, and Berry to the west. The **panorama★★** from the esplanade of porte César (318m) affords a view of the little northern Sancerre villages dotting the route des Vignobles (Wine Route) from St-Satur to St-Gemmes (don't miss the *circuit* that goes down to St-Satur). A walk through the old town affords some charming surprises. With regard to the wine, the surest bets in **AOC Sancerre** are the **Domaines** (estates) **Vacheron** and **Henri Bourgeois**, families which have had roots here since time immemorial *(see Shopping Guide)*. The new **Maison des vins** (Wine House) can also help with your purchases.

Leave Sancerre heading SW on D 7, then turn right on D 923. At the crossroads, don't miss the remarkable **view★★** of Sancerre, the vineyards, St-Satur and the Loire Valley. The road goes through a sea of grape vines, then winds down the high chalky-clay hills known as *terres blanches* (white ground) where the vineyards produce full-bodied wines. *Turn right towards Chavignol.* The road goes through **Chavignol** which produces the famous *crottin* – a goat's cheese that can be soft, hard or extra mature, and goes wonderfully with Sancerre.

Continue on D 183 to St-Satur, then cross the Loire and turn right onto D 553. The road runs into the Appellation Pouilly-sur-Loire area, which includes 50ha of Chasselais which produce the actual **Appellation Pouilly-sur-Loire**, and 950ha of Sauvignon which produce the famous Pouilly-Fumé.

The **Château de Tracy** (15C-16C) is not open to visitors, but you can taste and purchase wines on the estate and catch a glimpse of the magnificent grounds with cedar trees standing among the vine stocks and a view stretching all the way to Sancerre *(see Shopping Guide)*.

At Bois-Gibault, take a right onto D 243 towards Les Loges. Watch for the fork to the left towards Les Loges under the railway bridge. **Les Loges** is a winegrowing hamlet which owes its name to the *loges de vigne*, small buildings used as shelters in the vineyards. Note the typical 19C winemakers' houses with vaulted cellars beneath the staircase.

Pouilly-sur-Loire

To get off to a good start in your exploration of Central Loire wines, go to the **Caves de Pouilly-sur-Loire** *(see Shopping Guide)*.

The **Pavillon du milieu de Loire**, on the banks of the river, has displays of valley wildlife and a room devoted to wine-growing. It also has information about the **reserve naturelle du Val-de-Loire** (nature preserve) and *(free)* brochures about the **sentiers du Milieu de Loire** (trails), two of which go through vineyards overlooking the Loire. ⟁ *Jul-Aug: 10am-12.30pm, 2-7pm; May-Jun and Sep-Oct: Wed-Mon 10am-12.30pm, 2-6.30pm; Nov-Mar: Sat-Sun 2-6pm; school hols (zones B and C): Wed-Mon 2-6pm. Closed Jan and 25 Dec. 4€ (6-18 yr-olds: 3€).* ☎ *03 86 39 54 54.*

Cross the bridge over the Loire and take D 59. Turn right (towards Sancerre) onto D 10 at Vinon.

After about 2km, turn left and head up the tiny steep road marked "route des Vignobles" which affords a magnificent **view★** of the Sancerre hills.

Turn left onto D 955, then right onto D 22.

La Borne

Known for its stoneware, this village has gained international recognition in the field of contemporary ceramics. Its fifty or so artists and craftsmen come from a variety of countries. Their work can be seen in numerous workshops, at the **Centre de creation céramique** and at the **Musée de la Poterie**. *mid-Mar-end Oct: Sat-Sun, public and school hols (zones B and C) 3-7pm; beginning Nov-beginning Jan: Sat-Sun, public and school hols (zones B and C) 2-6pm. No charge.* ☎ *02 48 26 96 21.*

Leave La Borne heading SW on D 46.

Morogues

The vineyards covering the slopes from Morogues to Menetou – the pride and joy of Berry viticulture – were among the most highly valued in France in the days of Jacques Coeur. Today they cover more than 400ha and produce fresh and spicy white wines, supple and fragrant reds, and fruity rosés.

Château de Maupas

⟁ *Guided Tours (45min) from Easter-end Sep: 2-7pm; Sun and public hols: 10am-12pm and 2-7pm. 6.50€ (children: 4€).* ☎ *02 48 64 41 71.*

The château, in the Maupas family since the time of Louis XV, contains an **impressive plate collection★** and also produces a good red Menetou.

Menetou-Salon

Guided Tours (1hr 15min) Jul-Sep: 10am-6.30pm; Apr-Jun and Sep-Oct: Sat-Sun 10am-6.30pm. 8.50€ (children: 4€). ☎ *02 48 64 80 16 or 02 48 64 80 54.*

Owned for a short time by Jacques Coeur, the **Château de Menetou-Salon** was rebuilt in the 19C. There is an antique car collection in the outbuildings.

To reach Bourges, leave Menetou on the D 59 towards Saint-Martin-d'Auxigny.

Sancerre and its vineyards.

Bourges★★★

The Cathédrale St-Étienne and the Palais Jacques Coeur, the heart and soul of Bourges, both benefited from a furrier's sons' love of fine architecture. An amazing businessman, Jacques Coeur (1395-1456) succeeded in amassing a fortune so large that he soon gained the trust of King Charles VII, and became the king's financier in 1439.

The **Cathédrale St-Étienne★★★**, a Unesco World Heritage site, was built in two stages (1195-1215 and 1225-60). Its **central portal** depicting the Last Judgment is a masterpiece of Gothic sculpture (13C). Don't miss the **stained glass windows★★★** (mostly early 13C), the **crypt★★** and the **astronomical clock★** dating from 1424.

The **Palais Jacques Coeur★★**, begun in 1443, is one of the finest civil buildings from the Gothic era. The captivating façade is richly decorated. The master and mistress of the house can be seen in the half-open simulated windows on either side of the festooned loggia, while the central turret is decorated with exotic trees – palms, oranges and dates – evoking the countries in the Orient to which Jacques Coeur travelled. His huge fortune allowed him to satisfy his love of beauty and the comforts of life, and the palace's furnishings attest to his extraordinary success in this regard. *Guided tours (1hr) Jul-Aug 9.30am-12.15pm, 2-6.15pm; Sep-Apr: 10am-12.15pm, 2-5.15pm. Closed 1 Jan, 1 May, 1 and 11 Nov, 25 Dec. 6.10€ (children under 17: no charge).* ☎ 02 48 24 79 41.

Other "musts" in Bourges include the **maisons à colombages★** (half-timbered houses, 15C-16C) in the old section of town north of the cathedral, the **promenade des Remparts★** (tour of the ramparts) and the **Musée Estève★★** (abstract art by Berri painter Maurice Estève, born in 1904). The Printemps de Bourges music festival *(3rd week in April)* draws singers from around the world.

Take N 76 out of Bourges towards the Quincy-Reuilly region.

Mehun-sur-Yèvre★

The shady promenade along the Canal du Berry – overlooking the remains of the castle of Jean de Berry and the church – is a lovely place for a walk in this pretty little town.

Berry porcelain manufacturers have been established in Foëcy, Noirlac and Mehun since the 19C. The **Pôle de la porcelaine** in Mehun, a pleasant glass building, contains a variety of unusual collector's items. *Jul-Aug: 10am-12pm, 2-6pm; May-Jun and Sep: Tue-Sun 2-6pm; Mar-Apr and Oct: Sat-Sun 2-6pm. 4.55€ (children under 10: no charge).* ☎ 02 48 57 06 19.

Quincy

AOC Quincy, stretching between Quincy and Brinay, boasts 204ha planted in Sauvignon grapes which produce a dry, subtle and elegant white wine which is usually at its best within two or three years. During the last weekend in August, Quincy hosts the Fêtes de l'Océan celebrating the marriage of seafood and wine.

Brinay

The little **church** contains an interesting series of 12C **frescoes★**, including a rare calendar of each month's labours (for September – a man trampling grapes in a large vat), and a representation of the Wedding at Cana alluding to the theme of wine.

In Brinay, take a left onto D 18ᴱ (route du Vignoble) towards Méreau. In Méreau, take a left onto D 918 in the direction of Lucy-sur-Arnon and Reuilly.

Reuilly

The **AOC Reuilly** vineyards, spread over both sides of the Arnon, cover 167ha producing remarkable dry and fruity white Sauvignon wines, as well as excellent quality rosés and reds from Pinot Gris and Pinot Noir. And why not visit the little **Musée de la Vigne et du Vin de Reuilly** devoted to winemaking materials. *5, r. Rabelais. Summer: Tue-Sun 10am-12pm, 2-6pm. No charge.* ☎ 02 54 49 24 94.

Touraine Wine Route

FROM VALENÇAY TO BLOIS

210km. Michelin Local map 323, A-F 1-4. See itinerary ② on the map on p. 280-281.

Valençay boasts two AOCs with its name – for its trimmed pyramid-shaped goat's cheese, and for its wines which, like those of Touraine, are made from Sauvignon and Chardonnay grapes.

Château and Parc de Valençay★★★

Jul-Aug: 9.30am-7.30pm; end Mar-end Jun and beginning Sep-Oct: 9.30am-6pm Château and show. 8.50€ (children: 4.50€). ☎ 02 54 00 10 66. *www.chateau-valencay.com*

Built around 1540, Valençay is a Renaissance gem. Bonaparte ordered Talleyrand to buy it in 1803 as a place for lavish receptions, and it is also a mecca for Napoleonic history. Sumptuously furnished, the château is surrounded by beautiful **grounds★**. Napoleon's maze, a small farm, a children's castle, picnic area and restaurant make Valençay one of the liveliest châteaux in the Loire Valley. A wine-tasting of Clos du château de Valençay concludes the short play evoking the sumptuous feasts prepared by chef Carême for Talleyrand's guests.

Take the route de Blois (D 956) out of Valençay. After Fontguenand, turn left towards Meusnes on the route des Vignobles Touraine-Val de Loire. This takes you out of AOC Valençay and into **AOC Touraine**.

With Meusnes to your right, continue on the signposted itinerary (signs show a bunch of grapes) which winds nicely through the vineyards. After crossing the Cher, turn left in Châtillon-sur-Cher and follow the route des Vignobles. The scenery alternates between vines and woods, then the panorama opens onto a sea of gently sloping vineyards.

On the way out of Noyers-sur-Cher, the route des Vignobles forks in two opposite directions. Leaving the road to Blois on your right, turn left onto the road to Saint-Aignan.

Saint-Aignan★

Saint-Aignan, which marks the border of Berry and Touraine, is dominated by a graceful Renaissance château and **collegiate church★**, a gem of Romanesque art (remarkable 12C-15C **frescoes★★**). As the point of departure for the Cher canal to Nitray (37), it is also a hub of river tourism in the region.

Take D 17 along the Cher towards Mareuil-sur-Cher. A few kilometres after Mareuil, turn left onto the route des Vignobles which leads up to a plateau covered with grape vines; then follow the road down into some winding, wooded valleys. The road takes you through Thésée-la-Romaine (Gallo-Roman site), then offers a superb panorama over the valley as it rises up to the winegrowing slopes of Monthou-sur-Cher. The **Château Gué-Péan** (16C-17C) stands in the little valley. Then head back to the banks of the Cher.

Bourré

At Bourré, the valley narrows. As is often the case in the Touraine and Saumur regions, the hills have been hollowed out by the former tufa quarries turned into troglodyte dwellings, wine cellars or mushroom beds, as here at the **Caves champignonnières des Roches**.

La Ville Souterraine★ is a lifelike reproduction of a village square carved out of the rock. *For both sites: tours (1hr) from mid-Jul to mid-Aug: every hr from 10am-6pm; from mid-Mar to mid-Jul and mid-Aug to mid-Nov: 10am-12pm, 2-6pm. 5.50€ (children 6-14: 3.60€). Bring warm clothing.* ☎ 02 54 32 95 33.

Montrichard★

Walk to the top of the **castle tower** in this little medieval town – the best place to appreciate the fine **panorama** over the valley. *Jun-Sep: 10am-6pm; Palm Sun-end May: Fri-Wed 10am-12pm, 2-5pm. Sound tours of the dungeon from Easter to end Sep. 5€. Mid-Jul to mid-Aug: tours with characters in costume at 4.30pm, night shows Fri and Sat (same period). 7€.* ☎ 02 54 32 05 10.

And in fine weather you can take a **boat ride** on the *Léonard de Vinci. Quai du Cher, 4100 Montrichard.* ☎ *02 54 75 41 53, www.ldv-bateau.com Jul-Aug: leaves at 3 and 5pm; mid-Apr to mid-Oct: Sat and Sun and public hols, leaves at 3 and 5pm. 9€.*

The **Caves Monmousseau** run for over 15km: a sequence of underground galleries in which to explore the various stages in making effervescent wine. *71 rte de Vierzon. Tours (1hr) Apr-Oct: 10am-6pm; Nov-Mar: daily except Sat-Sun and public hols 10am-12pm, 2-5pm. Closed 23 Dec-2 Jan. 2.75€.* ☎ *02 54 32 35 15.*

Château de Chenonceau★★★

Mid-Mar to mid-Sep: 9am-7pm; mid-end Sep: 9am-6.30pm; beginning-mid Mar and beginning-mid Oct: 9am-6pm; mid-end Oct and mid-end Feb: 9am-5.30pm; beginning-mid Feb and beginning-mid Nov: 9am-5pm; mid-Nov to end Jan: 9am-4.30pm. 9.50€ château, gardens and Wax Museum (children 7-18: 8€). ☎ *0 820 20 90 90. www.chenonceau.com*

A Renaissance treasure built over the Cher River, Chenonceau has been nicknamed "the Ladies' castle" for having nearly always belonged to women, including Catherine de Medici and Diane de Poitiers, the beautiful and insidiously powerful mistress of François I and Henri II. The **gardens★★** and the banks of the Cher provide lovely views of the château. Picnic areas by the moat.

The château's vineyards (30ha) produce nice little wines which can be tasted at the **Cave des Dômes** from March to the 1st weekend in November. ☎ 02 47 23 90 07.

Leave Chenonceaux on D 40 in the direction of Civray-de-Touraine, then towards Amboise (D 31). 3km before Amboise on the left stands the **Pagode de**

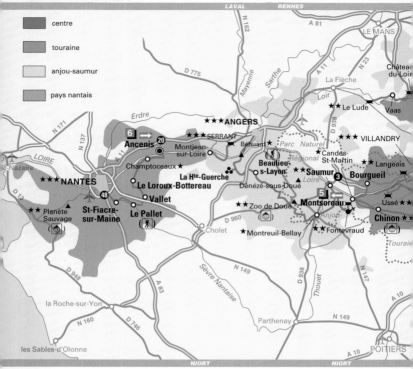

Chanteloup★. The Duc de Choiseul had this superb *chinoiserie* built here in the 18C – the only vestige of the château. Picnicking allowed on the grounds. *Jul-Aug: 9.30am-7.30pm; Jun: 10am-7pm; May and Sep: 10am-6.30pm; Apr: 10am-12pm, 2-6pm, Sat and Sun and public and School hols: 10am-6pm; Oct-Nov: Sat and Sun and public hols 10am-5pm. Last entrance 30min before closing. 6.30€ (children: 4.30€).* ☎ *02 47 57 20 97.*

Amboise★★

This town on the banks of the Loire, which has preserved its ancient feudal structure, is dominated by the most Italian of the Loire châteaux, where François I held extravagant parties, organised by Leonardo da Vinci. But the golden age of Amboise was in the 15C, when Charles VIII brought in artists and craftsmen from Italy to renovate the **château★★** where he had spent his childhood. The inside contains an exceptional collection of Gothic and Renaissance furniture. There is a splendid **view★★** from the terrace. Don't miss the **Chapelle St-Hubert**, where Da Vinci is buried. In summer there's a superb sound and light show. *Jul-Aug: 9am-7pm; Apr-Jun: 9am-6.30pm; mid to end Mar and Sep-Oct: 9am-6pm; beginning-mid Nov: 9am-5.30pm; mid-Nov to Jan: 9am-12pm, 2-4.45pm; Feb to mid-Mar: 9am-12pm, 1.30-5.30pm. Closed 1 Jan, 25 Dec. 7.50€ (children 7-14: 4.20€)* ☎ *08 20 20 50 50. www.chateau-amboise. tm.fr*

For a pleasant setting in which to sample Touraine-Amboise wines, try the **Caveau des Vignerons d'Amboise** at the foot of the château *(see Shopping Guide).*

The **château du Clos-Lucé★★** is the house where Leonardo da Vinci spent the last three years of his life. Along with the Master's bedroom, it contains 40 reconstructions of his "fabulous machines". A magnificent show in the **Parc Léonardo da Vinci** – full of fun and magic – takes you on a discovery of the eclectic genius of this artist-engineer-architect, while videos and thematic booths in the hall take you on a deeper journey into the world of this true Renaissance man. *Jul-Aug: 9am-8pm; Apr-Jun and Sep-Oct: 10am-7pm; Feb-Mar and Nov-Dec: 10am-6pm; Jan: 10am-5pm. Closed 1 Jan, 25 Dec. 11€ (children: 6.50€).* ☎ *02 47 57 00 73.*

Leave Amboise on D 751 in the direction of Montlouis. The road runs along the Loire, providing frequent peeks of the river, its islands and golden sand banks. The pretty little village of **Lussault-sur-Loire** is where the **AOC Montlouis** begins, stretching between the Loire and Cher rivers.

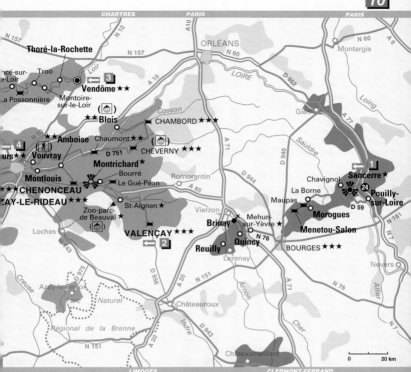

Montlouis -sur-Loire

This little town is built in terraces over the tufa slopes with their hollowed-out cellars. The Maison des vins, which is scheduled to open in 2005 on quai Albert-Baillet, is across from the cooperative. The **Domaine de la Taille aux Loups** *(see Shopping Guide)* offers a selection of *moelleux*, dry and fizzy Montlouis wines.

The **Château de la Bourdaisière**, set among the vineyards near Montlouis on the route d'Amboise *(also a guesthouse, see practical information)*, grows over 400 varieties of tomatoes in its **vegetable garden★**. *Tours (45min) Jun-Sep: 10am-7pm; Apr-May and Oct: 10am-12pm, 2-6pm. 6.50€ (children 8-18: 5.50€). Free access to grounds and vegetable garden.* ☎ *02 47 45 16 31. www. chateaulabourdaisiere.com*

Leave Montlouis on the D 751, which runs alongside the Loire to Vouvray.

Vouvray

Whether sparkling or still, dry, medium or slightly sweet, **Vouvrays** are among the most famous white wines from Touraine. The little town built in terraces on white tufa contains a number of ancient winegrowing houses which are more or less troglodyte caves. Be sure to go around the town on the route des Vignobles, which will take you in particular to the **Caves des Producteurs de Vouvray**, **Clos Naudin** and **Domaine Huet** *(see Shopping Guide)*.

⬧ Follow the GR 33 on two marked trails *(6-18km)* to explore the town's architecture and the panoramas over the Loire and its vineyards. Walk on to **Rochecorbon** where the hillside overlooking the river is dotted with troglodyte caves. The rich houses and palm trees – due to a microclimate – give it an air of the Mediterranean Riviera. This is where the **Marc Brédif** cellars are. Hollowed out between the 8C and 10C, these 2km-long caves contain over a million bottles, the oldest of which date from 1873. The course is well-designed, with an oenological game. *Dégustation-vente* (tasting/sales) of Vouvray, Chinon, Bourgueil and Saumur-Champigny. *87 quai de la Loire, 37210 Rochecorbon,* ☎ *02 47 52 50 07. Apr-Oct: 10.30am-12.30pm, 3-6pm. 4.50€.*

The **Château Moncontour** (late 15C-18C), which Balzac was eager to buy and where he set certain scenes in his story *La Femme de trente ans*, has very old vineyards and a modern *chai* (wine storehouse). Its wonderful Musée du Vin contains an amazing assortment of over 2 000 tools! *Les Patys, 37210 Vouvray,* ☎ *02 47 52 60 77. Summer: 9-11am, 2-6pm. 4€.*

Head E out of Vouvray on the Route touristique de la Vallée de la Brenne (D 46). Go past Vernou-sur-Brenne (many cellars and charming old houses) and continue up to Chançay. The **Château de Jallanges** is a pretty brick-and-white-stone Renaissance building overlooking vineyards and lovely grounds. *Mar-Oct: 10am-12pm, 2-6pm. 7€ (children: 5€).* ☎ *02 47 52 06 66. www.chateaudejallanges.fr*

After a few kilometres you'll come to the Renaissance gardens of the **Château de Valmer** on a remarkable terraced site overlooking the Brenne. The troglodyte chapel has 16C stained-glass windows, and the château produces its own Vouvray. *Beginning-Jul to mid-Sep: Tue-Sun 10am-7pm; May-Jun and mid to end Sep: Sat and Sun and public hols 2-7pm. 7.50€. (children under 16: no charge).* ☎ *02 47 52 93 12.*

Go back down D 79, then turn left onto D 1. The road runs along the Vallée de la Cisse and through **AOC Touraine-Amboise**, which spreads over both banks of the Loire. *In Pocé-sur-Cisse, take a left onto the Route du Vignoble (D 431) and climb up to the beautiful plateaux covered with vineyards, then come back down to Limeray.*

After a few kilometres, the road leaves Indre-et-Loire and enters Loir-et-Cher, taking you into **AOC Touraine-Mesland** via the town of Monteaux. The Route du Vignoble rising through the hills to the picturesque village of **Mesland** offers a fine **view** of the Château de Chaumont on the other side of the Loire.

Château de Chaumont-sur-Loire★★

2nd week in May to mid-Sep: 9.30am-6.30pm; Apr and 1st week in May and mid-end Sep: 10.30am-5.30pm; Oct-Mar: 10am-12.30pm, 1.30-5pm. Last entrance 30min before closing. Closed 1 Jan, 1 May, 1 and 11 Nov, 25 Dec. 6.10€ (children under 18: no charge). 1st Sun of every month: no charge. ☎ *02 54 51 26 26.*

This feudal-looking château, built from 1445-1510, was already influenced by the Renaissance. It was first owned by Catherine de Medici and Diane de Poitiers. Later on, Napoleon exiled Madame de Staël here.

The **grounds** are magnificent. *From 9am to dusk. Closed 1 Jan, 1 May, 1 and 11 Nov, 25 Dec. No charge.* ☎ *02 54 51 26 26.*

The château's farm houses the **Conservatoire international des parcs et jardins et du paysage** (International Conservatory of parks, gardens and landscaping), where the Festival international des jardins is held from mid-May to mid-October, drawing thousands of visitors. *Information,* ☎ *02 54 20 99 20. www.chaumont-jardins.com*

Leaving the Loire Valley and its tufa houses with slate roofs at Candé-sur-Beuvron, you head southeast to Valaire and the winegrowing area of Sologne. Asparagus and strawberries are grown here in addition to grapes. **AOC Cheverny** extends for more than 2 000ha (but only 488ha in production) on the left bank of the Loire from the Sologne around Blois to the Orléanais border. There are many grape varieties in this mainly sandy terroir. The Cheverny "style" was created from a blend of these.

Château de Cheverny★★★

Tours (45min) Jul-Aug: 9.15am-6.45pm; Apr-Jun and Sep: 9.15am-5.15pm; Oct-Mar: 9.15am-5pm; Nov-Feb: 9.45am-5pm. Dog feeding times: beginning Apr to mid-Sep at 5pm; mid-Sep to end Mar: at 3pm except Tue, Sat-Sun and public hols. 6.10€ (château and grounds), 10.50€ (château and permanent exhibition), 10.80€ (château and special tour of grounds and canal). ☎ *02 54 79 96 29. www.chateau-cheverny.com*

The château was built between 1604 and 1634, and the land surrounding it has been in the same family since 1388. Wonderfully furnished and maintained, it is a remarkable example of the classical style.

⬚ Young visitors and cartoon fans may find something familiar about the building: it was the model for the famous Château de Moulinsart – or Marlinspike in English – in the *Tintin* books: there's a permanent exhibition in the outbuildings about the young hero's adventures. The grounds (100ha) can be visited in an electric car or by boat on the canal. Children are fascinated by feeding time at the **kennel** with its 90 dogs.

The road goes through **Cour-Cheverny**, the heart of **AOC Cour-Cheverny**, reserved for white wines made with the Romorantin *cépage*. *Head NE on D 102; then turn left onto D 112 at Bracieux.* The road takes you through the **Parc de Chambord** and its natural hunting preserve.

Château de Chambord★★★

Apr-Sep: 9am-6.15pm; Oct-Mar: 9am-5.30pm. Last entrance 30min before closing. Closed 1 Jan, 1 May, 25 Dec. 7€ (children under 18: no charge). 1st Sun of every month (Oct-Mar): no charge. ☎ *08 25 82 60 88 (special rate). www.chambord.org*

Chambord, built from 1518-45 and probably initially designed by Leonardo da Vinci, has 440 rooms, 365 fireplaces and 83 staircases! Surrounded by 5 000ha of grounds, the château is a Unesco World Heritage site. Don't miss the superb sound and light show and the equestrian arts show in the Maréchal de Saxe stables in summer. The Chambord estate **grounds** offer a variety of activities from bicycle and horseback rides, roller-skating, horse-drawn carriage rides, boat trips on the Cosson and excursions to hear the calls of the rutting stags.

Blois★★

With its pedestrian streets, winding alleys, townhouses, gardens and terraces, Blois is wonderfully suited to walking tours. Wonderful too is the **Maison de la Magie Robert-Houdin★**, which takes you into a giant kaleidoscope, an illustrated room and a **Théâtre des Magiciens★** (Magicians' Theatre). ♿ *Jul-Aug: 10am-12.30pm, 2-6.30pm; Apr and All Saints Day holidays: 10am-12.30pm, 2-6pm; May-Jun and Sep: Tue-Sun 10am-12pm, 2-6pm. (30min) shows daily. Closed Oct-Mar. 7.50€ (children 6-11: 4.50€). ☎ 02 54 55 26 26. www. maisondelamagie.fr*

Some of the names associated with the **Château de Blois★★★** include Louis XII who brought in the first signs of Italian art in around 1500; Catherine de Medici, who had a cabinet with 237 sculpted panels which, according to Alexandre Dumas, contained secret drawers for poison; Henri III, who had his rival the Duc de Guise assassinated; and Gaston d'Orléans, who commissioned the famous architect Mansart to work there. The **Musée des Beaux-Arts** is located on the first floor of the **aile Louis XII** (Louis XII wing). *Apr-Sep: 9am-6pm; Sep-Mar: 9am-12.30pm, 2-5.30pm. Last entrance 30min before closing. Closed 1 Jan, 25 Dec. 6.50€ (children: 2€). 1st Sun of every month (Nov-Mar): no charge. ☎ 02 54 90 33 33. www.ville-blois.fr*

Regional wines can be tasted and purchased at the **Maison des vins de Loir-et-Cher** on Place du château *(see Shopping Guide).*

"Le pays des châteaux à vélo" (Cycling round château country) offers 300km of safe and well-marked cycling tours around Blois, Chambord and Cheverny, including two through the vineyards. Maps and itineraries are available at regional tourist offices or on the web at www.chateauxavelo.com

FROM VENDÔME TO LUDE

95km. Michelin Local Map 317, K-P 2-3. See itinerary ③ *on the map on p. 280-281.*

Vendôme★★

Vendôme, a "little Venice" full of hidden charms, is worth visiting at night. *Night-time torchlight tours through the heart of Vendôme (1hr 30min) in Jul-Aug: Thu at 10pm. 4€ leaving from the Office de tourisme (Tourist Office). ☎ 02 54 77 05 07.*

It can even be visited in a boat full of flowers that takes you out on the Loir to explore the Porte d'Eau (Water Gate) and the *chevet* of the abbey-church. *47 r. de la Poterie, 02 54 77 05 07. Jul-Aug: 2.30-7pm. Boats leave from the Embarcadère (landing stage) du Moulin Perrin, off rue du Change. 4€ (information available across from the landing stage).*

Go W on D 2 out of Vendôme. Turn left onto D 5 in Villiers-sur-Loir, then D 67 towards Thoré and an immediate left after the bridge over the Loir. The road goes through the village of **Rochambeau**, built partly into the rock.

Thoré-la-Rochette

The heart of the **appellation Coteaux-du-Vendômois**. The former station – now containing the **Maison du vin et des produits des terroirs vendômois** – is the point of departure for the **Train touristique de la vallée du Loir,** which takes you to Troo on a 36km trip with a number of stops. *Guided trip (3hr) from Thoré to Troo. Contact Mr Claude Germain, Mairie, 41100 Thoré-la-Rochette, ☎ 02 54 72 80 82.*

The road goes through **Lavardin★**, where the ruins of a feudal castle stand above the town.

Leave for Montoire on the pleasant little road that runs along the left bank of the Loir.

Montoire-sur-le-Loir

Montoire would much rather not be remembered for its most "historic" moment – the meeting of Hitler and Pétain at its railway station in 1940 – and offers more pleasant sights in the here and now: its old houses, a beautiful bridge over the Loir and the adorable **Chapelle St-Gilles★** decorated with superbly coloured **frescoes★★**. **Musikenfête**, a museum/show of traditional music, has over 500 instruments which you can listen to on headphones. *Espace de l'Europe, quartier Marescot. Mar-Sep: Tue-Sun 10am-12pm, 2-6pm; Oct-Dec: Tue-Sun 2-6pm. ☎ 02 54 85 28 95 or 02 54 72 60 91.*

Troo

Troo, a troglodyte village overlooking the Loir, is full of terraced houses connected by little streets, stairs and mysterious alleyways. Opposite is the charming **St-Jacques-des-Guérets** church which has preserved some exquisitely fresh Byzantine-looking **murals★** (12C-13C).

Proceed on D 917 and turn left at Sougé onto the signposted Route Touristique towards Artins. Turn right onto D 10, then right again onto the route de l'Isle Verte; after 100m, turn left onto the road that runs in front of the Château du Pin.

From the bridge opposite the château you can see upstream to **Isle Verte**, at the confluence of the Loir and "its friend the Braye", where Ronsard wanted to be buried. The **church** in **Couture-sur-Loir** (Gothic chancel with Angevin vaulting) contains the tombs of Ronsard's parents.

Manoir de la Possonnière★

Open visits in the morning, guided tours in the afternoon (50min) Jul-Aug: 10am-7pm;
end Mar to end Jun and beginning Sep to mid-Nov: Fri, Sat-Sun, Mon and public hol
2-6pm. Last entrance 1hr before closing. 6€ (children under 12: no charge). ☎ 02 5
85 23 30.

This is where the poet Pierre de Ronsard, leader of the Pléiade group, was bor
in 1524.

Go back to Couture and take D 57 N over the Loir. Turn left.

Poncé-sur-le-Loir

Poncé is a town with character. It has a Renaissance château and a remarkabl
collection of 12C frescoes in its church. The **Centre de Création artisanale "Le**
Moulins de Paillard" is a craft centre devoted to pottery and glassblowing. &
Beginning-May to mid-Sep: Tue-Sat 10am-12pm, 2-7pm; rest of the year: Tue-Sat 2-6pm
Closed Jan and public hols. 4.20€. ☎ 02 43 44 45 31.

The **Château de Poncé**, built in 1542, has a magnificent vaulted **Renaissance**
staircase★★ sculpted with a rarely equalled sense of whimsy and perspective
The garden is adorned with an arbour and a maze. The dovecote's 1 800 niche
and turning ladders have been preserved. The outbuildings contain the Musée du
Folklore Sarthois. *Apr to mid-Nov: 2-6.30pm, Fri, Sat and public hols 10.30am-noon*
2-6.30pm. 5.50€. ☎ 02 43 44 45 39.

Follow the route du Vignoble (D 919). It takes you to Ruillé-sur-Loir and Lhomme, in
the heart of **Appellation Jasnières**, about which Curnonsky said that "three times
a year it produces the best white wine in the world". In summer, the **Musée de la**
Vigne in **Lhomme** organises walks through the vineyards. ☎ 02 43 44 43 62.

Château-du-Loir

The keep is the only vestige of the feudal castle which gave the town its name. **St**
Guingalois Church contains a 17C Pietà and panels from the Flemish Manneris
School. Stretching out not far from the town is the magnificent forest of Bercé.

Take D 10 out of Château-du-Loir towards Château-la-Vallière. Turn right onto C 2
towards La Bruère-sur-Loir immediately after the bridge at Nogent. Take D 11, then
right onto D 30 towards Vaas.

Vaas

Houses, little gardens, the church and washing houses are all next to each othe
on the banks of the Loir. Don't miss the **Moulin à blé de Rotrou**, a former flour
mill, on the left before the bridge. *Guided tours Jul-Aug: 2-5.30pm. 3.20€.* ☎ 02 43
46 70 22.

Turn left onto D 305, which goes past the **Cherré archaeological site**. This 1C and
2C AD Gallo-Roman ensemble contains a temple, thermae, two other buildings
and an attached reddish sandstone **theatre**.

Château du Lude★★

& *Jul-Aug: grounds accessible 10am-12.30pm, 2-6pm, guided tours of the château (45min*
2-6pm; Apr-Jun and Sep: grounds, daily except Wed 10am-12pm, 2-6pm, guided tours o
the château daily except Wed 2-6pm. 6€. ☎ 02 43 94 60 09. www.lelude.com

Le Lude, a magnificent château on the banks of the Loir, has several faces. Its
large round towers are Medieval and Gothic, its furnishings, dormer windows and
medallions are Italian Renaissance, and its harmonious riverside façade is Louis
XVI. The furniture inside is exceptional.

FROM TOURS TO ST-NICOLAS-DE-BOURGUEIL

125km. Michelin Local Map 317, J-N 4-6. See itinerary **4** *on the map on p. 280-281.*

Tours★★

Tours has preserved no less than three old neighbourhoods: **old Tours★★★** with
the Place Plumereau and its Medieval and Renaissance houses, the **quartier Saint-**
Julien★ in the centre of town, and the **quartier de la cathédrale★★** further east
with the archbishop's palace. The **Musée des vins de Touraine**, with its tools
stills, wine presses and costumes, is located in the storeroom of St. Julien's church
(12C). *Daily except Tue 9am-12pm, 2-6pm (last entrance 30min before closing). Closed*
1 Jan, 1 May, 14 Jul, 1 and 11 Nov, 25 Dec. 2.60€. ☎ 02 47 61 07 93.

Take D 88 W out of Tours. The road passes near the **Prieuré de Saint-Cosme★**
where Ronsard is buried. *Apr-Sep: 9am-7pm; Oct-Mar: 9.30am-12.30pm, 2-5pm.*
Closed 1 Jan, 25 Dec. 4.50€ (children 12-18: 3€). ☎ 02 47 37 32 70.

Continue on D 88, then turn left at l'Aireau-des-Bergeons. In **Savonnières** you can
visit the amazing petrified caves with their rock formations next to a petrified
waterfall, a cemetery, Gallo-Roman remains and objects currently in the process
of petrification. *Guided Tours (1hr) Apr-Sep: 9am-6.30pm; beginning Feb to end*
Mar and beginning Oct to mid-Nov: 9.30am-12pm, 2-6pm; mid-Nov to mid-Dec: daily
except Thu 9.30am-12pm, 2-5.30pm. Closed mid-Dec to beginning winter break. 5.20€.
☎ 02 47 50 00 09. www.grottes-savonnieres.com

Gardens and Château de Villandry★★★

The **gardens★★★** at Villandry are a magnificent recreation of the architectural layout adopted in the Renaissance under the influence of the Italian gardeners brought to France by Charles VIII. *Mid-Jun to mid-Sep: 9am-7.30pm; Apr to mid-Jun and mid-end Sep: 9am-7pm; Oct: 9am-6.30pm; Mar: 9am-6pm; Feb and first 2 weeks Nov: 9am-5.30pm; mid-Nov to Jan: 9am-5pm. 5€, 7.50€ château and grounds. (children: 3.50€, 5€).* ☎ *02 47 50 02 09. www.chateau villandry.com*

Built in the 16C around the original dungeon, the **château★★** is decorated with Spanish furniture and an interesting collection of paintings.

Street sign in Tours.

Mudéjar ceiling★ room. *Jul-Aug: 9am-6.30pm; Apr-Jun and Sep-Oct: 9am-6pm. Mar: 9am-5.30pm; first 2 weeks Feb and first 2 weeks Nov: 9am-5pm; Christmas hols: 9.30am-4.30pm. Closed the rest of the year. Guided Tours (2hr) except in Feb, Dec, Sun from May-Sep (brochures provided). 7.50€ (château and grounds).* ☎ *02 47 50 02 09. www.chateauvillandry.com*

Continue on D 7 to Lignières, then cross the bridge towards Langeais.

Château de Langeais★★

Mid-Jul to end Aug: 9.30am-7pm; beginning Apr to mid-Oct: 9.30am-6.30pm; mid-Oct to end Mar: 10am-5.30pm. Closed 25 Dec. 6.50€ (children: 4€). ☎ *02 47 96 72 60.*

The imposing medieval fortress of Langeais has made it through the centuries intact. The richly furnished **apartments★★★** evoke the atmosphere of seigniorial life in the 15C and early Renaissance.

Head back S over the Loire and take an immediate right onto D 16.

Château d'Ussé★★

Guided Tours (45min) Apr-Sep: 9.30am-6.30pm; mid-Feb to end Mar and beginning Oct to 11 Nov: 10am-12pm, 2-5.30pm. 9.80€. ☎ *02 47 95 54 05.*

Built in the 15C, this château was the inspiration for Charles Perrault's *Sleeping Beauty.* 📷 It also has a very interesting **game room★**. Princess Aurora, Carabossa and Prince Charming are all there on display, as you walk down the covered way.

Rivarennes

The village used to have sixty ovens for making *poires tapées* ("beaten pears"). Today you can taste one of these delicious local specialities in a troglodyte cave, **La Poire Tapée à l'Ancienne**. *R. de Quinçay, 37190 Rivarennes,* ☎ *02 47 95 45 19. www.poiretapees.com 10am-12pm, 2-7pm.*

This is in **Appellation Touraine-Azay-le-Rideau**, a relatively small vineyard (100ha), but with an original *encépagement*: Chenin for the whites and a Grolleau *assemblage* for the rosés.

Marnay: Musée Maurice-Dufresne★

♿ *May-Sep: 9.15am-6.45pm; Feb-Apr and Oct-Nov: 9.15am-5.45pm; Closed Dec-Jan. 10€ (children: 5€).* ☎ *02 47 45 36 18.*

📷 This museum, located in the verdant setting of a former paper mill, has a collection of over 3 000 old machines displayed in a wonderful – almost Surrealist – bric-à-brac manner. Pieces include Blériot's 1909 airplane, a 1792 guillotine, a 1908 Russian sleigh, an 1850 fire engine, a 1912 steam engine, a 1959 Morgan car and military vehicles from the two World Wars turned into farm machinery.

Turn right out of the museum (onto D 120, then D 57) to reach Azay.

Château d'Azay-le-Rideau★★★

Jul-Aug: 9.30am-7pm; Apr-Jun and Sep: 9.30am-6pm; Oct-Mar: 10am-12.30pm, 2-5.30pm. Last entrance 45min before closing. Closed 1 Jan, 1 May, 25 Dec. 6.10€ (children under 18: no charge), no charge 1st Sun of every month (Nov-Mar). ☎ *02 47 45 42 04. www. monum.fr*

A Renaissance gem built in the 16C on an island in the Indre, Azay contains extremely rich decorations and furnishings, in particular its **tapestries★**. But everything here – the trees and the handsome architecture, reflected in the glassy water – is absolutely dazzling.

Go S out of Azay, cross the bridge over the Indre and turn left onto D 17, then right onto D 57. The road goes through **Villaines-les-Rochers**, *a picturesque troglodyte village which became the capital of basketry, then* **Crissay-sur-Manse**, *a postcard-*

pretty village with old tufa houses – with square (15C) turrets, mullioned window and hidden gardens – dominated by the imposing ruins of the château (15C).

Continuing west on D 21 takes you into **Appellation Chinon** – Rabelais country The vineyards, which stretch for over 2 000ha on both sides of the Vienne take over completely along the road through Panzoult, Cravant-les-Coteaux an Chinon.

Chinon★★

Chinon rises in terraced rows between the Vienne river and chalky slope crowned by an impressive **medieval fortress★★**, which is open to visitors. *Apr-Sep 9am-7pm; Oct-Mar: 9.30am-5pm. Closed 1 Jan, 25 Dec. 6€ (children 12-18: 4.50€ ☎ 02 47 93 13 45.*

The "Circuit-Découverte" brochure *(available at the Tourist Office)* is a good guid to **old Chinon**.

The **Caves Painctes**, mentioned in Rabelais' tales of Pantagruel, still attract thei share of devotees of the vine. Induction ceremonies for the Bons Entonneur (Rabelaisian singers) take place there several times a year *(Jan, Jun, Sep and Dec* during a gala evening and show. By booking early enough in advance, you migh well have a chance to take part in these Rabelaisian festivities! *Secrétariat de l Confrérie, Imp. Des Caves-Painctes, 37500 Chinon, ☎ 02 47 93 30 44.*

🎦 The **Musée du Vin et de la Tonnellerie** (Wine and Cooperage Museum features life-size robots of characters such as Rabelais and his disciples who teac you about vineyard work, the winemaking process and making casks. *Enquire a the Tourist Office.*

Now it's time for some wine-tasting at **Caves Couly Dutheil** or **Cave Montplaisi** *(see Shopping Guide).*

The **Maison de la rivière** offers a variety of traditional boat rides, such as cruise at the confluence of the Loire and Vienne rivers, à la carte cruises and planne theme rides. *12 quai Pasteur. Jul-Aug: daily except Mon 10am-12.30pm, 2-6.30pm, Sa Sun and public hols 3-6.30pm; Easter-end Jun and Sep: daily except Mon 10am-12.30pm 2-5.30pm, Sat-Sun and public hols 2-5.30pm. Closed 1 May. 3€. ☎ 02 47 93 21 34.*

4.5km W of Chinon *(D 8)*, on the right, is the **Château de Coulaine**, open to visi tors *(see Shopping Guide)*. Turn right onto D 749. By making a slight detour throug **Beaumont-en-Véron**, you can taste and buy a wide selection of Chinon wine at estate prices at the **Maison des vins et du tourisme** *(see Shopping Guide)*. It competent and dynamic guides will provide you with a wealth of informatio about vineyard tours in the area.

Back on D 8, you will soon come to Savigny-en-Véron and D 7. As you cross the bridge there is a view of the superb **site★** of Candes-St-Martin, at the confluences of th Loire and Vienne, flanking the Plaine du Véron.

Candes-Saint-Martin★

The **collegiate church★**, built in the 12C-13C on the site where St Martin died i 397, was equipped with defences in the 15C. A small path *(to the right of the churc* leads up to the top of the hillside and a beautiful panorama. Rue St-Martin belov the church leads to the riverbank.

Leave Candes on D 7, which crosses the Vienne bridge and runs along the Loire. Tak the first bridge on the left to reach Bourgueil (D 749). The **Appellations Bourguei** and **Saint-Nicolas-de-Bourgueil** are linked by the same *cépage* (Cabernet Franc) which is mainly distinguished by its terroirs – gravel near the river and tufa o the slopes.

Bourgueil

Bourgueil – famous for its wine, whose ruby-colour and delightful qualities wer praised by Rabelais – contains an ancient **winemaking abbey** founded in th late 10C. It was one of the richest in Anjou, possessing vineyards all along it slopes. Today it houses the Musée des Arts et traditions Populaires (Folk Art an Traditions Museum). *At the eastern end of town, on the road to Restigné. Guide Tours (1hr) Jul-Aug: daily except Tue 2-6pm; Apr-Jun and Sep-Oct: Sun and public hol 2-6pm. 5€. ☎ 02 47 97 72 04.*

The **Maison des vins de Bourgueil** has a small selection of wines and provide information on the interesting vineyard walking path which goes through th winegrowing slopes of Benais *(a few kilometres E of Bourgueil)*; you might also tr the **Domaine Yannick Amirault** *(see Shopping Guide)*.

Leaving Bourgueil, head for **Chevrette** where the **Cave Touristique du Pays d Bourgueil** and its Wine Museum are located. *Apr-Sep: 9.30am-5.30pm. ☎ 02 4 97 72 01.*

Saint-Nicolas-de-Bourgueil

Wines are tasted over dinner in the excellent restaurant at the Caveau de Vignerons Le Saint Nicolas Gourmand, and can be bought in the adjoining cella which sells all varieties of Saint-Nicolas-de-Bourgueil. You could also try th **Domaine Olivier** *(see Shopping Guide)*.

Anjou-Saumur Wine Route

About 170km from Montsoreau to Montjean-sur-Loire (Maine-et-Loire). Michelin Local Map 317, D-J 4-5. See itinerary 5 on the map on p. 280-281.

This tour takes you through AOCs Saumur, Layon and Savennières.

Montsoreau

Montsoreau is famous for its (15C) **château** – in a "fortress with comforts" style – which is reflected in the Loire. Audiovisual exhibition, **"Les Imaginaires de Loire"**. *May-Sep: 9am-7pm; Oct to mid-Nov and Feb-end Apr: 2-6pm. Last entrance 45min before closing. Closed rest of year. 7.70€ (children: 4.80€). ☎ 02 41 67 12 60. www.chateau-montsoreau.com*

Take D947 S towards Fontevraud.

Abbaye de Fontevraud★★

Jun-Sep: 9am-6.30pm; Apr-May and Oct: 10am-5.30pm. Closed 1 Jan, 1 and 11 Nov, 25 Dec. 6.10€ – 7.50€) in season. ☎ 02 41 51 71 41. www.abbaye-fontevraud.com

This royal abbey – and burial place of the Plantagenets – is one of the greatest monastic complexes in France. Despite being converted into a prison from 1904 to 1963 (writer Jean Genêt was once a prisoner here) and undergoing other damage, it has preserved several pure gems of Angevin architecture such as its abbey-church noted for the lightness of its arches, **polychrome effigies★** and impressive **kitchen★★**.

St Michel's Church★ (12C-15C), in the village, contains some exceptional **works of art★**.

Go back to Montsoreau, turn left onto D 947 towards Saumur. The slopes along this road are lined with troglodyte dwellings, White Renaissance houses, cellars and former quarries, often converted into mushroom-beds. The ones at **Saut-aux-Loups** – on the way out of Montsoreau – show the various stages of mushroom culture; they also have delicious *galipettes*, large mushrooms baked in bread ovens, which you can taste (in season). ♿ *Guided Tours (1hr) Jul-Aug: 10am-6.30pm; Mar-Jun and Sep to mid-Nov: 10am-12pm, 2.15-6pm. 4.90€. (children 6-14: 3.40€). ☎ 02 41 51 70 30. www.troglo-sautauxloups.com*

Turquant

This is where **Appellation Saumur-Champigny** begins, covering 1 490ha in 9 town districts. To see the vineyards, you must climb up the hillside. 🚶 The GR3 and GR36 long-distance hiking routes go right through the vineyards.

Stop at **La Grande Vignole**, a rare example of a seigniorial troglodyte abode with a *fuye* (dovecote) and 16C chapel. *Apr-Sep: 10am-6pm; Oct: Thu and Fri 2-6pm, Sat-Sun 10am-6pm. No charge. ☎ 02 41 38 16 44 or 02 41 52 90 84, www.filliatreau.fr*

In nearby Val-Hulin, the **Troglo des pommes tapées** is doubly worth a visit for its superbly decorated 19C-style cellar, and for its *pommes tapées*, the tasty local speciality which was a big hit in the 1880s when the phylloxera crisis forced winemakers to convert to another crop. *Guided Tours (1hr) Jul-Aug: daily except Mon 10am-12pm, 2.30-6pm; May-Jun and Sep: Sat-Sun and public hols 10am-12pm, 2.30-6pm. 5€. ☎ 02 41 51 48 30.*

Parnay

The delicious little **Romanesque Church** perched on top of the hillside amid the vineyards provides a great opportunity for a lovely walk. There is an ornithological preserve across from the village on a sand bank in the Loire.

Souzay-Champigny

Lift up your gaze and admire Marguerite d'Anjou's **castle**, connected by a turret to a 13C-14C troglodyte abode. The village is also known for its Clos Cristal (it now belongs to the Hospices de Saumur) with trellised vines climbing over a wall – in order to have their roots facing north and their tops facing south.

Saumur★★

The Château de Saumur, perched atop its tufa hillside, looks like a medieval miniature from the illuminated pages of the *Très Riches Heures du duc de Berry*. Renowned for its famous sparkling wines, the town also has strong connections with France's horse-breeding industry.

The winding little streets between the château and the bridge in **old Saumur★** have kept their medieval layout. Almost unchanged since its reconstruction (late 14C), the **château★★** conceals a richly ornamented and comfortable abode behind its fortress-like exterior. It contains the **Musée d'Arts décoratifs★★** and the **Musée du Cheval★** (Horse Museum). *Château closed for renovations. Visits of the grounds only: Apr-Oct daily except Tue 10am-1pm, 2-6pm; rest of year: daily except Tue 10am-12.30pm, 2-5.30pm. Guided Tours available all year round with advance booking (Apr-Oct). 2€. (children under 11: no charge). ☎ 02 41 40 24 40.*

The **Maison du vin de Saumur**, a model in its genre, contains a wealth of information on wine and wine tourism *(see Shopping Guide)*.

Don't leave town without visiting one of the many cellars located in Saumur itself where the wines with fine bubbles are slowly talking on their full character. The most curious is probably the **Caves Louis de Grenelle**, a town-beneath-the-town. Guided tours followed by a tasting with commentary. A fun place for learning about wines and wine-growing. *20 r. Marceau, BP 206, 49415, Saumur,* ☎ *02 41 50 17 63, www.caves-de-grenelle.fr May-Oct guided tours (1hr 20min) 9.30am-6.30pm; 2-6pm; Oct to Mar guided tours Mon-Fri 9am-12pm; 1.30-6pm. Closed 1 May, Christmas and New Year's Day. 2.50€.*

Saint-Hilaire-Saint-Florent

The **Caves Bouvet-Ladubay** are among the most interesting – with cellars hollowed out of the cliff. Wine-tasting school open to all wine-lovers. Exceptional collection of labels. Contemporary art gallery. ⅙ *Guided Tours (1hr) Jun-Sep: 8.30am-7pm, Sun 9.30am-7pm; Oct-May: 9am-12.30pm, 2-6pm, Sat 9.30am-12.30pm, 2-6pm, Sun and public hols 9.30am-12.30pm, 2.30-6pm. Closed 1 Jan, 25 Dec. 1€.* ☎ *02 41 83 83 83. www.bouvet-ladubay.fr*

Go back to the roundabout across from the Château de Saumur and take the Route Touristique towards Champigny and Fontevraud through the vineyards (D 145). After the Aunis farm, an important Resistance centre for Saumur cadets during the Second World War, turn right towards Chaintre and Varrains, one of the smallest townships in **Appellation Saumur-Champigny**, but the one with the largest number of winemakers.

In Samoussay, take the first left towards Saint-Cyr-en-Bourg. The road goes past the **Cave des Vignerons de Saumur**, which has over 10km of underground galleries. Here you can find out about the history of the vineyards, wine-making secrets and a whole range of Saumur wines including Saumur brut, Crémant-de-Loire, Saumur-Champigny, Cabernet-de-Saumur, etc. *Guided tours (1hr) May-Sep 10am-12.30pm, 2-7pm; Oct-Apr: daily except Sun 9.30am-12.30pm, 2-6pm. Closed 1 and 11 Nov, 25 and 31 Dec. 2.50€.* ☎ *02 41 53 06 18.*

Château de Brézé★★

Guided Tours Apr-end Sep: 10am-6.30pm; Oct-Dec and Feb to end Mar: daily except Mon 2-4.45pm, Sat-Sun 10am-6pm. Closed Jan, 24-25 Dec. 6.80€, château, 7.10€ underground, 11€ château and underground. ☎ *02 41 51 60 15. www.chateaude-breze.com*

This elegant Renaissance château, remodelled in the 19C, elegantly furnished and surrounded by a sea of vineyards, has a secret – its fabulous **troglodyte complex★★**! Over a kilometre of underground trails with wine cellars, a press for the famous Brézé white wines, cellars – including three which have been turned into a painted "cathedral" **chamber★**, a **bakery★**, and the largest known underground fortress!

Drive towards Montreuil-Bellay, then turn right (D 178) towards St-Just-in-Dive, then left (D 162). **Le Coudray-Macouard** – full of little medieval streets lined with 15C-18C houses, a château, church and many cellars – is one of the most picturesque villages in Anjou.

Go S on the little road that runs along the Thouet.

Montreuil-Bellay★

Verdant banks washed by the Thouet, old streets, ancient houses and gardens, fortified surrounding walls and gates all give Montreuil-Bellay true medieval charm. The Medieval kitchen in the **château★★**, a lovely 15C home, has been pre-

In the Layon hills.

served. *Guided tours (1hr) Apr-Oct: 10am-6pm (last entrance 30min before closing). 7€.* ☎ *02 41 52 33 06.*

Take the bridge over the Thouet (towards Doueé-la-Fontaine) out of Montreuil-Bellay and turn left onto D 88 towards Sanziers, then right onto D 178.

Le Puy-Notre-Dame

Throngs of pilgrims came to the 13C **collegiate church** during the Middle Ages to venerate the Virgin Mary's belt, brought back from Jerusalem in the 12C. You can learn all about the mysteries of silkworms at the **Musée de la Soie Vivante** in this village. *Guided tours (1hr 15min) May-11 Nov: 10am-12pm, 1.30-6pm, Sun and Mon 2-5pm; rest of year upon request. 4.20€. (children: 2.50€).* ☎ *02 41 38 28 25.*

To the west of Le Puy, the D 178 is lined with vineyards as far as the eye can see. It goes through the pretty little village of Argentay, then into **Appellation Coteaux-du-Layon** at Verchers-sur-Layon. Coteaux-du-Layon is a subtle and delicate white wine – *moelleux* or *liquoreux* – produced with the Chenin Blanc or Pineau-de-la-Loire *cépages* harvested in late September when the grapes start to be covered with noble rot. The appellation extends over 1 200ha and 27 townships on the Layon, a small tributary of the Loire. The six local areas with particularly well-exposed soil which can tag the AOC onto their name as a guarantee of quality are Rochefort, St-Aubin-de-Luigé, St-Lambert, Beaulieu, Faye and Rablay. Certain very specific wines from the Butte de Chaume in the Rochefort township have had the right to use the **Appellation Chaume** label since 2003.

From Concourson the road climbs up the steep slopes covered with vine stocks all the way to St-Georges-sur-Layon, a former mining town.

Take a left onto D 84 and continue to Tigné, then go N on D 167.

Martigné-Briand

The **château**, ravaged by the Vendée wars, has nevertheless preserved some magnificent remains of its flamboyant 16C splendour. It is best seen when it comes to life on the first Sunday in October, as host to the Vendanges de la Belle Époque.

Turn left onto D 125. **Thouarcé** is in the heart of **AOC Bonnezeaux** (90ha). This "divine nectar" blending aromas of candied fruit with undertones of minerals and honey, is only produced on three small, steep slopes with full southern exposure. Gathered in successive pickings to get the best out of the noble rot, this vintage gives full, mellow wines which combine intensity, complexity, freshness and elegance as they age.

Rablay-sur-Layon boasts a 15C Tithing House *(Maison de la Dîme)* in the Grand-Rue and a 17C building which houses artists' workshops.

Beaulieu-sur-Layon

This other small wine-making town, which dominates the Layon slopes (viewpoint indicator), has preserved a few Mansart houses as well as 13C frescoes in the church.

🚶 A former railway line has been turned into a hiking path along the Layon for 25km.

The **Château Pierre-Bise** makes an excellent Chaume *premier cru* and affords an exceptional panorama *(see Shopping Guide).*

Go west out of town and turn right onto D 55 to reach the **Caveau-Musée du Vin**, which has a collection of old Anjou wine bottles and glasses. *Jun-Aug: 10am-12pm, 2-6pm, Sun 10am-1pm; Sep-May: Mon-Fri 2-5pm. Inquire at the Tourist office. No charge.* ☎ *02 41 78 65 07.*

The road goes down into a valley where cellars and quarries have been dug out of the rock face. In a locality called **Pont-Barré** there is a pretty view over the Layon's narrowing course and the ruins of a Medieval bridge where a violent battle took place in 1793 between the Royalists *(Blancs)* and Revolutionaries *(Bleus). Get back on N 60 and follow it S.*

Saint-Lambert-du-Lattay

🏛 The **Musée de la Vigne et du Vin d'Anjou**, set up in the Coudraye storerooms, evokes the world of Angevin winemaking, featuring winemaking and cooperage tools, illustrations and a collection of wine presses. In a room called *l'Imaginaire du Vin* you get to use your eyes, nose and taste buds. There is also an observation and exploration game called *Les Clefs du Musée* (The Keys to the Museum) designed especially for children (7-14). *Jul-Aug: 11am-1pm, 3-7pm; Apr-June and beginning Sep-11 Nov: Sat-Sun and public hols 2.30-6.30pm. 4.80€. (children: 3.15€).* ☎ *02 41 78 42 75.*

The hilly, winding St-Aubin-de-Luigné road is lined with Butte de Chaume vineyards where the famous **Quarts-de-Chaume** wines are produced on a few rare parcels of land. *Turn left onto D 106 just before St-Aubin, then right.*

Château de la Haute-Guerche

Jul-Aug: 9am-12pm, 2-6pm. No charge. ☎ *02 41 78 41 48.*

This fortress built during the reign of Charles VII and ruined by the Vendée wars, once housed the lords to whom the Chaume lands belonged. They rented them out in return for payment in kind of the best quarter of the vineyard's harvest, which is where the Quarts-de-Chaume appellation's name comes from.

Go back to St-Aubin and turn right onto the little road that leads to La Haie-Longue.
Take the **Corniche Angevine★** (D 751 cliff road) with a view over the entire width of the valley. At **La Haie-Longue** there is a remarkable **view★★** of the Loire and its *boires*, expanses of water sprawling out lazily under the silvery light. As you leave town, there is a chapel devoted to Notre-Dame-de-Lorette and a monument to René Gasnier, a pioneer of aviation. Further on, **Rochefort-sur-Loire** has preserved a few old houses, but its fame mainly comes from the slopes overlooking the town, a privileged few of which have the Quarts-de-Chaume and Chaume Premier Cru Coteaux-du-Layon Appellations. The **Domaine des Baumard**, 150m from the church, has Quarts-de-Chaume, Savennières and other wines *(see Shopping Guide)*.

Béhuard★

The charming island of Béhuard grew up around a rock, on top of which sits the little **Church of Notre-Dame**. Built in the 15C by Louis XI, it became a popular destination for pilgrimages to the Virgin Mary, protector of travellers. Have a walk around the old village with its 15C and 16C houses, and along the wayside cross.

Savennières

The village **church** has a pretty Romanesque *chevet* with sculpted modillions and a southern portal from the same period. Note the herringbone-brick ornamentation on the (10C) shale wall of the nave.

The **AOC Savennières** terroirs, perched atop the steep slopes overlooking the Loire, have very well-exposed soil composed of shale, Volcanic seams and sand. They produce great whites which are mainly converted into dry, full-bodied and rich wines with an invigorating final note and intense, complex aromas. There are two world-class Savennières vintages: Coulée-de-Serrant and Roche-aux-Moines.

Grown with biodynamic methods since 1980, the famous Coulée-de-Serrant stretches over 7ha of steep slopes overlooking the Loire. The **Domaine Vignobles de la Coulée de Serrant** contains a former monastery, the ruins of a former fortified castle and a path with Celtic cypresses *(see Shopping Guide)*.

After tasting some of the Savennière and Anjou wines at the **Domaine du Closel**, in the very heart of Savennières, you can visit the English-style gardens (with a picnic area) and vineyards using a map with explanations of the terroir, landscape and growing methods. *1 pl. du Mail, 49170 Savennières,* ☎ *02 41 72 81 00. 9am-12.30pm, 1.30-7pm. 6€. Reservations required.*

The road that runs along the Loire towards **Epiré** climbs up through the vineyards over the small but deep valley of a Loire tributary. The **Château de Chamboureau**, with one of the oldest vineyards in Appellation Savennières, is a lovely 15C home *(see Shopping Guide)*.

After La Pointe the road follows the banks of the Maine on to Angers.

Angers★★★

Angers' gigantic medieval fortress is a reminder that it was once the capital of a kingdom comprising England and Sicily. Built by St Louis from 1228-38, the **château★★★** narrowly escaped destruction during the Religious Wars. Only the tops of its 17 towers were taken off. Its greatest jewel, the **Apocalypse Tapestry★★★** (14C), originally 133m long and 6m high, is a colourful, grandiose illustration of the Revelations of St John. The royal abode contains a superb collection of 15C and 16C tapestries, including the **Tapestry of the Passion** and **mille-fleurs tapestries★★**. *May-Aug: 9.30am-6.30pm; Sep-Apr: 10am-5.30pm. Guided tours of the dungeon cells. (1hr) at 10.15am, 11.15am, 2.15pm and 3.15pm. last entrance 45min before closing. Closed 1 Jan, 1 May, 1 and 11 Nov, 25 Dec. 6.10€. (children under 18: no charge).* ☎ *02 41 87 43 47. www.monum.fr*

For a last look at some tapestries, don't miss the **Musée Jean-Lourçat et de la Tapisserie contemporaine★★**. It occupies the **Hôpital St-Jean★**, founded in 1174, and contains a series of tapestries by Jean-Lourçat (1892-1966) entitled *Le Chant du monde★★* (Song of the World). *Jun-Sep: 10am-7pm; Oct-Jun: daily except Mon 10am-12pm, 2-6pm. Closed 1 Jan, 1 May, 1 and 11 Nov, 25 Dec. 4€.* ☎ *02 41 05 38 37 or 02 41 05 38 38 (Tue-Fri 1.30-5pm). www.angers.fr*

While walking through **old Angers★** to take in its many monuments – the **Cathédrale Saint-Maurice★** (12C-13C, 16C), half-timbered 16C houses such as the **Maison d'Adam★**, Église Saint-Serge (13C chancel), **the Galerie David d'Angers★**

and the **Hôtel Pincé★** – you may want to stop for a break in one of the many gardens in this city known for its flowers and green spaces, including the Jardin des Plantes, the Jardin du Mail and the Arboretum. And to keep up on wines, there's the **Maison du vin de l'Anjou** *(see Shopping Guide)*. The **Académie des vins du Val de Loire** offers training courses, intensive workshops, special appointments, lectures and wine tastings. *Hôtel des Vins La Godeline, 73 r. Plantagenêt, BP 52327, 49023 Angers Cedex 02, ☏ 02 41 87 62 57, www.interloire.com*

Take N 23 W out of Angers.

Château de Serrant★★★

Guided tours (1hr) Jul-Aug: 9.45am-5.15pm, beginning Feb hols-end Jun and Sep: 9.45am-12pm, 2-5.45pm. Oct-Dec: Wed-Sun 9.45am-12pm, 2-5.15pm. Closed rest of year. 9€. ☏ 02 41 39 13 01.

Begun in 1546, this Renaissance château contains some magnificent **apartments**. The furniture collection is so rich and of such high quality that it has been classified as a historical monument, which is a first.

Take D 961 S out of St-Georges-sur-Loire. In summer, the little **Train touristique Chalonnes par vignes et vallées** takes you down the old streets of **Chalonnes-sur-Loire** and up the vineyards' steep paths, offering superb panoramas of the Layon hills. *Jul-Aug: 10am-7pm. Length 1hr 15min. 5.50€. Information and reservations ☏ 02 41 78 14 90 or 02 41 78 25 62.*

Take D 751 W. The road follows the edge of the plateau, interspersed with little valleys. This is the **Appellation Coteaux-de-la-Loire** area. Perched atop a promontory, **Montjean-sur-Loire** houses a museum evoking former activities in the region such as working with hemp, the Loire as a working river, lime kilns and coal mines. *Closed temporarily.*

The Pays Nantais

About 170km from Ancenis to Nantes (Loire-Atlantique). Michelin Local Map 316, G-I 3-5. See itinerary **6** *on the map on p. 280-281.*
This tour takes you through the Saumur, Layon and Savennières AOCs.

Ancenis

This is the **Appellation Coteaux-d'Ancenis** area, where Ancenis was long a very active port for transporting wine. The Vignerons de la Noëlle group of producers cultivates 350ha of vineyards and produces Gros-Plant and Coteaux d'Ancenis.

Take D 763 S out of Ancenis.

Liré

Liré is renowned for the poet Joachim du Bellay (1522-60), who sang the praises of his native village in a famous sonnet while on a journey to Rome. The **Musée Joachim-du-Bellay**, in a 16C dwelling, has preserved mementos relating to the poet. *Jul-Aug: 10.30am-12.30pm, 2.30-6pm, Apr–Jun and Sep-Oct: Wed-Sun 10.30am-12.30pm, 2.30-6pm, Sat 2.30-6pm; Mar: Sun 2.30-5.15pm. Guided tours at 11am, 3 and 5 pm. Closed Easter Mon. 4.20€. ☏ 02 40 09 04 13. www.musee-du-bellay.fr.st*

Go W on D 751 to reach Liré.

Champtoceaux★

This is a wonderful **site★** perched on top of a peak overlooking the Loire Valley. The **Promenade de Champalud★★**, behind the church, gives a panoramic view of the river divided into branches and vast sandy islands. From there you can visit the ruins of the citadel destroyed in 1420, as well as an old river toll.

Turn left onto D 7 after La Varenne. Climbing up to the plateau away from the Loire, you enter **AOC Muscadet-Sèvre-et-Maine** country, one of the densest vineyards in the Loire Valley. It owes its name to the Petite Maine and the Sèvre Nantaise which run through it.

Le Loroux-Bottereau

After forming a crack corps during the 1793 insurrection, the inhabitants of this town brought down the wrath of Turreau, who had it destroyed in 1794. Le Loroux has managed to preserve a 13C fresco in the church: there is a fine view of the vineyards from its tower. Get a copy of the free *Bienvenue dans nos caves* brochure at the Tourist Office, which lists the winemakers in the region who open their cellars in rotation. The topoguide *Randonnées, Détours en vignoble* is also on sale there. *Take D 307 (route du Vignoble) in the direction of Vallet.* A small road on the left leads to the **Moulin du Pé**; from the top, there is a beautiful view of the Goulaine vineyards and marshes. The **Domaine de l'Écu** at Le Landreau is also open to visitors *(see Shopping Guide)*.

Head SE on D 37.

Shopping Guide

INFORMATION

Bureau des vins d'Anjou et de Saumur
– *Hôtel des Vins La Godeline - 73 r.
Plantagenêt - BP 2327 - 49023 Angers
Cedex 02 -* ☎ *02 41 87 62 57.*

**Conseil interprofessionnel des vins de
Nantes** – *Maison des vins - Bellevue - 44690
La Haye-Fouassière -* ☎ *02 40 36 90 10 -
www.muscadet.org*

Syndicat viticole de Pouilly – *2 r. des
Écoles - 58150 Pouilly-sur-Loire -* ☎ *03 86
39 06 83*

**Bureau interprofessionnel des vins
du Centre** – *9 rte de Chavignol - 18300
Sancerre -* ☎ *02 48 78 51 07 - www.vins-
centre-loire.com*

Bureau des vins de la Touraine – *12 r
des Étienne-Pallu - BP 61921 - 37019 Tours
Cedex 1 -* ☎ *02 47 60 55 00.*

OVERVIEW

CHARACTERISTICS

Central Loire Wines – White wines:
subtle and crisp Sauvignons with aromas
of gunflint, fruit (citrus, blackcurrant, litchi,
guava), flowers, plants (broom, rhubarb) and
musk. Red wines: full-bodied Pinot Noirs
which linger on the palate with distinct
aromas of Morello cherries, violets and
exotic wood in young wines, maturing with
age towards cherries in brandy, game and
truffles.

Touraine Wines – White wines: luminous
and aromatic Sauvignons with aromas of
broom, honeysuckle and exotic fruit. Chenin
Blanc wines with fine bubbles: aromas of
brioche, green apples and honey. Light
and fresh red wines from Gamay grapes.
Vouvrays have aromas of acacia, roses and
citrus developing undertones of candied
apricot, quince and, in particular, honey.
Jasnières and Coteaux-du-Loir have floral
and fruity aromas evolving into dried fruit
and honey. Chinon, Bourgueil and Saint-
Nicolas-de-Bourgueil: on gravelly soil they
give light reds which are highly aromatic (red
berries); on clay, flint and tufa, they produce
full-bodied and well-structured wines
maturing with aromas of dark berries, mild
spices and game.

Anjou and Saumur Wines – Red wines:
aromas of red berries, irises and violets. Fresh
and highly aromatic Anjou-Gamays with
undertones of fruit drops. White Saumurs
with aromas of fruit and white flowers and
subtle mineral undertones. Saumur Brut
and Crémant-de-Loire have aromas of white
fruit, balm, hazelnuts and almonds. White
Anjous: aromas ranging from honey and
apricots from regions of slate soil to more
floral combinations when Sauvignon and/or
Chardonnay grapes are present. Coteaux-
du-Layons produce strong, complex scents
of acacia honey with aromas of citronella
and candied fruit. Bonnezeaux, Quarts-de-
Chaumes and Savennières: strong, complex
scents with aromas of flowers, white
and exotic fruit (linden and anise for the
Savennières) maturing with undertones of

exotic wood, dried or candied fruit,
honey and almonds, with a pronounced
mineral quality.

Pays Nantais Wines – Muscadet: fresh,
with light, *perlant* bubbles when they are
matured on the lees; scents are discreetly
floral and fruity, sometimes minerally. Gros-
Plant: a crisp white wine.

S. Sauvignier / MICHELIN

STORAGE

The amount of time a Loire wine can
be stored varies considerably with the
climate. A cool year will produce dry,
acidic wines to be consumed rapidly,
while a hot summer and autumn will
often result in rich wines with a greater
ageing potential. Even among Muscadets,
which are thought to be for rapid
consumption, some vintages may be kept
for 10 years. Within the same appellation,
the kind of soil may also influence storage
time. Regarding the Bourgueil, Saint-
Nicolas-de-Bourgueil and Chinon, for
example, the wines from gravelly soil are
at their best when young, whereas those
grown on tufa soils improve with age
and may be kept for several decades.
Likewise, Sancerres and other wines
made with Sauvignon Blanc grapes
mature rapidly when grown on chalky
soil, while those grown on marly and
flinty clay soils take longer to come into
their own and have a greater storage
potential (2-5 years, and sometimes 10
or more).

Saumur Bruts, Crémants and Mousseux
should ordinarily be consumed within 2 or
3 years. Wines with the greatest ageing
potential (several decades) include – for
the best vintages – Jasnières, Coteaux-du-
Layons, Montlouis moelleux, Vouvrays, as
well as Bonnezeaux, Quarts-de-Chaumes
and Savennières (minimum 8-year storage
potential).

PRICES

Very good Touraine, Anjou and Pays Nantais
wines can be found for less than 5€. On
average, they range from 5-8€ and 15-20€,
but certain Pouilly-Fumés, Sancerres and
Chinons can run over 30-40€. The best

Bonnezeaux, Quarts-de-Chaume, Savennières and Vouvrays can reach 45-75€ when already aged.

BUYING

WINE MERCHANTS

La Cave de Louis XII – *10 r. Émile-Laurens - 41000 Blois - ☎ 02 54 74 28 18 - Tue-Sat 8.30am-12.30pm, 2.30-7pm.* Mr. Morin's cellar possesses some valuable bottles of wine from local producers – Menetou-Salons, Muscadets – as well as a fine selection of wines from Languedoc, the Rhone Valley, Burgundy and Bordeaux. A plus: the selection of delicatessen items and cheeses.

Aux Trésors de Bacchus – *Nouvelle-Place - 18300 Sancerre - ☎ 02 48 54 17 45 - www.fournier-pere-fils.fr - open in summer 10am-7pm; in winter 10am-6pm.* This cellar is owned by a winemaker who is extremely knowledgeable about the wines from his region. In addition to his own bottles, he offers Sancerres, Pouilly-Fumés and Coteaux-du-Giennois, all estate-bottled and chosen with great care. A fine selection of Burgundies, Bordeaux, Champagnes and wines from the Loire.

Aux Saveurs de la Tonnelle – *4 r. de la Tonnelle - 49400 Saumur - ☎ 02 41 52 86 62 - Tue-Sat 9.30am-1pm, 2.30-7.30pm, Sun 9.30am-1pm.* This shop prides itself on its rigorous selection of the best Loire Valley vintages: Chinons, Menetou-Salons, Sancerres, Saulur-Champignys, Rosé-d'Anjou, Vouvrays, Coteaux-du-Layon, etc. Treasures from other French vineyards – such as a 1988 Pommerol or a 1995 Haut-Médoc – are also to be found.

Les Belles Caves – *15 pl. des Halles - 37000 Tours - ☎ 02 47 38 73 18 - Tue-Sat 9.30am-12.30pm, 3-7pm.* This fine cellar has an interesting choice of Loire Valley wines. The friendly owner has carefully selected many treasures for his clients. Many people enjoy his "wine in bulk" corner with Bourgueil, Chinon and Anjou wines. Whisky, spirits and Champagnes are also well-represented in the 1 000 different bottles sold in the shop.

MAISONS DES VINS

The maisons des vins – wine centres – have the advantage of offering a good selection of wines from their appellation at estate prices. They also provide valuable information on the vineyards.

Maison du vin de l'Anjou – *5 bis pl. Kennedy - 49100 Angers - ☎ 02 41 88 81 13 - www.interloire.com - May-Sep: Tue-Sun 9am-1pm, 3-6.30pm; Oct-Apr: Tue-Sat 9.30am-1pm, 5-6.30pm. Closed Jan-Feb and public hols.*

Maison des vins et du tourisme – *14 r. du 8-Mai-1945 - 37420 Beaumont-en-Véron - ☎ 02 47 58 86 17 - Tue-Sat 9.30am-12.30pm, 2.30-6.30pm. Closed Christmas and New Year's Day.*

Maison des vins de Loir-et-Cher – *11 pl. du Château - 41000 Blois - ☎ 02 54 74 76 66 - Mon-Fri 9am-12pm, 2-5pm. Closed Christmas, New Year's Day, 1 and 11 Nov.*

Maison des vins de Bourgueil "Jean Carmet" – *18 pl. de l'Église - 37140*

Bourgueil - ☎ 02 47 97 92 20 - 15 May-15 Sep: Tue-Sat 10am-12.30pm, 3-7pm; mid-Sep to mid-May: 2-6pm, Sat 10am-12pm, 2-6pm.

Maison des vins de Loir-et-Cher – *11 pl. du Château - 41000 Blois - ☎ 02 54 74 76 66 - Mon-Fri 9am-12pm, 2-5pm. Closed Christmas, New Year's Day, 1 and 11 Nov.*

Maison des vins de Nantes – *BP 33 - Bellevue - 44690 La haye-Fouassière - ☎ 02 40 36 90 10 - Mon-Fri 8.30am-12.30pm, 2-5.45pm (Sat 11am-6pm in Jul-Aug) - closed on public hols.*

Maison du vin de Saumur – *Quai Lucien-Gautier - 49400 Saumur - ☎ 02 41 38 45 83 - mdesvins-saumur@interloire.com - Apr-Sep: Mon 2-7pm; Tue-Sat 9.30am-1pm, 2-7pm, Sun 9.30am-1pm; Oct-Mar: Tue-Sat 10am-1pm, 2-6.30pm - closed mid-Jan to mid-Feb.*

Maison du Muscadet – *4 rte d'Ancenis - 44330 Vallet - ☎ 02 40 36 25 95.*

WINEGROWING COOPERATIVES

Caveau des vignerons d'Amboise – *Pl. Michel-Debré - 37400 Amboise - ☎ 02 47 57 23 69 - mid-Mar to mid-Nov: 10am-7pm.* Whites, rosés, reds, and traditional, Champagne-style wines from twelve winemakers are presented here. Other local products for sale.

La Cave Montplaisir – *Quai Pasteur - 37500 Chinon - ☎ 02 47 93 20 75 - 15 Mar to 15 Nov: Mon-Sat 10am-12.30pm, 2.30-7.30pm, Sun 11am-12.30pm, 2.30-7.30pm.* This huge (2 500m²) cellar belongs to 3 winemakers from the area. After visiting the maze of tunnels dug out of the tufa walls – full of bottles, casks and tuns – try a Chinon, Saumur or Touraine rosé at the tasting bar.

Caves de Pouilly-sur-Loire – *39 av. des Tuileries - 58150 Pouilly-sur-Loire - ☎ 03 86 39 10 99 - caves.pouilly.loire@wanadoo.fr - Mon-Fri 8am-12pm, 2-6pm, Sat 9am-12.30pm, 2-6pm, Sun in season 10am-12.30pm, 2.30-6.30pm.* This cellar, created in 1948, now has 100 members and is one of the main producers of Pouilly-Fumé and Coteaux-du-Giennois. The shop has a long bar for tasting their white wines with that typical terroir flavour.

Caves des Producteurs de Vouvray – *"La Vallée Coquette" - RN 152 betsween Tours and Amboise - 37210 Vouvray - ☎ 02 47 52 75 03 - www.vouvray-cp.com - daily 9am-12.30pm, 2-7pm - closed 1 Jan and 25 Dec.* You can see how Vouvrays are made – both effervescent and still – without necessarily walking the entire two kilometres of tunnel-cellars hollowed out of the tufa. Wines from the cooperative and other Loire Valley producers for sale. Tastings.

ESTATES

Château Pierre-Bise – *49750 Beaulieu-sur-Layon - ☎ 02 41 78 31 44 - daily 8am-12pm, 2-6pm - by appointment.* This family-owned vineyard, reopened in 1974, covers 54ha planted mainly in Chenin grapes (35ha), as well as Cabernet Francs and Cabernet-Sauvignons (18ha). Yields are low, planting/ripening is done naturally and the vines are pruned. Grapes are harvested manually in successive pickings. A long ageing period follows slow fermentation without yeast or chaptalisation.

Château de Coulaine – *2 r. de Coulaine - 37420 Beaumont-en-Véron - ☎ 02 47 98 44 51 - chateaudecoulaine@club-internet.fr* This château, in the same family for several centuries, has 16ha. The vineyard has been organic since 1997. The vines (Cabernet Franc and Chenin) are rooted in flinty clay, chalky clay or sandy soil. The grapes are treated with a long maceration period, and some vintages are aged in oak barrels.

Domaine Yannick Amirault – *5 pavillon du Grand-Clos - 37140 Bourgueil - ☎ 02 47 97 78 07 - Mon-Sat 8am-12pm, 2-6pm - by appointment only.* The vineyard is planted in flinty clay and gravelly soil. The Cabernet Francs vines get plenty of sunshine due to their southern exposure. The grapes are converted into wine in thermo-regulated vats.

Domaine Pinard – *42 r. St-Vincent - 18300 Bué - ☎ 02 48 54 33 89 - Mon-Sat 9am-12pm, 2-6.30pm - by appointment.* This family vineyard has been handed down from father to son since 1789. It has 15ha of Sauvignon and Pinot Noir. Always striving to maintain high standards, they practise manual harvesting, pneumatic pressing, fermentation with automatic temperature control, pumping up the lees, filtering and estate-bottling.

Domaine Patrick Baudouin – *Princé - 49290 Chaudefonds-sur-Layon - ☎ 02 41 78 66 04 - contact@patrick-baudouin-layon. com - by appointment.* After working at several different jobs, Patrick Baudouin took over the family estate created by his great-grandparents in the 1920s. He replanted the vineyards and, eight years later, bought and restructured an old wine storehouse surrounded by fallow slopes. His estate of 10ha in production, including 7ha planted with Chenin and 3ha of Cabernet Franc and Sauvignon, stretches over the townships of Chaudefonds-sur-Layon, St-Aubin-de-Luigné, Rochefort-sur-Loire and St-Germain-des-Près. In 2004 the estate entered its third year since converting to organic gardening.

Caves Couly Dutheil – *12 r. Diderot - 37500 Chinon - ☎ 02 47 97 20 20 - info@coulydutheilchinon.com - by appointment.* This prestigious vineyard, run by maîtres de chai (cellar masters) Pierre and Jacques Dutheil, produces light, fruity wines, and has just celebrated its 75th anniversary. Take a moment to try them in their tasting room.

Domaine de l'Écu – *La Bretonnière - 44430 Le landreau - ☎ 02 40 06 40 91 - bossard. guy.muscadet@wanadoo.fr - daily except Sun and public hols 9am-12pm, 2-6pm. by appointment.* This 21ha family vineyard is planted in Melon-de-Bourgogne (16ha) for Muscadet, Folle Blanche (2ha) for Gros Plant du Pays Nantais, Cabernet (2ha) for red vin de pays, and Chardonnay (1ha) for the traditional method. The vineyard has been biodynamic since 1992.

Domaine François Chidaine – *5 Grande-Rue - Husseau - 37270 Montlouis-sur-Loire - ☎ 02 47 45 10 20 - françois.chidaine@wanadoo.fr - daily except Sun in winter 10am-12pm, 2.30-7pm.* The estate's Chenin vines are planted on various flinty-clay and chalky plots. The biodynamic vineyard is grown traditionally, using ploughing, training, and manual harvesting. In 2002 François and Manuella Chidaine joined in with Nicolas Martin to buy an additional 10ha of vineyards, making a total of 26ha, in the Appellation Vouvray area.

Château de Tracy – *Tracy-sur-Loire - 58150 Pouilly-sur-Loire - ☎ 03 86 26 15 12 - tracy@wanadoo.fr* This estate has been in existence since 1396. The 27ha vineyard is planted with Sauvignon and divided into two kinds of terroir - chalky Kimmeridgian and flinty clay. The vineyard has been cultivated using environmentally conscious *"lutte raisonnée"* techniques since 1994. The vines – 23 years old on average – are harvested manually. Wines then age in stainless steel vats for a year.

Domaine des Baumard – *La Giraudière - 8 r. de l'Abbaye - 49190 Rochefort-sur-Loire - ☎ 02 41 78 70 03 - contact@baumard. fr - Mon-Sat 10am-12pm, 2-5.30pm - by appointment.* Old documents attest to the Baumard family's winemaking in Rochefort-sur-Loire since 1634. During the 1950s and 1960s, Jean Baumard turned his property into a state-of-the-art estate. Today, his son Florent proposes a wide range of wines - dry, *moelleux*, sparkling Crémants-de-Loire and even brandy made from Coteaux-de-Loire. The forty hectares of vineyards are grown with rational control.

S. Sauvignier/MICHELIN

Domaine des Rochelles – *12 chemin des Rochelles - 49320 St-Jean-des-Mauvrets - ☎ 02 41 91 92 07 - jy.a.lebreton@wanadoo. fr - Mon-Sat 9am-12pm, 2-6pm - by appointment.* In 1977 Jean-Yves Lebreton took over this estate created by his great-grandfather Édouard, which had been handed down through the generations. The vineyard has 58ha, including 38 planted in Cabernet Franc and Cabernet-Sauvignon, 10 in Chenin and 10 in Sauvignon, Chardonnay and Grolleau. The vineyard is grown with rational control.

Domaine Henri Bourgeois
– Chavignol - 18300 Sancerre - ☎ 02 48 78 53 20 - domaine@henribourgeois.com - 9am-12pm, 2-6pm - by appointment. The estate, located on the best slopes in Sancerre, has been in the Bourgeois family for ten generations. In 1950 the vineyard only had 2ha. Today it covers 65ha spread over chalky clay, flinty and Kimmeridgian marl soil. The estate acquired a modern wine storehouse and a new tasting cellar in 2004.

Domaine Vacheron – 1 r. du Puits-Poulton - 18300 Sancerre - ☎ 02 48 54 09 93 - vacheron.sa@wanadoo.fr The 38ha of this family-owned vineyard – clustered around the hillock of Sancerre – are planted in Pinot Noir for the reds and Sauvignon for the whites. The sloping terrain and limited production provide proper maturation for the grapes and intensify the aromas of the terroir. The reds are aged in oak barrels for about twelve months.

Vignoble de la Coulée de Serrant
– Château de La Roche-aux-Moines - 49170 Savennières - ☎ 02 41 72 22 32 - coulee-de-serrant@wanadoo.fr Mon-Sat 8.30am-12pm, 2-5.45pm. This vineyard has 14ha. The Coulée-de-Serrant alone covers an AOC of 7ha, the exclusive property of the Joly family. The vineyard has been grown biodynamically since 1980.

Château de Chamboureau – Épiré - 49170 Savennières - ☎ 02 41 77 20 04 - Mon-Sat 10am-12pm, 2-6pm - by appointment. This vineyard has 25ha, 20 in production. Pierre and Hervé, two of the eleven children of Michel and Anne Soulez, run the estate with one of their grandchildren, Hugues Daubercies, a maître de chai and oenologist. The wine-making process is traditional, with slow fermentation for three to five months in oak barrels. Fermentation and ageing are done in barrels with over two wines for up to twelve months, then in vats up to eighteen months.

Château de Villeneuve – 3 r. Jean-Brevet - 49400 Souzay-Champigny - ☎ 02 41 51 14 04 - Mon-Sat 9am-12pm, 2-6pm. The estate has belonged to the Chevallier family since 1969. The 25ha of 30-35-year-old vines with Cabernet Franc and Chenin grapes are rooted in chalky-clay Turonian soil. The harvest is by hand. Wines are aged in wood vats, 500-litre casks and barrels.

Domaine des Roches Neuves – 56 bd St-Vincent - 49400 Varrains - ☎ 02 41 52 94 02 - thierry-germain@wanadoo.fr - 8am-12pm, 2-6pm - by appointment. Wine has been grown on this estate since 1850 with 22ha planted in Cabernet Franc and Chenin. In the new vat room, the grapes are very carefully sorted out before being picked off their stems and put in wooden vats.

Domaine Huet – 11 r. de la Croix-Buisée - 37210 Vouvray - ☎ 02 47 52 78 87 - huet.echansonne@wanadoo.fr - Mon-Sat 9am-12pm, 2-6pm - by appointment. This family-run estate was created in 1928. Since 1990, Noël Pinguet's 35ha of vineyards have been cultivated biodynamically, using only Chenin Blanc grapes. The harvest is done manually, in successive pickings. Half of the vines are 30-50 years old. The wine is aged six months in oak barrels and in stainless steel vats.

Domaine du Clos Naudin – 14 r. de la Croix-Buisée - 37210 Vouvray - ☎ 02 47 52 71 46 - Mon-Sat 9am-12pm, 2-6pm - by appointment. Philippe Foreau has remained faithful to his grandparents' methods of earthing in autumn and unearthing in spring. Chemical weed-killers are prohibited. Grapes are fermented for two months with no yeast or chaptalisation, and are converted into wine in small barrels.

Vallet

This is the capital of Muscadet, so don't miss a visit to the **Maison du Muscadet**. The **Château de Fromenteau** has made tours of its winemaking operation even more fun by designing a maze in the vineyard. 44330 Vallet, ☎ 02 40 36 23 75. Jul-Aug: afternoons. Otherwise, by appointment. 5€ (children: 4€).
The road goes through **Mouzillon**, which celebrates the Nuit du Muscadet in early July. It also has a factory making Petits Mouzillons biscuits to go with the Muscadet. ZA des Quatre-Chemins (the biscuit factory is by the roadside), 44330 Mouzillon, ☎ 02 40 33 77 77. Mar-Dec: guided tours (25min) Mon-Sat 9am-12pm, 2-6pm.
Take a right in the direction of Le Pallet.

Le Pallet

At the **Musée du Vignoble Nantais** there are over 1 000 tools and machines (from the 17C to the present) evoking the life of a winemaker. In the "five-senses" room you can explore the diversity of wine through fun experiments. After which you'll need to do some "lab work" by tasting a glass of Muscadet. ♿ Mid-June to mid-Sep: 11am-6pm; beginning Mar to mid-Jun and mid-Sep to 11 Nov: 2-6pm; guided tours available daily at 4pm in summer, and Sun at 4pm the rest of the year. Closed 1 Nov. 4€ (children under 12: no charge) ☎ 02 40 80 90 13.
🚶 The 7km trail marked by an orange rectangle leaves from the Chapelle Saint-Michel and meanders through the surrounding vineyards.

La Haye-Fouassière

The town's three claims to fame are Muscadet, the LU biscuit factory and fouace, a cake shaped like a star with six points, which goes wonderfully with Muscadet and can be found at the **Maison des Vins de Nantes** (see Shopping Guide).

Saint-Fiacre-sur-Maine

This township has the highest density of vineyards in France. It is also the birth-place of Sophie Trébuchet, the mother of Victor Hugo who trampled the grapes in his grandfather's wine press.

Nantes★★★

Nantes is the historic capital of the Dukes of Brittany, and the city has retained two major monuments from that magnificent era: the **cathedral★** (begun in 1434 and finished in 1891), with a very pure Gothic **interior★★** containing the **tomb of François II★★**, and the **Château des Ducs de Bretagne★★**, a powerful fortress dating mainly from its reconstruction by François II (1466). *Currently under restoration. To organise a visit, call ☎ 02 51 17 49 00.*

The other great architectural era in Nantes was the 18C-19C, when the city derived its wealth from the slave trade, then turned to industry after it was abolished. The former **île Feydeau★** and the **Quartier Graslin★** attest to that prosperity.

Exploring the Caves

In Doué and its environs the cellars were dug underground, in the plains, rather than out of the hillside.

Village troglodytique Rochemenier (Rochemenier Troglodyte Village)

In Louresse, 6km N of Doué on D 69 and D 177. Apr-Oct: 9.30am-7pm; Feb-Mar and Nov: Sat-Sun and public hols 2-6pm. 4.50€ (children 7-16: 2.40€). ☎ 02 41 59 18 15.

The visit is comprised of two troglodyte farms (abode and outbuildings) abandoned since about 1930.

Maisons troglodytes de Forges (Forges Troglodyte Houses)

5.5km N of Doué on D 214. Jun-Sep: 9.30am-7pm; Mar-May and Oct: 9.30am-12pm, 2-6pm (Oct 6.30pm). 4.50€. ☎ 02 41 59 00 32.

This hamlet, restructured following excavations in 1979, was once occupied by three families, then abandoned in 1940.

Caverne sculptée de Dénezé-sous-Doué (Sculpted Caves)

5.5km N of Doué on D 69. Jun-Aug: 10am-7pm; Sep-Oct: 10am-6pm; Apr-May: 2-6pm. Closed Mon (except public hols). 4€ (children: 2.5€). ☎ 02 41 59 15 40. Dress warmly, temperatures are typically c 14°C.

This cave, its walls covered with hundreds of unusual figurines, has long remained a mystery. After studying the costumes, musical instruments and attitudes, archaeologists have dated it from the 16C. It is thought to have housed a secret community of stone carvers whose works illustrate their initiation rites.

In the Footsteps of Famous Authors

Du Bellay, Ronsard, Rabelais, Balzac and Julien Gracq are just some of the many famous authors who were born, or lived, in the Loire Valley. Here are some more places – worth a visit – with links to writers, in addition to the ones mentioned throughout the guide.

In the footsteps of Balzac at the Château de Saché

7km E of Azay-le-Rideau on D 84. Apr-Sep: 9am-7pm; Oct-Mar: 9.30am-12.30pm, 2-5.30pm. Closed 1 Jan, 25 Dec. 4.5€ (children 12-18: 3€). ☎ 02 47 26 86 50.

Balzac, born in Tours in 1799, loved coming to Saché; at the time it was a 23hr journey from Paris! In the 19C, this 16C and 18C house belonged to a friend of the writer, Monsieur de Margonne. It is surrounded by beautiful grounds with true romantic charm, which inspired the pages of his *Lily of the Valley*. Several rooms contain manuscripts and various mementoes relating to Balzac's stays here.

In the footsteps of Rabelais at La Devinière

7km SW of Chinon on D 117. Apr-Sep: 9am-7pm; Oct-Mar: 9.30am-12.30pm, 2-5pm. Closed 1 Jan, 25 Dec. 4.50€ (children 12-18: 3€). ☎ 02 47 95 91 18.

It was at this charming farm that François Rabelais, the son of a Chinon lawyer, was born in 1494. You can visit the bedroom of the writer who created Gargantua and see the little museum illustrating his life and work.

Fun and Games for the Children

Child's Play – There are more than 50 places in Anjou and Touraine – including castles, museums, animal parks and underground sites – which offer exploration games and other activities specially designed to make visits more fun for children. For a complete list of places, ask for the *(free)* brochure from the Tourist office for Anjou *(pl. Kennedy, BP 32147, 49021 Angers Cedex 02, ☎ 02 41 23 51 51, www. anjou-tourisme.com)* or Touraine *(9 r. Buffon, BP 3217, 37032 Tours Cedex, 02 47 31 47 48, www.tourism-touraine.com).*

Zoo-parc de Beauval★

4km S of Saint-Aignan on D 675. ♿ Beginning Apr to mid-Nov: 9am-dusk; mid-Nov to end Mar: 10am-12pm, 2-6pm. 15€ (children 3-10: 10€). ☎ 02 54 75 50 00. www. zoobeauval.com

In this 22ha park full of flowers and a variety of landscapes (Amazonian forest, Savannah, waterways, tropical greenhouses, etc) live 4 000 animals, including many rare species such as manatees, white tigers with blue eyes, white lions, koalas, kookaburras, etc. It also has black panthers, pumas, hyenas, marmosets, gorillas and orangutans, crocodiles and turtles, parrots and giraffes. Shows with birds of prey in free flight, and sea-lions.

Aquarium du Val de Loire★

8km W of Amboise on D 751. Take D 283 as you leave Lissault-sur-Loire and follow the signs. ♿ Mid-Jul to mid-Aug: 10am-8pm; beginning Apr to mid-Jul and mid-end Aug: 10am-7pm; end Jan to end Mar, beginning Sep to mid-Nov and Dec: 10.30am-6pm. Closed 3 weeks in Jan after Christmas hols and from mid-Nov to All Saints Day holidays. 12€, ticket including mini-châteaux 19.50€ (children 4-14: 8€, 13€). ☎ 0 825 08 25 22. www.aquariumduvaldeloire.com

This handsome aquarium with a highly modern design is noted for its many freshwater fish, including gudgeons and minnows, pike, carp, trout and salmon. It has both little-known local species and astonishing tropical ones. Among the attractions are tunnels with pike and sturgeon, shark tunnels and an unusual fish petting pool.

Parc des Mini-Châteaux

Take D 81 S out of Amboise. ♿ Mid-Jul to mid-Aug: 10am-8pm; beginning Apr to mid-Jul and mid-end Aug: 10am-7pm; Sep: 10.30am-7pm; beginning Oct to beginning Nov: 10.30am-6pm. 12€, ticket including Aquarium 19.50€ (children 4-14: 8€, 13€). ☎ 0 825 08 25 22. www.mini-chateaux.com

All the most beautiful châteaux, mansions and homes in the Loire valley are here to see in this 2ha park – reproduced in models on a 1/25 scale. In the evening they are lit up.

Zoo de Doué★★

On the way out of Doué, on the route de Cholet. Jul-Aug: 9am-7.30pm; spring and autumn: 9am-7pm; winter: 10am-6.30pm. Closed from All Saints Day to Feb hols. 13€ (children under 10: 8€). ☎ 02 41 59 18 58. www.zoodoue.fr

The zoo is located at an exceptional troglodyte **site★** with former conchiferous stone quarries containing "cathedral-ceiling" caves and lime kilns. Acacia and bamboo trees, waterfalls and boulders create a natural environment for the 500 animals – often endangered species that live in partial freedom here. Vultures, leopards, snow leopards and penguins are among the stars.

Planète Sauvage (Wild World)★★

20km SW of Nantes on D 723, D 751, then D 758. ♿ Jul-Aug: 10am-5.30pm; Apr-Jun and Sep: 10am-5pm; Mar and beginning Oct-11 Nov: 10am-4pm. 16€ (children 3-12: 10€). ☎ 02 40 04 82 82. www.planetesauvage.com

Driving through the 10km-long safari trail – in a bush and savannah habitat – provides a close-up view of animals like hippopotami, elephants, bison, tigers, lions and giraffes. The safari village, reached on foot, is a bush village setting with activities such as a reptile arch, miniature animal farm and a sea-lion show.

Take a chirping cicada, whisk in a little sun and an idle sprawl on the beach, add some hundred-year-old vine stocks, a dash of Mediterranean blue and a few olive trees, and then open a bottle of rosé. There you have it – the ideal Provençal cocktail! Provence seems to have been specially created for growing vines. The Greeks, who founded ancient Massalia 2 600 years ago, had the right idea when they brought with them France's first vines. The transplants were successful, and today, France's oldest vineyard is also one of the country's finest and most varied, producing not only the famous rosés but also some renowned reds and whites. Stretching from Les Alpilles to the hills behind Nice, the vineyards symbolise the timeless roots of Provence, offering a view of the sea at every turn.

Terroir

Michelin Local Maps 340 and 341 – Alpes-Maritimes (06), Bouches-du-Rhône (13) and Var (83).

Surface area: 110 000ha. Production: 5 million hectolitres a year.

The wines of Provence owe much of their character to the Mediterranean climate: 3 000 hours of sunshine a year, the *mistral* wind that drains the soil, and very little rain. Then there is the varied relief, which gives each appellation its originality. From east to west, from Les Alpilles to Nice, the soil types are as follows: limestone in Les Alpilles chain and the Aix hills, Cretaceous limestone around Cassis, siliceous limestone in Bandol, siliceous soil in the Massif des Maures, and red sandstone in a strip from Toulon to St-Tropez.

Grape varieties

In Provence there are as many colourful grape varieties as there are landscapes. Traditionally, the wines are made by blending several grape varieties.

For the rosés and reds, there is the Grenache variety (one of the most widespread in Southern France), as well as Syrah, Carignan, Tibouren (a specifically Provençal type, used mainly for rosés), Cinsault, Mourvèdre (the chief type in Bandol, which only thrives at the seaside), Braquet and Folle Noire (only in the Bellet vineyard) and Castet (in the Aix-en-Provence and Palette areas). For the whites, the varieties include Rolle and Vermentino (both of Ligurian origin), Ugni Blanc (an old Provençal type), Sémillon, Clairette, Sauvignon, Marsanne, and Bourboulenc Blanc (for the mellow touch).

Appellations

Côtes-de-Provence – With 21 000ha and a million hectolitres, this appellation makes up the main vineyard in Provence. It stretches over a third of the Var, extends all the way to Marseille, and has an enclave in Alpes-Maritimes. It is mainly known for its rosés (80% of the production).

Coteaux-d'Aix-en-Provence – The second largest appellation in Provence in terms of volume is in the limestone area between the River Durance, Les Alpilles and Montagne Sainte-Victoire. The main type of wine produced is rosé (65%).

Terraced vineyards above Cassis.

Baux-de-Provence – This small appellation has been separated from the AOC Coteaux-d'Aix-en-Provence since 1995, and stretches out below the olive groves of Les Alpilles.

Bandol – The king of Provençal reds is produced in eleven municipalities spread out over a cirque of hills sheltered from the *mistral* wind, overlooking the sea.

Cassis – The vineyard, perched on a cirque of hills, spreads down in terraced fields or *restanques* towards the seaport of Cassis, producing a dry, fruity white wine.

Coteaux-Varois – These wines, of which 80% are rosés, are only produced in the Var, around Brignoles, the old summer residence of the Counts of Provence.

Palette – This is one of France's smallest appellations. Grown on the outskirts of Aix-en-Provence, it produces a smooth, tannic red, sometimes referred to as the "Claret of Provence".

Bellet – This is a tiny appellation nestled in the St-Roman-de-Bellet area, on the hills behind Nice. Bellet wines are only known to a privileged few.

Background

The cradle of wine – Provence's vines were brought to the area in around 600 BC by the Phoenicians (Greeks from Asia Minor). They have prospered through the ages thanks to support from various quarters, including the Romans – Caesar is believed to have given Provençal wine to his legionaries on their return from conquering the Gauls – monastic orders, aristocrats and Good King René of Anjou. The latter, who was Count of Provence from 1447 to 1480, so encouraged the growth of the vineyards that he was dubbed the Wine-Grower King. In the early 20C the vineyards suffered from overproduction, and the lower quality of the wines had a lasting impact on their image. Since then the wine-growers have made a considerable effort, reducing yield, concentrating on smoothness, and limiting overexposure to the sun. The recent arrival of outside investors has marked a revival. These "foreigners" *(estrangers)* see new financial possibilities in the Provençal vineyards. The sector employs more than 20 000 people, but is faced with increasing pressure from developers.

Everything's rosy in the vineyard – Rosé is still the major wine produced in Provence, accounting for 60% of the output. Provence alone produces 8% of the world's rosés. In France rosé is looked upon as a simple summer barbecue wine, but it enjoys a higher status abroad, especially in the United States and Japan, where it is the ambassador product for Provence.

Local expressions – Provence has its own vocabulary when it comes to wine. An *avis* is a vine shoot, a *tine* is a vat, and a *crotte* a cellar. One of the grape varieties is known as twisted tail *(pecoui-touar)* or magpie's 'knee' *(ginou d'agasso)* because its bunches of grapes grow on stalks shaped like these.

Hill Wines of Provence

Between the chain of Les Alpilles to the west and the massif of La Sainte-Baume to the east, superb vineyards cling to limestone heights, dotted among fields of olives and lavender. This wine trail goes from Baux-de-Provence to Aix-en-Provence, through the AOC areas of **Baux-de-Provence**, **Coteaux-d'Aix-en-Provence** and the tiny but famous **Palette** appellation.

LES ALPILLES

43km. Michelin Local Map 340, D-E3. See itinerary **1** *on the map on p. 306-307.*

The wine-growers of Les Alpilles are a favoured lot: they have earned appellation status for their reds and rosés (which have been classified AOC **Baux-de-Provence** since 1995, while the whites remain AOC Coteaux-d'Aix) and they work in an exceptional setting. Their particular section of timeless Provence consists of blinding white clayey limestone that rises in waves and spreads over the land for about thirty kilometres. Below the crests, a sea of vineyards and olives trembles from the blast of the *mistral* wind. The magnificent wine-growing estates dotted over eight municipalities consist of old family properties that have been handed down from generation to generation. The wine produced is mainly red, although most places go in for a little white or rosé too.

Saint-Rémy-de-Provence★

Whatever the access road you choose, you pass through vineyards to get to St-Rémy. The small town beautifully symbolises the essence of Provence, with its boulevards shaded by plane trees, its network of winding alleyways and its old houses that have often been converted into art galleries. **Place de la République** stands beside the ring road and livens up the centre with outdoor cafés and colourful market days. When the stalls are taken down, the square becomes a car park.

Take the time to stroll through the alleys to see the impressive **Collegiate church of St-Martin** (which contains a lovely polychrome organ case), **Nostradamus's Birthplace** (with only the façade remaining) and the stylish private mansions.

Leave St-Rémy heading W on D 99, then turn left onto D 27. On the way, you drive alongside the AOC Baux-de-Provence vineyards on the northern slopes of Les Alpilles.

Directory

WHERE TO EAT

AROUND BANDOL

Le Clocher – *1 r. Paroisse - 83150 Bandol -* ☎ *04 94 32 47 65 - le.clocher@wanadoo.fr - Closed 10 to 24 Jan, 10 to 30 Nov, Wed and lunchtime June-Sep – 13€ lunch - 26/35€.* This friendly little restaurant in old Bandol has a terrace and a dining room which, in style at least, brings to mind one of the local cafés. The delicious local recipes have been updated for contemporary tastes, and make you forget all about the crowds in the pedestrian quarter.

La Farigoule – *2 pl. du Jeu-de-Paume - 83330 Le Castellet -* ☎ *04 94 32 64 58 - Closed 3 weeks in Nov, and Tue and Wed in winter - Booking essential in summer - 18/32€.* Nestling in the heart of the village, this restaurant has a fine dining room decked out in Provençal colours and a host of curios. Grilled fare sizzles away in the open fireplace. Pleasant terrace shaded by a vine arbour.

AROUND CANNES

Le Comptoir des Vins – *13 bd de la République - 06400 Cannes -* ☎ *04 93 68 13 26 - contact@comptoirdesvins.com – Closed Feb, Mon evening, Tue evening, Wed evening, Sun and public holidays – 22.50/30€.* Monsieur Bitton runs the wine shop at the front while Madame Bitton serves simple, copious dishes in the little restaurant at the back. You can have a glass of wine with each dish or choose a bottle (at a reasonable price) directly from the shop shelves.

La Gousse d'Ail – *11 av. de Grasse - 06220 Vallauris -* ☎ *04 93 64 10 71 – Closed 1 to 15 July, 25 Oct to 10 Nov, Tue evening in winter, Tue lunchtime and Sun lunchtime in summer, Sun evening and Mon – 23/33€.* The name alone (The Clove of Garlic) conjures up *aïoli* (garlic mayonnaise), rosemary, anchovies, *rascasse* (scorpion fish) and *rouille* (spicy Provençal sauce for accompanying fish). The decor is rustic and the atmosphere friendly. This is a family-run establishment that makes it a point of honour to serve carefully prepared regional cuisine at affordable prices.

CASSIS

Le Cabanon de Papi – *5 r. Brémond - 13260 Cassis – In winter, open for lunch and dinner daily except Mon; in summer only open in the evenings, closed Jan -* ☎ *04 42 01 09 09 - 15/25€.* Hidden away in a quiet alley a stone's throw from the harbour, this has a young friendly feel to it, spruce decor, and one can eat on the terrace or inside. Provençal and Corsican specialities served with Cassis wines. The garlic sausage *tian* (oven-baked gratin) is to die for!

AROUND HYÈRES

Le Bacchus *Gourmand – Maison des vins des côtes de Provence - N 7 - 83460 Arcs-sur-Argens -* ☎ *04 94 99 50 20 - Sep-June closed Wed, Sun and Tue evening, July-Aug closed Wed and Fri lunchtime - 37/49€.* The restaurant is on the first floor of the wine centre (Maison des vins des Côtes de Provence), and serves gourmet Provençal fare with the inevitable Côtes-de-Provence wines. It also runs gourmet theme weekends featuring scallops, asparagus, game dishes and more.

Le Bistrot à l'Ail – *22 av. Georges-Clemenceau - 83250 La Londe-les-Maures -* ☎ *04 94 66 97 93 – Closed Dec, lunchtime in summer, Wed lunchtime, Mon and Tue – 28€.* Young Cédric Gola takes care of the cooking and his wife the guests. They serve beautifully presented Provençal fare made from market-fresh produce. You are sure to enjoy your meal here, whether on the tiny terrace looking onto the street or in the dining room.

Le Jardin Provençal – *18 av. Georges-Clemenceau - 83250 La Londe-les-Maures -* ☎ *04 94 66 57 34 - Closed 15 Dec to 20 Jan, Tue lunchtime and Mon- 28/40€.* It's worth coming here just to see the Provençal garden that surrounds the restaurant's delightful shady terrace. In summer it's advisable to book, so as not to miss out on the local fare: mullet salad, creamy mussels with garlic, loin of lamb with parsley, and scrumptious desserts.

Le P'tit Clos – *27 av. Riondet - 83400 Hyères -* ☎ *04 94 35 75 29 – Closed Wed, Mon lunchtime and Sun evening - 16/35€.* This tiny restaurant – with only seven tables – is a pure delight. The chef, Frédéric Chiron creates marvels: asparagus with summer truffles and tomato compote with basil, fillet of duck breast with savory sauce and bean purée, pears with thyme, and cocoa sorbet. You are given a warm welcome, and the decor is bucolic with hollyhocks on the wall and artificial "lawn" mats on the tables.

NICE

Grand Café de Turin – *5 pl. Garibaldi - 06100 Nice -* ☎ *04 93 62 29 52 – 19.82/30.49€.* This has been an institution in Nice for more than two hundred years. It is a large café with a simple, friendly setting where the seafood is served at reasonable prices. The fresh, generous portions, the terrace giving onto the street (heated in winter), and the lively atmosphere all make the place extremely pleasant. Non-stop service until 11pm.

Au Rendez-vous des Amis – *176 av. de Rimiez, aire St-Michel - 06100 Nice -* ☎ *04 93 84 49 66 - rdvdesamis@msn.com – Closed Feb school holidays, 19 Oct to 10 Nov, Tue in winter and Wed -* ✉ *- 21.50/24.50€.* Isabelle and Thierry welcome you to their colourful restaurant as if they were having you for a meal at home. Isabelle takes care of the starters and desserts while Thierry cooks the flavoursome main dishes from the South. Not a wide choice – which means the ingredients are very fresh – but the fixed menu is reasonably priced.

ST-RÉMY-DE-PROVENCE

Lézard Vin – *12 bd Gambetta - 13210 St-Rémy-de-Provence -* ☎ *04 90 92 59 66 – June-Sep: Mon-Sat 11am-4pm, 6.30pm-midnight; Oct-May: weekend lunchtime and evenings; winter: daily except Wed.* This wine bar with its eclectic decor has a friendly atmosphere and a good selection of local wines. It also has a pleasant terrace and offers musical entertainment. Sandwiches and light snacks available. Wines can be bought to take away.

Grain de Sel – *25 bd Mirabeau - 13210 St-Rémy-de-Provence -* ☎ *04 90 92 00 89 - jean-philipe.garcia@wanadoo. fr – Closed Tue evening, Thur evening, Sat lunchtime, Sun lunchtime and Wed - ⊟ - 17/28€.* This small restaurant has a successful mix of modern furniture, light grey colours and rococo-style lights. As for the food, the chef focuses fully on local products, adding a refined personal touch. The informal service and background jazz music invite you to prolong your stay.

Le Jardin de Frédéric – *8 bd Gambetta - 13210 St-Rémy-de-Provence -* ☎ *04 90 92 27 76 – Closed mid-Jan to mid-Feb, Mon lunchtime and Sun except public holidays – 24.50/28.50€.* The woman who runs the restaurant is also an artist and her paintings hang on the walls of the warm dining room, part of which is vaulted. She is often inspired by the Provençal repertoire of recipes to make her carefully prepared dishes.

SALON-DE-PROVENCE

Le Craponne – *146 allée de Craponne - 13300 Salon-de-Provence -* ☎ *04 90 53 23 92 - Closed 8 to 31 Aug, 24 Dec to 5 Jan, and Wed evening - 21/34€.* This restaurant has a good reputation among the locals and serves traditional fare with a family touch: chef's terrine, calf's head in *gribiche* sauce (vinaigrette with chopped boiled eggs, gherkins, capers and herbs), entrecôte steak *à la bordelaise* (with a red wine sauce), duck in orange sauce, and home-made cakes and pastries. In summer you can eat in the little courtyard, and enjoy the peace and shade.

WHERE TO STAY

AROUND AIX-EN-PROVENCE

Château du Petit Sonnailler – *13121 Aurons -* ☎ *04 90 59 34 47 - www.petit-sonnailler.com - 3 rooms: 58/65€.* This is hidden among the vineyards in the hills around Aix. It is located on a working wine-growing estate and takes you back several centuries. There's a crenellated 12C tower which contains a bedroom – our favourite – with medieval wooden panelling, plus a former guard room where breakfast is served (in fine weather you can eat on the terrace) and a grand staircase. You can also visit the cellars for a wine tasting.

Maison d'hôte La Quinta des Bambous – *Chemin des Ribas - 13100 St-Marc-Jaumegarde -* ☎ *04 42 24 91 62 – www.laquintadesbambous.free.fr - 3 rooms: 100/110€.* This unusual villa stands facing the northern slopes of Montagne Sainte-Victoire. Its design combines contemporary rigour and Far-Eastern aesthetics. The rooms (each with private bathroom) are decorated with plant motifs and Japanese-inspired artworks created by the woman who runs the hotel. The peacefulness of the place can be enjoyed on the private terraces, in the bamboo garden and in the long swimming pool on the edge of the forest.

BANDOL

Chambre d'hôte Villa Lou Gardian – *646 rte de Bandol - 83110 Sanary-sur-Mer - A 50, Bandol exit -* ☎ *04 94 88 05 73 - ⊟ - 4 rooms: 68/78€.* Despite the closeness of the road, the rooms in this recently built villa are relatively quiet. They are air-conditioned, colourful and simply decorated. The place has a huge flower garden with hundred-year-old trees, a large swimming pool and a tennis court.

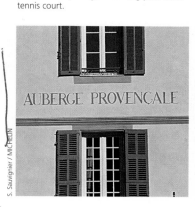

S. Sauvignier / MICHELIN

Chambre d'hôte Les Cancades – *1195 Chemin de la Fontaine-de-Cinq-Sous - 83330 Le Beausset - 3km E of Le Castellet. Just across from the supermarket on N 8, take Chemin de la Fontaine-de-Cinq-Sous -* ☎ *04 94 98 76 93 - ⊟ - 4 rooms: 60/70€.* A steep, narrow track leads to the wooded residential area where the owner of this hotel, a retired architect, has set up his Provençal mas. The fine, handsomely furnished rooms, the suite, the park, the swimming pool and the summer kitchen are all blissfully quiet and relaxing.

AROUND BRIGNOLES

La Cordeline – *14 r. des Cordeliers - 83170 Brignoles -* ☎ *04 94 59 18 66 – www.lacordeline.com – Booking essential - 5 rooms: 65/98€ - meals 25€.* This handsome 17C mansion is a haven of peace right in the centre of town. Fine family furniture adorns the huge rooms. As soon as day breaks you can enjoy breakfast with home-made jams on the terrace, in the shade of the climbing vine.

Chambre d'hôte Château de Vins – *83170 Vins-sur-Caramy - 9km NE of Brignoles on D 24, on the road to Thoronet -* ☎ *04 94 72 50 40 – Closed Nov to Apr - ⊟ - 5 rooms: 46/70€.* This fine 16C building with four turrets has soberly appointed rooms all named after musicians. The place has been renovated by the dedicated and energetic landlord, and hosts cultural events, concerts, music lessons and exhibitions in the summer.

CAGNES-SUR-MER

⊜⊜ **Les Jardins Fragonard** – *12 r. Fragonard - 06800 Cagnes-sur-Mer -* ☎ *04 93 20 07 72 -* ⌿ *- 4 rooms: 55/85€ - meals 16€.* This fine 1925 villa stands in a peaceful park planted with Mediterranean species on the heights above Cagnes. The large rooms have been decked out in bright Provençal colours and some have cane furnishings. Depending on the season, you can have breakfast on the terrace or at the large table in the dining room where evening meals may also be served.

AROUND HYÈRES

⊜⊜ **Chambre d'hôte L'Aumônerie** – *620 av. de Fontbrun - 83320 Carqueiranne -* ☎ *04 94 58 53 56 - guidesdecharme.com – Closed 1 to 15 Aug -* ⌿ *- Booking advisable - 4 rooms: 60/120€.* This house, which once belonged to a naval chaplain, is blissfully quiet and likes to keep things that way. The decor in the rooms is restrained. You can have breakfast in bed or on the terrace shaded by maritime pines. Don't miss the garden that leads to the private beach and the sea.

SALON-DE-PROVENCE

⊜⊜ **Chambre d'hôte Domaine du Bois Vert** – *Quartier Montauban - 13450 Grans - 7km S of Salon-de-Provence on D 16 and then D 19 towards Lançon -* ☎ *04 90 55 82 98 - Closed 5 Jan to 15 Mar -* ⌿ *- 3 rooms: 60/72€.* This drystone *mas,* or farmstead, stands in a garden of oak and pine trees beside a river. Its garden-floor rooms are decorated in the Provençal style, with red hexagonal floor tiles, exposed beams and antique furniture. Depending on the season, breakfast is served in the large living room or on the terrace.

GOURMET SHOPPING

Gastronomie Provençale – *N 7 - Celony - 13100 Aix-en-Provence -* ☎ *04 42 21 14 22 -* *gastronomieprovencale2@wanadoo. fr – Mon to Fri 8am-12pm, 1-5pm - Closed 24 Dec to 5 Jan and public holidays.* This small family establishment, set up in 1957, owes its renown to the Provençal recipe for potted thrush *(terrine de grive),* which it has updated for contemporary tastes. It has expanded into other flavours, with pheasant, moufflon, ostrich and Corsican *figatelli* (pork liver sausage). It also sells cooked dishes, sauces, oils, and fruit in muscatel.

Le Mas de l'Olivier – *2 r. de la Ciotat - 13260 Cassis -* ☎ *04 42 01 92 41 - Jan: Fri to Sun 10.30am-12.30pm, 2.30-6pm; Feb-Mar: Mon to Wed 2.30-6pm, Thur to Sun 10.30am-12.30pm, 3-6.30pm; Apr-Dec: Tue to Sun 10.30am-12.30pm, 3-6.30pm, Mon 3-6.30pm.* This small shop in an alley in the town centre sells herbes de Provence, carefully selected varieties of olive oil, several types of olives, anchovy sauce *(anchoïade),* tapenade (an olive and caper paste), garlic vinegar and all sorts of delicacies. Soap, coloured fabrics and essential oils are also on sale.

Boutique de l'Abbaye de Lérins – *At the harbour station - 06400 St-Honorat (island) -* ☎ *04 92 99 54 00 - www. abbayedelerins.com - Daily 10.10am-12.15pm, 2-5pm - Closed 8 Nov to 8 Dec.* The shop sells books and a good many products that have either been made on the spot or come from other abbeys – wine, *lavandin* (hybrid lavender), honey and the famous Lérina liqueur made from 45 aromatic plants.

Miel de Provence – *Grand-Draille Nord - La Galine - 13210 St-Rémy-de-Provence -* ☎ *04 90 92 28 88 – Mon to Sat 8.30am-12.30pm, 2.30-7pm, Sun 8.30am-12.30pm.* Brun & Fils have kept bees for five generations. They are passionately interested in their trade and follow through every step in the honey-making process. Among their products are honey, pollen, sweets and fabulous home-made *pain d'épices* – a sort of gingerbread.

Les Baux-de-Provence★★★

Driving along the D 27, a delightfully winding secondary road, you round yet another bend and suddenly come upon a spectacular **site★★★**. The bare rock spur of Les Baux stands detached from Les Alpilles, with vertical ravines on either side. On the top is a fortified castle lying in ruins, and old stone houses. The vines have been replaced by a weird landscape (home to the mineral bauxite), where the rock takes on fantastic shapes, as if chiselled by some wild stonecutter.

On arriving in the village (pedestrianised throughout) go through Porte Mage gateway, and then take the street on the left to place Louis-Jou. It is always better to come here in low season, when the place is quieter. The deserted **alleyways** catapult you into a different age. Take a look at the three rooms with pointed vaulting in the former town hall or the **hôtel de ville** dating from the 17C. A street on the right, La Calade, leads to Porte d'Eyguières, which is decorated with coats of arms and used to be the town's only entrance gate. Leading off from the corner of La Calade, rue de l'Église runs to **place St-Vincent★**, where there is a beautiful view of the Fontaine valley and the Val d'Enfer. The **Romanesque Church of St-Vincent★** is flanked on the left by a graceful lantern of the dead. The simple church, which was partly carved out of the bedrock in the 12C, is surprisingly light inside.

Leave Les Baux heading SE on D 27, then turn left onto D 5. The 17C **Mas de la Dame** comes into view, looking like an island lost in a sea of vines and olives. It stands in a cirque of limestone hills at the foot of Les Baux, making a fine picture – one that was immortalised by Van Gogh in 1889. The painting has disappeared, stolen from its owner in the 1960s. However, the estate itself, which produces both wine and olive oil, has had a happier fate. It is run by the two granddaughters of the original owner, and its wine (red, white and rosé) is a success. Go into the cellar and decide for yourself, savouring the site as you do so; it is one of the most beautiful in Les Alpilles. *D 5, 13520 Les Baux-de-Provence,* ☎ *04 90 54 32 24, masdeladame.com 8.30am-7pm. Closed New Year's Day and Christmas.*

Head back along D 5 in the opposite direction. At Maussane-les-Alpilles turn left onto D 17.

Mouriès

With 80 000 olive trees, Mouriès prides itself on having the highest density of olive-growers in the South of France. One only has to pay a visit to the **Moulin à Huile Coopératif du Mas Neuf** to be convinced. Whatever the flavour, subtle or fiery, the AOC olive oil from the Baux-de-Provence valley scoops up the medals in tasting competitions. *13890 Mouriès,* ☎ *04 90 54 32 37. Daily except Sun afternoon, 9am-12pm, 2-6pm.*

Head N on D 24. At the end of the road, turn right onto D 99. 3km further on, turn left and follow the signs to Château Romanin. On the northern slopes of Les Alpilles, **Château Romanin** stands isolated in the middle of vines, olives and almond trees (it also produces its own olive oil). The tasting cellar is buried in the rock, under the ruins of a 13C Knights Templars' castle, which is flanked by a monumental wine-maturing storehouse modelled on a cathedral. Outside, there is a fine view of Mont Ventoux and Les Alpilles. 🚶 A **walking trail** *(an easy, 25min walk)*, takes you past 11 instructive panels explaining about vines and the biodynamic methods used in wine-growing. *Rte de Cavaillon, 13210 St-Rémy-de-Provence,* ☎ *04 90 92 45 87, contact@romanin.com Apr-Sep: 9.30am-7pm, Oct-Mar: 9.30am-1pm, 2-6pm. Closed Sun, Christmas and New Year's Day.*

Take D 99 back to St-Rémy-de-Provence. On the way you can stop at a little place called La Galine to buy wine from **Domaine Hauvette** *(see Shopping Guide)*.

THE AIX-EN-PROVENCE AREA

Around 90km from St-Chamas to Meyreuil. Michelin Local map 340, F-H 3-5. See itinerary **2** *on the map on p. 306-307.*

What was once the stronghold of Good King René of Anjou is now that of the noble wine-growing *bastides*. The vineyards stretch over 4 000ha and 49 municipalities, against the rugged background of Montagne Sainte-Victoire. Many wine-growing estates in the heart of what is now a highly urbanised area have managed to preserve the atmosphere of a much earlier age. The vineyards are bounded to the north by the River Durance and the Trévaresse range, and stretch east to the Salon area and the Étang de Berre. The country to the south of Aix-en-Provence is home to the small Palette appellation.

St-Chamas

This curious village is the last fishing port (apart from Martigues) on the **Étang de Berre★**. A few small boats testify to a once flourishing activity which is now limited to two or three families that still go out to catch eels and grey mullet. St-Chamas is also where you will see troglodyte houses *(private)*, with their enormous picture windows right in the middle of the cliff face.

Leave St-Chamas heading SE on D 10.

The vineyards on the north and west shores of the Étang de Berre offer an extra-ordinary contrast with the gigantic petrochemical installations. Here the wines have AOC **Coteaux-d'Aix-en-Provence** status. You can try them out at **Domaine Calissanne** *(see Shopping Guide)*.

After the intersection between D 21 and D 10, you come to Château Virant. This estate consists of more than 100ha of vines, about 20ha of olive trees, an enormous cellar, and red, white and rosé wines that have stood the test of time. *Rte de St-Chamas, 13680 Lançon-de-Provence,* ☎ *04 90 42 44 47, www.chateauvirant.com 8am-12pm, 1.30-6.30pm (public holidays 8.15am-12pm, 2.30-6.30pm).*

Return to the crossroads and take D 21 on the right. The road begins to rise and after 1.6km you come to a small pass where a track leads to a rocky escarpment *(do not take the steps up to the viewing table; access is dangerous)*. There are fine views of the Étang de Berre, the vineyards and the fields of greenhouses that cover the plain.

In Lançon head N on D 15. Who has ever been to the Massif des Costes, apart from a few unusually curious locals? This is a good example of a small, exceptional wine-growing area tucked away from the tourist trail and bursting with Provençal character.

Pélissanne

Every Sunday morning a large market is held on place Roux-de-Brignoles, in front of the town hall. Fruit and vegetable growers, wine-growers and potters abound. Why not buy some local produce that you can enjoy peacefully in Parc Maureau, just beside the square? Then stroll through the alleyways in the old centre, which forms a perfect circle, to see 17C, 18C and 19C houses.

Don't leave before stocking up at the **Moulin des Costes**. This beautiful 17C stone mill has recently been put back into action, producing oil and flour. It also sells tapenade paste, olives, olive wood items and pottery. *445 chemin de St-Pierre, 13330 Pélissanne, ☎ 04 90 55 30 00. Wed 3-7pm, Sat 9am-12pm, 3-7pm.*

Aurons

From its lookout point, this "doll's village", set right in the middle of the massif, which rises to a height of 394m, affords a good view of the region and its vineyards. The place seems bathed in peace and quiet.

D 22B then winds its way through vineyards, orchards and olive groves to **Vernègues**. The town is in two parts, new and old. The new is below, with dead straight streets. The old is above, and was destroyed by an earthquake in 1909, the worst France has ever known (46 people died and 250 were injured). The neighbouring villages still bear the scars.

Head for La Roque-d'Anthéron on D 22.

La Roque-d'Anthéron

This village will delight music lovers, as it is here that the Château de Forbin, a fine 17C building, holds the International Piano Festival every summer.

One kilometre away, below D 563, **Silvacane Abbey★★** stands on the banks of the Durance. It is a wonderful example of the plain Cistercian beauty that flourished in Provence in the 13C. Its style is surprisingly spare, and its lines noble. The site was already occupied by monks from Marseille in the 11C and then improved by the Cistercians when it was affiliated with their Order. The abbey's prosperity declined through the ages to such an extent that it was converted into a farm after the Revolution. The State bought the buildings in 1949 and gradually began restoring them. Today the church, cloisters and conventual buildings are open to the public. *Jun-Sep: 10am-6pm, Oct-May: daily except Tues 10am-1pm, 2-5pm. Closed 1 Jan, 1 May, 25 Dec. 6.10€. ☎ 04 42 50 41 69 www.monum.fr*

D 543 leads to **Rognes**, where the vines and the wine-growers' cooperative greet you as soon as you enter the village, reminding you that most of the inhabitants make a living from wine-making.

Saint-Cannat

If you can, come here on a Wednesday morning when the market livens up the main square. Plane trees provide shade and the bistros overflow. The only downside to this cheerful Provençal setting is the din from the traffic on the nearby N 7.

However, once you are out of town and off the N 7, a small bend and a few hundred yards of gravel track catapult you into another world, **Château de Beaupré**. This graceful 18C Provençal *bastide* has been in the hands of Baron Double's family since 1890 *(see Shopping Guide)*.

Continue along N 7 to Aix-en-Provence. Go through town by following the boulevards around the centre, and then head E to Meyreuil, taking N 7 and then D 58H to the right.

Château Simone

13590 Meyreuil. No possibility of tours but there is a shop: see Shopping Guide.

Welcome to the tiny kingdom of a wine sometimes referred to as the "Claret of Provence". Château Simone, the main and oldest producer of one of France's smallest AOC appellations, **Palette**, is worth a special trip. Even if you cannot see the magnificent vaulted cellar or taste the wine (red, white and rosé) you can still take a quick look at the elegant estate, set up by Carmelites from Aix-en-Provence in the 16C. The original *bastide* was altered under Napoleon III. It looks over formal gardens and 21ha of vines growing on limestone scree. All

A bottle of Château Simone.

S. Sauvignier/MICHELIN

the wines are matured for at least two years in wooden casks. René Rougier, the present owner of the property, which was bought by his great-great-grandfather, is a passionate wine-grower and landscape gardener. He hopes to replant some vines in a little valley, "just for the pleasure of looking at them".

Seaview Vines from Cassis to Nice

FROM CASSIS TO BANDOL

Around 140km starting from Cassis. Michelin Local Map 340, I-K 6-7. See itinerary ③ on the map on p. 306-307.

Cassis⌂

Beyond the vineyards, you see the sea. Cassis is a small lively fishing port and renowned wine-producing centre. Its 13 privately owned wine companies are famous for their excellent white wine – dry, delicate and fruity.
Clos Sainte-Magdeleine and the **Maison des Vins** *(see Shopping Guide)* will tell you all you want to know about AOC Cassis, one of the oldest appellations in France (1936).
The pleasure of the wine is enhanced by Cassis's magnificent **site★**. The summer resort has grown in an amphitheatre between Cap Canaille and the *calanques* (inlets), bathed in a lovely light that inspired artists such as Matisse, Derain, Vlaminck and Dufy.
Before leaving Cassis, why not go on a **boat trip** to see the **calanques★★**. *Les Bateliers de Cassis: ☎ 04 42 01 90 83 or 04 42 01 71 17 (Tourist office). Boat trip (45min) to the Port-Miou, Port-Pin and En-Vau calanques, with no stops. 11€. Other trips: 5 calanques (1hr) or 8 calanques (1hr 30min). Observation of underwater life by night, mid-July to mid-Aug.*
There's also the sea bed to explore and the beaches to enjoy *(see the "Into the Deep Blue Sea" section at the end of the chapter)*. When the sun goes down, the ideal place to try the delicious local seafood is on the quays.
🛈 The Tourist office provides brochures on walks through the vineyards.
Continue along D 559 towards Bandol. At Les Lecques exit, turn left onto D 66. Here you enter the Bandol appellation area, one of the first AOCs in France (1941). The vines cover about 1 400ha between St-Cyr-sur-Mer, Le Castellet and Ollioules, stretching from the Sainte-Baume massif to the sea. The appellation owes its special quality to the regional microclimate: a lot of sunshine (3 000 hours a year), good rainfall, mainly in autumn and winter, and limestone soil with a south-facing prospect that benefits from the gentle sea breeze. Although Bandol produces whites and rosés, its reputation has been made by its reds. The main grape variety, Mourvèdre (not normally grown much in France), produces wonders here. Then it's just a question of maturing the wine in oak casks for 18 months, and ageing it for five years or more to bring out its generous personality.

La Cadière-d'Azur

The 13C Peï Gate, in front of the town hall leads to the old streets that lend the place so much charm. This very old hill town with its ruined ramparts seems to stand guard against its ancient rival, Le Castellet, perched on a hill opposite. From the eastern end of the village there is a fine **view★** inland over Le Castellet and on to the Sainte-Baume massif.
Leave the village on D 66 and turn immediately right onto a narrow road signposted "Chemin de l'Argile". This pretty wine road crosses through countryside where the soil type is clay *(argile)*, particularly suitable for Mourvèdre vines. The grapes need moisture to ripen, and the clay retains the water. The area produces well-known wines that are deep and silky. Take the time to stop at one of the AOC Bandol estates that line the road, for instance **Domaine Bunan-Moulin des Costes** *(see Shopping Guide)*.
At the end of the road, turn left onto D 559B. 1.5km further on, at a bend, turn right at the sign to "Domaine Ray Jane".

Domaine Ray Jane, Musée de la Tonnellerie et des Outils Vignerons (Museum of Coopers' and Wine-Growers' Instruments)

83330 Le Plan-du-Castellet, ☎ 04 94 98 64 08. Daily except Sun 8.30am–noon, 2-7pm (6.30pm in winter). Tour of the museum for clients only, by appointment.
The Constant family has converted part of the cellar into a private museum. The wine-grower himself takes clients on a tour of his collection, to see 19C coopers' instruments, 18C stills, a grape basket used for festive occasions, and a reconstruction of a Provençal kitchen. Each item has been dated and bears a hand-written label, making for a wonderfully unusual and educational tour.
Return to D 559B, then turn left onto D 226.

Le Castellet★

Several films have been made in this attractive village perched on a wooded hill. The old stronghold has well-preserved ramparts, a carefully restored 12C church and a castle, parts of which date back to the 11C. Many of the houses were built in the 17C and 18C. From beyond the gate on place de la Mairie there is a fine view of the northern slopes of the wine-growing area, which is protected from the mistral wind by the Sainte-Baume massif. As far as wine is concerned, don't miss **Domaine de l'Olivette** *(see Shopping Guide)*.

Head for Le Beausset on D 26.

The ridge road runs alongside vines planted in terraced fields or *restanques*. At Le Beausset, try the wines at **Domaine de l'Ermitage** *(see Shopping Guide)*.

Just beyond the roundabout (as you bypass Le Beausset on D 26) turn right. A narrow road winds its way through olive groves, orchards and vineyards dotted with clumps of broom and cypress trees. It leads to **Chapelle Notre-Dame du Beausset-Vieux**, where the terrace affords a **sweeping panorama★** that takes in Le Castellet, the Sainte-Baume massif, Gros Cerveau and the coast from Bandol westwards to La Ciotat. From here you can make out the different wine-growing areas, with the AOC Bandol wines on the hills, and the local wines *(vins de pays)* and table wines on the plains.

N 8 heads down to **Ollioules**, which specialises in the cut-flower trade and also in wine-growing. *From Ollioules, take D 11 to Sanary-sur-Mer and then D 559 to Bandol.*

côtes-de-provence

coteaux-d'aix-en-provence

baux-de-provence

bandol

cassis

coteaux-varois

palette

bellet

Bandol⌂

Bandol developed into a holiday destination in the 19C thanks to the railway. Four beaches of fine sand make it popular today. The marina lies in a cove, bordered by **Allée Jean-Moulin★** and Allée Alfred-Vivien lined with pine trees, palms and bright flower-beds.

BETWEEN THE CÔTES-DE-PROVENCE AND COTEAUX-VAROIS VINEYARDS

Around 170km from Hyères to St-Tropez. Michelin Local Map 340, L-O 5-7. See itinerary 4 on the map on p. 306-307.

The AOC **Côtes-de-Provence** vineyard is Provence's largest. The appellation covers 84 municipalities, three départements (Bouches-du-Rhône, Var and Alpes-Maritimes) and 19 000ha. The area is right in the heart of Mediterranean Provence, stretching up the valleys of the Arc and the Argens, and running alongside the *calanques* and beaches from Marseille to Nice. Of the 12 winds that blow here, the *mistral* is the most famous and is believed to ward off disease. Red, white and rosé wines are made, but rosé is way ahead of the others, accounting for 80% of the production. The AOC Côtes-de-provence vineyard is cut geographically in half by the **Coteaux-Varois** appellation around Brignoles, which stretches over a limestone area to the foothills of Montagne Sainte-Baume, and covers 2 200ha and 28 municipalities.

Hyères★

Hyères is home to eight Côtes-de-Provence wine-growing estates, including **Château de Mauvanne** *(see Shopping Guide)*. The town has charming medieval streets. Go through the **Porte Massillon** gateway and up rue Massillon. Once the main street of the old town, this is now a bustling shopping street with fruit and vegetable stalls and many Renaissance doorways. On place Massillon, the 12C tower, **Tour St-Blaise**, the fortified apse of a Knights Templar commandery, holds temporary exhibitions. *Climb up the steps and go along rue Ste-Catherine.* From the terrace on place St-Paul there is a good **view★** of the town, the peninsula, and the islands of Porquerolles, Port-Cros and Le Levant.

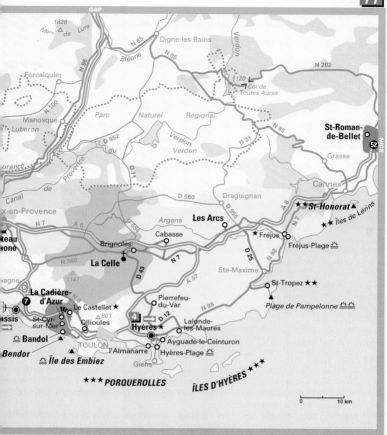

The Hyères vineyard stretches from the coast south of town, to the foothills of the **Massif des Maures★★★** north of town. By taking N 98 east, you get to the pleasant seaside resort of **Lalonde-les-Maures**, which is also an important wine centre: its immediate hinterland has no less than 23 estates, including **Château Les Valentines** and **Château Ste-Marguerite** *(see Shopping Guide)*. D 88 goes through the **Borrels** vineyards, making for a pleasant drive past a host of wineries tucked away among the vines, pine trees and olive groves. The road opens onto D 12. Take this north to **Pierrefeu-du-Var**, another wine-growing town with 14 estates and a wine cooperative. Here you can stop at a number of places, such as Domaine de la Tour des Vidaux, which also offers accommodation and an evening meal for residents *(see Shopping Guide)*.

Head W on D 14, then take D 43 to La Celle, not far from Brignoles.

Abbaye de La Celle

Apr-Sep: guided tours (45min) 9am-12.30pm, 2-6.30pm, Sat-Sun 9am-12.30pm, 2-6.30pm; Oct-Mar: 9am-12pm, 2-5pm, Sat 9am-12pm, 2-5.30pm, Sun 10am-12pm, 2-5.30pm (last tour 1hr before closing). Closed 1 Jan, 1 May, 1 and 11 Nov, 25 Dec. 2.30€. ☎ 04 94 59 19 05. www.la-celle.fr

This 11C-12C Romanesque building was sold during the Revolution and converted into a farm before becoming a luxury hotel. Today it is owned by the Var County Council and is being restored. The abbey church, cloisters and cloister garden, chapterhouse and storeroom, now a sacristy, may be visited. The austere, fortress-like Chapel of Ste-Perpétue has a single, cul-de-four nave. Inside, there is a Catalan Christ, executed with striking realism, as well as two Baroque altarpieces and the sarcophagus of Garsende de Sabran.

The wine centre, **Maison des vins Coteaux-Varois** is located within the Abbaye de La Celle precinct, in a magnificent 12C building, of which part has been superbly fitted out to display local produce. 80 wine-growers are represented here, for red, white and rosé wines, and the abbey's own modest production is also on show. It is a pleasure to stroll through the prestigious site, and see the conservation vineyard with its 88 grape varieties, or the different exhibitions that are put on here. *The wine centre has brochures on three discovery trails of the Coteaux-Varois* *vineyards that can be done by car.* ☎ *04 94 69 33 18, cotvarois@aol.com Winter: Mon to Sat 10am-12pm, 2-6pm; summer: Mon to Sat 10am-12pm, 3-7pm, Sun and public holidays 10am-12pm.*

Brignoles

The maze of narrow, twisting streets in old Brignoles now forms the central district of what has become a lively town, set in the heart of the Coteaux-Varois vineyards.

In this appellation area, as in that of Côtes-de-Provence, rosé wine is by far the most common, accounting for 80% of the production. The vines grow on hillier relief, at an average altitude of 350m (sometimes 500m), where the climate is of a Piedmont type, cold in winter, and hot and dry in summer.

In Brignoles itself, south of place Carami, picturesque old streets lead into the **old town**. It's worth taking a stroll along rue du Grand-Escalier with its arches, rue St-Esprit, and rue des Lanciers, in which there is a **Romanesque house** with twin windows.

The regional museum, **Musée du Pays Brignolais** is housed in a building that dates in part from the 12C, formerly the **Palace of the Counts of Provence**. The tower stands high above the town *(viewing table)*. In the guardroom is the 2C **Gayole tombstone★**, believed to be the oldest Christian monument of ancient Gaul, although the iconography – a fisherman, an anchor, a shepherd with a sheep, celestial trees, and a personified sun – still testifies to the Graeco-Roman polytheistic tradition. There is also a **crib**, created in 1952 in the Provençal tradition. *Apr-Sep: Wed-Sat 9am-12pm, 2.30-6pm, Sun 9am-12pm, 3-6pm; Oct-Mar: Wed-Sat 10am-12pm, 2.30-5pm, Sun 10am-12pm, 3-5pm. Closed 1 Jan, Easter Sunday, 1 May, 1 Nov, 25 Dec. 4€.* ☎ *04 94 69 45 18.*

Head E out of Brignoles on N 7, then turn left onto D 79. Lining the road to the village of **Cabasse** are six Coteaux-Varois estates, stretching out along a valley carpeted with vines out of which rise old Provençal buildings. **Domaine Gavoty** makes for an interesting stop *(see Shopping Guide)*.

Head S from Cabasse on D 13, then take N 7 to Les Arcs.

Les Arcs

The town, nestling in the heart of vineyards that produce excellent wines, vies with Brignoles for the title of capital of the Côtes-de-Provence area. It is dominated by the old Parage quarter and the ruins of Château de Villeneuve, which is the starting point for the Provence wine trail.

The wine centre, **Maison des vins Côtes-de-Provence** is the headquarters of the Côtes-de-Provence appellation. Its main aim is to promote the wine, with some 800 sorts on show (including 80 for laying down) classified according to five growing areas. There is a modern tasting area where 16 different wines may be tasted free of charge every week. Specialist advice is on hand, and regional foods are sold. Upstairs there's a gourmet restaurant, Le Bacchus. One Saturday a month an introductory session on wine-tasting is held, naturally featuring Côtes-de-Provence wines *(23€, 4hr). N 7, 83460 Les Arcs,* ☎ *04 94 99 50 20, www.caveaucp.fr Daily Apr-Sep; closed Sun from Oct to end Mar.*

Domaine Sainte-Roseline produces prestigious wines *(see Shopping Guide)*.

From Les Arcs, take N 7 for 5.5km towards Fréjus, then turn right onto D 25 to Ste-Maxime. There take N 98 along the coast, then branch off to St-Tropez (41km).

Before arriving in St-Tropez itself, stop off at the **Village des Maîtres Vignerons de la Presqu'île de St-Tropez** at La Foux roundabout. This large shop sells wine made by a group of eight estates and a cooperative *(see Shopping Guide)*.

St-Tropez★★

Everybody is familiar with the jet-set image of "St-Trop", with its pastel coloured houses, its hills, rocky headlands and fine beaches. But fewer people associate it with the local vineyards spread among umbrella pines and heather.

The **harbour★★** teems with life. A cosmopolitan crowd gathers here, to stroll past the yachts of all shapes and sizes. In summer the craft seem to be moored less for any serious seafaring activity than for the opportunity to be seen. On the waterfront and in the neighbouring streets, dominated by the church's colourful bell-tower, the traditional pink and yellow houses have been converted into cafés and ice-cream parlours, restaurants, clothes shops and luxury boutiques.

In the early 20C St-Tropez was painted by great artists whose works are kept in the **Musée de l'Annonciade★★**. The museum is housed in a 16C chapel, a stone's throw from the harbour yet peacefully removed from the bustle of the town. On display are masterpieces of late 19C-early 20C painting, for the most part wonderful interpretations of the area as it was at the time. The Pointillists are represented by, among others, Signac, with his sparkling blue *Orage*. The Fauves are represented by Matisse, Van Dongen, Braque, and Marquet, and the Nabis group by Vuillard and Vallotton. *July-Oct: daily except Tue 10am-1pm, 3-10pm, Dec-June: daily except Tue 10am-12pm, 2-6pm. Closed Nov, 1 Jan, 1 May, Ascension, 25 Dec. 4.50€, 5.50€ during temporary exhibitions (July-Oct).* ☎ *04 94 97 04 01.*

A Few More Unusual Vineyards

WINE AND THE ISLANDS

Île de Porquerolles★★★

Access from Giens Peninsula: TLV (Transports Littoral Varois), Port de la Tour-Fondue, 83400 Giens, ☎ 04 94 58 21 81. 15€ return ticket. Regular services year round to Porquerolles. Boat trips to two of the islands (Porquerolles and Port-Gros) July-Aug, daily except Sat-Sun and public holidays.

Off the coast of Hyères are what are known as the Golden Islands (Îles d'Or) – Porquerolles, Port-Cros and Le Levant – forming the southernmost part of Provence. There are three wine-growing estates on Porquerolles, producing red, white and rosé Côtes-de-Provence wine. The most famous, **Domaine de la Courtade**, provides a good opportunity for a ramble *(cars are not allowed on the islands)* among the pine trees and the vines *(see Shopping Guide).*

Île des Embiez⚓

13 to 24 crossings a day (8min) from Le Brusc landing stage to Six-Fours. 9€ return ticket (children 3-12: 6€ return ticket). Enquire at Société Paul Ricard, ☎ 04 94 10 65 20 or 0 890 711 183. www.paul-ricard.com

Opposite Bandol, on Île des Embiez, 10ha of vines planted by the late Paul Ricard, of *pastis* fame, produce 29 000 bottles a year of red, rosé and white.

Île de Bendor⚓

Departures every 30min in summer. Crossing time 7min. 7€ return ticket. ☎ 04 94 29 44 34.

On Île de Bendor, formerly owned by the late Paul Ricard, a curious **Exposition des Vins et Spiritueux** displays 8 000 bottles of wine, aperitifs and liqueurs from 52 different countries, as well as a collection of crystal glasses and decanters. *Jul-Aug: Sun-Tue and Thu-Fri 10am-12.30pm, 3-7pm, Wed and Sat 3-7pm. Closed Sep-June. No charge.* ☎ 04 94 29 44 34.

Îles de Lérins★★

Access: Société Planaria, Abbaye de Lérins, Île St-Honorat, ☎ 04 92 98 71 38. Shuttle service from Cannes (Quai Lauboeuf) every hour: 8am-12pm, 2-4.30pm (May-Sep: every hour except 1pm, return trip 6pm; winter: no boats at 11am). 9€ return ticket (children: 5€).

Opposite Cannes, on **Île St-Honorat★★**, the wine is produced by monks, according to age-old tradition. It is sold at the **Boutique de l'Abbaye de Lérins**.

THE BELLET VINEYARD

Michelin Local Map 341, E5. Leave Nice heading W on N 98, then take N 202 to the right. After St-Isidore, turn off to the right and head for St-Roman-du-Bellet.

The tiny (50ha) and extremely old (3C BC) vineyard that makes up the AOC **Bellet** appellation spreads up in terraces or *restanques* on steep slopes of limestone scree in the municipality of Nice, among the Bellet hills looking over the Var plain. The vineyard benefits from a favourable amount of sunshine and its own microclimate, with the *mistral* and *tramontane* winds blowing almost uninterruptedly along the valley. The vineyard's fifteen or so wine-growers are spread over a residential area in family estates producing reds, rosés and whites. The latter are the best, with notes of lime and honey, but are expensive. The wines are sought after by connoisseurs, and go well with Nice specialities, such as *socca*, a chickpea flour pancake, *pissaladière*, a cross between a pizza and an onion tart, or vegetable *tian*, an oven-baked gratin dish. Most of the producers are in **St-Roman-de-Bellet**. Château de Bellet is the appellation's flagship wine *(see Shopping Guide).*

Epic Settings in the Sun

Plateau des Antiques★★ in St-Rémy-de-Provence

Apr-Aug: 9am-7pm; Sep-Mar: daily except Mon 10.30am-5pm. Closed 1 Jan, 1 May, 1 and 11 Nov, 25 Dec. 6.10€ (children under 18: no charge). ☎ 04 90 92 64 04.

The once prosperous city of Glanum lies amid pine and olive trees one kilometre south of St-Rémy. It was abandoned after Barbarian invasions at the end of the 3C, but two magnificent monuments – the mausoleum and commemorative arch – remain, together with the archaeological site of **Glanum★**.

Apart from the pinecone finial that once crowned its dome, the 18m-high **mausoleum★★**, one of the finest of its kind in the Ancient Roman world, has survived virtually intact. We know today that it was not a tomb, but a monument built in memory of the deceased, around 30 BC. Note the low reliefs of hunting and battle scenes on the four sides of the podium.

Shopping Guide

INFORMATION

Syndicat des Vins des Coteaux d'Aix
– Maison des agriculteurs - 22 av.
Henri-Pontier - 13626 Aix-en-Provence
Cedex 1 - ☎ 04 42 23 57 14 - www.
coteauxaixenprovence.com

Maison des Vins de Bandol – 22 allée
Alfred-Vivien - 83150 Bandol - ☎ 04 94 29
45 03 - www.vins-de-bandol.com – From
June to the end of Sep: daily except Sun
afternoon 10am-12.30pm, 3-7pm; from the
end of Sep to the end of May: daily except
Wed and Sun 10am-12pm, 3-6.30pm. This
wine centre has grown out of the Syndicat
des Vignerons de Bandol and is mainly
concerned with giving information on the
local AOC wines.

Syndicat des Vignerons de Bellet – 06200
St-Roman-de-Bellet - ☎ 04 93 37 81 57 -
www.vinsdebellet.com

Syndicat des Vignerons de Cassis
– Château de Fontcreuse - 13 rte P.-Imbert
- 13260 Cassis - ☎ 04 42 01 71 09.

OVERVIEW

CHARACTERISTICS

The rosés of Provence are fresh and fruity,
go down well, and can be enjoyed by
wine buffs and non-specialists alike. The
reds are less well known but are becoming
increasingly popular. They can be supple
with a fruity balance of ripeness and
acidity, with red berry flavours. The region
also produces reds for storage, which are
structured and expressive, matured in
tuns and barrels. Provence's whites only
make up a small percentage of the overall
production but are not to be dismissed:
they are complex and aromatic, and
sometimes smell of the garrigue or of white
fruit, with notes of honey and dried fruit.
Two rare appellations complete the range
of Provence wines: Palette (near Aix) and
Bellet (near Nice), just as small as they are
famous.

STORAGE

Baux-de-Provence – Red, 5-10 years, rosé
2-3 years.
Coteaux-d'Aix-en-Provence – Red, 10-15
years, rosé and white, 2-5 years.
Cassis – White, up to 10 years.
Palette – Red, 10-15 years.
Côtes-de-Provence – Red, 5-10 years, rosé
and white should be drunk within a year.
Coteaux-Varois – Red, up to 10 years, rosé
should be drunk young, white, 2-3 years.
Bellet – Red, 10-15 years, white, 2-10 years.

PRICES

Baux-de-Provence – 8€ to 11€.
Coteaux-d'Aix-en-Provence – 3€ to 8€.
Cassis – 5€ to 10€.
Bandol – 10€ to 25€.
Palette – 11€ to 25€.
Côtes-de-Provence – 3€ to 11€.
Coteaux-Varois – 5€ to 11€.
Bellet – 11€ to 15€.

BUYING

WINE MERCHANTS AND WINE CENTRES

Le Tonneau de Bacchus – 296 av. du
11-Novembre - 83150 Bandol - ☎ 04 94
29 01 01 - tonneaubacchus@wanadoo.
fr – Tue-Sat 9.30am-12.30pm, 4-8pm,
Sun morning until noon, daily in July-Aug
– closed mid to end Jan. The enthusiastic
caviste (cellarmaster) offers a wide choice of
Bandol wines, as well as wines from other
parts of France. Ask for the programme
on wine courses and the theme evenings
organised in the adjoining restaurant, La
Table de Bacchus. Tasting sessions for wine
or olive oil.

La Cave de Forville – 3 marché Forville
- 06400 Cannes - ☎ 04 93 39 45 09 - www.
caveforville.com Wines made by small-scale
producers are given a lot of space in this
shop. Mr Ferrante and his business partner,
both experienced sommeliers select their
wines after careful tasting. The bottles sold
here come from all over France, and include
some prestigious vintages and a good choice
of Bordeaux wines.

Le Chai Cassidain – 6 r. Séverin-Icard
- 13260 Cassis - ☎ 04 42 01 99 80 – Wed-
Sun 10am-1pm, 4-8.30pm, Tue 4-8.30pm,
open daily in summer. 13 whites, 2 reds
and 5 rosés from the Cassidain vineyard are
sold here along with major wines such as
Palette, as well as Côtes-du-Rhône, Côtes-
de-Provence and wines from other parts
of France. This is a friendly shop run by an
extremely knowledgeable caviste. On some
days, snacks are served with the tastings.

La Maison des Vins – Rte de Marseille
- 13260 Cassis - ☎ 04 42 01 15 61 - www.
maisondesvinscassis.com – Mon-Sat 9am-
12.30pm, 2.30-7.30pm, Sun 9am-12.30pm
– Closed public holidays in winter. With their
AOC status dating from 1936, the Cassis
vineyards cover an area of about 170ha,
comprising 14 estates producing mainly
white wine (80% of the production). La
Maison des Vins sells wines from 11 of them,
selected for their quality. Local, regional and
national wines are also on sale.

Le Petit Village – At La Foux – near the
shopping centre, on the outskirts of Gassin
- 83580 St-Tropez - ☎ 04 94 56 40 17 -
www.mavigne.com - June-15 Sep: Mon-Sat
8.30am-1pm, 2.30-7.30pm, rest of the year:
Mon-Sat 8.30am-12.30pm, 2.30-6.30pm.
This large shop is the showcase for the chief
wine-growers of the St-Tropez peninsula.
It sells wine from a group of eight estates,
including the prestigious Château de
Pampelonne, and from a cooperative in the
Toulon hinterland (Cave St-Roch-les-Vignes
in Cuers). Tasting sessions free of charge.

ESTATES

Château Sainte-Roseline – 83460 Les Arcs-
sur-Argens - ☎ 04 94 99 50 30 - chateau.
sainte.roseline@wanadoo.fr Formerly the
abbey of La Celle Roubaud, Château Sainte-
Roseline is named after a prioress who

became a protégée of Pope John XXII. It was the latter who originated the prestigious vineyard that now spreads over 100ha, and grows many varieties of grapes. The Château is taking all possible steps to concentrate on the different kinds. Efforts are continuing in the wine stores on three levels. For instance, after the grapes have gone through two manual sorting processes, they are then moved on to the next stage by gravity, which ensures better protection. In 2003 a new vinification plant for red wine was installed and has meant wider use of the *pigeage* technique (pushing down the crust that forms on the fermenting grapes) and the adoption of wooden casks for making their most prestigious products. The Château has been awarded Cru Classé status.

Domaine Gavoty – *83340 Cabasse* - ☎ *04 94 69 72 39* - *domaine. gavoty@wanadoo. fr*. The property has belonged to the Gavoty family since 1806, handed down from generation to generation. Roselyne took over from her father, Pierre, in 1985. Today the vineyard stretches over 53ha and grows Rolle, Grenache, Cinsault, Syrah and Cabernet grapes. There are seven white vintages and several old red ones, all made naturally without any additional use of wood.

Domaine Bunan – Moulin des Costes – *83740 La Cadière-d'Azur* - ☎ *04 94 98 58 98* - *www.bunan.com – April to Sep: daily 8am-12pm, 2-7pm; Oct to March: Mon-Sat 8am-12pm, 2-6pm*. This estate in the middle of vines, pines and olive trees produces AOC Bandol and Côtes-de-Provence wines. With its still dating from 1920, it also makes an old marc with stemmed grapes, and a white brandy distilled from marc. Lastly, don't leave without having tried the home-made olive oil, *tapenade* or honey.

Domaine de l'Olivette – *Chemin de l'Olivette* - *83330 Le Castellet* - ☎ *04 94 98 58 85* - *info@domaine-olivette.com* The property has been in the family since the 18C, expanding over the generations to its present size of 55ha. The vines are mainly planted on the hills around Le Castellet. The property uses the latest techniques and is also advised by a wine laboratory that follows up the wine-making process from the time the grapes are ripe to the time the wine is bottled.

Clos Sainte-Magdeleine – *Av. du Revestel* - *13260 Cassis* - ☎ *04 42 01 70 28* - *jsack@club-internet.fr* The estate was set up at the end of the 19C and has belonged to the Zafiropulo family since 1920. It consists of 9ha of vines for white wine and 3ha for tenant farming.

Domaine de l'Hermitage – *Chemin de Rouve* - *83330 Le Beausset* - ☎ *04 94 98 71 31* - *www.domainesduffort.com* - *Winter: Mon-Fri 9am-12pm, 2-6pm; summer: Mon-Sat 9am-12pm, 3-7pm – Closed public holidays*. This family business consists of 70ha of very carefully tended vines, which are pruned back short and treated using ecologically responsible methods. Half of the vineyard produces AOC Bandol wine, aged for at least eighteen months in large oak casks, and the other half is given over to Côtes-de-Provence wine. The star product is a rosé that has won a gold medal.

SCA Château de Mauvanne – *2805 rte de Nice* - *83400 Hyères* – *Mon-Sat (daily in summer) 9am-12pm, 2-6pm* - ☎ *04 94 66 40 25* - *chateaudemauvanne@free.fr* In 1999 following the advice of Yves Morard, his wine-specialist in Lebanon, who also owns an estate in the Vaucluse, Bassim Rahal bought Château de Mauvanne, thus adding to what he already owned in Lebanon – a vineyard of more than 200ha. Of his 50ha in France, 43 are devoted to vines, with the Grenache, Syrah, Cinsault, Mourvèdre and Tibouren varieties for the reds and rosés, completed by Carignan and Cabernet-Sauvignon; and Rolle, Ugni Blanc and Clairette for the whites. The vineyard is cultivated using ecologically responsible methods, and the grapes are harvested by both hand and machine. The vinification and maturing are carried out traditionally in vats, while the top of the range reds are matured in wood casks. Table wine is also produced on the property.

SCEA Domaine de la Courtade – *83400 Porquerolles (island)* - ☎ *04 94 58 31 44* - *lacourtade@terre-net.fr* This vineyard was created in 1983, as a result of a meeting between a manufacturer, Henri Vidal, who had been in love with Île de Porquerolles since his childhood, and a wine specialist from Alsace, Richard Auther, passionately fond of scuba diving. Today the property has 25ha of vines and an olive grove of more than 800 trees, some of which are over 100 years old.

S. Sauvignier / MICHELIN

Château Calissanne – *13680 Lançon-de-Provence* - ☎ *04 90 42 63 03* - *daily 9am-7pm (1pm on Sun) – By appointment*. Château Calissanne, a property of 1 000ha, has 105ha of vines. Syrah, Cabernet-Sauvignon, Mourvèdre, Grenache, Clairette, Sémillon and Sauvignon are planted on calcareous colluvial deposits at sea level. The vineyard is cultivated using ecologically responsible methods and much of the harvest is done manually. The wines are then matured in oak casks: ten to fourteen months for the Prestige wine, and between sixteen and eighteen for the Clos de Victoire.

Château Les Valentines – *Quartier Les Jassons - rte de Collombrières - 83250 La Londe-les-Maures -* ☎ *04 94 15 95 50 - www.lesvalentines.com – Mon-Sat 9am-12.30pm, 2-7pm – Closed public holidays.* The owners of this attractive winery with its Provençal colours have worked relentlessly to give a new lease of life to their 23ha of vines, some of which are over 80 years old. Their first grape harvest dates back to 1997, producing mainly rosés and reds. First and foremost, one should taste the Bagnard wine, AOC Côtes-de-Provence.

Château Sainte-Marguerite – *Le Haut-Pansard - 83250 La Londe-les-Maures -* ☎ *04 94 00 44 44 - www.chateausaintemarguerite.com – Mon-Fri 9.30am-12.30pm, 2-6pm, Sat Apr-Sep – Closed public holidays.* This beautiful property lined with palm trees cultivates 50ha that produce some 250 000 bottles a year, 75% of which end up on the tables of great restaurants. On offer are several AOC Côtes-de-Provence wines, including Esprit de Sainte-Marguerite and Château Hermitage St-Martin.

Château Simone – *Chemin Simone - 13590 Meyreuil -* ☎ *04 42 66 92 58 - www.chateau-simone.fr – Mon-Sat 9am-12pm, 2-6pm – Closed public holidays.* With its 17ha lost in the middle of the pines, the Château Simone vineyard, which has had AOC Palette status since 1948, is one of the smallest in France. It produces a smooth tannic red, sometimes referred to as the "Claret of Provence", as well as some rosé and a white with an unusual bouquet. The wines may not be tasted.

Château de Bellet – *440 chemin de Saquier - St-Roman-de-Bellet - 06200 Nice -* ☎ *04 93 37 81 57 - chateaudebellet@aol.com* The Château, a four-century old family property, is the jewel of the Bellet appellation. This is where Ghislain de Charnacé, grandson of Baron de Bellet, grows 9ha of vines. He loves the land and fervently defends an old grape variety called Braquet.

Domaine La Tour des Vidaux – *Quartier Les Vidaux - 83390 Pierrefeu-du-Var -* ☎ *04 94 48 24 01 - tourdesvidaux@wanadoo.fr* Spurred on by his love of wine, Paul Weindel took over this 24ha property in 1996. He launched into improving the place, installing his own wine-making plant. The vines are grown on schist soil on the southern slopes of the Massif des Maures.

The grape varieties are Grenache, Syrah, Cabernet-Sauvignon, Cinsault, Carignan and Tibouren for the reds and rosés, and Clairette and Ugni Blanc for the whites. The latest techniques are used throughout the property, in combination with traditional methods for the wine-making, using mainly French oak 25hl-50hl tuns, and to a lesser extent, barrels.

Château de Beaupré – *N 7 - 13760 St-Cannat -* ☎ *04 42 57 33 59 - chbeaupré1@aol.com* The property was set up by Christian Double's grandfather in 1890, and consists of 42ha today. For several years now, in conjunction with the regional association of sommeliers, a special wine has been made for red and rosé, called Clos des Sommeliers. Château de Beaupré produces reds, rosés and whites, including a Collection du Château wine, which is fermented in new barrels and then matured in the same barrels for three months before being bottled.

Château Pradeaux – *676 chemin des Pradeaux - 83270 St-Cyr-sur-Mer -* ☎ *04 94 32 10 21 - chateaupradeaux@wanadoo.fr – 9am-12pm, 3-6pm – By appointment Sun and public holidays.* Cyrille Portalis and his wife Magali have been running this 26ha property (of which 21ha are used for wine) since 1983. The vines are grown on clayey limestone soil, with Mourvèdre, Grenache and Cinsault grape varieties. The grapes are harvested by hand and the wine-making process is traditional: the grapes are pressed lightly so as not to damage the skins, and the wine is matured in oak casks.

Domaine Hauvette – *La Haute-Galine - 13210 St-Rémy-de-Provence -* ☎ *04 90 92 03 90.* Dominique Hauvette took over here in 1988. The 14ha property is run as an organic vineyard, with the grapes being harvested by hand and the vinification carried out traditionally. 40 000 bottles are produced a year.

WINE FESTIVALS

Bandol – Fête du millésime (festival of the year's vintage), 1st Sun in Dec.

Cassis – Cassis wine festival, *ban des vendanges* (declaration of the date of the grape harvest), 1st Sun in Sep.

Hyères – Les Vignades, tasting and sale of wine, 3rd Sat in July.

Rognes – Coteaux-d'Aix wine festival, late May.

The **Arc municipal★** on the main route to the Alps marked the entrance to Glanum. Its perfect proportions and the exceptional quality of its carved decoration show Greek influence. Note the lovely festoon of fruit and leaves, and inside, the finely-carved hexagonal coffered ceiling. On the sides, men and women captives can be seen, down by the victors' booty. The despondency of these figures is well rendered.

Musée de Tauroentum in St-Cyr-sur-Mer

8km W of Bandol on D 559. From St-Cyr-sur-Mer, drive along the coast towards La Madrague, in the direction of Les Lecques port. June-Sep: daily except Tue 3-7pm; Oct-May: Sat-Sun and Easter school holidays 2-5pm. Closed 1 Jan, 25 Dec. 3€. ☎ *04 94 26 30 46.*

St-Cyr, situated close to the AOC Bandol vineyards, is home to the remains of Tauroentum, the only Roman villa beside the sea on France's Mediterranean coast. The museum stands between Les Lecques and La Madrague and has been carefully built on the 1C foundations of a fine mansion. Excavations have unearthed three black and white mosaics, kilns for potters and tile makers, funerary items, family utensils, glass, and cabled marble columns.

Walk through the Roman town of Fréjus★

33km NE of St-Tropez on N 98. The tour on foot takes about 1hr 30min-2hr as the ruins are scattered over a large area. Leave the car in the car park on place Agricola.

In the 2C the amphitheatre or **Arènes★** could accommodate approximately 10 000 spectators. Today the original tiered seating has crumbled but the place is still used in summer for shows and bullfights: Picasso came here to watch. Impress the regulars with the fact that Fréjus is the world's easternmost bullfighting venue! *Apr-Oct: Mon and Wed-Sat 10am-1pm, 2.30-6.30pm; Nov-Mar: Mon and Wed-Fri 10am-12pm, 1-5.30pm, Sat 9.30am-12.30pm, 1.30-5.30pm. Closed 1 to 15 Jan, 1 May, 25 Dec. 5€ (under 12s no charge).* ☎ 04 94 51 83 83. *www.ville-frejus.fr*

Rue Joseph-Aubenas then avenue du Théâtre-Romain lead to the **theatre**, where you can still see the radial walls on which the arches supporting the tiers of seats once rested. Inside, the orchestra pit is visible, as is the slot into which the curtain was lowered. *Apr-Oct: daily except Sun 10am-1pm, 2.30-6.30pm; Nov-Mar: daily except Sat-Sun 10am-12pm, 1.30-5.30pm. Closed 1 and 15 Jan, 1 May, 25 Dec. No charge.* ☎ 04 94 53 58 75.

From the theatre, go up the street to the **aqueduct**. The water for Fréjus was collected at Mons, 40km away. The aqueduct reached the city level with the ramparts, and the water was then channelled around the town as far as the water tower *(castellum)* from which the distribution conduits started. This walk ends on the other side of the town centre, at **Porte d'Orée**, a fine archway, most likely some of the remains of the harbour baths. The different vestiges in the immediate area recall that Roman Fréjus was first and foremost a port created by dredging and deepening a lagoon.

Into the Deep Blue Sea

Cassis⚓

There are three natural beaches, all fine for children: **Grande-Mer** (♿, *showers, toilet facilites, lockers, pedalo hire)*, **Bestouan** *(showers, toilet facilites, air mattress hire)*, and **Corton** *(small-scale sailing base)*.

Bandol⚓

The seaside resort of Bandol is classified as a *Station nautique*, testifying to the variety and quality of the activities on offer (such as the diving centre on Île de Bendor). There are four main sand beaches: Centrale, Casino, Lido to the east, and the well-sheltered Rènecros facing west.

Around Hyères

There are 20km of beaches, all supervised in summer. **Almanarre** stretches along the salt marshes of Étang des Pesquiers. It is a sand beach popular with families.

Hyères-Plage⚓ resort lies beside a small forest of umbrella pines. Its beaches include Hippodrome, Capte and Bergerie, stretching all the way to Giens Peninsula. The water is shallow until you get about 60m from the shore.

Ayguade-le-Ceinturon, the old port of Hyères is now a seaside resort. It stands between two sand beaches, one on boulevard du Front-de-Mer, in front of the camp sites, and the other on avenue des Girelles.

St-Tropez

The **beaches around St-Tropez**⚓⚓ are truly heavenly, with their fine sand and rocky creeks where umbrella pines burst with kernels in summer. You are spoilt for choice over a stretch of 10km, and if you feel energetic, can reach the beaches on foot, along the coast path that goes round the peninsula to Cavalaire Bay.

There are no traffic jams out to the close and relatively peaceful **Bouillabaisse beach** (ideal for windsurfing when the *mistral* blows), to the west, or the shaded **Graniers beach** *(access via rue Cavaillon)* to the east, on the way to Cannebiers Bay, a well-favoured beach between the citadel and the rocks. Further east is **Les Salins beach** *(access via avenue Foch)*. The most appealing and the most fashionable are the **Pampelonne beaches**⚓⚓ well-sheltered from the mistral wind. They are often private, and cater to every taste: Club 55 to dance the night away, or Nioulargo for the smart set.

Fréjus

Between Port-Fréjus and Pédégal Bridge, along the seafront promenade, **Fréjus-Plage**⚓ extends for more than a kilometre in a lovely wide beach of fine sand. Further west, **Aviation beach** is long and sandy.

La Vallée du Rhône

The Rhône Valley

From Vienne, head downstream along the banks of the Rhône: for the last two thousand years its meandering course has been bordered by some of the most renowned and spectacular of France's vineyards. Stretching over 250 communes and 6 départements between Vienne and Nîmes, the region is one of the most diverse in France and divides into two distinct geographical areas. The northern part between Vienne and Valence is striking for its sheer south facing slopes although the climate remains continental; the southern part, from Montélimar to the Luberon, is redolent of the Mediterranean with vines growing in arid soil between olive groves and lavender fields.

The terroirs

Michelin Local Maps 327, 331, 332 and 339 – Ardèche (07), Drôme (26), Gard (30), Haute-Loire (42), Rhône (69) and Vaucluse (84).
Surface area: 81 292 ha. Production: 3.6 million hl a year.

Running for over 200km from north to south, the terroirs are astonishingly varied, incorporating a climatic and geological diversity which is exemplified by the region's Côtes du Rhône wines. The Mediterranean climate brings with it the Mistral, a harsh wind which is necessary and beneficial to the development of the vine. Caused by the difference in air pressure between north and south, the Mistral brings with it seasonal heavy rains and exceptional sunshine. From Vienne to Avignon and from the Cévennes to the foothills of the Alps, the Rhône has created a complex and varied terrain, whilst its sediment has enriched the local soil.

The wines

As complex and varied as the terroir, the region's wines are predominantly reds (90% of the AOCs, 6% rosés and 4% whites), and split into four main sub-groups: the regional appellation Côtes du Rhône, the Côtes du Rhône villages (covering 90 communes of which 16 bear the appellation "village", including Valréas and Cairanne), 13 Crus (the finest of all, of which 8 are located in the northern part), and finally the young Rhône Valley appellations (Côtes du Luberon, Costières de Nîmes, Coteaux de Tricastin, Côtes du Ventoux, and the Diois appellations). Two further Crus complete the jigsaw: the sweet Beaumes de Venise and Rasteau wines.

The Côtes du Rhône AOC regulations permit the use of 21 grape varieties, of which 8 are white. Some are employed as the principal ingredient (Syrah, Grenache, Mourvèdre, Viognier, Marsanne, Roussanne, Bourboulenc, Clairette), while others play a secondary role (Cinsault, Carignan, Cournoise, Picpoul etc). The northern Côtes du Rhône reds are generally all Syrahs. To the south, the climatic and geological variety means greater diversity: 13 grape varieties are permitted in Châteauneuf-du-Pape! Notably, the Muscat blanc à petits grains grape is only used in the naturally sweet Beaumes de Venise.

Useful Tips

In the northern area, head up the minor roads which wind between Côte-Rôtie, Condrieu, Saint-Joseph and Crozes-Hermitage for spectacular views over France's steepest vineyards.

The prestigious Côte-Rôtie vineyard overlooking the Rhône.

Here, buying direct from the producer will only mean a 10% discount. They are reluctant to compete against their wine merchants, who can sometimes offer cheaper prices at wine fairs or through special promotional deals. On the other hand, the producers are the only people to speak to if you really want to find out the details of their methods, terroirs and cellars.

Background

Cultivated since Antiquity, the vineyards of the Rhône valley are today divided into two distinct areas. The north, with its astonishingly steep terraces, has granite hillsides covered by vines from Ampuis (south of Vienne) to Saint-Peray (north of Valence), a 200km ribbon of greenery enveloping the Rhône. Machinery is unsuitable for its terraces which are supported by low stone walls, and virtually all work is done by hand, or sometimes even by helicopter. The combination of geography, poor soil geology and the south and southeast facing prospect makes for some rarefied wines with a smoky, spicy character which are much sought-after by connoisseurs.

Beyond Valence, the landscape changes entirely: a vine-free strip of 50km separates the northern Côtes du Rhône from the south. From Donzères to Avignon, a huge plain extends as far as the eye can see, from the Coteaux du Gard to the west to the Luberon and Mont Ventoux to the east. The exceptional sunshine and the richness of the sub-soil (thanks to the alluvial deposits which have built up all along the Rhône's banks) make for some good quality wines.

The Northern Côtes du Rhône

THE VERTIGINOUS VINEYARDS

75km from Ampuis (Rhône) to St-Péray (Ardèche). Michelin Local Map 327, H-1 7-9 and 331, K-L 3-4. See Itinerary **1** *on the map on p. 324. This route follows the N 86, unless indicated otherwise.*

Ampuis

Accounting for 90% of the appellation's production, the capital of the Côte-Rôtie extends along the right bank of the Rhône. First recorded in the 1C BC – Pliny the Elder and Plutarch were later to praise **Côte-Rôtie**, "the wine of Vienne" – its vineyards were held to be the oldest in Gaul. They are surrounded by incredibly steep terraces supported by low stone walls, this vertiginous backdrop extends away above the rooftops of the village. The domaine Etienne Guigal has a good reputation *(see Shopping Guide)*.

From place de l'Église, follow the D 615 towards Les Haies to head up through the Côte-blonde vineyards. After 3km, every turn provides breathtaking scenery. On the way back down there are fine views of the château, now occupied by one of the region's largest wine merchants. Although not open to the public, it has a fine Renaissance façade (16C) on the banks of the Rhône. If you've ever wondered what sort of wine to serve with Christmas or Thanksgiving dinner, this is the place to find out: it was here, in 1553, that the first turkeys were eaten in France!

Condrieu

The Condrieu appellation produces an excellent white wine from the Viognier grape. This wine has become widely known thanks to the local busy port on the Rhône. Condrieu blanc is delicious with some local goat's cheese.

The paths used by the wine growers of bygone times are known as *coursières* to the townsfolk. The tourist office sells a guide to three trails of between 3km and 6km, offering fine views over the vineyards.

A less energetic option by car is to follow the *belvédère* signposts on the D 124 uphill towards **Semons** *(parking)* from the Condrieu north exit. From the church (18C) square, the pano-

---

WINE GROWERS OR MOUNTAINEERS?

From Ampuis to l'Hermitage, the northern Côtes du Rhône is distinguished by its steep slopes, sometimes as precipitous as 80% (4 in 5). Laid out in terraces supported by low stone walls, its vineyards seem to defy gravity. The steepness of these granite hillsides precludes any use of machinery, so all work continues to be done by hand. Down in the vineyards on the plain, one man can tend to 10-15ha. In the northern Côtes du Rhône, one man can only work two hectares. The sole concession to modernity is the French wine industry's only monorail, which can be seen at the Ampuis Sud junction (domaines Barge et Montez): of Swiss construction, this transport system has opened up an extremely steep area for cultivation. Thanks to this, equipment, wine harvests and manpower have travelled effortlessly up and down since 2003. Here, there are also many all-terrain vehicles in evidence: far from being a motoring fashion statement, they are essential for reaching the vines along battered tracks.

Directory

WHERE TO EAT

AROUND BONNIEUX

😊😊 **La Flambée** – Place du 4-Septembre – 84480 Bonnieux – ☎ 04 90 75 82 20 – closed Jan –16/23€. Grilled meats, pizzas from a wood oven and other specialities – daube provençale, pain de chèvre, truffles, game – are served in this family restaurant which remains impervious to the fads of fashion. Rustic dining room and terrace with view over the Cavalon valley. Reasonably priced.

😊😊 **L'Antiquaire** – 9 Rue du Grand-Pré – 84160 Lourmarin – ☎ 04 90 68 17 29 – closed 19 Jan-9 Feb, 15 Nov-5 Dec, Sun evening, Tue lunch, and Mon from Oct to Apr – 18€ lunch – 28/39€. This pretty stone building's sign is reminiscent of the work of Henri Bosco, one of Lourmarin's bards. Even more evocative of the region than his work is the menu, which includes the typical local flavours of marinated olives, artichokes, bream and bouillabaisse. It's worth booking in advance.

AROUND CONDRIEU

😊 **Bistrot à Vins de Serine** – Place de l'Église – 69420 Ampuis – ☎ 04 74 56 15 19 – closed 1-15 Sep, Sun and Tue-Thu evenings – 🍴 – 12/15€. As the name implies, this is an opportunity to taste some interesting wines as well as having a meal. In summer, guests are served on the terrace with a vineyard view.

😊😊 **Reclusière** – 14 Route Nationale – 69420 Condrieu – ☎ 04 74 56 67 27 – closed 18 Feb-11 Mar and Tue – 🍴 – 18/44€. On entering this merchant's house, guests find themselves in bright dining rooms decorated with pictures. Traditional cuisine with a modern twist courtesy of the chef and his team.

😊😊 **Alain Charles** – Route Nationale – 42410 Chavanay – ☎ 04 74 87 23 02 – closed 2-10 Jan, 16 Aug-7 Sep, Sun evenings and Mon except public holidays – 🍴 – 19/55€. A good stopping point for gourmets following the Côtes du Rhône route. Behind its welcoming façade awaits a friendly team of staff who ensure their guests have a pleasant meal. Elegant and rather original decor is the backdrop for classic cuisine dictated by seasonal availability.

AROUND NÎMES

😊 **Del Sud** – 10 Rue Littré – 30000 Nîmes – ☎ 04 66 67 22 50 – Tue-Sat – 🍴 – 11/19€. This shop-restaurant in the city centre has everything that the Mediterranean does best: a plethora of produce available over the counter, and light dishes (poisson à la plancha, rognons à la libanaise and filet de bœuf à l'origan, among others) to enjoy over a glass of wine on the terrace.

😊😊 **Wine Bar Chez Michel** – Square de la Couronne – 30000 Nîmes – ☎ 04 66 76 19 59 – closed Sat lunch, Mon lunch and Sun – 🍴 – 18/20€. If the name were not sufficient to indicate a theme, a glance at the menu and decor will instantly confirm initial suspicions: the table bases are made from barrels and over 250 wines are on offer to accompany the cuisine.

😊😊 **Aux Plaisir des Halles** - 10 Rue Littré – 30000 Nîmes – ☎ 04 66 36 01 02 – closed 3 Feb-1 Mar, 24 Oct-9 Nov, Sun and Mon – 19€ lunch – 22/45€. The talk of the town; beyond its discreet façade the ambience is one of contemporary chic, both on the well presented terrace and in the fine cuisine itself. The excellent wine list offers an interesting regional selection.

😊😊 **Le Bouchon et l'Assiette** – 5 bis Rue de Sauve – 30000 Nîmes – ☎ 04 66 62 02 93 – closed 2-17 Jan, 29 Apr-2 May, 29 Jul-23 Aug, Tue and Wed – 15€ lunch – 24/29€. Guests have a choice of fine dining room with stone walls or a more intimate smaller room in this warm, refined ambience decorated with antiques. As much care is taken over the wines and menu as is evident in the decor; astonishingly reasonable prices.

S. Sauvignier / MICHELIN

AROUND NYONS

😊 **Au Délice de Provence** – 6 La Placette – 84600 Valréas – ☎ 04 90 28 16 91 – closed 28 Jun-4 Jul, Tue evening and Wed – 15/36€. A stone built house with two recently renovated dining rooms, where guests can savour regional cuisine carefully prepared from the freshest ingredients: gigot de lotte, filet de canette, agneau à la provençale, rillettes de truite de mer, savarin aux pruneaux…

😊😊 **Charrette Bleue** – Route du Gap – 26110 Nyons – ☎ 04 75 27 72 33 – closed 6 Dec to late Jan, Tue from Sep to Jun, Sun evening from Oct to Mar and Wed – 🍴 – 23/36€. The sign of this pretty stone farmhouse with tiled roof is evocative of the autobiographical works of local writer René Barjavel. Tasty regional dishes may be enjoyed out on the terrace or in the dining room with exposed beams. Worth a visit.

AROUND ORANGE

😊 **Rom'antique** – Place Silvain – 84100 Orange – ☎ 04 90 51 67 06 – closed first week in Feb, first week in Mar, Sat lunch and Mon – 11.50/27.50€. A friendly, family run operation, with the daughter running the kitchen, occasionally assisted by her father, while her mother, the proprietor, welcomes guests and serves regional cuisine and excellent desserts. Ask for a table on the terrace, which will provide a view of the Roman theatre.

☕ **Le Yaca** – 24 Place Silvain – 84100 Orange – ☎ 04 90 34 70 03 – closed 28 Oct-24 Nov, Tue evening and Thu – 12/22€. The colourful dining room is partially vaulted; a surprising find close to the Roman theatre. Generous portions of simple cuisine at reasonable prices. Book in advance.

☕ **Le Pistou** – 15 Rue Joseph-Ducos – 84230 Châteauneuf-du-Pape – ☎ 04 90 83 71 75 – closed Jan, 23-30 Jun, Sun evening, Mon and evenings from Nov to Easter except Sat – 15/26€. A small establishment in the centre of town, on an alley leading to the Papal fortress. The menu is displayed on a blackboard, including many local specialities: try paupiette d'agneau au basilic or monkfish in bouillabaisse sauce.

☕☕ **Le Jardin d'Adrien** – 58 Cours Aristide-Briand – 84100 Orange – ☎ 04 90 50 63 04 – closed Tue evening and Thu – 15€ lunch – 25/35€. Attractive little restaurant with a bright dining room decorated with photos of Mediterranean pines. Shady summer terrace within its own courtyard. Traditional cuisine with southern influences, of which rabbit with thyme and swordfish with fennel are two flavourful examples.

☕☕ **Hostellerie Château des Fines Roches** – Route des Sorgues – 84230 Châteauneuf-du-Pape – ☎ 04 90 83 70 23 – closed 21 Nov-23 Dec – 30/75€. Atop a hill overlooking vineyards, Benoît Joulian's establishment offers provençale cuisine rich in aromas and colour (brochette de rognons poêlés au romain, saint-pierre rôti à l'huile d'olive), served in the dining room or on the panoramic terrace.

ST-PAUL-TROIS-CHÂTEAUX

☕☕ **L'Esplan** – Place de l'Esplan – 26130 St-Paul-Trois-Châteaux – ☎ 04 75 96 64 46 – closed 15 Dec-15 Jan, Sun evening from 30 Sep to 30 Jan and lunch – 🖃 – 20/46€. Behind the fine façade is a dining room in pastel tones and an inner courtyard shaded by an old palm tree. A mouth-watering menu full of detail, reflecting the chef's passionate approach; cuisine incorporating herbs, vegetables and seasonal produce from his own garden.

AROUND VAISON LA ROMAINE

☕ **Saint-Hubert** – Le Village – 84340 Entrechaux – ☎ 04 90 46 00 05 – closed 26 Jan-12 Mar, 27 Sep-9 Oct, Tue-Wed – 12.50/44.50€. Run by the same family since 1929, this establishment focuses on traditional cuisine; virtually every dish has a classic quality to it, from the terrines maison to the filet de perche à la provençale, served under an arbour in summer.

☕ **Auberge d'Anais** – 84340 Entrechaux – 5km SE of Vaison towards St-Marcellin on the D 54 and then the D 938 – ☎ 04 90 36 20 06 – closed 23 Dec-1 Feb, evenings except Fri and Sat from Nov to Feb and Mon from Mar to Oct – 10€ lunch – 15/28€. Surrounded by vines and olive trees, this establishment has many regulars who value its appetising cuisine, own wine, and good service. The chef uses local produce and has a seasonal truffle menu. A few guest rooms and a swimming pool.

☕☕ **Auberge de la Bartavelle** – 12 Place Sus-Auze – 84110 Vaison-la-Romaine – ☎ 04 90 36 02 16 – closed 15 Jan-3 Feb, 1-15 Nov and Mon – 20/28€. Inside, this centrally located establishment has the air of a private residence: wood floors, summer holiday photos and a picture window providing plenty of light. The menu is composed of traditional dishes with a southern influence including aubergine tart and pieds et paquets – a local speciality of tripe and sheep's trotters which is an acquired taste, to say the least!

☕☕ **Le Brin d'Olivier** – 4 Rue Ventoux – 84110 Vaison la Romaine – ☎ 04 90 28 74 79 – closed 26 Jan-3 Feb, 8-18 Mar, 7-25 Jun, 28 Sep-15 Oct, 1-9 Dec, 22-29 Dec, lunch from Jun to Sep, Sat lunch, Thu lunch, Tue evening and Wed – 25/50€. A pleasant Provençal establishment with a short yet well chosen menu, including gaspacho de tomates fraiches aux petites crevettes and a duo de brochettes à l'aïoli and cinnamon crème brûlée. Attractive olive tree on the terrace.

☕☕ **Les Florets** – Route des Dentelles – 84190 Gigondas – ☎ 04 90 65 85 01 – closed 1 Jan-15 Mar, Mon evening and Tue Nov-Apr and Wed – 24/37€. Deep in the countryside at the foot of the Dentelles de Montmirail, this pleasant establishment has been run by the same family for three generations. Tasty local cuisine accompanied by their own wines, namely Gigondas, Vacqueyras and Côtes du Rhône. Delightful shady terrace.

☕☕ **Mas de Bouvau** – Route de Cairanne – 84150 Violes – ☎ 04 90 70 94 08 – closed 2-31 Jan, 20-30 Dec, evenings Nov-Feb, lunch Jul-Aug, Sun evening, Tue lunch and Mon – 25/38€. A traditional Provençal farmhouse transformed into a restaurant. Although the decor is only vaguely in keeping with local tastes, the menu has plenty of regional specialities such as croustillant de chèvre chaud à la tapenade and tranche de gigot d'agneau aux herbes and home-made pâtisseries.

☕☕ **La Maison** – Quartier Piolon – 84340 Beaumont-de-Ventoux – ☎ 04 90 65 15 50 – closed 1 Oct-9 Apr, Mon-Tue from Sep to Jun and lunch from 12 Jul to 31 Aug – 28€. A well restored farmhouse in a small village surrounded by vineyards and orchards. A charming terrace shaded by lime trees precedes a dining room in yellow hues where Provençal cuisine prevails, including aubergines confites and tian d'agneau. Three small yet pleasant guest rooms.

WHERE TO STAY

AROUND BONNIEUX

⊜⊜ **Chambre d'Hôte La Maison des Sources** – *Chemin des Fraisses – 84360 Lauris – 4.5km SW of Lourmarin on the D 27 – ☎ 04 90 08 22 19 or 06 08 33 06 40 – open all year –⊬– 4 rms: 62/82€ – meal 25€.* At the foot of the Luberon, this old farm is hidden away among vines, orchards and olive trees, with a cliff dotted by cave dwellings for a backdrop. It has limewashed rooms, with a vaulted dining room and lounge. Garden.

AROUND CONDRIEU

⊜⊜ **La Domaine de Clairefontaine** – *Chemin des Fontanettes – 38121 Chonas-l'Amballan – ☎ 04 74 58 81 52 – domainede clairefontaine@yahoo.fr – closed 12 Dec-15 Jan – ▯ –28rms: 45/115€ – ⌴ 12€ – restaurant 35/100€.* Once a retreat for the bishops of Lyon, this old building (1766) has characterful accommodation and offers sophisticated cuisine served in refined surroundings. Delightful annex and terrace overlooking beautiful parkland planted with ancient trees.

DIE

⊜⊜ **Hotel des Alpes** – *87 Rue Camille-Buffardel – 26150 Die – ☎ 04 75 22 15 83 – hoteldesalpesdie@wanadoo.fr – 24rms: 43/47€ – ⌴ 6€* Those seeking to experience the home of Clairette need look no further than this 14C coaching inn. Spacious accommodation, which has been gradually restored; the ideal base from which to explore the streets of Die.

AROUND NÎMES

⊜⊜ **Passiflore** – *1 Rue Neuve – 30310 Vergeze – ☎ 04 66 35 00 00 – 11rms: 51/60€ – ⌴ 7€ – restaurant 25€.* Run by an English couple, this 18C farmhouse has a cosy lounge area, and attractive restaurant and breakfast room decorated in Provençal style. The quiet well presented accommodation overlooks a verdant inner courtyard.

NYONS

⊜⊜ **Hôtel Picholine** – *Promenade Perrière – 26110 Nyons – 1km N of Nyons on Promenade des Anglais – ☎ 04 75 26 06 21 – picholine26@wanadoo.fr - closed 7 Feb-1 Mar and 24 Oct-17 Nov – ▯ – 16rms: 55/69€ – ⌴ 7.50€ – restaurant 22.50/39€.* A tranquil spot in the Nyons hills, this large edifice on a private road has a garden with swimming pool shaded by the light foliage of olive trees and a pleasant terrace likely to induce apathy. Functional rooms, some of which have balconies.

ORANGE

⊜⊜⊜ **Mas des Aigras** – *Chemin des Aigras – 84100 Orange – ☎ 04 90 34 81 01 – masdesaigras@free.fr - closed 1-15 Jan, 26 Oct-11 Nov, Tue, Wed and Sat lunch from Apr to Sep – ▯ – 13rms: 75/106€ – ⌴ 11€ – restaurant 26/50€.* An attractive farmhouse in pale stone among vines and fields not far from Orange. Its charming young owners have improved the accommodation's decor and introduced air conditioning. The cuisine uses organic produce.

AROUND ST-PAUL-TROIS-CHÂTEAUX

⊜⊜ **Gite du Val des Nymphes** – *Domaine de Magne – 26700 La Garde-Adhémar – 1km along the Chapelle-du-Val-des-Nymphes road – ☎ 04 75 04 44 54 – ▱ – 5rms: 48/65€ – meal 18€.* Surrounded by its own land, this Tricastin fruit farm is a delight. The accommodation is in an independent building and overlooks orchards. Meals are served in a fine vaulted dining room decorated with antique tools and old photographs.

S. Sauvignier / MICHELIN

AROUND VAISON LA ROMAINE

⊜ **Chambre d'Hôte La Farigoule** – *Le Plan-de Dieu – 84150 Violès – 7km W of Gigondas on the D 80 towards Orange and then the D 8 and the D 997 towards Violès – ☎ 04 90 70 91 78 – closed Nov-Mar –▱ – 5rms: 35/55€.* This 18C winemaking estate has retained its original charm. The rooms, reached via a fine staircase and decorated with antique furniture, are individually named after famous Provençal authors, whose works are available for guests to read. Breakfast is served in an attractive vaulted room. Garden, cycle hire.

⊜⊜ **Les Géraniums** – *Place de la Croux – 84330 Le Barroux – ☎ 04 90 62 41 08 – les.geraniums@wanadoo.fr - ▯ – 22rms: 45/50€ – ⌴ 8€ – restaurant 23/46€.* This imposing stone house sits at the heart of a fortified village dominating the Comtat plain. The impeccably kept rooms are furnished in rustic style. Generous local cuisine served on the large terrace or in the dining room, decorated with pictures painted by an appreciative guest.

⊜⊜ **Hotel Garance** – *Ste-Colombe – 84410 Bédoin – 4km E of Bédoin on the Mont Ventoux road – ☎ 04 90 12 81 00 – hotelagarance@aol.com – closed 15-30 Nov – ▱– 13rms: 45/65€ – ⌴ 7€.* A restored farmhouse at the heart of a small village surrounded by vines and orchards. The rooms have modern furnishings, Mediterranean colour schemes and original flooring. Those at the back have views of Mont Ventoux. Breakfast served on the terrace in summer. Swimming pool.

⊜⊜ Chambre d'Hôte Mas de la Lause
– Chemin de Geysset – 84330 Le Barroux
– ☎ 04 90 62 33 33 – closed 15 Nov-15
Mar – 5rms: 50/71€ – meal 16.50€. Built
in 1883, this farmhouse is tucked away
among vines and apricot trees. Restored in
contemporary style, its rooms retain their
Provençal colour scheme. Prepared using
local produce, the robust cuisine is served in
the dining room or outside under an awning,
overlooking the château.

⊜⊜ Domaine des Tilleuls – Route du
Mont Ventoux – 84340 Malaucene –
☎ 04 90 65 22 31 –
info@domainedestilleuls.com - ✉
– 20rms: 70/85€ – ☕ 8€. This former
silkworm farm now offers Provençal style
accommodation in pastel tones with
tiled floors and shimmering fabrics. Air
conditioning is not necessary, the 18C
stone walls ensuring a cool ambience. Ask
for a room overlooking the 12ha park.

SHOPPING

A. Blachère – Route des Sorgues – 84230
Châteauneuf-du-Pape – ☎ 04 90 83 53 81 –
Apr-Sep: Mon-Sat 10am-7pm – closed public
holidays. Founded by the Blachère family
in 1835, this is one of Provence's oldest
artisan distilleries. It specialises in making
beverages from the local scrubland flora;
Élixir du Mont Ventoux, Comtadine, Vieux
Marc de Provence and aperitif Lou Gardian
are among its creations. Enjoyable stuff, but
proceed with caution!

Le Moulin Autrand-Dozol – Promenade
de la Digue, le Pont-Roman – 26110 Nyons
– ☎ 04 75 26 02 52 – www.moulin-dozol.
com - Mon-Sat 9am-12pm, 2-6.30pm. As
a result of new safety regulations, the mill
has been idle since 1998. Now a shop and
museum, visitors can acquire the local AOC
olive oil (traditionally cold pressed), as well
as soaps, tapenades, honey, spices and other
local produce.

ramic **view** reveals a loop in the Rhône dominated by vine-covered slopes, and
the farmland of the plains where orchards and dairy farming, on the right bank,
and cereal crops, on the left, predominate.
From Condrieu, head S on the N 86, then turn right onto the D 34.

Saint-Michel-sur-Rhône

On the banks of the Rhône, the village is home to the **Château Grillet AOC**, one
of the rarest in France, being made exclusively by **Château Grillet** *(signposted)*, a
vineyard of a mere 3ha producing a much sought-after white wine. Tasting is not
on offer, but the wine is for sale *(see Shopping Guide)* and visitors can admire the
turreted chateau beside its vineyard.
Return to the N 86 and head S before turning right onto the D 503 towards Malleval.

Malleval

The 16C houses of this village are surrounded by vines and oak trees. From the
belvédère *(picnic tables and information boards)* there is a fine view over the salt
store, *commanderie*, church (11C apse), and the ruins of the keep. Malleval is at the
heart of the **Saint-Joseph appellation**: covering 26 communes, these vineyards
sit between the Condrieu and Côte-Rôtie AOCs to the north and Cornas to the
south.
Near the cemetery at the top of the village the vines are especially impressive as
they rise vertically uphill. The orchards on the outskirts of the village are evidence
of the area's thriving market gardening activities, set within the boundaries of the
Pilat Regional Park.
Return to the N 86 and head S.

Saint-Desirat

Located in the Distillerie Gauthier, the **Musée de l'Alambic★** traces the history of
the mobile distillers. Farmers used to enjoy a special dispensation allowing them
to make up to 10 litres of brandy for their personal consumption. In 1960, this loo-
phole was closed and the mobile distillers were replaced by regulated commercial
distilleries. Film footage, a fine collection, information boards and reconstructions
allow the visitor to understand the processes involved, with a tasting opportunity
rounding off the visit in an agreeable fashion. The distillery offers its products for
sale, notably its speciality poire Williams eau-de-vie.
*Jul-Aug: 8am-7pm, Sat-Sun and public holidays 10am-7pm (last admission 1hr before
closing); Sep-Jun: 8am-12pm, 2-6.30pm, Sat-Sun and public holidays 10am-12pm,
2-6.30pm. Closed 1 Jan and 25 Dec. No charge. ☎ 04 75 34 23 11.*

Tournon-sur-Rhône★

Situated at the foot of striking granite hills, Tournon is a busy market town. Shady
quaysides, the ramparts of the old castle and hilltop ruins make for a quintessen-
tial Rhône Valley scene. Built by the lords of Tournon, the château dates from the
14C and 15C. The inner courtyard is accessed via a venerable set of double doors.
Inside, the Musée Rhodanien focuses on the Rhône's water traffic and boatmen, as
well as local figures such as the sculptor Gimond, a pupil of Maillol, the publisher
Charles Forot, and the Ardèche engineer Marc Seguin who in 1825 built the first

metal suspension bridge over the river; demolished in 1965, it was subsequently reconstructed using more modern structural techniques. Its revolutionary cabled column system is still in use in the United States. *Jul-Aug: 10am-12pm, 2-6pm; from mid-Mar to May and Sep-Oct: Thu-Tue 2-6pm; Jun: daily 2-6pm. Closed 1 May. 3.50€.* ☎ *04 75 08 10 30*

On leaving, head to the **terraces★** for a splendid view over the town and the Rhône. **Vini Découverte** offers cellar visits, wine tastings and guided walks through the vineyards, either for a half-day or over two days. The daily trips include transport in 9-seater vehicles; subject to a minimum 4 people. *13 Place Auguste-Faure, 07300 Tournon-sur-Rhône,* ☎ *04 75 07 23 05, vini-decou verte.com*

Cross over the Seguin footbridge to Tain-l'Hermitage, leaving behind the slopes of Saint Joseph and entering the appellations **Hermitage** and **Crozes-Hermitage**, up on the hill and down on the plain respectively.

Tain-l'Hermitage

Home to the famous Hermitage and Crozes-Hermitage appellations (the latter, extending to some 1 300ha, is the largest vineyard of the northern Côtes du Rhône) this large and peaceful town has a multitude of wine cellars, and a vine covered hillside overlooks its streets. A stone's throw from the river, there are some lovely walks to enjoy – perhaps after a drink at the Café de Nice (*closed Tue*) situated on the banks of the Rhône (fine views of Tournon). On the right bank heading north, the Promenade Robert-Schumann hugs the river for over 1km with panoramic views of Tournon.

🚶 Down in the far left corner of Place du Taurobole, Rue de l'Hermitage opens onto a steep paved pathway (*20mins there and back*) leading to the *belvédère* Pierre Aiguille and the chapelle Saint Christophe; from here there are fine views over the Hermitage vineyards, the river and the Ardèche département. Note the geography, ideally suited to winemaking; shielded from chill north winds, the south facing slopes benefit from a Mediterranean microclimate.

A fine choice of wines is available from the **Cave Coopérative de Tain-l'Hermi-tage** and from **Paul Jaboulet Aîné** *(see Shopping Guide).*

Head S out of Tournon along Rue du Dr-Cadet and Rue Greffieux towards Saint Romain-de-Lerps.

Panoramic route★★★

Following a ridge, this route offers some extraordinary views. The steep twisting climb is dizzying. Soon the entire Valentinoise plain is visible, the Vercors ridge away to the east. A little further along, the Gorges du Doux open up to the right.

In the village of Plats on the plateau, turn left onto the GR 42 at the war memorial. Note the "tower" of St-Romain-de-Lerps on leaving the village.

Panorama of Saint-Romain-de-Lerps★★★

Two viewing platforms have been sited on either side of a little chapel close to the "tower", surmounted by a transmitter mast. The expansive view takes in 13 *départements* and is one of the most impressive in the Rhône valley.

From St-Romain-de-Lerps, the D 287 leads downhill to St-Péray and offers some remarkable views of the Valence basin.

Saint-Péray

Valence's principal suburb, the large town of St-Péray sprawls between housing estates and vineyards. Along with **AOC Cornas** (red wines), 2km north on the N 86 (visit the **Domaine Alain Voge** in **Cornas** – *see Shopping Guide*), the **appellation Saint-Péray** is the last of the vineyards of the northern Côtes du Rhône. Some good deals are on offer at **Domaine du Tunnel** *(see Shopping Guide).*

As a parting gesture, climb to the **ruins of the château de Crussol,** where the **site★★★** offers a last chance to see the Valence plain, the Vercors and the Alps.

CLAIRETTE DE DIE

One day excursion, 150km there and back from Valence. Michelin Local Maps 332, F 5. Die also appears on the map on p. 324.

Sited in a hollow surrounded by mountains and high hills, the city is well off the beaten track and most easily approached from the west, a winding climb along the Drôme valley. Opt instead for the twisting minor roads and head over either the Chaudière, Rousseau or Menée pass to reach the Diois, an attractive landscape of vines, fruit trees and lavender to which Die has given its name. The city is surrounded by vineyards where Clairette and Muscat are the predominant varieties. Ripened in the Drôme sun, these grapes make some memorable sparkling wines.

Die★

An important crossroads in Antiquity, Die is today a small market town best known for the production of **Clairette-de-Die**; a good example of this sweet sparkling white wine can be obtained from **Cave de Die Jaillance** *(see Shopping Guide)*. The other local AOC is **Chatillon-en-Diois**, producing red and white wines in a mountain setting, its vineyards clinging to the slopes of the 2 000m Glandasse massif.

The itinerary takes in the **Roman ramparts**, 3m-thick walls which in the 3C stretched for some 2km. Their remains can be followed from the northeast of the town, by the tourist office at **Porte St-Marcel**, to the Cathedral (its wrought iron bell tower is a landmark on approaching Die). Its doorways are embellished by carved capitals depicting biblical scenes (Cain and Abel, sacrifice of Abraham) to the north, and scenes of combat (men and griffon, water nymph and crocodile) to the west and south.

The Town Hall is the former bishop's palace. Inside the **Chapelle St-Nicolas**, an 11C private oratory, note the fine 12C mosaic work depicting the Universe. *Guided tours (30 min) Tue 2pm and Fri 11.30am. 2€. ☎ 04 75 22 03 03.*

The Southern Côtes du Rhônes

Olive trees, terraced farming, cypresses... beyond Montélimar one is undoubtedly in Provence, and no longer in the same Rhône valley as one was around St-Péray. Likewise, the wines are different. The southern Côtes du Rhône has a separate identity, its vineyards governed by a Mediterranean climate, chalky soil and the mistral. The vines themselves also differ from those further north: instead of being trained on vertical supports known as *échalas*, they are trimmed in a manner which resembles a hand emerging from the soil. It is almost entirely a vast plain on the banks of the Rhône, stretching over four départements (Ardèche, Drôme, Vaucluse and Gard).

TOUR OF THE VINEYARD VILLAGES

160km from La Garde-Adhémar (Drôme) to Lirac (Gard). Michelin Local Map 332, B-D 7-9. See Itinerary **2** *on the map on p. 324.*

La Garde-Adhémar

Although not within the Coteaux-du-Tricastin AOC, this village set high above the Tricastin plain is worth a visit for its picturesque limestone houses, vaulted alleyways and winding lanes spanned by arches. An important stronghold of the Adhémar family in the Middle Ages, its **Romanesque church★** is notable for its two apses and the attractive silhouette of its two storey octagonal bell tower surmounted by a squat pyramid. Close

Clairette-de-Die Vineyard.

B. Kaufmann / MICHELIN

by, the **Chapelle des Pénitents** has 12C twin west windows, visible from the church square. Inside the chapel there is an exhibition dedicated to La Garde-Adhémar, and an audio-visual presentation entitled *Le Tricastin en images* focusing on the region. *On request at Club Unesco. No charge. ☎ 04 75 04 41 58.*

From the terrace there is a fine **view★** over the plain, dominated by the Vivarais foothills, most notably the Dent de Rez. Below is the **Jardin des Herbes**, where over 200 species of aromatic and medicinal plants are cultivated. *No charge. Rejoin the D 158 and head S.*

Saint-Paul-Trois-Châteaux

The village is surrounded by the vineyards of **AOC Côteaux-du-Tricastin**. Comprising five red grape varieties, the appellation takes in 21 communes. The vines flourish among lavender fields, olive groves and of course truffle oaks, since the truffle is one of the other great natural resources of the Tricastin plain. The route leads to the **Cathedral★**, built in the 11C and 12C, a fine example of Provençal Romanesque architecture.

Located in the tourist office behind the apse of the cathedral, the **Maison de la Truffe et du Tricastin** is an exhibition of posters, showcases and a video presentation on the cultivation and marketing of truffles. Tricastin's "black diamond" is a highly prized – and very costly – ingredient in many tasty local dishes. In the vaulted cellars below, wines from the Tricastin hills are on display, along with a selection of antique winemaking equipment.

Jun-Sep: 9am-12pm, 3-7pm, Sun 10-12pm, 3-7pm, Mon 3-7pm (last admission 1hr before closing); Oct-Nov and Mar-May: Tue-Sat 9am-12pm, 2-6pm, Mon 2-6pm; Dec-Feb 9am-12pm, 2-6pm, Sun 10am-12pm, 2-6pm, Mon 2-6pm. Closed public holidays. 3.50€. ☎ *04 75 96 61 29.*

Head SE on the D 59 before turning right onto the D 59A. Beyond Saint-Restitut, the **route des carrières** leads across a limestone plateau, passing truffle oaks and open-cast quarries, worked between the 18C and the 20C.

Saint-Restitut: Storeroom of the Dauphins

At the end of the road. Mid-Mar to late Sep: Wed-Sun 10.30am-7pm, Tue morning. 4€. Guided tours (1hr) subject to prior booking. ☎ *04 75 08 10 30. www.cellier-des-dauphins.com*

A temple to the wines of Tricastin, the storeroom's huge cellars house the region's various *Crus*. Vineyard exhibition and tour of the cellars by miniature train.

Return to the D 59 and turn right.

Suze-la-Rousse

The principal town of Medieval Tricastin, the alleyways of Suze wind up the left bank of the Lez. Behind its substantial walls, the town's *calades* (fine Renaissance houses), massive Romanesque church, 17C *halle aux grains*, and old town hall with attractive 15C and 16C façade make this a rewarding place for a stroll.

An imposing **château** sits atop the Colline de la Garenne. This is reached by a path through a 30ha truffle oak plantation. The exterior of the 14C building is a fine example of Medieval military architecture, while its interior was remodelled during the Renaissance, as was the inner courtyard. *Jul-Aug: guided tours (45min) 9.30-11.30am, 2-6pm; Sep-Jun: 9.30-11.30am, 2-5.30pm (Nov-Mar: Wed-Mon). Closed 1 Jan, 25 Dec. 3.10€.* ☎ *04 75 04 81 44.*

The château is home to the **Université du Vin**; incorporating a laboratory and tasting room, it offers long and short wine courses. At the foot of the château, the vine garden is a collection of around 70 grape varieties which allows students and visitors to examine seasonal changes in the plants. *26790 Suze-la-Rousse,* ☎ *04 75 97 21 30, www-universite-du-vin.com Introduction to wine tasting weekend 320-325€, one day combined wine and cookery course 125€, fine wine tasting day 300€.*

Head E out of Suze towards Visan on the D 251 before joining the D 161. Beyond Visan head SE on the D 20.

Chapelle Notre-Dame-des-Vignes

May-Oct: 10-11.30am and 3-5.30pm. ☎ *04 90 41 90 50.*

In the chancel of this 13C chapel is a painted wooden statue of the Virgin, the focus of a pilgrimage on 8 September each year. According to legend, it was discovered by a winemaker in a field. Removed to the parish church, the statue miraculously turned up in the same field on three further occasions. The chapel was erected in response to this miracle.

Return to Visan and head N towards Valréas on the D 976.

Valréas

Although well within the Drôme département, this small town producing **Côtes-du-Rhône-Villages** is part of the Vaucluse département, an anomaly which it has shared with its neighbours Grillon, Richerenches and Visan since 1791. Together they are known as the *"Enclave des Papes"*, a reference to their one-time allegiance to the Avignon popes and a unique territorial distinction in France.

In the town, the **Tour de Tivoli** is all that remains of the ramparts, today superseded by a ring of shady planted boulevards. At the heart of the alleyways forming the old town are some fine old buildings. The **town hall** has a majestic 15C façade overlooking Place Aristide-Briand. The south door of the church of **Notre-Dame-de-Nazareth** is a good example of Provençal Romanesque architecture. On Place Pie a fine wrought-iron grille opens onto an alley leading to the 17C **Chapelle des Pénitents-Blancs**. The chancel has carved stalls and a beautiful coffered ceiling. *Visits upon request at the tourist office,* ☎ *04 90 35 04 71.*

Also known as the tour de l'Horloge, the tour du château Ripert dominates the garden; from the terrace there is a fine **view** over old Valréas and the Tricastin hills.

Head E on the D 541 towards St-Pantaléon-les-Vignes.

St-Pantaléon-les-Vignes

🚶 Laid out by the wine makers of the appellation Côtes-du-Rhône-Villages-St-Pantaléon-les-Vignes and **Rousset-les-Vignes**, the **Sentier des Terroirs** has two trails (*2hr30min each, or both can be tackled for a 5hr walk*) which wind through pleasant vineyards surrounded by olive groves, lavender fields, pines and oaks. Along the paths are bottle shaped signs, each relating to a chapter in the free guide *(available from the cellars and town halls of the two villages)* detailing the vines, the flora, the countryside and soil.

Continue along the D 541, then turn right onto the D 538 to Nyons.

Nyons

Down on the Tricastin plain yet well protected by the mountains, the town sits at the mouth of the Eygues valley. Brought by the Greeks 2 500 years ago, the olive tree thrives here on account of the mild climate. From November to February, the oil mills are operational; some continue to employ traditional methods. The **Musée de l'Olivier** focuses on the history of olive cultivation and oil manufacture. *Avenue des Tilleuls.* ⸓ *10.30-11.30am, 2.30-5.30pm. Public holidays: ring ahead. 2€. No charge on Journée du Patrimoine.* ☎ *04 75 26 12 12.*

The humpbacked **Pont Roman★** (or Vieux Pont) was built in the 13-14C. Its 40m arch is one of the most striking in the Midi.

Join the D 94, heading right towards Tulette. Beyond Pont-de-Mirabel, turn right onto the D 190 to reach Vinsobres.

Vinsobres

Perched high above the Eygues valley, this attractive village produces **Côtes-du-Rhône-Villages-Vinsobres**. Steep lanes, old stone houses and vaulted passageways are sandwiched between two churches, one Protestant (at the top of the village), one Catholic (at the bottom). From the square in front of the former, there is a fine **view** over the vineyards and the mountains of Garde-Grosse and Ventoux.

⚑ There are a number of **signposted routes** starting from the tourist office allowing cyclists and walkers to explore the area's vineyards, olive groves, orchards and lavender fields.

Rejoin the D 94 and continue in the direction of Tulette.

Saint-Maurice-sur-Eygues

At the top of this sleepy Drôme Provençale village beneath plane trees is Domaine Viret (signposted), known for its traditional organic wine making on a 50ha vineyard surrounded by oaks and pines. For the last few years, Alain and Philippe Viret have been busy with an ambitious and unusual project: to construct a cellar using the architectural philosophy of the ancient world and the same methods employed by the builders of medieval cathedrals... *26110 St-Maurice-sur-Eygues,* ☎ *04 75 27 62 77, viretwine@aol.com 9am-12pm, 3-7pm.*

Continue along the D 94 before turning left at the first junction (D 20), before turning right onto the D 51 towards Cairanne. The route heads through vineyards, leading away from the Baronnies mountains and past the Col du Debat before revealing a panorama over the Dentelles de Montmirail and Mont Ventoux.

Cairanne

Known for its red wine with a powerful bouquet, this old village overlooking vineyards high in the Vaucluse is the capital of the **Côtes-du-Rhône-Villages** appellation. From the lanes between its two chapels dedicated to **St-Roch** (1726) and **Notre-Dame des Excès** (1631), both erected in response to plague outbreaks, there are fine **views★** over vineyards to the Dentelles de Montmirail and Mont Ventoux.

⚑ The tourist office provides a free booklet suggesting walks through the old village and the vineyards. ⸓ *04 90 30 76 53.*

The **Domaines Richaud** and **l'Oratoire St-Martin** produce some good wines *(see Shopping Guide)*. The **Parcours Sensoriel de la Cave de Cairanne** is an unmissable experience for those seeking to learn about the wines of the Rhône valley in general and appellation Côtes-du-Rhône-Villages-Cairanne in particular. This interactive sensory exhibition (children will not be bored) is located in the cellars of the Cairanne co-operative. Vistors can make their own way round or be guided by a sommelier (who will provide tips on tasting). Combined wine and chocolate events are held in conjunction with the Castelin de Châteauneuf-du-Pape chocolate factory *(30€ per person, reservation in advance). Route de Bollène, 84290 Cairanne,* ☎ *04 90 30 82 05, www.cave-cairanne.fr Mon-Sat 9.30am, 10.30am, 3pm and 4.30pm. 6€ (under 12s no charge). Prior booking advised.*

The **Écurie du Muzet** gives riders the opportunity to enjoy the vineyard from the saddle (or alternatively by horse drawn carriage). Itinerary includes a ride through the vines, a guide to tasting in the Côtes-du-Rhône-Villages-Cairanne cellars and a visit to the Parcours Sensoriel de la Cave de Cairanne. *Quartier le Muzet, 84290 Cairanne,* ☎ *04 90 46 12 99 or 06 09 88 38 14, ecuriesdumuzet@aol.com Day trip 85€ (horseback), 70€ (carriage) with lunch.*

Head E on the D 69 towards Rasteau.

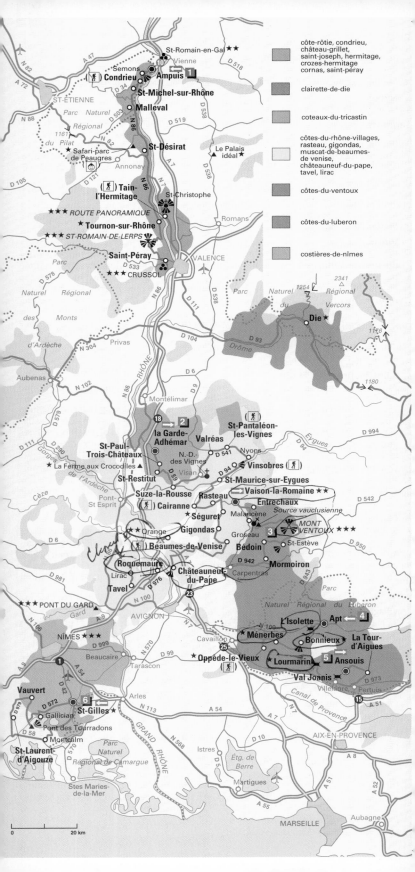

Rasteau

Two attractions draw visitors here: the sweet wine AOC **Rasteau**, produced from vines growing 300m up in the foothills of the Baronnies massif, and the **Musée des Vignerons**, with its collection of antique winemaking tools and bottles. ⚒ *Jul-Aug: 10am-6pm; Easter to late Jun and Sep: 2-6pm. Closed Sun and Tue, early Oct to Easter. 3€.* ☎ *04 90 83 71 79.*

Continue to the village of Roaix, then head right towards Séguret on the D 88.

Séguret★

On entering this beautiful village rising in tiers at the foot of a hill, head on from the main street into a vaulted passageway which leads past the attractive 15C Comtadine des Mascarons fountain, the 14C belfry, and the 12C church of St-Denis. From the information board point in the square, there is a good view of the Dentelles and the Comtat plain. A ruined Medieval castle and a network of steep lanes lined with old houses add to the charm of the place and encourage visitors to linger. The vineyards produce **Côtes-du-Rhône-Villages-Séguret**, reds with a hint of almonds and aromatic rosés, which may be sampled at **Domaine du Cabasse** *(see Shopping Guide)*.

On leaving Séguret, head left onto the D 23 towards Sablet, then proceed along the D 7 and the D 79.

Gigondas

Against the backdrop of the Dentelles de Montmirail, this peaceful town is well known for **AOC Gigondas**, a full bodied red wine made from the Grenache grape and one of the big names in the lower Rhône valley along with Châteauneuf-du-Pape. There are numerous tasting and direct buying opportunities, notably at **Domaine Les Goubert** and at **Caveau du Gigondas** *(see Shopping Guide)*. A climb to the top of the ramparts is rewarded with a sublime **view★** over vineyards and the Cévennes.

Follow the D 7 to Beaumes-de-Venise.

Beaumes-de-Venise

In the southern foothills of the Dentelles de Montmirail, this large village derives its name from the caves overlooking it (BAUME is the Provençal word for cave) and a variant of Venaissin. The subtly aromatic and famous **Muscat-de-Beaumes-de-Venise** hails from here, as visitors arriving along the D 7 will realise: to the right of the first roundabout is the imposing **Cave Cooperative des Vignerons de Beaumes-de-Venise** *(see Shopping Guide)*; adjacent to the shop is an exhibition tracing the history and character of the local AOC. Also worth a visit is **Domaine de Durban** (Leydier et Fils – *see Shopping Guide*).

🏛 The Cave des Vignerons and the tourist office provide directions to **two signposted trails** *(with explanatory boards on viticulture)* which wind around the Dentelles exploring the Trias terroir (one of four geological areas in which Beaumes de Venise grows); a 9km red circuit (3hr 30min) and a 4km green circuit (1hr 40min).

Head S on the D 90. Turn right onto the D 55 at Aubignan, then right again onto the D 950. Before reaching the N 7, fork right onto the D 72 which crosses over the motorway. Then turn left onto the D 68 towards Châteauneuf-du-Pape.

Châteauneuf-du-Pape

The Avignon Papacy's involvement in Châteauneuf's vineyards led to the adoption of the town's current name in the 18C. Ruined by the phylloxera outbreak in 1866, the vineyards were subsequently replanted, and in 1923 the local wine growers laid down strict rules to guarantee quality, including territorial limits, grape dimensions, choice of grape varieties (13 permitted), and production techniques. Today, 300 vineyards grow 3 300 ha of vines. Châteauneuf's bottles proudly display their papal origins, with a tiara and the crossed keys of St Peter chased into the glass.

From the papal fortress, there is a superb **view★★** of the Rhône valley, Roquemaure and the château de l'Hers, Avignon with the Rocher des Doms and the Papal Palace rising from the Alpilles; also visible is the Luberon, the Vaucluse plateau, Mont Ventoux, the Dentelles de Montmirail, the Baronnies massif, and the Montagne de la Lance.

1km from Châteauneuf on the Sorgues road, **Château La Nerthe** is the appellation's oldest vineyard *(see Shopping Guide)*.

Before stopping for a tasting at **Maison des vins Vinadéa** *(see Shopping Guide)*, a visit to the **Musée du Vin** is a must. The wine's production process is traced, from the soil types through to the work of the wine makers, with details of the varieties along the way (extensive collection of antique winemaking equipment). Visitors will learn that Châteauneuf-du-Pape is the cradle of French AOCs, thanks to Baron le Roy, a local landowner who, along with the Bordeaux Senator Jean Capus, brought about the 1935 legislation creating the AOC system. *Cave L-C Brotte-Père*

Anselme. Early Apr to mid- Oct: 9am-1pm, 2-7pm; mid Oct to early Apr: 9am-12pm, 2-6pm. Closed, 1 Jan, 25 Dec. No charge. ☎ 04 90 83 70 07. www.brotte.com

Head out of the village towards Roquemaure on the D 17, before forking right at the "circuit touristique" signpost. An ideal motoring excursion, this 8km circuit winds round the steep minor roads as they weave between the vineyards, giving a rare close up view of the unusual terroir that constitutes **Châteauneuf-du-Pape**, the driest of the Rhône valley. Its reddish soil is strewn with large rounded pebbles. The sun's heat it absorbs by day benefits the vines by night, thereby optimising the ripening grapes. The route takes in numerous domaines where you may stop for a tasting.

Head W out of Châteauneuf-du-Pape on the D 17. Turn left onto the D 976 which crosses over the Rhône.

Roquemaure

This large winemaking town retains some old houses, including that of Cardinal Bertrand near the church. The Tour des Princes de Soubise is the most important remnant of the château where Clement V, the first Avignon pope, died on 20 April 1320. On the opposite bank, the château de l'Hers with its machicolated tower seems to stand guard over its precious vineyard.

Every year, the weekend nearest to 14 February witnesses festivities, including a commemoration of the arrival of the relics of St Valentine in the village. These were purchased in Rome by a winemaker in 1868 and offered to the parish to protect the local vines against the phylloxera outbreak.

> ### THE POPE'S FAVOURITE TIPPLE
> Pliny the Elder referred to Muscat de Beaumes de Venise as early as the 1C, but it was the Avignon Pope Clement V who secured its place in posterity; such was his liking for Muscat that he had 70ha of vines planted on the hillsides of Beaumes de Venise. After the Papacy's return to Rome, the vineyard fell into abeyance; production did not start again until the end of the 19C and it was not until 1943 that it achieved AOC status. The grapes are still hand picked from the trained vines. The appellation today covers some 500ha of well established terraces in hilly terrain. Its unusual flavour is derived from the Muscat blanc à petit grain grape, giving an exotic floral bouquet. Used for cooking and a popular aperitif, Muscat is a great accompaniment to foie gras, strong flavoured dishes, puddings and Roquefort.

Located in Château de Clary, the **Académie du Vin et du Goût** was revived in 2003 by wine and olive oil enthusiasts and has become a cultural centre dedicated to wine and gastronomy. The traditional interior has been retained, with the inclusion of specialist pale wood furniture used for tasting courses, cookery lessons and gastronomic events. *Château de Clary, 30150 Roquemaure, ☎ 04 66 33 04 86. Afternoon's tasting 50€, whole day 235€ (includes 18 wines and lunch), weekend 417€. Prior booking advised.*

Head SW on the D 976.

Tavel

Sited on the left bank of the Rhône, this Côtes du Rhône Gardoises village is renowned for its long-established rosé. Fuller-bodied and darker than the wines of Provence, it became the first rosé to be accorded **AOC status** in 1936. Its 900ha of vineyards are all within the *commune*, a striking terroir composed of rounded pebbles, sand and chalky soil. Quite apart from its viticulture, Tavel has another claim to fame: its quarries, now exhausted, supplied the stones used for the Statue of Liberty's foundations.

The Dentelles de Montmirail in the vicinity of Gigondas, surrounded by vines.

Shoppers need look no further than **Domaine de la Mordorée** *(see Shopping Guide)*. The circuit des Vignobles is a pleasant drive, punctuated by milestones hewn from the local rocks, with a viewing point (picnic area) from where a fine panorama of the vines and village may be enjoyed.

North of Tavel on the D 26 is **Lirac,** the centre of an **AOC** which produces robust reds and rosés.

CÔTES DU VENTOUX

75km from Vaison-la-Romaine to Carpentras (Vaucluse). Michelin Local Map 332, D-E 8-9. See Itinerary 3 *on the map p. 324.*

At a height of 1 909m, the "Géant de Provence" is classified by Unesco as a biosphere reserve, with its eponymous vineyard below it. Encompassing some 51 communes (7 700ha) from Vaison-la-Romaine in the north to Apt in the south, it produces fruity wines characterised by a pleasant balance between freshness and elegance.

From Vaison-la-Romaine head SE on the D 938. After 3.5km, turn left onto the D 54.

Entrechaux

Once property of the bishops of Vaison, the village is dominated by the hilltop ruins of its château. There are also two estates here where **appellation Côtes-du-Ventoux** wines may be tasted.

Return to Malaucène road via D 13.

Malaucène

The 14C fortified church replaced a Roman building and was once part of the town ramparts; inside there is a Provençal Romanesque nave and beautiful carved musical instruments in the 18C organ loft.

Adjacent to the church, Porte Soubeyran leads to the **old town**: its old houses, fountains, wash-houses, oratories, and at its centre an old belfry crowned by a wrought iron bell tower make this an atmospheric spot. To the left of the church, a path leads to the Calvary, from where there are fine views of the Drôme mountains and Mont Ventoux.

Turn left onto the D 974.

Chapelle Notre-Dame-du-Groseau

This chapel is all that remains of a Benedictine abbey, a daughter house of St Victor de Marseille. The square building *(closed to the public)* is the chancel of the 12C abbey, its nave having been destroyed.

Source Vauclusienne du Groseau

To the left of the road, water pours forth from several fissures at the foot of a steep slope (over 100m) to form a clear pool beneath fine trees. The Romans built an aqueduct to carry water from here to Vaison-la-Romaine.

The route climbs northwards up the steepest face of Mont Ventoux, passing pastureland and pine woods near the Mont Serein refuge. From the viewing point beyond the Ramayettes hut, there is a fine **view★** of the Ouvèze and Groseau valleys, the Baronnies massif and the summit of La Plate.

The panorama becomes broader as the route climbs, revealing the Dentelles de Montmirail and the heights of the western Rhône and the Alps. After two broad bends, the route reaches the summit.

Summit of Mont Ventoux★★★

The peak is the site of a military radar station and to the north a radio mast. From the platform on the south side, there is a vast **view★★★** (information board) from the Pelvoux massif to the Cévennes via the Luberon, the Ste-Victoire peak, the Estaques hills, Marseille, the Étang de Berre, the Alpilles, the Rhône valley and (in good weather) the Canigou.

The descent is down the south face; constructed in 1885, the original hairpin route drops from 1 909m to 310m at Bédoin in just 22km.

Saint-Estève

From the bend, until recently a nightmarish challenge for participants in the Ventoux motor race (discontinued in 1973), there is a **view★** to the right of the Dentelles de Montmirail and the Comtat, with the Vaucluse plateau to the left.

Bédoin

Home to four winemaking *domaines*, the picturesque streets in this hilltop village lead to a Jesuit-style church.

Mormoiron

The **Musée de la Musique Mécanique** has an interesting collection of items, allowing visitors to see and more importantly hear a serinette dating to 1740, a grand orchestrion from 1900 (9 instruments), a carousel organ and several barrel organs. *Easter to late Sep: guided tour (1hr, last admission 1hr before closing) 10am, 11.15am, 3pm, 4.15pm and 5.30pm; early Dec to Easter: Sun, 3pm, 4.15pm and 5.30pm.* ☎ 04 90 61 75 91.

Head W on the D 942 to Carpentras.

THE CÔTES DU LUBERON

On the left bank of the Rhône and halfway between the Alps and the Mediterranean is the mountainous barrier of the Luberon, a landscape of vineyards which dominate the region's economy. Between Calavon and Durance, some 3 800ha of north and south facing slopes are given over to **AOC Côtes du Luberon**, producing an annual average of 160 000hl, 60% of which is red. The alpine influence on the climate explains why a significant proportion (22%) of its output is white. The Luberon's wines are full-bodied and characterful with a wild and fruity bouquet. Smooth and heady, they make for excellent autumn and winter drinking.

There are two proposed itineraries, the first in the Petit Luberon on the northern side of the massif, the other to the south in the Basse Durance.

The Petit Luberon

41km from Apt to Cavaillon (Vaucluse). Michelin Local Map 332, E-F 10-11. See Itinerary 4 *on the map on p. 324.*

Apt

Known for its ochre and crystallised fruit, Apt is a pleasant backwater. The quiet charm of its alleyways and its busy Saturday morning market, its stalls laden with fruit and vegetables, Provençal fabrics, infinite varieties of honey and craftware, invite the visitor to linger far longer than planned.

Head W out of Apt on the D 3 towards Bonnieux and continue for 6km.

Chateau de l'Isolette

Rte de Bonnieux, 84400 Apt, ☎ 04 90 74 16 70, www.chateau-isolette.com Mon-Sat 8.30-11.30am, 2-5.30pm. Closed between Christmas and New Year and public holidays.

Against this magnificent backdrop, visitors can indulge in some tasting and direct buying in the cellars before visiting the little winemaking museum. The family who assembled this collection (no charge during wine tasting) allow their clients to visit it.

Bonnieux★

Perched on a hillside, the village dominates the valley where the Petit Luberon gives way to the Grand Luberon. **Haut-Bonnieux** is approached along the vaulted Rue de la Mairie from Place de la Liberté, a steep climb leading to a terrace below the old church. From this point, there is a delightful **view★** of the Calavon valley, with the precipitous village of Lacoste to the left, while to the right Gordes and Roussillon stand out from red rocks in the direction of the Vaucluse plain.

On rejoining the D 36, a visit can be paid to the **Musée de la Boulangerie**, an interesting exhibit exploring the baker's trade through utensils and documents. *Jul-Aug: 10am-1pm, 3-6.30pm; Apr-Jun and Sep-Oct: 10am-12.30pm, 2.30-6pm. Closed Tue, early Nov to late Mar, 1 May. 3.50€. ☎ 04 90 75 88 34.*

The small, family run **Château la Canourgue** produces a good Côtes-du-Luberon *(see Shopping Guide).*

Head S out of Bonnieux on the D 3 before turning left onto the D 109. The road winds up the side of the Petit Luberon with Bonnieux to the rear before **Lacoste** looms into view; the jagged walls of its imposing ruined castle have been partially rebuilt; it once belonged to the Sade family. Imprisoned on numerous occasions and condemned to death in his absence, the infamous Marquis de Sade sought refuge here in 1774.

Ménerbes★

Also perched on a rocky outcrop, Ménerbes is largely responsible for the Luberon's ever increasing popularity. It is an architectural gem, with narrow alleys, imposing residences and attractive squares. Tucked away behind high walls, the houses built by the merchant class now belong to film stars and millionaires, and many have hosted writers and artists including Picasso, Nicolas de Staël, Albert Camus and Peter Mayle. Through such famous names Ménerbes has acquired an international reputation and, unlike some of its neighbours, it has not succumbed to the commercial pressures of tourism. Here, an atmosphere of lively conviviality prevails, perhaps best experienced in the café Le Progrès in Place Albert-Roule.

Located in the **Domaine de la Citadelle**, the **Musée du Tire-Bouchon** is well worth seeing. A collection of over 1 000 corkscrews from around the world, it pays tribute to this often overlooked item, without which the ritual that is wine would not be the same... *On the way out of Ménerbes, 2.5km on the D 3 towards Cavaillon. Domaine de la Citadelle. Apr-Oct: 10am-12pm, 2-7pm; Nov-Mar: Mon-Fri (closed public holidays) 9am-12pm, 2-6pm, Sat 10-12pm, 2-6pm. 4€ (no charge for under 15s). ☎ 04 90 72 41 58. www.musee-tirebouchon.com*

Head S on the D 3 before joining the D 188.

Oppède-le-Vieux★

Park in the car park just beyond the village before exploring on foot.

Occupying an impressive **site★** on a spur, this village hewn into the rock was until recently partly in ruins, but has experienced a revival in its fortunes thanks to the efforts of artists and literary figures who have striven to restore it without detracting from its authenticity. From the ancient Place du Bourg, climb to the upper village, surmounted by its collegiate church and the ruins of its château. From the terrace in front of the church, there is a fine **view★** of the Coulon valley, the Vaucluse plateau and Ménerbes.

🛈 Created with the assistance of the Parc Naturel Régional du Luberon, the **Sentier des Vignerons d'Oppède** is an excellent way to get to know the local terroir. *1hr 30min of easy walking. Departure point: close to the oratoire St-Joseph in Oppède. Guidebook available from tourist office and Maison du Parc. There is a similar walk from Curcuron to the S.* The route, marked by signs depicting a bunch of grapes, heads through the vineyards at the foot of Oppède. Along the way are five explanatory boards detailing the grape varieties and winemaking techniques. Pleasant at any time of year, but most interesting during harvest time in September and October.

Head NW on the D 176 and the D 3 and D 2 to the left to reach Cavaillon.

The Basse Durance

42km from Ansouis to Lourmarin (Vaucluse). Michelin Local Map 332, F-G 11. See Itinerary ⑤ on the map on p. 324.

Ansouis

Both a fortress and a residence, the 13C **château★** has two principal attractions: its extraordinary collection of copper pans in the huge kitchens, and its bucolic terrace overlooking hanging gardens. *Jul-Sep: guided tour 2.30-6pm (last admission 30min before closing); Easter holidays to late Jun and Oct: Wed-Mon 2.30-6pm (last admission 1hr before closing). 6€ (children 3€). ☎ 04 90 09 82 70.*

After absorbing the atmosphere by wandering the alleyways of this sleepy country town, visitors can conclude with a tasting at **Château Tuchâteaun** *(see Shopping Guide).*
Those in search of the unusual should visit the **Musée Extraordinaire**, where an underwater cave has been recreated, com-

Perched on a hillside, Bonnieux is a typical Luberon village.

plete with corals bathed in a blueish light; a curious find in winegrowing country, the cave reflects the fact that the Luberon region was once beneath the oceans. *Apr-Sep: guided tour (30min) 2-7pm; Mar and Oct-Dec: 2-6pm. Closed Tue, Jan-Feb, 25 Dec. 3.50€. ☎ 04 90 09 82 64.*

Head NE out of Ansouis on the D 37 before turning right onto the D 135 towards La Tour-d'Aigues.

La Tour-d'Aigues

Destroyed in an accidental fire in 1780 and sacked by revolutionaries in 1792, the ruined château at the centre of the village makes for a scenic backdrop. What remains of the exterior, notably the monumental gateway and richly decorated façade, shows the splendour of this 16C Renaissance residence. Inside there is a keep and a small chapel, while the cellars house two interesting museums, one dedicated to Faïence, the other to rural life. *Jul-Aug:10am-1pm, 2.30-6.30pm, Sun 2.30-6pm; Apr-Jun and Sep-Oct: 10am-1pm, 2.30-6pm, Sun and Mon 2-6pm, Tue 10am-1pm; Nov-Mar: 10am-12pm, 2-5pm, Sun and Mon 2-5pm, Tue 10am-12pm. Closed 1 Jan, 24-26 Dec and 31 Dec. 4.50€ (children under 8 : no charge). ☎ 04 90 07 50 33. www.chateaulatourdaigues. com*

Given that la Tour d'Aigues is at the heart of the appellation Côtes-du-Luberon, wine buffs might wish to visit **Bastide de Rafinel** *(see Shopping Guide).*

Take the D 956 to Pertuis then head W on the D 973. Before reaching Villelaure, turn right following the signs for Château Val Joanis.

Pertuis: Jardin du Château Val Joanis

Garden visit followed by wine tasting (Côtes-du-Luberon). Apr-Oct: 10am-7pm. Christmas market on 4-5 Dec. No charge. ☎ 04 90 79 88 40. www.val-joanis.com

Behind the cellars of this winemaking estate are fine terraced gardens laid out on three levels, the first a kitchen garden, the second a flower garden, and the third given over to ornamental trees. Running along its left hand side is a rose arbour, while to the right is an olive grove. Exuding peace and tranquillity, this garden is an island of colour among a sea of vines.

Rejoin the D 973. In **Cadenet**, *wickerwork is the subject matter of the* **Musée de la Vannerie**: *on the Durance, the village was once renowned for this activity, harvesting willow trees which grew on the banks of the river. ♿ Apr-Oct: Wed-Mon 10am-12pm, 2.30-6.30pm. Closed 1 May. 3.50€. ☎ 04 90 68 24 44.*

Lourmarin★

In an exceptional location, Lourmarin is known for its **château★**, built during the 15C and the Renaissance. If you only plan to visit one château in the region, it should be this one, with its fine wood panelled and stone galleries in the old wing, and superb rooms richly decorated with Renaissance style furniture. The grand staircase, ending dramatically with a slender pillar supporting a stone cupola, is another architectural highlight. *Jul-Aug: guided tours 10am, 11am, 3pm, 4pm, 5pm, 6pm; May-Jun and Sep 10am, 11am, 2.30pm, 3.30pm, 4.30pm, 5.30pm; Mar-Apr and Oct: 11am, 2.30pm, 3.30pm, 4.30pm; Nov-Dec and Feb; 11am, 2.30pm, 4pm; Jan: weekend afternoons. Independent visits during Jul-Aug 10-11.30am, 3-6pm. Closed 1 Jan, 25 Dec. 5€ (children under 10: no charge). ☎ 04 90 68 15 23.*

Round off with a tasting at **Château Constantin-Chevalier** *(see Shopping Guide).* A worthwhile final stop in the Côtes du Luberon is **Château St-Pierre de Méjans** at Puyvert, not far from Lourmarin *(2km to the SW on the D 27).*

THE COSTIÈRES DE NÎMES

60km from St-Gilles (Gard). Michelin Local Map 339, K-L 6-7. See Itinerary ⑥ on the map on p. 324.

St-Gilles★

Gateway to the Camargue, this important winemaking centre is well known for its **former abbey church of St-Gilles**, a veritable masterpiece whose façade includes some of the finest examples of Provençal Romanesque statuary. It is difficult today to fully appreciate the significance of this abbey at its peak; imagine the chancel of the former abbey church extending beyond the existing chancel and, to the south, the cloisters with their courtyard surrounded by the chapterhouse, refectory, kitchens and basement storerooms. This great medieval monument fell victim to the Wars of Religion; what remains is its fine **façade★★** (including some of the best Romenaesque sculpture in the South of France), vestiges of the chancel and the **crypt★**. *Ancient chancel, spiral staircase and crypt: open every day, contact Bureau d'Acceuil aux Monuments, Place de la Republique (opposite the church on the left). 3.50€. ☎ 04 66 87 41 31. www.ot-st-gilles.fr*

Head SW out of St Gilles on the N 572 towards Montpellier. Flanked by slopes, the route cuts through **AOC Costières-de-Nimes** country; to the left are the Scamandre and Charnier, where reeds are harvested.

Turn left onto the D 779. At **Gallician**, a classic winemaking town, **Château Mas Neuf** *(see Shopping Guide)* is worth a visit.

In Gallician, turn right onto the minor D 381, then left onto the D 104 to the Canal du Rhône at Sète.

Pont des Tourradons

There is an interesting **view★** from this marshland bridge, taking in typical Petite Camargue landscape; the dead-straight canal, lakes and reed beds, a marriage of land and sky in silence and solitude. Long horned black bulls graze peacefully in the landscape; one of the best places to experience the true atmosphere of the Camargue.

Head back along the D 104 then turn right onto the D 352.

Vauvert

Today a suburb of Nîmes, this large winemaking village retains its historic centre, its covered market having been converted into an exhibition centre.

Head W on the N 572. Before Aimargues, turn left onto the D 979 towards Aigues-Mortes.

Saint-Laurent-d'Aigouze

Worth a visit in this large winemaking village is its bullfighting arena erected under the shade of plane trees in the square by the church (the sacristy seems to serve as an enclosure for bulls), where traditional contests take place to mark its feast day *(late Aug).*

Continue along the D 979 before turning left onto the D 58. The route heads through the sandy-earthed fields of wine and asparagus country. Here and there are large farmhouses under shady pine trees.

After 9.5km, turn left onto the minor D 179 towards Montcalm and St-Gilles. In Montcalm are the ruins of a huge 18C residence and, out among the vineyards, a farmhouse chapel dating from the same era.

Return to St-Gilles on the D 179 crossing the marshland of the Camargue Gardoise.

The Rhône and the Romans

Nîmes★★★

When Roman legionaries established a colony here in 31 BC, they built 16km of imposing perimeter walls. Situated on the Domitian Way, the settlement was embellished by fine buildings: a forum with the Maison Carrée to the south, an amphitheatre, a circus, baths and fountains fed by an aqueduct (of which the Pont du Gard is the most impressive vestige). The town reached its height in the 2C, with a population of 25 000 and a building programme which included Plotinius' basilica and the Fontaine district.

Nîmes' **amphitheatre★★★** (late 1C-early 2C) differs from its counterpart at Arles in its detail. The best preserved Roman amphitheatre anywhere, it is a two storey limestone structure of 60 arcades. Inside, an ingenious system of corridors, stairways, galleries and vomitoria allowed spectators to exit the amphitheatre within a few minutes. *Mid-Mar to mid-Oct: 9am-7pm; mid-Oct to mid-Mar: 10am-5pm. Closed 1 Jan, 1 May, 25 Dec and performance days. 4.65 €. ☎ 04 66 76 72 77.*

The best preserved of Roman temples, the **Maison Carrée★★★** dates from the reign of Augustus (late 1C BC). The purity of line, proportions and fluted columns suggest a Greek influence; above all, it owes its charm to its almost fragile character, in keeping with the city's other monuments. *Mid-Mar to mid-Oct: 9am-7pm; mid-Oct to mid-Mar: 10am-5pm. Closed 1 Jan, 1 May, 25 Dec. No charge.*

In Gallo-Roman times, the area now covered by the **Jardin de la Fontaine★★** was the site of baths, a theatre and a temple. Laid out by an 18C military engineer, the garden follows the plan of the ancient Nemausus fountain. To the left of the fountain is the temple of Diana, destroyed in 1577 during the Wars of Religion; surrounded by greenery, it makes for a romantic backdrop. The verdant Mont Cavalier is crowned by the symbol of the city, the **Tour Magne★**, the most imposing vestige of the Roman perimeter walls. This three storey polygonal tower is 34m high. *Apr-Sep: 9am-6.30pm; Oct-Mar: 9am-4.30pm. Closed 1 Jan, 1 May and 25 Dec. 2.40€. ☎ 04 66 58 30 00.*

Vienne: Gallo-Roman city of Saint-Romain-en Gal★★

2km S of Lyon. Mar-Oct: 10am-6pm; Nov-Feb: 10am-5pm. Closed Mon, 1 Jan, 1 May, 1 Nov, 25 Dec. 3.80€ (no charge for children). ☎ 04 74 53 74 02.

On the right bank of the Rhone, excavations of the site have unearthed a built up area with opulent villas, shops, artisans' workshops and baths. The most impressive finds are on show in the **Museum★**, including the **Dieux Oceans mosaic★**; the mosaics are the principal feature of this site. These floor decorations, often inspired by mythology, give an insight into the tastes of their original owners. Thus, the Orpheus mosaic affirms the triumph of culture over nature. The exceptional **Échassiers wall painting★** demonstrates the refinement of the interior decoration. Lastly, the **Punishment of Lycurgus mosaic★** is a beautiful example of the artistic excellence of the Gallo-Roman period.

Orange★★

Literally the gateway to the city, the **triumphal arch★★** marks the northern approach to Orange, situated on the Via Agrippa, the road linking Lyon and Arles (on entering the town along the N 7; free parking at the crossroads). Remarkable for its size (the third largest surviving arch at 19.21m high, 19.57m wide and 8.40m deep), it is also the best preserved of its kind; the north side is particularly complete in its decoration. Built around 20 BC and subsequently dedicated to Tiberius, it commemorates the exploits of the veterans of the Second Legion. Composed of three archways flanked by columns, and originally surmounted by a bronze chariot and two trophies, it has two peculiarities; the triangular pediment above the central archway and the two attic storeys.

Built during the reign of Augustus (sometimes known as Octavian) the **théâtre antique★★★** is the only Roman theatre to retain its stage wall intact, an imposing structure some 103m long and 36m high. Its upper storey is composed of two rows of corbels with holes which held the poles supporting the *velum*, an awning to shelter spectators from the sun. The semicircular cavea could accommodate up to 7 000 people, ranged in accordance with their status. Below, the orchestra had rows of movable seats for high ranking spectators. The stage, fitted with wooden flooring under which the machinery was kept, is 61m wide and 9m deep.

Shopping Guide

INFORMATION

Inter Rhône, interprofession des vins AOC Côtes du Rhône et vallee du Rhône – *6 Rue des Trois-Faucons – 84024 Avignon Cedex 1 – ☎ 04 90 27 24 00 – www.vin-rhone.com*

Syndicat des Côtes du Ventoux – *Route de Velleron – 84975 Carpentras Cedex – ☎ 04 90 63 36 50.*

Syndicat des Côtes du Luberon – *90 Boulevard St-Roch – BP12 – 84240 La Tour d'Aigues – ☎ 04 90 07 34 40.*

OVERVIEW

CHARACTERISTICS

With complex bouquets, the wines from the northern part are more refined and sought after (Côte Rôtie, Condrieu, Hermitage). The southern wines are simpler and more quaffable, the reds often heady (Côtes du Rhône Villages Cairanne is a good example), the rosés lively and fresh (Tavel), and the whites fruity and smooth (Cairanne). The five southern Crus, including the complex, strong and velvety red Châteauneuf du Pape, are in no way inferior to their northern counterparts. Further south, the reds of Costières de Nîmes are light country wines, the reds of Côtes du Luberon full bodied (the whites have a floral bouquet), and the Côtes du Ventoux reds fine and quaffable. Low in alcohol, the sparkling, slightly sweet Clairette de Die is a gem.

PRICES

Wines of the northern Côtes du Rhône – Côte-Rôtie: 15-40€; Condrieu: 15-23€; Château Grillet: 30-38€; St Joseph: 10-15€; Hermitage: 35-40€. These prices reflect the effort required to successfully grow vines on the steep northern slopes. The grapes are harvested by hand and skilled workers are hard to come by. Simpler to produce, Croze-Hermitage from down on the plain costs between 5€ and 11€.

Wines of the southern Côtes du Rhône – Simpler and more quaffable, southern wines start around 5€. Châteauneuf du Pape: 11-15€; Tavel: 5-8€; Costières de Nîmes: 3-8€; Côtes du Luberon: 5-11€; Côtes du Ventoux: 5-8€; Clairette de Die: 5-8€.

STORAGE

Wines of the northern Côtes du Rhône - Côte-Rôtie: 5-15 years; Condrieu blanc: drink young, no more than 2-3 years; Château Grillet: white best drunk young, but can develop a certain class when aged (2-10 years); St Joseph: whites or reds are best drunk fairly young; Hermitage: well suited to laying down.

Wines of the southern Côtes du Rhône – All fairly young drinking wines : good news for those without cellars. Châteauneuf du Pape: red 5-20 years, white 1-10 years; Costières de Nîmes: red 4-5 years, white and rosé best drunk young; Côtes du Luberon: red 5 years, rosé 2 years, white 3 years; Clairette de Die: ready for immediate drinking.

BUYING

WINE MERCHANTS

La Bouteillerie – *43 Rue Nationale – 69420 Condrieu – ☎ 04 74 59 84 96 – rhone-millesimes@wanadoo.fr* - Tue-Sat 9am-12pm, 2-7pm, Sun 10am-12.30pm – closed first week in Jan. A vast range of wines, all of which the boss, M. Gérin, knows like the back of his hand. In layman's terms he explains the great local names like Côte-Rôtie and Condrieu, as well as lesser wines; worth listening to.

Caveau St-Vincent – *Place du Seigneur – 30126 Tavel – ☎ 04 66 50 24 10 –* 9.30am-12.30pm, 2.30-7pm – closed public holidays and Jan-Feb. An air conditioned cellar in the centre of the village, the ideal spot to get acquainted with France's premier rosé. Local produce for sale. Attractively decorated former stables with original manger and troughs.

COOPERATIVES

Cave Coopérative des Vignerons de Beaumes de Venise – *Quartier Ravel – 84190 Beaumes de Venise – ☎ 04 90 12 41 00 –* 8.30am-12.30pm (noon in winter), 2-7pm (6pm in winter). Plenty of Muscat and also the lesser known reds, rosés and whites of the Côtes du Rhône Villages Beaumes de Venise. The cooperative has over 150 members producing 55 000 hl per year.

"Vinadéa" Maison des Vins – *8 Rue du Mar. Foch – 84230 Châteauneuf du Pape – ☎ 04 90 83 70 69 – www.vinadea.com* - May-Jun: 10am-1pm, 2-7pm; Jul-Aug: 10am-7pm; Nov-Feb: 10am-12.30pm, 2-6pm; closed 1 week late Jan, 25 Dec and 1 Jan. A former stables with attractive stonework and beams, offering wines from 80 Châteauneuf du Pape vineyards; tastings with advice on offer. Books and gifts.

Cave de Die Jaillance – *Avenue de la Clairette – 26150 Die – ☎ 04 75 22 30 15 – www.jaillance.com* - 9am-12pm, 2-7pm – closed 1 Jan, 25 Dec. The choice and quality on offer takes in not only Clairette de Die, but also Crémant de Die and Châtillon en Diois wines. The guided cellar tour, followed by a tasting, is an ideal introduction for wine beginners.

Cave des Vignerons d'Estézargues – *Route des Gres – 30390 – Estézargues – ☎ 04 66 57 03 64 – les.vignerons. estezargues@wanadoo.fr* - Mon-Sat 8am-12pm, 2-6pm – booking essential. Representing ten winemakers, including Andézon, Bacchantes, Les Génestas, Grès Saint-Vincent, La Montagnette, Périllière and Pierredon, whose traditionally manufactured organic produce reflects the local grape varieties and terroir.

Caveau Gigondas – *Place du Portail – 84190 Gigondas – ☎ 04 90 65 82 29 –* 10am-12pm, 2-6.30pm, closed 1 Jan, 25 Dec. Open all year and run by an association of around fifty winemakers, this is an opportunity for visitors to taste a wide variety of Crus without feeling obliged to buy. Each bottle is the product of a single winemaker; advice available from the staff.

Cave de Tain l'Hermitage – *22 Route de Larnage – 26601 Tain l'Hermitage –* ☎ *04 75 08 20 87 – cellars:* ☎ *04 75 08 91 86 – commercial.france@cave-tain-hermitage.com* With 400 members producing 55 000hl annually from 1 100ha, this is one of the region's most important cooperatives, covering five appellations and a vin de pays; some rare vintages available which no wine merchant could obtain. Founded in 1933, since when it has continuously strived to improve quality.

DOMAINES

Domaine Étienne Guigal – *N 86 – 69420 Ampuis –* ☎ *04 74 56 10 22 – contact@guigal.com - Mon-Fri 8am-12pm, 2-6pm – ring ahead.* Guigal is one of Côte-Rôtie's best-known names thanks to the relentless efforts of Étienne Guigal and his son Marcel, and rightly enjoys international renown. The wine is made to allow grape variety and terroir to shine through; oenologist Philippe, son of Marcel, is the third generation to become involved. They have added two other northern vineyards to their empire, namely the former domaine Jean-Louis Grippat (Saint-Joseph and Hermitage) and the former domaine de Vallouit (Côte-Rôtie, Hermitage, Saint-Joseph and Crozes-Hermitage).

Domaine du Château Turcan – *Route de Pertuis – 2km from Ansouis on the D 56 – 84690 Ansouis –* ☎ *04 90 09 83 33 – www.chateauturcan.com - Apr to mid Jun: Mon-Sat 9.30am-12pm, 2.30-6.30pm; 15 Jun to late Sep: Mon-Sat 9.30am-12.30pm, 3-7pm, Sun in Aug – closed public holidays.* Covering 25ha in the lower Luberon, Château Turcan not only produces red, rosé and white Crus from 6 different grape varieties, but also has its own museum with over 2 000 winemaking utensils from the 16C to the present day, plus one of the oldest presses in France.

SCEA Leydier et Fils – Domaine de Durban – *84190 Beaumes de Venise –* ☎ *04 90 62 94 26 – Mon-Sat 9am-12pm, 2-6pm (5.30pm in winter) – closed public holidays.* The footpath which winds through Domaine de Durban's 119ha offers some fine views. Visitors receive a warm welcome from the Leydier family who will happily elaborate on their two house Crus: the Côtes du Rhône Villages Beaumes de Venise – a dry white wine – and the famous muscat.

Château La Canorgue – *Route du Pont Julien – 84480 Bonnieux –* ☎ *04 90 75 81 01 – Mon-Sat 9am-12pm, 2.30-5.30pm, ring ahead in winter.* The owner of this small family owned vineyard operates on strictly organic principles, resulting in a low yield. The wines are aged in oak barrels and bottled at the château.

Domaine de l'Oratoire Saint-Martin – *Route de St-Roman – 84290 Cairanne –* ☎ *04 90 30 82 07 – Mon-Sat except public holidays 8am-12pm, 2-7pm.* The Alary family has been involved in winemaking since 1692. Since 1982, Frédéric and Francois have cultivated these 25ha on the hillsides of St-Martin; the vines, some of which are over a century old, are harvested by hand. Open vats are used for their Côtes du Rhône Villages, closed vats for their Côtes du Rhône. The cellars with oak barrels have been in operation for over 150 years.

Cellars of Château de Courson.

Domaine Richaud – *Route de Rasteau – 84290 Cairanne –* ☎ *04 90 30 85 25 – Mon-Fri 9am-12pm, 2-6pm.* Since arriving here in 1974, Marcel Richaud has strived to fulfil the potential of these 45ha including the construction of a cellar for his vintages. Always eager for improvement, he endeavours to "understand" the terroirs in order to best exploit them.

Château de Curson – *26600 Chanos-Curson –* ☎ *04 75 07 34 60 – chateaucurson@freesurf.fr* Once owned by Diane de Poitiers, this château has become a jewel in the Crozes-Hermitage crown in the hands of Étienne Pochon, who has run it since 1988. Covering 14.6ha, the vineyard grows Syrah, Marsanne and Roussanne grapes.

Domaine Courbis – *Route de St-Romain – 07130 Chateaubourg –* ☎ *04 75 81 81 60 – domaine-courbis@wanadoo.fr - Mon-Fri 9am-12pm, 2-6pm, Sat and public holidays ring ahead.* Steep Ardèche slopes and fine bunches of grapes ripening in the sun; little has changed here since it became the seat of the Courbis family in the 16C. The 26ha vineyard produces a number of Crus, including the rare Cornas sabarotte (5-6 000 bottles per year), made in accordance with traditional methods.

Château La Nerthe – *Route de Sorgues – 84230 Châteauneuf-du-Pape –* ☎ *04 90 83 70 11 – www.chateau-la-nerthe.com - 9am-12pm, 2-5.30pm.* This château has Châteauneuf-du-Pape's oldest cellars. Its wines are highly esteemed and the prices reflect this, although visitors should not be put off. A real treat, worthy of a detour.

Domaine Alain Voge – *4 Impasse de l'Équerre – 07130 Cornas –* ☎ *04 75 40 32 04 – Mon-Fri 9-11.30am, 2-5.30pm.* The fourth generation of his family to be engaged in winemaking, Alain Voge

J. Damase / MICHELIN

has 12ha of hillsides planted with well-established vines, some of which are 70 years old. Eco-friendliness underlies the production. The grapes are harvested by hand; the wines are aged in barrels from Bordeaux and Burgundy.

Château Mas Neuf – *30600 Gallician* - ☎ *04 66 73 33 23* – *lucbaudet@chateaumasneuf.com* Luc Baudet's 62ha vineyard grows Syrah, Carignan, Grenache Noir, Mourvèdre and Roussanne grapes (he also grows 1ha of olives). Some of his wines are then aged for six to nine months in barrels. The vines grow in sandy, silt-laden "microterroirs". Production environmentally sound lines.

Domaine Les Goubert – *84190 Gigondas* – ☎ *04 90 65 86 38* – *jpcartier@terrre-net.fr* 23ha split over five communes growing between 150 and 400m up; Jean-Pierre Cartier was the first Gigondas winemaker to use new barrels. A Côtes du Rhône Villages Sablet is also made.

Château Constantin-Chevalier – *84160 Lourmarin* – ☎ *04 90 68 38 99*. Growing Syrah, Grenache and Carignan for reds and rosés, and Clairette, Ugni Blanc and Vermentino for whites in limestone/clay soil with rounded pebbles, the château extends over 20ha. Harvested by hand, the grapes are processed in temperature controlled vats using carbonic maceration; the wine is aged in vats and mature timber barrels.

Domaine de Piaugier – *3 Route de Gigondas* – *84110 Sablet* – ☎ *04 90 46 96 49* – *piaugier@wanadoo.fr* - *Mon-Sat 9am-12pm, 2-6pm – phone ahead*. The latest in a long line of winemakers, Jean-Marc Autran has been in charge here since 1985. His first vintages were created in the cellars built by his great-grandfather in 1947. Today, the 30ha vineyard includes a wide variety of terroirs. The grapes are processed in bunches and aged in concrete vats and barrels.

Domaine de Cabasse – *Route de Sablet* – *84110 Séguret* – ☎ *04 90 46 91 12* – *info@domaine-de-cabasse.fr*- *Mon-Fri (open every day Apr-Oct) 8am-12pm, 2-5pm*. Nicolas has recently stepped into the sloes of his father, Swiss agricultural engineer Alfred Haeni, whose love for the area and wine inspired him to produce appellation Côtes du Rhône Villages (Sablet and Séguret) and Gigondas reds, rosés and whites on this 20ha vineyard. The grapes are hand picked and graded before processing and ageing in vats and barrels for between eight months and two years depending on vintage and grape variety.

Domaine Delas Frères – *ZA de l'Olivet* – *07300 St-Jean-de-Muzols* – ☎ *04 75 08 60 30* – *jacques-grange@delas.com* - *Mon-Fri 9.30-12pm, 2.30-6.30pm – ring ahead*. Founded in 1835 and now comprising 14ha, the vineyard grows Syrah, Marsanne and Roussanne. *"Lutte raisonnée" (see p. 25)* principles are the rule here, and harvesting is by hand; processing takes place in concrete vats for red and stainless steel vats for whites. The wines are then aged in barrels and vats for up to 26 months.

Domaine du Tunnel – *20 Rue de la République* – *07130 St-Péray* – ☎ *04 75 80 04 66*. Covering 5.5ha, the vineyard grows Marsanne, Roussanne and Syrah in a varying mix of limestone, clay and granite soil. The *"lutte raisonnée" (see p. 25)* approach has seen herbicides banished. The grapes are hand picked. The reds are aged in barrels, the whites in a combination of stainless steel vats and barrels.

Paul Jaboulet Aîné – *Les Jalets – BP46 – La Roche de Glun – 26600 Tain l'Hermitage* – ☎ *04 75 84 68 93* – *info@jaboulet.com* - *ring ahead*. Founded by Antoine Jaboulet in 1834, this family business has a 100ha vineyard and also runs a wine merchants, dealing not only in some of the best known names in the northern Côtes du Rhône (Hermitage, Côte-Rôtie and Saint-Péray), but also southern wines like Châteauneuf-du-Pape and Gigondas. Its cellars are located in the Roman mines at Châteauneuf-sur-Isère.

Domaine de la Mordorée – *Chemin des Oliviers – 30126 Tavel* – ☎ *04 66 50 00 75* – *8am-12pm, 1.30-5.30pm – ring ahead*. Christophe Delorme turned his back on a family business manufacturing diving suits to devote himself to vines and winemaking. 38 parcels of land in eight communes totalling 55ha are harvested by hand. In 2001 a new tasting cellar was opened, and 2004 saw the planting of Condrieu vines.

S.Sauvignier / MICHELIN

Bastide de Rafinel – *84240 La Tour d'Aigues* – ☎ *04 90 07 48 61*. Bought as a ruin in 1980, and subsequently completely restored by Marie-Odile Ducrest; sited on the southern slopes of the Luberon, the 5ha vineyard is at an altitude of 300m. Grenache, Roussanne, Vermentino, Ugni Blanc, Syrah and Carignan grow in calcareous clay rich in cobalt and molasse. Harvesting is done by hand and the whites are aged in barrels.

Chateau Grillet – *42410 Verin* – ☎ *04 74 59 51 56*. Founded by her Neyret-Gachet ancestors, Isabelle Baratin-Canet runs this 3.4ha exclusively Viognier vineyard, planted in granitic sand on steep terraces. The wines are aged in vats and oak barrels. This vineyard is unique in France for being an appellation in its own right.

The stage wall had a rich decorative scheme composed of marble facing, stucco, mosaics, several tiers of columns, and niches for statues including that of Augustus, now returned to its original position. The wall has three doors: at the centre the royal door (for the principal actors), and two side doors (for minor actors). *Jun-Aug: 9am-8pm; Apr-May and Sep: 9am-7pm; Mar and Oct: 9am-6pm; rest of the year: 9am-5pm (last admission 15min before closing). 7.50€ (combined ticket with Musée Municipal).* ☏ *04 90 51 17 60.*

Roman ruins at Vaison-la-Romaine★★

Jun-Sep: Puymin 9.30am-6.30pm, Villasse 10am-12pm, 2.30-6.30pm; Mar-May: Puymin 9.30am-6pm, Villasse 10am-12pm, 2.30-6pm; Oct-Feb: 10am-12pm, 2-5pm. Closed Jan, 25 Dec, Villasse closed Tue morning. 7€ (children: 2.50€), ticket also admits to other monuments). ☏ *04 90 36 02 11.*

Spread over 15ha, this vast expanse of ruins allows the visitor to get a real understanding of daily life in the ancient settlement of Vasio. The excavated area covers the outskirts of the Gallo-Roman city, while its centre (the Forum and immediate vicinity) lies under the modern town. Presently, the excavations are progressing towards the cathedral in La Villasse district and around the Puymin hill, where a shopping quarter and a sumptuous house **(Peacock villa)** with mosaic decoration have been unearthed. On the northern side of the ancient city are the ruins of the baths (some 20 rooms – not open to the public), in use until the late 3C.

Pont du Gard★★★

24km NE of Nîmes on the N 86 and then the D 19. Free access to the bridge. Parking on either side 7-1am. 5€ (no time limit), no charge if you purchase a day pass which includes entrance to the cinema, museum and children's activities (8-20€).

One of the wonders of Roman architecture, this 1C masterpiece has bronzed stonework, a strange air of lightness, a backdrop of hills covered in verdant Mediterranean flora, and the green waters of the Gardon, all of which combine to create a vision of splendour. The Romans attached great importance to the quality of the water supplied to their cities; the Pont du Gard formed part of the 50km Nîmes aqueduct, channelling water from its source near Uzès with an average drop of 34cm per kilometre and provided 20 000m³ to the city per day. Constructed of massive blocks weighing 6 to 8 tonnes which were hauled over 40m up into position, the structure is composed of three storeys of arches resting on top of each other.

The Exotic and the Unusual

The Palais Idéal★ at Hauterives

38km NE of Tain l'Hermitage on the N 7 and then the D 51. Jul-Oct: 9am-12.30pm, 1.30-7.30pm; Apr-Jun and Sep: 9am-12.30pm, 1.30-6.30pm; Feb-Mar and Oct-Nov: 9.30am-12.30pm, 1.30-5.30pm; Dec-Jan: 9.30am-12.30pm, 1.30-4.30pm. Closed 1 Jan, 25 Dec and mid to late Jan. 5€ (children: 3.50€). ☏ *04 75 68 81 19.*

Set in the middle of its garden, the 10m-high Palais Idéal is a 300m² building enCrusted with bizarre decoration and inlaid with inscriptions, verses and dedications and epigrams. It was the brainchild of a local postman, Ferdinand Cheval, who spent 33 years constructing it.

The eastern front is the most unusual, with huge female idols made of reddish pebbles. Imitation plants sit cheek by jowl with evocations of oriental and medieval palaces. The interior is a mass of galleries and grottoes. Narrow stairs lead to an upper platform, the centre of a fantasy world which gave food for thought to the Surrealists.

The building is best seen in the evening, when the well-arranged lighting highlights the architecture to best effect.

The Crocodile Farm★ at Pierrelatte

8km NW of St-Paul-Trois-Chateaux on the D 59. ♿ *Early Mar to late Sep: 9.30am-7pm; early Oct to late Feb: 9.30am-5pm. 8.30€. (children: 6€).* ☏ *04 75 04 33 73.*

Warm water from the Tricastin nuclear power plant is supplied to this hothouse with its tropical garden and crocodile farm. A variety of species from around the world – caymans, American alligators and Cuban crocodiles among them – are kept in a number of large ponds. Further on, the enormous hothouse gives visitors a taste of the exotic. The many footbridges are good vantage points from which to admire the lush vegetation, colourful and noisy birdlife, and over 300 Nile crocodiles basking on banks or swimming silently in the dark water.

Safari-Parc de Peaugres★

36km NW of Tournon on the N 86, D 82 and N 82. Late Jun to Aug: 9.30am-6pm; Mar-May and early Sep to late Oct: 10am-5pm, school holidays, weekends and public holidays 9.30am-5pm; late Oct to early Feb: visitors on foot only 10.30am-4.30pm, school holidays and public holidays 10am-4.30pm. Closed 25 Dec. 16€ (children: 3-12: 10.50€). Out of season: check opening times. ☎ *04 75 33 00 32. www.safari-peaugres. com*

⊙ Laid out on either side of the N 82 at the foot of the Pilat massif, this 30-year-old animal park is home to over 400 mammals, 300 birds and around 100 reptiles. The events programme is available at the entrance.

By car – *Comply with safety regulations.* The road winds through four separated enclosures allowing close up views of monkeys, zebras, bears, bison, camels, buffalo, yaks, hippopotamus, deer and elephants.

On foot – The park's collection includes aquatic birds, giraffes, ostriches and antelopes. In the cellars of the château is a vivarium housing lizards, caymans, boa constrictors, pythons and frogs. The monkey house has mandrills, marmosets, orang-utans and lemurs. Lions, tigers and cheetahs can also be observed close up thanks to a glass tunnel. A pool is home to some sea lions and a small colony of penguins.

Off the Beaten Track

From Roman Roads to the Autoroute du Soleil and Marseille-bound TGVs, everything in the Rhône Valley seems to follow the flow of the river, speeding you north or south. But there's plenty to discover away from the region's cultural superhighways. These two little detours off the N86 offer a picturesque look at the region from a different angle, by car and on foot.

PARC NATUREL RÉGIONAL DU PILAT

Created in 1974, the park covers 65 000ha of very diverse countryside: forests of beech, fir plantations, open plateau pastureland and rolling hills, and swift streams at the bottom of deep valleys.
Turn off N68 at Chavanay and follow the D7 W to Pélussin.

Pélussin

Park on place Abbé-Vincent in front of the hospital. Walk down rue Dr-Soubeyran and take rue de la Halle on the left.
The old covered market provides a view of the Rhône plain and the town. Go through a fortified gatehouse and turn left. Note the ancient chapel and castle.

Maison du Parc

Easter to mid-Nov: 9.30am-12.30pm, 2pm-6pm (Sat-Sun 6.30pm); mid-Nov to Easter: 10am-12.30pm, 2pm-6pm (Fri 5pm). Closed Tue morning, Sat afternoon out of season. Moulin de Virieu, Pélussin. ☎ *04 74 87 52 00. www.parc-naturel-pilat.fr*
In addition to organising exhibitions and special events, the park's main information centre gives full details of its three nature trails, each forming a 3-4km loop, and eight themed hikes, to be followed over the course of a day or two. Of these, the Jean-Jacques Rousseau trail, linking Condrieu and La Jasserie, traces the philosopher's links with the area and his botanical interests. A 22km floral trail takes the rambler from the Mediterranean vegetation of the Malleval region to the subalpine formation of the Crêt de Perdrix. The ornithological trail, running from St-Chabin to St-Pierre-de-Bœuf, is best attempted between mid-May and mid-June, when many of the 90 featured species of birds can be seen; these range from mallard on St-Pierre Lake to crossbills in the fir forests and rock bunting out on the gorse heath.
Follow D63 W, then S.
From Faucharat viewpoint there are lovely views of the Régrillon Valley, the Rhone Valley and Pélussin.

Crêt d'Œillon★★★

15min on foot there and back. At the Croix de l'Œillon pass, take the road on the right leading to the turn-off to a private road, ending at the television relay station. Park in the car park. At the top, walk to the left around the fence: the viewing table is on the eastern end of the promontory, at the foot of a monumental cross.
▸ The panorama, from a height of 1 370m, is one of the most spectacular in the Rhône Valley. In the foreground, beyond the rocks of the Pic des Trois Dents, there is a bird's-eye view of the Rhône Valley, from Vienne to Serrières. In the distance, to the east, the view stretches right to the beginning of the Alps, south-east to Mont Ventoux and north-east to the Jura.
Return to the D63, continue for 11km.
The road meanders to and fro through lines of fir trees and broom-covered moorland.
Continue E as D63 joins D8ᴬ, then turn right on to D8, towards La Jasserie.

Le Crêt de la Perdrix★

15min on foot there and back. At the top of the climb, park near the path leading to the ridge.

⚐ The grass-covered summits of the Crêt de la Perdrix and the Crêt de l'OEillon both bristle with strangely eroded granitic rocks, known locally as *chirats*. The view from this second crest, which is less breathtaking though slightly higher at 1 432m, takes in the peaks of Mézenc, Lizieux, Meygal and Gerbier-le-Jonc.

Return by the same route, or via D8 and D503 to Malleval, or head S to join N82, then E to Serrières.

VALLÉE DE L'EYRIEUX

Turn off N68 at La Voulte or Beauchastel.

Beauchastel

This listed village is nestled at the foot of its ruined castle: climb up through the narrow alleys and covered streets to the terrace by the Maison du Patrimoine and enjoy the pretty view of St-Laurent-du-Pape and the valley.

Rejoin D21 and head towards St-Laurent-du-Pape.

St-Laurent-du-Pape

This attractive little town has always been regarded as the gateway to the valley, perhaps because of its bridge which spans the river. Swift but sparse in summer, the waters of the Eyrieux are famous for their sudden spates after the autumn storms, when the steep slopes of its upper course send the rainwater rushing through a succession of narrows, basins and gorges: the rate of flow can reach a phenomenal 3600m³ per second.

Take D266 N from St-Laurent. Turn off at the sign for the Serre de Pepeyrier ridge. Park about 250m along the road towards the television relay station, and climb up to the edge of the ridge.

View from Serre du Pepeyrier★

15min on foot there and back.

⚐ There is a beautiful view of the mouth of the Eyrieux and its orchards, and of the Rhône Valley.

Continue 5km along D266.

As the road rises, two panoramic bends offer impressive views, first of the Rhône, then of the Eyrieux.

A track, off D286 to the left, leads to the Château de Pierre-Gourde. Park at a pass, in sight of the ruins.

Château de Pierre-Gourde★★

This medieval castle, now a craggy ruin, adds to the austere but impressive feeling of the **site★**. At the foot of the peak on which the keep was built lie the remains of the main building, parts of the fortified curtain wall, and traces of the old feudal village. To the left of the ruins, a rocky terrace commands a fine, all-round view of the Trois-Becs, the Baronnies and, opposite, the jagged backbone of Croix de Bauzon.

Return to St-Laurent by the same route and rejoin the valley road in the direction of Cheylard.

This section of the D120, which passes a succession of roadside orchards, is at its most beautiful at the end of March. The peach trees burst into full spring blossom and the extraordinary symphony of colour – from pale pink to rich cerise and purple – spreads up from the lower valley.

At St-Sauveur-de-Montagut, take the D102, before the bridge, and follow the course of the Eyrieux's tributary, the Gluyère, towards St-Pierreville.

The road runs along the Gluyère Valley, where a beach has been laid out. The drive, following the course of the river almost the whole way, gives lovely views of this stark, wild, but beautifully natural landscape. The road is nearing the edge of the area known locally as les Boutières, still sustained in part by its traditional industries of cattle-rearing and forestry.

St-Pierreville

If the Eyrieux Valley is the land of the peach tree, St-Pierreville is the local capital of the chestnut! Grown at altitudes up to 800m, it is not a crop that lends itself to mechanised cultivation, and you may well see locals filling their wide wicker baskets by hand during the October harvest. At other times of the year, the exhibition at the **Maison du Châtaignier** offers a thorough introduction: you'll be able to discuss the merits of the *comballe* and *garinche* varieties like a connoisseur! *Guided tours 1hr 15min. Jul-Aug, Sun-Fri, 11am-12.30pm, 2.30pm-6pm; Jun, Sep-Nov, Wed and Sun, 2pm-6pm. 3.35€.* ☎ 04 75 66 64 33.

Savoie and Bugey

The area between lakes Geneva and du Bourget and the river valleys of the Ain and Isère is chequered with small vineyards, occupying the sunniest slopes of the Alpine foothills. In the Ain region, the Bugey wine-growing district nestles in a deep bend in the Rhone, on the southernmost fringe of the Jura. In Savoie, it is only because of winter-sports tourism that the vineyards have remained economically viable, but this does not mean that Savoie wines are of no value except as an accompaniment to fondues and raclettes. The wide range of grape varieties ensures the production of some quality wines, which are well worth seeking out in a region famed for its magnificent scenery.

Terroirs
Michelin Local Map 328 and 333 – Haute-Savoie (74), Savoie (73) and Ain (01).
Area: 2 500ha of vineyards in Savoie, 500ha in the Bugey district.
Production: 144 000hl, both areas combined.
The vines are in most cases grown on scree from glacial moraines. The climate is of continental/mountain type, with cold winters and mild to hot summers. It rains in spring and autumn, but there is plenty of sunshine all the year round.

Wines
Savoie – The **vin-de-savoie** appellation (AOC) is awarded to a number of Crus: Ripaille, Crépy, Marin and Marignan (Lake Geneva sector), Chautagne and Frangy (Rhone valley sector), Montmélian, Cruet, Chignin-Bergeron, Arbin, Abymes and Apremont (Montmélian sector); the white wines, which predominate in the region, are produced from the Altesse, Chardonnay and Jacquère grape varieties, the reds and rosés from Gamay, Mondeuse and Pinot Noir.
The **roussette-de-savoie** appellation applies to wines made from the Altesse grape.
The **ayze mousseux** appellation is given to a sparkling white wine produced from the Gringet and Roussette-d'ayze varieties.
The **seyssel** appellation produces another white made from Altesse grapes.

Bugey – The **vin-du-bugey** appellation (AOVDQS) applies mainly to white wines. They include Cerdon, Montagnieu and Manicle, and are made from the Altesse, Chardonnay and Molette grape varieties.

Useful tip
Given the local climate, the best times to explore this region are summer and early autumn.

The Savoie Wine Route

THE VINEYARDS OF LAKE GENEVA
16km from Thonon-les-Bains to Douvaine (Haute-Savoie). Michelin Local Map 328, K-L 2-3. See itinerary **1** *on the map on p. 341.*

Vineyards at the foot of Mont Granier, to the west of Montmélian.

Directory

WHERE TO EAT

IN BELLEY

⊜☺ **Auberge La Fine Fourchette** – N 504 - 01300 Belley - ☎ 04 79 81 59 33 - closed 21 Dec to 10 Jan, Sun evening and Mon - 🍴 - 22/52€. The large windows of the restaurant, tastefully decorated in a classical/rustic style, look out onto the Rhone Canal and open countryside. If weather permits, eat out on the terrace, which also has fine views. Whatever you choose from the menu, you can be sure of being served good traditional food in generous portions.

AROUND CERDON

⊜☺ **Bernard Charpy** – 1 r. Croix-Chalon - 01460 Brion - ☎ 04 74 76 24 15 – closed 18 to 24 May, 7 to 30 Aug, 26 Dec to 3 Jan, Sun and Mon - 🍴 - 23/43€. A charming chalet-style building just outside Nantua, though quenelles of pike with the renowned local sauce are no longer on the menu. Bernard Charpy presents an attractive traditional cuisine, with a good choice of fish which changes with the seasons. A bonus: affordable prices, easy on the bank balance…

AROUND SEYSSEL

⊜ **Auberge de la Cave de la Ferme** – R. du Grand-Pont - 74270 Frangy – ☎ 04 50 44 75 04 – closed Sun and Mon - 14€. The owners of this inn produce Savoie wines (Roussette, Mondeuse) and marc brandy. The cuisine also has a regional emphasis with some delicious cheese and pork-meat specialities to savour in an unpretentious rustic setting.

IN MONTMÉLIAN

⊜ **St-Vincent** – Au Gaz – 73800 Montmélian – ☎ 04 79 28 21 85 - 🍴 - 13/45€. A friendly restaurant on the main street of this village famous for its gently sparkling white wine. In their delightful vaulted dining room or on the pretty terrace overlooking the vineyards, the owners serve appetising classic dishes, accompanied by a fine list of wines.

⊜☺ **Viboud** – 73800 Montmélian – ☎ 04 79 84 07 24 – closed 23 Jun to 17 Jul, 30 Dec to 15 Jan, Sun evenings, Mon and Tue - 🍴 7/25€. This is one of the most highly regarded restaurants in Montmélian: the cuisine is simple and tasty, and the prices will not give you a heart attack. The menu changes every day, and the chef uses only fresh produce.

IN THONON-LES-BAINS

⊜ **Le Bétandi** – 2 r. des Italiens – 74200 Thonon-les-Bains – ☎ 04 50 71 37 71 – closed 24 Dec and 1 Jan – 10.67/28.20€. The decor of this small restaurant near the town centre is reminiscent of an old Savoyard farmhouse. The menu features some typical regional specialities: the inevitable fondues (Savoyard, farmer's wife and Piedmontese versions), tartiflettes and dishes such as chargrilled reblochonade.

⊜☺ **St-Charles** – 69 av. Gén.-de-Gaulle - 74200 Thonon-les-Bains – ☎ 04 50 83 09 26 – closed Sun evening and Mon - 🍴 25/40€. In winter, hearty eaters install themselves in the modern, brightly painted dining room, warmed by an open fire. In fine weather, they sit on the sunny terrace beside the flower garden. Whatever the season, they can enjoy excellent little traditional dishes prepared with fresh produce.

HOTELS AND CHAMBRES D'HÔTE

AROUND BELLEY

⊜ **Chambre d'hôte Les Charmettes** – La Vellaz, St-Martin-de-Bavel - 01510 Virieu-le-Grand - 11km N of Belley by N 504 to Chazey-Bons then D 31C – ☎ 04 79 87 32 18 - 🍴 3 rm: 33/40€. You can be assured of a pleasant stay in the magnificently restored former stables of this delightful farmhouse, typical of the Bugey. The bedrooms are charming and comfortable; one is equipped for the disabled. Cooking facilities available. Peaceful country setting.

AROUND CERDON

⊜☺ **Chambre d'hôte de Bosseron** – 325 rte de Genève - 01160 Neuville-sur-Ain - 8km NE of Pont-d'Ain on N 84 – ☎ 04 74 37 77 06 – closed Nov to Mar - 🍴 4 rm: 48/58€. This property is set in a fine 2ha park on the banks of the Ain. The house has character (carefully selected furniture, harmonious decor) and individually designed bedrooms. The outbuildings have been renovated to house a fitness centre, billiard room and kitchen for summer use. Friendly welcome.

AROUND MONTMÉLIAN

⊜☺ **Auberge Au Pas de l'Alpette** – Bellecombe - 38530 Chapareillan - 7km SW of Montmélian by N 6 and N 90 – ☎ 04 76 45 22 65 – closed end Nov, Sun evening and Wed - 🍴 - 13 rm: 41/45€, ☕ 7€, 12/34€. This isolated mountain inn in the heart of the Chartreuse massif offers an exceptional view of Mont Blanc. Warm atmosphere. Simple, clean attic rooms. At table, you can feast on raclettes, fondues and young goat with morel mushrooms, in the panelled dining room or out on the terrace.

AROUND THONON-LES-BAINS

⊜☺ **l'Ombre des Marronniers** – 17 pl. de Crête - 74200 Thonon-les-Bains – ☎ 04 50 71 26 18 - info@hotel-maronniers.com - closed 30 Apr to 3 May and 24 Dec to 3 Jan - 🅿 – 17 rm: 49/60€, ☕ 6.50€, 13/30€. In this picturesque chalet surrounded by a delightful garden, ask for one of the four Savoyard-style rooms, real little bijou apartments. The others are well maintained but, like the restaurant, a little old-fashioned-looking. Suitable for families.

Thonon-les-Bains♨♨

Thonon is renowned for its waters: those of its spa, reputed to be good for the kidneys, and those of Lake Geneva, with its magnificent landscapes. But do not let all this water distract you from the other good things in Thonon. Be sure to try some delicious fillets of locally caught perch with a glass of vin de ripaille. On the shores of **Lake Geneva★★★**, take a walk in the **Rives** district, down towards the harbour. Then return to the town centre by the **funicular railway**, from which there are unrestricted views of the area. *Jul-Aug: 8am-11pm; mid-Apr to Jun and Sep: 8am to 9pm; Oct to mid-Apr: 8am-12.30pm, 1.30pm-6.30pm, Sun 2pm-6pm (3min, every 15min). 1€ there and back.* ☎ *04 50 71 21 54.*

On reaching the Place du Château, go and see the **Musée du Chablais**, which occupies part of the Château de Sonnaz (17C): it houses a collection of local history exhibits, remains of the area's prehistoric lake-dwelling civilisation and Gallo-Roman artefacts. *Jul-Aug: 10am-12pm, 2.30pm-6.30pm (visitors admitted until 30min before closing time); Sep-Jun: daily except Mon and Tue 2.30pm-6.30pm. Closed Nov-Feb and public hols. 2€.* ☎ *04 50 71 56 34.*

Return to Rives by car and follow the Quai de Ripaille, at the end of which you can turn left into the driveway leading to the château.

Domaine de Ripaille★

The buildings of the **castle-monastery** of Ripaille, their roofs clad in bright-coloured tiles, rise above serried ranks of vines which produce a highly regarded white Chasselas. The complex, so distinctive of this region, evokes the most brilliant period of the House of Savoy. The interior is decorated in neo-Gothic style. After crossing the mulberry courtyard, you can visit first the wine press then the 17C kitchen. *Jul-Aug: guided tour (1hr) 11am, 2.30-4.45pm (every 30 min); Feb-Mar and Oct-Nov: 3pm. Closed Dec-Jan. 6€, children: 3€).* ☎ *04 50 26 64 44.*

The **Forest** of Ripaille covers an area of 53ha. From its waymarked paths you can watch roe deer. The trees in the **arboretum** were planted between 1930 and 1934. Nearby, in a clearing, stands a national monument to the Righteous, erected in homage to the men and women of Savoie who risked their lives escorting Jews to Switzerland during the Second World War. *May-Sep: 10am-7pm; Oct-Apr: 10am-4.30pm. Visitors admitted until 1hr before closing time. Closed Mon and Dec. No charge.* ☎ *04 50 26 28 22.*

Travel E from Ripaille, taking the D 32 to Marin.

Marin

There is a small vineyard in the village growing Chasselas grapes. Marin maintains memories of the old tradition of growing vines against the trunks of hollowed-out chestnut trees 6 to 8m high, known as crosses.

Return to Thonon by the N 5 and continue on the same road to Douvaine.

As you go through **Sciez**, you will see vineyards laid out on the steep banks of Lake Geneva. These produce Marignan wines – nothing to do with the famous French defeat of the Swiss at Marignano (1515).

The **Abbey of Filly** (11C), west of Sciez, has the oldest wine cellar in Savoie, still producing a good white wine.

The vineyards of **Crépy** produce white Chasselas wines. They are covered by an AOC appellation which also applies to the small area south of Douvaine around Loisin, Massongy and Baillason. The monks of Notre-Dame de Filly are said to have perfected the technique of making these *perlant* (gently sparkling) wines. Fruity in character, they go well with fried fish from the lake.

FOLLOWING THE RHONE

Approximately 150km from Frangy (Haute-Savoie) to Miolans (Savoie). Michelin Local Map 328, H-J 4-7. See itinerary **2** *on p. 341.*

A good part of the Savoie wine-growing district stretches along the valley of the upper Rhone in a landscape which is undulating but not yet mountainous. The vineyards are generally scattered, but more densely packed around the charming villages, many of which boast their own particular Cru.

Frangy

"I found the wine of Frangy so excellent that I would have been ashamed to remain tight-lipped in such fine company", wrote Jean-Jacques Rousseau in his *Confessions* concerning a tipple that has been produced here since the 11C. You are in the heart of **Roussette** country.

Leave Frangy and travel S on the D 910 for 3km then turn right onto the D 31 towards Desingy, continue via Usinens, then Challonges, reaching Seyssel by the D 14 and D 992. Vineyards are more in evidence around Desingy. The countryside becomes hillier in the vicinity of Usinens and Challonges, pretty wine-growing villages where Roussette is grown. From the church at Bassy, there is a fine view of the Seyssel dam.

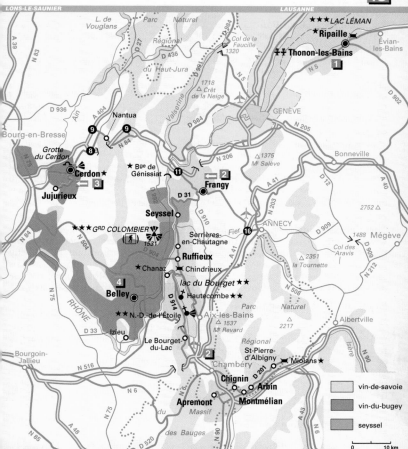

Seyssel

Cut in half by the Rhone, Seyssel is unusual in straddling two départements: Ain and Haute-Savoie. The town has given its name to the **Seyssel AOC** appellation, the oldest in Savoie, though there is no mention of its vineyards before the 11C. Seyssel is renowned for this sparkling wine made from Altesse and Molette grapes. The best wine-growing areas are north of the town, around Corbonod.

The environment and history of the region are very well illustrated at the Maison du haut Rhône, which shows films and stages temporary exhibitions. *10 rte d'Aix-les-Bains.* & *Mid-Jul to mid-Aug: 10am-1pm, 2.30pm-6pm; beginning May to mid-Jul and mid-Aug to end Oct: daily except Mon, Tue 10am-12pm, 2pm-5.30pm. 3€ (children 8-16: 2€).* ☎ *04 50 56 77 04.*

Travel S on the D 991. After Châteaufort, turn left and climb the hill to Motz, then come back on the D 56, a pleasant road with fine views of the Chautagne and the Lac du Bourget. The western part of the Chautagne is marshland planted with poplars, while the eastern part consists of sunny slopes planted mainly with Gamay. Producing almost a quarter of the wine covered by the AOC Vin-de-Savoie appellation, the vineyards stretch from Motz, in the north, to Chindrieux, in the south.

Serrières-en-Chautagne

Distinctive of this area are a number of fortified houses and castles.
🔲 Take time to walk the Châtaignier footpath *(2hr 30min there and back, starting from Serrières, difference in level 250m).* This detour takes in the curious neo-Gothic château of Lapeyrouse and reveals some fine views.

Ruffieux

Among the vineyards rises the **Château de Mécoras** (12C-16C), a fine specimen of medieval architecture. The **Cave de Chautagne** sells a score of different wines and houses a small museum of wine-making tools and equipment. *73310 Ruffieux,* ☎ *04 79 54 27 12, www.cave-de-chautagne.com*

Chindrieux

The **Château de Châtillon** stands on a site which controlled the main routes of Roman Gaul. The walls date from the 13C. *Easter to All Saints: guided tour (45min) Wed: 2pm-5pm. 3€ (children under 12: no charge).* ☎ *04 79 54 28 15.*

While in Chindrieux, visit the **Rucher de Chautagne** a bee-keeping establishment selling delicious mountain honeys. *Lachat, 2233 rte du Sapenay,* ☎ *04 79 54 20 68.*

Continue on the D 991, then turn right onto the D 914, before taking the D 18. The road wends its way through the reed-beds and poplars of the Chautagne marshlands, with views of vineyards on the hillsides.

Savières Canal

4km long, this canal provides a natural overflow for the waters of the Lac du Bourget, channelling them into the Rhone, and a safety valve for the "raging bull" floods of Provence. It is unusual in that at times its water flows in the opposite direction: when the snows melt in the spring, and during heavy rainfall in autumn, the rising waters of the Rhone flow back into the lake, which thus plays a balancing role.

Chanaz★

This charming village, home to many craftsmen, was a popular stopping place when working boats still plied the Savières Canal: inns which once served the bargees have revived the old tradition. Do not miss the rare walnut-oil mill, still in operation.

Continue on the D18 to Hautecombe Abbey. The road follows the banks of the **Lac du Bourget★★***, with splendid views of the eastern shoreline and Aix-les-Bains.*

Royal abbey of Hautecombe★★

It was here in this romantic setting that the sovereigns of the House of Savoy chose to be buried: it remains an excellent place to reflect on the history of the region amid its unforgettable scenery. The exuberantly decorated **church** was restored in the 19C in the troubadour Gothic style. The interior is a profusion of marble, stuccowork and illusionist painting (trompe-l'oeil). The thirty or so tombs of the princes of Savoy are adorned with 300 statues. Down below, beside the lake, is a huge boat-storage shed (12C) projecting into the water. It is said to be unique in France.

Return the way you came and, when you reach the D 914, turn left.

Chapelle Notre-Dame-de-l'Étoile

15min on foot there and back. The signposted driveway leading to the chapel is on a wide bend in the D914. From the platform in front of the building there is a **view★★** of the lake – looking out towards the charming curve of the Bay of Grésine – and also its mountain setting, with the Grand Colombier to the north and the Allevard massif to the south.

Le Bourget

Le Bourget was the main port of Savoie until 1859. A steam-boat service connected it with Lyon via the Savières Canal and the Rhone.

The **church** was built over a crypt which may date from the Carolingian era. Inside, the **frieze★** from the former *jubé* (rood screen), now set into the walls of the apse, is regarded as the masterpiece of 13C sculpture in Savoie.

Free access all year round; Jul-Aug, guided tour 10am-6pm; ask at the tourist office. ☎ *04 79 25 01 99.*

The **Château Thomas II** *(near the mouth of the Leysse)* was a simple hunting lodge belonging to the counts of Savoy. Meetings were held there to make and break family and diplomatic alliances. *Mid-Jul to end Aug: guided tour (1hr 30min) Wed. 4pm on request at the tourist office. 5€.* ☎ *04 79 25 01 99.*

Take the eastern route round Chambéry and join the N 6 in the Montmélian direction. After Challes-les-Eaux, turn left onto the D 5, then right onto the D 21.

Chignin

You will have become familiar with all the region's wines when you have visited this village, which lends its name to Chignin wines, mainly whites made with the Jacquère grape. The name should not be confused with Chignin-Bergeron, which applies only to white wines made with Roussanne grapes, the Savoie whites most suitable for ageing. There are plenty of wineries in this area, including the **André and Michel Quénard** estate *(see Shopping Guide).*

Travel S on one of the roads which joins the N 6, turn left for a short distance then immediately left again towards Apremont.

Apremont

Apremont is a highly regarded name identifying white wines made principally from the Jacquère grape; they are the best possible accompaniment to a Savoyard fondue. Apremont, lying at the foot of Mont Granier, derives its name from the

13

Shopping Guide

Overview

CHARACTERISTICS

Reds – Gamay wines are generally fairly light in colour, while those made from Mondeuse are darker. Berry fruit and fresh pepper notes can be detected in the bouquet.

Dry whites – The Jacquère and Chardonnay wines are paler with greenish highlights, Chasselas wines yellower. They have an aroma of citrus and exotic fruits, with a hint of mint when still young. Some are gently sparkling *(perlant)*.

Sparkling wines – Pale in colour with yellow highlights, not aggressively sparkling, with toasted brioche and hazelnut flavours. Cerdon is sweet and fruity.

AGEING

Reds – Rarely keep for more than three years, with the exception of good Mondeuse vintages.

Dry whites – Should be drunk young. Some Chasselas and Chardonnay wines will last for 3 to 5 years. Chignin-Bergeron will keep for up to 10 years.

PRICES

From 3 to 8€.

Buying

COOPERATIVE WINERIES

Le Vigneron Savoyard – *Rte du Crozet - 73190 Apremont -* ☎ *04 79 28 33 23 - vigneron.savoyard@wanadoo.fr* This cooperative sells a full selection of regional wines.

Les Vignerons des Terroirs Savoyards – *R. Antoine-Besson - 73800 Montmélian -* ☎ *04 79 65 22 01.* A cooperative which produces all types of red and white wines.

Caveau Bugiste – *01350 Vongnes -* ☎ *04 79 87 91 11 – 9am-12pm, 2pm-7pm.* The speciality of this venerable but welcoming institution is a red Manicle, Brillat-Savarin's favourite *Cru*.

ESTATES

Domaine Louis Magnin – *90 chemin des Buis - 73800 Arbin -* ☎ *04 79 84 12 12.* The Louis Magnin estate is a small family business. Since 1978, it has been run by Louis and Béatrice Magnin, third-generation growers. The 6ha vineyard is planted with Altesse, Roussanne and Mondeuse vines. The grapes are harvested by hand and traditional vinification techniques are used.

André et Michel Quénard – *Torméry - 73800 Chignin -* ☎ *04 79 28 12 75 - Mon, Tue, Thu and Fri 9am-11.30am, 1.30pm-4.30pm by appointment.* The stony, steeply sloping Torméry hillside is the best local vineyard. Its 20ha of vines benefit from a privileged sunny position. This unique terroir produces a white Chignin from Jacquère grapes. Its reputation was already established in the 11C, when it was described as producing *"optimi vini"*: "excellent wines". Today, the flourishing vineyard is being extended with the planting of vines

producing Chignin-Bergeron whites; and with Mondeuse, to produce a typically Savoyard red *vin de garde*.

Domaine Bouvet – *Le Villard – 73250 Fréterive -* ☎ *04 79 28 54 11 – 8am-12pm, 1.30pm-6.30pm – by appointment Sun.* Established in 1991, the estate is laid out on the hillsides of the Combe de Savoie, where they are protected from north winds by the Bauges massif. The area is planted with vines almost 30 years old: Jacquère, Cabernet Sauvignon, Chardonnay, Roussanne, Roussette, Mondeuse, Gamay and Pinot Noir. Vinification is performed in heat-regulated vats and, in the case of wines that are to age, the wine is matured in barrels.

Domaine Noël Dupasquier - *Aimavigne - 73170 Jongieux -* ☎ *04 79 44 02 23 - Mon-Sat – by appointment.* This estate is located in one of Savoie's most tucked-away villages. Benefiting from the area's microclimate and varied soils (part pebbly, part limestone scree), the regional grape varieties thrive on arid slopes. They are grown using chemically non-interventionist methods and vinified in the traditional manner, without added yeast.

Domaine Jean Perrier et Fils – *ZA Plan du Cumin - 73800 Les Marches -* ☎ *04 79 28 11 45 - vperrier@vins-perrier.com - Mon-Fri 9am-12pm, 2pm-6pm – by appointment Sat.* A major wine-grower and merchant, Gilbert Perrier is the brains of this estate, which has been in his family for one hundred and fifty years. Assisted by his three sons, he runs a 35ha vineyard producing Apremont, Abymes, Chignin, Chignin-Bergeron and Arbin wines from Gamay, Pinot and Mondeuse vines.

GAEC Maison Angelot – *01300 Marignieu -* ☎ *04 79 42 18 84 – 9am-12pm, 3pm-7pm – by appointment.* In the family since the beginning of the 20th century, the estate was taken over in 1987 by Philippe Angelot, who was joined by his brother that same year. Managed in an eco-friendly way, the vineyard consists of 23ha, 60% planted with white grape varieties (Chardonnay, Roussette, Aligoté) and 40% with vines producing reds and rosés (Gamay, Pinot, Mondeuse). The plots are south-south-east facing, at altitudes of between 200 and 350m.

P. Jausserand / MICHELIN

Latin *asper montis*, "rough mountain". The name of the local Abymes (abysses) wines recalls an earthquake which killed thousands of people in the 13C. These wines are very similar to Apremont, but with slightly more pronounced citrus flavours. You can buy them at the **Vigneron Savoyard** cooperative *(see Shopping Guide)*.

Follow the D 12 southward towards Marches. This area also produces some good wines from the Mondeuse grape, for instance those grown on the **Jean Perrier et Fils estate**, in the hamlet of Saint-André near **Marches** *(see below)*.

Montmélian

Though the former fortress was demolished in 1706, Montmélian still has some fine tall houses, with courtyards linked by covered passageways.

Montmélian is in the centre of a wine-growing region, whose scattered vineyards produce Savoie's most highly regarded wines. The **Musée régional de la Vigne et du Vin** provides an excellent introduction to the subject. *46 r. Jean-Pierre-Veyrat. Jul-Sep: daily except Mon am, Sun am and public hols, 10am-12pm, 2pm-6.30pm; Oct-Jun: Wed and Fri 2pm-5.30pm. 4€. ☎ 04 79 84 42 23. www.montmelian.com*

You can then go and put your newly acquired knowledge to use at the **Vignerons des Terroirs Savoyards** cooperative *(see Shopping Guide)*.

Arbin

Some powerful Mondeuse wines with a well-justified reputation are produced around this small village, somewhat spoilt by creeping development. The wines of the **Louis Magnin** estate are a good example *(see Shopping Guide)*.

Near Arbin, the village of **Cruet** is better known for its white Jacquère wines, but it also produces some good red Arbin.

Leave Arbin and drive E on the D 201. The **Combe de Savoie**, the northern section of the "Alpine furrow", is the name given to the valley of the Isère between Albertville and the Chambéry, where it is crossed by another valley. This is an exclusively agricultural region. The sun-drenched little towns from Montmélian to St-Pierre-d'Albigny stand among orchards, surrounded by vineyards and fields of maize and tobacco.

Saint-Pierre-d'Albigny

Historic gateway to the Bauges massif, St-Pierre-d'Albigny occupies a superb elevated position overlooking the coomb. There are many fine old buildings, including family mansions and fortified houses.

Join the D 911 for 800m, then turn right onto the D 101. Leave your car in the car park at Miolans, 100m out of the village.

Château de Miolans★

Jul-Aug: 10am-197pm; May-Jun and Sep: 10am-12pm, 1.30pm-7pm, Sun 1.30pm-7pm; Apr: w.-endweekends and public hols 1.30pm-7pm; school hols and All Saints' Day: 1.30pm-7pm. 6€ (children: 3€). ☎ 04 79 28 57 04.

Standing proudly on its platform of rock, 200m above the Combe de Savoie, the castle was used to keep watch over the routes of the Bauges, the Tarentaise and the Maurienne regions from 923 to 1523. It was then converted into a state prison (1559-1792). With its four lateral turrets, the castle keep, which housed the prison cells, imprints itself on the mind's eye. There is an unusual **covered way★**, which served a defensive purpose: its embrasures covered the approach to the castle for almost 200m.

The Bugey Wine Route

Nestling in a deep bend in the upper Rhone in the southern part of the Ain *département*, the Bugey district is an attractive part of France, boasting grandiose landscapes, a living rural tradition and a cuisine which makes the most of the region's dairy products, freshwater fish, fruits, truffles and, of course, wines. Its greatest claim to gastronomic fame, however, is its famous son, Jean-Anthelme Brillat-Savarin, author of the witty compendium of culinary anecdotes *La Physiologie du goût* (The Physiology of Taste), who was born in Belley. To the north of his home town in one of three fairly scattered areas of vineyards in the region; the other two are to be found around Cerdon and Montagnieu.

THE CERDON AREA

20km from Cerdon to Jujurieux (Ain). Michelin Local Map 328, F4. See itinerary ③ on the map on p. 341.

Cerdon★

In a magnificent setting of caves, narrow gorges and stunning viewpoints, Cerdon has lent its name to a unique sparkling rosé, slightly sweet and low in alcohol. The village is best visited on foot. Its narrow streets are set off by fountains and stone bridges. A copper workshop established on the site of a former mill continues to work sheet-copper using 19C techniques. ♿ *May-Sep: guided tour (1hr) 10am, 11am, 2pm, 3pm, 4pm and 5 pm; Oct-Apr and school hols: weekends and public hols 10am, 11am, 2pm, 3pm, 4pm and 5pm. Shop: 9am-12pm, 1.30pm-6.30pm, weekend and public hols 9.30am-12pm, 2pm-6.30pm. Closed 1 Jan, 25 Dec. 4.50€. ☏ 04 74 39 96 44. www.cuivreriedecerdon. com.*

Take the N 84 east out of Cerdon in the direction of Nantua. On the way, you will come to a **belvedere★★** offering all-round views of the landscape and vineyards of the upper Bugey. If you are tempted to take a 100 km/kph ride earthwards on

The old copper workshop in Cerdon.

G. Magnin / MICHELIN

a steel cable, stop off at **Fantasticable**; you land in vineyards, after a very rapid flight over Cerdon. *Enquire in advance, because this activity depends on weather conditions. Jul-Aug: 10am-12pm, 1.30pm-7pm; Easter to Jun and Sep to All Saints: Sat-Sun, public hols and 3-day weekends 10am-12pm, 2pm-6pm. 25€.* ☏ *04 74 39 96 44.*

Grotte du Cerdon (Cerdon cave)

At Labalme-sur-Cerdon. Jul.-Aug: guided tour (1hr 15min, last dep 1hr before closing time) 10am-6pm; Apr-Jun: 12.30pm-6pm and beginning Sep to mid-Oct: weekend and public hols 1pm-5pm. 5.80€ (children: 4.20€). Picnic area. ☏ 04 74 37 36 79. www. les-grottesdu-cerdon.com

The tour follows the course of a dried-up underground river. The tunnel, featuring fine rock formations, leads to a cavern with a 30m arch opening onto the outside world.

Return to Cerdon and take the D 63 SW towards Jujurieux. The road runs in valley bottoms with slopes clothed in vines. The little village of **Mérignat** is home to some welcoming and talented wine-growers.

Jujurieux

Though it has lost some of its former glory, this village with its thirteen châteaux still has some reminders of its silk-weaving heritage, in particular the **Bonnet Silkworks**: you can visit the collections and workshops of this former silk mill. ♿ *Mid-Jun to mid-Sep: guided tour (1hr), on request daily except Tue 10am-12pm, 2.30pm-6pm, Sat-Sun 2.30pm-6.30pm (last admission 1hr before closing time). 4.50€ (children: 3.50€). ☏ 04 74 37 23 14.*

Here, wine-growing whas always been a supplementary activity for the factory workers but, now the industry has disappeared, it has become an important source of income.

THE BELLEY WINE-GROWING AREA

10km from Belley to Lavours (Ain). Michelin Local Map 328, H6. See itinerary ④ on the map on p. 341.

North of Belley, the last of the eastern slopes rising from the Lavours marshlands are home to some of the best Bugey wines.

Belley

The chief town of the Bugey district preserves the memory of its most famous son, the jurist and philosopher of taste Jean-Anthelme Brillat-Savarin (1755-1826), who wrote: "Inviting someone means being responsible for his happiness all the time he is under one's roof". These are the words inscribed beneath the sculpted bust of him, at the north end of the Promenoir. His family home is at 62 Grande-Rue.

The **Cathedral of St John the Baptist**, almost totally rebuilt in the 19C, still has its 12C north doorway. Inside, the vast **choir★** (1473) is still intact. The 18C bishop's palace is said to have been built to plans by Jacques-Germain Soufflot, the architect of the Panthéon in Paris.

Take the D 69 NE out of Belley, then the D 69C. All along this road are wineries where you will receive a warm welcome, such as the **Maison Angelot** at **Marignieu** *(see Shopping Guide).*

Continue on the D 69C, then turn left onto the D 37. **Vongnes** is the main village in this area, where the **Caveau Bugiste** is worth visiting *(see Shopping Guide).*

Drive N to Ceyzérieu, then turn right towards Aignoz.

Lavours marshland nature reserve

🔱 A raised walkway 2 400m long takes you right into the heart of the marsh, a world of its own. At the **Maison du marais**, you can learn all about this aquatic environment and its biological diversity. Unrestricted access to the raised walkway all the year round. *Apr-Sep: daily; Feb-Mar and Oct-Nov: Sat, Sun. Closed Dec-Jan. Telephone for information about visiting times. 5€ (children: 3.50€).* ☎ 04 79 87 90 39.

Natural and Man-made Wonders

Grand Colombier★★★

24km NW of Ruffieux via the D 904, then the D 20. 🔱 Rising to a height of 1 531m, the Grand Colombier is the highest mountain in the Bugey. Two summits are easily accessible on foot: to the north, a rounded vantage point on which there is a cross *(30min on foot there and back; viewpoint indicator)*; to the south, a summit, with a sharp drop on the west side, where there is a triangulation point *(45 min on foot there and back)*.

From both points, there are magnificent all-round views of the Jura, the Dombes, the Rhone valley, the Massif Central and the Alps.

Génissiat Dam★

10km NW of Frangy via the D 314, then the D 14 and the D 214. This dam, commissioned in 1948, created an artificial lake 23 km long in the course of the Rhone (53 million m³), much used by pleasure boats in summer. To visit the surrounding area, leave your car in the car park beside the commemorative monument. On the first terrace is a kiosk with explanatory display panels for the benefit of tourists.

Remembering Heroes

In the heart of the Bugey, a mountainous area protected by the valleys of the Rhone and Ain and controlling some major road and rail routes, resistance fighters began setting up camp in 1943. They established their headquarters in the Valromey, which in February 1944 was the target of a German attack. At dawn on 5 February, 5 000 Germans surrounded the massif then, in lorries, on foot or on skis, climbed to attack the plateaux of Hauteville, Retord and Brénod. Snow made operations difficult, but the resistance fighters were forced to disperse after local skirmishes. From 6 to 12 February, the villages and local folk suffered enemy violence and reprisals. After it had re-formed, the Resistance was again the object of an enemy sweep, covering the whole of the Bugey, in July. The attacking force comprised 9 000 men supported by planes and light artillery. The *maquisards* then broke up into small groups and withdrew to the remotest mountain hide-outs.

Nantua: Ain and Haut-Jura Museum of the Resistance and Deportation★

20km NE of Cerdon via the N 84. May-Sep: daily except Mon 10am-1pm, 2pm-6pm; rest of the year on weekdays if booked ahead. Closed Dec. 4€ (children under 14: no charge). ☎ 04 74 75 07 50.

The old prison in Nantua, where resistance fighters were held, houses this museum, which really brings the past to life. Skilfully illustrated by **tableaux★**, with audioguide commentary by former *maquisards* and a British soldier, the varied collections evoke the atmosphere of the 1940s, the Occupation, the Resistance and its organisation, and the Deportation. The visit ends with a montage of films from the period *(18min)*, complemented by contemporary songs, a collection of propaganda posters, and two temporary exhibition rooms.

Izieu

21km SW of Belley via the D 992, then the D 19D. The name of this village is associated with one of the most heart-rending tragedies of the Second World War. A colony of Jewish children had found refuge in a hamlet about 800m beyond the village. On 6 April 1944 the Gestapo from Lyon arrested the 44 children, and their 7 teachers, because they were Jews. One person escaped in the course of the raid. Only one returned from concentration camp.

In 1987, after Klaus Barbie was sentenced for this crime against humanity, a **Memorial Museum★** association devoted to the Izieu children was founded by Sabine Zlatin, who directed the colony in 1943 and 1944. The main house is laid out to illustrate daily life in this short-lived place of refuge – its refectory, partly restored classroom and its dormitories. The barn houses an exhibition tracing the history of the children and their parents under the Nazi regime. The *magnanerie* (where silk worms were bred) is now an archive and conference centre (audiovisual commentary). *Mid-Jun to mid-Sep: 10am-6.30pm; mid-Sep to mid-Dec and mid-Jan to mid-Jun: 9am-5pm, Sat, Sun and public hols 10am-6pm. 4.60€ (children under 10: no charge).* ☎ 04 79 87 21 05.

Le Sud-Ouest

The Southwest

From the Pyrenean foothills to the Rouergue region and from the Dordogne Valley to the Toulouse area, people display their local character with pride and a certain panache. This is D'Artagnan and Cyrano country, where rebellion and nobility go hand in hand and good living is an art, performed with refinement and inspired by a sure sense of identity. As you travel along, you will discover the gentle hills of Périgord Pourpre, the fertile hillsides of Gascony, the River Lot lovingly meandering round the Cahors vineyards, the medieval cities of the Gaillac region, the mountains of Béarn and of the Basque country and the dales of Rouergue. Vineyards are less prominent here than in other regions. Yet, in this land of plenty, orchards, pastures, farmyards and cereal fields offer a wide choice of delicacies to be served with fine wines.

Terroirs

Michelin Local Maps 329, 336, 337, 338 and 342 – Aveyron (12), Dordogne (24), Gers (32), Lot (46), Lot-et-Garonne (47), Pyrénées-Atlantiques (64), Tarn (81).
Areas and production: Bergerac 9 600ha, yield 431 000hl; Buzet 2 000ha, yield 73 000hl; Cahors 4 450ha, yield 200 300hl; Côtes-de-Duras 2 000ha, yield 114 000hl; Côtes-du-Frontonnais 2 400ha, yield 82 000hl; Côtes-du-Marmandais 1 650ha, yield 85 600hl; Côtes-de-St-Mont 850ha, yield 48 000hl; Gaillac 3 100ha, yield 165 500hl; Irouléguy 210ha, yield 7 400hl; Jurançon 1 000ha, yield 50 000hl; Madiran 1 300ha, yield 70 000hl; Marcillac 150ha, yield 7 000hl; Monbazillac 2 000ha, yield 48 000hl; Pacherenc-du-Vic-Bilh 250ha, yield 8 400hl.
The temperate oceanic climate has a continental influence: relatively mild winters, wet springs, hot summers and sunny autumns. Soils consist of clay or chalky clay near the Dordogne and Lot rivers, gravel or gravelly sand in the Garonne area, stone and sand in Gascony.

Wines

Red wines – Bergerac, Côtes-du-Marmandais, Côtes-de-Duras, Buzet: Cabernet Franc, Cabernet-Sauvignon, Merlot and Malbec grape varieties. Cahors: Malbec variety. Gaillac: Braucol, Syrah, Merlot, Négrette, Gamay and Cabernet-Sauvignon grapes. Madiran: Tannat variety. Irouléguy: Cabernet Franc, Cabernet-Sauvignon and Tannat grapes. Côtes-de-St-Mont: Tannat, Fer-Servadou, Cabernet Franc and Cabernet-Sauvignon grapes. Marcillac: Gamay, Jurançon Noir and Merlot grapes. Côtes-du-Frontonnais: Cabernet Franc, Cabernet-Sauvignon, Cinsault Noir and Gamay grapes.

Dry and sweet white wines – Bergerac, Monbazillac, Côtes-du-Marmandais, Côtes-de-Duras, Buzet: Sémillon, Sauvignon and Muscadelle varieties. Gaillac: Mauzac, Len-de-l'El, Ondenc, Sauvignon and Muscadelle grapes. Côtes-de-St-Mont, Pacherenc-du-Vic-Bilh: Courbu, Clairette, Arrufiac, Gros-Manseng, Petit-Manseng, Sémillon and Sauvignon grapes. Jurançon: Gros-Manseng, Petit-Manseng and Courbu grapes.

Château de Monbazillac.

WHERE TO EAT

AROUND BERGERAC

🍴 **Le Plat dans l'Assiette** – *18 r. du Mourrier – 24100 Bergerac – ☎ 05 53 24 25 26 – closed Sun and Mon – reservations advisable – 12/23.50€.* It's unusual to see a typical Lyon tavern out West in foie gras country! The decor may not be really striking – bistro furniture, numerous trinkets, advertising signs, pictures and piano – but the influence of the ancient Gaulish capital on Périgord becomes obvious when you look at the menu and the wine list.

🍴🍴 **La Tour des Vents** – *Au Moulin-de-Malfourat – 24240 Monbazillac – 3km W of Monbazillac along D 14E – ☎ 05 53 58 30 10 – closed early Jan to early Feb, Sun evening, Wed evening and Mon Sep-Jun – 23/51€.* This haven of peace built beneath a ruined windmill suggests tradition and a gentle way of life. The dining room and terrace offer a fine view of the Bergerac vineyards. The tasty and plentiful cuisine, accompanied when appropriate by a very pleasant Monbazillac, is the other strong point of the establishment.

🍴🍴 **L'Enfance de Lard** – *Pl. Pélissière – 24100 Bergerac – ☎ 05 53 57 52 88 – closed Tue – reservations required – 24/42€.* A cosy atmosphere pervades the tiny, rustic yet pretty dining room of this restaurant located on the edge of an attractive square of Old Bergerac. This, added to the charming welcome and the refined cuisine, easily explains why the place is often packed.

AROUND CAHORS

🍴🍴 **La Garenne** – *Route de Brive – St-Henri – 46000 Cahors – ☎ 05 65 35 40 67 – closed Feb, 1-15 Mar, Mon and Tue evenings except Jul-Aug, and Wed – 16.50/44€.* This building in typical Quercy style was once used as stables. Stone walls, exposed timberwork, fine furniture in local style and old rural objects make up a pleasant rustic decor. However, La Garenne's strong point is its tasty cuisine which offers a wide choice of regional specialities.

🍴🍴 **Le Rendez-Vous** – *49 r. Clément-Marot – 46000 Cahors – ☎ 05 65 22 65 10 – closed 29 Apr to 14 May, 28 Oct to 12 Nov, Sun and Mon – 21.50€.* If you fancy eating tasty, trendy dishes without spending a fortune, the Rendez-Vous is the place. The colourful contemporary decor blends well with the old stone walls of the dining room and its mezzanine extension. Attractive menu. Reservations advisable.

🍴🍴 **Les Templiers** – *46900 Le Montat – 8km S of Cahors along N 20 and D 47 – ☎ 05 65 21 01 23 – closed 15 Jan to 10 Feb, 1-12 Jul, Sun and Mon evenings and Tue – 22.60/42.50€.* The building once housed a commandery of the Knights Templars. At least that's what the locals say…Today the two fine vaulted rooms of the restaurant which has taken possession of the premises offer attractive surroundings to regular and passing guests who enjoy the hearty local cuisine.

🍴🍴🍴 **Hostellerie le Vert** – *46700 Mauroux – ☎ 05 65 36 51 36 – closed 12 Nov to 13 Feb – 40€.* This hotel – a former wine-growing estate out in the middle of the Quercy countryside – offers its guests red-carpet treatment: a dining room with character featuring fine beams, stone walls and antique furniture, and distinctive bedrooms along the same lines. The most unusual of these is in the former cellar.

AROUND CONDOM

🍴🍴 **Moulin du Petit Gascon** – *Route d'Eauze – écluse de Gauge – 32100 Condom – ☎ 05 62 28 28 42 – closed 3 weeks in Nov, Sun evening and Mon mid-Sep to mid-Jun – lunch 12€ – 18/36€.* A secluded country place one would wish to keep a secret… A small charming lock along the River Baïse, an old mill camped on the river bank and, adjacent to the former lock-keeper's house, a restaurant with a terrace serving a tasty regional cuisine. There are jazz concerts on summer evenings.

🍴🍴 **Chez Simone** – *Pl. des Champions-de-France – 32250 Montréal – ☎ 05 62 29 44 40 – closed Feb school hols, Sun evening, Mon and Tue – lunch 15€ – 25/45€.* M Daubin, the jovial owner of this village inn since 1992, extends a particularly friendly welcome to the numerous gourmets who come to enjoy his typically regional cuisine. The elegant dining room brightened up by colourful murals offers conviviality with its authentic family atmosphere.

AROUND DURAS

🍴🍴 **Auberge du Moulin d'Ané** – *Route de Gontaud – 47200 Virazeil – 7km east of Marmande along D 933 then D 267 – ☎ 05 53 20 18 25 – closed Wed except Jul-Aug, and Tue – reservations advisable – 23/37€.* This old 17C stone mill in the heart of the countryside welcomes its guests on its veranda, offering a view of the tumbling waters of a cascade, or in its rustic-style dining room and delights them with regional specialities or traditional dishes which change with the seasons and the availability of fresh produce.

AROUND GAILLAC

🍴 **Hostellerie du Vieux Cordes** – *Haut-de-la-Cité – 81170 Cordes-sur-Ciel – ☎ 05 63 53 79 20 – closed Jan – 14.50/33€.* An old monastery in the heart of the splendid medieval city crowning the Puech de Mordagne: this means a stopover with undeniable character. Take a table on the terrace or in the attractive patio and enjoy the regional cuisine in which salmon and duck are prominent. Some of the bedrooms were recently refurbished.

🍴 **La Table du Sommelier** – *34 pl. Thiers – 81600 Gaillac – ☎ 05 63 81 20 10 – closed Sun except Jul-Aug, and Mon – 15/30€.* With its rich convivial setting combining rustic tables, wooden chests and wine-growing tools, La Table du Sommelier has definitively won over those who love good wine and thoroughly enjoy good food.

14

The key to success? A clever choice of imaginative dishes and a highly appealing wine list.

⊜⊜ **La Falaise** – Route de Cordes – 81140 Cahuzac-sur-Vère – 11km N of Gaillac along D 922 – ☎ 05 63 33 96 31 – closed 3-31 Jan, Sun evening, Wed lunch and Mon – lunch 21€ – 30/38€. On the way out of the village, a small ordinary façade hides two particularly pleasant dining rooms, extending onto a charming terrace shaded by willows. Here you can enjoy mouth-watering traditional dishes accompanied by generous, ruby-coloured Gaillacs.

⊜⊜ **Les Sarments** – 27 r. Cabrol (behind the abbey of St-Michael) – 81600 Gaillac – ☎ 05 63 57 62 61 – closed 25 Apr to 3 May, 19 Dec to 10 Jan, 21 Feb to 7 Mar, Sun and Wed evenings and Mon – 23/46€. This former wine storehouse, located in the centre of the old town, a stone's throw from the Maison des vins, features red-brick vaulting dating from the 14C and 16C. The menu offers a choice of traditional dishes and, as expected, the wine list presents a wide selection of Gaillacs.

AROUND MARCILLAC

⊜ **Le Lion d'Or** – 6 Tour-de-Ville – 12140 Entraygues-sur-Truyère – ☎ 05 65 51 40 44 – closed 2-15 Jan, Sun evening and Mon in low season – lunch 11€ – 14/24€. The new owners have retained the attractive features of the Lion d'Or: a seasoned rustic decor, colourful furnishings and a pleasant shaded terrace. In the kitchen, the owner uses fresh produce only while his wife proposes four set menus as well as a more ambitious selection of dishes.

⊜⊜ **Auberge du Fel** – Au Fel – 12140 Entraygues-sur-Truyère – ☎ 05 65 44 52 30 – closed 3 Nov to 31 Mar, lunchtime except Sat, Sun, school and public holidays – 18/36€. The view of the surrounding countryside from this old house overlooking the River Lot will enhance your discovery of the gourmet dishes, often flavoured with herbs: even the homemade ice creams include not just mint but also basil and thyme flavours.

⊜⊜ **Ferme-auberge de Mejanassère** – 12140 Entraygues-sur-Truyère – 4km east of Entraygues along D 42 – ☎ 05 65 44 54 76 – closed Oct to end of Mar – ⌷ – reservations required – 21€. This farm is believed to date back to Gallo-Roman times. Today, its fine local cuisine, its bread baked in a wood-fired oven, its terrace overlooking the vineyards across the valley, its attractive guest rooms and its self-catering cottage combine to make it a charming place to stay.

IN NERAC

⊜⊜ **Aux Délices du Roy** – 7 r. du Château – 47600 Nérac – ☎ 05 53 65 81 12 – closed Wed – 16/60€. Nestling beneath the castle of the House of Albret, this convivial family restaurant offers a small rustic dining room, recently painted in blue and yellow and enhanced by colourful furnishings. In the kitchen, M Sarthou, the owner-chef, skilfully blends seafood and traditional recipes.

AROUND PAU

⊜ **La Michodière** – 34 r. Pasteur – 64000 Pau – ☎ 05 59 27 53 85 – closed 28 Jul to 24 Aug, Sun and public holidays – lunch 12€ – 14/24€. From the ground-floor dining room, there is a view of the kitchen where the chef is busy preparing delicious dishes selected according to the availability of fresh produce. Lobster sauce corail and duck's liver escalope Michodière-style are reliable and popular choices.

É. Larribère / MICHELIN

⊜⊜ **Les Terrasses de Beaumont** – Parc Beaumont – 64000 Pau – ☎ 05 59 11 21 07 – ⌷ – 16€. Local people flock into this warm contemporary decor to try the appetising selection of regional dishes prepared by Stéphane Carrade: roast duck with coriander, roast leg of lamb with thyme and lemon, breaded pig's trotter with mustard, etc.

⊜⊜ **La Table d'Hôte** – 1 r. du Hédas – 64000 Pau – ☎ 05 59 27 56 06 – closed Christmas hols, Mon except evening in Jul-Aug, and Sun – 20/26€. The chef's cuisine, served in an attractive rustic dining room, is mainly based on regional recipes and products, revealing the finer aspects of the Béarn tradition. On the wine list, Jurançons and Madirans are prominent, as they blend admirably well with regional dishes.

⊜⊜ **Au Fin Gourmet** – 24 av. Gaston-Lacoste – 64000 Pau – ☎ 05 59 27 47 71 – closed Feb school hols, 26 Jul to 9 Aug, Sun evening, Wed lunchtime and Mon – lunch 16€ – 24/46€. Entering this elegant restaurant, nestling at the foot of the funicular and surrounded by a luxuriant bamboo garden, is like going back in time to the Belle Époque: wrought-iron furniture, green plants, round tables… Le Fin Gourmet knows how to receive its guests and delight gourmets with its delicious trendy recipes.

⊜⊜ **Arcé** – Route du Col-d'Ispéguy – 64430 St-Étienne-de-Baïgorry – ☎ 05 59 37 40 14 – closed mid-Nov to mid-Mar, Wed lunchtime and Mon 15 Sep to 15 Jul except public hols – 23/35€. The greenery surrounding the house, the typical white façade highlighted by red shutters, the pretty terrace shaded by plane trees, the rippling water of the river, the warm family welcome…The food? Well, you certainly won't want to leave once you've experienced the chef's tasty and copious cuisine!

AROUND ST-JEAN-PIED-DE-PORT

Pecoïtz – *Route d'Iraty – 64220 Aincille – 7km SE of St-Jean-Pied-de-Port along D 933 and D 18 – ☎ 05 59 37 11 88 – closed 1 Jan to 15 Mar and Fri Oct to May – 15/30€.* Convivial restaurant promoting the fine specialities of Basque cuisine, including ham piperade and chicken basquaise, cooked with tomatoes and sweet peppers. Prepared with dedication, these regional dishes release their full flavour when they are accompanied by a special bottle of Irouléguy. A few plain but clean bedrooms.

Central – *1 pl. Charles-de-Gaulle – 64220 St-Jean-Pied-de-Port – ☎ 05 59 37 00 22 – closed 15 Dec to 1 Mar, Mon evening and Tue Mar to Jun – 18/42€.* The dining room of the Central is an elegant veranda overlooking the Nive, extended in summer by a small terrace located directly over the water. In the kitchen, the chef carefully prepares appetising specialities inspired by regional recipes.

WHERE TO STAY

AROUND BERGERAC

La Flambée – *153 av. Pasteur – 24100 Bergerac – ☎ 05 53 57 52 33 – ▣ – 21 rooms: 72/80€ – ☛ 8€ – meal 17/32€.* This old house is situated on the outskirts of what was once the tobacco capital of France. The spacious rooms have distinctive features and are named after the local wine-growing estates. Those located in the annexe are more plainly decorated but enjoy the use of private terraces opening on to the park planted with trees. Fine swimming pool, tennis.

Manoir Grand Vignoble – *Le Grand-Vignoble – 24140 St-Julien-de-Crempse – ☎ 05 53 24 23 18 – grand. vignoble@wanadoo.fr – closed 14 Nov to 26 Mar – ▣ – 44 rooms: 82/109€ – ☛ 9€ – meal 23/45€.* This 17C manor house is surrounded by a vast 43ha. The main building houses the dining room (regional cuisine and local wines: Pécharmant, Bergerac) as well as about ten rooms, some with four-poster beds. Other rooms, located in the outbuildings, boast a contemporary decor and more space.

Château Lespinassat – *Route d'Agen – 24100 Bergerac – 3km SE of Bergerac along N 21 – ☎ 05 53 74 84 11 – 4 rooms: 140/290€ – meal 40€.* This handsome example of 18C architecture is reflected in the waters of a pond in the middle of superb parkland. The delightful interior decoration includes antique furniture, graceful mouldings, silky draperies, attractive fireplaces and fine parquet flooring. Large fully equipped bedrooms. Swimming pool.

AROUND CAHORS

Hôtel À l'Escargot – *5 bd Gambetta – 46000 Cahors – ☎ 05 65 35 07 66 – closed Feb school hols, Dec and Sun in low season –*

9 rooms: 48.50/54€ – ☛ 6€. This hotel, situated near the Tour Jean-XXII (named after Jacques Duèze, a native of Cahors, elected Pope in 1322), is housed in the former palace erected by the Pope's family. It contains functional rooms with colourful furniture and a refurbished breakfast room.

Hôtel Source Bleue – *Le Bourg – 46700 Touzac – 8km west of Puy-l'Évêque along D 811 – ☎ 05 65 36 52 01 – sourcebleue@wanadoo.fr – closed 16 Nov to 9 Apr – ▣ – 17 rooms: 65/89€ – ☛ 7€ – meal 20/27€.* The "blue stream", which originally sprang up on the south bank of the Lot, mysteriously moved, around 1950, to the north bank among the ancient paper mills later turned into a hotel and restaurant. Elegant rooms with distinctive features. Traditional cuisine served in a 17C outbuilding set up as a dining room.

Bellevue – *Pl. Truffière – 46700 Puy-l'Évêque – ☎ 05 65 36 06 60 – closed 15-30 Nov and 15 Jan to 15 Feb – 11 rooms: 68/85€ – ☛ 8€.* This hotel, built on a spur overlooking the Lot, is appropriately named. The spacious rooms boast a contemporary style with distinctive features. Inventive cuisine and splendid view of the valley from the Côté Lot restaurant. Regional dishes at L'Aganit.

S. Sauvignier / MICHELIN

AROUND CONDOM

Paix – *24 av. des Thermes – 31150 Barbotan-les-Thermes – ☎ 05 62 69 52 06 – hotel.paix@wanadoo.fr – closed 12 Nov to 17 Mar – ▣ – 32 rooms: 45/64€ – ☛ 7€ – meal 16/26€.* Recent building close to the church and the spa centre. The attractive, well-kept rooms are furnished in a functional style. Plain decor and family-hotel atmosphere in the restaurant offering a selection of traditional dishes (dietary menus on request).

Logis des Cordeliers – *R. de la Paix – 32100 Condom – ☎ 05 62 28 03 68 – reception@logisdescordeliers.com – closed 3 Jan to 5 Feb – ▣ – 21 rooms: 46/68€ – ☛ 6€.* This recent building situated in a peaceful district away from the town centre has functional rooms. Those with a balcony overlooking the swimming pool are more pleasant. Friendly welcome.

⊜⊜⊜ **Les Trois Lys** – 38 r. Gambetta – 32100 Condom – ☎ 05 62 28 33 33 – hoteltroislys@wanadoo.fr – closed Feb – 🅿 – 10 rooms: 110/150€– ⊡ 9€. The rooms of this elegant 18C mansion are air-conditioned and distinctive, often featuring antique furniture and sometimes a fireplace. Fine swimming pool at the back with a terrace on the side for lounging. Traditional cuisine served in the refurbished dining room. Cosy bar/smoking-room.

AROUND DURAS

⊜ **Les Rives de l'Avance** – Moulin-de-Trivail – 47430 Ste-Marthe – ☎ 05 53 20 60 22 – 🅿 – 16 rooms: 33.60/47.30€ – ⊡ 5.40€. This hotel, built in peaceful, green surroundings, on the edge of the small River Avance and close to a water-mill, offers an unexpected pastoral stopover near the motorway. Functional, colourful rooms.

⊜⊜ **Le Capricorne** – 1 r. Paul-Valéry – 47200 Marmande – ☎ 05 53 64 16 14 – closed 17 Dec to 2 Jan – 🅿 – 34 rooms: 51/57€ – ⊡ 7.50€. This modern building camped on the edge of the main road houses bright soundproofed rooms, which were recently refurbished. In the dining room decorated in a contemporary style and extended by a small terrace, you will be offered a choice of traditional dishes served with a local Marmandais wine.

AROUND GAILLAC

⊜⊜ **Hôtel Verrerie** – R. de l'Égalité – 81600 Gaillac – ☎ 05 63 57 32 77 – contact@la-verrerie.com – 🅿 – 14 rooms: 47/62€ – ⊡ 7.50€ – meal 21/35€. A tiny museum illustrates the history of this 200-year-old building, which was a glassworks – as the name suggests – and then a pasta factory before becoming a hotel. Of its modern, practical rooms, the best are those overlooking the park, which has a fine bamboo plantation. The bright dining room leads out on to a pleasant terrace.

⊜⊜ **Chambre d'hôte Aurifat** – 81170 Cordes-sur-Ciel – ☎ 05 63 56 07 03 – aurifat@wanadoo.fr – closed mid-Dec to mid-Feb – ⊿ – 4 rooms: 48/70€. A delightful place within walking distance of a famously attractive town. This former 13C timber-framed brick watchtower with adjacent dovecot has been beautifully restored: the rooms (all non-smoking) are pretty and the terraced garden overlooks the nearby fields.

AROUND MARCILLAC

⊜ **Chambre d'hôte Cervel** – Route de Vinnac – 12190 Estaing – ☎ 05 65 44 09 89 – closed 15 Nov to 30 Mar – ⊿ – 4 rooms: 40/49€ – meal 15€. This hillside farmhouse belongs to a friendly couple in love with their region. The rooms are extremely comfortable and the menu offers imaginative regional dishes. You'll love the visits to the resident goats, and the cups of highly scented Aubrac tea.

⊜⊜ **St-Fleuret** – 12190 Estaing – ☎ 05 65 44 01 44 – auberge.st.fleuret@wanadoo.fr – closed 15 Nov to 15 Mar, Sun evening and Mon in low season – 14 rooms: 44/47€ – ⊡ 6€ – meals 17/48€. This former 19C post-house contains modern rooms overlooking the garden or the old town dominated by a picturesque castle. Large country-style dining room heated by a fireplace, where guests are invited to discover regional specialities including the famous aligot, a combination of mashed potatoes and Tomme cheese.

IN NERAC

⊜ **Chambre d'hôte Le Domaine du Cauze** – 47600 Nérac – 2.5km east of Nérac along D 656 towards Agen – ☎ 05 53 65 54 44 – cauze.pope@wanadoo.fr – reservations required – 4 rooms: 46/53€ – meal 23/24€. Convivial farmhouse perched on a green hilltop which, when the weather is clear, affords a glimpse of the edge of the Landes forest. The rooms vary, some are filled with furniture found in antique shops, others with family items or modern, functional units. In fine weather meals are served in the arbour.

AROUND PAU

⊜ **Hôtel Central** – 15 r. L.-Daran – 64000 Pau – ☎ 05 59 27 72 75 – closed 20-26 Dec – 28 rooms: 30.80/56.20€ – ⊡ 6€. You will be made welcome in this small hotel situated in the town centre. The size and level of comfort of the rooms vary; they are gradually being refurbished and given distinctive features; some offer a wireless Internet connection; soundproofing is good and they are well kept.

⊜⊜ **Hôtel de Gramont** – 3 pl. Gramont – 64000 Pau – ☎ 05 59 27 84 04 – hotelgramont@wanadoo.fr – closed 20 Dec to 4 Jan – 34 rooms: 48/82€ – ⊡ 8€. This post-house is believed to date back to the 17C and to be the oldest hotel in Pau. The rooms have distinctive features and some antique furniture. Those on the top floor are less spacious but were recently refurbished.

AROUND ST-JEAN-PIED-DE-PORT

⊜⊜ **Hôtel Central** – Pl. Charles-de-Gaulle – 64220 St-Jean-Pied-de-Port – ☎ 05 59 37 00 22 – closed 15 Dec to 1 Mar – 12 rooms: 56/77€ – ⊡ 8€ – meal 18/42€. As its name implies, this hotel is well situated in the lively part of town. A 200-year-old staircase leads to slightly old-fashioned or recently brightened-up rooms, all of them adequately soundproofed.

MARKETS

Bergerac – Sat morning.
Cahors – Wed and Sat mornings.
Condom – Wed morning, covered market.
Gaillac – Tue, Thu and Sat mornings.
Marmande – Tue, Thu and Sat mornings.
Pau – Every morning, covered market.
St-Jean-Pied-de-Port – Mon, pl. du Gén.-de-Gaulle.

...ent of vineyards in the Southwest, we deliberately left out specific ... in our opinion, were less interesting from a tourist's point of view, ...s-du-Brulhois, Côtes-du-Frontonnais, Tursan and Béarn.

Background

An amazing variety of wines – Historically, the mosaic of vineyards scattered across the southwest quarter of France have at least one thing in common: for centuries, all were excluded from the market place by Bordeaux. Anxious to preserve their special trade agreements with northern Europe, the Bordeaux wine-growers invented all kinds of cunning taxes and regulations to avoid competition from inland wines. For instance, wines from Bergerac, Cahors, Gaillac and Agen were only allowed into the port of La Lune in Bordeaux once Bordeaux wines had been sold and shipped. Their quality often suffered as a result and, in addition, they were heavily taxed by consuls in Bordeaux and Libourne.

Fortunately, the development of the railway and road networks enabled wines from the Southwest to break free without losing their identity in the process: the region has preserved a number of ancient grape varieties, some of which were probably already being cultivated long before the arrival of the Romans.

Bergerac Country

Around 130km starting from Bergerac (Dordogne). Michelin Local Map 329 B-E 6-7. See round tour **1** *on the map on p. 354-355.*

The Guyenne region was dominated by the English crown during the height of the Middle Ages. Outside the fortified walls of the its medieval towns, or *bastides*, vineyards alternate with orchards of plum trees, pastures and woods, where there always seems to be a good place to enjoy a meal and a fine bottle. The Bergerac vineyards are the most extensive of the whole southwest, both in volume and area. They stretch some 50km from west to east along the north bank of the Dordogne, briefly crossing over to the hillsides on the opposite bank, south of Bergerac. Sweet or extra sweet white wines long dominated production but, for the past 25 years, the volume of red wines has been double that of white wines. All 90 municipalities in the Bergerac area are entitled to the **Bergerac** AOC which includes around ten local classifications.

Bergerac★

The historic capital of the middle Dordogne Valley is the link between Bordeaux and the inland areas. Bergerac owes a lot to Edmond Rostand who chose it as the birthplace of his voluble hero Cyrano, as charming as the local wines.

Old Bergerac★★ is situated next to the **former harbour** where the trading boats, known as *gabares*, used to moor to unload wood from the upper valley and load wine casks bound for Bordeaux. Strolling along the narrow streets, you will discover old timber-framed houses. One of these has been turned into the **Musée regional du Vin et de la Batellerie★: cooperage**, an ancient craft which played an important role in the economy of the area, is illustrated here and inland water transport comes to life through various models of *gabares*.

Mid-Mar to mid-Nov, Mon-Fri, 10am-noon, 2-5.30pm, Sat, 10am-noon, Sun, 2.30-6.30pm. 2€. ☎ 05 53 57 80 92.

A fine Renaissance residence houses the **Musée du Tabac★★**, which reveals the extraordinary story of tobacco: once extensively cultivated in the Bergerac region, it has now almost entirely disappeared. *& Tue-Fri, 10am-noon, 2-6pm, Sat, 10am-noon, 2-5pm, Sun, 2.30-6.30pm. Closed public hols, Sat afternoon and Sun from mid-Nov to mid-Mar. 3€. ☎ 05 53 63 08 12.*

The former **Cloître des Récollets** *(access via quai Salvette)* today houses the **Maison des vins de Bergerac**: the monks' cellar is now the meeting place of the Consuls de la Vinée Brotherhood, whereas exhibitions about wine *(see Shopping Guide)* are held in the **cloister building** (12C-17C).

Drive NE out of Bergerac along N 21. On the outskirts of Bergerac, the **Pécharmant** vineyards, exclusively devoted to the production of rich red wines, climb up the hillsides framing the Caudau Valley.

Return to Bergerac and follow D 933 S.

This is the beginning of the **Monbazillac** appellation, reserved for sweet white wines. It covers a hillside area extending over 2 500ha on the south bank of the Dordogne and includes the region's oldest vineyards, appreciated by the Dutch as early as the 17C because the wines travelled well. Monbazillac wines are made from grapes affected by what is called "noble rot" and collected manually through successive harvests. The process is the same as at Sauternes *(see Bordelais)*.

The buildings of the **Monbazillac cooperative** are about 4km from Bergerac.

Turn left onto D 14 then right onto D 13.

Château de Monbazillac★

Jul-Aug, 10am-7.30pm; Jun and Sep, 10am-12.30pm, 1.30-7pm; May and Oct, 10am-12.30pm, 2-6pm; Apr, 10am-noon, 2-6pm; Nov-Mar, daily except Mon, on request. Closed Jan. 5.49€ (children: 2.59€). ☎ 05 53 61 52 52.

The architectural style of this building erected circa 1550 is a blend of military austerity and Renaissance elegance. Inside, the **Great Hall** is adorned with a monumental fireplace and 17C Flemish furniture and tapestries. The wine storehouse, giving on to the main courtyard, has been turned into a restaurant. The **Musée du Vin** contains, among other exhibits, ancient wine-making and harvesting implements.

Several renowned estates are situated west of the château, among them **Château Tirecul La Gravière** *(see Shopping Guide)*.

Continue to Monbazillac then turn right onto D 14E. On the site of the 15C **Moulin de Malfourat**, a viewing table, perched on top of a 180m-high hill, provides details of the **panorama★** encompassing the vineyards as far as the eye can see.

D 14E joins D 933; turn right then immediately left onto D 17. The road runs through **Pomport**, a small municipality of the Monbazillac area, which produces some of the best Monbazillacs such as those of **Château Le Fagé**.

Drive to Sigoulès via D 17. **Sigoulès** boasts a 16C church and above all the most important **cooperative** in the Bergerac region *(see Shopping Guide)*.

Drive NW out of Sigoulès along D 15 then turn left onto D 14 and left again onto D 4 to Saussignac.

Saussignac

This village, camped on a hillside, is surrounded by vineyards of the same name. The Côtes-de-Saussignac vines produce only sweet and extra sweet white wines. The **Côtes-de-Saussignac AOC** was "revived" by a handful of Britons among the many who have settled in the region.

Drive back along D 4 then turn left onto D 14.

Sainte-Foy-la-Grande

This former *bastide* (founded by Alphonse de Poitiers in 1255) is a wine-growing centre with the lively atmosphere of a trading town. It has a chequer-board plan, a square surrounded by arcades and many old houses, dating from the Middle Ages, the Renaissance or the 17C. The banks of the Dordogne, beneath the ruins of the ramparts, are perfect for a romantic stroll.

Leave Ste-Foy W along D 936. Drive to a place called Tête Noire and turn right.

Montcaret

The site beneath the fine Romanesque church was occupied in Gallo-Roman times by a large **villa** with a peristyle, an atrium and its own **baths**. Particularly remarkable are the heating system, which worked by means of draughts, and the well-preserved 4C **mosaics★**, which comprise sixteen squares decorated with aquatic motifs. *Late May to late Sep, 9.45am-12.30pm, 2-6.30pm (last admission 45min before closing); Oct-Mar, daily except Sat, 10am-12.30pm, 2-5.30pm. Closed 1 Jan, 1 May, 1 and 11 Nov, 25 Dec. 4.60€. (children: no charge). ☎ 05 53 58 50 18.*

Leave Montcaret N towards St-Michel-de-Montaigne.

Château de Montaigne

Jul-Aug, guided tours of the tower (45min), 10am-6.30pm; May-Jun and Sep-Oct, daily except Mon and Tue, 10am-noon, 2-6.30pm; Jan-Apr and Nov-Dec, daily except Mon and Tue, 10am-noon, 2-5.30pm; school hols, 10am-noon, 2-5.30pm. Closed 25 Dec, 1 Jan and from 5 Jan to 3 Feb. 5€. ☎ 05 53 58 63 93.

Memories of **Michel Eyquem**, lord of Montaigne (1533-92), still haunt the **tower-library** where he dictated the *Essays* to his secretary. The beams are engraved with Greek and Latin maxims selected by the philosopher.

The present château, a fine late-19C, neo-Renaissance building, has replaced Montaigne's former residence, destroyed by fire. Walk round the edifice to admire the charming landscape of vineyards and woodland. The wines produced by the vineyards of the estate are on sale at the reception.

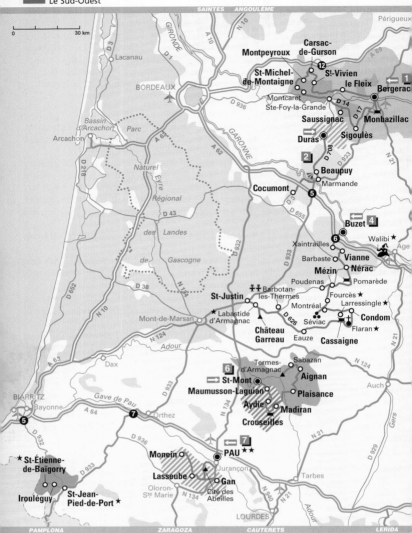

Drive NW along D 9 then turn right onto D 21 and right again onto D 10 to Montpeyroux. Between St-Michel-de-Montaigne and Fougueyrolles in the east, the hillsides produce dry white **Montravel** wines as well as sweet and extra sweet white wines classified as **Haut-Montravel** and **Côtes-de-Montravel**. The whole district also produces red and white Bergerac and Côtes-de-Bergerac wines.

Montpeyroux

There is a fine view of the area from this isolated hilltop village. Note the west front of the Romanesque **church**, surrounded by the churchyard: its lower parts feature modillions with unusual bawdy motifs. Nearby, an elegant 17C-18C **castle** comprises a main building with two pavilions at right angles flanked by round towers.

Leave Montpeyroux NE. The road leads to the **Gurson recreation area**, offering opportunities for fishing and activities on the beach. Above are the ruins of **Gurson castle** (11C-14C) camped on a hill planted with vines.

Carsac-de-Gurson

This village, surrounded by vineyards, boasts a fine Romanesque church. **La Grappe de Gurson cooperative** offers a selection of local wines.

Leave Carsac E on D 32, then, 2km further on, turn right onto a minor road leading to St-Vivien.

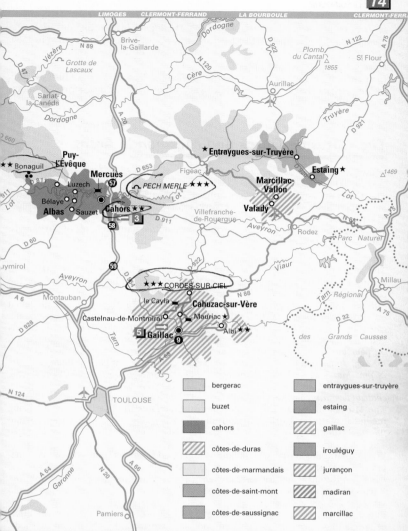

Saint-Vivien

You can buy wine from the **St-Vivien et Bonneville cooperative**, housed in an unusual neo-medieval building *(see Shopping Guide)*.

Turn left just before Vélines, then right past the gymnasium.

Les jardins de Sardy★

Easter to mid-Nov, 10am-6pm. 6€ (children over 10: 2€). ☎ *05 53 27 51 45.*

Italian and English in influence, these splendid gardens, where colours blend and fragrances mingle, were intended to increase people's sense of smell (in the **Cour des senteurs**) as well as visual awareness. This creation, which bears an Italian and English influence, has fully reached its goal. Château de Sardy overlooks 5ha of hillside vineyards. A good-quality Bergerac produced in small quantity *(visit of the wine storehouse on request)*.

Drive on to Vélines, then turn left onto D 32E2 towards Fougueyrolles and Le Fleix.

Running on top of the plateau, the small road winds through vineyards, past some of the finest estates in Bergerac country, such as **Château Roque-Peyre** *(accommodation)* in **Fougueyrolles**. Its owner is one of the wine-growers who initiated the recent red **Montravel** appellation, produced from small yields and fully matured in barrels.

Le Fleix

In this small town on the banks of the Dordogne, historically linked to the Protestant faith, the treaty ending the seventh War of Religion was signed in 1580. The Protestant church is housed in a former castle in the town centre.

Drive E to Prigonrieux along D 32.

In spite of its name, the tiny **Rosette** appellation, located on the hillsides overlooking **Prigonrieux**, only produces sweet white wines with a strong bouquet.

Return to Bergerac along D 32.

The Côtes de Duras and Marmande Areas

40km from Duras to Cocumont (Lot-et-Garonne). Michelin Local Map 336 C-D 1-3. See itinerary ② *on the map on p. 354-355.*

The **Côtes-de-Duras** AOC covers around 2 000ha following on the Entre-Deux-Mers appellation. These wines are very similar to Bordeaux wines and include, in particular, excellent dry and sweet white wines.

The road runs through undulating countryside dotted with orchards of plum trees; once dried, the plums become the famously delicious Agen prunes.

Duras

The dukes of Duras inspired Marguerite Donadieu, whose father was a native of nearby Pardaillan, to take Duras as her pen name. In her book *Les Impudents*, the castle is mentioned under the name of Ostel.

Built in 1308, the original castle had eight towers. In 1680 it was remodelled into a country residence then suffered a lot during the Revolution. A tour of the castle includes the guard-room, the kitchen, the bakery, the well, the dungeons and, of course, the whispering room. Four **museums** provide ample information on palaeontology, wine-growing and wines, cereals, arts and crafts and daily life. *Jul-Aug, 10am-7pm (last admission 1hr before closing); Jun and Sep, 10am-12.30pm, 2-7pm; Mar-May and Oct, 10am-noon, 2-6pm; Nov-Feb, Sat-Sun and school hols, 10am-noon, 2-6pm; Closed 1 Jan, 1 Nov, 25 Dec. 5€. ☎ 05 53 83 77 32. www. chateau-de-duras.com*

The **Musée-conservatoire du Parchemin** illustrates the making of books using medieval methods. In the scriptorium, you will even be able to try your hand! *Jul-Aug: 11am-1pm, 3-8pm; Apr-Jun and Sep: 3-6pm. 6€ (children: 3€). ☎ 05 53 20 75 55. www.museeduparchemin.com*

The **Maison des vins**, which houses the Association of Côtes-de-Duras winegrowers, provides information about the estates which are open to the public and has 160 different wines for sale, though without the possibility of tasting any; the **Berticot cooperative** sells a very fine Sauvignon made from the grapes of old vines *(see Shopping Guide)*.

End your visit of Duras on a sweet note by calling at **Éts Guinguet**, where all kinds of specialities based on prunes and chocolate are made by traditional methods. *Route de Montségur, 47120 Duras, ☎ 05 53 83 72 47.*

Leave Duras S along D 708 towards Marmande. The **Côtes-du-Marmandais** AOC extends on both sides of the Garonne, around Marmande, and covers an area of 1 000ha. The bulk of the production comes from local cooperatives.

Beaupuy

There is a superb view of the Garonne Valley from this village which boasts a lovely 13C church. Below, **Les Vignerons de Beaupuy cooperative** sells a fine selection of red wines *(see Shopping Guide)*.

Marmande

Marmande is renowned for its plums, peaches, melons, tobacco and above all its tomatoes. The town is not exactly beautiful but it conveys an impression of opulence.

The **Église Notre-Dame** (13C-16C) contains a 17C Entombment on the left near the entrance. On the south side of the church, there is a Renaissance cloister with French-style gardens.

Leave Marmande S via the bridge across the Garonne, turn right onto D 116 then left onto D 3 and drive 14.5km to Cocumont.

Cocumont

⚑ The municipality of Cocumont offers a **discovery trail** across the vineyards. This walk, which affords magnificent viewpoints, will also offer you an insight into the mysteries of the wine-grower's craft.

The area used to produce white wines, but today the Cocumont vineyards are mainly devoted to red wines. The **Élian Da Ros estate** is worth a visit.

The Cahors Wine Road

90km starting from Cahors (Lot). Michelin Local Map 337 C-E 4-5. See round tour **3** *on the map on p. 354-355.*

The vineyards of the **Cahors** AOC follow the meanders of the Lot and climb up on to the plateaux stretching along the river between Cahors and Soturac.
Explore both banks of the Lot and discover historic villages, impressive castles and numerous magnificent views of one of the most beautiful valleys in France. Cahors wines are exclusively red.

Cahors★★

The monuments of Cahors reveal a great deal about its past and its atmosphere in centuries gone by. All the ingredients of a pleasant visit are gathered here: a little history and culture, the peaceful banks of the Lot, the surrounding wooded hills with their precious truffles, good food and full-bodied wines.

Spanning the Lot, **Pont Valentré★★** is a kind of fortress guarding the river crossing and is regarded as the emblem of Cahors. Built in 1308, it was considerably remodelled when Viollet-de-Duc undertook its restoration in 1879. As for the **Cathédrale St-Étienne★★**, its construction began in the 11C and it owes its fortress-like appearance to the work commissioned by its successive bishops. The **north doorway★★**, depicting the Ascension, is the former Romanesque doorway of the west front; erected in 1135, it shows the influence of the Languedoc School. Inside the Cathedral, there is a marked contrast between the well-lit nave and the chancel decorated with stained glass and paintings. The Renaissance **cloister★** is adorned with elaborate carvings. The **Cathedral district★** is the most picturesque part of town with its narrow streets and old houses. The 13C **Église St-Barthélemy**, situated in the upper part of the old town, features a fine rectangular belfry-porch. From the nearby terrace, there is a lovely view of the Cabessut suburb and the Lot Valley. Follow rue de la Barre to the **Barbican** and **Tour St-Jean★** (also known, rather grimly, as the Tower of the Hanged Men), the finest fortified buildings in Cahors.

Vineyards near Cahors.

Drive NW out of Cahors along D 8 towards Luzech. The **Cap Nature** Site in **Pradines** organises recreational activities up in the trees, suitable for the whole family. *Mid-Jun to mid-Sep, 10am-5.30pm; Mar to mid-Jun and mid-Sep to mid-Nov, Wed, Sat-Sun, 10am-5pm. 16€ (children under 16: 15€).* ☎ 05 65 22 25 12.

The town's imprint vanishes from the landscape when you reach **Douelle**, a former stopover for inland water transport, where staves used for making barrels, known as *douelles*, were unloaded. Fine view of the Lot.

Turn right in Largueil. The **Côtes d'Olt cooperative** in **Parnac** initiated the revival of Cahors wines after the severe frosts of 1956.

Rejoin D 8 and turn right then left onto D 23. Drive through St-Vincent-Rivière-d'Olt and continue to Cambayrac. Cambayrac lies beyond the hamlet of Cournou, in a pleasant landscape of vineyards and arid plateaux.

Cambayrac

The **church** features a belfry-wall reminiscent of a French policeman's hat. Inside, the Romanesque apse was adorned in the 17C with a rare Classical-style decoration of marble and stucco.

Sauzet is in truffle country, on the southern border of the Cahors vineyards.

Drive N to Albas along D 37.

Albas

This small town, which used to be the seat of the bishops of Cahors, has retained the remains of the Episcopal castle and narrow streets lined with old houses. **Château Eugénie**, situated in the hamlet of La Rivière-Haute, is one of the best estates for this appellation *(see Shopping Guide).*

Follow D 8 to Bélaye.

Bélaye

This village stands on top of a high cliff towering over the Lot. From the upper square, there is a panoramic **view★** of the valley. Elegant houses recall the times when Bélaye formed part of the fief of the bishops of Cahors. A cello festival takes place in the church during the first week in August.

Grézels

The bishops of Cahors owned the Lot Valley between Cahors and Puy-l'Évêque and Grézels marked one of the boundaries of their fief. In the 12C, they therefore erected the **Château de la Coste** to guard the entrance to their land. A small Wine Museum is housed inside. *3-6pm. 4€. ☎ 05 65 21 34 18 or 05 65 21 38 28.*

Continue along D 8. The Pont de Courbenac offers the best overall **view** of the town of Puy-l'Évêque.

Puy-l'Évêque

This small town is built on terraces on the north bank of the Lot; the old ochre-coloured stone houses nestle round the keep and the **Église St-Sauveur**, once part of the defence system. The magnificent **doorway** is adorned with statues.

The only remaining part of the Episcopal castle is the 13C, 23m-high keep towering above the former outbuildings of the Episcopal palace. Admire the panoramic **view** of the valley from the **Esplanade de la Truffière**, next to the keep.

Clos Triguedina is one of the fine wines of the area *(see Shopping Guide)*.

If you follow the Lot Valley, west of Puy-l'Évêque, you will come across some of the famous estates of the Cahors region, such as **Château Lamartine** in **Soturac** *(see Shopping Guide)*.

Leave Puy-l'Évêque E along D 811.

Prayssac

Lively in summer, this small town lying beneath Calvayrac castle overlooks one of the tighter meanders of the Lot, enclosing the **Clos de Gamot** vineyards which produce good wines *(see Shopping Guide)*.

⚡ The **Dolmens discovery trail** to the north-east leads to many megaliths *(itinerary available from the tourist office)*.

Drive to Luzech along D 9.

Luzech

Crowned by its castle keep, Luzech occupies a magnificent site tucked inside a superb loop of the Lot, with the oppidum of Impernal to the north and the Pistoule promontory to the south.

From the top of Impernal Hill, the **panorama★** encompasses Luzech and its surroundings slicing through the plain like a ship's prow and the Lot winding between rich crops. From the terrace of the 12C **keep**, there is a bird's-eye view of the town. Stroll through the **old town** and explore the district around place des Consuls which has retained its medieval look. Housed in the fine vaulted cellar of the 13C Consuls' residence *(tourist office)*, the **Musée archéologique Armand-Viré** retraces the rich past of the site. Some items dating back to Roman times are exceptional. *Jul-Aug, Mon-Fri, 9am-12.30pm, 2-5.30pm, Sat, 9.30am-12.30pm, 2-4pm, Sun, 10am-noon; Sep-Jun, daily except Sat afternoon, Sun and Mon, 9.30am-12.30pm, 2.30-5.30pm. Closed from Christmas to early Jan and public hols. 2€. ☎ 05 65 20 17 27.*

Drive on to Cahors along D 9 and D 145. The narrow road follows the meanders of the Lot and goes through **Caix** with its splendid water sports centre offering swimming and various water sports. **Domaine de Lagrézette**, a handsome Renaissance building in **Caillac**, produces some of the finest (and most expensive) Cahors wines. The underground cellars and the barrel storehouse, which is 55m long and 19m high, can be visited. *46140 Caillac, ☎ 05 65 20 07 42, lagrezette-adpsa@club-internet.fr 10am-7pm. No charge.*

Rejoin D 145 and drive on to Mercuès.

Château de Mercuès

It occupies a remarkable site overlooking the north bank of the Lot. Mentioned as early as 1212, extended in the 14C and 15C, the fortress became a country residence in the 16C and later the seat of the bishops of Cahors: it was restored in the 19C. Today it is a hotel-restaurant. The vineyard of the château is renowned. Cellars and storehouses can be visited. *Cellars open Jul-Aug, Tue-Sun, 9.30am-1.30pm, 2.30-6.30pm. Closed Tue and Wed mornings. ☎ 05 65 20 00 01.*

Armagnac and Floc-de-Gascogne

Armagnac is obtained by distilling white wines made from Colombard, Ugni, Baco and Folle Blanche grape types. The process must take place without interruption at the latest on 30 March following the harvest. The white eau-de-vie (spirit) is then kept in oak casks where it acquires its colour and matures for a variable length of time. There are three main categories according to age: the "3 Stars" or "3 Crowns" have spent at least eighteen months maturing in casks; the "VO" (Very Old) and "VSOP" (Very Superior Old Pale) have matured for at least four and a half years; as for the "XO", "Hors d'âge", "Napoléon", "Extra", they are at least five and a half years old.

Floc-de-Gascogne, produced in Armagnac country, is a fortified wine made from a mixture of fresh must, containing at least 170g of sugar per litre, with Armagnac at a strength of 52°. The alcohol makes it possible to stop the fermentation of the must which thus retains its sugar. Floc can be either white or rosé.

Around Gascony

About 215km from Buzet-sur-Baïse (Lot-et-Garonne) to Labastide-d'Armagnac (Landes). Michelin Local Map 336 A-E 4-6. See itinerary **4** *on the map on p. 354-355.*
A trip through the Buzet, Armagnac and Côtes de Gascogne vineyards.

Buzet-sur-Baïse

The Buzet vineyards cover some 2 000ha along both banks of the river Garonne, between Marmande and Agen. Revived in the 1960s thanks to **Les Vignerons de Buzet** cooperative, the vineyards produce red and rosé wines from Bordeaux vines, and also a few white wines. The Vignerons de Buzet estate produces all the varieties of wines qualifying for the **Buzet** AOC. It offers a tour of the maturing storehouse which contains 4 000 barrels and an informative slide show. A visit to the cooperage reveals all the subtleties of the barrel-makers craft, and of the wood itself. *47160 Buzet-sur-Baïse, ☎ 05 53 84 74 30, buzet@vignerons-buzet.fr 10.30am-4pm. By appointment in winter.*

From Buzet, follow D 108 S to Xaintrailles.

South of the Garonne Valley, between the Gers and the Baïse, vineyards have been devoted to the production of **Armagnac** for centuries. In the land of musketeers, of good food and of rugby, people know how to enjoy themselves. The Festival de jazz in Marciac, Festival des bandas in Condom and the Tempo Latino in Vic-Fezensac are essential summer entertainment.

The production of Armagnac extends over three specific areas: Bas-Armagnac in the west, where soils are acid and sandy; Haut-Armagnac in the east and the north, where chalky soils prevail; Ténarèze in the centre where soils are a mixture of clay, chalk and sand.

Xaintrailles

From the top of this village, there are splendid **views** of the Garonne Valley and of the Landes Forest. The 12C castle was rebuilt in the 15C by Jean Poton de Xaintrailles, a comrade-in-arms of Joan of Arc.

Drive E to Vianne along D 141.

Vianne

The fortifications of this former English *bastide*, founded in 1284, are almost intact and it has retained its distinctive chequer-board plan. Glassmaking is the traditional activity and there are glass-blowers and glass-cutters still working here.

Follow D 642 S, cross the Baïse and drive on to Barbaste.

Barbaste

On the east bank of the Gélise stands the **Moulin de Henri IV** with its four square towers of uneven height. The mill once defended the old ten-arch **Romanesque bridge** which is still standing.

◉ As you enter the **Château Imaginaire**, you step into another world, intended to make you forget reality. You are told stories as you move along an interactive trail highlighted by an original setting, encountering holograms and 3-D pictures along the way. &. *Jul-Aug, 10am-noon, 2-7pm (Tue and Thu, 9pm); Apr-Jun, Sep-Oct, Christmas and Feb school hols, 2-6pm. 8€ (children 5-11: 6€). ☎ 05 53 97 25 15. www.chateau-imaginaire.com*

D 930 leads to Nérac.

Nérac

Jeanne d'Albret, Henri IV's mother, set up in Nérac an important centre for the promotion of humanist ideas and the Protestant faith. The poet Clément Marot described the place as "a refuge more pleasant than freedom". A tour of the **old town★** includes **Sully's house** (second half of the 16C), **Pont Vieux**, old houses with typical loggias and **Pont Neuf** affording a fine view of the river banks. The

Promenade de la Garenne, along the Baïse, offers a very pleasant walk beneath one-hundred-year-old oak trees. Jeanne d'Albret's Renaissance **castle** has only retained one of its original four wings as well as a stair turret. Its **museum** houses archaeological collections. *Jun-Sep, 10am-noon, 2-7pm; Oct-May, 10am-noon, 2-6pm. Closed Mon. 4€.* ☏ 05 53 65 21 11.

Château du Frandat produces Buzet wine, Armagnac and Floc *(see Shopping Guide)*.

Leave Nérac S along the Condom road (D 930). 6.5km further on, behind a screen of greenery on the right, stands Pomarède castle.

Château de Pomarède

Mid-Jul to mid-Sep, guided tours (30min), 9am-noon, 2-6pm; mid-Sep to mid-Jul, apply to the owner. 4€. Château de Pomarède, 47600 Moncrabeau, ☏ 05 53 65 43 01.

This 17C-18C Gascon-style manor features a dovecot, a wine storehouse, stables and a saddlery.

Rejoin the road and turn right onto D 149 1km further on.

Mézin

This hilltop place is a centre of wine-growing and cork-making. The 11C **Église St-Jean-Baptiste** features a composite style. The **Musée du Liège et du Bouchon** illustrates the times when Mézin was one of the capitals of cork-making. ♿ *Jul-Sep, 10am-noon, 2-7pm (last admission 30min before closing); Apr-Jun and Oct, 2-6pm. Closed Mon and public hols (except 14 Jul and 15 Aug). 3.50€ (children under 18: no charge).* ☏ 05 53 65 68 16.

Drive W out of Mézin along D 656. As you leave, note on your left a Gascon dovecot perched on pillars.

Poudenas

This village, crisscrossed by steep streets, is dominated by a 16C-17C **castle** featuring a fine Italian-style façade. ♿ *Mid-Jul to end of Aug, guided tours (1hr), daily except Mon 3-6pm. 5€.* ☏ 05 53 65 78 86.

From the old bridge, there is a lovely view of the castle, the church tower and the Hôtellerie du Roy Henry with its wooden gallery.

Return to Mézin and turn right onto D 5 running into D 29.

Fourcès★

This attractive circular *bastide*, one of the most charming villages of the Gers area, is popular with artists and craftsmen. The lofty 15C-16C **castle** stands alongside the Auzoue where water lilies grow in summer. Today it is a renowned hotel and restaurant. An array of colours brightens up the small town on the last weekend in April, when the spring-flower market is on.

Montréal

This *bastide*, founded in 1256, has retained its fortified Gothic church and its central square lined with arcaded houses; one of these has been turned into an interesting **Musée archéologique** *(access via the tourist office)* displaying finds from the Séviac site *(see below).* ♿ *Jul-Aug, 10am-12.30pm, 2-6.30pm; Sep and Jun, 10am-12.30pm, 2-6pm. Apply beforehand to the tourist office. No charge, ticket combined with the Gallo-Roman Villa in Séviac.* ☏ 05 62 29 42 85.

Follow the signposting to the Séviac site, west of Montréal.

Inside an Armagnac storehouse...

Villa gallo-romaine de Séviac

Jul-Aug, 10am-7pm; Mar-Jun and Sep-Nov, 10am-noon, 2-6pm. Guided tours (1hr) available. 4€ (children under 12: no charge), ticket gives admission to the Musée archéologique in Montréal. ☏ 05 62 29 48 57. www.seviac-villa.fr.st

Excavations have revealed the foundations of a luxury 4C Gallo-Roman villa, as well as various remains testifying to a permanent occupation of the site from the 2C to the 7C. The extensive baths of the villa include rooms heated by hypocaust (an underfloor heating system), a swimming pool and several pools lined with marble and decorated with exceptionally fine mosaics.

Follow D 15 towards Condom as far as Larressingle.

S. Sauvignier/MICHELIN

Larressingle★

This walled-in 13C gem is the favourite haunt of artists and craftsmen. A spiral staircase links the three storeys of the ruined **keep**. The fortified Romanesque **church** has been reduced to two adjoining chancels. Walk round the fortifications along the path running outside the walls. ⊙ You will discover the **Cité des machines du Moyen-Âge**, a 13C siege camp, realistically reconstructed at the foot of the fortifications. ⚐ *Jul-Aug, 11am-7pm (1hr guided tours available in Jul-Aug only, at 11.30am, 3, 4.30 and 5.30pm); May-Jun and Sep, daily except Wed, 11am-5.30pm; Oct-Apr, daily except Wed, 2-5pm. Closed 24 Dec to 7 Jan. 1.50€ (guided tours: 4.70€).* ☏ *05 62 68 33 88.*

A shop, situated opposite the main entrance to the village, sells regional products, local wines and Armagnac from nearby farms.

Condom

The historic capital of the Armagnac and Ténarèze areas has the appearance of a small bourgeois city proud of its trading activities, of its administrative status (*sous-préfecture*) and of its name...which is a source of stifled amusement for English-speaking visitors. Every summer, the town enthusiastically livens up to the sound of brass bands during the Festival des bandas.

The **Cathédrale St-Pierre★**, with its impressive square tower, dates from the early 16C and is one of the last great Gothic buildings to be erected in the Gers region. Adjoining the eastern gallery of the **cloisters★**, St Catherine's Chapel, now a public passageway, has attractive polychrome keystones.

Those who appreciate Armagnac and Floc are spoilt for choice. By way of an introduction to the subject, visit the **Musée de l'Armagnac** *(rue Jules-Ferry)* which displays a rare collection of implements, an array of cooperage tools, bottles made by Gascon gentlemen-glassmakers and various stills. *Apr-Oct, 10am-noon, 3-6pm; Nov-Mar, 2-5pm. Closed Mon, Tue and public hols. 2.20€.* ☏ *05 62 28 47 17.*

For a more practical approach, call at **Maison Ryst-Dupeyron**, housed in the fine 18C Hôtel de Cugnac. This establishment offers a visit of the 18C wine storehouse. The tour includes audio-visual presentations and a free tasting. *1 rue Daunou. Jul-Aug, guided tours (1hr), 9am-noon, 2-6pm, Sat-Sun and public hols, on request. Closed 1 Jan. No charge.* ☏ *05 62 28 08 08.*

Leave Condom S along D 930.

Abbaye de Flaran★

Jul-Aug, 9.30am-7pm; Feb-Jun and Sep-Dec, 9.30am-12.30pm, 2-6pm. Closed 3 weeks in Jan, 1 May, 25 Dec. 3.80€, no charge on the 1st Sun of the month (Nov-Mar). ☏ *05 62 28 50 19.*

Admire the simplicity and austerity of this beautiful Cistercian abbey: owned by the Gers *département*, it holds first-class temporary exhibitions year in, year out. Built between 1180 and 1210, the **church** features double capitals with very simple ornamentation. The **cloister** is reached via the church. The west gallery alone is original (late 14C); it is covered with timberwork. The **gardens** are in two sections: one is laid out in the French style and the other, near the old mill, grows herbs and medicinal plants.

Drive NW to Cassaigne along D 142.

Château de Cassaigne

⚐ *Jul-Aug, 10am-7pm; mid-Sep to early Feb and end of Feb to mid-Jun, daily except Mon, 9am-noon, 2-6pm. No charge.* ☏ *05 62 28 04 02. www.chateaudecassaigne.com*

The former country residence of the bishops of Condom dates from the 13C. The visit includes a tour of the wine storehouse and a slide show relating the history of the château, wine-growing and the origins of Armagnac. There are interesting 16C kitchens. Don't forget to taste the local product after admiring the vineyards.

D 208 and D 931 lead to Gondrin and Eauze.

The fine Romanesque church in **Mouchan** is worth a visit. **Gondrin** is an attractive *bastide* surrounded by vineyards. Gourmets will want to call at the **Ferme du Cassou**, where they can find just about all the delights of the Gers. *Route de Vic-Fezensac, 32330 Gondrin,* ☏ *05 62 29 15 22. 8am-noon, 2-6pm. Discovery and tasting on Wed morning in Jul-Aug.*

Eauze

The capital of Bas-Armagnac is the ancient Elusa, the region's main city in Gallo-Roman times, which have left their mark. The sandy soils of Bas-Armagnac are reckoned to produce the best wines for distillation. Wine-growers, who have signposts along the roads, also sell Côtes-de-Gascogne local wines. **Château du Tariquet** is well known for its fruity white wine; it is one of the largest wine-growing estates in France *(see Shopping Guide)*.

Place d'Armagnac is a picturesque square lined with arcaded houses. The 15C **Cathédrale St-Luperc** is a typical example of southern Gothic architecture.

The prime exhibit of the **Musée archéologique** is the **Gallo-Roman treasury** of Eauze: coins and jewellery encrusted with precious stones.   *Jun-Sep, 10am-12.30pm, 2-6pm; Feb-May and Oct-Dec, 2-5pm (mornings on request). Closed Tue, Jan, 1st weekend in July, public hols. 4€, No charge on the 1ˢᵗ Sun of the month (Nov-Mar).* ☎ *05 62 09 71 38.*
Continue to Barbotan-les-Thermes along D 626 and D 656.

Barbotan-les-Thermes ‡ ‡

The hot underground springs, renowned for the treatment of leg complaints, have encouraged the growth of exotic plants in the **park** surrounding the spa establishment: a pleasant place for a stroll before visiting the 12C **church**.
In summer, **Uby Lake**, situated south of the town, offers its shores, laid out as a recreation area, to anyone wishing to take a dip.
Continue to Labastide-d'Armagnac along D 626.

On the right before reaching Labastide, a path leads to **Notre-Dame-des-Cyclistes** Chapel, dedicated to cycling enthusiasts who, in the words of the prayer to protect them, "travel all across the Lord's beautiful Creation". It's a charming spot and makes a perfect stop for a picnic.

Labastide-d'Armagnac★

Lovely *bastide* founded in 1291. Place Royale is surrounded by old timber-framed houses surmounting a row of arcades bedecked with climbing roses. Impressive 15C bell-tower.

Saint-Justin

This is the oldest *bastide* in the Landes region (1280). It already existed at the time of Henri IV.
Return to Labastide-d'Armagnac, follow D 626 towards Cazaubon then turn right and drive 3.5km along D 209.

Écomusée de l'Armagnac – Château Garreau

Apr-Oct, Mon-Fri, 9am-noon, 2-6pm, Sat, 2-6pm, Sun and public hols, 3-6pm; Nov-Mar, Mon-Fri, 9am-noon, 2-6pm. 4€. ☎ *05 58 44 88 38.*
This important estate has set up a wine-growers' museum displaying implements and old stills. A pleasant trail will enable you to discover the local aquatic fauna and an experimental wood where ceps are cultivated. A shop sells produce from the estate.

The Gaillac Area

80km starting from Gaillac (Tarn). Michelin Local Map 338 C-D 6-7. See tour 5 *on the map on p. 354-355.*
The hillsides of the Gaillac area, dotted with fairy-tale villages, are reminiscent of Tuscany and offer a gentle transition from the Atlantic to the Mediterranean influence. The Gaillac area, extending over 3 700ha west of Albi, has been a wine-growing region since Roman times. There is a wide variety of grape types, which explains why just about every kind of wine is produced here: sparkling, dry and sweet white wines, red and rosé wines, all entitled to the **Gaillac** AOC.

Gaillac

To explore the town, stroll through the network of narrow winding streets lined with old houses forming a harmonious blend of brick and wood.
⏱ The Hauts de Gaillac hike *(5hr, 18km medium difficulty)* offers the opportunity of discovering the surrounding vineyards. *Map available at the tourist office.*
Construction work on the **abbey church of St-Michel** began in the 11C and lasted until the 14C. The former abbey buildings house the **Maison des vins de Gaillac** which provides information on the vineyards, as well as the possibility of tasting and buying wine from some one hundred producers *(see Shopping Guide).*
The **Musée des Arts et Traditions populaires**, housed in the same building, displays archaeological collections and illustrates the crafts connected with wine-growing.   *Jul-Aug, 10am-1pm, 2-7pm; the rest of the year, 10am-noon, 2-6pm. Closed 1 Jan, 1 May, 1 Nov, 25 Dec. 2.30€. Pass available for the 3 museums, 3€, valid one year.* ☎ *05 63 41 03 81.*
The **Moulin** and **René Rieux** estates are renowned for their good value for money *(see Shopping Guide).*
Leave Gaillac N along D 922 towards Cahuzac-sur-Vère.

Cahuzac-sur-Vère

This former stronghold has some of the most renowned estates of the Gaillac area, in particular **Domaine des Tres Cantous**, famous for its remarkable Vin d'Autan and Vin de Voile. Robert Plageoles, an erudite enthusiast, speaks very

poetically about his wines. *81140 Cahuzac-sur-Vère, ☎ 05 63 33 90 40, Robert-bernard-plageoles@wanadoo.fr Jun-Aug, 8am-noon, 3-7pm; Sep-May, 8am-noon, 2-4pm, Sat-Sun and public hols by appointment.*
D 21 leads SE to Mauriac castle.

Château de Mauriac★

May-Oct, guided tours (1hr), 3-6pm; the rest of the year, Mon-Sat, on request, Sun, 3-6pm. 6€ (children: 4€). Apply to M Emmanuel Bistes, ☎ 05 63 41 71 18. www.bistes.com

Partly dating from the 14C, this castle has a fine harmonious façade. The tour includes several ground-floor rooms displaying paintings by artist Bernard Bistes, the owner of the castle. The first-floor rooms have all been restored and furnished in different styles and colour schemes.

Follow D 21 then turn left onto D 30. The road runs through vineyards to **Cestayrols** where **Domaine de Lacroux** produces an excellent red *(see Shopping Guide)*. The 15C church in **Noailles** boasts a fine vaulted chancel.

Drive N along D 30, then turn right onto D 922.

Cordes-sur-Ciel★★★

This medieval town occupies a splendid **site★★** on a height overlooking the Cérou Valley. Sometimes called the "town with a hundred Gothic arches", Cordes is a timeless city, made all the more beautiful by the sunlight playing on the pink and grey hues of its sandstone façades.

Visiting Cordes means breathing in the atmosphere of this old city, strolling through the narrow cobbled streets among exceptionally fine 13C-14C **Gothic houses★★**, admiring the carved ornamentation of their façades and the often highly original window displays made by craftsmen!

Maison Prunet, located in the centre of the fortified town, houses the **Musée de l'Art et du sucre**, truly a mini-paradise – or a trial of temptation – for anyone with a real sweet tooth! Mostly displayed in glass cases are works of art made entirely of sugar. *Jul-Aug, 9am-7pm; Apr-Jun and Sep-Oct, 10am-noon, 2-6.30pm; Nov-Dec and Feb-Mar, daily except Mon, 10am-noon, 2.30-6pm. Closed Jan. 2.30€ (children: 1.55€). ☎ 05 63 56 02 40.*

Drive S along D 922 towards Gaillac, then, 8km further on, turn right to Le Cayla castle.

Le Cayla

This typical Languedoc manor house was the family home of **Eugénie de Guérin** (1805-48) and her brother **Maurice** (1810-39), both romantic poets and writers; the **Musée Maurice-et-Eugénie-de-Guérin** is devoted to them. The peaceful surroundings and the faithfully reconstructed living quarters are a moving commemoration of the writers. *May-Sep, guided tours (1hr), 10am-noon, 2-6pm; Oct-Apr, daily except Mon, 2-6pm. Closed Tue, 1 Jan, 1 May, 1 and 11 Nov, 25 Dec. 2€, no charge on the 1st Sun of the month (Oct-Apr). ☎ 05 63 33 90 30.*

Continue along the same road until you join up with D 1; turn right then left onto D 4. The road runs through landscapes where vineyards give way to woodland. The 14C church in **Vieux** contains beautiful frescoes.

Castelnau-de-Montmiral

This picturesque village is an ancient 13C *bastide*, perched on a rocky spur. It is easy to imagine what an important look-out position this must have been: the name Montmiral derives in part from *mirer*, meaning "to see" in Occitan. From its rich past, the *bastide* has retained some old houses, skilfully restored. On the west and south sides of **place des Arcades**, surrounded by arcades, there are two 17C houses. In the 15C parish **church**, note the **gem-encrusted cross-reliquary★** of the counts of Armagnac, known as the "Montmiral Cross", a fine example of 13C religious gold and silver work.

Château de Mayragues produces fine Gaillac wines *(see Shopping Guide)*.

Return to Gaillac along D 964.

The Rivière-Basse Area

75km starting from St-Mont (Gers). Michelin Local Map 336 B-C 7-8. See round tour **6** *on the map on p. 354-355.*

This undulating region heralds the Pyrenees. Situated southwest of the Gers and encroaching on the Hautes-Pyrénées, the vineyards of the **Madiran** AOC, with their characterful reds, are some of the most renowned in Gascony. **Pacherenc-du-Vic-Bilh**, grown in the same area, is a usually sweet and occasionally dry white wine. **Côtes-de-St-Mont**, on the border of the Madiran area, are pleasant white, red and rosé wines. These three appellations owe a lot to the dynamism of local cooperatives.

Shopping Guide

INFORMATION

Comité interprofessionnel des vins du Sud-Ouest – *BP 18 – 31321 Castanet-Tolosan* – ☎ *05 61 73 97 06 – www.vins-du-sud-ouest.com*

Conseil interprofessionnel des vins de la région de Bergerac – *1 r. des Récollets – BP 426 – 24104 Bergerac Cedex* – ☎ *05 53 63 57 57 – www.vins-bergerac.fr*

Union interprofessionnelle du vin de Cahors – *430 av. Jean-Jaurès – 46000 Cahors* – ☎ *05 65 23 22 24.*

Union interprofessionnelle des vins des Côtes de Duras – *Maison du vin – D 668 – 47120 Duras* – ☎ *05 53 20 20 70 – www.cotesduras.com*

Bureau national interprofessionnel de L'Armagnac AOC – *11 pl. de la Liberté – BP 3 – 32800 Eauze* – ☎ *05 62 08 11 00 – www.armagnac.fr*

Syndicat des vins VDQS entraygues-le-fel – *Les Buis – 12140 Entraygues-sur-Truyère* – ☎ *05 65 44 50 45.*

Syndicat des vins AOVDQS estaing – *L'Escalière – 3 r. Flandres-Dunkerque – 12190 Estaing* – ☎ *05 65 44 75 38.*

Commission interprofessionnelle du Vin de Gaillac – *Maison des vins – abbaye St-Michel – 81600 Gaillac* – ☎ *05 63 57 70 60 – www.vins-gaillac.com*

OVERVIEW

CHARACTERISTICS

Bergerac, Côtes-de-Duras, Côtes-du-Marmandais, red Buzet – Light ruby to dark purple. Aromas: red berries, blackcurrant, green pepper developing into prune and truffle.

Dry white Bergerac – Light straw to golden green. Aromas: bitter almond and citrus fruit developing into coffee.

Sweet Bergerac – Light straw to golden copper. Aromas: iodine, roasted almond, wild strawberry.

Cahors – Dark purple. Aromas: blackberry, black berries, spices, maturing into truffle and prune. Very tannic when young, becoming more supple with age.

Red Gaillac – Carmine to purple red. Aromas: red berries, pepper and spices.

Sweet Gaillac – Straw-coloured when young, turning to caramel when very old. Aromas: exotic fruit, pear, candied fruit maturing into iodised and spicy flavours.

Dry Jurançon – Light straw to golden green. Aromas: citrus fruit, lime and exotic fruit developing into honey.

Sweet Jurançon – Straw to golden yellow. Aromas: candied citrus fruit, honey and roasted almond.

Red Irouléguy – Vermilion to dark ruby. Aromas: green pepper and berries.

STORAGE

Red wines – 5 to 10 years depending on quality. Longer for Madiran, Côtes-de-Bergerac and Cahors wines.

Dry white wines – 3 to 5 years for most wines. Montravel wines and some of the Gaillacs keep longer.

Sweet and extra sweet white wines – Monbazillac, Haut-Montravel and some sweet Gaillacs keep very well for over 10 years.

PRICE

Most classified wines sell between 3 and 11€.

Monbazillac, Jurançon, sweet Gaillac, Cahors and Côtes-de-Bergerac wines from 8€.

BUYING

WINE MERCHANTS

L'Art et le Vin – 17 Grand'Rue – 24100 Bergerac – ☎ 05 53 57 07 42 – Tue-Sat, 9am-12.30pm, 2-7pm. The claret-coloured façade of this shop close to the covered market is in itself an indication: you are entering a place dedicated to the world of wine. The selected classified wines, kept in wooden boxes, come essentially from small local wine-growers, whose production is followed year after year: it's worth asking about their Pécharmant, Bergerac and Monbazillac.

Atrium – Route de Toulouse – 46000 Cahors – ☎ 05 65 20 80 80 – Mon-Sat, 8am-12.30pm, 2-7.30pm; Jul-Aug, daily, 8am-8pm. This is the headquarters of the Atrium chain, whose concept of storehouse-shop entirely dedicated to wine and to the promotion of the vineyards of Southwest France is most original. The shop offers a selection from each region and, in particular, a good choice of Cahors, Madiran, Gaillac and Buzet wines.

COOPERATIVES

Cave des Vignerons de Beaupuy – *47200 Beaupuy* – ☎ *05 53 76 05 10 – Mon-Sat, 9am-noon, 2.30-6pm.* Good selection of Côtes-du-Marmandais red wines.

La Grappe de Gurson – *24610 Carsac-de-Gurson* – ☎ *05 53 82 81 50 – Mon-Sat, 9am-noon, 2-6pm.* This cooperative provides a good insight into Bergerac wines and offers very good value for money.

Cave Berticot – *Route de Ste-Foy-la-Grande – 47120 Duras* – ☎ *05 53 83 75 47 – berticot@wanadoo.fr – daily, 8am-noon, 2-6pm – by appointment.* Set up in 1965, the Berticot cooperative includes around

S. Sauvignier/MICHELIN

one hundred wine-growers. The vineyards cover 750ha planted with Merlot, Cabernet-Sauvignon and Sémillon grapes.

The vines are grown in mixed soils of clay and limestone, using environmentally conscious methods, by 30 to 35% of the producers. The cooperative uses thermo-regulated vats. The wines are matured in barrels for six to twelve months or in stainless-steel vats for six to eighteen months. White wines are left to mature on the lees for three to nine months.

Cave cooperative de Jurançon – *53 av. Henri-IV – 64290 Gan – ☎ 05 59 21 57 03 – www.cavedejurancon.com – Jun-Aug, Mon-Sat, 1-7.30pm, Sun, 9.30am-12.30pm, 3-7pm ; Sep-May, Mon-Sat 8am-12.30pm, 1.30-7pm (Jan 6.30pm).* Excellent wines and reception.

Cave de Monbazillac – *Route d'Eymet – 24240 Monbazillac – ☎ 05 53 63 65 06 – monbazillac@chateau-monbazillac.com – Mon-Sat, 8am-noon, 2-6pm.* The cooperative, which forms part of the Musée du Vin offers the best wines of this appellation. A corner is set aside for tasting, allowing visitors to test their nose, and, in the area devoted to the discovery of the terroir, a few wine-making secrets are revealed.

Côtes d'Olt – *Caunezil – 46140 Parnac – ☎ 05 65 30 71 86 – som@cotesolt.com.* These wines are made from 25-year-old vines situated in an exceptionally fine terroir. The cooperative, which includes 250 wine-growers, was set up in 1947. For an area covering 45ha, there are as many as 2 000 maturing barrels and between one and a half and two million bottles going through the ageing process.

Cave cooperative des Vignerons du Pays basque – *Route de St-Jean-Pied-de-Port – 64430 St-Étienne-de-Baïgorry – ☎ 05 59 37 41 33 – daily, 9am-noon, 2-6.30pm – Oct-May, closed Sun – guided tours on request (3€).* The cooperative produces most of the Irouléguy AOC and sells many first-rate wines.

Les Producteurs Plaimont – *Route d'Orthez – 32400 St-Mont – ☎ 05 62 69 62 87.* Today, the cooperative has 1 000 members and vineyards covering 2 500ha. Harvesting is done by hand and vinification by settling. A great many wines are matured in oak casks for six to fourteen months. The cooperative owns more than 5 000 barrels one third of which is renewed every year.

Les viticulteurs réunis de St-Vivien et Bonneville – *La Reynaudie – 24230 St-Vivien – ☎ 05 53 27 52 22 – Mon-Sat, 9am-noon, 2-6pm.* This cooperative has a choice of red and white Bergeracs, as appealing as their price.

Cave cooperative – *24240 Sigoulès – ☎ 05 53 61 55 00 – Mon-Sat, 9am-noon, 2-5.30pm.* Almost all the appellations of the Bergerac region can be found here.

Caves des Vignerons du Vallon – *RN 140 – 12330 Valady – ☎ 05 65 72 70 21 – Mon-Sat, 9am-noon, 2-6pm – closed Sun and public hols.* This cooperative, which includes some forty wine-growers from Valady

and the surrounding area, only sells Marcillac AOC wine. Made from the Fer-Servadou grapes, locally known as mansois, this wine has a fine red colour, raspberry, blackcurrant or bilberry aromas and is both smooth and rich.

WINE CENTRES

Maison des vins de Bergerac – *2 pl. Cayla, quai Salvette – 24100 Bergerac – ☎ 05 53 63 57 55 – contact@vins-bergerac.fr – high season, 10am-7pm; low season, Tue-Sat 10.30am-12.30pm, 2-6pm.*

Maison des vins des côtes de Duras – *Route de Marmande – 47120 Duras – ☎ 05 53 94 13 48 – www.cotesdeduras. com – Jul-Aug, 9am-noon, 2-7pm ; Sep-Jun, Mon-Fri, 9am-noon, 2-5.30pm.*

Maison des vins de Gaillac – *Caveau S-Michel – Abbaye St-Michel – 81600 Gaillac – ☎ 05 63 57 15 40 – maison.vins. gaillac@wanadoo.fr – Jul-Aug, 10am-1pm, 2.30-7pm ; the rest of the year, 10am-noon, 2-6pm – closed Christmas, New year, 1 May and 1 Nov.*

ESTATES

Château Eugénie – *Rivière-Haute – 46140 Albas – ☎ 05 65 30 73 51 – couture@chateaueugenie.com.* This château, which has been a family estate for 500 years, owns 30ha of hillside terraced land. The vineyards get a lot of sunshine. The traditional combination of grape varieties includes Auxerrois, Merlot and a little Tannat. Vinification is also traditional; wines are then matured in oak casks and bottled on the estate.

Domaine du Crampilh – *64350 Aurions-Idernes – ☎ 05 59 04 00 63 – madirancrampilh@aol.com – Mon-Sat, 9am-noon, 2-6pm – by appointment.* The 28ha of the estate consist of siliceous and clayey soils; 23ha are planted with Tannat, Cabernet-Sauvignon and Cabernet Franc grapes to produce red wines; 5ha are planted with petit and gros manseng to produce white wines.

Château d'Aydie – Vignobles Laplace – *64330 Aydie – ☎ 05 59 04 08 00 – pierre.laplace@wanadoo.fr.* In 1961, the Laplace family pioneered bottling on the estate. Pierre Laplace's four children then abandoned polyculture to devote themselves entirely to wine-growing. Today, the estate includes 55ha of vineyards planted on mixed soils composed either of chalk and clay or silica and clay. Madiran wines are matured in barrels for eighteen months.

Château de Mayragues – *12km NE of Gaillac along D 964 then D 15 – 81140 Castelnau-de-Montmiral – ☎ 05 63 33 94 08 – www.chateau-de-mayragues.com – Mon-Sat, 9am-7pm – closed Sun except for reservations, and Christmas.* There are many reasons why one should visit this château: its fortified architectural style (14C and 16C), its hilly surroundings, its vineyards (bio-dynamic wine growing) and its Gaillac wines: red, rosé, white, sparkling and slightly sparkling wines. Two guest rooms and a self-catering cottage available.

Château de Lacroux – *81150 Cestayrols* – ☎ *05 63 56 88 88 – chateaudelacroux@wanadoo.fr – Mon-Sat 8am-noon, 2-7pm – by appointment.* Ten generations of wine-growers have worked on the estate since 1746! They began selling their wine in 1982. The vineyard, cultivated using *"lutte raisonnée"* methods, is planted with Duras and Braucol grape varieties for red wines and with Mauzac and Len-de-l'El for white wines. It covers a chalky-clay hillside area of 38ha facing south-southeast.

Domaine Élian Da Ros – *Laclotte – 47250 Cocumont* – ☎ *05 53 20 75 22.* This family estate was taken over in 1997 by Élian Da Ros who, one year later, built his own storehouse and left the cooperative. Today the vineyard covers 16ha planted with Merlot, Cabernet-Sauvignon, Cabernet Franc, Cot, Abouriou and Syrah varieties for red wines and with white and grey Sauvignon and Sémillon for white wines. Two-thirds of the vines are between 25 and 30 years old and are grown by organic methods on sedimentary clay, gravelly clay and chalky clay. Harvesting is done by hand and the grapes are sorted in the vineyard. Wines are matured in large casks and barrels for twelve to twenty months depending on the vintage and the year.

EARL David Fourtout – *Les Verdots – 24560 Conne-de-Labarde* – ☎ *05 53 58 34 31 – fourtout@terre-net.fr – Mon-Sat 9am-noon, 2-7pm.* This family estate extends over 33ha planted with Merlot, Malbec, Cabernet Franc and Cabernet-Sauvignon varieties for red wines and with Sémillon, Sauvignon and Muscadelle for white wines. The red varieties thrive on chalky soil where the rock stratum nears the surface; the white varieties prefer a clayey soil. In a deliberate move to provide quality while safeguarding the environment, the estate has invested in a specialised waste-processing plant.

Cave de Crouseilles – *64350 Crouseilles* – ☎ *05 59 68 10 93 – May-Sep, Mon-Sat, 9am-1pm, 2-7pm, Sun, 10am-7pm ; Oct-Apr , Mon-Sat, 9.30am-12.30pm, 2-6pm, Sun, 1-6pm.* In less than 50 years, the Crouseilles cellar, established in the château of the same name, has acquired an unquestionably high reputation in the profession. In the shop and tasting area, you will discover the red Madiran and the dry or sweet Pacherenc-du-Vic-Bilh which are the prize appellations of this estate.

Clos Bellevue – *Chemin des Vignes – 64360 Cuqueron* – ☎ *05 59 21 34 82 – Mon-Fri 8-11.30am, 2-5pm.* Le Clos has been in the hands of the Muchada family since the Revolution! Jean Gérard took control of the estate in 1972 and decided to make his own wine and to bottle it on the premises. His son Olivier took over from him in 2002. A conscientious wine-grower, he now runs the 40ha estate, including a 9ha vineyard. The soil is a mixture of chalk and clay with a lot of stones. The vineyard is planted with Gros Manseng (60%), Petit Manseng (37%), Tannat and Cabernet Franc (3%) grape varieties, grown by environmentally responsible methods. Harvesting is done by hand in small crates and, every year, Olivier Muchada sells wine made after the *vendanges vertes*. The wine is made in thermo-regulated vats then matured on the lees.

Château du Tariquet – *32800 Eauze* – ☎ *05 62 09 87 82 – contact@tariquet.com.* Today, the estate is not only renowned for its Bas-Armagnac and Floc-de-Gascogne, but also for its Côtes-de-Gascogne local wine. The search for quality and a controlled yield from the vines have promoted the production of well-known and appreciated wines. Traditional vinification also allows for a refined production.

Domaine René Rieux – *1495 Route de Cordes – 81600 Gaillac* – ☎ *05 63 57 29 29 – Mon-Sat (except Sat morning), 9am-5pm.* The estate comprises a 20ha hillside vineyard planted on chalky-clay soil. The cultivation methods – working the soil, adding organic soil treatments – are intended to enhance the characteristics of the terroir and grape varieties. Harvesting is done by hand and the grapes are carried in crates or small trailers before being lightly pressed while still whole. Wines in the Harmonie range are traditionally fermented in vats, whereas wines in the Concerto range are fermented and matured in casks. Lastly, sparkling wines in the Symphonie range are made according to the Méthode Gaillacoise with natural yeast and without addition of liqueur.

Domaine du Moulin – *Chemin de Bastié – 81600 Gaillac* – ☎ *05 63 57 20 52 – do mainedumoulin@libertysurf.fr – Mon-Sat, 9.30am-noon, 2-7pm, Sun, by appointment.* The Hirissou family has been running this estate for nine generations. The present owner invites you to taste, among others, his Vieilles Vignes Rouge vintage – awarded a prize at the Concours des vins de Gaillac – in his fine tasting cellar, located on a hillside in the middle of the vineyard.

Domaine du Cros – *12390 Goutrens* – ☎ *05 65 72 71 77 – pteulier@domaine-du-cros.com – Mon-Sat, 9am-1pm, 2-7pm – by appointment.* Philippe Teulier, the main force behind the revival of this vineyard which nearly disappeared, is a remarkable wine-grower. His estate, which, in 1984, covered only 3ha, now extends over 25ha exclusively planted with Mansoi, the local name of the Fer-Servadou grape variety. Vinification, lasting twenty to twenty-five days, takes place in stainless-steel, thermo-regulated vats. The wine is matured in barrels for eighteen months before being bottled.

Domaine Arretzea – *64220 Irouléguy* – ☎ *05 59 37 33 67.* This terraced mountain vineyard is cultivated by organic methods certified by Écocert: no chemical fertilizer is used; on the other hand, weeding is done mechanically, organic insecticides are used and compost freely added.

Domaine de Cabarrouy – *Chemin Cabarrouy – 64290 Lasseube* – ☎ *05 59 04 23 08 – Mon-Sat (except Mon* *morning)*, *9am-12.30pm, 2-7.30pm – by appointment.* Patrice Limousin and Freya Skoda, who once made Muscadet wine, fell in love with this chalky-clay hillside and have gradually replanted it since 1988. Today, the vineyard extends over 5.5ha, including 3ha planted with Petit Manseng and 2.5ha with Gros Manseng. Harvesting is done by hand through successive selections. Sainte-Catherine and Extrême vintages are made and matured in oak casks for a minimum of eighteen months.

Château Tirecul La Gravière – *24240 Monbazillac – ☎ 05 53 57 44 75 – bruno. bilancini@cario.fr – Mon-Fri, 9am-noon, 2-6pm.* Situated in the heart of Périgord Pourpre, the vineyard stretches over 10.5ha in the Côte-de-Monbazillac area. The estate has been run by Bruno and Claudie Bilancini since 1992. In accordance with the regional wine-making tradition, it is mainly planted with Muscadelle grapes to which are added some Sémillon and Sauvignon varieties. From the 2000 vintage onwards, the estate has been producing a dry white wine. Bruno and Claudie also own Château La Feuilleraie in Pomerol.

Domaine Bru-Baché – *R. Barada – 64360 Monein – ☎ 05 59 21 36 34 – Mon-Sat, 9am-noon, 2-6pm – by appointment.* The 8ha vineyard of this estate, extending on the Casterasses hillsides overlooking the village of Monein, thrives on sedimentary clay. Claude Loustalot, anxious to respect the terroir and to use natural cultivation and vinification methods, runs his estate on *"lutte raisonnée"* lines. Harvesting is done by hand. Wines are matured in oak casks for sixteen to eighteen months.

Clos Uroulat – *Quartier Trouilh – 63360 Monein – ☎ 05 59 21 46 19 – Mon-Sat, by appointment.* Charles Hours is an oenologist who created this estate in 1983 with the help of his daughter Marie. The vineyard, extending over 7.5ha, is planted with Gros and Petit Manseng varieties thriving on chalky pudding-stone. Following the manual harvest, the grapes are fermented and the wine is then matured in oak casks. Some wines are made from sun-dried grapes.

Domaine Cauhapé – *Quartier Castet – 64360 Monein – ☎ 05 59 21 33 02 – domainecauhape@wanadoo.fr.* Henri Ramonteu is a top Jurançon wine-grower whose hillside vineyard extends over 40ha. Gros and Petit Manseng are grown on gravelly and stony soils consisting of clay and silica. The late harvest coincides with the first snowfalls.

Château du Frandat – *Route d'Agen, D 7 – 47600 Nérac – ☎ 05 53 65 23 83 – daily, 9am-noon, 2-6pm – closed early Nov to end of Mar except by appointment and Sun.* This estate is proud to make three different products all classified as AOC: red, rosé and white Buzet wines, rosé and white Floc-de-Gascogne and Armagnac. Tour of the storehouse and free tasting.

Clos de Gamot – *46220 Prayssac – ☎ 05 65 22 40 26 – maisonjouffreau@wanadoo.fr – Mon-Fri, by appointment, Sat-Sun, 9am-noon, 2-7pm.* Part of the 12ha Clos de Gamot estate boasts vines over 116 years old and still producing. The vineyard is exclusively planted with the auxerrois grape variety, which grows on soils containing silica and clay mixed with pebbles and flint. Wine-growing is traditional: ploughing, no chemical herbicide, harvesting by hand etc.

Château Le Fagé – *Le Fagé – 24240 Pomport – ☎ 05 53 58 32 55 – info@chateau-le-fage.com – Mon-Fri, 8am-noon, 2-6pm, Sat-Sun, by appointment.* In 1983, François Gérardin took control of the estate, which has been owned by his family for three hundred years; he was joined by his son Benoît in 2000. Situated on the northern slopes of Monbazillac, the 39ha vineyard is mainly planted with Merlot (70%) to which are added Cabernet Franc, Cabernet-Sauvignon and Malbec for the production of red wine; and with Sémillon, Sauvignon and Muscadelle for the production of white wine. Harvesting is done by hand for sweet wines and by machine for dry white wines and red wines. Vinification and maturing are traditional: concrete vats and barrels are used for the red Cuvée Prestige.

Clos Triguedina – *Jean-Luc-Baldès – 46700 Puy-l'Évêque – ☎ 05 65 21 30 81 – Mon-Sat, 9am-noon, 2-6pm.* The Baldès family has been in the wine-growing business for eight generations and continues to run this 60ha estate with passion and know-how. Clos Triguedina, which the estate produces, is one of the top names of the Cahors AOC and one of the most award-winning wines in Quercy. Tour of the cellar, storehouse and family museum.

S. Sauvignier / MICHELIN

Ferme Abotia – *Ispoure – 64220 St-Jean-Pied-de-Port – ☎ 05 59 37 03 99 – abotia@wanadoo.fr – Mon-Sat, 8am-noon, 2-6pm.* This estate has been run by the Errecart family for several generations; the present owners use their know-how to perfect two top products of the Basque gastronomy: an excellent Irouléguy AOC, twice a prize-winner at the Concours Général Agricole, and prime farmhouse pork sold in an unusual way.

Château Lamartine – *46700 Soturac – ☎ 05 65 36 54 14 – chateau-lamartine@wanadoo.fr – Mon-Sat, 9am-noon, 2-6pm, Sun, by appointment.* Alain Gayraud's grand-father, Édouard Serougne, was one of the wine-growers who brought about the revival of Cahors wine. Founded in 1883, the estate now consists of 30ha of vines growing on arid terraced soils. A restoration programme of the storehouses has been undertaken in a deliberate effort to maintain high quality.

Château de Viella – *Route de Maumusson – 32400 Viella – ☎ 05 62 69 75 81.* Situated within the boundaries of the municipality of Viella, this hillside vineyard extends over 25ha of pebbly-clay soil planted with Petit Manseng, Tannat and Arrufiac grape varieties enjoying plenty of sunshine. Harvesting is done by hand; the grapes then spend a long time in the vats before being left to mature in new casks.

Château du Cèdre – *Bru – 46700 Vire-sur-Lot – ☎ 05 65 36 53 87 – chateauducedre@wanadoo.fr – Mon-Sat, 9am-noon, 2-6pm.* Pascal and Jean-Marc Verhaeghe, who combine their exceptional know-how with their wish to respect the terroir and have a constant concern for quality, are excellent in their field. The vineyard, extending over 25ha, is cultivated without using weedkiller. Wine-making process includes treading and stalking of the whole harvest sorted by hand. The estate also produces a basic table wine.

Festivals

Albas – "Le Bon air est dans les caves", Sat after Ascension Day. **Duras** – Fêtes des vins, 2nd weekend in Aug.
Gaillac – Fêtes des vins, 2nd weekend in Aug.
Madiran – Fête du vin, 14-15 Aug.
Nérac – Fête du vin, 2nd weekend in Aug
Viella – Harvest of the New-Year's-Eve at midnight.

Saint-Mont

This village, with its picturesque narrow streets, is dominated by an 11C-13C abbey church boasting beautiful Romanesque capitals. However, its main attraction is the **Cave des Producteurs Plaimont**. This important association of cooperatives initiated the return of part of the Armagnac vineyards to the production of quality wines *(see Shopping Guide)*.

Drive S along D 946 then turn left onto D 262 towards Viella.

The road overlooks the vineyards and offers superb views extending as far as the Pyrenees. The village of **Viella** is known for its fine 18C **Château de Viella**.

Continue E along D 136 towards Maumusson-Laguian.

Maumusson-Laguian

Château Lafitte-Teston is worth a visit: the splendid cellar of the estate is built over an impressive underground barrel storehouse. *32400 Maumusson-Laguian, ☎ 05 62 69 74 58. Mon-Sat, 9am-12.30pm, 1.30-7pm.*

Follow a minor road S onto D 317 towards Aydie.

Aydie

Aydie is the largest municipality of the Madiran AOC. The **Château d'Aydie-Vignobles Laplace** is well-known for the quality of its wines and its friendly welcome *(see Shopping Guide)*.

Continue along D 317.

Crouseilles

The **Château de Crouseilles**, a fine 18C building, typical of Béarn, belongs to the local cooperative and its 250 members *(see Shopping Guide)*.

Madiran

The Madiran AOC vineyards were established in the 11C by Benedictine monks, near the village which gave them its name. The vast 12C **abbey church**, built over a remarkable crypt, is still standing. The **Maison des vins du Pacherenc et du Madiran** has been set up in the former priory, next to the church. It offers information about the vineyards as well as a wine tasting and the sale of locally produced wine in rotation. *65700 Madiran, ☎ 05 62 31 90 67. Mid-Jun to mid-Sep, Mon-Fri, 9am-6.30pm, Sat 9am-2pm, 3.30-6.30pm, Sun, 2.30-6.30pm; mid-Sep to mid-Jun, Mon-Sat 8.30am-12.30pm, 1.30-5.30pm.*

Drive NE along D 58, turn left onto D 935, then right onto D 946 to Plaisance.

Plaisance

This small, peaceful town boasts a 14C square lined with half-timbered houses. The St-Mont and local cooperatives both belong to the Union des Producteurs Plaimont and therefore sell the same wines *(see Shopping Guide)*.

Drive N out of Plaisance via D 3 and turn right onto D 20.

Aignan

Situated on the fringe of a vast forest, Aignan castle, famous for its production of Armagnac, has retained a few traces of its medieval past: a square surrounded by covered galleries resting on wooden pillars, half-timbered houses and a Romanesque church with a beautiful carved doorway.

Sabazan

This hilltop village is worth a detour on account of its remarkably lofty Romanesque church. Admire the hoarding (corbelled timberwork at the top of a tower or curtain wall, enabling the besieged to drop all kinds of missiles on the attackers having reached the foot of the wall) crowning the bell tower.

Termes-d'Armagnac

The fortress of Thibaut de Termes (1405-67), one of Joan of Arc's comrades-in-arms, has lost its keep and part of the main building. On the south platform, reached via a dark, steep spiral staircase, you will see the wax figures of the **Musée du Panache gascon**: Gascon musketeers (starting with D'Artagnan), Henri IV, and Thibaut's departure are the prize exhibits. *Jun-Sep, Wed-Mon, 10am-7.30pm, Tue, 3-7.30pm; the rest of the year, Wed-Mon, 2-6pm. Closed 1 Jan, 25 Dec. 4€ (children: 3.50€). ☎ 05 62 69 25 12. www.toursdetermes.com*
From the top of the 39m-high keep, there is a fine **panorama★** of the Adour Valley and the Pyrenees.
Return to St-Mont via Riscle.

Jurançon

55km from Pau to Monein – (Pyrénées-Atlantiques). Michelin Local Map 342 J-K 3. See itinerary ⑦ on the map on p. 354-355.
The name of Henri IV has been linked with Jurançon and its vineyards ever since the lips of the future king were moistened with a drop of southern wine at his christening. The Jurançon vineyards extend over the steep slopes of the Pyrenean foothills south of Pau. The tall vines form a charming landscape against the background of the Pyrenees. The **Jurançon AOC** only produces dry and sweet white wines.

Pau★★

This is Henri IV's elegant native town. A funicular links the upper town *(place Royale)* and the lower town *(railway station). No charge.*
From the **boulevard des Pyrénées★★**, a magnificent **panorama★★** extends over the Pyrenees range, from the Pic du Midi de Bigorre to the Pic d'Anie.
Plaques fixed to the balustrade show the summits directly opposite and their respective heights.
The 14C **castle★★** was built on the orders of Gaston Phoebus, Count of Foix, a hot-tempered but cultured man best remembered for his treatise on hunting, the *Livre de la Chasse*. Overlooking the fast-flowing river, the fortress has lost its military aspect, in spite of its brick keep. Remodelled into a Renaissance palace by Marguerite d'Angoulême, it was extensively restored in the 19C, in the time of Louis-Philippe and Napoleon III. The **apartments** include a series of richly decorated rooms housing a superb collection of **tapestries★★★**. The **King's bedroom** contains Henri IV's amazing cradle: a turtle shell from the Galapagos Islands! *Mid-Jun to mid-Sep, guided tours (1hr 15min), 9.30am-12.15pm, 1.30-5.15pm; Apr to mid-Jun and mid-Sep to Oct, 9.30-11.45am, 2-5pm; Nov-Mar, 9.30-11.45am, 2-4.15pm. Closed 1 Jan, 1 May, 25 Dec. 4.50€, no charge on the 1ˢᵗ Sun of the month. ☎ 05 59 82 38 07. www.musee-chateau-pau.fr*
East of the castle lies the old town, where a network of picturesque streets lined with antique shops and restaurants offers a pleasant stroll.
Leave Pau S along N 134. The village of **Jurançon** now forms part of the conurbation and there are very few vineyards to be seen.
Drive NW along D 2. In **Laroin**, you could visit the Souch estate, particularly renowned and cultivated by bio-dynamic methods.
Turn left onto the winding D 502.

La Cité des Abeilles

Jul-Aug, 2-7pm (last admission 1hr before closing); Apr-Jun, Sep to mid-Oct, All Saints and Feb school hols, Tue-Sun 2-7pm, mid-Oct to Mar, Sat-Sun and public hols, 2-6pm. Closed mid-Dec to mid-Jan. 5.50€ (children: 3.75€). ☎ 05 59 83 10 31. www.citedesabeilles.com
Ⓖ Devoted to bees and their environment, this educational open-air museum offers a nature trail along a hillside abounding in melliferous plants.
Turn left onto a minor road running into D 217; turn left then right onto D 230.
The **Chapelle-de-Rousse** area is one of the main centres of Jurançon wine, with many estates surrounding extremely beautiful residences. **Clos Lapeyre** houses a Musée de la Vigne et du Vin in its cellars. Ⓘ A thematic trail offers a pleasant stroll through the vineyard. *La Chapelle-Rousse, 64110 Jurançon, ☎ 05 59 21 50 80. Mon-Sat, 9am-noon, 2-6pm. By appointment. No charge.*
Continue S towards Gan via a minor road on the right.

Gan

The **Gan cooperative** was largely responsible for the revival of Jurançon wine in the 1970s *(see Shopping Guide)*.

Follow D 24 W to Lasseube.

Lasseube

This large village is typical of Pyrenean villages. The church and the old village houses are in 16C Gothic style. Located on the southern boundary of the Jurançon AOC, Lasseube nevertheless boasts a few fine estates such as the **Domaine de Cabarrouy** *(see Shopping Guide)*.

Leave Lasseube N along D 34 towards Monein.

The road runs through the vineyards between Lacommande and Monein. The imposing **Église St-Blaise** (12C-18C) in **Lacommande** features an amazing number of different styles; note, in particular, the Hispano-Arab vaulting in the north chapel. **Clos Bellevue** in **Cuqueron** produces good wines *(see Shopping Guide)*.

Monein

Monein is proud of having one of the best Jurançon vineyards; you will be able to judge for yourself at the **Confrérie du Jurançon** (Jurançon Brotherhood). ♿ *Guided tours (30min), daily except Sun, Mon and public hols, 9.30am-noon, 2.30-7pm. No charge.* ☎ *05 59 21 34 58.*

It is in the Monein area that you are likely to find the finest sweet Jurançons, often harvested at the beginning of winter, as is the case in the **Cauhapé**, **Bru-Baché** and **Clos Uroulat estates** *(see Shopping Guide)*.

Irouléguy

For this area, we have suggested a tour of the most interesting towns and villages in the appellation. These are marked on the map on p . 354-355 and on Michelin Local Map 342 D-E 3-4.

Located in the Pyrénées-Atlantiques, close to St-Jean-Pied-de-Port and Spain, **Irouléguy** is the only appellation on the French side of the Basque country. Vines grow on steep slopes in a mountainous landscape, but not above 400m.

Saint-Jean-Pied-de-Port★

The citadel restored by Vauban guards the town with its red sandstone walls.

Rue de la citadelle, running down to the Nive, is lined with 16C and 17C houses. N°41, known as the **bishops' prison**, houses an exhibition devoted to the way of St James in medieval times. *Jul-Aug, 10am-7pm; Apr-Jun and Sep-Oct, 11am-12.30pm, 2-6.30pm. Closed Tue. 3€ (children under 10: no charge).*

Situated in rue de l'Église, the Gothic **Église Notre-Dame** features fine sandstone pillars.

The bastion of the **citadel** offers a panoramic view of the whole Saint-Jean Valley and its lovely villages (viewing table).

A splendid *bastide*, of Navarre-influenced design, stands in the middle of the vineyards of the **Brana estate**, one of the rare independent producers in this area. It offers a fine selection of Irouléguy wines and a remarkable pear brandy. *3 bis av. du Jaï-Alaï, 64220 St-Jean-Pied-de-Port,* ☎ *05 59 37 00 44. Mon-Fri, 10am-noon, 2.30-6.30pm. By appointment. Admission charge.*

Situated in the village of **Irouléguy** *(on D 15, between St-Jean-Pied-de-Port and St-Étienne-de-Baïgorry)*, the **Arretxea estate** is a good place to visit *(see Shopping Guide)*.

Saint-Étienne-de-Baïgorry★

11km W of St-Jean-Pied-de-Port along D 15. This typical Basque village is at the very centre of the Irouléguy appellation, as you can conclude from a visit to the **Cave coopérative des Vignerons du Pays basque** *(see Shopping Guide)*.

Built in the 18C over a remodelled Romanesque base, the **Église St-Étienne★** is interesting on account of its three storeys of galleries, a style particular to the Basque country.

Vineyards of the Aveyron Region

We do not suggest an itinerary but a tour of towns and villages of the Aveyron vineyards instead. These are marked on the map on p. 354-355 and on Michelin Local Map 338 G4 H3.

Marcillac, Estaing, Entraigues-le-Fel, Côtes-de-Millau... the Aveyron vineyards are a patchwork of small appellations which kept on going in spite of the onslaught of phylloxera, and survive on "faisses", arid terraces cultivated by a handful of tough wine-growers. These vineyards are all the more interesting since they are located in magnificent surroundings, in the Tarn Gorges and Lot Valley.

Marcillac vineyards on the red soil of Rouergue.

Marcillac

The small **Marcillac** AOC covers a mere 160ha planted with the Fer-Servadou variety, known here as Mansois, which produces red wines only. The **Cros estate** in **Goutrens** *(12.5km SW of Marcillac along D 962 and D 43)* is one of the main producers *(see Shopping Guide)*.

Marcillac-Vallon – *17km NW of Rodez along D 901.*
Lying at the bottom of a sheltered valley, the village has fine old houses with cellars. Here, wine was once kept in goatskins rather than barrels, and used to be carried by mules.
Every year at Whitsuntide, the feast of Saint-Bourrou is celebrated in the chapel of **Notre-Dame-de-Foncourieu** *(1km N of the town)*; during this amazing feast, wine-growers welcome the appearance of the first buds on the vines.

Valady – *6km southwest of Marcillac along D 962.*
The **Vignerons du Vallon** cooperative is located here, in the very heart of the Marcillac appellation *(see Shopping Guide)*. The manor, an old 13C building with a stone-slab roof, houses a small museum of local arts, crafts and daily life.

Estaing and Entraygues-le-Fel wines (VDQS)

Estaing★ – *40km N of Rodez along D 988 to Espalion, then D 920.*
Nestling inside a loop of the Lot, the **castle**, dominated by its 14C-15C keep, guards a group of old houses with stone-slab roofs. It is home to a religious community. The 15C **church** facing the castle boasts a superb bell tower.
The **Vignerons d'Olt** grow the entire production of this small appellation (14ha) consisting of special red and white wines made from a combination of chenin and Mauzac varieties. *Route de Nayrac, 12190 Estaing, ☎ 05 65 44 04 42.*

Entraygues-sur-Truyère★ – *17km NW of Estaing along D 920.*
Situated at the exit of the splendid Gorges de la Truyère, Entraygues is a small picturesque city and a sports and leisure resort (canoeing-kayaking, rambling). The 20ha vineyard produces fruity white and red wines. It extends over sunny terraced hillsides bordering the River Lot.

Gourmet Delights

In an area which is so rich in gastronomic specialities, you may want to try your hand at a cookery course.

Gers

Loisirs-Accueil Gers – The Gers Loisirs-Accueil service *(Maison de l'agriculture, Route de Tarbes, BP 178, 32003 Auch Cedex, ☎ 05 62 61 79 00, Fax 05 62 61 79 09)* offers several ways to discover the local gastronomy: a package including the visit of wine storehouses, a market tour and a day's cooking practice; a foie gras weekend in a farm including an introduction to the art of carving a goose and preparing foie gras; a course with a top chef of the Ronde des Mousquetaires. *www.gers-tourisme.com*

Lot-et-Garonne

L'Atelier des Sens – *Restaurant Les Loges de L'Aubergade, 52 r. Royale, 47270 Puymirol, ☎ 05 53 95 31 46.* Cookery courses combined with tastings, visits to producers of local products and discussions around a gastronomic theme.

est

eil Dordogne – *25 r. du Prés.-Wilson, BP 2063, 24002 Périgueux Cedex,* 0 24 or 05 53 35 50 05. Courses in the preparation of foie gras, cookery courses in learning all about truffles and mushrooms.

Lot

Loisirs-Accueil Lot – *Pl. François-Mitterrand, 46000 Cahors,* ☎ *05 65 53 20 90. www.reservation-lot.com* Detailed list of courses (preparing foie gras, discovering truffles, vineyards and the terroir) and registration.

Pyrénées-Atlantiques
Hôtel de la Reine Jeanne – *44 r. du Bourg-Vieux, 64300 Orthez,* ☎ *05 59 67 00 76 or 05 59 65 03 06.* This course offers an introduction to traditional farm cooking. *Organised from mid-Oct to end of Apr.*

Going Back in Time

Prehistory in the Pech-Merle cave★★★
32km E of Cahors along D 663, D 662 and D 41. Mid-Apr to Oct, guided tours (1hr); ticket office open 9.30am-noon, 1.30-5pm. Visit limited to 700 visitors per day (reservations advisable 3 days in advance in Jul-Aug). 7€ (children: 4.50€), ticket combined with the Prehistory Museum. ☎ *05 65 31 27 05. www.pechmerle.com*
During the tour of the cave, you can admire beautiful concretions as well as rock carvings and paintings between 16 000 and 20 000 years old. The **Chapelle des Mammouths** is decorated with drawings of bison and mammoth. In the lower part of the prehistoric gallery, a panel is decorated with the silhouettes of two horses, patterned all over and around with dots and hand prints.

The Middle Ages at Bonaguil castle★★
18km NW of Puy-l'Évêque; drive along D 811 to Duravel then follow the signposting. Jun-Aug, 10am-6pm, Apr-May, 10.30am-1pm, 2.30-5.30pm; Sep, 10.30am-1pm, 2.30-5pm; Feb-Mar, 11am-1pm, 2.30-5.30pm; Oct, 11am-1pm, 2.30-5pm; Nov, school hols, Sun and public hols, 11am-1pm, 2.30-5pm; Dec, school hols, 2.30-5pm. Closed Jan, 25 Dec. 4.50€ (children 7-16: 3€). ☎ *05 53 71 90 33.*
This splendid medieval fortress, on the borders of Quercy and Périgord Noir, is one of the most perfect specimens of 15C-16C military architecture. Enter the castle through the barbican, a huge bastion which represented the first line of defence. The second line of defence comprised the Grosse Tour (Great Tower), one of the largest of its kind ever built in France. Towering over both lines of defence, the keep was the watch and command station. The complex included shops and facilities which granted the castle complete autonomy in the event of a siege... but the castle was never put to the test.

The 19C in Albi, Musée Toulouse-Lautrec★★
23km E of Gaillac via D 988 and N 88. Jul-Aug, 9am-6pm; Jun and Sep, 9am-noon, 2-6pm; Apr-May, 10am-noon, 2-6pm; Mar and Oct, daily except Tue, 10am-noon, 2-5.30pm; Jan-Feb and Nov-Dec, daily except Tue, 10am-noon, 2-5pm. Closed 1 Jan, 1 May, 1 Nov, 25 Dec. 4.50€ (children under 14: no charge). ☎ *05 63 49 48 70. www.musee-toulouse-lautrec.com*
Henri de Toulouse-Lautrec was born into a wealthy aristocratic family in Albi in 1864. His childhood was marred by two accidents which left him deformed and he left Albi for Montmartre in 1882. Valentin le Désossé, La Goulue, Bruant, Jane Avril, people he met in brothels and cabarets became his models. A superb draughtsman, he observed and sketched with brilliant, often trenchant precision and expression, allowing his charcoal strokes to show beneath the paint.
Over one thousand works bequeathed by the artist's parents are exhibited here. Even though many key paintings may be absent, the stock displayed is most interesting.

Family fun at Walibi Aquitaine★
4km SW of Agen along D 656. 15 Jul to 8 Aug and 23-29 Aug, 10am-7pm; 9-22 Aug, 10am-8pm (11pm on 21 Aug); Jun to mid-Jul and 30-31 Aug, 10am-6pm; Apr-May and Sep, Sat-Sun and public hols, 10am-6pm; Oct, Sat-Sun, 11am-6pm. Please check. 22.50€ (children 3-11: 17€). ☎ *05 53 96 58 32. www.walibi.com*
This recreation park offers an entertaining day out to the whole family. Turning, rolling, sliding... there is something for visitors of all ages. You can whirl round in giant coffee cups, go down the raging Radja River or watch the musical fountains (650 moving fountains) and the trained seals performing acrobatics.

Index

Director	David Brabis
Editorial	Nadia Bosquès
English Edition	Mike Brammer, Theo Gott, Alison Hughes, Blandine Lecomte, Grace Coston
Practical Information	Theo Gott, Alison Hughes
Mapping	Alain Baldet, Michèle Cana, Cécile Lisiecki
Picture Editor	Stéphane Sauvignier, Éliane Bailly, Jacqueline Pavageau
Lay-out	Didier Hée
Artwork	Marc Pinard, Didier Broussard, Bernard Dumas
Graphics	Christiane Beylier à Paris 12^e
Cover	Michel Cortey, Wag Interactive 13210 St-Rémy-de-Provence
Production	Pierre Ballochard, Renaud Leblanc
Marketing	Ellie Danby
Sales	John Lewis (UK), Robin Bird (USA)
Public Relations	Gonzague de Jarnac, Paul Cordle
Advertising	Manchette Publicité - 4, rue Rouget-de-Lisle 92793 Issy-les-Moulineaux Cedex ☎ 01 40 93 23 93

Contact

The Green Guide
Michelin Travel Publications
Hannay House
39 Clarendon Road
Watford Herts WD17 1JA
United Kingdom
☎ 01923 205 240
Fax 01923 205 241
www.viaMichelin.com
TheGreenGuide@uk.michelin.com

Acknowledgements

Rémi Bellissant, Patrick Berger,
Nadia Bourgne, Philippe Catz,
Damien Delattre, Aurélien Massé,
David Ridgway, Olivier Schvirtz

© Données domaines / Guide Fleurus des Vins